# THE UNITED NATIONS AND FREEDOM OF EXPRESSION AND INFORMATION

There are a multitude of UN legal instruments which pertain to the rights of freedom of expression and information, and this book is the first to comprehensively map them and their function. It details the chequered history of rights within the UN system, and evaluates the suitability of the system for overcoming contemporary challenges and threats to the rights. Leading scholars address key issues, such as how the rights to freedom of expression and information can come into conflict with other human rights, and with public policy goals, such as counter-terrorism. The book's institutional focus comprises five international treaties, UNESCO and the UN Special Rapporteur on freedom of expression. Relevant for academics, lawyers, policy-makers and civil society actors, it also examines how new communication technologies have prompted fresh thinking about the substance and scope of the rights to freedom of expression and information.

TARLACH MCGONAGLE is a senior researcher at the Institute for Information Law in the Faculty of Law at the University of Amsterdam.

YVONNE DONDERS is Professor of International Human Rights and Cultural Diversity and Executive Director of the Amsterdam Center for International Law in the Faculty of Law at the University of Amsterdam.

Professor Kevin Boyle †, to whom this book is dedicated.
(Photo courtesy of the University of Essex)

# THE UNITED NATIONS AND FREEDOM OF EXPRESSION AND INFORMATION

Critical Perspectives

Edited by

TARLACH MCGONAGLE

and

YVONNE DONDERS

CAMBRIDGE UNIVERSITY PRESS

**CAMBRIDGE**
**UNIVERSITY PRESS**

University Printing House, Cambridge CB2 8BS, United Kingdom

Cambridge University Press is part of the University of Cambridge.

It furthers the University's mission by disseminating knowledge in the pursuit of education, learning and research at the highest international levels of excellence.

www.cambridge.org
Information on this title: www.cambridge.org/9781107083868



First published 2015

*A catalogue record for this publication is available from the British Library*

*Library of Congress Cataloguing in Publication data*
The United Nations and freedom of expression and information : critical perspectives / edited by Tarlach McGonagle, Yvonne Donders.
pages cm
ISBN 978-1-107-08386-8 (Hardback)
1. Freedom of expression. 2. Freedom of information (International law)
3. International law and human rights. 4. United Nations. I. McGonagle, Tarlach, editor.
II. Donders, Yvonne, editor.
K3253.U55 2015
342.08′53–dc23 2014044893

ISBN 978-1-107-08386-8 Hardback

# CONTENTS

# DEDICATION AND APPRECIATION

The present volume is the culmination of a broader research project, also entitled, 'The United Nations and freedom of expression and information: critical perspectives', originally conceived of and run by Kevin Boyle and the editors of the present volume. It was born in a flurry of enthusiasm, excitement and ambition. The project aimed to (and did) provide an expert forum to contribute to the Human Rights Committee's then ongoing process of drafting a new General Comment on Article 19 of the International Covenant on Civil and Political Rights. The expert papers presented at that conference, as revised and realigned, aimed to fill a gap in existing scholarship. On completion of the project and the publication of this volume, the former enthusiasm, excitement and ambition remain, but they have become clouded in a very deep and enduring sense of sadness and loss. Our dear friend Kevin Boyle passed away in December 2010 and this book is dedicated to his memory.

After we had decided to dedicate the book to Kevin, further sadness followed. Two contributors to this volume, Karol Jakubowicz and Lucy Smith, passed away in 2013. We would also like to set out our profound appreciation of them and their work and we feel truly honoured to be able to include their chapters in the present edited collection.

For decades, through his prolific scholarship and his extensive, high-level contributions to the Council of Europe's media-related policy-making, Karol Jakubowicz was a leading player in a veritable 'media revolution in Europe'.[1] He had a great ability to generate, articulate, explore and operationalize ideas. He was always 'ahead of the curve', always pursuing the principles, with the clear-sightedness to see through the dizzying technological changes and appreciate the constant fundamental democratic, cultural and social issues behind them.

[1] K. Jakubowicz, *Media Revolution in Europe: Ahead of the Curve* (Strasbourg: Council of Europe, 2011).

Lucy Smith's very distinguished academic career included many prestigious academic and other public appointments, including President of the University of Oslo and successive memberships of the Committee on the Rights of the Child. In recognition of her outstanding scholarship, she was awarded honorary doctorates by several universities across the world.

The preparation of this book proved a protracted process, and during the finalization stage, in particular, we were spurred on by the hope that the collection as a whole would be a fitting showcase for the excellent contributions that Kevin, Karol and Lucy made to the book project and a result of which they would have been proud.

## Professor Kevin Boyle

Professor Kevin Boyle was an internationally renowned human rights lawyer, scholar and activist whose curriculum vitae includes numerous glittering legal and academic achievements.[2] It also offers a rich narrative of his life's engagement with people, structures and processes and his ability to promote human rights agendas and to drive legal reform. But Kevin was much more than his impressive professional résumé suggests. To his students, he was first and foremost an inspiring educator and mentor; to others, a highly effective adviser, advocate, political strategist or diplomat, as the situation required. Those who have been taught by him or who have worked with him will have experienced and appreciated at first-hand the personal qualities that made him much more than the sum of his professional parts.[3]

Kevin graduated in law at Queen's University Belfast (1965) and obtained a diploma in criminology from Cambridge (1966). He then became a law lecturer at Queen's and spent a year at Yale (1972). After his spell at Queen's, in 1978, he took up a chair in law at University College Galway (now known as the National University of Ireland, Galway), where he established the Irish Centre for the Study of Human Rights in 1980. In 1986, Kevin left Galway to become founding Director of the NGO, ARTICLE 19 – the Global Campaign against Censorship

[2] For detailed overviews of Kevin's career path, see N. Rodley, 'Kevin Boyle obituary', *Guardian*, 2 January 2011; 'Kevin Boyle. Man of law committed to equality, social justice', *The Irish Times*, 1 January 2011.

[3] B. Petranov, 'In Memoriam. Kevin Boyle – Strong Link in the Chain', 7 *SUR – International Journal on Human Rights* 13 (2010), 184–7.

(subsequently known as the 'Campaign for Free Expression', and currently using the slogan, 'Defending freedom of expression and information'). After his departure from Galway, Kevin retained an active interest in freedom of expression and media freedom in Ireland, collaborating with Marie McGonagle (National University of Ireland, Galway) to produce a number of reports, policy papers, submissions to the Irish Law Reform Commission and other documents on a variety of press freedom issues, including a blueprint and draft code of practice leading to the establishment of the first Irish Press Council in 2007.

Kevin's early years at the helm of ARTICLE 19 were coloured by the organization's engagement with freedom of expression and information issues in the former Soviet bloc and China; themes like defamation, the protection of journalists and hate speech, and perhaps most famously, the defence of Salman Rushdie after a fatwa was issued against him by Ayatollah Khomeini in 1989, following the publication of his novel, *The Satanic Verses.* Kevin was Chairman of the International Committee for the Defence of Salman Rushdie and his publishers, a campaign spearheaded by ARTICLE 19 and American PEN.[4] Throughout his career, Kevin always insisted on the synergies between the right to freedom of expression and the right to equality and non-discrimination. While appreciating the real-life tensions and frictions between both rights, he remained a firm believer in the power of free speech and counter-speech for combating hate speech.[5]

In 1989, Kevin was appointed professor of law at the University of Essex, to be joined there the following year by Nigel Rodley, appointments which ushered in a period of consolidation of the University's human rights profile. Kevin served as Director of the University's internationally acclaimed Human Rights Centre through the 1990s into the

[4] See further: ARTICLE 19, 'History and Achievements', www.article19.org/pages/en/history-achievements.html, last accessed 5 June 2014. See also: ARTICLE 19, 'Death of ARTICLE 19 Founding Director: Kevin Boyle (1943–2010)', Statement, 6 January 2011.

[5] 'Overview of a Dilemma: Censorship versus Racism' and 'Religious Intolerance and the Incitement of Hatred', in S. Coliver (ed.), *Striking a Balance: Hate Speech, Freedom of Expression and Non-discrimination* (United Kingdom: ARTICLE 19/University of Essex, 1992), 1–8 and 61–71, respectively; (with A. Baldaccini) 'A Critical Evaluation of International Human Rights Approaches to Racism', in S. Fredman (ed.), *Discrimination and Human Rights: The Case of Racism* (Oxford University Press, 2001), 135–91; 'Hate Speech: The United States Versus the Rest of the World?', 53 Me. L. Rev. 487 (2001); 'The Danish Cartoons', 24 *Netherlands Quarterly of Human Rights* 2 (2006), 185–91. Kevin also played a very influential role in the drafting of *The Camden Principles on Freedom of Expression and Equality* (London: ARTICLE 19, April 2009).

new century, and again in 2006–7, periods during which the Centre went from strength to strength.[6] Kevin always believed very firmly in the importance of multidisciplinary approaches to the study of human rights and he had been instrumental in setting up the University's MA programme (Theory and Practice of Human Rights). It was therefore very fitting that precisely that MA was conferred on Kevin as an honorary degree by the University in July 2010. The National University of Ireland, Galway, posthumously awarded him an honorary doctorate in laws in recognition of his life's work in September 2011.

A practising barrister, Kevin argued many – sometimes landmark – cases before national and international courts. His most famous cases before the European Court of Human Rights include: *Donnelly & Others* v. *the United Kingdom* (with co-counsel, Hurst Hannum), *Jersild* v. *Denmark* and *Bladet Tromso & Stensaas* v. *Norway*. However, he is perhaps most readily associated with his litigation on behalf of Kurds in Turkey, which he carried out with his colleague at Essex, Françoise Hampson. In recognition of their work for the Kurdish Human Rights Project, they were jointly named UK Human Rights Lawyer of the Year by the NGO, Liberty (the National Council for Civil Liberties in England and Wales) and the *Law Society Gazette* in 1998.

Kevin was a prominent figure in the Northern Ireland Civil Rights Movement, especially in its early years. He saw and articulated the need for law-based approaches for promoting human rights. He later spent a year (2001–2) as senior adviser to Mary Robinson while she was United Nations High Commissioner for Human Rights. It was a very eventful year as he took up the position immediately after the Durban World Conference on Racism and the September 11 attacks. He was also Chair of Minority Rights Group International (2007–10).

Kevin took ill shortly before he was scheduled to travel to the Netherlands in April 2010. He was due to give one of the key presentations at a conference in Amsterdam that he had been instrumental in getting off the ground: the United Nations and Freedom of Expression and Information: Critical Perspectives. This is a global, complex, politically sensitive topic, shaped by intra-institutional positioning over more than half a century. The topic was suitably ambitious and it fed his great appetite for challenging topics. He was always a man for big issues; new

[6] See further, K. Boyle, 'Twenty-Five Years of Human Rights at Essex', 5 *Essex Human Rights Review* (1) (July 2008), 1–15.

approaches to big issues; new ideas about big issues, and inevitably, new big issues.

This is reflected in his major publications (as editor and contributor): *New Institutions for Human Rights Protection*; (with Mary Robinson) *A Voice for Human Rights*; (with Tom Hadden) *Northern Ireland: The Choice*; (with Tom Hadden) *Northern Ireland: A Positive Proposal*; (with Juliet Sheen) *Freedom of Religion & Belief: World Report 1997*; (with David Beetham) *Introducing Democracy: 80 Questions and Answers*. He was a much-valued editorial/advisory board member of various leading journals, such as the *Netherlands Quarterly of Human Rights*, *Human Rights Quarterly* and *Religion and Human Rights*.

There was a unique complementarity in Kevin's various professional activities, but he always seemed to have a keen sense of the potential and limitations of each. The *festschrift* to mark his retirement from the University of Essex, edited by his colleagues, Geoff Gilbert, Françoise Hampson and Clara Sandoval, could not have had a more apt title: *Strategic Visions for Human Rights: Essays in Honour of Professor Kevin Boyle*. It is a clear recognition of his ability to think above, around and beyond existing structures, disciplines and ideas. Conor Gearty captures this ability of Kevin's eloquently, describing it as a seemingly 'new way to do law: get on top of all the stuff, the cases, the statutory provisions, the complex scholarship... and then deploy them not to mystify and stifle the people, but rather to empower and therefore to enrich them'.[7]

Kevin is missed very dearly for the professional integrity, commitment and ability that characterized his whole career. He is missed just as dearly for the sincerity, warmth and contagious enthusiasm that defined him as a person.

The esteem in which Kevin is held by family, friends, colleagues, and former students across the globe, is clear from the surge of tributes after his death.[8] There is striking, but unsurprising, consistency in the content and tone of the tributes. The consistency is striking because of the sheer range of activities in which Kevin was involved over several decades. People would have met him and got to know him in very different contexts and periods, but the impression he made on them was constant.

7 C. Gearty, 'Doing human rights: Three lessons from the field', in G. Gilbert, F. Hampson and C. Sandoval (eds.), *Strategic Visions for Human Rights: Essays in Honour of Professor Kevin Boyle* (London: Routledge, 2011), 54–66, 54.

8 Memorial websites include: www.ehraa.org/; www.nuigalway.ie/law/Kevin_Boyle.

The consistency is unsurprising because it was always the same Kevin. He was someone who did his best for others and had their best interests at heart; someone whose support and encouragement carried so many, many people distances we could never have contemplated on our own.

*Tarlach McGonagle and Yvonne Donders*
*Faculty of Law*
*University of Amsterdam*

# NOTES ON CONTRIBUTORS

ANTOINE BUYSE is full professor of human rights and Director of the Netherlands Institute of Human Rights of Utrecht University, the Netherlands. He holds an MA in history and a Ph.D. in law, both *magna cum laude*, from Leiden University. His doctoral thesis focused on the right to post-conflict housing restitution for refugees and other displaced persons. He is editor-in-chief of the *Netherlands Quarterly of Human Rights* and he hosts a blog on the ECHR (echrblog.blogspot.com). His research interests include the ECHR, human rights in post-conflict situations and situations of transition, housing rights and freedom of expression. Buyse is also a member of the Young Academy, the special branch for highly talented young scholars of the Royal Netherlands Academy of Arts and Sciences.

SYLVIE COUDRAY has been working at UNESCO for almost twenty-five years. She is the Chief of Section for Freedom of Expression in the Division of Freedom of Expression and Media Development. Her first assignment was to generate public awareness and foster advocacy to promote freedom of the press as an essential component of any democratic society, notably through the organization of the World Press Freedom Day and the UNESCO World Press Freedom Prize, as well as the UN Plan of Action on the Safety of Journalists and the Issue of Impunity. At the normative level, she has been actively involved in the planning and organization of a series of regional seminars on promoting pluralistic and independent media. At the operational level, she took part actively in the media assistance programmes to draw up master plans for restructuring the media landscape in the aftermath of national reconciliations. She has an M.Sc. in History (Sorbonne) and an M.Sc. in media and communication (Institut Français de Presse). She has edited several publications in various media-related fields such as media and new communication technologies, media and terrorism, and media in conflict areas.

HELEN DARBISHIRE is founder and director of the Madrid-based organization Access Info Europe. She is a human rights activist who has worked on promotion of the right of access to information since 1993, working with organizations such as ARTICLE 19 and the Open Society Foundations. Helen has provided expertise to a wide range of NGOs and IGOs, including UNESCO, the Council of Europe, the OSCE, and the World Bank. She is a founder and two-term chair (2004–10) of the global Freedom of Information Advocates Network. She is also on the board of various CSOs, including Fundación Civio (Spain), DATA (Uruguay), Diritto di Sapere (Italy), and the Request Initiative (UK), and is a Fellow of the Open Forum Academy.

YVONNE DONDERS is Professor of International Human Rights and Cultural Diversity and Executive Director of the Amsterdam Center for International Law at the Faculty of Law of the University of Amsterdam. Dr Donders graduated from Utrecht University in international relations and holds a Ph.D. from the Law Faculty of Maastricht on human rights and the right to cultural identity. Her research interests include public international law, international human rights law, in particular economic, social and cultural rights and human rights and cultural diversity. She teaches courses on international law and international human rights law and gives lectures on cultural rights and cultural diversity. She is currently a member of the National Commission for UNESCO, member of the Human Rights Committee of the Advisory Council on International Affairs, member of the Editorial Board of the *Netherlands Quarterly of Human Rights*, member of the board of the Royal Netherlands Society of International Law and President of the Dutch United Nations Association.

KAROL JAKUBOWICZ † worked as a journalist and executive in the Polish press, radio and television for many years. Dr Jakubowicz was Vice-President, Television, Polish Radio and Television; Chairman, Supervisory Board, Polish Television and Head of Strategic Planning and Development at Polish Television, and then Director, Strategy and Analysis Department, the National Broadcasting Council of Poland, the broadcasting regulatory authority (2004–6). He also taught at universities in Poland and abroad. He was also senior adviser to the chairman of the National Broadcasting Council, the broadcasting regulatory body of Poland. He was Chairman of the Intergovernmental Council of the Information for All Programme, UNESCO (2008–10). He was a member of the Council of the Independent Media Commission of Kosovo (2007–8). He was active in the Council of Europe, in part as former Chairman of the Committee of Experts on Media Concentrations and Pluralism (1995–6), Vice-Chairman and Chairman of the Standing Committee on Transfrontier Television (1995–2002), and as Chairman of the Steering Committee on the Media and New Communication Services (2005–6).

TARLACH MCGONAGLE is a senior researcher at the Institute for Information Law (IViR), Faculty of Law, University of Amsterdam and at the School of Human Rights Research in the Netherlands. Dr McGonagle was awarded a Ph.D. by the University of Amsterdam (2008) for his thesis examining the interface between freedom of expression and minority rights under international law. He regularly writes expert reports for various branches of the Council of Europe, OSCE, other IGOs and NGOs. He is currently Rapporteur of the Council of Europe's Committee of Experts on protection of journalism and safety of journalists. He was an invited expert speaker at the Thematic Discussion on 'Racist Hate Speech' organized by the UN Committee on the Elimination of Racial Discrimination in 2012. He is academic coordinator of IViR's specialized master's programme, *Informatierecht*, at the University of Amsterdam.

TOBY MENDEL is a lawyer and the founder and Executive Director of the Centre for Law and Democracy, a Canadian-based international human rights NGO that focuses on providing legal expertise regarding foundational rights for democracy. Prior to that, he was Senior Director for Law at ARTICLE 19 for twelve years. He has provided peak-level expertise, including in the area of legal drafting, on these rights to a wide range of actors including the World Bank, UNESCO, UNDP, Council of Europe, OSCE, ABU and various other intergovernmental bodies, as well as numerous governments and NGOs in countries all over the world. Before joining ARTICLE 19, he worked as a senior human rights consultant with Oxfam Canada and as a human rights policy analyst at the Canadian International Development Agency. He has published extensively on a range of freedom of expression, right to information, communication rights and refugee issues, including comparative legal and analytical studies on public service broadcasting, community broadcasting, privacy, the right to information and regulation of broadcasting.

MICHAEL O'FLAHERTY is Established Professor of Human Rights Law and Director of the Irish Centre for Human Rights, National University of Ireland, Galway. Prior to that Professor O'Flaherty was Chief

Commissioner of the Northern Ireland Human Rights Commission and Professor of Applied Human Rights and Co-director of the Human Rights Centre, University of Nottingham. He is a former member (2004–12) and Vice-chairperson of the UNHRC. He read law at University College Dublin (BCL), theology and philosophy at the Gregorian University, Rome (B.Ph., STB), international relations at the University of Amsterdam (MA, MPhil.) and is a Solicitor of the Irish Courts. From 2009–11 he was Rapporteur for development of the UN Human Rights Committee's General Comment No. 34 on Article 19 ICCPR. O'Flaherty initiated the Dublin Process on the Strengthening of the UN Human Rights Treaty Body System (2009–11) and was rapporteur for its Dublin Outcome Document. He has led a number of other applied research projects, such as 'Consolidating the Profession: The Human Rights Field Officer' (2004–9), which generated the Guiding Principles for Human Rights Field Officers and the Statement of Ethical Commitments for Human Rights Officers. He was Rapporteur for the Yogyakarta Principles on the Application of Human Rights in Relation to Sexual Orientation and Gender Identity (2007). O'Flaherty was a member of the UN Expert Group on Human Rights Indicators and is a Fellow of the Royal Society of the Arts. He also advises many international and regional intergovernmental and NGOs and is a member of editorial boards of journals and advisory committees of human rights organizations worldwide.

SEJAL PARMAR (LLB (hons), LSE; Ph.D. Law, EUI, Florence) is Assistant Professor of Law, Central European University, Budapest. Before taking up her current position in 2012, Dr Parmar was Senior Legal Officer at ARTICLE 19, for over four and a half years. In that role she wrote numerous position papers, statements, analyses and amicus briefs and delivered oral presentations, statements and trainings to a broad range of intergovernmental, governmental and non-governmental audiences. Her work has focused on the relationship between freedom of expression and the right to information, on the one hand, and other rights (e.g., equality, freedom of religion) on the other. She has led ARTICLE 19's legal and policy work on UN human rights bodies' resolutions on 'defamation of religions', the interpretation of Article 20 ICCPR on incitement to hostility, discrimination and violence, domestic blasphemy and incitement laws, as well as advocacy of the Camden Principles on Freedom of Expression and Equality. She has also developed ARTICLE 19's policy positions on climate change, development and the right to health, and legal bans on the wearing of the full face veil. Parmar has also been a Visiting Lecturer in International Human Rights Law at Queen Mary, University of London. Her publications include articles on freedom of expression, the relationship between international and EU human rights law and the EU Charter of Fundamental Rights. She is currently a member of the Advisory Council of Advocates for International Development (A4ID).

SIR NIGEL RODLEY KBE is Professor of Law and Chair of the Human Rights Centre at the University of Essex, current Chairperson of the United Nations Human Rights Committee and President of the International Commission of Jurists. Rodley obtained an LLB from the University of Leeds (1963), an LLM from Columbia University (1965), an LLM from New York University (1970) and a Ph.D. from the University of Essex (1993). In 1973, Rodley became the first Legal Adviser of the International Secretariat of Amnesty International, a position he held until 1990; during the same period he taught public international law at the London School of Economics and Political Science. In 1990 he was appointed Reader in Law at the University of Essex, becoming Professor of Law in 1994. He was Dean of the School of Law (1992–5) and has been Chair of the Human Rights Centre since 2004. Rodley served as UN Special Rapporteur on torture (1993–2001). Since 2001 he has been a member of the UN Human Rights Committee (Vice-Chair 2003–4; 2009–10). He was elected a Commissioner of the International Commission of Jurists in 2003 and is a member of Council of its British Branch, JUSTICE. He is a Patron of Freedom from Torture (the Medical Foundation for the Care of Victims of Torture) and REDRESS. Rodley was awarded a KBE in the 1998/99 New Year's Honours List, 'for services to human rights and international law'. He received an honorary LLD from Dalhousie University in 2000 and in 2005 received (jointly with Professor Theodoor Van Boven and Judge Pieter Kooijmans) the American Society of International Law's Goler T. Butcher medal for 'outstanding contributions to . . . international human rights law'.

MARTIN SCHEININ is Professor of Public International Law at the European University Institute in Florence (2008–). Prior to that (1998–2008), he was Armfelt Professor of Constitutional and International Law, and Director of the Institute for Human Rights, Åbo Akademi University, Finland. He served as a member of the UNHRC from 1997–2004 and was the first UN Special Rapporteur on the protection and promotion of human rights and fundamental freedoms while countering terrorism (2005–11). He was also the Chairperson of the International Law Association Committee on Human Rights Law and Practice (1997–2008).

LUCY SMITH † Dr Juris, Professor Emeritus, University of Oslo, was a university lecturer at the Law Faculty, University of Oslo, from 1965, full professor from 1987, and President (Rector) of the University (1993–2000). Her primary field of research was child rights issues, on which she was an active writer and spokesperson since the 1970s, and especially since her doctoral treatise in 1980. Returning to the Law Faculty in 2000, she became Chair of the Board of the Norwegian Center on Human Rights. She continued her engagement in university governance on the international level as Vice-President of the European University Association for several years. She was a member of the UN Committee on the Rights of the Child (2003–9). After retiring as a professor in 2005, she retained her office at the University, and continued her writing and tutoring on child rights. She has published books and articles (mainly in Norwegian) on child law, company law and contract law, and has lectured in many universities around the world. Smith was a member of the Norwegian Academy of Science and Letters and an honorary doctor of Copenhagen, Uppsala and Sungkyankwan Universities.

PATRICK THORNBERRY is Emeritus Professor of International Law at Keele University, and currently a Visiting Fellow and tutor at Kellogg College, University of Oxford. He was a member of the UN Committee on CERD (2001–14). Professor Thornberry is a former Chairman of Minority Rights Group International. His many publications in the field of international human rights law evidence a particular focus on the rights of minorities and indigenous peoples at global and European levels, as well as on issues of racial discrimination, self-determination and autonomy. Professor Thornberry's interests are aptly summarized in the title of the Festschrift – Minorities, Peoples and Self-determination – presented to him in 2005 by an international group of colleagues. In 2006 he was awarded a CMG (Companion of St Michael and St George) by HM Queen Elizabeth II for services to international human rights. Professor Thornberry chaired the UN Forum on Minority Issues in 2014 which was dedicated to the theme of preventing and addressing violence and atrocity crimes against minorities.

ELIZA VARNEY is a senior lecturer in Law at Keele University. Dr Varney completed her LLB at the University of Hull (1999), her LLM in Romania (2001) and her Ph.D. at the University of Hull (2006). Varney's research is in disability equality, focusing on access to goods and services (particularly information and communication technologies) and on the implementation of the CRPD. She is a member of the Socio-Legal Studies Association, a member of the Society of Legal Scholars and a Fellow of the Higher Education Academy.

AIDAN WHITE is the Director of the Ethical Journalism Network, based in London where he is currently working with the Media Diversity Institute. He has worked as a journalist in the UK with newspapers including the *Guardian* and the *Financial Times* and is a former member of the British Press Council. From 1987 to 2011 he was the General Secretary of the International Federation of Journalists based in Brussels. He is a founder of the International Freedom of Expression exchange and the International News Safety institute.

# FOREWORD

The United Nations Charter speaks at several points of the objective of promoting 'human rights and fundamental freedoms', notably Articles 1(3), 55, 62(2) and 76. We do not often stop to consider in what the human rights sub-group of 'fundamental freedoms' consists. Without necessarily intending to be comprehensive, I take them to include as a hard core the freedom of opinion and expression and the intimately related freedoms of assembly and association. As observed by Prince Zeid Ra'ad Al Hussein, the new United Nations High Commissioner for Human Rights, in his opening statement to the Human Rights Council's 27th Session, on 8 September 2014, that was also his first formal public address: 'Freedoms of expression, association and peaceful assembly are rights that enable people to share ideas, form new thinking, and join together with others to claim their rights.'

In many countries, these freedoms can be and are taken for granted; often to the point of insistent focus on the problems associated with their exercise, rather than on the importance of their content. They are not, of course, taken for granted in societies or situations in which they are especially needed and may be under challenge. The challenges may come from the law, or from action outside the law. One has only to think of the fate of all too many journalists whose legitimate professional activities brought them harassment, detention, torture or even death at the hands of those who feel threatened by truth. They know the meaning of freedom of expression.

Kevin Boyle first came to prominence as a leader of the Northern Ireland Civil Rights Association early in the 'troubles'. His activities were not without risk, at least from unofficial sectors committed to retaining the discriminatory 'legal' privileges that the majority population of that province enjoyed. Kevin knew the importance of the fundamental freedoms at first-hand. So, Kevin was the colleague who would introduce post-graduate human rights students at the University of Essex to the issue of freedom of expression. But he did not have a simplistic view of the issue. Another key interest of his was the question of non-discrimination, a principle that could come into apparent conflict with freedom of speech.

It was a dichotomy he thrived on, one of his books being about hate speech.[1] One of his leading cases was the *Jersild* case[2] before the European Court of Human Rights, which ensured that the law distinguished between prohibited racist speech and the need for honest broadcast news.

Kevin was one of the prime movers behind the conference that formed the basis for the chapters of this book. It was a stimulating conference, of which I had the pleasure and privilege of chairing a session. It was well timed, as the UN Human Rights Committee was engaged in drafting a 'General Comment' on Article 19 of the International Covenant on Civil and Political Rights (freedoms of opinion and expression). It provided stimulating material for this particular Human Rights Committee member's contributions to the Committee's discussions.

It is thus appropriate that one of the book's chapters deals centrally with what became General Comment No. 34 (2011). It follows a masterly introduction to the field of the UN's involvement with freedom of expression. These chapters set the scene for a broad-ranging canvassing of the complexities of the scope and nature of the right to freedom of expression and information.

It is sad that Kevin did not live to see the appearance of this book. It could not be more fitting that it be dedicated to him.

*Sir Nigel Rodley*
*Professor of Law and Chair of the Human Rights Centre,*
*University of Essex*
*Chair, UN Human Rights Committee*
*September 2014*

1 S. Coliver (ed.), with K. Boyle and F. D'Souza (contributing eds.), *Striking a Balance: Hate Speech, Freedom of Expression and Non-discrimination* (United Kingdom: ARTICLE 19/ University of Essex, 1992).

2 *Jersild* v. *Denmark*, Judgment of the European Court of Human Rights of 23 September 1994, Series A no. 298.

# SELECTED ABBREVIATIONS AND ACRONYMS

| | |
|---|---|
| ACHPR | African Commission on Human and Peoples' Rights |
| ACHR | American Convention on Human Rights |
| CEDAW | Convention on the Elimination of All Forms of Discrimination against Women |
| CERD | [UN] Committee on the Elimination of Racial Discrimination |
| CESCR | [UN] Committee on Economic, Social and Cultural Rights |
| CM | [CoE] Committee of Ministers |
| CoE | Council of Europe |
| COs | Concluding Observations |
| CRC | Convention on the Rights of the Child |
| CRPD | Convention on the Rights of Persons with Disabilities |
| ECHR | European Convention on Human Rights |
| ECommHR | European Commission of Human Rights |
| ECtHR | European Court of Human Rights |
| ECOSOC | [UN] Economic and Social Council |
| EU | European Union |
| GC | General Comment |
| GR | General Recommendation |
| HRC | [UN] Human Rights Committee |
| HR Council | [UN] Human Rights Council |
| IACHR | Inter-American Commission on Human Rights |
| IACtHR | Inter-American Court of Human Rights |
| ICANN | Internet Corporation for Assigned Names and Numbers |
| ICCPR | International Covenant on Civil and Political Rights |
| ICERD | International Convention on the Elimination of All Forms of Racial Discrimination |
| ICESCR | International Covenant on Economic, Social and Cultural Rights |
| ICTs | information and communication technologies |
| IGO | Intergovernmental organization |
| IPDC | [UNESCO] International Programme for the Development of Communication |
| ITU | International Telecommunication Union |

| | |
|---|---|
| NGO | non-governmental organization |
| NWICO | New World Information and Communication Order |
| OAS | Organization of American States |
| OHCHR | Office of the [UN] High Commissioner for Human Rights |
| OIC | Organisation of Islamic Cooperation |
| OSCE | Organisation for Security and Co-operation in Europe |
| RFOM | [OSCE] Representative on Freedom of the Media |
| UDHR | Universal Declaration of Human Rights |
| UN | United Nations |
| UNCHR | United Nations Commission on Human Rights |
| UNGA | United Nations General Assembly |
| UNESCO | United Nations Educational, Scientific and Cultural Organization |
| WIPO | World Intellectual Property Organization |
| WSIS | World Summit on the Information Society |

# ACKNOWLEDGEMENTS

This edited collection is the culmination of a broader, identically-titled research project, initiated by the editors and the late Prof. Kevin Boyle, to whom this book is dedicated. The editors would like to express their gratitude for the generous financial support for the project provided by: the Sigrid Rausing Trust; the Dutch Ministry of the Interior and Kingdom Relations (Constitutional and Legislative Affairs); the Royal Netherlands Academy of Arts & Sciences (KNAW); the Faculty of Law, University of Amsterdam, and the University of Essex. The project was managed very efficiently by the office managers of the three collaborating institutions, Anja Dobbelsteen, Martine van Trigt and Anne Slowgrove. Valuable research assistance for the initial phase of the project was provided by Chris Burnett, Stefan Kulk, Mirjam Streng and Celine Vossen. The editors would also like to thank David Goldberg for generously providing a wealth of historical UN documents and references.

In the editorial phase, valuable assistance was provided by Valeria Boshnakova, Denise van Schie and, in particular, Mathijs Meutgeert, who very patiently converted most of the book's chapters into house style. The editors are very grateful to Elizabeth Spicer, Sarah Green and Jessica Murphy at Cambridge University Press for their commitment to this book and their efficiency in overseeing the production process.

Thanks are also due to Anouschka Boswijk for designing the cover image, *Das Ungreifbare*, and to Kylie Sayer at the Human Rights Centre, University of Essex, for helping to procure a suitable photo of Kevin Boyle.

Michael O'Flaherty's chapter in this volume was previously published as: 'Freedom of Expression: Article 19 of the International Covenant on Civil and Political Rights and the Human Rights Committee's General Comment No 34', 12 *Human Rights Law Review* (No. 4, 2012), 627–654. The editors gratefully acknowledge Oxford University Press' permission to republish the article in revised form in this volume.

# 1

## The development of freedom of expression and information within the UN: leaps and bounds or fits and starts?

TARLACH MCGONAGLE

### 1 Introduction

This chapter tells the story of how the rights to freedom of expression and information have been shaped by the United Nations' (UN) institutional dynamics over the years. It is an abridged version of the story because it does not purport to offer a full institutional history of those rights – a version which would require meticulous analysis of the workings of various committees over a protracted period of time. Instead, the chapter gives an account of how the growth of the rights to freedom of expression and information has been both stimulated and stymied by different factors in the particular institutional context of the UN. It traces the broad contours of the two rights by connecting the largest conceptual, normative, historical and institutional dots. This sketching exercise sets out the parameters not only of the present chapter, but of the book as a whole.

The chapter opens with a brief exploration of the contiguous nature of the rights to freedom of expression and information. This necessarily involves reflection on the instrumental role that the media and new communications technologies can play in the realization of both rights in practice. The remainder of the chapter has an overtly institutional focus. Its next three substantive sections correspond to three broad – roughly chronological, but occasionally overlapping – phases in the development of freedom of expression and information at the UN. Each period is denoted by its key features or aspirations: trailblazing, consolidation and expansion, and the quest for coherence and consistency. Various thematic challenges have presented themselves during these periods, a number of which are woven into the chapter's narrative. Finally, after offering some substantive conclusions, the chapter will explain the objectives and structure of the book as a whole.

As suggested by the chapter's title, the development of the rights to freedom of expression and information has had a chequered history within the UN. Bold rhetoric characterized the UN's initial approach to the protection of the rights, but the promise of that rhetoric was soon thwarted by the escalation of Cold War politics. The enshrinement of the rights, first in Article 19 of the Universal Declaration of Human Rights (UDHR or Universal Declaration) and then in Article 19 of the International Covenant on Civil and Political Rights (ICCPR), provided hard-and-fast bases for the later consolidation and expansion of the right. Relevant provisions in subsequent treaties have tended to replicate or build on Article 19, ICCPR, for instance, by applying its core principles to specific groups or thematic concerns (e.g., the rights of children and persons with disabilities).

As well as expanding the scope of the rights to freedom of expression and information, later treaties have also helped to ensure that the rights are interpreted in an evolutionary manner that reflects societal and technological developments. In the same vein, the Human Rights Committee's General Comment No. 34 on Article 19, ICCPR,[1] adopted in 2011 – nearly thirty years after its previous General Comment on the same article – seeks to provide a comprehensive, coherent and modern interpretation of the scope and content of these rights. General Recommendation No. 35 on racist hate speech, adopted by the Committee on the Elimination of Racial Discrimination (CERD) in 2013, has a similar purpose and potential in respect of relevant provisions of the International Convention on the Elimination of All Forms of Racial Discrimination (ICERD).

Besides treaty law, various other institutional forces contribute on an ongoing basis to the development of these rights. The UN Educational, Scientific and Cultural Organization (UNESCO, a specialized agency of the UN) and the UN Special Rapporteur on the promotion and protection of the right to freedom of opinion and expression (a specialized mandate) are good examples of such institutional forces.

## 2 Freedom of expression and information: contiguous rights

### *2.1 Conceptual considerations*

Circumspection is required when describing the relationship between the rights to freedom of expression and information. Their relationship is

[1] HRC, General Comment No. 34: Article 19 (Freedoms of opinion and expression), UN Doc. CCPR/C/GC/34, 12 September 2011.

contiguous and complicated; logical and paradoxical. It is characterized by mutual dependencies. Freedom of expression and information contribute to the opinion-forming process in different ways. Information is the basis for expression that seeks to communicate with and persuade others, as well as for participation in public affairs. In that sense, information can be seen as antecedent to expression. However, expression can also produce and disseminate information, which suggests a more complex and symbiotic relationship. The availability and accessibility of information are prerequisites for any well-functioning democratic society. The most commonly advanced rationales for freedom of expression suggest, if only implicitly, that freedom of information is subsumed in freedom of expression. Normative articulations of the right to freedom of expression similarly tend to style it as a compound right, comprising the rights to freedom of opinion, and to seek, receive and impart information and ideas.

Theoretical justifications for the protection of freedom of expression are numerous, rich and varied.[2] Each of the theories has 'explanatory power' and 'serious weaknesses' and there is a 'synergy among the various explanations for freedom of expression that is lost when the discussion deals with the strengths and weaknesses of a single theory'.[3] It therefore makes sense not to seek to ground freedom of expression in any 'unitary principle'[4] but to be cognizant of the 'full panoply of justifications'.[5] Those justifications tend to style freedom of expression as a vital vector for the advancement of individual autonomy or self-fulfilment, or for the advancement of democratic practices or societal interests. The main rationales for freedom of expression could be briefly summarized as: self-fulfilment/individual autonomy; the advancement of knowledge/discovery of truth/avoidance of error; effective participation in democratic society; self-government; distrust of government/slippery

[2] See generally: E. Barendt, *Freedom of Speech*, 2nd edn (Oxford University Press, 2005); F. Schauer, *Free Speech: A Philosophical Enquiry* (Cambridge University Press, 1982); W. Sadurski, *Freedom of Speech and Its Limits* (Dordrecht/Boston/London: Kluwer Academic, 1999); T. M. Scanlon, 'A Theory of Freedom of Expression', in T. M. Scanlon, *The Difficulty of Tolerance* (Cambridge University Press, 2003), 6–25; T. I. Emerson, *Toward a General Theory of the First Amendment* (New York: Random House, 1966).

[3] L. A. Powe, Jr., *The Fourth Estate and the Constitution: Freedom of the Press in America* (University of California Press, 1991), 240.

[4] F. Schauer, 'Free Speech and the Argument from Democracy', in J. R. Pennock and J. W. Chapman (eds.), *Liberal Democracy: Nomos XXV* (New York University Press, 1983), 242. See also, Schauer, *Free Speech*, 14.

[5] Powe, *Fourth Estate*, 240.

slope arguments. Other justifications include: societal stability and progress; tolerance and understanding/conflict prevention or resolution, and the enablement of other human rights.

Any analysis of the rights to freedom of expression and information would be incomplete without due consideration of the position, role and freedom of the media/press and other communication and information technologies. The media play a crucial instrumental role in the realization of the right to freedom of expression. In practice, information and ideas are circulated widely by the media and debate is conducted extensively in the media. By virtue of their reach, speed, influence and impact, more often than not, the media are the most effective means of receiving, imparting and seeking information and ideas. But the media are much more than just sheets of typed paper or 'wires and lights in a box';[6] they select, push, frame and manage (editorial) content. These are all complementary roles that generate considerable power and influence for the media in society. Thus, the media (as traditionally understood) have come to be regarded as 'an essential dimension of contemporary experience'[7] and as 'the central *institution* of a democratic public sphere'.[8]

The media's importance stems from both their role as society's public watchdog or the Fourth Estate, monitoring and checking misuse and abuse of power by the State and other powerful forces in society. It also stems from the media's ability to create forums in which democratic deliberation and debate on matters of public interest can take place. This can be termed participation *through* the media. Another important dimension to participation (albeit one that is less widely appreciated) is participation *in* the media, i.e., in media decision-making structures and processes. The distinction between participation in and through the media is important,[9] particularly for disadvantaged or disenfranchised groups in society. Participation in the media implies 'participation in the production of media output (content-related participation) and in media

[6] E. R. Murrow, 'Wires and lights in a box' speech, Radio Television News Directors Association Convention, Chicago, 15 October 1958, www.rtdna.org/content/edward_r_murrow_s_1958_wires_lights_in_a_box_speech#.U6ljALRRaXg (last visited 23 June 2014).

[7] R. Silverstone, *Why Study the Media?* (London: Sage, 1999), 1. See also, P. Dahlgren, *Television and the Public Sphere: Citizenship, Democracy and the Media* (London: Sage, 1995), 155.

[8] (emphasis per original). C. E. Baker, 'Viewpoint Diversity and Media Ownership', *Federal Communications Law Journal* 60(3) (2009), 654.

[9] N. Carpentier, *Media and Participation: A Site of Ideological–Democratic Struggle* (Bristol/Chicago: Intellect, 2011), 66–70.

organizational decision-making (structural participation)', which enhances the potential for members of different groups in society to influence how they are represented in the media.[10] Self-representation and empowerment are strengthened through participation in the media.

Advances in information and communications technologies have transformed the media environment of the past and they clearly have far-reaching consequences for how information and ideas are disseminated and processed. The internet holds unprecedented potential for multidirectional communicative activity: unlike traditional media, it entails relatively low entry barriers. The participatory architecture of Web 2.0 is particularly conducive to sharing information and ideas and participating in public debate. Whereas in the past it was necessary to negotiate one's way through the institutionalized media in order to get one's message to the masses, this is no longer the case. There is reduced dependence on traditional points of mediation and anyone can, in principle, set up a website or communicate via social media. While there are no guarantees that an individual's message will actually reach wide audiences, the capacity to communicate on such a scale clearly does now exist.

Given the interactive and many-to-many character of social media,[11] it is difficult to position them in a traditional institutional or institutionalized media setting; rather, they operate around existing institutionalized media. In different ways, they complement, enhance, compete with, challenge and even disrupt traditional media. Besides social media, other Internet-based actors, e.g., search engines, also determine the shape of freedom of expression and information today. The media are therefore no longer the main moderators of public debate or the main gatekeepers of the information highways and byways. The complexity of the evolving media, communication and information ecosystem poses a gamut of new regulatory dilemmas.[12] It also calls for a thorough reappraisal of traditional understandings of the rights to freedom of expression and information in order to ensure their optimal application in the evolving ecosystem.

[10] *Ibid.*, 68.

[11] See generally, E. Siapera, *Understanding New Media* (Los Angeles, CA: Sage, 2012) and C. Fuchs, *Social Media: A Critical Introduction* (London: Sage, 2014).

[12] See generally, K. Jakubowicz, *A New Notion of Media?: Media and Media-Like Content and Activities on New Communications Services* (Strasbourg: Council of Europe, April 2009).

### 2.2 *Freedom of expression and information in an emergent institutional framework*

These conceptual and terminological considerations, conflations and confusions have been centrally relevant to the UN's engagement with the rights to freedom of expression and information. Indeed, they predate it: in his famous 'Four Freedoms' State of the Union address in 1941, Franklin Delano Roosevelt looked forward to 'a world founded upon four essential human freedoms': freedom of speech and expression, freedom of worship, freedom from want and freedom from fear.[13] The Four Freedoms later had a palpable influence on the preamble of the Universal Declaration of Human Rights. It has been reported that Roosevelt, while thinking through these freedoms in closed circles before delivering his famous address, identified freedom of information as a fifth freedom, distinguishing between 'freedom of knowledge, freedom of information' and 'freedom to express oneself'.[14] This could suggest that Roosevelt saw both the commonalities and distinctions of both rights and was trying to figure out whether it would be best to calibrate them as an integrated right or as separate rights.

Writing in 1953, Salvador P. López – then UN rapporteur on freedom of information, explained that the *term*, '"freedom of information" is a relatively new one', while the *concept* 'is old, being little more than the aggregate of the more familiar antecedent principles of freedom of thought, freedom of expression and freedom of the Press'.[15] On such a reading, 'freedom of information' is taken to cover a cluster of related freedoms.

Over the years, the two terms have not been used entirely consistently across the UN. The term, freedom of information, was initially in vogue and it was taken to cover freedom of expression, before that approach was inverted so that freedom of expression (covering freedom of information), became the dominant phrase. The adoption of the Universal Declaration of Human Rights appears to have been the major catalyst for this shift in terminological preferences. Freedom of expression remains the conventionally used term today and its dominance is attested to by its

[13] F. D. Roosevelt, 'The four freedoms', State of the Union Message, 6 January 1941.

[14] J. H. Burgers, 'The Road to San Francisco: The Revival of the Human Rights Idea in the Twentieth Century', *Human Rights Quarterly* 14 (1992), 468–9.

[15] S. P. López, *Freedom of Information*, Report by the Rapporteur on Freedom of Information, UN ECOSOC, Official Records, 16th Session, Supp. No. 12 (New York: United Nations, 1953), 2.

prevalence in the texts of relevant international human rights treaties. Freedom of information tends to be subsumed into a more capacious understanding of freedom of expression. Nevertheless, 'freedom of information' has since acquired the autonomous meaning of 'freedom of access to information' and has itself become a conventionally used term in its own right.[16]

## 3 Trailblazing

### *3.1 Towards a Universal Declaration of Human Rights*

The architects of the post-war international order were charged with a most daunting task. They had to overcome their fear of the past and create robust institutions that would embrace the future. They had to write bold texts that would provide universal guarantees of a panoply of human rights for everyone without distinction everywhere. It was significant that references to universal human rights were included in the Charter of the United Nations.[17] The inclusion of such references constituted authoritative grounding for the further development of human rights, even if the Charter 'did not say what those rights may be, and no one knew whether any rights really could be said to be universal, in the sense of being acceptable to all nations and peoples, including those not yet represented' in the UN.[18] It is also noteworthy that the potential of the human rights provisions is trammelled by the provisions for the protection of national sovereignty.[19] These observations have led to the Charter's human rights provisions being called 'a glimmering thread in a web of power and interest'.[20]

That thread was promptly picked up during the drafting of the Universal Declaration of Human Rights. The right to freedom of expression posed particularly acute challenges. With long and venerable traditions in civilizations across the world, the right has also been persistently honoured in the breach. There was no real blueprint for its affirmation, at least not at the universal level. Given the tabula rasa nature of the drafting exercise, the drafters sought inspiration from a wide range of

[16] See generally, M. McDonagh, 'The Right to Information in International Human Rights Law', *Human Rights Law Review* 13:1 (2013), 25–55.

[17] See, for example, Articles 1, 13, 55 (*juncto* 56), 62 and 68.

[18] M. A. Glendon, *A World Made New: Eleanor Roosevelt and the Universal Declaration of Human Rights* (New York: Random House, 2001), 19.

[19] *Ibid.* [20] *Ibid.*

legal, political, religious and philosophical sources. They looked at international precedents – such as they were[21] – as well as practices from the national level. They needed to formulate a provision that would do justice to the differentiation inherent in prevalent understandings of what the right entails, yet provide a textual basis for its consistent interpretation and effective realization in practice.

In 1948 the UN General Assembly proclaimed the Universal Declaration of Human Rights as 'a common standard of achievement for all peoples and all nations'. The very idea of a universal declaration of human rights was tremendously ambitious and ground-breaking, but so, too, was its content. Some of the drafters, like Eleanor Roosevelt, harboured the hope that it 'may well become the international Magna Carta of all men everywhere'.[22] Yet, its ambition was modest in other respects, creating moral obligations, not legal ones. It is declaratory and exhortatory in character and sought to contribute to the bigger project of a full-blown international bill of human rights. Although the Universal Declaration does not purport to be legally binding, the majority of its provisions have come to acquire legally binding status through customary international law. In that sense its actual impact has surpassed its original, formal ambition.

Article 19 of the Universal Declaration is probably the best-known free expression provision in any international instrument and it is certainly the firmest foundation stone in the UN's protection of freedom of expression. It sets out the right to freedom of expression as follows:

> Everyone has the right to freedom of opinion and expression; this right includes freedom to hold opinions without interference and to seek, receive and impart information and ideas through any media and regardless of frontiers.

At first glance, it appears to be unequivocal and to broker no exceptions or restrictions. Such a reading of the provision would be erroneous, however. The Declaration's 'integrated articles' should not be read as a

[21] For a succinct overview of 'Freedom of Information prior to the United Nations', see López, *Freedom of Information*, 4–6; K. Nordenstreng and T. Seppä, 'The League of Nations and mass media: the rediscovery of a forgotten story', Paper presented at the 15th Conference of the International Association for Mass Communication Research (IAMCR), Section of International Communication session 'Communication and Peace; The Role of the Media in International Relations', New Delhi, 27 August 1986.

[22] Cited in Glendon, *World Made New*, 166 and in J. P. Humphrey, *Human Rights & the United Nations: A Great Adventure* (New York: Transnational, 1984), 73.

'string of essentially separate guarantees'.[23] The drafters of the Universal Declaration deliberately opted to condense the notion of restrictions on rights in Articles 29 and 30, rather than repeat them in respect of each of the rights they govern. A general, catch-all limitations clause is structurally tidier, but it has nevertheless resulted in the limitations being almost hidden in Article 29(2).[24] This should not, however, be seen as downplaying their importance as they 'turn up in the front line in all the conventions and in the practice of their implementation'.[25] Articles 29 and 30 read as follows:

> Article 29
>
> 1. Everyone has duties to the community in which alone the free and full development of his personality is possible.
> 2. In the exercise of his rights and freedoms, everyone shall be subject only to such limitations as are determined by law solely for the purpose of securing due recognition and respect for the rights and freedoms of others and of meeting the just requirements of morality, public order and the general welfare in a democratic society.
> 3. These rights and freedoms may in no case be exercised contrary to the purposes and principles of the United Nations.
>
> Article 30
>
> Nothing in this Declaration may be interpreted as implying for any State, group or person any right to engage in any activity or to perform any act aimed at the destruction of any of the rights and freedoms set forth herein.

Article 30 is a prohibition of abuse of rights clause, designed to prevent any provisions in the Declaration from being invoked in a manner contrary to its letter or spirit. It has become typical for such 'safety-valve' clauses to be included in international human rights treaties.[26]

Besides these more general and sweeping restrictions, specific restrictions on the right to freedom of expression are also foreseen by the articles protecting other rights, e.g., privacy. The interplay between freedom of expression and privacy can, in practice, lead to limitations on either right. For instance, Article 12 of the Universal Declaration states:

[23] Glendon, *A World Made New* (2001), 239.

[24] T. Opsahl, 'Articles 29 and 30: The Other Side of the Coin', in A. Eide, G. Alfredsson, G. Melander, L. A. Rehof and A. Rosas, with the collaboration of T. Swinehart (eds.), *The Universal Declaration of Human Rights: A Commentary* (Norway: Scandinavian University Press, 1992), 459.

[25] *Ibid.*

[26] See, for example, Article 5, ICCPR and Article 5, ICESCR.

'No one shall be subjected to arbitrary interference with his privacy, family, home or correspondence, nor to attacks upon his honour and reputation. Everyone has the right to the protection of the law against such interference or attacks.' The latter sentence envisages situations in which the law could restrict the right to freedom of expression in order to protect individuals against attacks on their honour and reputation.

Similarly, Article 7 concerns equality before the law, non-discrimination and equal protection of the law. The second of its two sentences reads: 'All are entitled to equal protection against any discrimination in violation of this Declaration and against any incitement to such discrimination.' The entitlement to protection against incitement to discrimination should be seen as another specified ground for the permissible limitation of the right to freedom of expression.

The UN's engagement with the rights to freedom of expression and information actually pre-dates the Universal Declaration of Human Rights. In one of its earliest Resolutions, the UN General Assembly demonstrated its awareness of the importance of information about its own activities; an early recognition of the importance of transparency for the fledgling organization.[27] In another of its earliest Resolutions, the UN General Assembly affirmed the fundamental importance of freedom of information, describing it as the 'touchstone' of all other human rights.[28] The main purpose of the Resolution was to call for an international conference on freedom of information, which was held in 1948.

### 3.2 *The UN Conference on Freedom of Information*

The UN Conference on Freedom of Information is one of the most neglected chapters in the history of the development of the rights to freedom of expression and information within the UN system. The concrete output of the Conference comprised: three draft conventions (most notably a draft Convention on Freedom of Information); draft articles on freedom of information for inclusion in the International Bill of Rights, and no fewer than forty-three Resolutions on different aspects

[27] UNGA Resolution 13(1), 'Organization of the Secretariat', 1 February 1946. Section II, entitled 'Information', opens with the acknowledgement that the UN 'cannot achieve its purposes unless the peoples of the world are fully informed of its aims and activities'. For commentary, see D. Goldberg, 'Freedom of information in the 21st century: bringing clarity to transparency', 14 *Communications Law* (2) (2009), 52.

[28] UNGA Resolution 59(1), 14 December 1946.

of freedom of information.[29] As such, the Conference was regarded at the time as 'a great success'[30] and afterwards as a 'high point in the United Nations discussions of freedom of information'.[31] However, the high expectations[32] raised by the Conference failed to be realized in its political aftermath. The Conference's centrepiece, the draft Convention on Freedom of Information, was never adopted and most of its resolutions failed to achieve any lasting impact. Its greatest impact remained behind the scenes, by supplying the drafters of the UDHR and the ICCPR with texts that were very close to the formulae ultimately adopted.

### 3.2.1 Draft conventions

The Conference proposed three draft conventions: a draft Convention on the Gathering and International Transmission of News; a draft Convention Concerning the Institution of an International Right of Correction, and a draft Convention on Freedom of Information. Of these, only one has been opened for signature and ratification: the Convention on the International Right of Correction. The Convention establishes the right of Contracting States to correct false information concerning their interests or, more accurately, have such information corrected. The Convention remains in force today, with seventeen States Parties, but is little known and ineffectual. The draft Convention on Gathering and International Transmission of News found itself in a curious legal limbo after its fate was formally tied to that of the draft Convention on Freedom of Information.[33]

There was a contextual cohesion to the design and drafting of the three conventions. While they were intended as an 'integral whole', it was clear that the draft Convention on Freedom of Information was the most important of the three – the 'keystone of the structure'.[34] It was composed of fourteen articles, but it was never adopted. Although the text of the draft Convention had been agreed upon in Geneva, it was not opened

[29] See further, Final Act, United Nations Conference on Freedom of Information, Geneva, Switzerland, 23 March–21 April 1948.

[30] Humphrey, *Human Rights & the United Nations*, 53.

[31] López, *Freedom of Information*, 11.

[32] Report, Seminar on Freedom of Information, Organized by the UN in cooperation with the Government of Italy, Rome, 7–20 April 1964, UN Doc. No. ST/TAO/HR/20, 16, para. 58.

[33] *Report on Rome Seminar on Freedom of Information* (1964), 17, para. 58; Humphrey, *Human Rights & the United Nations* (1984), 81–2 and 96; López, *Freedom of Information*, 15.

[34] López, *Freedom of Information*, 15.

for signature and ratification there and then. Instead, a political decision was made to refer the three draft conventions to the Economic and Social Council (ECOSOC) and to all governments invited to the Conference for 'study' and 'comments', respectively.[35] The ECOSOC would then 'examine' the draft conventions 'in light of' governmental comments before submitting them to the UN General Assembly for approval before opening them for signature by States. It was thought that such a step would lend greater 'prestige and authority' to the draft conventions.[36] However, in reality the subsequent delay gave opponents of the draft Convention on Freedom of Information (in particular) time to mobilize and Cold War politics then quickly froze any prospect of progress towards its adoption and ratification.[37]

During the Cold War, ideological battle lines were resolutely drawn around the nature and scope of the right to freedom of expression.[38] The role of the media proved particularly contentious, with the US and other Western States pitting themselves against the USSR and Eastern-bloc States on the question of whether 'the media of information have a primary responsibility to work positively for the cause of peace and to combat the "remnants of fascism"'.[39] The former trenchantly opposed the idea, whereas the latter staunchly supported it. More fundamentally, there were irreconcilable differences of opinion on the underlying question of the calibration of 'the rights and freedoms as against the duties and responsibilities involved in the concept of freedom of information.'[40] Those conceptual differences and enmities became increasingly politicized and polarized over time. This resulted in a protracted 'dialogue between the deaf',[41] characterized by 'continual finger-pointing by American and Soviet UN representatives at the respective weaknesses of their countries'.[42]

Besides the adversarial relationship between Eastern and Western coalitions of States, post-1945 'world communication politics' were also shaped by differences between Northern and Southern groups of States.[43] The emergence of 'a large number of new, post-colonial states' in Asia

[35] Resolution No. 43, United Nations Conference on Freedom of Information.
[36] Humphrey, *Human Rights*, 53. [37] *Ibid.*
[38] For excellent accounts and analyses, see López, *Freedom of Information*, 11–15ff. and H. Eek, *Freedom of Information as a Project of International Legislation: A Study of International Law in Making* (Uppsala: A.-B. Lundequistska Bokhandeln, 1953), 10–23.
[39] López, *Freedom of Information*, 11. [40] *Ibid.*
[41] Humphrey, *Human Rights & the United Nations*, 53.
[42] Glendon, *World Made New*, 36.
[43] C. J. Hamelink, *The Politics of World Communication* (London: Sage, 1994), 23.

and Africa led to the 'development of larger and more heterogeneous constituencies that began to bring an increasingly diversified set of claims to the diplomatic negotiations.'[44] Fledgling post-colonial States were particularly anxious to restructure the 'international provision of information': '[I]n their struggle to become sovereign entities they confronted, in addition to political and economic dependencies, the cultural legacy of former colonial relations.'[45]

The entrenched positions of the rival ideological camps also manifested themselves in institutional structures. Under the auspices of ECOSOC, two sub-commissions were set up, focusing on the prevention of discrimination and the protection of minorities, and on freedom of information and the press. The former was established at the urging of the Soviet bloc States and the latter, at the urging of Great Britain, France and the United States. The Sub-Commission on freedom of information and the press was disbanded by ECOSOC in 1951, a development which has been viewed as a major setback for the UN's overall efforts to protect and promote the right to freedom of expression.[46] Various attempts were made over the years to reinstitutionalize freedom of expression/information, through the instatement of a dedicated committee or rapporteur, but largely to little or no avail.[47]

Formally, the draft Convention on Freedom of Information remained a recurrent item on the UN General Assembly's agenda for years to come, but in practice it was no longer prioritized. Sporadic interest was shown in the draft text over the years, but not enough to create the momentum needed to get the draft Convention off the ground. Ultimately, the draft Convention ceased to be even a formal agenda item in the UN General Assembly in the course of the 1970s.[48] The draft Convention arguably became a siren song for the drafters of the ICCPR, distracting them from their own text. Eager to achieve synergies with the pending Convention on Freedom of Information, they routinely tried to anticipate the draft Convention's likely approach and content.[49]

The Conference on Freedom of Information would appear to have generated some interest in contemporary legal scholarship, particularly

[44] *Ibid.*, 23–4. [45] *Ibid.*, 24. [46] Humphrey, *Human Rights & the United Nations*, 21.

[47] *Ibid.*, 56 and *Report on Rome Seminar*, 21–2, paras. 82–3.

[48] For details of this process, see T. McGonagle, *Minority Rights, Freedom of Expression and of the Media: Dynamics and Dilemmas* (Antwerp: Intersentia, 2011), 175–6.

[49] See generally, M. Bossuyt, *Guide to the 'Travaux Préparatoires' of the International Covenant on Civil and Political Rights* (Dordrecht: Martinus Nijhoff, 1987), 373–402.

in the United States,[50] where the Hutchins Commission's influential report, *A Free and Responsible Press*, was published in 1947.[51] Over the years, a number of extensive reports and studies on freedom of expression/information, some of which were conducted under the auspices of the UN, has led to intermittent revivals of interest in the Conference and the draft Convention on Freedom of Information. Those reports can be seen as mapping and pulse-taking exercises.[52] Typically, they would document and analyse the practice of freedom of expression at the international and national levels, inventorize problems and make recommendations.[53] However, like the Conference and draft Convention, they failed to achieve significant or lasting traction.

The abortive nature of the draft Convention has thus denied it the level of critical scrutiny to which it would have been subjected if it had been formally adopted. Study of the different drafts may therefore seem academic, sterile or fanciful. Yet, the different versions of the text reveal the pressing political priorities and hardening political positions of the times, many of which continue to resonate today. For instance, one of the 'necessary restrictions' on freedom of expression introduced by the UN General Assembly's further development of the draft text, concerned 'attacks on founders of religions'.[54] Had the draft Convention been adopted and entered into force, that provision would surely have proved dispositive for the controversy that followed the publication in 2005 by the Danish newspaper, *Jyllands-Posten*, of twelve cartoons of the Prophet Mohammed.[55]

[50] See, for example, C. Binder, 'Freedom of Information and the United Nations', *International Organization* 6(2) (May 1952), 210–26; E. D. Canham, 'International Freedom of Information', *Law & Contemp. Probs.* 14 (1949), 584–98; Z. Chafee, Jr., 'Legal Problems and Freedom of Information in the United Nations', *Law & Contemp. Probs.* 14 (1949), 545–83; J. B. Whitton, 'The United Nations Conference on Freedom of Information and the Movement against International Propaganda', *American Journal of International Law* 43(1) (Jan. 1949), 73–87.

[51] The ('Hutchins') Commission on Freedom of the Press, *A Free and Responsible Press* (University of Chicago Press, 1947).

[52] See, for example, Eek, *Freedom of Information*; López, *Freedom of Information*; *Report on Rome Seminar*.

[53] For example, the full, formal description of López's 1953 *Freedom of Information* report is: 'A report on contemporary problems and developments, with recommendations for practical action'.

[54] For details and discussion, see McGonagle, *Minority Rights*, 375ff.

[55] For commentary, see K. Boyle, 'The Danish Cartoons', *Netherlands Quarterly of Human Rights* 24(2) (2006), 185–91.

Furthermore, in the period following the Second World War, the 'phenomenon' or practice of radio-jamming (disrupting or preventing the reception of radio signals) directed at broadcasts emanating from rival States was common.[56] It was very much a feature of the Zeitgeist's (international) political preoccupation with harmful broadcasting, propaganda, false information and the right of correction. The determination to devise regulatory responses to the practice informed the deliberations at the Conference on Freedom of Information and prompted various General Assembly Resolutions over the years, as well as a wider debate on the legitimacy and effectiveness of 'information intervention' generally.[57] The radio-jamming debates of the past resonate strongly in the cyber-security debates of the present and many of the central legal questions remain *de rigueur* today.

### 3.2.2 International Bill of Rights

The Conference proposed a formula for the freedom of expression provision in the UDHR that was very close to the one ultimately adopted. The textual differences between the draft and adopted texts are negligible. For example, 'shall have' became 'has' and 'shall include' became 'includes'. In both cases, the modal auxiliary verb 'shall' was dropped in favour of the present tense, thereby swapping a sense of (future) compulsion for a sense of immediacy perhaps more fitting for a declaratory text like the UDHR. Furthermore, whereas the draft text referred to the right to 'freedom of thought and expression', the adopted text refers to 'freedom of opinion and expression'. The phrase 'by any means' in the Conference's formula eventually made way for 'through any media'.

The text proposed by the Conference for inclusion in the draft Covenant on Human Rights (later to become the ICCPR) did, however, differ in some significant regards from the adopted text. The text proposed by the Conference reads, in full:

> 1. Every person shall have the right to freedom of thought and the right to freedom of expression without interference by governmental action; these rights shall include freedom to hold opinions, to seek, receive and impart information and ideas, regardless of frontiers, either orally, by written or printed matter, in the form of art, or by legally operated visual or auditory devices.

[56] Hamelink, *Politics of World Communication*, 24, 27 and 137–9.

[57] *Ibid.* On 'information intervention', see J. F. Metzl, 'Information Intervention: When Switching Channels Isn't Enough', *Foreign Affairs* 76(6) (Nov./Dec. 1997), 15–20.

2. The right to freedom of expression carries with it duties and responsibilities and may, therefore, be subject to penalties, liabilities or restrictions clearly defined by law, but only with regard to:
   (a) Matters which must remain secret in the interests of national safety;
   (b) Expressions which incite persons to alter by violence the system of government;
   (c) Expressions which directly incite persons to commit criminal acts;
   (d) Expressions which are obscene;
   (e) Expressions injurious to the fair conduct of legal proceedings;
   (f) Infringements of literary or artistic rights;
   (g) Expressions about other persons natural or legal which defame their reputations or are otherwise injurious to them without benefiting the public;
   (h) The systematic diffusion of deliberately false or distorted reports which undermine friendly relations between peoples and States;

A State may establish on reasonable terms a right of reply or a similar corrective remedy.

3. Measures shall be taken to promote the freedom of information through the elimination of political, economic, technical and other obstacles which are likely to hinder the free flow of information.
4. Nothing in this article shall be deemed to affect the right of any State to control the entry of persons into its territory or the period of their residence therein.

The differences between the proposed and adopted texts can be grouped into three main categories: overall approach; the presence of additional components in the draft text, and differences of conceptual and terminological emphasis. The greatest difference in the overall approach of the respective texts concerns legitimate restrictions on the right. The draft text *enumerates* a list of 'penalties, liabilities or restrictions' in detailed fashion, whereas the adopted text (see below) *describes* the range of permissible 'restrictions' in a much more succinct fashion.

This overall approach in the draft text partly explains the presence of additional elements, besides the enumerated restrictions. Those elements include the provisions for States to: establish a right of reply or similar corrective remedy; promote freedom of information by eliminating obstacles, and control entry to and residence in their territories.

The different emphases concern, first, specifications in the draft text that were not retained in the adopted text, and second, specifications absent in the draft text, but subsequently introduced into the adopted text. Examples of the former include: 'without interference by governmental action' (as opposed to 'without interference' *tout court*); 'legally operated visual or auditory devices' (as opposed to the more open-ended formula, 'any other media of his choice'), and 'penalties, liabilities or restrictions' (as opposed to the less cumbersome phrase 'certain restrictions'). Examples of the latter include 'information and ideas *of all kinds*' (emphasis added) and '*special* duties and responsibilities' (emphasis added).

### 3.2.3 Resolutions

The forty-three Resolutions adopted by the UN Conference on Freedom of Information were grouped into six chapters, as summarized in the following overview:

| Chapter | Title | Resolutions | Main/significant focuses |
|---|---|---|---|
| I | General principles | 1–4 | Fundamental right to freedom of information; right of access to sources of information; diversity of sources, moral obligations, condemnation of propaganda; aims of friendship, understanding and peace; combating racial and national hatred and prejudice |
| II | Measures to facilitate the gathering and international transmission of information | 5–24 | Free movement and admission into foreign territories; possible definition of foreign correspondent; non-discriminatory access to news (sources and material); no censorship unless concerning military security; practical cooperation; development of news agencies; role of press and agencies in reporting on States' efforts to promote peace, etc. |
| III | Measures concerning the free publication and reception of information | 25–38 | Libel laws; media ownership and control; cost of radio sets and related taxation; technical needs of war-torn countries; teaching of journalism; international code and court of honour; guaranteeing independence and |

(*cont.*)

| Chapter | Title | Resolutions | Main/significant focuses |
|---|---|---|---|
| | | | economic security of news personnel |
| IV | Continuing machinery to promote the free flow of information | 39 | Terms of reference for Sub-Commission on Freedom of Information and of the Press |
| V | Miscellaneous | 40–41 | — |
| VI | Possible modes of action by means of which the recommendations of the Conference can best be put into effect | 42–43 | All documents passed by Conference referred to ECOSOC for 'study' Governments invited to comment on draft Conventions proposed by Conference |

The foregoing overview gives a flavour of the preoccupations of the period. It should be pointed out that most of the provisions concerned institutional or professional organizations, networks or individuals, e.g., the press and news agencies. The free flow of information and the mobility of information professionals across geopolitical boundaries was a point of tension as the free flow principle sat uneasily with contemporaneous sensitivities about individual States' sovereignty and security. It is noteworthy that such sensitivities have never really disappeared, just like other dominant issues highlighted in various resolutions: questions of media diversity/pluralism; concentration of media ownership; the chilling effect of libel laws; the desirability and feasibility of defining a 'journalist', etc.

Many of the resolutions pay attention to the material and procedural obstacles to the operation of foreign correspondents. There is also considerable attention for practical forms of cooperation between the press and agencies, which could enhance the free flow of information. Examples include the exchange and pooling of sources and resources, as well as various capacity-building measures.

It is interesting to note the recurrent provision for a right of reply in various resolutions and other texts adopted at the Conference. No such provision was ultimately included in the ICCPR or in any other subsequent UN treaty containing provisions on freedom of expression. Regional human rights treaties differ in their approaches. Such a provision has, for instance, been incorporated into the Inter-American Convention on Human Rights (Article 13) as an integral component of the right to freedom of expression. No such component is envisaged in the European Convention on Human Rights, although references have been made to the importance of the right of reply in the case-law of the European Court of Human Rights, and other standard-setting work by the Council of Europe promotes a right of reply.[58] The African Charter on Human and Peoples' Rights does not provide for a right of reply either.

## 4 Consolidation and expansion

Article 19 of the Universal Declaration of Human Rights has already been described above as the firmest foundation stone in the UN's system of protection for freedom of expression and information. But its purpose was never intended to be anything more than foundational. Article 19, ICCPR, is the veritable centrepiece of the edifice that has been constructed on Article 19 of the Universal Declaration. Owing to this status, Article 19, ICCPR, has come to exercise centrifugal influence on the development of the rights to freedom of expression and information, at two levels. First, it does so at the level of norm-setting, and second at the level of interpretation. Its value for, and influence on, other treaties (norm-setting) is explored in the next two subsections, while the importance and impact of the Human Rights Committee's General Comment No. 34 on the right to freedom of opinion and expression will be dealt with in section 5.

### *4.1 Consolidation*

Article 19 of the ICCPR fleshes out the key principles articulated in Article 19 of the UDHR and couples them to the duties, responsibilities and restrictions that shape the exercise of relevant rights in practice. It reads:

> 1. Everyone shall have the right to hold opinions without interference.
> 2. Everyone shall have the right to freedom of expression; this right shall include freedom to seek, receive and impart information and ideas of all kinds, regardless of frontiers, either orally, in writing or in print, in the form of art, or through any other media of his choice.

[58] For overviews, see T. McGonagle, *Minority Rights*, 540–5; R. Ó Fathaigh, 'The Recognition of a Right of Reply under the European Convention', *Journal of Media Law* 4(2) (2012), 322–32.

3. The exercise of the rights provided for in paragraph 2 of this article carries with it special duties and responsibilities. It may therefore be subject to certain restrictions, but these shall only be such as are provided by law and are necessary:
   (a) For respect of the rights or reputations of others;
   (b) For the protection of national security or of public order (ordre public), or of public health or morals.

A careful reading of the text of Article 19 reveals that the apparently unobtrusive reference to 'special duties and responsibilities' is its lynchpin. The importance of this phrase cannot be overstated: it links the broad enunciation of the right to freedom of expression with permissible restrictions on the right. It legitimates certain restrictions on the right, as long as they are provided by law and are necessary. Like the European Convention on Human Rights (Article 10), but unlike equivalent provisions in various other international human rights instruments, Article 19, ICCPR does not specify to whom the duties and responsibilities are directed. The UDHR refers to 'the community' (Article 29); the American Convention on Human Rights refers to 'family', 'community' and 'mankind' (Article 32) and the African Charter on Human and Peoples' Rights refers to 'family and society, the State and other legally recognized communities and the international community' (Article 27).

The drafters of the ICCPR considered freedom of expression to be both a 'precious heritage' and a 'dangerous instrument'[59] and this prompted them to include a reference to the duties and responsibilities that accompany the exercise of the right. The apprehension inherent in this vision of freedom of expression can be seen as both recognition of, and a response to, the particular power wielded by mass media and especially the misuse and abuse of that power. There was a perceived need for a '*corrigendum* to the wide recognition of the freedom' of expression.[60] Given the divisiveness of the question of the right to freedom of expression and accompanying duties and responsibilities,[61] it is quite remarkable that this phrase was included at the heart of Article 19 at all, never mind with the intensification assured by the adjective, 'special', which goes further than equivalent phrases in relevant provisions of regional human rights treaties such as the European

[59] *Ibid.*

[60] H. C. Krüger, 'Use of the Media to Promote and Infringe Human Rights', in K. E. Mahoney and P. Mahoney (eds.), *Human Rights in the Twenty-first Century* (The Hague: Kluwer, 1993), 743–56.

[61] Bossuyt, *Guide to the Travaux of the ICCPR*, 386–7.

Convention on Human Rights (Article 10). The insertion of the adjective, 'special', was deliberate, even if the precise motives for its insertion are unclear.[62] It seems plausible that the adjective 'special' was intended to insist on the specific nature of the power of the media.

In contradistinction to the text proposed by the UN Conference on Freedom of Information for inclusion in the ICCPR, the definitive text of Article 19 gives a very terse formulation of the permissible restrictions on the right to freedom of expression. It countenances only a narrow range of grounds for restricting the right (although arguably, 'rights of others' is quite open-ended, and terms like 'national security', 'public order' and 'public morals' are all susceptible to expansive interpretation). The drafters ultimately opted for a brief clause setting out general limitations to the right.[63] One argument against including a lengthy list of specific limitations was that no such catalogue of limitations 'could ever be sufficiently exhaustive to cover all situations'.[64] Another argument against a detailed list was that such a level of specificity would be too long and therefore inappropriate for inclusion in a general covenant on civil and political rights; such a list would be better suited for inclusion in a Convention on Freedom of Information[65] (the draft version of which was still in a state of political abeyance at the operative time).

Article 19, ICCPR must be read in conjunction with Article 20, ICCPR, which prohibits propaganda for war, as well as advocacy of different types of hatred 'that constitutes incitement to discrimination, hostility or violence'.[66] It is noteworthy that Article 20, unlike other substantive articles in the ICCPR, does not set out a right as such. Instead, it sets out further restrictions on other rights (most notably the right to freedom of expression), thereby prompting Nowak to label it 'an alien element in the system of the Covenant'.[67] It provides for further restrictions by explicitly requiring that certain conduct 'shall be prohibited by law'.[68] As such, Article 20 is widely regarded as providing

[62] *Ibid.* [63] For details of the deliberations during the drafting process, see *ibid.*, 387–8.
[64] *Ibid.*, 388. [65] *Ibid.*
[66] Article 20, ICCPR reads: '1. Any propaganda for war shall be prohibited by law. 2. Any advocacy of national, racial or religious hatred that constitutes incitement to discrimination, hostility or violence shall be prohibited by law.'
[67] M. Nowak, *U.N. Covenant on Civil and Political Rights – CCPR Commentary*, 2nd rev. edn (Kehl: Engel, 2005), 468.
[68] See further, D. McGoldrick, *The Human Rights Committee: Its Role in the Development of the International Covenant on Civil and Political Rights*, 2nd edn (Oxford: Clarendon, 1994), 480.

for the further restriction of the right to freedom of expression and has even been called 'practically a fourth paragraph to Article 19'.[69] Indeed, during the drafting of the ICCPR, the draft article that ultimately became Article 20 was realigned so that it would immediately follow Article 19, thereby emphasizing the close relationship of the two articles.[70] The Human Rights Committee's General Comment No. 34 clarifies that the two articles are 'compatible with and complement each other' and that the acts addressed in Article 20 are all subject to Article 19(3).[71] It also states firmly that restrictions on the right to freedom of expression should not 'go beyond what is permitted in [article 19] paragraph 3 or required under article 20'.[72]

Article 19, ICCPR has served both as a source of inspiration and as a model for many comparable provisions in other treaties. Sometimes, corresponding provisions in other treaties are almost carbon copies of Article 19, ICCPR, e.g., Article 13 of the Convention on the Rights of the Child (CRC)[73] and Article 13 of the International Convention on the Protection of the Rights of All Migrant Workers and Members of Their Families.[74] Indeed, it is worth mentioning in passing that the latter provision essentially merges Articles 19 and 20, ICCPR, into one article, which underscores the tightness of the relationship between those articles, as explained in the preceding paragraph.

### 4.2 *Expansion*

Besides the process of consolidation of the right to freedom of expression (in particular) and freedom of information within the UN treaty system, the right has also been undergoing a process of expansion. The latter

[69] K. J. Partsch, 'Freedom of Conscience and Expression, and Political Freedoms', in L. Henkin (ed.), *The International Bill of Rights: The Covenant on Civil and Political Rights* (New York: Columbia University Press, 1981), 227; Nowak, *CCPR Commentary*, 477; UN Human Rights Committee General Comment No. 11 – Prohibition of propaganda for war and inciting national, racial or religious hatred (Article 20), 29 July 1983 and General Comment No. 34. For more detailed discussion, see McGonagle, *Minority Rights*, 272–6.

[70] Article 26 of the Human Rights Commission's draft of 1954 had originally been positioned at the very end of the substantive provisions contained in the draft text. See further, Nowak, *CCPR Commentary*, 470; Bossuyt, *Guide to the ICCPR*, 398.

[71] UN HRC General Comment No. 34, para. 50.

[72] *Ibid.*, para. 49.

[73] Although Article 13, CRC omits references to the right to hold opinions without interference (cf. Article 19(1), ICCPR) and to the duties and responsibilities that go hand-in-hand with the exercise of the right to freedom of expression (cf. Article 19(3), ICCPR).

[74] UNGA Resolution 45/158 of 18 December 1990.

process has benefited from the former: the consolidation of the right facilitates the concerted exploration of its implications in specific thematic contexts and for specific groups. One obvious example of this is the ICCPR's sister covenant, the ICESCR. Two other pertinent examples are the CRC and the Convention on the Rights of Persons with Disabilities (CRPD), each of which contains discreet focuses on different aspects of the right to freedom of expression, tailored to the specific needs of their respective target groups of rights-holders.

Among the provisions of the ICESCR most readily associated with the right to freedom of expression, are Article 15 (the rights to take part in cultural life; to enjoy the benefits of scientific progress and its applications, and to benefit from the protection of the moral and material interests resulting from any scientific, literary or artistic production/authorship) and Article 13 (the right to education). However, as Yvonne Donders documents in Chapter 3 of this volume, informational aspects of the right to freedom of expression – as well as the more autonomous right of access to information – are also centrally implicated in the realization of a number of other economic, social and cultural rights, e.g., the right to an adequate standard of living (Article 11) and the right to health (Article 12). The central importance of accessibility of different types of information, as Donders also points out, is routinely recognized by the Committee on Economic, Social and Cultural Rights, e.g., in its General Comments.

Article 17, CRC, opens up a new dimension to the right to freedom of expression, by focusing specifically on the instrumental role of the media in providing particular types of content that are necessary or suitable for children. It reads:

> States Parties recognize the important function performed by the mass media and shall ensure that the child has access to information and material from a diversity of national and international sources, especially those aimed at the promotion of his or her social, spiritual and moral well-being and physical and mental health.
>
> To this end, States Parties shall:
>
> (a) Encourage the mass media to disseminate information and material of social and cultural benefit to the child and in accordance with the spirit of article 29;[75]
> (b) Encourage international co-operation in the production, exchange and dissemination of such information and material from a diversity of cultural, national and international sources;

75 [Editors' note] Article 29 concerns the direction of education of the child.

(c) Encourage the production and dissemination of children's books;
(d) Encourage the mass media to have particular regard to the linguistic needs of the child who belongs to a minority group or who is indigenous;
(e) Encourage the development of appropriate guidelines for the protection of the child from information and material injurious to his or her well-being, bearing in mind the provisions of articles 13 and 18.[76]

Thus, as explained in detail by Lucy Smith in Chapter 5 of this volume, Article 17 seeks to tread the fine line between the *freedom* of children to access diverse information and material (including online) and the *protection* they need from information and material that could harm them. The abundance and accessibility of both beneficial and harmful content online presents additional complexities for striking the right balance between these often contradictory priorities. One of the CRC's guiding principles – the best interests of the child – is instructive for this balancing act.

In the same vein, the CRPD also contains novel, detailed provisions on the right to freedom of expression and information which are attuned to present-day technological realities. For example, Article 9, CRPD, entitled 'Accessibility', calls on States Parties to the Convention to take appropriate measures, *inter alia*, to:

2(f) Promote other appropriate forms of assistance and support to persons with disabilities to ensure their access to information;
2(g) Promote access for persons with disabilities to new information and communications technologies and systems, including the Internet;
2(h) Promote the design, development, production and distribution of accessible information and communications technologies and systems at an early stage, so that these technologies and systems become accessible at minimum cost.

Article 21, CRPD, entitled 'Freedom of expression and opinion, and access to information', is even more detailed:

> States Parties shall take all appropriate measures to ensure that persons with disabilities can exercise the right to freedom of expression and opinion, including the freedom to seek, receive and impart information and ideas on an equal basis with others and through all forms of communication of their choice, as defined in article 2 of the present Convention, including by:

[76] [Editors' note] Article 13 concerns freedom of expression and Article 18 concerns parental responsibilities for the upbringing and development of the child.

(a) Providing information intended for the general public to persons with disabilities in accessible formats and technologies appropriate to different kinds of disabilities in a timely manner and without additional cost;
(b) Accepting and facilitating the use of sign languages, Braille, augmentative and alternative communication, and all other accessible means, modes and formats of communication of their choice by persons with disabilities in official interactions;
(c) Urging private entities that provide services to the general public, including through the Internet, to provide information and services in accessible and usable formats for persons with disabilities;
(d) Encouraging the mass media, including providers of information through the Internet, to make their services accessible to persons with disabilities;
(e) Recognizing and promoting the use of sign languages.

This provision is informed by the specific needs of persons with disabilities concerning their ability to enjoy the rights to freedom of expression and information, especially insofar as their enjoyment of those rights is predicated on, or facilitated by, communications technologies. It has been observed that:

> Where the exercise of a liberty depends upon technology, access to that technology largely determines the substantive liberty of the actor. Sometimes this is because the liberty in question cannot be enjoyed in any form without a general level of technology.[77]

These observations are particularly apposite for persons with disabilities. Article 21, CRPD points up the need for information and communications technology to be suited to the needs of persons with disabilities, otherwise their right to freedom of expression and information is unlikely to be effective in practice. In Chapter 6 of this volume, Eliza Varney provides a very detailed and nuanced examination of Article 21 and other provisions of the CRPD. She shows very convincingly that the letter and spirit of those provisions are crucially important for ensuring that persons with disabilities have full and equal access to information and are thereby able to participate effectively in public life.

Whereas the above treaties have led to an expansion of the scope of freedom of expression within their respective fields of application, other treaties have appeared to contribute to its contraction. For example, relevant provisions of ICERD (i.e., Articles 4 and 5), trammel the scope

[77] J. M. Balkin, 'Some Realism about Pluralism: Legal Realist Approaches to the First Amendment', *Duke Law Journal* 39(3) (1990), 375, 406.

of the right in order to prevent racial discrimination. As ICERD was adopted prior to the ICCPR, its Articles 4 and 5 draw on Article 19 of the UDHR (as opposed to Article 19, ICCPR). ICERD is widely – and correctly – perceived as an outlier among other international human rights treaties that contain provisions governing the relationship between freedom of expression and hate speech, insofar as Article 4, ICERD, creates more far-reaching obligations for States Parties than comparable provisions in other treaties. Article 4, ICERD, requires States to render several offences, including specific types of expression, *punishable* by law, whereas Article 20 of the ICCPR requires that a narrower range of types of expression be *prohibited* by law. The offences/types of expression set out in Article 4 are:

- all dissemination of ideas based on racial superiority;
- all dissemination of ideas based on racial hatred;
- incitement to racial discrimination;
- all acts of violence against any race or group of persons of another colour or ethnic origin;
- incitement to such acts;
- the provision of any assistance to racist activities, including the financing thereof.

States' obligations under Article 4 are to be discharged 'with due regard to the principles embodied in the Universal Declaration of Human Rights and the rights expressly set forth in article 5 of this Convention', including the right to freedom of expression. Had this 'due regard' clause not been so astutely inserted into Article 4's opening paragraph, most of the enumerated measures would have been deemed incompatible with the right to freedom of expression.[78] CERD's interpretation of Article 4 has been characterized by a traditional reluctance to engage in a detailed, contextualized way with freedom of expression issues,[79] but the adoption of General Recommendation No. 35 on racist hate speech shows a more sophisticated understanding of the dynamics of freedom of expression and the role of the media and Internet.[80]

The foregoing brief panorama of UN treaty provisions on the rights to freedom of expression and information reveals that each of the relevant

[78] For further analysis, see McGonagle, *Minority Rights*, 280–90.

[79] See further, P. Thornberry, 'Confronting Racial Discrimination: A CERD Perspective', *Human Rights Law Review* 5(2) (2005), 239–69.

[80] See further, section 5.1.2, and in particular, Patrick Thornberry in this book (Chapter 4).

treaties tends to emphasize different aspects of the rights. It also reveals that Article 19 ICCPR, is the central reference point for comparable provisions of other UN treaties. That status explains why the UN Human Rights Committee's General Comment No. 34 on Article 19 ICCPR, was always destined to resonate beyond the ICCPR itself. Whether synergic or frictional, the interplay between these various treaty provisions on freedom of expression have, at all times, significant bearing on how the right is understood and applied in practice. As will be seen in the next section, other institutional forces also help to shape the contours of the rights.

## 5 Quest for coherence and consistency

On the back of processes of consolidation and expansion, the challenge for the rights to freedom of expression and information at the UN today is to ensure their effective implementation and coherence and consistency in their interpretation. The previous section reviewed a constellation of treaties and the concordance and idiosyncratic accentuations of their main provisions on freedom of expression, information and the media. The present section will shift the attention from the *drafting* of treaties to the *interpretation* of treaties, which can also have a determinative impact on the realization of the rights in question. It will then look further at a range of non-treaty dynamics shaping these rights. In the penumbra of these treaties, other mechanisms and procedures and their interplay seek to ensure that the rights to freedom of expression and information – in all their various emphases – are realized coherently and consistently in practice. This section will conclude with a brief consideration of the swirl of issues and challenges dominating debates on the rights to freedom of expression and information today.

### *5.1 Evolving interpretations of freedom of expression and information*

A General Comment (GC) or General Recommendation (GR) focuses on a specific theme(s) or treaty provision(s) and it is usually the leading source of interpretative guidance for the treaty in question.[81] A GC or GR

[81] See further, P. Alston, 'The Historical Origins of the Concept of "General Comments" in Human Rights Law', in L. Boisson De Charzournes and V. Gowlland-Debbas (eds.), *The International Legal System in Quest of Equity and Universality* (Leiden: Martinus Nijhoff, 2001), 763–76.

typically reflects the accumulated experience and expertise of a given treaty's oversight body on the subject matter of the GC or GR. One GC and one GR are singled out here as being especially relevant for advancing coherence and consistency in the interpretation of UN treaty-based guarantees for freedom of expression, information and the media. They are the Human Rights Committee's GC No. 34 and CERD's GR No. 35.

#### 5.1.1 The Human Rights Committee's General Comment No. 34

In a much-anticipated development, the United Nations' Human Rights Committee adopted its GC No. 34 on Article 19 (freedoms of opinion and expression) of the ICCPR at its 102nd session on 21 July 2011.[82] GC No. 34 replaces the Committee's earlier GC No. 10 on Article 19, ICCPR, which was adopted in 1983[83] and did not anticipate the current reality of a globalized communications environment dominated by Internet-based technologies.

GC No. 34 reiterates the interrelationship between freedom of expression and other rights safeguarded by the ICCPR, e.g., privacy, religion, association and assembly, electoral and participatory rights, minority rights, etc. It stresses that all branches of the State are under an obligation to respect freedom of opinion and expression and it recalls that freedom of *opinion* cannot be subject to exception or restriction. It uses a very extensive set of examples to demonstrate the broad scope of freedom of *expression*.

GC No. 34 recognizes (and explains) the importance of ensuring a free, independent and diverse media in democratic society. States are specifically called upon to guarantee the operational, editorial and financial independence of public service broadcasting services. The need for States to appreciate the emergence of, and foster the independence of, new media (e.g., 'internet and mobile based electronic information dissemination systems')[84] is also emphasized. States are moreover urged to ensure access of individuals to those new media.

[82] For commentary by the Rapporteur on the General Comment, Michael O'Flaherty, see Chapter 2 in this book. For further commentary, see A. de Zayas and Á. R. Martín, 'Freedom of Opinion and Freedom of Expression: Some Reflections on General Comment No. 34 of the UN Human Rights Committee', *Netherlands International Law Review* 59 (2012), 425–54.

[83] UN HRC General Comment No. 10 – Freedom of expression (Article 19), 29 July 1983.

[84] General Comment No. 34, para. 15.

The right of access to information held by public bodies is considered in detail and in order to give effect to that right, States are encouraged to 'proactively put into the public domain Government information of public interest'.[85] States should furthermore 'make every effort to ensure easy, prompt, effective and practical access to such information'.[86]

The lengthiest sections of the GC are those dealing with Article 19(3) – restrictions on the right to freedom of expression, and the limitative scope of those restrictions in specific areas. The former elaborates in detail on the specific conditions subject to which restrictions on freedom of expression may be permitted: the restrictions must be provided by law; be based on one of the grounds set out in Article 19(3)(a) and (b), and conform to the strict tests of necessity and proportionality. The latter scrutinizes the scope of permissible restrictions in specific contexts, such as political discourse, media regulation, journalism, counter-terrorism and defamation. It stipulates, for instance, that blasphemy laws and laws penalising the expression of opinions about historical facts are incompatible with the ICCPR.

In respect of the media, the GC repeatedly states that restrictions on freedom of expression must comply with the requirements of Article 19(3) (e.g., licensing processes; new media), or finds particular restrictions to be presumptively impermissible (e.g., the penalization of a media outlet (or prohibition of a website or information dissemination system) solely for criticising the government; generic bans on the operation of certain websites). The promotion of media pluralism is strongly advocated.

### 5.1.2 CERD's General Recommendation on racist hate speech

CERD adopted its GR No. 35, entitled 'Combating racist hate speech', during its 83rd session in August 2013.[87] This is CERD's most explicit and detailed engagement with racist hate speech to date.[88] GR No. 35 is significant not only for its detailed engagement with racist hate speech, but also because it aligns ICERD's provisions on freedom of expression more closely with those of other international legal standards, in particular Article 19, ICCPR. As already mentioned, ICERD has traditionally had an outlier status among international human rights treaties in

85 *Ibid.*, para. 19. 86 *Ibid.*

87 CERD, General Recommendation No. 35 – Combating racist hate speech, Doc. No. CERD/C/GC/35, 23 September 2013.

88 For details of other GRs dealing with the topic, see para. 3 of GR No. 35.

respect of freedom of expression because of its heavy reliance on the criminalization of (certain types of) expression in order to combat racism. GR No. 35 recognizes that ICERD is a living instrument and that it must be better synchronized with other treaties and informed by contemporary understandings of racist hate speech – its causes, manifestations and impact.

In keeping with this line of thinking, the GR explores a range of strategies against racist hate speech other than the criminalization of expression, i.e., civil and administrative law measures. It acknowledges that there is inherent differentiation within the notion of 'racist hate speech', which means that different remedies and responses are appropriate. It emphasizes the need to examine contextual factors, such as content/form, climate, position/status of speaker, reach, objectives,[89] when determining what sort of remedies or responses are best suited to combating particular types of racist hate speech. The multiple and differentiated measures envisaged by the Convention for combating racist hate speech include teaching, education, culture and information (Article 7 ICERD).[90] In this respect, it can be said to have rediscovered the 'neglected pillar'[91] of ICERD.

It is against this background that the GR's media-specific provisions have been crafted. The GR stresses that 'informed, ethical and objective media, including social media and the Internet, have an essential role in promoting responsibility in the dissemination of ideas and opinions'.[92] States should therefore put in place 'appropriate legislation for the media in line with international standards' and 'encourage the public and private media to adopt codes of professional ethics and press codes that incorporate respect for the principles of the Convention and other fundamental human rights standards'.[93]

It states that 'media representations of ethnic, indigenous and other groups ... should be based on principles of respect, fairness and the avoidance of stereotyping'.[94] The media should furthermore 'avoid referring unnecessarily to race, ethnicity, religion and other group characteristics in a manner that may promote intolerance'.[95] It recognizes that 'local empowerment through media pluralism facilitates the emergence

[89] *Ibid.*, para. 15. [90] See also: *ibid.*, paras. 8 and 9.
[91] S. Farrior, 'The Neglected Pillar: The "Teaching Tolerance" Provision of the International Convention on the Elimination of All Forms of Racial Discrimination', *ILSA J. Int'l & Comp. L.* 5 (1999), 291–9.
[92] CERD GR No. 35, para. 39. [93] *Ibid.* [94] *Ibid.*, para. 40. [95] *Ibid.*

of speech capable of countering racist hate speech'.[96] For that reason, it advocates 'facilitation of access to and ownership of media by minority, indigenous and other groups ... including media in their own languages'.[97] It also 'encourages self-regulation and compliance with codes of ethics by Internet service providers'.[98]

#### 5.1.3 Overall impact of General Comments and Recommendations

In a highly influential article which was first published in 1984, Philip Alston called for 'quality control' when 'conjuring up new human rights'.[99] He wrote:

> Recognition of the essential dynamism of the notion of human rights inevitably requires a willingness to consider the need to proclaim additional human rights. The challenge is to achieve an appropriate balance between, on the one hand, the need to maintain the integrity and credibility of the human rights tradition, and on the other hand, the need to adopt a dynamic approach that fully reflects changing needs and perspectives and responds to the emergence of new threats to human dignity and well-being.[100]

The challenge identified by Alston is applicable not only to the recognition of new rights, but also to the (dynamic) interpretation of existing rights, for example through General Comments or Recommendations. The challenge becomes that of ensuring that the interpretation of existing international normative standards is: (1) faithful to the original and inherent logic and purpose of those standards, and (2) reflective of, and responsive to, changing (international) legal frameworks and ambient societal situations.

The Human Rights Committee's GC No. 34 and CERD's GR No. 35 have modernized the interpretation of their respective treaty provisions on freedom of expression and information, by recognizing the relevance of media and Internet. GC No. 34 is already proving to have a similar centrifugal influence at the interpretative level as Article 19 ICCPR has had at the norm-setting level: it is being widely quoted by other treaty-monitoring bodies and non-treaty mechanisms and procedures. GR No. 35, for its part, realigns ICERD more closely with other international

[96] *Ibid.*, para. 41. [97] *Ibid.* [98] *Ibid.*, para. 42.
[99] 'Conjuring up New Human Rights: A Proposal for Quality Control', *American Journal of International Law* 78 (1984), 607–21.
[100] *Ibid.*, 609.

human rights treaties such as the ICCPR, in respect of the interpretation of its provisions on freedom of expression. These two examples are perhaps more striking than general comments or recommendations adopted by other treaty-monitoring bodies, but that should not downplay the importance of the latter.

Since 2000, all General Comments adopted pursuant to the ICESCR have contained references to the right to information.[101] Some of these references describe the interrelationship of the right to information with other human rights and the enabling role it can play in the realization of other human rights. Some of the references focus on the importance of the accessibility of information concerning particular human rights, both in terms of its availability and its suitability (e.g., in particular languages or formats). The corresponding State obligation to disseminate different kinds of information is another focus. In the context of the CRC, General Comment No. 12, 'The right of the child to be heard', describes the fulfilment of a child's right to information, *inter alia*, via the mass media, as a prerequisite for the effective realization of the right to express his/her views.[102]

## *5.2 Freedom of expression and information beyond treaty law*

### 5.2.1 Specialized agencies

A number of the UN's so-called 'specialized agencies' – autonomous organizations that are connected to the UN by virtue of special agreements – conduct activities that relate to the rights to freedom of expression, information and the media and Internet. The International Telecommunication Union (ITU), UNESCO and the World Intellectual Property Organization (WIPO) are the most obvious examples.

The ITU is the UN's specialized agency for information and communications technologies. The ITU's main goals include the allocation of global radio spectrum and satellite orbits, the development of technical standards to ensure interconnection between networks and technologies and the improvement of accessibility of ICTs for disadvantaged communities worldwide. It is an important institutional stakeholder in the framing of international regulation and policy concerning network

[101] This point is borrowed from Yvonne Donders (Chapter 3 in this book).

[102] General Comment No. 12, 'The right of the child to be heard', 20 July 2009, para. 82. This point is borrowed from Lucy Smith (Chapter 5 in this book).

neutrality and Internet governance.[103] It played a leading role in the organization of the World Summit on the Information Society (WSIS). The WSIS took place in two phases – in Geneva (2003) and in Tunis (2005) – and it led to two sets of outcome documents.[104] The central aim of the WSIS was to:

> build a people-centred, inclusive and development-oriented Information Society, where everyone can create, access, utilize and share information and knowledge, enabling individuals, communities and peoples to achieve their full potential in promoting their sustainable development and improving their quality of life, premised on the purposes and principles of the Charter of the United Nations and respecting fully and upholding the Universal Declaration of Human Rights.[105]

There has been an extensive implementation, follow-up and review process to the WSIS[106] and it is also relevant to note that pursuant to the WSIS, the Internet Governance Forum (IGF) was established as a new – open and multi-stakeholder – forum for the discussion of public policy issues related to Internet governance. While the IGF lacks formal decision-making powers, its multi-stakeholder governance approach (following through on the approach taken at the WSIS), has been hailed as a 'major conceptual innovation'[107] and a 'real innovation in international politics'.[108] Notwithstanding its innovative character, the IGF is also seen as a 'fragile experiment' and it faces 'major challenges'.[109] Indeed, even the participatory promise of the WSIS involved various complications and frictions in practice. It was 'a laboratory for developing and implementing new modes of governance, struggling between the promise of a multi-stakeholder environment, in which all actors can

[103] Various aspects of these issues are teased out by Karol Jakubowicz in Chapter 10 in this book.

[104] 'Building the Information Society: A Global Challenge in the New Millennium', Declaration of Principles, World Summit on the Information Society, Geneva, Doc. No. WSIS-03/GENEVA/DOC/4-E, 12 December 2003; Tunis Commitment, World Summit on the Information Society, Tunis, Doc. No. WSIS-05/TUNIS/DOC/7-E, 18 November 2005.

[105] 'Building the Information Society', Declaration of Principles, para. 1.

[106] For an overview, see www.itu.int/wsis/index.html (last visited 23 June 2014). Details of the WSIS+10 Review event, hosted by UNESCO, are provided by Sylvie Coudray, in Chapter 7 in this book.

[107] B. de la Chapelle, 'The Internet Governance Forum: How a United Nations Summit Produced a New Governance Paradigm for the Internet Age', in C. Möller and A. Amouroux (eds.), *Governing the Internet – Freedom and Regulation in the OSCE Region* (Vienna: OSCE Representative on Freedom of the Media, 2007), 19–26, 25.

[108] W. Kleinwächter, 'The History of Internet Governance', in *Ibid.*, 41–64, 63.

[109] de la Chapelle, 'Internet Governance Forum', 26.

participate equally, and the attempts by many governments to retain a dominant role for the state'.[110]

UNESCO is mandated by its Constitution to 'promote the free flow of ideas by word and by image', in order to advance 'the mutual knowledge and understanding of peoples for the higher cause of peace and security'.[111] UNESCO's promotion of freedom of expression would therefore appear to be motivated by instrumental rather than intrinsic reasons.[112] It employs a variety of strategies and techniques in discharging its mandate, e.g., legal/regulatory, ethical and professional standard-setting; advocacy and awareness-raising; capacity development.[113] It has made an enduring contribution to the development of the right to freedom of expression by explicitly focusing on the importance for democracy, culture and (economic) development of (access to) media and communications technologies.

This contribution was not achieved without major setbacks and fierce controversies, however. In the late 1970s and early 1980s, UNESCO became the forum in which debates about the New World Information and Communication Order (NWICO) were waged. The NWICO agenda sought to promote a more equitable international communication order and a truly free flow of information at the global level. To those ends, it sought to advance the concept of a 'right' to communicate, socially responsible journalism and other mechanisms for the circulation of information and ideas; it favoured the democratization of (international) communications structures and processes (e.g., by making them more participatory in character) and strongly linked communicative rights to the whole development agenda. One set of protagonists in the debate, the newly decolonized States, challenged the cultural imperialism of the existing international communications system. For them, the debate was an extension of the struggle to 'develop a New International Economic Order and shake off dependencies in the economic realm'.[114] NWICO's vision was very much shaped by the contemporary geopolitical cleavages between North and South and East and West, which were perpetuated in culture, communications and commerce. The

[110] A. Hintz, *Civil Society Media and Global Governance: Intervening into the World Summit on the Information Society* (Münster: Lit Verlag, 2009), 267.
[111] K. Nordenstreng, 'Myths about Press Freedom', *Brazilian Journalism Research* 3(1) (2007), 20, drawing on Articles 2(a) and 1 UNESCO Constitution.
[112] For critical analysis and an explanation of the significance of this point, see *ibid.*, 20–2.
[113] For detailed insights into these approaches, see Chapter 7 in this book.
[114] Hintz, *Civil Society Media*, 58ff.

pursuit of the NWICO's objectives proved highly polemical and led to bitter political rifts within UNESCO, with long-term consequences, such as the withdrawal of the United States and the United Kingdom from the organization. A defining moment in the debate was the publication of the famous Report of the MacBride Commission, which made a valiant attempt to synthesize and reconcile the divisive positions within the debate.[115]

The close relationship between freedom of expression and cultural diversity has been to the fore of UNESCO's standard-setting activities, featuring centrally in, *inter alia*, its Declaration on Cultural Diversity[116] and the UNESCO Convention on the Protection and Promotion of the Diversity of Cultural Expressions.[117] The Convention seeks to protect and promote the diversity of cultural expressions and to create an appropriate environment in which cultures can thrive. It also links such diversity to intercultural interaction and dialogue, and development issues. Although a number of the legal obligations for Contracting States are weak-worded, the Convention is of symbolic importance in so far as it provides a cultural and human rights counterfoil to trade and economic approaches to cultural activities, goods and services.

Likewise, UNESCO's standard-setting texts regularly emphasize the role of the media in serving broad public policy objectives, consistent with the organization's constitutional mandate. Examples of such objectives include: strengthening peace, international understanding; combating racism, apartheid and incitement to war,[118] and using satellite broadcasting to enhance the free flow of information, education and cultural exchange.[119]

Other highlights among its activities include the pivotal roles of its Director-General and International Programme for the Development of Communication (IPDC) in international campaigns for the protection of

115 See S. MacBride *et al.*, *Many Voices One World: Towards a New More Just and More Efficient World Information and Communication Order* (London: UNESCO, 1980).

116 UNESCO Declaration on Cultural Diversity, 2 November 2001.

117 UNESCO Convention on the Protection and Promotion of the Diversity of Cultural Expressions, 20 October 2005 (entry into force: 18 March 2007).

118 UNESCO Declaration on Fundamental Principles concerning the Contribution of the Mass Media to Strengthening Peace and International Understanding, to the Promotion of Human Rights and to Countering Racialism, Apartheid and Incitement to War, 28 November 1978.

119 UNESCO Declaration of Guiding Principles on the Use of Satellite Broadcasting for the Free Flow of Information, the Spread of Education and Greater Cultural Exchange, 15 November 1972.

journalists. The UN Plan of Action on the Safety of Journalists and the Issue of Impunity is particularly noteworthy.[120] The Plan of Action is the outcome of a process initiated by the Intergovernmental Council of the IPDC in 2010. The IPDC is a multilateral UN forum that aims to mobilize the international community to discuss and promote media development in developing countries. It has a central role in monitoring the follow-up to the killings condemned by UNESCO's Director General and it has adopted a number of Reports and Decisions on the topic. The key objective of the Plan of Action is to work 'toward the creation of a free and safe environment for journalists and media workers in both conflict and non-conflict situations, with a view to strengthening peace, democracy and development worldwide'.[121] The Plan of Action emphasizes the instrumentality of journalists' freedom and safety for peace, democracy and development. Its underlying justification is to 'uphold the fundamental right of freedom of expression and, in so doing, to ensure that citizens are well informed and actively participate in society at large'.[122]

The WIPO describes itself on its website as 'the global forum for intellectual property services, policy, information and cooperation'.[123] Its primary aims are to 'to promote the protection of intellectual property throughout the world through cooperation among States and, where appropriate, in collaboration with any other international organization' and to 'ensure administrative cooperation among the Unions [designed to promote the protection of intellectual property]'.[124]

International regimes for the protection of intellectual property rights on the one hand, and human rights on the other hand, have developed with limited cross-fertilization and cross-referencing.[125] Two models have been distinguished to describe their relationship, one conflictual and the other more conciliatory.[126] The conflict model pits copyright and

[120] The UN Plan of Action on the Safety of Journalists and the Issue of Impunity, the 1st UN Inter-Agency Meeting on the Safety of Journalists and the Issue of Impunity, Doc. No. CI-12/CONF.202/6, 14 September 2011.

[121] *Ibid.*, para. 4.1. [122] *Ibid.*, para. 2.1. [123] wipo.org (last visited 23 June 2014).

[124] Article 3, Convention Establishing the World Intellectual Property Organization, UNTS No. I-11846, opened for signature, 14 July 1967; entry into force, 26 April 1970.

[125] P. Torremans, 'Copyright (and Other Intellectual Property Rights) as a Human Right', in P. L. C. Torremans (ed.), *Intellectual Property and Human Rights (Enhanced Edition of Copyright and Human Rights)* (Alphen aan den Rijn: Kluwer Law International, 2008), 196. See generally the other chapters in the same volume.

[126] *Ibid.*, 196–7.

intellectual property rights against human rights, in particular, the rights to freedom of expression and information as well as economic, social and cultural rights. Advocates of this approach tend to consider human rights as having a more fundamental status than intellectual property rights. The second, 'compatibility', model perceives both sets of rights as seeking to achieve an appropriate 'private–public rights balance':

> On the one hand there is a need to define the scope of the private exclusive right that is given to authors as an incentive to create and as recognition of their creative contribution to society broadly enough to enable it to play its incentive and recognition function in an appropriate and effective way, whilst on the other hand there is the broader interest of society that the public must be able to have adequate access to the fruits of authors' efforts.[127]

Whatever the preferred conceptual framing of their relationship, in practice, the objectives of intellectual property and those of freedom of expression and information are often competing.[128]

### 5.2.2 Specialized procedures

In 1993, the Human Rights Commission appointed a UN Special Rapporteur on the promotion and protection of the right to freedom of opinion and expression, mandated to gather all relevant information on, and report on, threats to the exercise of the right in practice and its actual violation.[129] The mandate for the Special Rapporteur was established following an influential report by Danilo Türk and Louis Joinet.[130] They envisaged that a Special Rapporteur would have the key task of assuring the 'protection of professionals in the field of information', a somewhat different emphasis to the mandate finally agreed upon. In 2008, the Special Rapporteur's mandate was renewed, revised and broadened to include, *inter alia* and somewhat controversially, the task of reporting on 'instances in which the abuse of the right of freedom of expression constitutes an act of racial or religious discrimination'.[131]

[127] *Ibid.*, 197.

[128] See generally, D. Gervais, 'Intellectual Property and Human Rights: Learning to Live Together', in Torremans, *Intellectual Property and Human Rights*, 3–23.

[129] UN Commission on Human Rights' Resolution 1993/45 of 5 March 1993.

[130] D. Türk and L. Joinet, 'The Right to Freedom of Opinion and Expression', Final Report, Conclusions and Recommendations, UN Doc. No. E/CN.4/Sub.2/1992/9/Add.1, 14 July 1992, 3.

[131] UN Human Rights Council Resolution 7/36 of 28 March 2008.

The Special Rapporteur undertakes several types of activities that contribute to enhancing understanding of the meaning of the right to freedom of expression in contemporary times. Toby Mendel's chapter in this book classifies and analyses those activities in an unprecedented level of detail. Among the most influential of those activities are the Special Rapporteur's annual reports to the UN Human Rights Council. The annual reports include thematic focuses which often deal with cutting-edge issues relating to freedom of expression, on which there is limited international jurisprudence or a lack of clarity or specificity in relevant legal standards. Examples include the safety of journalists (including online journalists) (2012)[132] and freedom of expression and the Internet (2013).[133] Interestingly, in the latter, the Special Rapporteur inches towards recognition of Internet access as a human right, but without travelling the full distance.[134]

Increasingly, the Special Rapporteur teams up with other Special Rapporteurs and specialized UN mandates to issue collective statements on current human rights issues and problems that include freedom of expression aspects. When a number of Special Rapporteurs present a united front like this, the political authority of their statements is augmented. A similar logic applies to the annual joint statements adopted by the Special Rapporteur together with equivalent or comparable specialized mandate-holders from the Inter-American Commission on Human Rights, the African Commission on Human and Peoples' Rights and the Organization for Security and Co-operation in Europe (the 'Specialized Mandates'). This thematic intergovernmental collaboration demonstrates how the role of the Special Rapporteur has evolved to transcend the UN's institutional structures. It has led to the forging of common approaches that enhance global understandings of what the right to freedom of expression entails. As such, the joint statements represent an essential prong to the Special Rapporteur's overall contribution to the 'progressive development of international standards relating to freedom of expression', as the title of Mendel's chapter so aptly puts it.[135]

[132] *Report of the Special Rapporteur on the Promotion and Protection of the Right to Freedom of Opinion and Expression*, UN Doc. A/HRC/20/17, 4 June 2012.

[133] *Report of the Special Rapporteur on the Promotion and Protection of the Right to Freedom of Opinion and Expression*, UN Doc. A/HRC/17/27, 16 May 2011.

[134] *Ibid.*, in particular, Section V 'Access to the Internet and the necessary infrastructure', paras. 60–6 and Section VI 'Conclusions and recommendations', B. 'Access to the Internet and the necessary infrastructure', paras. 85–8.

[135] See Chapter 8 in this volume.

### 5.3 *Issues and challenges*

By now, it should be clear that prior understandings of the right to freedom of expression and information are being challenged by transformative advances in media and communication technologies, as discussed by Aidan White.[136] Individuals' ability to effectively exercise their right to seek, receive and impart information and ideas is increasingly determined by technological considerations, in particular access to the Internet and to the abundance of content and services available on the Internet. A diversity of new actors has emerged and become influential in the media and communications sector, such as social-networking services, search engines, news-aggregating sites, blogs, content-sharing sites, wikis, etc. These technological developments have societal implications which sometimes call for specific normative responses, including from the UN. The process of attuning the UN's various standards and mechanisms to these developments and their implications is an ongoing one, as Karol Jakubowicz demonstrates in Chapter 10 in this volume.

In their 10th Anniversary Joint Declaration, entitled 'Ten Key Challenges to Freedom of Expression in the Next Decade', the Specialized Mandates identify the following key 'threats' [*sic*] to freedom of expression: mechanisms of government control over the media; criminal defamation; violence against journalists; limits on the right to information; discrimination in the enjoyment of the right to freedom of expression; commercial pressures; support for public service and community broadcasters; security and freedom of expression; freedom of expression on the Internet, and access to information and communications technologies. The range of threats included in this list bears out the Joint Declaration's preambular assertion that 'some of the historic challenges to freedom of expression have still not been addressed successfully, while new challenges have arisen due to technological, social and political developments'.[137]

Two other preambular references in the same Joint Declaration – recognizing the 'enormous potential of the Internet as a tool for realizing the right to freedom of expression and to information' and the 'unique nature' of the medium and the need to ensure that freedom of expression is guaranteed online – presaged the focus of subsequent Joint Declarations by the Specialized Mandates. The Joint Declarations adopted since

[136] See Chapter 11 in this volume.

[137] The Specialized Mandates, Joint Declaration: Ten Key Challenges to Freedom of Expression in the Next Decade, 3 February 2010.

2010 have shown a vivid awareness of the growing importance of the Internet for freedom of expression. Their focuses have, for instance, included freedom of expression and the Internet (2011)[138] and the protection of freedom of expression and diversity in the digital terrestrial transition (2013).[139]

The Joint Declaration on freedom of expression and the Internet focuses on the applicability of general principles and traditional legal issues (e.g., criminal and civil liability) to the Internet, as well as a range of specific technological issues, i.e., intermediary liability; filtering and blocking; network neutrality and access to the Internet. These focuses are largely representative of where contemporary debates on freedom of expression and information are at. Of course, other focuses of contemporary debates include age-old concerns for media freedom and pluralism; the safety and protection of journalists and others contributing to public debate; the nature and scope of permissible restrictions on the rights to freedom of expression and information; the nature and scope of the duties and responsibilities that govern the exercise of the rights to freedom of expression and information, etc.

Overarching all of these historic and new issues, challenges, opportunities and threats, a number of questions or axes for further reflection remain. The first axis for further reflection arises from the 'universal, indivisible and interdependent and interrelated' character of all human rights, as reaffirmed, *inter alia*, by Article 5 of the Vienna Declaration of 1993.[140] This approach insists on the presumptive coherence of rights and provides an integrated conceptualization of human rights within which the relationship of other rights with the rights to freedom of expression and information should be considered. The right to freedom of expression is often described as an enabler of other human rights. While it can be instrumental in the realization of other rights, paradoxically it can also be at odds with them in certain specific circumstances. The right to freedom of religion is a case in point. Privacy and data protection are other good examples. The interplay between freedom of expression and various other human rights is sure to continue to shape the scope of

138 The Specialized Mandates, Joint Declaration on Freedom of Expression and the Internet, 1 June 2011.

139 The Specialized Mandates, Joint Declaration on the Protection of Freedom of Expression and Diversity in the Digital Terrestrial Transition, 3 May 2013.

140 World Conference on Human Rights – The Vienna Declaration and Programme of Action (1993).

the right to freedom of expression in practice; the judicious management of that interplay will remain a work in progress.

The second axis is closely related to the first. It concerns the role of inter-treaty relationships in shaping the scope of the right to freedom of expression and information. What potential is there for cross-fertilization between (interpretations of) relevant provisions in generalist treaties (e.g., ICCPR) and thematically focused treaties (e.g., CRC, CRPD)? To what extent should what we understand as the traditional 'core' of the right to freedom of expression be expanded to incorporate emerging, thematically coloured interpretations of the right?

The third axis for further reflection concerns the dynamic interpretation of existing rights. According to the 'living instrument' doctrine, treaties should not remain 'static and lifeless',[141] but rather grow with the times and therefore 'be interpreted in the light of present-day conditions'.[142] With its responsive character, this teleological approach to treaty interpretation can render treaties more enduring and 'future-proof' than when other interpretative techniques, like originalism, are espoused. Acknowledgement of the organic growth of treaties paved the way for the Human Rights Committee's GC No. 34 and CERD's GR No. 35 to reinvigorate tired understandings of the right to freedom of expression in the contexts of the ICCPR and ICERD, respectively. The General Comment and Recommendation reflect how new technological capabilities and uses have reshaped contemporary communicative realities, as well as their resultant impact on the rights to freedom of expression and information.

The fourth axis concerns the influence of UN standards at the regional level. With what Kevin Boyle has termed 'the emergence of a global village of precedent',[143] it is apposite to enquire as to the level of interaction or dialogue that underpins the drafting and interpretation of legal norms at the global and regional levels. In Chapter 14 in this volume, Antoine Buyse examines the nature and extent of such judicial dialogue in respect of global and regional human rights mechanisms in freedom of expression cases. His meticulous analysis focuses in particular

[141] Brennan, J., dissenting, in *Marsh* v. *Chambers*, 463 US 783 (1983), 817.

[142] *Tyrer* v. *the United Kingdom*, Judgment of the European Court of Human Rights of 25 April 1978, Series A, no. 26, para. 31; *Matthews* v. *the United Kingdom*, Judgment of the European Court of Human Rights of 18 February 1999, para. 39.

[143] Kevin Boyle, untitled address, 8 December 1999, Human Rights Centre, University of Essex, England.

on the dialogical interaction between the UN Human Rights Committee and the European Court of Human Rights. Despite an abundance of case law, he concludes that there is a scarcity of dialogue.

## 6 Conclusion

This chapter sets out to tell a story about the historical, ongoing and projected growth of a cluster of rights within an institution. The early years of the UN saw the tentative development of an ostensibly coherent international human rights system within which the right to freedom of expression would be protected and promoted. But as the fledgling organization tried to spread its wings, the Cold War set in and halted its flight. Efforts to promote and protect the rights to freedom of expression and information endured particularly serious setbacks. For all the progress registered at the 1948 Conference on Freedom of Information, the bulk of its output (three draft conventions, draft provisions for the International Bill of Rights and forty-three political resolutions) failed to get off the ground. The growth of the rights to freedom of expression and information was therefore anything but steady and linear.

Nevertheless, the enshrinement of important guarantees of the right to freedom of expression in the International Bill of Rights did lead to the consolidation of the right at the global level. A phase of expansion followed as other international treaties emerged which also contain provisions on the right to freedom of expression and approach in ways consistent with their own specific objectives. These developments have led to a strengthening of the core of the rights to freedom of expression and information, as well as shifting emphases and changing parameters beyond its core. One crucial development – not least in the context of this book's main focus – has been the increased autonomy acquired by the right to freedom of information. It can no longer be viewed merely as a constituent element of the right to freedom of expression; it has come into its own as a full-blown right of access to information which continues to enjoy a close, contiguous relationship with the right to freedom of expression.

As the rights to freedom of expression and information continue to develop, a major challenge for the UN is to ensure that maximum coherence and consistency is achieved in the approaches taken by all of its relevant standards and mechanisms. As this chapter and book show, there is considerable institutional breadth in the range of relevant UN standards and mechanisms: besides treaty-based bodies, various other mechanisms can also influence the expansion or contraction of the rights in different ways, e.g., UNESCO, the Special Rapporteur and the ITU. Each of the treaty-based and other mechanisms has its own mandate/ priorities, dynamics and level of dynamism, which underscores the importance of the ongoing quest for coherence and consistency.

Even in the brief foregoing analysis, one can note the surprising endurance of priority themes and problems and an institutional inability to resolve them. Many of the thematic preoccupations of the past have demonstrated their staying power over the years or re-emerged as thematic priorities of the present: State surveillance, distrust of new communications technologies, national security, duties and responsibilities, the power of the media, etc. It must then be concluded that the history of the UN's development of the rights to freedom of expression and information has been characterized as much by leaps and bounds as it has by fits and starts. This chequered past is 'still present' and the future is 'in the making'.[144]

## 7 Objectives and structure of the book

### *7.1 Objectives*

This book's primary aim is to make a valuable and timely contribution to existing academic literature on UN standards and mechanisms dealing with the rights to freedom of expression and information. It seeks to fill a gap in existing scholarship by providing a critical and uniquely comprehensive examination of the various UN approaches to the rights to freedom of expression and information. Instead of taking an approach that is treaty, mechanism or issue specific, the focus of this book spans the full breadth of UN instruments and procedures dealing with freedom of expression and information. It embraces a wide range of pressing, substantive issues relating to freedom of expression and information and examines how they are dealt with across the UN system. The complex, dynamic relationship between freedom of expression and information and the media and Internet is a recurrent theme throughout the book.

The book first sets out to map in detail and contextualize the vast body of UN (legal) standards and mechanisms that are relevant for the

[144] This sentence borrows a couple of subheadings from the MacBride Report (1980), 3 and 10, which was the epicentre of one of the most tumultuous incidents in the history of the UN's engagement with the right to freedom of expression.

protection and promotion of the rights to freedom of expression and information. It tries to gauge the overall coherence of those standards and mechanisms and identifies and explains significant divergences between them. It explores the relationship between the rights to freedom of expression and information and other human rights. It also examines a selection of urgent and emergent themes that are prompting fresh thinking about the substance and scope of the right to freedom of expression and information. One such theme is the ever-evolving relationship between freedom of expression and information and the (traditional and new) media. It reflects on the suitability of relevant UN standards and mechanisms for confronting and negotiating contemporary challenges and threats to the right to freedom of expression and information. Finally, the book also reflects on the extent to which relevant UN standards and mechanisms have influenced equivalent regional standards and mechanisms.

The book comprises contributions from internationally recognized academic and civil society experts with keen insights into, and in many cases, first-hand experience of, the operational dynamics of the UN system.

### *7.2 Structure*

The book opens with this introductory chapter (by Tarlach McGonagle), which traces the development of the rights to freedom of expression and information within the UN system for the protection of human rights. It provides the requisite historical, institutional and thematic contextualization at the very outset. The chapter's title, 'The development of freedom of expression and information within the UN: leaps and bounds or fits and starts?', seeks to capture a sense of the triumphs and failures that have defined the UN's engagement with the rights to freedom of expression and information over the years. After this overarching chapter, the rest of the book is organized into two parts, focusing on institutional aspects and thematic aspects of the rights to freedom of expression and information, respectively.

Part I, entitled 'UN normative and institutional approaches to the protection of freedom of expression and information', offers an across-the-board examination of how selected UN treaties/treaty bodies guarantee the rights to freedom of expression and information. The treaties have been selected on the basis of their important provisions on the rights to freedom of expression and/or information. The treaties in question focus on: civil and political rights; economic, social and cultural rights; the elimination of all forms of racial discrimination; the rights of the child, and the rights of persons with disabilities.

Each of the chapters foregrounds one or more of the salient features of the approach taken by the treaties' respective monitoring bodies. Thus, Chapter 2 by Michael O'Flaherty, who was the Human Rights Committee's Rapporteur for the drafting of GC No. 34, focuses on the precedential value of the ICCPR in 'Interpreting freedom of expression and information standards for the present and the future'. Yvonne Donders in Chapter 3 on the ICESCR, chooses as her central focus, 'Accessibility and the right to information'. Chapter 4 on ICERD, written by Patrick Thornberry, who was CERD's Rapporteur for the drafting of GR No. 35, concerns itself above all with 'The prohibition of "racist hate speech"'. Lucy Smith's Chapter 5 on the CRC deals with a range of specific issues implicated in 'Freedom of expression for children'. The mainstay of Eliza Varney's chapter on the CRPD is the role of that convention in 'Ensuring full and equal access to information' for persons with disabilities (Chapter 6).

Besides these treaty-based approaches, the particular contribution of UNESCO to the promotion of 'Freedom of expression, information and the media' is also given careful consideration by Sylvie Coudray (Chapter 7). Part I's final focus is the role played by the UN Special Rapporteur on the Right to Freedom of Opinion and Expression; a role that is aptly described by Toby Mendel as one of 'Progressive development of international standards relating to freedom of expression' (Chapter 8).

Part II, entitled 'Selected thematic focuses', identifies and critically examines a number of cutting-edge themes relating to freedom of expression and information. As such, it casts off from the institutional moorings of Part I, but does not lose sight of them. This allows for more in-depth scrutiny of key and emergent issues than is often possible within the strictures of treaty-monitoring or institutional agenda-setting.

The chapters by McGonagle and Donders demonstrate that in many UN treaties, the right to freedom of information tends to be subsumed in a wide embracing formulation of the right to freedom of expression, but that it has also managed to extricate itself from the grip of those formal formulations and evolve into a right of access to information. Part II opens with a timely and insightful exploration of key challenges for the continued development of the right to information. Written by Helen Darbishire, 'Ten challenges for the right to information in the age of mega-leaks', delves into current debates on, *inter alia*, the public interest in disclosure of information held by States' authorities and the confidentiality of diplomatic communications (Chapter 9). The Snowden revelations have emphatically underscored the pressing nature of these challenges.

Another central challenge for the rights to freedom of expression and information today and in the future is the impact of information and communication technologies (ICTs) on the realization of both rights in practice. The (regulation of the) changing media in safeguarding the right to freedom of expression is therefore dealt with by Karol Jakubowicz in Chapter 10, 'Early days: the UN, ICTs and freedom of expression'. The title of the chapter is suggestive of one of the chapter's main findings: despite the UN's renewed, recent flurry of engagement with ICTs and their relationship with the rights to freedom of expression and information, it really is a case of 'early days' for that engagement. One can therefore expect future phases of consolidation and expansion, as in the UN's previous engagement with mass media.

In such a dramatically reconfigured media ecosystem, new challenges and opportunities inevitably arise for traditional media and journalism. Drawing on his professional experiences as former Secretary General of the International Federation of Journalists and as current Director of the Ethical Journalism Network, Aidan White examines these issues with great verve, insights and authority in Chapter 11, 'A new vision of values, accountability and mission for journalism'.

The sometimes frictional interplay between the right to freedom of expression and other rights, values or interests, also features prominently in the book. For instance, Martin Scheinin in Chapter 13, 'Limits to freedom of expression: lessons from counter-terrorism', draws on his experiences as former UN Special Rapporteur on the Protection and Promotion of Human Rights and Fundamental Freedoms while Countering Terrorism, and provides a highly topical case study of such frictions.

The analysis in Part I illustrates the power of institutional and political forces to influence understandings of the legitimacy of restrictions on the rights to freedom of expression and information. Sejal Parmar subjects those forces to critical scrutiny in Chapter 12, 'Uprooting "defamation of religions" and planting a new approach to freedom of expression at the UN'. The controversial 'defamation of religions' campaign temporarily achieved significant traction within the UN in recent years.

A recurrent concern of this book is the impact of relevant UN standards, across the UN and further afield in other regional systems for the protection of human rights. While implicit or incidental in several chapters, this concern is rendered explicit in the final chapter in Part II: Antoine Buyse's 'Tacit citing: the scarcity of judicial dialogue between the global and the regional human rights mechanisms in freedom of expression cases' (Chapter 14).

## Literature

Alston, P. 'The Historical Origins of the Concept of "General Comments" in Human Rights Law', in L. Boisson De Charzournes and V. Gowlland-Debbas (eds.), *The International Legal System in Quest of Equity and Universality* (Leiden: Martinus Nijhoff, 2001), 763–76.

'Conjuring up New Human Rights: A Proposal for Quality Control', *American Journal of International Law* 78 (1984), 607–21.

Baker, C. E. 'Viewpoint Diversity and Media Ownership', *Federal Communications Law Journal* 60(3) (2009), 651–71.

Balkin, J. M. 'Some Realism about Pluralism: Legal Realist Approaches to the First Amendment', *Duke Law Journal* (1990), 375.

Barendt, E. *Freedom of Speech*, 2nd edn (Oxford University Press, 2005).

Binder, C. 'Freedom of Information and the United Nations', *International Organization* 6(2) (May 1952), 210–26.

Bossuyt, M. *Guide to the 'Travaux Préparatoires' of the International Covenant on Civil and Political Rights* (Dordrecht: Martinus Nijhoff, 1987).

Boyle, K. 'The Danish Cartoons', *Netherlands Quarterly of Human Rights* 24(2) (2006), 185–91.

Burgers, J. H. 'The Road to San Francisco: The Revival of the Human Rights Idea in the Twentieth Century', *Human Rights Quarterly* 14 (1992), 447–77.

Canham, E. D. 'International Freedom of Information', 14 *Law & Contemp. Probs.* (1949), 584–98.

Carpentier, N. *Media and Participation: A site of ideological-democratic struggle* (Bristol/Chicago, IL: Intellect, 2011).

Chafee, Jr., Z. 'Legal Problems and Freedom of Information in the United Nations', *Law & Contemp. Probs.* 14 (1949), 545–83.

Chapelle, B. de la 'The Internet Governance Forum: How a United Nations Summit Produced a New Governance Paradigm for the Internet Age', in C. Möller and A. Amouroux (eds.), *Governing the Internet – Freedom and Regulation in the OSCE Region* (Vienna: OSCE Representative on Freedom of the Media, 2007), 19–26.

Dahlgren, P. *Television and the Public Sphere: Citizenship, Democracy and the Media* (London: Sage, 1995).

Eek, H. *Freedom of Information as a Project of International Legislation: A Study of International Law in Making* (Uppsala: A.-B. Lundequistska Bokhandeln, 1953).

Emerson, T. I. *Toward a General Theory of the First Amendment* (New York: Random House, 1966).

Farrior, S. 'The Neglected Pillar: The "Teaching Tolerance" Provision of the International Convention on the Elimination of All Forms of Racial Discrimination', *ILSA J. Int'l & Comp. L.* 5 (1999), 291–9.

Fuchs, C. *Social Media: a critical introduction* (London: Sage, 2014).

Gervais, D. 'Intellectual Property and Human Rights: Learning to Live Together', in P. L. C. Torremans (ed.), *Intellectual Property and Human Rights (Enhanced Edition of Copyright and Human Rights)* (Alphen aan den Rijn: Kluwer Law International, 2008), 3–23.

Glendon, M. A. *A World Made New: Eleanor Roosevelt and the Universal Declaration of Human Rights* (New York: Random House, 2001).

Goldberg, D. 'Freedom of Information in the 21st Century: Bringing Clarity to Transparency', *Communications Law* 14(2)(2009), 50–6.

Hamelink, C. J. *The Politics of World Communication* (London: Sage, 1994).

Hintz, A. *Civil Society Media and Global Governance: Intervening into the World Summit on the Information Society* (Münster: Lit Verlag, 2009).

Humphrey, J. P. *Human Rights & the United Nations: A Great Adventure* (New York: Transnational, 1984).

('Hutchins') Commission on Freedom of the Press, *A Free and Responsible Press* (University of Chicago Press, 1947).

Jakubowicz, K. *A New Notion of Media?: Media and Media-Like Content and Activities on New Communications Services* (Strasbourg: Council of Europe, April 2009).

Kleinwächter, W. 'The History of Internet Governance', in C. Möller and A. Amouroux (eds.), *Governing the Internet – Freedom and Regulation in the OSCE Region* (Vienna: OSCE Representative on Freedom of the Media, 2007), 41–64.

Krüger, H. C. 'Use of the Media to Promote and Infringe Human Rights', in K. E. Mahoney and P. Mahoney (eds.), *Human Rights in the Twenty-first Century* (The Hague: Kluwer, 1993), 743–56.

MacBride, S. *et al. Many Voices One World: Towards a New More Just and More Efficient World Information and Communication Order* (London: UNESCO, 1980).

McDonagh, M. 'The Right to Information in International Human Rights Law', *Human Rights Law Review* 13(1) (2013), 25–55.

McGoldrick, D. *The Human Rights Committee: Its Role in the Development of the International Covenant on Civil and Political Rights*, 2nd edn (Oxford: Clarendon, 1994).

McGonagle, T. *Minority Rights, Freedom of Expression and of the Media: Dynamics and Dilemmas* (Antwerp: Intersentia, 2011).

Metzl, J. F. 'Information Intervention: When Switching Channels Isn't Enough', 76 *Foreign Affairs* (No. 6, November/December 1997), 15–20.

Murrow, E. R. 'Wires and lights in a box', speech, Radio Television News Directors Association Convention, Chicago, 15 October 1958, www.rtdna.org/content/edward_r_murrow_s_1958_wires_lights_in_a_box_speech#.U6ljALRRaXg, last visited 23 June 2014.

Nordenstreng, K. 'Myths about Press Freedom', *Brazilian Journalism Research* 3(1) (2007), 15–30.

Nordenstreng, K. and T. Seppä, 'The League of Nations and mass media: the rediscovery of a forgotten story', paper presented at the XV Conference of the International Association for Mass Communication Research (IAMCR), Section of International Communication session on 'Communication and Peace: The Role of the Media in International Relations', New Delhi, 27 August 1986.

Nowak, M. *U.N. Covenant on Civil and Political Rights – CCPR Commentary*, 2nd rev. edn (Kehl: Engel, 2005).

Ó Fathaigh, R. 'The Recognition of a Right of Reply under the European Convention', *Journal of Media Law* 4(2) (2012), 322–32.

Opsahl, T. 'Articles 29 and 30: The Other Side of the Coin', in A. Eide, G. Alfredsson, G. Melander, L. A. Rehof and A. Rosas, with the collaboration of T. Swinehart (eds.), *The Universal Declaration of Human Rights: A Commentary* (Norway: Scandinavian University Press, 1992), 449–70.

Partsch, K. J. 'Freedom of Conscience and Expression, and Political Freedoms', in L. Henkin (ed.), *The International Bill of Rights: The Covenant on Civil and Political Rights* (New York: Columbia University Press, 1981), 209–45.

Powe, Jr., L. A. *The Fourth Estate and the Constitution: Freedom of the Press in America* (University of California Press, 1991).

Roosevelt, F. D. 'The four freedoms', State of the Union Message, 6 January 1941.

Sadurski, W. *Freedom of Speech and Its Limits* (Dordrecht/Boston/London: Kluwer, 1999).

Scanlon, T. 'A Theory of Freedom of Expression', in T. M. Scanlon, *The Difficulty of Tolerance* (Cambridge University Press, 2003), 6–25.

Schauer, F. *Free Speech: A Philosophical Enquiry* (Cambridge University Press, 1982).

'Free Speech and the Argument from Democracy', in J. R. Pennock and J. W. Chapman (eds.), *Liberal Democracy: Nomos XXV* (New York University Press, 1983), 241–56.

Siapera, E. *Understanding New Media* (Los Angeles, etc.: SAGE, 2012).

Silverstone, R. *Why Study the Media?* (London, etc.: SAGE Publications, 1999).

Thornberry, P. 'Confronting Racial Discrimination: A CERD Perspective', *Human Rights Law Review* 5(2) (2005), 239–69.

Torremans, P. 'Copyright (and Other Intellectual Property Rights) as a Human Right', in P. L. C. Torremans (ed.), *Intellectual Property and Human Rights*

*(Enhanced Edition of Copyright and Human Rights)* (Alphen aan den Rijn: Kluwer Law International, 2008), 195–215.

Whitton, J. B. 'The United Nations Conference on Freedom of Information and the Movement against International Propaganda', *American Journal of International Law* 43(1) (Jan. 1949), 73–87.

Zayas, A. de and Á. R. Martín, 'Freedom of Opinion and Freedom of Expression: Some Reflections on General Comment No. 34 of the UN Human Rights Committee', *Netherlands International Law Review* 59 (2012), 425–54.

## Treaty bodies' General Comments/Recommendations

### CRC

General Comment No. 12: The Right of the Child to Be Heard, 20 July 2009.

### CERD

General Recommendation No. 35 – Combating Racist Hate Speech, Doc. No. CERD/C/GC/35, 23 September 2013.

### HRC

General Comment No. 10 – Freedom of Expression (Article 19), 29 July 1983.

General Comment No. 11 – Prohibition of Propaganda for War and Inciting National, Racial or Religious Hatred (Article 20), 29 July 1983.

General Comment No. 34: Article 19 (Freedoms of opinion and expression), UN Doc. CCPR/C/GC/34, 12 September 2011.

### UNESCO

UNESCO Declaration on Cultural Diversity, 2 November 2001.

UNESCO Declaration on Fundamental Principles concerning the Contribution of the Mass Media to Strengthening Peace and International Understanding, to the Promotion of Human Rights and to Countering Racialism, Apartheid and Incitement to War, 28 November 1978.

UNESCO Declaration of Guiding Principles on the Use of Satellite Broadcasting for the Free Flow of Information, the Spread of Education and Greater Cultural Exchange, 15 November 1972.

*Report of the Special Rapporteur on the Promotion and Protection of the Right to Freedom of Opinion and Expression*, UN Doc. A/HRC/20/17, 4 June 2012.

*Report of the Special Rapporteur on the Promotion and Protection of the Right to Freedom of Opinion and Expression*, UN Doc. A/HRC/17/27, 16 May 2011.

*The Specialized Mandates*

Joint Declaration: Ten Key Challenges to Freedom of Expression in the Next Decade of 3 February 2010.

Joint Declaration on Freedom of Expression and the Internet of 1 June 2011.

Joint Declaration on the Protection of Freedom of Expression and Diversity in the Digital Terrestrial Transition, 3 May 2013.

## Miscellaneous

*Conferences*

Final Act, United Nations Conference on Freedom of Information, Geneva, Switzerland, 23 March–21 April 1948.

World Conference on Human Rights – The Vienna Declaration and Programme of Action (1993).

'Building the Information Society: A Global Challenge in the New Millennium', Declaration of Principles, World Summit on the Information Society, Geneva, Doc. No. WSIS-03/GENEVA/DOC/4-E, 12 December 2003; Tunis Commitment, World Summit on the Information Society, Tunis, Doc. No. WSIS-05/TUNIS/DOC/7-E, 18 November 2005.

*Reports*

Türk, D. and Joinet, L. *The Right to Freedom of Opinion and Expression*, Final Report, Conclusions and Recommendations, Doc. No. E/CN.4/Sub.2/1992/9/Add.1, 14 July 1992.

*Report, Seminar on Freedom of Information, Organized by the UN in Cooperation with the Government of Italy*, Rome, 7–20 April 1964, Doc. No. ST/TAO/HR/20.

López, S. P. *Freedom of Information*, report by the Rapporteur on freedom of information, UN ECOSOC, Official Records, 16th Session, Supp. No. 12 (New York: United Nations, 1953).

## UN Resolutions

UN Human Rights Council Resolution 7/36 of 28 March 2008.

UN Commission on Human Rights' Resolution 1993/45 of 5 March 1993.

UNGA Resolution 45/158 of 18 December 1990.

UNGA Resolution 59(1), 14 December 1946.

UNGA Resolution 13(1), 'Organization of the Secretariat', 1 February 1946.



# PART I

## UN normative and institutional approaches to the protection of freedom of expression and information

2

# International Covenant on Civil and Political Rights: interpreting freedom of expression and information standards for the present and the future

MICHAEL O'FLAHERTY

## 1 Introduction

This chapter is concerned with an examination of the manner in which Article 19 of the International Covenant on Civil and Political Rights is interpreted and applied in the practice of the Human Rights Committee, with a particular focus of attention on the development of the 2011 General Comment (General Comment No. 34) on the provision. That discussion is set in a context of an examination of the role that freedom of expression plays for democracy and the enjoyment of other human rights.

## 2 Origins and significance of freedom of expression

On the eve of his imprisonment in China, the Nobel laureate, Liu Xiaobo wrote that 'Freedom of expression is the basis of human rights, the source of humanity and the mother of truth. To block freedom of speech is to trample on human rights, to strangle humanity and to suppress truth.'[1] Liu Xiaobo's powerful affirmation of the status of freedom of expression is well grounded both in history and in contemporary experience.

Michael O'Flaherty, 'Freedom of Expression: Article 19 of the International Covenant on Civil and Political Rights and the Human Rights Committee's General Comment No 34', *Human Rights Law Review* 12(4) (2012), 627–54. By permission of Oxford University Press.
Thanks are expressed to Pei-Lun Tsai for her assistance in completing the notes for this chapter.

[1] C. Coonan, 'China condemns "insult" of award for jailed dissident Liu Xiaobo', *The Independent*, 9 October 2010.

The right to freedom of expression has ancient roots.[2] Expression was important to the ideas of Aristotle – with the human considered as the *zoon politicon* or political animal. There are claims that early Islamic thought also gave a high value to what we might call 'free speech'. For instance, the Islamic scholar Hugh Goddard argues that the modern conception of academic freedom of expression originates in the *madrasas* (Islamic religious schools) of the ninth century.[3] Later, the fathers of enlightenment philosophy elevated this freedom to a very high level indeed. We all know Voltaire's remark, 'Sir, I do not share your views but I would risk my life for your right to express them' (albeit it is sometimes suggested the quote is misattributed).[4] John Stuart Mill helped to shape our modern understanding of the parameters of an entitlement to seek, receive and impart information and ideas. He also addressed the manner in which such rights may be limited by the State where their exercise would constitute a direct threat to society.[5]

Liberal theorists identified freedom of expression as essential to democracy and good governance.[6] This perception is still very much alive: the United Nations (UN) Human Rights Committee has described freedom of expression as being 'of paramount importance for any democratic society'.[7]

The identification of a relationship of freedom of expression and democracy brings into relief some philosophical tension. Enlightenment thought maintained an ambiguous double classification of freedom of expression as inhering in the person as an autonomous subject and as a right in the service of society (thus the French Declaration of the Rights of Man and the Citizen (1789) identifies freedom of expression as a right of man but limits its exercise to citizens).[8] Marx would later seize with

[2] T. D. Jones, *Human Rights: Group Defamation, Freedom of Expression and the Law of Nations* (Leiden: Martinus Nijhoff, 1998), 34–7.

[3] H. Goddard, *A History of Christian–Muslim Relations* (Edinburgh University Press, 2000), 100.

[4] O. Bakircioglu, 'Freedom of Expression and Hate Speech', *Tulsa Journal of Comparative and International Law* 16 (2008), 1.

[5] J. S. Mill, *On Liberty* (London: Watts, 1929), 92–115.

[6] P. Norris, *Driving Democracy: Do Power-Sharing Institutions Work?* (Cambridge University Press, 2008), 186.

[7] HRC, *Tae Hoon Park* v. *Republic of Korea*, Communication No. 628/1995, 3 November 1998, para. 10.3.

[8] M. Nowak, *U.N. Covenant on Civil and Political Rights: CCPR Commentary*, 2nd rev. edn (Kehl am Rein, Germany: N.P. Engel, 2005), 438.

approval on the Declaration's category of citizens' rights and, as Manfred Nowak puts it, thereby 'laid the cornerstone for the conflict between bourgeois and socialist human rights theory'.[9]

This conflict came to play an important role in the eventual articulation of international human rights law, with a tension between States that saw human rights primarily as tools for social progress and those that perceived human rights to be validated on the basis of the autonomy and subjectivity of the person. The former point of view is well illustrated by the statement of the Soviet Union expressed during the drafting of the International Covenant on Civil and Political Rights (ICCPR) that rights of political liberty were to be guaranteed only, 'in accordance with the principles of democracy and in the interest of strengthening international cooperation and world peace'.[10]

Ultimately, though, socialist perceptions came to play little decisive role in the articulation of a right of freedom of expression in UN forums. In 1946, the General Assembly, at its first session, declared that [freedom of information] is 'a fundamental human right . . .The touchstone of all the freedoms to which the United Nations is consecrated'.[11] The articulation of the right, two years later, in Article 19 of the Universal Declaration of Human Rights (UDHR), is consistent with this understanding: 'Everyone has the right to freedom of opinion and expression; this right includes freedom to hold opinions without interference and to seek, receive and impart information and ideas through any media and regardless of frontiers.'[12]

Here we have a bold and unconditional restatement of the classic liberal position. Subsequent legal instruments remained largely true to the liberal understanding, and the sheer extent of references to the right is indicative of the high importance accorded to it. Its first expression in treaty form was in Article 10 of the European Convention on Human Rights (1950).[13] There followed Article 5 of the Convention on the

[9] *Ibid.*, 438–9.

[10] M. J. Bossuyt, *Guide to the 'Travaux Préparatoires' of the International Covenant on Civil and Political Rights* (Leiden: Martinus Nijhoff, 1987), 374.

[11] GA, *Resolution 59(1): Calling of an International Conference on Freedom of Information*, UN Doc. A/RES/59(I), 14 December 1946, adopted at its 1st session.

[12] UN GA, Resolution 217 (III): Universal Declaration of Human Rights, 10 December 1948, Art. 19.

[13] Convention for the Protection of Human Rights and Fundamental Freedoms as Amended by Protocols No. 11 and No. 14, Rome, 4 November 1950, entered into force 3 September 1953, CETS 5, Art. 10.

Elimination of All Forms of Racial Discrimination (1965),[14] and, finally, in 1966, Article 19 of the ICCPR (1966).[15] Two additional regional provisions followed: Article 13 of the American Convention on Human Rights (1969)[16] and Article 9 of the African Charter on Human and Peoples' Rights (1981).[17] The right is expressed with specific reference to children and in notably vibrant terms at Articles 12 and 13 of the Convention on the Rights of the Child (1988).[18] Hard-law provisions are mirrored by myriad soft-law references. Such texts include the outcome document of the World Summit on Information Society (December 2003)[19] the Inter-American Declaration of Principles of Freedom of Expression, (2000)[20] and the Declaration of Principles on Freedom of Expression in Africa (2002).[21] It is notable that intergovernmental organisations have established special procedures mandates for promotion of the right, including, the special rapporteurs on freedom of expression and/or media of the UN,[22] the Organization for Security and Co-operation in Europe (OSCE),[23] the Organization of American States (OAS)[24] and the African Commission on Human and Peoples' Rights.

The high importance accorded to freedom of expression in international law and related discourse is not just a matter of philosophy or ideology. As a matter of empirical observation it can be seen that free

[14] International Convention on the Elimination of All Forms of Racial Discrimination, 21 December 1965, entered into force 4 January 1969, 660 UNTS, 195, Art. 5.

[15] International Covenant on Civil and Political Rights, New York, 16 December 1966, entered into force 23 March 1976, 999 UNTS, 172, Art. 19.

[16] American Convention on Human Rights, 'Pact of San José', Costa Rica, adopted 22 November 1969, entered into force 18 July 1978, OAS TS No. 36, Art. 13.

[17] African Charter on Human and Peoples' Rights, Banjul, Gambia, 27 June 1981, entered into force 21 October 1986, OAU Doc. CAB/LEG/67/3 rev. 5, Art. 9.

[18] Convention on the Rights of the Child, New York, 20 November 1989, entered into force 2 September 1990, 1577 UNTS 3, Arts. 12 and 13.

[19] Declaration of Principles: Building the Information Society: A Global Challenge in the New Millennium, Doc. No. WSIS-03/GENEVA/DOC/4-E, 12 December 2003.

[20] Inter-American Commission on Human Rights (IACHR), Inter-American Declaration of Principles on Freedom of Expression, adopted by the Inter-American Commission on Human Rights at its 108th Regular Session, 19 October 2000.

[21] African Commission on Human and Peoples' Rights (ACHPR), Declaration of Principles on Freedom of Expression in Africa, ACHPR /Res. 62(XXXII)02, 23 October 2002.

[22] United Nations Commission on Human Rights (CHR), Resolution 1993/45: Right to Freedom of Opinion and Expression, UN Doc. E/CN.4/1993/122, 5 March 1993.

[23] Organization for Security and Co-operation in Europe (OSCE), Permanent Council, *Decision 193: Mandate of the OSCE Representation on Freedom of the Media*, 5 November 1997.

[24] Declaration of Santiago, Second Summit of the Americas, 18–19 April 1998.

expression is essential to the good working of the entire human rights system.[25] It is sometimes described as a multiplier or *meta* right because of its role in enabling enjoyment of so many other rights.[26] Political participation rights, for instance, would be meaningless without the exchange of ideas.[27] Cultural rights are to a large extent enjoyed through expression.[28] The rights to assembly and association would mean little if they did not include an entitlement to engage with others.[29] We may ask the question, though, as to whether the link is only, or predominantly, with civil and political rights. At first sight it may not be so obvious what relevance this right may have with regard to enjoyment of such economic and social rights as health and housing.[30] However, with a little probing it is obvious that the equitable enjoyment of these rights is not possible without the respectful giving and receiving of information between duty bearer and rights holder, without the participation of the rights holder in decisions that affect his or her welfare.[31] Amartya Sen goes so far as to suggest that no country that vigorously ensures freedom of expression will experience famine.[32] Insights such as these lie behind the prominent place accorded to freedom of expression in recent theories of the rights-based approach to development (RBAD). It is notable, for instance, how centrally and obviously critical free expression is to the implementation of core RBAD principles, including accountability, transparency and empowerment.[33]

[25] K. Boyle, 'Thought, Expression, Association, and Assembly', in D. Moeckli *et al.* (eds.), *International Human Rights Law* (Oxford University Press, 2010), 266.

[26] M. O'Flaherty, 'Article 19 UDHR: contemporary challenges and opportunities for freedom of expression', lecture at the Carr Centre for Human Rights Policy, Kennedy School of Government, Harvard University, 4 March 2009; www.hks.harvard.edu/cchrp/events/2009/month03/article19.pdf (last accessed 12 March 2014).

[27] HRC, General Comment No. 25: The Right to Participate in Public Affairs, Voting Rights and the Right of Equal Access to Public Service (Art. 25), UN Doc. CCPR/C/21/Rev.1/Add.7, 12 July 1996.

[28] Committee on Economic, Social and Cultural Rights (CESCR), General Comment No. 21: Right of Everyone to Take Part in Cultural Life (Art. 15, para. 1 (a), of the International Covenant on Economic, Social and Cultural Rights), UN Doc. E/C.12/GC/21, 21 December 2009.

[29] Boyle, 'Thought, Expression', 257–8.

[30] See Chapter 3 in this book.

[31] B. I. Hamm, 'A Human Rights Approach to Development', *Human Rights Quarterly* 23–4 (2001), 1005 and 1018–20.

[32] A. Sen, *Development as Freedom* (Oxford University Press, 1999), 16.

[33] United Nations Educational, Scientific and Cultural Organization (UNESCO), 'World Press Freedom Day 2008 Concept Paper: Freedom of Expression, Access and Empowerment'; www.unesco.org/new/fileadmin/MULTIMEDIA/HQ/CI/WPFD2009/pdf/wpfd2008_concept+engl.pdf (last accessed 17 March 2014).

## 3 Article 19, paragraphs 2 and 3, ICCPR

As is addressed elsewhere in this book, freedom of expression is subject to an array of assaults, abuses, concerns and protection gaps. The addressing of these requires multifaceted action from many actors. For instance, it demands ongoing monitoring and reporting; persistent advocacy; education about the role of freedom of expression in society; putting in place of self-regulatory frameworks for journalists; exploration of non-criminal strategies to combat hate speech; law reform; judicial restraint; accountability for human rights violations; and policy development regarding the free expression rights of the child. It also calls for innovative transnational approaches.[34]

Crucial to the effectiveness of all such responses will be the existence of a strong normative framework in the form of international human rights law in support of freedom of expression. One should thus enquire as to whether the existing standards are adequate to their function. The present chapter frames a response to that question around the principal global expression of the right in Article 19 (paragraphs 2 and 3) of the ICCPR and the work of the Human Rights Committee.

ICCPR Article 19, paragraphs 2 and 3, read:

> 2. Everyone shall have the right to freedom of expression; this right shall include freedom to seek receive and impart information and ideas of all kinds, regardless of frontiers, either orally, in writing or in print, in the form of art, or through any other media of his choice.
> 3. The exercise of the rights provided for in paragraph 2 of this article carries with it special duties and responsibilities. It may therefore be subject to certain restrictions, but these shall only be such as are provided by law and are necessary: (a) for respect of the rights or reputation of others; (b) for the protection of national security or of public order (*ordre public*), or of public health or morals.

[34] See Council of Europe Commissioner of Human Rights, *Ethical Journalism and Human Rights*, CommDH (2011) 40, 8 November 2011, https://wcd.coe.int/ViewDoc.jsp?id=1863637; W. H. Dutton, A. Dopatka, M. Hills, G. Law and V. Nash, *Freedom of Connection, Freedom of Expression: The Changing Legal and Regulatory Ecology Shaping the Internet* (UNESCO, 2011); Joint Declarations of the United Nations Special Rapporteur on the Promotion and Protection of the Right to Freedom of Opinion and Expression, Organization of American States Special Rapporteur on Freedom of Expression, the Representative on Freedom of the Media of the OSCE, and the Rapporteur for the African Commission on Human and Peoples' Rights (for extensive analysis, see Chapter 8 in this book); Article 19, Freedom of Expression: Enforcement, www.article19.org/pages/en/enforcement.html (all websites last accessed 4 April 2014).

Bearing in mind that the topic of freedom of opinion came to be addressed separately from freedom of expression (in paragraph 1 of Article 19), the formulation of paragraph 2 is notably close to that in the UDHR. Furthermore, when one considers that the schema of the treaty required that a specific restrictions provision (paragraph 3) be included (since, unlike in the case of UDHR, the treaty does not contain a general restriction provision), it can be concluded that freedom of expression as articulated in Article 19, ICCPR, is faithful to the right as found in the Universal Declaration. Such fidelity did not come about without extensive debate. As with all other provisions of the Covenant, the language addressing freedom of expression was subject to protracted review over a drafting period that lasted from 1947 until 1966 (albeit Article 19 was agreed in its final form in 1961, on a vote at the 3rd Committee of the General Assembly of 82 to 1, with 7 abstentions).[35] Numerous proposals were made for significant variants on the UDHR formulation.[36] At least in the first phase of drafting, very many of these were fermented in the context of a UN Conference on Freedom of Information and an ultimately fruitless drafting process for a convention on that topic.[37]

Some of the drafting proposals remain of interest even at this remove. Reference has already been made to efforts of the Soviet Union to introduce words that would instrumentalise freedom of expression in the service of international cooperation and world peace.[38] Another suggestion, initially supported by many States, including the USA and the UK, would have limited the scope of the right through a stipulation that electronically broadcast expression would only be protected to the extent that it was by means of 'legally operated visual and auditory devices'.[39] With regard to another proposal, that remains of interest because of its tangential relevance to the contemporary discussion as to whether Article 19 embraces a right of access to information (discussed below), negotiators ultimately rejected the proposal of India and others, that the word 'seek' in the term, 'to seek, receive and impart information', should be replaced with the word 'gather'.[40] Not all of the unsuccessful proposals regarding the scope of the right were intended to narrow it. For instance, a French proposal would have had the right carry with it an explicit duty on States to promote it and remove obstacles to its realisation.[41]

35 Bossuyt, *Guide to the 'Travaux Préparatoires'*, 401.
36 *Ibid.*, 373–4, 381–3 and 386–93.
37 *Ibid.*, 374–5. See further in this regard, Chapter 1 in this book.
38 *Ibid.*, 374.
39 *Ibid.*, 383.
40 *Ibid.*, 384.
41 *Ibid.*, 381.

Negotiations on the extent to which the right might be restricted were particularly fraught and lasted throughout the drafting process. Already in 1947, the drafting committee felt unable to decide between a brief generalised statement of permissible restrictions on the right or a lengthy detailed listing.[42] Instead it referred alternative drafting proposals for the attention of the Commission on Human Rights. It identified proposals for twenty-five permissible restrictions regarding, *inter alia*, disclosures arising out of marital and personal relations, profanity in public places, and commercial and economic matters.[43] Early proponents of such an extensive listing included the Union of South Africa,[44] and another significant source was the proceedings of the Conference on Freedom of Information.[45] By the 1960s, the Soviet bloc had become the champion of extensive restrictive language, such as with regard to racist speech and expression that manifested class prejudice – with proposals tabled unsuccessfully by the Soviet Union and Yugoslavia.[46] Ultimately, the 3rd Committee, by 71 votes to 7, with 12 abstentions, adopted the generalised language to be found in paragraph 3 of Article 19.[47]

Before leaving this brief review of the *travaux préparatoires* it is relevant also to take note of the drafting of the one provision of the ICCPR that specifically requires States to restrict forms of expression, Article 20. It reads:

> 1. Any propaganda for war shall be prohibited by law.
> 2. Any advocacy of national, racial or religious hatred that constitutes incitement to discrimination, hostility or violence shall be prohibited by law.

In the scheme of the Covenant, this provision is a curiosity, imposing an obligation but not creating a right. It had a troubled passage through negotiation. The proponents of such a provision (principally the Soviet Union and other States of the Communist bloc) argued that the forms of expression at issue are so pernicious and dangerous that they require an explicit prohibition.[48] Opponents, such as the USA, expressed concern that such a provision could stifle expression and encourage censorship, including prior censorship, and that, in any case, paragraph 3 of Article 19 was sufficient to empower States to regulate such speech.[49] It was also observed that some of the terms under consideration for inclusion in the article, such as 'incitement to discrimination (and) hostility', were

[42] *Ibid.*, 374–5. [43] *Ibid.*, 375. [44] *Ibid.*, 375–6. [45] *Ibid.*, 374–5.
[46] *Ibid.*, 393–4. [47] *Ibid.*, 401. [48] *Ibid.*, 407. [49] *Ibid.*, 406–7.

unclear and would be difficult to interpret and apply.[50] During the protracted debate the proposal underwent considerable change – such as with the disappearance of the suggestion that the provision require the criminalisation rather than just the prohibition of the impugned forms of expression[51] and the late addition (in 1961) of the prohibition on war propaganda.[52] States that spoke to the issue of the relationship of the provision with Article 19 made clear that it did not serve to exclude the application of Article 19 with regard to the impugned forms of expression – rather it added an additional requirement on the State to take particular forms of action against such expression.[53] On a suggestion of Chile, the close nexus of the two articles was acknowledged with a repositioning of the provision immediately after Article 19 (previously it had constituted Article 26 of the draft Covenant).[54] Ultimately, the contested nature of Article 20 was reflected in the vote for its adoption at the 3rd Committee: 52 in favour, 19 against and 12 abstentions.[55]

## 4 Articles 19 and 20 in the practice of the HRC, 1977–2010

Article 19 comprises two elements regarding freedom of expression: a statement of the right and a list of the contexts in which its exercise may be limited. The statement is broad: encompassing a right to 'seek, receive and impart information and ideas of all kinds, regardless of frontiers, either orally, in writing or in print, in the form of art, or through any other media'. The words, 'of all kinds', are not to be found in the equivalent article of the European Convention on Human Rights.[56] Commentators have taken from them that every communicable type of subjective idea and opinion is embraced[57] – a view confirmed by the Human Rights Committee in *Ballantyne et al.* v. *Canada*.[58] Committee jurisprudence has also affirmed that the right covers political expression,[59] and, in *Ballantyne*, commercial speech,[60] albeit according a higher level of protection to the former.[61]

[50] *Ibid.*, 407–8. [51] *Ibid.*, 403. [52] *Ibid.*, 407–8. [53] *Ibid.*, 398. [54] *Ibid.*

[55] *Ibid.*, 410. See further, concerning Article 20, ICCPR, Chapter 1 in this book.

[56] ECHR, Art. 10. [57] Nowak, *U.N. Covenant on Civil and Political Rights*, 443–4.

[58] HRC, *Ballantyne, Davidson, McIntyre* v. *Canada*, Nos. 359/1989 and 385/1989, 5 May 1993, para. 11.3.

[59] HRC, *Primo José Essono Mika Miha* v. *Equatorial Guinea*, Communication No. 414/1990, 10 August 1994, para. 6.8.

[60] *Ballantyne et al.* v. *Canada*, para. 11.3.

[61] HRC, *Zeljko Bodrozić* v. *Serbia and Montenegro*, Communication No. 1180/2003, 23 January 2006, para. 7.2.

Committee jurisprudence has frequently affirmed the applicability of Article 19 to journalistic expression and the Committee has a long practice of addressing both direct attacks on journalists[62] and State efforts to limit journalistic space.[63] It is interesting that, in an otherwise very scant General Comment on Article 19 (General Comment No. 10, 1983), the Committee stated that, 'because of the development of modern mass media, effective measures are necessary to prevent such control of the media as would interfere with the right of everyone to freedom of expression'.[64] This aspect is reinforced by the absence from Article 19 of the stipulation to be found in the European Convention that the right is to be protected, without interference by 'public authority'. Finally, in 2004, the Committee had the opportunity to find a violation of Article 19 on the basis of the confiscation of an artwork and the imprisonment of the artist, in *Hak-Chul Sin* v. *Republic of Korea*.[65]

One may conclude from this overview of Committee practice that Article 19 put in place a broad protection with a wide sweep that embraces all verbal and artistic expression. Committee practice, however, left open such questions as to the extent to which Article 19 covers other forms. While in *Kivenmaa* v. *Finland* the Committee held that Article 19 protects such non-verbal expression as the unfurling of a banner,[66] in *SG* v. *France*, it refused to recognise the politically motivated defacement of road signs as a form of expression.[67] This oddity led Sarah Joseph *et al.* to wonder what status graffiti might have (maybe art?).[68] In *Baban* v. *Australia* the Committee was invited to consider a hunger strike to be a form of protected expression. While it appeared to be willing to consider such a proposition, it disposed of the claim on the basis of inadmissibility.[69] In the early case of *LTK* v. *Finland*, the Committee decided that the act of refusal to perform military service was not a form

[62] HRC, *Philip Afuson Njaru* v. *Cameroon*, Communication No. 1353/2005, 14 May 2007.

[63] HRC, *Rakhim Mavlonov and Shansiy Sa'di* v. *Uzbekistan*, Communication No. 1334/2004, 29 April 2009.

[64] HRC, General Comment No. 10: Freedom of expression (Art. 19), 29 June 1983, para. 2.

[65] HRC, *Hak-Chul Sin* v. *Republic of Korea*, Communication No. 926/2000, 19 March 2004, paras. 7.2 and 8.

[66] HRC, *Auli Kivenmaa* v. *Finland*, Communication No. 412/1990, 10 June 1994, para. 9.3.

[67] HRC, *SG* v. *France*, Communication No. 347/1988, 15 November 1991, para. 5.2.

[68] S. Joseph, J. Schultz and M. Castan, *The International Covenant on Civil and Political Rights: Cases, Materials, and Commentary* (Oxford University Press, 2004), 521.

[69] HRC, *Omar Sharif Baban* v. Australia, Communication No. 1014/2001, 18 September 2003, para. 6.7.

of expression.[70] Interestingly, though, in *Myung-Jin Choi and Yeo-Bum Yoon* v. *Republic of Korea* (2006), it accepted that the same act could constitute a manifestation of religion or belief,[71] leading us to speculate that *LTK* might be decided differently post 2006. And then, what of the expression of identity through forms of clothing or other bodily adornment? The Committee had an opportunity to explore this when it decided *Hudoybergonova* v. *Uzbekistan* (2004), a case of a female student who was not permitted to wear a hijab at a State-run educational facility and who complained of violations of Articles 18 (freedom of religion) and 19. The Committee found a violation under Article 18 and declined to also examine the claim under Article 19.[72] Another open question concerned the application of Article 19 with regard to forms of expression of gender identity – a matter of obvious importance for those who are transgender.

One further aspect of the scope of freedom of expression may be considered – it is the outcome of the curious finding in *Zündel* v. *Canada* (2003) that a failure to give a Holocaust-denying journalist access to a press conference facility in a parliamentary building that was available to other journalists did not raise issues under Article 19, since the article does not confer a right to free expression in any particular location. The Committee observed that there is no 'unfettered right of any individual or group to hold press conferences within the Parliamentary precincts. . .the Committee notes that the author remained at liberty to hold a press conference elsewhere'.[73] This seems an unfortunate decision on a number of grounds, including that it does not take account of the special significance of the event taking place in so nationally prestigious a location. It unduly limits the scope of application of Article 19, particularly since the Committee could have still determined a non-violation without limiting the scope of freedom of expression by instead having recourse to the application of the article's limitation provisions. It may more generally be observed that laws on genocide denial appear to have tended to trigger discomfort on the part of the Committee   in *Faurisson* v. *France* (1996) – a case concerning the imposition of a criminal penalty under the Gayssot Act – a statute penalising denial of the existence of the Holocaust – the Committee

[70] HRC, *LTK* v. *Finland*, Communication No. 185/1984, 9 July 1985, para. 5.2.

[71] HRC, *Yeo-Bum Yoon and Myung-Jin Choi* v. *Republic of Korea*, Communications Nos. 1321/2004 and 1322/2004, 23 January 2007, para. 8.3.

[72] HRC, *Raihon Hudoyberganova* v. *Uzbekistan*, Communication No. 931/2000, 8 December 2004, para. 5.3.

[73] HRC, *Ernst Zündel* v. *Canada*, Communication No. 953/2000, 29 July 2003, para. 8.5.

considered that while the penalty, in the specific circumstances of the actions of Mr Faurisson, did not constitute a violation of Article 19, it suggested that the statute itself constituted an excessive restriction on freedom of expression.[74] We will return to this issue later in the chapter.

Another area of uncertainty with regard to the reach of Article 19 has concerned the extent of the entitlement to access information. Until 2009, this had not been addressed in the jurisprudence of the Human Rights Committee, albeit it had suggested elements of such an entitlement in a number of Concluding Observations.[75] In 2006, the Inter-American Court of Human Rights, in *Claude Reyes et al.* v. *Chile*, held that Article 13 of the American Convention on Human Rights 'protects the right of all individuals to request access to State-held information, with the exceptions permitted by the restrictions established in the Convention'.[76] Since then, the European Court of Human Rights recognised a limited right of public access to information in the context of court proceedings.[77] The Committee's first opportunity to consider the matter arose in the case of *Mavlonov and Sa'di* v. *Uzbekistan*. On that occasion, a majority of the Committee considered that a member of the public has the right to receive journalistic information, 'as a corollary of the specific function of a journalist and/or editor to impart information'.[78] This contentious basis for recognition of a right to receive information was subject to the dissent of two members who observed that '(t)he Committee's literalist reading [of article 19(2)] would require it to treat every potential recipient of any information or ideas that have been improperly suffered [*sic*] under article 19 as a victim.'[79] In another problematic case of 2009, this time concerning information held by the State, the Committee rejected at the admissibility stage a claim that a refusal to provide an author with information about the application of

74 HRC, *Robert Faurisson* v. *France*, Communication No. 550/1993, 16 December 1996, para. 9.3.

75 HRC, Concluding Observations on Azerbaijan, UN Doc. CCPR/C/79/Add.38, 3 August 1994, para. 18; Ukraine; Ireland; Lithuania.

76 IACHR, *Claude-Reyes et al.* v. *Chile*, Merits, Reparations and Costs, Judgment, Series C No. 151, 19 September 2006, para. 77.

77 ECtHR, *Társaság a Szabadságjogokért* v. *Hungary* (Appl. No. 37374/05), 14 July 2009. See further Chapters 3 and 9 in this book.

78 HRC, *Mavlonov and Sa'di* v. *Uzbekistan*, Communication No. 1334/2004, 19 March 2009, para. 8.4.

79 *Ibid.*, at Appendix, separate opinions of Committee members Sir Nigel Rodley and Mr Rafael Rivas Posada; see also the Concurring Opinion of Mr G. L. Neuman in *Toktakunov* v. *Kyrgyzstan*, Communication No. 1470/2006, 21 April 2011.

the death penalty constituted a violation of Article 19. The Committee observed that, 'the author has not explained why exactly he, personally, needed the information in question; rather he contended that this was a "matter of public interest"...the present communication constitutes an *actio popularis* and...is inadmissible'.[80] This approach was clarified (or moderated) in *Toktakunov* v. *Kyrgyzstan* where, on similar facts, an author's claim was found to be admissible since he, as a legal consultant at a human rights organisation that had a 'watchdog' function, had demonstrated that he 'as an individual member of the public, was directly affected by the refusal of the State party's authorities to make available to him, on request, the information on use of the death penalty'.[81]

Turning to the list of the contexts in which the exercise of the right to freedom of expression may be limited, a number of issues arise. In the first instance, the reference to, 'special duties and responsibilities', an undoubted oddity in the general scheme of the Covenant, seems to give no particular cause for concern as it does not constitute a distinct restriction. Instead, it has been argued that it serves to emphasise the duty of the State to take positive measures to ensure an adequate space in society for free expression – for instance by ensuring that media not be controlled by monopoly interests.[82] Likewise, the absence of a provision, as found in the European Convention, that restrictions be, 'necessary in a democratic society', does not appear to have caused any difficulty in practice (with the Committee, as we have seen, frequently invoking the role freedom of expression plays in ensuring a democratic society). The permissible purposes for restriction are notably fewer than those listed in the European Convention. Thus there is no mention of restrictions in the interest of territorial integrity or public safety, for the prevention of disorder or crime, for preventing the disclosure of information received in confidence, and for maintaining the authority and impartiality of the judiciary.[83]

Notwithstanding the relatively brief list of reasons for restriction one might assume that the provision has the potential to unravel the protected right. The point was well put by late Committee member Rajsoomer Lallah: 'recourse to restrictions that are, in principle, permissible under Article 19, paragraph 3, bristle with difficulties, tending to

[80] HRC, *S. B.* v. *Kyrgyzstan*, Communication No. 1877/2009, 25 August 2009, para. 4.
[81] *Toktakunov* v. *Kyrgyzstan*, at para. 6.4.
[82] HRC, Concluding Observations on Russian Federation, UN Doc. CCPR/CO/79/RUS, 1 December 2003, para. 18.
[83] ECHR, Art. 10.

destroy the very existence of the right sought to be restricted' (*Faurisson* v. *France*).[84] However, practice has been encouraging. Jurisprudence has demonstrated that restrictions must be necessary and proportionate to the goal sought to be achieved and that this is a determination that is not the exclusive prerogative of the State (*Gauthier* v. *Canada*).[85] In *Gauthier* and subsequent cases, the Committee stipulated that the State must specify and justify the precise nature of the threat posed by the exercise of freedom of expression by an individual (*Kim* v. *Republic of Korea*).[86] In the 2005 decision in *Bodrozic* v. *Serbia and Montenegro*, a case of criminal libel proceedings against a journalist who criticised a well-known public figure, the responsibility of the State to justify the limitation in its specific circumstances was reaffirmed. The Committee also took the opportunity to observe that 'in circumstances of public debate in a democratic society, especially in the media, concerning figures in the political domain, the value placed by the Covenant upon uninhibited expression is particularly high'.[87] This recalled the finding of a violation in *De Moraes* v. *Angola* (2005) on the basis of the imprisonment of a journalist who had published comments critical of the head of State. The Committee considered that: 'the severity of the sanctions imposed on the author cannot be considered as a proportionate measure to protect public order or the honour and the reputation of the President, a public figure who, as such, is subject to criticism and opposition'.[88] In *Colman* v. *Australia* (2006), the fining and eventual imprisonment of a person who failed to obtain the required permit before delivering an innocuous speech at a shopping mall was found to be wholly disproportionate to the legitimate interest of the State in regulating the delivery of addresses in public places.[89] We find many other examples of a strict approach of the Committee in Concluding Observations. For example, it has frequently criticised the extent of

[84] *Robert Faurisson* v. *France*, Individual opinion by Rajsoomer Lallah (concurring), para. 13.

[85] HRC, *Robert Gauthier* v. *Canada*, Communication No. 633/1995, UN Doc. CCPR/C/65/D/633/1995, 5 May 1999, para. 13.6.

[86] *Ibid.*, para. 13.6 and HRC, *Keun-Tae Kim* v. *Republic of Korea*, Communication No. 574/1994, 4 January 1999, para. 12.5.

[87] *Bodrozić* v. *Serbia and Montenegro*, para. 7.2.

[88] HRC, *Rafael Marques de Morais* v. *Angola*, Communication No. 1128/2002, 18 April 2005, para. 6.8.

[89] HRC, *Patrick Coleman* v. *Australia*, Communication No. 1157/2003, 10 August 2006, para. 7.3.

limitation of freedom of expression in counter-terrorism legislation,[90] defamation laws[91] and blasphemy provisions.[92]

Concern has been expressed regarding restrictions on the grounds of protection of public morals. In the early case of *Hertzberg* v. *Finland* (1982), the Committee found no violation of Article 19 in the failure of the State to interfere with the banning by its broadcasting company of programme segments dealing with issues of homosexuality. The Committee stated that: 'public morals differ widely. There is no universally applicable common standard. Consequently, in this respect, a certain margin of discretion must be accorded to the responsible national authorities.'[93] This is the only case in which the Committee has invoked such a margin of discretion – which seems to mirror the margin of appreciation doctrine so favoured by the European Court of Human Rights. It has been rightly criticised by Sarah Joseph *et al.* who have observed that the purpose of the European approach – the resolution of situations where there is no common ground within all the State Parties – is inapplicable to the situation under the Covenant where globally common practice is inevitably a rare thing.[94] The Committee, in the subsequent case of *Sohn* v. *Republic of Korea*, appeared, albeit not explicitly, to reverse itself on the matter when it affirmed that it reserves to itself an assessment of whether, in any given situation, there were circumstances justifying restriction of the right rather than deferring to national authorities on the matter.[95]

Turning to the consideration of Article 20, the Committee in *Faurisson* and in *Ross* v. *Canada*, affirmed that the provision addresses forms of aggravated abuse that would all fall foul in any case of Article 19(3).[96]

[90] HRC, Concluding Observations on the United Kingdom, UN Doc. CCPR/C/GBR/CO/6, 21 July 2008 and Concluding Observations on the Russian Federation, UN Doc. CCPR/CO/79/RUS, 6 November 2003.

[91] HRC, Concluding Observations on the United Kingdom, UN Doc. CCPR/C/GBR/CO/6, 21 July 2008; Concluding Observations on Italy, UN Doc. CCPR/C/ITA/CO/5, 24 April 2006 and Concluding Observations on the Former Yugoslav Republic of Macedonia, UN Doc. CCPR/C/MKD/CO/2, 3 April 2008.

[92] HRC, Concluding Observations on the United Kingdom: the Crown Dependencies of Jersey, Guernsey and the Isle of Man, UN Doc. CCPR/C/79/Add.119, 27 March 2000 and Concluding Observations on Kuwait, UN Doc. CPR/CO/69/KWT, 27 July 2000.

[93] HRC, *Leo Hertzberg* v. *Finland*, Communication No. 61/1979, 2 April 1982, para. 10.3.

[94] Joseph *et al.*, *International Covenant on Civil and Political Rights*, 527–8.

[95] HRC, *Jong-Kyu Sohn* v. *Republic of Korea*, Communication No. 518/1992, 3 August 1995, para. 10.4.

[96] HRC, *Faurisson* v. *France* and *Malcolm Ross* v. *Canada*, Communication No. 736/1997, 26 October 2000.

Otherwise, it has provided little guidance in the period under review, or since, and many uncertainties persist. For instance, what constitutes 'propaganda' and what situations does the word 'war' address? Manfred Nowak makes an argument to limit the scope of the word, 'propaganda', by means of an application of the interpretative rules contained in the Vienna Convention on the Law of Treaties,[97] but his approach is somewhat speculative.

The term, 'war', on the other hand has been interpreted by the Committee as being restricted to, 'an act of aggression or breach of the peace contrary to the Charter of the United Nations'.[98] While one may wonder how this meaning might apply in practice – since the act of propaganda will commonly precede the conflict and thus any determination of its status under the Charter – this is nevertheless a useful restriction of the term.

With regard to the second element of the article, a number of interpretative problems arise, as was foreseen during the drafting of the provision.[99] For instance, what meaning should be given to such terms as 'advocacy', 'incitement' and 'hostility'? Most of these issues remain open and we can only speculate that they refer to forms of abuse at a level of seriousness that may exceed those addressed in Article 19. Other questions concern the relationship of Articles 19 and 20. Here, as previously observed, we do find guidance. What is less clear is when a matter should be dealt with under Article 19 and when under Article 20. This was the context for the separate opinion of Mr Lallah in *Faurisson*, referred to earlier, where he considered that the case should have been disposed of under Article 20 rather than by invocation of the limitation clauses of Article 19.[100]

The roles and interplay of Articles 19 and 20 are particularly pertinent to the question of permissible responses to abusive attacks on religions.[101] This is one of the major contemporary controversies, as we see from the furore around threats triggered by the writings of Salman Rushdie,[102] the

[97] Nowak, *U.N. Covenant on Civil and Political Rights*, 472.

[98] HRC, General Comment No. 11: Prohibition of Propaganda for War and Inciting National, Racial or Religious hatred (Art. 20), UN Doc. HRI/GEN/1/Rev.1 at 12, 29 July 1983, para. 2.

[99] Bossuyt, *Guide to the 'Travaux Préparatoires'* (1987), 406–8.

[100] *Faurisson* v. *France*, Individual opinion by Rajsoomer Lallah (concurring), para. 11.

[101] For extensive analysis of this topic, see Chapter 12 in this book.

[102] M. M. Slaughter, 'The Salman Rushdie Affair: Apostasy, Honor, and Freedom of Speech', *Virginia Law Review* 79 (1993), 153.

publication of the Danish cartoons,[103] recent Dutch movies[104] and so on. A number of States have argued that these types of acts of disrespect of religion should be dealt with through a new international prohibition of defamation of religions.[105] So far, the topic has been aired principally in political forums of the UN, such as the Human Rights Council[106] and the General Assembly,[107] where the relevant resolutions adopted in 2011 suggest that the positions of those States that advocated on the topic are moderating.[108] The issues raised are complex. On the one hand there is the need to protect the right of religious freedom, a right no less important than any other contained in international human rights law. There is also the need to take account of the very real distress that much comment causes to people of faith. However, on the other hand, the proposed 'defamation' route has given cause for serious concern. In the first place, the notion of defamation of religion is utterly alien to the human rights system, in that it would protect an idea or belief rather than the individual who holds that belief.[109] Second, it may force a State to determine which religious beliefs may be expressed.[110] Third, it would constitute an internationalisation of blasphemy laws with a potentially dramatic effect on freedom of expression.[111] For instance, it could prove to be a tool for the repression of peoples of minority faith or no faith or whose lifestyle

[103] H. J. Steiner *et al.*, *International Human Rights in Context: Law, Politics, Morals*, 3rd edn (Oxford University Press, 2007), 659–65.

[104] J. Nijboer and K. Soeters, 'Death of a Filmmaker: Freedom of Expression and Tolerance under Siege', the 13th BOBCATSSS Symposium, 31 January–2 February 2005, Budapest.

[105] R. J. Dobras, 'Is the United Nations Endorsing Human Rights Violations?: An Analysis of the United Nations' Combating Defamation of Religions Resolutions and Pakistan's Blasphemy Laws', *Georgia Journal of International & Comparative Law* 37 (2009), 339.

[106] HR Council, Resolution 13/16: Combating Defamation of Religions, UN Doc. A/HRC/RES/13/16, 15 April 2010.

[107] GA, Resolution 64/156: Combating Defamation of Religions, UN Doc. A/RES/64/156, 8 March 2010.

[108] HR Council, Resolution 16/1: Combating Intolerance, Negative Stereotyping and Stigmatization of, and Discrimination, Incitement to Violence and Violence Against, Persons Based on Religion or Belief, UN Doc. A/HRC/RES/16/18, 24 March 2011 and GA, Resolution 66/167: Combating Intolerance, Negative Stereotyping and Stigmatization of, and Discrimination, Incitement to Violence and Violence Against, Persons Based on Religion or Belief, UN Doc. A/RES/66/167, 19 December 2011.

[109] S. Parmar, 'The Challenge of "Defamation of Religions" to Freedom of Expression and the International Human Rights', *European Human Rights Law Review* 3 (2009), 365. See also her contribution in the present book (Chapter 12).

[110] L. Bennett Graham, 'Defamation of Religions: The End of Pluralism?', *Emory International Law Review* 23 (2009), 75–6.

[111] R. J. Dobras, 'Is the United Nations Endorsing Human Rights Violations?' (2009), 366–7.

offends the tenets of a State's dominant faith. Taking account of such considerations as these, it is important then to assess whether the existing legal provisions are capable of providing adequate protection to religions. The present author would suggest that they are. In the framework of individual rather than 'institutional' human rights, Article 19, as we have seen, clearly countenances restrictions on expression for purposes of respecting religiously held beliefs and practices. Article 20 expressly addresses expression intended to generate religious hatred. What is more, the Covenant, at Article 18, protects religious belief and practice, and, at Articles 2 and 26, it prohibits religious discrimination. The interplay of these provisions would appear to be sufficient to provide international legal protection from forms of expression that constitute extreme assaults on the religious beliefs and practices of any person.[112]

At this point we can draw some conclusions from this review of practice up to 2010 about the state of the law. It is clear that Article 19 is a reasonably sturdy provision. It has a wide reach and restrictively formulated limitation clauses. The Human Rights Committee has interpreted it in a manner that favours a wide enjoyment of free expression and it has applied the restriction clauses narrowly. Of course, there remain open questions. Some of the elements, particularly of Article 20, are unclear. The jurisprudence, inevitably, only addressed a small range of issues and, notwithstanding the many additional indications to be found in the Committee's Concluding Observations, there remained areas of uncertainty regarding the scope and application of the article. Furthermore, in some cases, the findings of the Committee were unconvincing and in need of review. Thus was set the context, in 2009, for the Committee's decision to develop a new General Comment on Article 19.

## 5 The role of general comments

General comments are, as Philip Alston puts it, the 'means by which a UN human rights expert committee distils its considered views on an

[112] This conclusion is supported by the comments of a number of speakers at an international expert workshop convened by the UN High Commissioner for Human Rights in October 2008. *Report of the Office of the UN High Commissioner for Human Rights, Expert Seminar on the links between Articles 19 and 20 of the International Covenant on Civil and Political Rights: 'Freedom of Expression and Advocacy of Religious Hatred that Constitutes Incitement to Discrimination, Hostility or Violence'* (Geneva, 2–3 October 2008), UN Doc. A/HRC/10/31/Add.3, 16 January 2009.

issue which arises out of provisions of the treaty, whose implementation it supervises, and presents those views in the context of a formal statement'.[113] The practice of the drafting of general comments is now widespread among the UN human rights treaty bodies, albeit, notwithstanding the remark of Alston, they do not all share a common understanding of the purpose or status of these instruments. In the case of the Human Rights Committee, the adoption of the comments is specifically mandated by Article 40 of the Covenant and the Committee intends that they constitute authoritative legal analysis of the provisions of the treaty, except to the extent that the text might indicate otherwise.[114] This analysis is based principally on the experience of the committee in applying the particular provisions that are at issue. The Committee considers that general comments carry considerable legal authority, adopted as they are by the body that is mandated to supervise implementation by States of the Covenant.[115] They have evolved over the years to be substantial and highly detailed commentaries on each aspect of a given article of the Covenant. They draw on all of the applicable jurisprudence of the Committee and take due account of its practice in the review of the periodic reports submitted by States Parties. They can also serve to relate the article under examination to the relevant contemporary human rights environment. Draft General Comments are subject to the comments of States and interested organisations and individuals.

As we have noted, a General Comment on Article 19 already existed, as did one on Article 20. However, they both date from the very early days of the Committee when the practice of providing detailed commentary had not yet been developed. And, of course, they cannot take account of the considerable jurisprudence since then. They have long been in need of updating. For these reasons, the decision of the Committee to develop the new General Comment on Article 19, was to be welcomed.

[113] P. Alston, 'The Historical Origins of "General Comments" in Human Rights Law', in L. Boisson De Charzournes and V. Gowlland-Debbas (eds.), *The International Legal System in Quest of Equity and Universality* (Leiden: Martinus Nijhoff, 2001), 764.

[114] HRC, Summary Record of the 2674th Meeting, 23 October 2009, UN Doc. CCPR/C/SR.2674, 9 August 2010, para. 2.

[115] HRC, General Comments Adopted by the Human Rights Committee under Article 40, Paragraph 4, of the International Covenant on Civil and Political Rights, UN Doc. CCPR/C/21/Rev.1, 19 May 1989.

## 6 The development of General Comment No. 34

The Human Rights Committee adopted the decision to develop the General Comment on Article 19, to replace General Comment No. 10, at its 94th session in March 2009.[116] It appointed the present writer to serve as rapporteur for development of the text. The rapporteur/present writer presented his draft text at the 97th session in October of that year.[117] The Committee reviewed that draft over the subsequent three sessions, by the end of which, in October 2010, a second revised draft was completed. That draft was then put for review and comment by States Parties to the ICCPR and any other interested organisations or individuals. The second draft,[118] together with these proposals, was presented to the Committee by the rapporteur/present writer for discussion at its 101st and 102nd sessions. The review concluded in July 2011 when General Comment No. 34 was adopted.[119]

The rapporteur/present writer's first draft,[120] the structure of which was retained in the final document, comprised fifty-six paragraphs, making it one of the lengthiest general comment texts ever considered by the Committee. It comprised general remarks, an examination of the scope of the two rights at issue – freedom of opinion and freedom of expression and a focused examination of the scope of three aspects of freedom of expression in particular – journalistic expression, access to information and political expression. There followed an examination of the application of paragraph 3 of Article 19. The draft then addressed the application of the paragraph 3 restrictions in the context of political expression, journalistic/media expression, counter-terrorism measures, defamation laws, blasphemy laws and 'memory laws'. The draft concluded with a six-paragraph examination of the relationship of Articles 19 and 20.

On the occasion of the introduction of his draft, the rapporteur/present writer explained his methodology.[121] He identified four sources

[116] HRC, *Report of the Human Rights Committee*, Vol. I, GA Official Records, 94th Session, Supplement No. 40, UN Doc. A/94/40, para. 41.

[117] HRC, Draft General Comment No. 34: Article 19, Draft Undertaken for the Human Rights Committee by Michael O'Flaherty, UN Doc. CPR/C/GC/34/CRP.1, 31 August 2009.

[118] HRC, Draft General Comment No. 34 (Upon Completion of the First Reading by the Human Rights Committee), UN Doc. CCPR/C/GC/34/CRP.5, 25 November 2010.

[119] HRC, Summary Record of the 2820th Meeting, 21 July 2011, UN Doc. CCPR/C/SR.2820, 15 August 2011, para. 86.

[120] Draft General Comment No. 34 by Michael O'Flaherty.

[121] HRC, Summary Record of the 2674th Meeting, para. 2.

for its content. The first of these was the existing general comment on Article 19, General Comment No. 10. He also indicated that, to the extent relevant, other general comments of the Committee had been taken into account. For example, he drew from General Comment No. 27 regarding the application of restriction clauses. The third source was the jurisprudence of the Committee as found in Views adopted on individual communications. The final source was the guidance to be found in Concluding Observations. Concerning the latter, he recalled that he was reverting to the practice of such referencing that had been commonplace in the Committee's general comments until falling into abeyance in recent years. He explained further that his reliance on existing practice of the Committee meant that examples given in support of various propositions sometimes seemed somewhat idiosyncratic and not necessarily the best vehicles to illustrate the application of the principle at issue. It would be for the Committee to determine whether these be retained in the draft or replaced by more appropriate examples.

With regard to the nature and purpose of the General Comment, the rapporteur/present writer indicated, in line with previous practice of the Human Rights Committee, that it should serve as a legal interpretation of Article 19 rather than a recommendatory or policy-level instrument, except to the extent that the text indicates to the contrary.[122] The language of the draft made clear which of its elements were considered to be of the nature of legally binding obligations. Where the application of the law was unclear or it was otherwise appropriate to avoid language of formal obligation that, also, was clearly indicated.

With regard to the structure of the draft, the rapporteur/present writer explained that it had not proved possible to develop a text that would simply be comprised of opening general remarks and then a detailed exegesis of the words of Article 19 as had previously been the case with comments of the Committee.[123] This was because it was impossible to locate all of the relevant guidance of the Committee with reference to specific elements of the article. This was especially the case with regard to the Committee's views on the application of paragraph 3. That paragraph identifies a number of grounds on which restrictions may be imposed. However, as a matter of practice, in the context of the individual communications procedure, States often fail to indicate which of the grounds is being relied on, instead either referring to them all or just

[122] *Ibid.* [123] *Ibid.*, para. 16.

making reference in general terms to the application of the overall paragraph. In many such cases the Committee, in its Views, follows suit. In order for the general comment to adequately capture the Committee's guidance in these situations, it was necessary to add a lengthy section that is arranged thematically around the principal contexts for such restrictions rather than by specific grounds as found in paragraph 3.

Finally, the rapporteur/present writer explained the inclusion of text regarding the relationship with Article 20.[124] He acknowledged that he had not been mandated to develop general comment guidance on that article. Nevertheless, he argued that some analysis should be included in the general comment because of the intimate nexus between the two provisions and the extent to which Article 20 may serve to restrict Article 19 rights.

## 7 Passage of the draft in the Committee: the first reading

Very many elements of the text that were debated in the first reading were then agreed without significant discussion in the second. Attention will be drawn here to some of the more notable of these. Comment on other elements that experienced significant adjustment in the second reading will be dealt with in the next section of this chapter. Reference is made only to the preponderance of the text that relates to freedom of expression, as that is the topic of this chapter.

Scope of the right: the Committee retained the broad language to the effect that freedom of expression embraces every form of idea and opinion capable of transmission to others, including views that may be deeply offensive.[125] In the view of the present writer it thus, implicitly, rejected the approach it had taken in *Zündel*, discussed above. However, following debate, and in the interest of consensus, it deleted text to the effect that forms of expression may, 'depending on the particular circumstances, include such forms as the choice of clothing or the wearing or carrying of a religious or other symbol, and a hunger strike'. This deletion was accepted by many Committee members on the understanding that the list of forms of expression must always be an open one that does not a priori exclude the deleted or any other forms.[126] Thus, for example, and

124 *Ibid.*, para. 2.

125 HRC, General Comment No. 34: Article 19 (Freedoms of opinion and expression) UN Doc. CCPR/C/GC/34, 12 September 2011, para. 11.

126 Human Rights Committee, Summary Record of the 2699th Meeting, 17 March 2010, UN Doc. CCPR/C/SR.2699, 3 May 2010, para. 101.

taking just one example put to the Committee by NGOs, it could embrace such forms of expression as a person's external indication of gender choice.

Access to information: the Committee agreed to the retention of a section on this topic, taking account of its own experience in reviewing periodic reports, the evolving practice at the regional level and the interpretation of the ICCPR by the UN Special Rapporteur on Freedom of Expression. As the text was subject to significant strengthening on the second reading, it is discussed further below.

The application of Article 19(3): the draft presented a detailed extrapolation of each of the requirements of the paragraph, whereby any restriction must be provided by law, be necessary and proportionate and only be for the specific purposes recognised in that paragraph (respect for the rights and reputation of others, protection of national security, public order, public health or morals).[127] The draft drew in part from the manner in which limitation clauses were addressed in General Comment No. 22 on freedom of movement,[128] and it offered the opportunity to set out in the most elaborated fashion yet undertaken, of the Committee's understanding of the operation of such provisions. In so doing it elaborated on the application of the restriction clause in a manner that also provides some guidance with regard to the similarly worded provisions of such other articles of the Covenant as those regarding the freedoms of movement, assembly and association.

Restriction of the rights: the draft's schema was accepted by the Committee with a number of adjustments to detail. Among the more notable elements of the finalised text were the provisions whereby 'it is not compatible with the Covenant for a restriction to be enshrined in traditional, religious or other such customary law';[129] the term 'rights' in Article 19(3) includes but is not restricted to 'human rights';[130] and, 'when a State party invokes a legitimate ground for restriction of freedom of expression, it must demonstrate in specific and individualized fashion the precise nature of the threat and the necessity and proportionality of the specific action taken, in particular by establishing a direct and immediate connection between the expression and the threat'.[131] That last element regarding the nexus between the expression and the threat

[127] General Comment No. 34, paras. 21–36.

[128] HRC, General Comment No. 22: The Right to Freedom of Thought, Conscience and Religion (Art. 18), UN Doc. CCPR/C/21/Rev.1/Add.4, 20 July 1993, para. 8.

[129] General Comment No. 34, para. 24. [130] *Ibid.*, para. 28. [131] *Ibid.*, para. 35.

was not in the original draft and sets a high bar for restrictions – it will be of interest to see whether it will be accepted by commentators.

Margin of appreciation: the Committee accepted the proposal in the draft to the effect that the scope of the right is, 'not to be assessed by reference to a "margin of appreciation"'.[132] It thus definitively confirmed its repudiation of the findings in *Hertzberg*.

Freedom of the media: this topic is addressed in considerable detail, drawing in the main from Concluding Observations. Both public and private monopolistic tendencies are addressed. For instance, following lengthy discussion, the following formula was agreed, 'States parties should take appropriate action, consistent with the Covenant, to prevent undue media dominance or concentration by privately controlled media groups in monopolistic situations that may be harmful to a diversity of sources and views'.[133] It was also decided to retain language of the draft that acknowledges the opening up of the journalistic function to, 'a wide range of actors, including professional full-time reporters and analysts, as well as bloggers and others who engage in forms of self-publication in print, on the internet or elsewhere'.[134]

Defamation: it was agreed to include language to the effect that, 'States parties should consider the decriminalization of defamation and, in any case, the application of the criminal law should only be countenanced in the most serious of cases and imprisonment is never an appropriate penalty'.[135]

The relationship of Articles 19 and 20: while it was agreed to keep a section to this effect the Committee decided, in the interests of consensus, to remove language that addressed the specificities of Article 20 and instead just to address issues of relationship with Article 19. It retained the paragraph to the effect that, 'what distinguishes the acts addressed in article 20 from other acts that may be subject to restriction under article 19, paragraph 3, is that for the acts addressed in article 20, the Covenant indicates the specific response required from the State: their prohibition by law. It is only to this extent that article 20 may be considered as *lex specialis* with regard to article 19.'[136] By means of the retention of this language it was reaffirmed that any expression that would require to be prohibited pursuant to Article 20 would also be of so grave a nature that its restriction would be permitted under Article 19(3). In other words,

[132] *Ibid.*, para. 36. [133] *Ibid.*, para. 40. [134] *Ibid.*, para. 44. [135] *Ibid.*, para. 47.
[136] *Ibid.*, para. 51.

Article 20 does not set any lower bar of protection for the specific forms of expression with which it deals.

## 8 Passage of the draft in the Committee – the second reading

For the second reading, the Committee had to hand the observations and recommendations received from States and other such interested Parties as NGOs and academics. No other treaty body submitted comments despite a request that had been made to them by the Committee.[137] Submissions were received from three of the special rapporteurs of the Human Rights Council, who asked that their submissions be treated as confidential. In total, some 75 submissions were received, containing more than 350 distinct comments and drafting suggestions.[138] In the view of the rapporteur/present writer, a great many of the comments were extremely useful and, if adopted, would render the text more rigorous and generally strengthen its provisions. Inevitably, there were also recommendations that were at odds with the schema that had already been adopted for the comments; that contradicted clear positions of the Committee or that, in some cases, were difficult to understand.

Seventeen States Parties made submissions, with the majority of them expressing support for the Committee's initiative and broadly welcoming the first draft – albeit with suggestions for its alteration. Notably, the USA made such a submission. As far as the present writer is aware, this is the first time that this State Party has submitted textual proposals for a General Comment of the Committee. Previous submissions had been made following adoption of such texts, as was the case with its very critical comments regarding General Comment No. 24 on the topic of reservations to the ICCPR.[139] The innovation may suggest a new willingness by this State Party to accept the utility of general comments. It might also be considered as reflective of the importance for that State of freedom of expression.

The management of the consideration of the large number of proposals proved to be a challenging task. While all Committee members

[137] Orally confirmed to the present writer by the Secretary of the Committee.

[138] HRC, Summary Record of the 2815th Meeting, 19 July 2011, UN Doc. CCPR/C/SR.2815, 26 July 2011, para. 2.

[139] Observations on General Comment No. 24 (52), on Issues Relating to Reservations Made upon Ratification or Accession to the Covenant or the Optional Protocols Thereto, or in Relation to Declarations under Article 41 of the Covenant, United States of America, UN Doc. 50/40, Annex VI, 3 October 1995.

had copies of the full file of materials, the rapporteur/present writer proposed to draw to the attention of the meeting all proposals of States Parties and of the Special Rapporteurs but only those of other actors where they constituted clear textual suggestions (as opposed to general observations).[140]

One of the first categories of recommendation that had to be considered by the Committee concerned the extent to which the draft general comment was thought to have disregarded the ways in which the internet has revolutionised communication. Numerous proposals were made to strengthen the text in this regard. Ultimately, the Committee opted for a framework paragraph:

> States parties should take account of the extent to which developments in information and communication technologies, such as internet and mobile based electronic information dissemination systems, have substantially changed communication practices around the world. There is now a global network for exchanging ideas and opinions that does not necessarily rely on the traditional mass media intermediaries. State parties should take all necessary steps to foster the independence of these new media and to ensure access of individuals thereto.[141]

This text, drawing in part on specific submissions, marks an unusual willingness by the Committee to engage with the interaction of technological advancement and the enjoyment of ICCPR rights.[142]

As has been mentioned earlier, the text on freedom of information was strengthened during the second reading, with account being taken of a number of NGO submissions. An explicit reference was added on the duty of the State to facilitate enjoyment of the right by, 'proactively put[ting] in the public domain Government information of public interest' and by providing that 'States parties should make every effort to ensure easy, prompt, effective and practical access to such information'.[143] Notably, the Committee avoided making reference in the body of the General Comment to the alleged nexus of freedom of information and the reference in Article 19(2) to a right to 'receive' information, as well as to any requirement that the right of access to public information may only reside in someone who demonstrates a distinct specific interest in accessing the information in question. It would thus appear that the

140 HRC, Summary Record of the 2815th Meeting, paras. 67–73.
141 General Comment No. 34, para. 15. 142 See further Chapter 1 in this book.
143 *Ibid.*, para. 19. For further examination, see Chapter 9 in this book.

Committee has distanced itself from the approach taken in *S.B.* and in *Toktakunov*.

Following extensive debate on a proposal by a national human rights institution,[144] the Committee made an addition to the text addressing restrictions to expression on the basis of morals. The draft already referred to General Comment No. 22 to the effect that, 'the concept of morals derives from many social, philosophical and religious traditions; consequently, limitations . . . for the purpose of protecting morals must be based on principles not deriving exclusively from a single tradition'.[145] Considering this guidance to be inadequate, the Committee agreed to add that '[a]ny such limitations must be understood in the light of universality of human rights and the principle of non-discrimination'.[146] This is an important clarification that lessens the scope for abuse of ICCPR rights through invocation of the protection of morals.

With regard to the other grounds for the restriction of freedom of expression (respect for the rights and reputation of others, protection of national security, public order, and public health), the Committee declined to elaborate definitions. In the first reading it had removed language to this effect from the draft submitted by the rapporteur/present writer. At the second reading, it declined to accept the many submissions proposing that there be such language. Committee members were understandably reluctant to erect strict definitions that might hamper legitimate future application of Article 19(3).[147] Nevertheless, in the view of the present writer, the Committee may thus have missed an opportunity to impede abusive invocation by States of the various grounds. Commentators may also be disappointed that the Committee, in its guidance regarding the term, 'rights and reputation of others', failed to address the complex and important issue of the relationship of Article 19 with such other Covenant provisions as Articles 17 (concerning privacy) and 18 (concerning freedom of religion or belief) – albeit elements of the relationship are touched on in the final sections of the text, as is noted below.

Two further adjustments to the text that occurred in the second reading may be mentioned – concerning blasphemy and 'memory' laws. The language of the first draft had addressed the topic of blasphemy in a

144 HRC, Summary Record of the 2815th Meeting, paras. 1–14.
145 General Comment No. 34, para. 32; General Comment No. 22, para. 8.
146 General Comment No. 34, para. 32.
147 Views of some individual members expressed informally to the present writer.

manner that was consistent with Committee practice. It only countenanced criminal blasphemy laws in the context of the application of Article 20 and it set rigorous requirements for non-criminal laws, including respect for Articles 2, 5, 18 and 26, and a prohibition on their use to penalise commentary on religious leaders or tenets of faith.[148] When read together with the prohibition of any restriction of freedom of expression by means of religious or traditional law, this draft, in effect, left little or no space for the operation of blasphemy laws. Notwithstanding this rigorous language, a number of NGOs made submissions very late in the day (during the Committee session) to the effect that this formula left open the possibility for grave violations of freedom of expression by States. It remains the view of the present writer that the NGOs considerably overstated their case. Nevertheless, their concerted lobby afforded the Committee the occasion to revisit the language whereby it declared that blasphemy laws were only compatible with the Covenant when enacted pursuant to the requirements in Article 20.[149] In a similar fashion, the Committee adjusted the provision on 'memory' laws, or 'laws that penalise the expression of opinions about historical facts', to the effect that they are never compatible with the ICCPR (thus overruling *Faurisson*).[150]

## 9 Conclusion

This chapter has reviewed the state of freedom of expression as found in the ICCPR, taking due account of the adoption of General Comment No. 34. The General Comment undoubtedly strengthens the framework for protection of the right by the Human Rights Committee, as well as by all other actors at national and international levels who seek to rely on the ICCPR. The General Comment also constitutes a significant contribution to the doctrine of the application of restriction clauses of the Covenant and other international human rights instruments. It has also to be acknowledged, as has been observed in this chapter, that the text is not beyond reproach: instances have been cited of what may have been missed opportunities to clarify the Committee's positions, as well as of a small number of excessive claims in terms of the state of the application of Article 19.

[148] Draft General Comment No. 34 by Michael O'Flaherty, para. 49; Draft General Comment No. 34 (Upon Completion of the First Reading), para. 50.

[149] General Comment No. 34, para. 48.

[150] *Ibid.*, para. 49.

The impact of the General Comment will rely to a great extent on how it is invoked in practice and how it will be received by States Parties. It is now in use by the Human Rights Committee and has been relied on in a number of recent Concluding Observations on State Party periodic reports,[151] as well as in views adopted under the Optional Protocol.[152] Early indications from beyond the practice of the Committee are encouraging. A number of civil society initiatives have cited it in advocacy and policy initiatives.[153] For instance, it is invoked to frame elements of a voluntary code of practice for the telecommunications industry.[154] Also, the present writer is aware that the International Telecommunications Union put references to the general comment before States that participated in the World Conference on International Telecommunications in December 2012.[155] Within the UN context, the General Comment has come before States on at least two occasions: at the biannual meetings of the Human Rights Committee with ICCPR States Parties in Geneva in October 2011 and at an informal briefing event that took place in New York in March 2012.[156] On both occasions State commentary was generally complimentary and there was an absence of specific criticism of any part of the text.

It is by taking account of reactions such as these that it will become possible to determine whether the Human Rights Committee – by means of the General Comment – has indeed re-fortified Article 19 and whether it has rendered the provision equal to the panoply of contemporary threats and challenges to freedom of expression. Or, to return to the broader context with which this chapter began, the test will be that of the

[151] e.g., HRC, Concluding Observations on the Islamic Republic of Iran, UN Doc. CCPR/C/IRN/CO/3, 29 November 2011, para. 27 and Concluding Observations on Yemen, UN Doc. CCPR/C/YEM/CO/5, 23 April 2012, para. 25.

[152] e.g., HRC, *Maria Tulzhenkova* v. *Belarus*, Communication No. 1838/2008, 17 January 2012, para. 9.2, n. 3.

[153] As reported orally by a representative of Open Society Justice Initiative to an informational event on General Comment 34 at United Nations Headquarters, New York, 27 March 2012.

[154] 'ACCESS Telco Action Plan: Respecting Human Rights: Ten Steps and Implementation Objectives for Telecommunications Companies', 4; https://www.accessnow.org/page/-/docs/Telco_Action_Plan.pdf (last accessed 17 March 2014).

[155] Correspondence on file with the present writer.

[156] United Nations Webcast, 'The Freedom of Expression and the Human Rights Committee's General Comment No. 34 (CCPR/C/GC/34)', event co-organised by the Permanent Missions of Kenya, the Netherlands and Uruguay, 27 March 2012, available at: www.unmultimedia.org/tv/webcast/2012/03/panel-discussion-the-freedom-of-expression-english.html (last accessed 17 March 2014).

extent to which it will contribute to the fulfilment of the vision of Liu Xiabo of (a country), 'being a land of free expression, where all citizen's speeches are treated the same; here, different values, ideas, beliefs, political views. . .here compete with each other and coexist peacefully; here majority and minority opinions will be given equal guarantees'.[157]

## Literature

Alston, P. 'The Historical Origins of "General Comments" in Human Rights Law', in L. Boisson De Charzournes and V. Gowlland-Debbas (eds.), *The International Legal System in Quest of Equity and Universality* (Leiden: Martinus Nijhoff, 2001).

Bakircioglu, O. 'Freedom of Expression and Hate Speech', *Tulsa Journal of Comparative and International Law* 16 (2008), 1–50.

Bennett Graham, L. 'Defamation of Religions: The End of Pluralism?', *Emory International Law Review* 23 (2009), 69–84.

Bossuyt, M. J. *Guide to the 'Travaux Préparatoires' of the International Covenant on Civil and Political Rights* (Leiden: Martinus Nijhoff, 1987).

Boyle, K. 'Thought, Expression, Association, and Assembly', in D. Moeckli *et al.* (eds.), *International Human Rights Law* (Oxford University Press, 2010), 257–79.

Dobras, R. J. 'Is the United Nations Endorsing Human Rights Violations?: An Analysis of the United Nations' Combating Defamation of Religions Resolutions and Pakistan's Blasphemy Laws', *Georgia Journal of International & Comparative Law* 37 (2009), 339–80.

Dutton, W. H., A. Dopatka, M. Hills, G. Law and V. Nash, *Freedom of Connection, Freedom of Expression: The Changing Legal and Regulatory Ecology Shaping the Internet* (Paris: UNESCO, 2011).

Goddard, H. *A History of Christian–Muslim Relations* (Edinburgh University Press, 2000).

Hamm, B. I. 'A Human Rights Approach to Development', *Human Rights Quarterly* 23(4) (2001), 1005–31.

Jones, T. D. *Human Rights: Group Defamation, Freedom of Expression and the Law of Nations* (Leiden: Martinus Nijhoff, 1998).

Joseph, S., J. Schultz and M. Castan, *The International Covenant on Civil and Political Rights: Cases, Materials, and Commentary* (Oxford University Press, 2004).

Mill, J. S. *On Liberty* (London: Watts, 1929).

Norris, P. *Driving Democracy: Do Power-Sharing Institutions Work?* (Cambridge University Press, 2008).

[157] Coonan, 'China condemns "insult" of award', 2010.

Nowak, M. *U.N. Covenant on Civil and Political Rights: CCPR Commentary*, 2nd rev. edn (Kehl am Rein: Engel, 2005).

O'Flaherty, M. 'Freedom of Expression: Article 19 of the International Covenant on Civil and Political Rights and the Human Rights Committee's General Comment No 34', *Human Rights Law Review* 12(4) (2012), 627–54.

Parmar, S. 'The Challenge of "Defamation of Religions" to Freedom of Expression and the International Human Rights', *European Human Rights Law Review* 3 (2009), 353–75.

Sen, A. *Development as Freedom* (Oxford University Press, 1999).

Slaughter, M. M. 'The Salman Rushdie Affair: Apostasy, Honor, and Freedom of Speech', *Virginia Law Review* 79(1) (1993), 153–204.

Steiner, H. J. *et al. International Human Rights in Context: Law, Politics, Morals*, 3rd edn (Oxford University Press, 2007).

## Journalistic articles

Coonan, C. 'China condemns "insult" of award for jailed dissident Liu Xiaobo', *The Independent*, 9 October 2010.

## UN documents

### *HRC*

General Comment No. 10: Freedom of expression (Art. 19), UN Doc. HRI/GEN/1/REV.6, 29 June 1983.

General Comment No. 11: Prohibition of Propaganda for War and Inciting National, Racial or Religious hatred (Art. 20), UN Doc. HRI/GEN/1/Rev.1, 29 July 1983.

General Comment No. 22: The Right to Freedom of Thought, Conscience and Religion (Art. 18), UN Doc. CCPR/C/21/Rev.1/Add.4, 20 July 1993.

General Comment No. 25: The Right to Participate in Public Affairs, Voting Rights and the Right of Equal Access to Public Service (Art. 25), UN Doc. CCPR/C/21/Rev.1/Add.7, 12 July 1996.

General Comment No. 34: Article 19: Freedom of Opinion and Expression, UN Doc. CCPR/C/GC/34, 12 September 2011.

Observations on General Comment No. 24 (52), on Issues Relating to Reservations Made upon Ratification or Accession to the Covenant or the Optional Protocols Thereto, or in Relation to Declarations under Article 41 of the Covenant, United States of America, UN Doc. 50/40, Annex VI, 3 October 1995.

Draft General Comment No. 34: Article 19, Draft Undertaken for the Human Rights Committee by Michael O'Flaherty, UN Doc. CPR/C/GC/34/CRP.1, 31 August 2009.

Draft General Comment No. 34 (Upon Completion of the First Reading by the Human Rights Committee), UN Doc. CCPR/C/GC/34/CRP.5, 25 November 2010.
General Comments Adopted by the Human Rights Committee under Article 40, Paragraph 4, of the International Covenant on Civil and Political Rights, UN Doc. CCPR/C/21/Rev.1, 19 May 1989.
Concluding Observations on Azerbaijan, UN Doc CCPR/C/79/Add.38, 3 August 1994.
Concluding Observations on Italy, UN Doc. CCPR/C/ITA/CO/5, 24 April 2006.
Concluding Observations on Kuwait, UN Doc. CPR/CO/69/KWT, 27 July 2000.
Concluding Observations on the Islamic Republic of Iran, UN Doc. CCPR/C/IRN/CO/3, 29 November 2011.
Concluding Observations on the Russian Federation, UN Doc. CCPR/CO/79/RUS, 1 December 2003.
Concluding Observations on the United Kingdom, UN Doc. CCPR/C/GBR/CO/6, 21 July 2008.
Concluding Observations on the United Kingdom: the Crown Dependencies of Jersey, Guernsey and the Isle of Man, UN Doc. CCPR/C/79/Add.119, 27 March 2000.
Concluding Observations on the Former Yugoslav Republic of Macedonia, UN Doc. CCPR/C/MKD/CO/2, 3 April 2008.
Concluding Observations on Yemen, UN Doc. CCPR/C/YEM/CO/5, 27–28 March 2012.
*Report of the Human Rights Committee*, Vol. I, GA Official Records, 94th Session, Supplement No. 40, UN Doc A/94/40.
Summary Record of the 2674th Meeting, 23 October 2009, UN Doc. CCPR/C/SR.2674, 9 August 2010.
Summary Record of the 2699th Meeting, 17 March 2010, UN Doc. CCPR/C/SR.2699, 3 May 2010.
Summary Record of the 2815th Meeting, 19 July 2011, UN Doc. CCPR/C/SR.2815, 26 July 2011.
Summary Record of the 2820th Meeting, 21 July 2011, UN Doc CCPR/C/SR.2820, 15 August 2011.

## *HR Council*

Resolution 13/16: Combating Defamation of Religions, UN Doc. A/HRC/RES/13/16, 15 April 2010.
Resolution 16/1: Combating Intolerance, Negative Stereotyping and Stigmatization of, and Discrimination, Incitement to Violence and Violence Against, Persons Based on Religion or Belief 8, UN Doc. A/HRC/RES/16/18, 24 March 2011.

## *General Assembly*

Resolution 59(1): Calling of an International Conference on Freedom of Information, UN Doc. A/RES/59(I), 14 December 1946, adopted at its 1st session.

Resolution 64/156: Combating Defamation of Religions, UN Doc. A/RES/64/156, 8 March 2010.

Resolution 66/167: Combating Intolerance, Negative Stereotyping and Stigmatization of, and Discrimination, Incitement to Violence and Violence Against, Persons Based on Religion or Belief, UN Doc. A/RES/66/167, 19 December 2011.

## *Other UN documents*

United Nations Commission on Human Rights (CHR), Resolution 1993/45: Right to freedom of opinion and Expression, UN Doc. E/CN.4/1993/122, 5 March 1993.

Committee on Economic, Social and Cultural Rights (CESCR), General Comment No. 21: Right of Everyone to Take Part in Cultural Life (art. 15, para. 1 (a), of the International Covenant on Economic, Social and Cultural Rights), UN Doc. E/C.12/GC/21, 21 December 2009.

*Report of the Office of the UN High Commissioner for Human Rights, Expert Seminar on the Links between Articles 19 and 20 of the International Covenant on Civil and Political Rights: 'Freedom of Expression and Advocacy of Religious Hatred that Constitutes Incitement to Discrimination, Hostility or Violence'* (Geneva, 2–3 October 2008), UN Doc. A/HRC/10/31/Add.3, 16 January 2009.

## **Miscellaneous**

African Commission on Human and Peoples' Rights (ACHPR), Declaration of Principles on Freedom of Expression in Africa, ACHPR /Res.62(XXXII)02, 23 October 2002.

Declaration of Principles: Building the Information Society: A Global Challenge in the New Millennium, Doc. No. WSIS-03/GENEVA/DOC/4-E, 12 December 2003.

Declaration of Santiago, Second Summit of the Americas, 18–19 April 1998.

Inter-American Commission on Human Rights (IACHR), Inter-American Declaration of Principles on Freedom of Expression, Adopted by the Inter-American Commission on Human Rights at its 108th Regular Session, 19 October 2000.

## Case law

### *HRC*

*Baban* v. *Australia*, Communication No. 1014/2001, 18 September 2003.
*Ballantyne, Davidson, McIntyre* v. *Canada*, Nos. 359/1989 and 385/1989, 5 May 1993.
*Bodrozić* v. *Serbia and Montenegro*, Communication No. 1180/2003, 23 January 2006.
*Coleman* v. *Australia*, Communication No. 1157/2003, 10 August 2006.
*Faurisson* v. *France*, Communication No. 550/1993, 16 December 1996.
*Gauthier* v. *Canada*, Communication No. 633/1995, UN Doc. CCPR/C/65/D/633/1995, 5 May 1999.
*Hertzberg* v. *Finland*, Communication No. 61/1979, 2 April 1982.
*Hudoyberganova* v. *Uzbekistan*, Communication No. 931/2000, 8 December 2004.
*Kim* v. *Republic of Korea*, Communication No. 574/1994, 4 January 1999.
*Kivenmaa* v. *Finland*, Communication No. 412/1990, 10 June 1994.
*LTK* v. *Finland*, Communication No. 185/1984, 9 July 1985.
*Marques de Morais* v. *Angola*, Communication No. 1128/2002, 18 April 2005.
*Mavlonov and Sa'di* v. *Uzbekistan*, Communication No. 1334/2004, 19 March 2009.
*Mika Miha* v. *Equatorial Guinea*, Communication No. 414/1990, 10 August 1994.
*Njaru* v. *Cameroon*, Communication No. 1353/2005, 14 May 2007.
*Park* v. *Republic of Korea*, Communication No. 628/1995, 3 November 1998.
*Ross* v. *Canada*, Communication No. 736/1997, 26 October 2000.
*SB* v. *Kyrgyzstan*, Communication No. 1877/2009, 25 August 2009, para. 4.
*SG* v. *France*, Communication No. 347/1988, 15 November 1991.
*Sin* v. *Republic of Korea*, Communication No. 926/2000, 19 March 2004.
*Sohn* v. *Republic of Korea*, Communication No. 518/1992, 3 August 1995.
*Toktakunov* v. *Kyrgyzstan*, Communication No. 1470/2006, 21 April 2011.
*Tulzhenkova* v. *Belarus*, Communication No. 1838/2008, 17 January 2012.
*Yoon and Choi* v. *Republic of Korea*, Communications Nos. 1321/2004 and 1322/2004, 23 January 2007.
*Zündel* v. *Canada*, Communication No. 953/2000, 29 July 2003.

### *ECtHR*

*Társaság a Szabadságjogokért* v. *Hungary* (Appl. No. 37374/05), 14 July 2009.

### *IACHR*

*Claude-Reyes et al.* v. *Chile*, Merits, Reparations and Costs, Judgment, Series C No. 151, 19 September 2006.

3

# International Covenant on Economic, Social and Cultural Rights: accessibility and the right to information

YVONNE DONDERS

## 1 Introduction

According to international human rights law, notably Article 19 of the International Covenant on Civil and Political Rights (ICCPR), the right to freedom of opinion and expression includes the freedom to seek, receive and impart information and ideas through any media and regardless of frontiers. In his report of 2000, the UN Special Rapporteur on Freedom of Opinion and Expression stated that the *freedom* of information was in fact a *right* to information and that this right was not just a component of freedom of expression, but a right in itself.[1] This status of the right to information was then reaffirmed by the United Nations Commission on Human Rights[2] – thus accepted by States – and is now widely accepted and recognized. The Human Rights Committee (HRC) included the right of access to information as a specific item in its General Comment No. 34 on freedom of opinion and expression.[3]

The rights to seek and to have access to information, as well as the right to receive information, have traditionally been developed in the context of civil and political rights. Information plays a central role in good governance and the democratic process. It advances participation and it is needed to properly monitor the government and to combat corruption. However, the right to information is also a significant

[1] *Report of the Special Rapporteur on the Promotion and Protection of the Right to Freedom of Opinion and Expression*, UN Doc. E/CN.4/2000/63, 18 January 2000, paras. 42, 15.

[2] United Nations Commission on Human Rights, Resolution 2000/38: The Right to Freedom of Opinion and Expression, 20 April 2000, para. 10(a).

[3] Human Rights Committee, General Comment No. 34, Article 19 (Freedoms of opinion and expression), UN Doc. CCPR/C/GC/34, 12 September 2011, paras. 18–19. See Chapters 1 and 2 in this book.

element in good governance regarding the implementation of economic, social and cultural rights, such as the right to education, the right to health, the right to food and the right to an adequate standard of living. Information plays a crucial role in securing access to facilities, goods and services in the field of, for instance, health and education and in allowing people to make informed choices in these areas. The right to information thereby contributes importantly to the enjoyment of these rights.

This chapter explores the interconnectedness between the right to information and economic, social and cultural rights as enshrined in the International Covenant on Economic, Social and Cultural Rights (ICESCR). The Committee on Economic, Social and Cultural Rights, which monitors the compliance with and implementation of the ICESCR, has maintained that access to information about relevant services and facilities is part of the normative content of several provisions, for instance the right to health and the right to work. This right to information accordingly brings several types of State obligations, including the negative obligation to allow access to information concerning economic and social facilities and services, but also in some instances positive obligations to promote, facilitate and provide access to, as well as actively distribute, information. This chapter will outline the normative content and corresponding State obligations of the right to information in relation to several economic, social and cultural rights, in particular the right to health. This chapter focuses on the interpretative and supervisory work of the CESCR, in particular its Concluding Observations as part of the State reporting procedure and its General Comments, but will also examine the work of other UN bodies and secondary sources. First, though, a brief introduction to the right to information and its development within international human rights law will be provided.[4] Since the work of several regional human rights bodies has been crucial in the elaboration of the right to information, these will also be analysed briefly.

## 2 The right to information: a brief introduction

### *2.1 Rationale and normative framework*

Freedom of information was recognized by the UN General Assembly (GA) as early as 1946. In its Resolution 59(1), the GA stated that 'freedom of information is a fundamental human right and ... the

[4] See Chapter 9 in this book.

touchstone of all the freedoms to which the UN is consecrated.'[5] Before, in another Resolution, the GA had pointed at the importance of the wide spreading of information about the UN and its functioning.[6] Both were meant to emphasize the importance of the free flow of information, mainly disseminated via the media, but it could not yet be seen as a recognition of the right to access information held by public authorities.[7]

The right to information is included in the Universal Declaration of Human Rights (UDHR), the ICCPR and also in regional human rights instruments, which are dealt with below. Article 19 UDHR states that the right to freedom of opinion and expression 'includes freedom to hold opinions without interference and to seek, receive and impart information and ideas through any media and regardless of frontiers'. Article 19 ICCPR affirms that the right to freedom of expression 'shall include freedom to seek, receive and impart information and ideas of all kinds, regardless of frontiers, either orally, in writing or in print, in the form of art, or through any other media of his choice'.

The right to freedom of expression, including the right to information can be limited by States in accordance with the limitation clause of Article 19(3) ICCPR. There it is indicated that:

> the rights provided for in paragraph 2 of this article carries with it special duties and responsibilities. It may therefore be subject to certain restrictions, but these shall only be such as are provided by law and are necessary: a. For respect of the rights or reputations of others; b. For the protection of national security or of public order (*ordre public*), or of public health or morals.

These provisions, and similar provisions in regional human rights instruments, have been interpreted and elaborated by the respective treaty bodies. Via different tools, including State reports and individual communications, these bodies have elaborated the contours of the right to information, including the entitlements of individuals, the obligations of States and the possible limitations of this right.

[5] GA, Resolution 59(1): Calling of an International Conference on Freedom of Information, 14 December 1946.

[6] GA, Resolution 13(1): Organization of the Secretariat, Annex I, Recommendations of the Technical Advisory Committee on Information concerning the Policies, Functions and Organization of the Department of Public Information, 13 February 1946.

[7] T. Mendel, *Freedom of Information: A Comparative Legal Study*, 2nd edn (Paris: UNESCO, 2008), 8.

Being part of the right to freedom of expression and with reference to the text of Article 19 ICCPR, 'through any media' implied that the right to information was originally considered mainly in relation to the free media and press freedom. Later on, the dimension of information held by public authorities was added, including the (alleged) obligations of these authorities to make such information available and/or distribute it actively, via media or other means. The right to have access to public information, or in other words the right to know, became a central part of the right to information.[8] In its General Comment No. 34, the HRC affirmed that Article 19(2) ICCPR 'embraces a right of access to information held by public bodies.'[9] Below, the focus is on this dimension of the right to information, since it is most relevant to economic, social and cultural rights.

The right to information is important for the public as well as the private domain. The right to information is one of the rights upon which free and democratic societies depend and a right that gives meaning to the right to participate. The recognition of the right to information confirms its importance for democracy and for the rule of law.[10] Information is crucial for participation in democratic decision-making processes, as well as for the assessment of public authorities' performance, to hold them accountable and prevent corruption. Therefore, public bodies should not keep information to themselves or distribute it as a discretionary gift, but 'as custodians of the public good', they should make it available and accessible to the people.[11]

Apart from being important for democratic and participation purposes, access to information is crucial for personal development and for individual decision-making. This is directly relevant also for economic, social and cultural rights. A good example of an area where access to information is crucial is health. The health of a society depends on

[8] ARTICLE 19, 'Access to Information: An Instrumental Right for Empowerment' (London, 2007), 5.

[9] HRC, General Comment No. 34 (2011), para. 18.

[10] *Report of the Special Rapporteur on the Promotion and Protection of the Right to Freedom of Opinion and Expression*, UN Doc. E/CN.4/2000/63, 18 January 2000, paras. 42, 15; S. Sedley, 'Information as a Human Right', in J. Beatson and Y. Cripps (eds.), *Freedom of Expression and Freedom of Information, Essays in Honour of Sir David Williams* (Oxford University Press, 2000), 241.

[11] T. Mendel, *Freedom of Information* (2008), 4; H. H. Perritt and C. J. Lhulier, 'Information Access Rights Based on International Human Rights Law', *Buff. Law Review* 45 (1997), 899.

information on clean water, sanitation, vaccines, statistics, etc., but also on information campaigns to prevent illnesses. But access to medical information also helps individuals to make informed decisions on medical treatment and the use of medication.[12]

### 2.2 *Normative content and State obligations*

The right to information has developed from a *freedom* to seek, receive and impart information, as it was described in the UDHR and the ICCPR, into a *right* to seek, receive and impart information. Consequently, the content of the right to information developed from a mere right of access to information to a right to actively *seek* and *receive* information.[13] The enlarged scope and content of the right to information as included in international human rights instruments have been elaborated by various international and regional supervisory bodies. They indicate the possible claim aspect of this right towards the State and thereby more broadly the obligations of States towards the beneficiaries of these rights.

#### 2.2.1 United Nations

In its General Comment No. 34, the HRC connects the right of access to information to other rights in the Covenant, thereby underlining the interdependence and interrelatedness of all human rights. For instance, the right of access to information in connection with Article 2 ICCPR on non-discrimination in the enjoyment of the rights in the Covenant implies a general right of information for all regarding their Covenant rights. Furthermore, the link between the right of access to information and Article 25 on political participation implies that the media should have access to public information and that the general public has the right to receive media output. The relation with Article 17 on respect for private life and privacy implies that individuals have the right to know which personal data is stored and which authorities have access to such data. The right of access to information in connection with Article 10 on

[12] Mendel, *Freedom of Information*, 4–5; ARTICLE 19, *Access to Information*, 10 and 17. See, also, ARTICLE 19, *The Free Flow Principles: Freedom of Expression and the Rights to Water and Sanitation* (London, 20 March 2014) available at: www.article19.org/data/files/medialibrary/37492/Right-to-Water-WEB.pdf (last accessed 25 March 2014).

[13] *Report of the Special Rapporteur on the Promotion and Protection of the Right to Freedom of Opinion and Expression* (2000), paras. 42, 15; Mendel, *Freedom of Information*, 3.

rights of persons deprived of their liberty and Article 14 on rights of the accused implies, for instance, access rights for these persons in relation to information relevant to them.[14]

According to the HRC, the right to information gives rise to several negative and positive obligations of States. In General Comment No. 34, they are formulated as follows:

> To give effect to the right of access to information, States parties should proactively put in the public domain Government information of public interest. States parties should make every effort to ensure easy, prompt, effective and practical access to such information. States parties should also enact the necessary procedures, whereby one may gain access to information, such as by means of freedom of information legislation. The procedures should provide for the timely processing of requests for information according to clear rules that are compatible with the Covenant. Fees for requests for information should not be such as to constitute an unreasonable impediment to access to information. Authorities should provide reasons for any refusal to provide access to information. Arrangements should be put in place for appeals from refusals to provide access to information as well as in cases of failure to respond to requests.[15]

These obligations to a large extent reflect the ideas that have been developed by various international bodies and institutions. For instance, in their Joint Declaration of 2004, the Special Rapporteurs on Freedom of Expression of the United Nations (UN), the Organization of American States (OAS) and the Organization for Security and Co-operation in Europe (OSCE) stated that the right to access information held by public authorities is a fundamental human right and its implementation should be guided by the principles of maximum disclosure and the presumption that all information is accessible, subject only to a narrow system of exceptions. The Special Rapporteurs reaffirmed that public authorities have an obligation to proactively publish information of public interest, even in the absence of a specific request.[16]

These principles were taken from the work of, *inter alia*, the NGO ARTICLE 19 on the right to information. ARTICLE 19 drafted a list of principles for national legislation on access to information. Among these principles were the principle of maximum disclosure; the obligation of public authorities to disclose key information, or information of public

[14] HRC, General Comment No. 34, para. 18. [15] *Ibid.*, para. 19.

[16] Joint Declaration by the UN Special Rapporteur on Freedom of Opinion and Expression, the OSCE Representative on Freedom of the Media and the OAS Special Rapporteur in Freedom of Expression (adopted 6 December 2004), 2.

interest; the principle of narrow exceptions which are clearly outlined, including the legitimate aims which may justify non-disclosure and tested by the criteria of harm and public interest; and the obligation to have procedural guarantees for the request for information, including strict time limits for the processing of requests and the cost of gaining access to information should not be so high as to deter potential applicants.[17]

Information in relation to economic, social and cultural rights, for instance the rights to health, education, social security or food, often concerns information of public interest. The question is, however, what the scope of 'public interest' is and to what extent more individual interests could also oblige public bodies to disclose information. And should the obligation of maximum disclosure be limited to information upon request, or does the right to information also imply that public bodies proactively publish and widely disseminate information on their own initiative? How does maximum disclosure work out in relation to the possible limitations of the right to information, in other words exceptions to disclosure, in relation to economic, social rights and cultural rights, for instance for the protection of privacy or public safety?

### 2.2.2 Council of Europe

The right to information and corresponding State obligations and possible limitations have also been dealt with by regional supervisory bodies. Some of these cases concern economic, social or cultural issues, notably health.

The European Court of Human Rights (ECtHR, or 'the Court') has consistently recognized that the public has a right to receive information of general or public interest. Most of the cases relate to press freedom serving to impart information and ideas, emphasizing the role of the media as a public watchdog.[18] The Court has however also recognized the role of NGOs in this respect.[19] The Court has been more cautious in its approach towards positive obligations of States Parties to provide or

[17] ARTICLE 19, 'The Public's Right to Know: Principles on Freedom of Information Legislation' (London, 1999). See also, Mendel, *Freedom of Information*, 31–40.

[18] ECtHR, *Sunday Times* v. *the United Kingdom* (Appl. No. 6538/74), Judgment of 26 April 1979, para. 65: 'Not only do the media have the task of imparting such information and ideas: the public also has a right to receive them' and para. 66: 'Article 10 (Art. 10) guarantees not only the freedom of the press to inform the public but also the right of the public to be properly informed.'

[19] ECtHR, *Österreichische Vereinigung zur Erhaltung, Stärkung und Schaffung eines wirtschaftlich gesunden land-und forstwirtschaftlichen Grundbesitzes* v. *Austria* (Appl. No. 39534/07), Judgment of 28 November 2013, para. 34.

disclose information. As regards access to information held by public authorities, the Court has consistently argued that the government does not have a general obligation to disclose information. At the same time, the government may not restrict a person from receiving information that others are willing to share.[20] The Court has argued that 'it is difficult to derive from the Convention a general right of access to administrative data and documents', but that the importance of the disclosure of such data and documents for the applicant's personal situation should be taken into account.[21] If a person has a special interest, the information may have to be disclosed. This line of reasoning was also confirmed in cases concerning, for instance, information on abortion, which is important for a woman's health, which implied that the State was to refrain from interference when a woman herself obtained such information.[22] The State may also not prevent in a disproportionate way the distribution of such information by third parties.[23]

More recently, the ECtHR seems to be willing to expand the scope of obligations in relation to the right to information. One example concerned the refusal by the Czech authorities to allow an environmental NGO access to administrative documents concerning a nuclear power station. The Court found this refusal an interference with the right to receive information as guaranteed by Article 10. However, it argued that this right may be limited and concluded that the refusal met the conditions of the limitations clause in Article 10(2).[24] The

[20] ECtHR, *Leander* v. *Sweden* (Appl. No. 9248/81), Judgment of 26 March 1987, para. 74: 'The Court observes that the right to freedom to receive information basically prohibits a Government from restricting a person from receiving information that others wish or may be willing to impart to him. Article 10 (Art. 10) does not, in circumstances such as those of the present case, confer on the individual a right of access to a register containing information on his personal position, nor does it embody an obligation on the Government to impart such information to the individual.'

[21] ECtHR, *Loiseau* v. *France* (Appl. No. 46809/99), Judgment of 18 November 2003, para. 7.

[22] ECtHR, *Open Door and Dublin Well Woman* v. *Ireland* (Appl. No. 14234/88; 14235/88), Judgment of 29 October 1992, para. 72: 'the injunction limited the freedom to receive and impart information with respect to services which are lawful in other Convention countries and may be crucial to a woman's health and well-being. Limitations on information concerning activities which, notwithstanding their moral implications, have been and continue to be tolerated by national authorities, call for careful scrutiny by the Convention institutions as to their conformity with the tenets of a democratic society.'

[23] ECtHR, *Women on Waves and Others* v. *Portugal* (Appl. No. 31276/05), Judgment of 3 February 2009, paras. 38–43.

[24] ECtHR, *Sdruženi Jihočeské Matky* v. *Czech Republic* (Appl. No. 19101/03), Admissibility Decision of 10 July 2006.

information in this case concerned a matter of public interest. While the Court was willing to accept that in principle States have a positive obligation to provide such information under Article 10, it also recognized possible limitations to this right. In the case of *OVESSG* v. *Austria* the Court concluded that the limitation criteria were not met and that Austria had violated Article 10 by completely refusing access to information on agricultural and forest land transactions, which was considered disproportionate to the legitimate aim.[25]

The (former) European Commission of Human Rights[26] and Court have also dealt with the right to information under Article 8 concerning the right to respect for private life. Interestingly, it seems that the Court is more willing to accept positive obligations for States to disclose information under Article 8. Relevant cases concerned the disclosure of information concerning health and environment. For instance, in the *Guerra* v. *Italy* case, the European Commission of Human Rights held that Italy had violated its obligations under Article 10 by withholding information on the risks of living close to a chemical plant. It argued that in cases of information concerning the protection of public well-being and health or danger to the environment, Article 10 placed a positive obligation on States to make information not only available, but to actively publish it.[27] The Court did not follow this interpretation of Article 10 and stayed in line with its previous jurisprudence, arguing that freedom of information 'cannot be construed as imposing on a State, in circumstances such as those of present case, positive obligations to collect and disseminate information of its own motion'.[28] It did, however, find a violation of Article 8. It reasoned that the right to respect for private life implied a right to information, if such information is relevant to the enjoyment of the right. In this case, the lack of information prevented people from

[25] ECtHR, *Österreichische Vereinigung zur Erhaltung, Stärkung und Schaffung eines wirtschaftlich gesunden land-und forstwirtschaftlichen Grundbesitzes (OVESSG)* v. *Austria* (Appl. No. 39534/07), Judgment of 28 November 2013, para. 47.

[26] The European Commission of Human Rights was a body of independent experts charged with determining whether cases should be admitted for consideration on merits by the European Court of Human Rights. It was disbanded on 1 November 1998 upon entry into force of Protocol No. 11 to the Convention for the Protection of Human Rights and Fundamental Freedoms, restructuring the control machinery established thereby, ETS No. 155, 11 May 1994.

[27] ECommHR, *Guerra and Others* v. *Italy* (Appl. No. 14967/89), Report adopted 29 June 1996.

[28] ECtHR, *Guerra and Others* v. *Italy* (Appl. No. 116/1996/735/932), Judgment of 19 February 1998, para. 53.

making a proper risk assessment, which prevented them from enjoying their rights related to private lives and home.[29] The Court came to a similar conclusion in a case concerning a methane explosion on a slum site in Istanbul in which thirty-nine people died. The Court concluded that Turkey had violated several provisions of the ECHR, among which Article 2 on the right to life. The Court applied its *Guerra* ruling concerning the right to information to Article 2 and concluded that insufficient measures had been taken to provide the inhabitants of the slums with information enabling them to assess the risks they might run as a result of the choices they had made.[30]

In another comparable case on risk assessment, the case of *McGinley and Egan* v. *United Kingdom*, the Court held that Article 8 implied an obligation on the State to establish a proper procedure for providing information on hazardous activities to exposed individuals. This case concerned nuclear testing, causing possible adverse consequences on the health of persons.[31] In the judgment of *Vilnes and Others* v. *Norway*, the Court went a step further by holding that under certain circumstances the State's obligation to provide access to information essential to assess health risks includes not only non-refusal to provide such information, but a duty to actively provide it, even if there is scientific uncertainty about the precise nature and extent of the risks.[32] In other words, the Court is ready to accept far-reaching positive obligations concerning the dissemination of information under Article 8 (and 2), in particular when it concerns potential health risks, whereas it has not (yet) been ready to accept such obligations under Article 10.

This changed somewhat with the judgment in the case of *Társaság* v. *Hungary*. In this case, the Court recognized a right to information under Article 10 in a more explicit way, but it did not accept a general positive obligation on State authorities to publish or disseminate information. The Court unanimously agreed that in cases of information of public interest, public authorities have an obligation not to impede such information so that others, in this case an NGO, could disseminate it. It argued that 'obstacles created in order to hinder access to information

[29] *Ibid.*, para. 60.

[30] ECtHR, *Öneryildiz* v. *Turkey* (Appl. No. 48939/99), Judgment of 30 November 2004, paras. 90 and 108.

[31] ECtHR, *McGinley and Egan* v. *United Kingdom* (Appl. Nos. 21825/93 and 23414/94), Judgment of 8 June 1998.

[32] ECtHR, *Vilness and Others* v. *Norway* (Appl. No. 52806/09), Judgment of 5 December 2013, para. 244.

of public interest may discourage those working in the media...from pursuing such matters. As a result, they may no longer be able to play their vital role as public watchdogs and their ability to provide accurate and reliable information.'[33] The Court confirmed this standpoint in relation to NGOs in the case of *OVESSG* v. *Austria*.[34]

The political bodies of the Council of Europe have also recognized the right to information. In a recommendation on information held by public authorities, the Committee of Ministers agreed that 'everyone within the jurisdiction of a member states shall have the right to obtain, on request, information held by the public authorities other than legislative bodies and judicial authorities'.[35] In another recommendation, the Committee of Ministers held that 'member states should guarantee the right of everyone to have access, on request, to official documents held by public authorities'.[36] These recommendations formed the basis for the adoption in 2008 of the European Convention on Access to Official Documents, the first binding international instrument recognizing a general right of access to official documents held by public authorities.[37] It should be noted, however, that the Convention also includes a long list of potentially legitimate aims for which this right may be limited, provided that the measures are provided by law, necessary in a democratic society and proportionate to the aim pursued.[38] The Convention has not yet entered into force, as it has only six of the ten necessary ratifications.[39]

### 2.2.3 The Organization of American States

The right to information, including positive obligations for States, is most explicitly recognized in the human rights system of the

[33] ECtHR, *Társaság a Szabadságjogokért* v. *Hungary* (Appl. No. 37374/05), Judgment of 14 April 2009, para. 38. See also, ECtHR, *Kenedi* v. *Hungary* (Appl. No. 31475/05), Judgment of 26 May 2009, paras. 42–5.

[34] ECtHR, *Österreichische Vereinigung zur Erhaltung, Stärkung und Schaffung eines wirtschaftlich gesunden land-und forstwirtschaftlichen Grundbesitzes (OVESSG)* v. *Austria* (Appl. No. 39534/07), Judgment of 28 November 2013, para. 41.

[35] Council of Europe, Committee of Ministers, Recommendation No. R(81)19 on Access to Information Held by Public Authorities, 25 November 1981.

[36] Council of Europe, Committee of Ministers, Recommendation No. 2 of the Committee of Ministers to Member States on Access to Official Documents, 21 February 2002.

[37] Council of Europe, Convention on Access to Official Documents, Tromsø, 18 June 2009, CETS No. 205, Art. 2.

[38] Convention on Access to Official Documents, 2009, Art. 3.

[39] On 1 February 2014, eight more States had signed but not ratified the Convention.

Organization of American States (OAS). Article 13 of the American Convention on Human Rights (ACHR)[40] includes the right to freedom of thought and expression including the freedom to seek, receive and impart information, similar to the European Convention on Human Rights. The Inter-American Court of Human Rights (IACtHR) expressed in an Advisory Opinion on Article 13 of the ACHR that the right to freedom of expression 'implies a collective right to receive any information whatsoever'.[41] This notion led to the full recognition of the right to access information held by public authorities in the case of *Claude Reyes and Others* v. *Chile*. The case concerned the authorities' refusal to provide information on a deforestation project authorized by the Chilean government, which could have prejudicial effect on the environment and sustainable development of Chile. The Court decided that:

> by expressly stipulating the right to 'seek' and 'receive' information, Article 13 of the Convention protects the right of all individuals to request access to State-held information, with the exceptions permitted by the restrictions established in the Convention. Consequently, this article protects the right of the individual to receive such information and the positive obligation of the State to provide it... The information should be provided without the need to prove direct interest or personal involvement in order to obtain it, except in cases in which a legitimate restriction is applied. The delivery of information to an individual can, in turn, permit it to circulate in society, so that the latter can become acquainted with it, have access to it, and assess it. In this way, the right to freedom of thought and expression includes the protection of the right of access to State-held information, which also clearly includes the two dimensions, individual and social, of the right to freedom of thought and expression that must be guaranteed simultaneously by the State.[42]

With this judgment, the Court defined a positive obligation for the State to disseminate information of general interest, whereby no direct interest of the receiver had to be proven. It also recognized that such information may be of interest not only to an individual, but to a larger community or society as a whole.

[40] American Convention on Human Rights, 'Pact of San José', Costa Rica, adopted 22 November 1969, entry into force 18 July 1978.

[41] IACtHR, *Compulsory Membership in an Association Prescribed by Law for the Practice of Journalism*, Advisory Opinion OC-5/85, 13 November 1985, para. 30.

[42] IACtHR, *Claude Reyes and Others* v. *Chile*, Series C No. 151, 19 September 2006, para. 77.

### 2.2.4 African Union

Within the African human rights system, the right to information is recognized in Article 9 of the African Charter on Human and Peoples' Rights.[43] It is interesting to note that the formulation of this provision is different from the similar provisions in the European and American Conventions on Human Rights. Article 9 starts with the phrase that every individual has the right to receive information, after which the second paragraph includes the freedom to express and disseminate opinions. The African Commission on Human and Peoples' Rights adopted in 2002 a Declaration of Principles on Freedom of Expression.[44] In this Declaration it is clearly stated that everyone has the right to access information held by public bodies. The Declaration further confirms that States not only have negative obligations, but also positive ones, for instance, even in the absence of a request, to actively to publish important information of significant public interest.[45] There have been no individual cases concerning the right to information before the African Commission on Human and Peoples' Rights, nor before the African Court on Human and Peoples' Rights.

### 2.2.5 Conclusion

In short, the core of the right to information is the right to have access to information, in particular, but not limited to, information of public interest. The State should ensure maximum disclosure, which implies first the negative obligation not to interfere with the free flow of information shared or disseminated by others. This is also linked to the fact that the right to information is part of the right to freedom of opinion and expression. The right to information may, however, also place positive obligations upon States to disseminate information, upon request as well as proactively, and to do so on a non-discriminatory basis. The scope of these positive obligations depends on the situation and the individual and community interests at stake. One may also wonder to what extent States are obliged to take special measures in relation to the (form of) information distributed, such as translating it

[43] African Charter on Human and Peoples' Rights, Banjul, Gambia, adopted 27 June 1981, entry into force 21 October 1986, OAU Doc. CAB/LEG/67/3 rev. 5, 21 ILM 58 (1982).

[44] ACHPR, Res.62(XXXII)02: Resolution on the Adoption of the Declaration of Principles on Freedom of Expression in Africa (2002), 23 October 2002.

[45] *Ibid.*, Art. IV.

into different languages, or making it accessible for disadvantaged groups such as persons with visual or cognitive disabilities.[46]

As indicated above, the right to information may be lawfully limited by States with the aim to protect the rights of others, national security, public order, or public health or morals. For instance, the right to information has to be balanced with the right to respect for privacy.[47] Respect for privacy relates not only to how State authorities obtain information, but also to how they safeguard, store and process it.[48] The ECtHR has defined several factors relevant to the collection, storage and use of information in relation to respect for privacy. These include the nature of the material disclosed (the more private or sensitive, the more care should be taken), the gravity of the threat or the social importance of the purpose for disclosure; and the gravity of the impact of disclosure for the persons involved. Moreover, a proper procedure should be in place for persons affected.[49] Respect for and protection of privacy are closely linked to the issue of confidentiality. Sometimes the public interest actually prevents public authorities from disclosing information. Examples could be information about security and intelligence operations. A balance has to be struck between the public interest in favour of not disclosing information and the countervailing interest of the public in receiving information about public authorities and their activities.[50] The current debates on the disclosure of classified information (WikiLeaks, Cablegate) show the complexity and delicacy of striking such a balance.

Limitations to the right to information in relation to economic, social and cultural rights could, for instance, be justified in order to respect and protect the right to privacy, for instance, the right to have personal health data treated with confidentiality or the right of health workers to have their privacy respected.

## 3 The right to information and economic, social and cultural rights

Although the right to information is incorporated in treaties containing civil and political rights – the ICCPR, the ECHR and the ACHR – it has a

[46] See Chapter 6 in this book.
[47] This right is incorporated in Article 17 ICCPR, in Article 8 ECHR and in Article 11 ACHR.
[48] D. Feldman, 'Information and Privacy', in Beatson and Y. Cripps (eds.), *Freedom of Expression*, 301 and 308.
[49] *Ibid.*, 313–16.
[50] R. Scott, 'Confidentiality', in Beatson and Cripps (eds.), *Freedom of Expression*, 267 and 274. See Chapter 9 in this book.

clear relevance for economic, social and cultural rights and this has been acknowledged by States, international supervisory bodies and scholars. The right to information is a good example of a right that is not only valuable in itself, but also as a right that unlocks and promotes the enjoyment of other human rights. It is not only a component of one right (to freedom of opinion and expression) and a right in itself, it also gives effect to other rights, assists in their realization and, in the case of economic, social and cultural rights, may be a precondition for their realization.[51] The right to information is also crucial for the realization and litigation of economic, social and cultural rights.[52] The right to information thereby embodies the principles of the indivisibility, interrelatedness and interdependence of all human rights.

The Committee on Economic, Social and Cultural Rights has explicitly recognized that the right to information is a component of the rights to health, water, work and cultural participation. The Committee monitors the implementation of the Covenant by the States Parties via a periodic State reporting procedure and, since 2013, an individual communication procedure.[53] For the reporting procedure, the Committee has adopted reporting guidelines, outlining which information States Parties should include in their reports. The right to information can be found in the guidelines as one of the topics to be addressed. The practice and experience of the Committee is laid down in so-called General Comments, in which it comments on specific treaty provisions or elaborates on the relationship between the treaty and specific themes or issues.[54] These General Comments are not legally binding upon States Parties, but they provide them with an authoritative interpretation of the provisions of the

[51] S. Jagwanth, 'The Right to Information as a Leverage Right', in R. Calland and A. Tilley (eds.), *The Right to Know, the Right to Live: Access to Information and Socio-Economic Justice* (Cape Town: Open Democracy Advice Centre, 2002), 13; Sedley, 'Information as a Human Right', 248.

[52] International Commission of Jurists, *Courts and the Legal Enforcement of Economic, Social and Cultural Rights – Comparative Experiences of Justiciability* (Geneva, 2008); Centre on Housing Rights and Evictions, *Litigating Economic, Social and Cultural Rights: Achievements, Challenges and Strategies* (Geneva, 2003), M. Daruwala and V. Nayak (eds.), *Our Rights, Our Information: Empowering Peoples to Demand Rights through Knowledge*, Commonwealth Human Rights Initiative (Paris: UNESCO, 2007).

[53] The individual communications procedure is laid down in GA, Resolution A/RES/63/117, Optional Protocol to the International Covenant on Economic, Social and Cultural Rights, 10 December 2008, entry into force 5 May 2013. On 1 February 2014, no individual communications had been submitted.

[54] *Report on the Working Methods of the Human Rights Treaty Bodies Relating to the State Party Reporting Process*, UN Doc. HRI/MC/2005/4, 25 May 2005, 28, para. 105.

Covenant. The Committee has included the right to information in several of its General Comments on specific economic, social and cultural rights.

### 3.1 *The right to information in General Comments on economic, social and cultural rights*

The Committee on Economic, Social and Cultural Rights has since several years firmly integrated the right to information in its elaboration and interpretation of the normative content and State obligations of various provisions of the Covenant. Interestingly, the right to information was not included in the General Comments on the right to food and the right to education, both adopted in 1999. All General Comments since include a reference to the right to information. The fact that the right to information was not explicitly mentioned in the General Comments on the rights to food and education does not mean that it is not important in relation to these rights. This is confirmed by the reporting guidelines. In these guidelines, States Parties are requested to include in their reports information on the implementation of the right to food, for instance, 'the measures taken to disseminate knowledge of the principles of nutrition, including of healthy diets'.[55] Dissemination of knowledge is closely related to the right to information.

The right to information was first included in the General Comment on the right to the highest attainable standard of health (right to health), adopted in 2000. It was indicated that the right to health is closely related to and dependent upon other rights, among which the right to access information.[56] The Committee further included access to information as a dimension of one of the elements of the normative content of the right to health, namely the accessibility of health facilities and services. Accessibility was described as having four overlapping dimensions: non-discrimination, physical accessibility, economic accessibility and *information accessibility*. The Committee noted that 'accessibility includes the right to seek, receive and impart information and ideas concerning health

[55] Committee on Economic, Social and Cultural Rights, *Guidelines on Treaty-Specific Documents to be Submitted by States Parties under Articles 16 and 17 of the International Covenant on Economic, Social and Cultural Rights*, UN Doc. E/C.12/2008/2, 24 March 2009, para. 45.

[56] Committee on Economic, Social and Cultural Rights, General Comment No. 14, The Right to the Highest Attainable Standard of Health (Article 12 of the ICESCR), UN Doc. E/C.12/2000/4, 11 August 2000, para. 3.

issues' and refers in that connection to Article 19(2) ICCPR.[57] The Committee, however, also warned that 'accessibility of information should not impair the right to have personal health data treated with confidentiality'.[58]

In all subsequent General Comments the Committee included access to information as part of the accessibility of the right, whereby it adjusted the specific elements to the provision concerned. In the General Comment on the right to water the Committee maintained that accessibility includes the right to seek, receive and impart information concerning water issues, without however referring to Article 19 ICCPR.[59] The Committee further stated under the heading of the implementation at national level that 'individuals and groups should be given full and equal access to information concerning water, water services and the environment held by public authorities or third parties.'[60] Moreover, States should give timely and full disclosure of information on the proposed measures that interfere with the right to water.[61]

In the General Comment on the right to work, the Committee maintained that 'accessibility includes the right to seek, obtain and impart information on the means of gaining access to employment through the establishment of data networks on the employment market at the local, regional, national and international levels'.[62] Again, no reference to Article 19 ICCPR was made.[63] The Committee further referred to the dissemination of information as one of the possible measures to implement strategies and programmes to eliminate employment-related discrimination 'with minimum resource implications'.[64] It further indicated

57 *Ibid.*, para. 12(b)iv. 58 *Ibid.*

59 Committee on Economic, Social and Cultural Rights, General Comment No. 15, The Right to Water (Articles 11 and 12 ICESCR), UN Doc. E/C.12/2002/11, 20 January 2003, para. 12(c)iv.

60 *Ibid.*, para. 48.

61 *Ibid.*, para. 56. See, also, ARTICLE 19, *Free Flow Principles*. The principles include the right to know, because 'information empowers people to pursue their rights to water and sanitation. This aspect of the right obliges governments and other duty bearers to proactively inform the population about issues relating to water and sanitation, water-related resources and management. It is the basis for transparency, accountability and good governance in all water and sanitation-related matters.'

62 Committee on Economic, Social and Cultural Rights, General Comment No. 18, The Right to Work (Article 6 ICESCR), UN Doc. E/C.12/GC/18, 6 February 2006, para. 12(b)iii.

63 It seems that the Committee on Economic, Social and Cultural Rights no longer wanted to explicitly refer to Article 19 ICCPR, but chose to include the right to (access) information more generally.

64 *Ibid.*, para. 12(b)i.

that States have a positive obligation to undertake educational and informational programmes to increase public awareness on the right to work.[65]

In the General Comment on the right to social security the Committee noted that the social security system should ensure the right to seek, receive and impart information on social security entitlements. Interestingly, it is explicitly stated that this right is not only to be ensured to individuals, but also to organizations.[66] At various points in the General Comment, the importance of the right of access to information and disclosure of information were emphasized, for instance in relation to social security services[67] and to prevent the denial of social security to certain groups.[68]

Another example of the adjustment of the right to information to the specific requirements of the right in question is the General Comment on the right to take part in cultural life. In this General Comment, the Committee noted under accessibility, the right of everyone to seek, receive and share information on all manifestations of culture, but it added that this information should be in the language of the person's choice.[69] The right to information was mentioned at several other points in the General Comment, for instance by emphasizing the link between the right to take part in cultural life and other human rights, such as the right to freedom of expression and the right to information.[70] Respect for freedom of expression includes expression in the languages of one's choice and the right to seek, receive and impart information and ideas of all kinds and forms: 'This implies the right of all persons to have access to, and to participate in, varied information exchanges.'[71]

From the reporting guidelines and the General Comments, it appears that the Committee on Economic, Social and Cultural Rights clearly recognizes the importance of the right (of access) to information for the implementation and enjoyment of several economic,

[65] *Ibid.*, para. 28.

[66] Committee on Economic, Social and Cultural Rights, General Comment No. 19, The Right to Social Security (Article 9 ICESCR), UN Doc. E/C.12/GC/19, 4 February 2008, para. 26.

[67] *Ibid.*, para. 27. [68] *Ibid.*, para. 35.

[69] Committee on Economic, Social and Cultural Rights, General Comment No. 21, The Right of Everyone to Take Part in Cultural Life (Article 15(1)a ICESCR), UN Doc. E/C.12/GC/21, 21 December 2009, para. 16(b).

[70] *Ibid.*, para. 43. [71] *Ibid.*, para. 46.

social and cultural rights. The Committee includes access to information as one of the essential elements of the implementation and enjoyment of these rights. It further appears that the States Parties not only have negative obligations not to interfere with the right to seek information, but that they also should actively provide access to information and/or disseminate information. It is interesting to see that in relation to the right to take part in cultural life, information is even to be accessed in a language of one's choice. This language issue is not included in relation to information concerning other rights. It is, however, imaginable that information on health issues or on social security systems should also be made available in different languages. The Committee has indeed confirmed this in its General Comment on non-discrimination, in which it stated that 'information about public services and goods, for example, should also be available, as far as possible, in languages spoken by minorities'.[72] Apart from minority languages, one can also think of special language facilities for persons with visual impairment or low levels of literacy. Interestingly, these issues are not addressed in the General Comment on persons with disabilities. This General Comment recognizes that States Parties have positive obligations to ensure that persons with disabilities can fully enjoy the rights in the Covenant, including 'special tailored measures', but no specific obligations in relation to (access to) information were included.[73]

The reporting guidelines and the General Comments are directly linked to the State reporting procedure and the dialogue between the Committee and States Parties on their implementation of the Covenant. It is therefore also interesting to look at this procedure in the elaboration of the right to information in relation to economic, social and cultural rights and the State obligations in this regard.

[72] Committee on Economic, Social and Cultural Rights, General Comment No. 20, Non-Discrimination in Economic, Social and Cultural Rights (Article 2(2) ICESCR), UN Doc. E/C.12/GC/20, 2 July 2009, para. 21.

[73] As included in paragraph 9: 'The obligation in the case of such a vulnerable and disadvantaged group is to take positive action to reduce structural disadvantages and to give appropriate preferential treatment to people with disabilities in order to achieve the objectives of full participation and equality within society for all persons with disabilities. This almost invariably means that additional resources will need to be made available for this purpose and that a wide range of specially tailored measures will be required.' Committee on Economic, Social and Cultural Rights, General Comment No. 5, Persons with Disabilities, UN Doc. E/1995/22, 9 December 1994. See Chapter 6 in this book.

### 3.2 *The right to information in Concluding Observations by the Committee on Economic, Social and Cultural Rights*

The importance attached to the right to information in relation to the implementation of economic, social and cultural rights is confirmed in the State reporting procedure. In this procedure, States Parties have to report periodically on how they have implemented the provisions of the Covenant. The Committee then critically assesses the report and enters into a dialogue with the State Party. NGOs are allowed to submit so-called shadow reports in which they can provide additional, often critical, information on the performance of the State Party. After the dialogue, the Committee adopts Concluding Observations, in which it highlights the good practices of the State Party as well as the remaining challenges for the implementation of the Covenant. The Concluding Observations are a selection of the many issues that have arisen in the reporting procedure. For this chapter, the Concluding Observations (COs) adopted between 2005 and 2012 were studied to see to what extent and how the Committee referred to the right to information.[74] It appears that it did so most often in relation to the right to health, in particular reproductive health.

For example, in the CO on Mauritania, the Committee encouraged the State in its combat against HIV and AIDS 'to disseminate information as to how HIV/AIDS can be effectively prevented, including by using condoms'.[75] The State Party seems to have a positive obligation in this regard. In the CO on Tanzania, the Committee recommends the State to take measures to address the high rate of teenage pregnancies, *inter alia*, 'through family planning information and services'.[76] Here the obligation is formulated less strongly but it is part of a wide range of measures to be taken.

Both early pregnancy and sexually transmitted diseases were also addressed in the CO on Slovakia. The Committee noted with concern that sexual and reproductive health education was not included in school curricula, which meant that youth was left uninformed about these issues.[77] Similar observations were made in respect of the Russian Federation, which

[74] A full study of the State reports as well as the summaries of the dialogues falls outside the scope of this chapter. The COs offered sufficient insight into the way the Committee refers to the right to information in relation to economic, social and cultural rights.

[75] Committee on Economic, Social and Cultural Rights, Concluding Observations on Mauritania, UN Doc. E/C.12/MRT/CO/1, 30 November 2012, para. 27.

[76] Committee on Economic, Social and Cultural Rights, Concluding Observations on Tanzania, UN Doc. E/C.12/TZA/CO/1-3, 30 November 2012, para. 24.

[77] Committee on Economic, Social and Cultural Rights, Concluding Observations on Slovakia, UN Doc. E/C.12/SVK/CO/2, 08 June 2012, para. 25.

was called upon to increase knowledge of and access to affordable contraceptive methods and to ensure that family planning information and services would be available to everyone, including in rural areas.[78] The CO on Cameroon also included that measures were to be taken, including information on birth control and family planning, to reduce infant and maternal mortality and to facilitate the access of women and girls to sexual and reproductive health services.[79] The Committee used similar language in its CO on the Philippines, where it explicitly found such information to be inadequate.[80] The CO on Sri Lanka also spoke of better inclusion of educational programmes and appropriate information on sexual and reproductive health in the curricula of the Sri Lankan education system.[81] The availability and accessibility of reproductive and sexual health information and services for everyone were also mentioned in the COs on Serbia[82] and India.[83]

Although the obligations were formulated cautiously and not always in explicitly positive terms, it is clear that the Committee considers education and information on sexual and reproductive health as falling under the various provisions of the Covenant, notably Articles 12 (right to health) and 13 (right to education) and that the States Parties have positive obligations in this regard.

The right to information in relation to the right to health has further raised several other points. In the CO on Kenya, the Committee recommended that the State Party take immediate measures to ensure that pregnant women with HIV/AIDS are not discriminated against and are informed about and have free access to antiretroviral medication during pregnancy, labour and after birth, including for their children.[84] In the

78 Committee on Economic, Social and Cultural Rights, Concluding Observations on the Russian Federation, UN Doc. E/C.12/RUS/CO/5, 1 June 2011, para. 30.

79 Committee on Economic, Social and Cultural Rights, Concluding Observations on Cameroon, UN Doc. E/C.12/CMR/CO/2-3, 23 January 2012, para. 27.

80 Committee on Economic, Social and Cultural Rights, Concluding Observations on The Philippines, UN Doc. E/C.12/PHL/CO/4, 2 December 2008, para. 31.

81 Committee on Economic, Social and Cultural Rights, Concluding Observations on Sri Lanka, UN Doc. E/C.12/LKA/CO/2–4, 09/12/2010, para. 34. Sri Lanka was also encouraged to speed up the adoption of a right to information act, para. 10.

82 Committee on Economic, Social and Cultural Rights, Concluding Observations on Serbia, UN Doc. E/C.12/UNK/CO/1, 1 December 2008, para. 30.

83 Committee on Economic, Social and Cultural Rights, Concluding Observations on India, UN Doc. E/C.12/IND/CO/5, 8 August 2008, para. 77.

84 Committee on Economic, Social and Cultural Rights, Concluding Observations on Kenya, UN Doc. E/C.12/KEN/CO/1, 1 December 2008, para. 32.

CO on Brazil, the Committee expressed its concern about child sex abuse and recommended that the State Party, *inter alia*, organize information campaigns for parents, communities and children.[85]

States Parties are also obliged to provide information in situations of health risks. The Committee in its CO on Serbia emphasized that minority and Roma families should be adequately informed about the health risks involved in living in an internally displaced persons camp and should be offered adequate alternative housing solutions that are culturally acceptable.[86] The rights to information, health and housing were connected here. The Committee recommended that the Republic of Korea ensure that adequate information on health risks relating to bottled drinking water was made available to the public.[87] The Committee called on the authorities in Kazakhstan to provide for more general public information campaigns on healthy lifestyles.[88]

The COs on Libyan Arab Jamahiriya[89] and China included a more general urge to respect and protect freedom of information and expression in these States Parties. In these COs, freedom of information and expression is linked to the right to take part in cultural life and the right to enjoy the benefits of scientific progress (Article 15). For instance, in the CO on China, the Committee noted with deep concern the restrictions placed on access to information with regard to academic research, foreign and domestic publications and the Internet.[90]

The Committee sometimes makes an explicit link between the rights to information and education, in particular information and education on human rights. For instance, it urged Libyan Arab Jamahiriya to ensure that information on human rights was disseminated effectively among the population.[91] Sometimes such education and information were

[85] Committee on Economic, Social and Cultural Rights, Concluding Observations on Brazil, UN Doc. E/C.12/BRA/CO/2, 12 June 2009, para. 22.

[86] Committee on Economic, Social and Cultural Rights, Concluding Observations on Serbia, UN Doc. E/C.12/UNK/CO/1, 1 December 2008, para. 29.

[87] Committee on Economic, Social and Cultural Rights, Concluding Observations on the Republic of Korea, UN Doc. E/C.12/KOR/CO/3, 17 December 2009, para. 32.

[88] Committee on Economic, Social and Cultural Rights, Concluding Observations on Kazakhstan, UN Doc. E/C.12/KAZ/CO/1, 01 July 2010, para. 36.

[89] Committee on Economic, Social and Cultural Rights, Concluding Observations on the Libyan Arab Jamahiriya, UN Doc. E/C.12/LYB/CO/2, 25 January 2006, para. 38.

[90] Committee on Economic, Social and Cultural Rights, Concluding Observations on China, UN Doc. E/C.12/1/Add.107, 13 May 2005, paras. 39 and 68.

[91] Committee on Economic, Social and Cultural Rights, Concluding Observations on the Libyan Arab Jamahiriya, UN Doc. E/C.12/LYB/CO/2, 25 January 2006, para. 38.

linked to specific communities. It recommended that the Libyan Arab Jamahiriya take measures in the field of education and information to 'encourage knowledge of the history, traditions, language and culture of the various groups, including the Amazigh community, existing within its territory'.[92] In the CO on Ecuador, the Committee expressed its concern that insufficient informational material has been translated into the various indigenous languages.[93]

The right to information is also linked to the right to an adequate standard of living as included in Article 11 ICESCR. In the CO on Ecuador, the Committee urged the State Party to establish channels for providing the public with information on the coverage of a voucher programme intended for persons living in extreme poverty, thereby increasing the protection of the right to an adequate standard of living.[94]

The fact that the right to information is not included in all Concluding Observations adopted by the Committee does not diminish the importance of this right for the implementation and enjoyment of economic, social and cultural rights. As stated above, COs are a selection of the topics discussed with the State Party and do not fully cover all issues at stake. The overview here does, however, confirm the link between the right to information and economic, social and cultural rights and it also broadly confirms that States have negative as well as positive obligations in this regard. The COs, issued for individual States Parties, confirm the picture arising from the General Comments and the reporting guidelines, which have a more general application for all States Parties.

## 4 In focus: the right to information and the right to health

The work of the Committee on Economic, Social and Cultural Rights shows that one of the economic, social and cultural rights where the right to information is of crucial importance is the right to health. It can indeed be argued that without the right to information, 'the ICESCR's guarantee of a right to health becomes devoid of meaning'.[95] Various UN bodies, including the Committee, have recognized the right to (access to)

[92] *Ibid.*, para. 43.
[93] Committee on Economic, Social and Cultural Rights, Concluding Observations on Ecuador, UN Doc. E/C.12/ECU/CO/3, 13 December 2012, para. 33.
[94] *Ibid.*, para. 23.
[95] G. A. Hoffman, 'In Search of an International Human Rights to Receive Information', *International and Comparative Law Review* 25(165) (2002–3), 174.

information as one of the critical underlying determinants of the right to health and a proper information system, with for instance appropriately disaggregated data, as a building block for a good health system.[96]

The strong link between the right to information and the right to health follows from the earlier conclusion that the right to information is particularly relevant if it concerns information of public interest. Public interest is often at stake in the case of (public) health. This is why the State has not only negative but also positive obligations to provide (access to) information which is relevant to the health of individuals or communities. The State should share information, not only upon request, but also without such a request, and should make information publicly available at its own initiative. Such information could concern many different health (related) issues: general health policies, health risks, specific ways of treatment, drugs, medication, sexual and reproductive health, etc. It also means that the State has a positive obligation to prevent and end all forms of discrimination in relation to (access to) information and to ensure that health information is made available to vulnerable groups, including women, children, minorities, indigenous peoples, persons with disabilities, elderly, etc.[97]

Such information concerning health is crucial at different levels: to broadly monitor State policies in a democratic process and to have knowledge about the general health situation in a country, but also more individually to be able to make informed choices in relation to health, to give informed consent to medical interventions and to promote one's own health.[98]

[96] *The Right of Everyone to the Enjoyment of the Highest Attainable Standard of Physical and Mental Health*, Report of the Special Rapporteur, Paul Hunt, UN Doc. E/CN.4/2004/49, 16 February 2004, paras. 28 and 68; *Report of the Special Rapporteur on the Right of Everyone to the Enjoyment of the Highest Attainable Standard of Physical and Mental Health*, Paul Hunt, UN Doc. A/HRC/7/11, 31 January 2008, paras. 45, 68(c) and 71. Other underlying determinants of health are access to safe water and adequate sanitation, an adequate supply of safe food, nutrition and housing, healthy occupational and environmental conditions and freedom from discrimination.

[97] Jagwanth, 'Right to Information', 7; see also: S. Coliver, 'The Right to Information Necessary for Reproductive Health and Choice under International Law', *American University Law Review* 44 (1994–5), 1283–6; *Report of the Special Rapporteur*, Paul Hunt, 16 February 2004, para. 39.

[98] Coliver, 'Right to Information Necessary', 1280 and 1288; *Report of the Special Rapporteur*, Paul Hunt, 31 January 2008, para. 40; M. Hartlev, 'Patient Rights', in B. Toebes, M. Hartlev, A. Hendriks and J. Rothmar Herrmann (eds.), *Health and Human Rights in Europe* (Antwerp: Intersentia, 2012), 130; T. Lemmens and C. Telfer, 'Access to Information and the Right to Health: the Human Rights Case for Clinical Trials Transparency', *American Journal of Law and Medicine* 38 (2012), 104–6.

Interesting in relation to the individual level is that the right to information also implies its opposite: the right not to be informed, or the right not to know. This right implies a negative obligation to respect the wish of a person not to receive information, such as genetic information, or not to be informed of the outcome of genetic testing.[99]

A particular area of health where information is crucial (and often lacking) is sexual and reproductive health. This was not only recognized by the Committee on Economic, Social and Cultural Rights, but also by the Special Rapporteur on the Right to Health and by scholars. Ensuring access to information on sexual and reproductive health is recognized as an obligation of immediate effect and a core obligation of States.[100] These two connotations show the importance attached to this right. While the ICESCR in Article 2 prescribes that the rights in the Covenant may be achieved progressively, States have several immediate obligations, such as ensuring non-discrimination.[101] It is interesting to see that access to information, even beyond non-discrimination, is considered an immediate obligation. The Committee has further elaborated the concept of 'core obligations' in relation to economic, social and cultural rights, which is the minimum essential level of protection that States should provide, irrespective of their economic and social development.[102] Apparently, access to information is considered to be such a core obligation.

It has further been established that ensuring access to information on sexual and reproductive health implies that States have negative and positive obligations. Negative obligations imply that States do not interfere with the dissemination of information by others, for instance on abortion services or birth control. Positive obligations include providing women with sufficient and reliable information and educating them on matters of sexuality and reproduction.[103] Another positive obligation in relation to health, which is also grounded in the rights to liberty and security and the prohibition of inhumane and degrading treatment, is the obligation not to perform or permit medical interventions, in particular

[99] Hartlev, 'Patient Rights', 132.

[100] *Report of the Special Rapporteur*, Paul Hunt, 16 February 2004, paras. 14, 18, 29 and 42; *Report of the Special Rapporteur*, Paul Hunt, 31 January 2008, para. 52.

[101] Committee on Economic, Social and Cultural Rights, General Comment No. 3 on the Nature of States Parties' Obligations (Article 2, para. 1 of the Covenant), UN Doc., E/1993/21, 1991, para. 9.

[102] *Ibid.*, para. 10.

[103] Coliver, 'Right to Information Necessary', 1299–300; J. Rothmar Herrmann, 'Reproductive Health', in Toebes *et al.* (eds.), *Health and Human Rights in Europe*, 145–76.

far-reaching interventions such as abortion or sterilization, without prior and informed consent.[104]

The right to information in relation to the right to health and health care is also a so-called 'patient right'.[105] Patient rights include the right to information and to confidentiality before and during treatment, including about health condition, treatment opportunities and possible negative effects of treatment, but also after treatment, including access to one's own files and to have information destroyed.[106]

As argued above, the right to information could be limited by the State, for instance to protect the rights of others. Limitations of access to information in relation to health can be envisaged to protect privacy. Health information may be sensitive and may have to be concealed to protect the privacy of a person, or the confidential relationship between the patient and health care providers.[107]

## 5 Concluding remarks

The right to information is formally part of the right to freedom of expression and as such included in the ICCPR and other instruments on civil and political rights. It has however gained broader meaning as being a right of its own. The right to information allows people to critically follow their authorities, as part of democracy, transparency, accountability and participation, but it also allows individuals and communities to make informed choices or to express informed consent on various matters.

The right to information is clearly linked to economic, social and cultural rights. It is more than part of the normative content of these

[104] Coliver, 'Right to Information Necessary', 1301–2. Article 7 ICCPR includes that 'no one shall be subjected without his free consent to medical or scientific experimentation'.

[105] Patient rights to information are internationally recognized in the Council of Europe Convention for the Protection of Human Rights and Dignity of the Human Being with regard to the Application of Biology and Medicine: Convention on Human Rights and Biomedicine, adopted 4 April 1997, Articles 5 and 10; the WHO Declaration of the Promotions of Rights of Patients in Europe, Copenhagen, 1994, Article 2; UNESCO Universal Declaration on Bioethics and Human Rights, adopted 19 October 2005, Articles 6, 22 and 23.

[106] Hartlev, 'Patient Rights', 111, 113 and 116. Information on treatment and medicines is often not in the hands of public authorities, but in the hands of private (pharmaceutical) companies. The question to what extent they have obligations to make such information available and accessible falls outside the scope of this chapter. See, on this issue: Lemmens and Telfer, 'Access to Information', 63–112.

[107] Hartlev, 'Patient Rights', 139.

rights; it is a determining factor in the enjoyment of these rights and one of the crucial elements for States in the implementation of these rights. The right to information thereby echoes the interrelatedness and interdependence of all human rights.

The right to information concerns the right to seek, receive and impart information, which is broadly grouped as the right of access to information. Such access not only concerns the media or other information providers, but it may also concern State authorities directly. In particular, in relation to information of public interest, individuals and communities have the right to receive such information and State authorities have the obligation to make such information available and accessible or to disseminate it actively.

The fact that the State should play an active role in providing (access to) information of public interest also follows from the specific character of these rights, as compared to civil and political rights. Most economic, social and cultural rights are drafted in a programmatic way. This means that they are not formulated as substantive rights for individuals (everyone has the right to...), but as assignments to States Parties (States Parties recognize the right to..., or undertake to respect and ensure the right to...). This formulation as well as the character of these rights imply that the obligations of States are not merely negatives ones of State abstention but also positive ones of State action.

Moreover, most economic, social and cultural rights concern (public) goods and services, such as education, food, water, housing, health care, etc. It is clear that information about the way a State has taken measures and has implemented policies in relation to these goods and services, as well as information about their availability is crucial for the beneficiaries of the rights. They can only truly enjoy these rights if they are sufficiently informed of their existence and their normative content and of the different laws, policies, measures, services and facilities available. It is only when individuals and communities are adequately and transparently informed that they can make choices about the way and extent to which they wish to enjoy their rights, for instance as to which education or health care they prefer, which possibilities there are for social security and which employment opportunities exist. Information also implies that the beneficiaries can critically assess these measures and policies and can hold their State accountable in case of non-respect or violation of these rights.

The fact that the right to information is an important part of the implementation of economic, social and cultural rights is confirmed by the work of the Committee on Economic, Social and Cultural Rights. The Committee has included the right to information in its reporting guidelines and in all its General Comments since the year 2000. It has also regularly included the right to information in its COs on various States Parties. The link between the right to information and economic, social and cultural rights is also confirmed in the work of other UN bodies, such as the Special Rapporteur on the right to health.

The fact that the right to information is a determinant factor of economic, social and cultural rights, in particular the right to health, implies that States have positive as well as negative obligations. They should not only make information available and accessible upon request, but they also have a positive obligation to disseminate information of public interest (pro) actively. This is confirmed in the HRC's General Comment No. 34, which lays down that States Parties should proactively put in the public domain government information of public interest. At the same time, the right to information may be limited, for instance to protect the rights of others, in particular their privacy, or national security.

A human rights approach to information implies that special measures may have to be taken to make information also accessible for vulnerable groups, such as persons with low levels of literacy or visual disabilities. One could also think of information in different languages, in particular those of minorities and indigenous peoples. And although the ways and modes of information sharing have also drastically changed with the developments in the information and communication technologies, the State should not forget those people who are not familiar or experienced with the internet or online tools. A holistic approach to the right to information is needed to make this right effective in practice for different groups in society.

It should be noted that the elaboration of the State obligations in relation to the ICESCR has so far taken place via the reporting procedure, including (reporting) guidelines, COs and General Comments. This procedure is focused on monitoring general policies and measures and does not concern individual or specific situations. The individual complaint procedure of the ICESCR has only recently come into force. As soon as individual complaints are examined by the Committee on Economic, Social and Cultural Rights, more concrete situations could be tested, as is already the case at the regional human rights courts. This will further clarify and strengthen the bond between the right to information and economic, social and cultural rights.

## Literature

ARTICLE 19, *Access to Information: An Instrumental Right for Empowerment* (London, 2007).

ARTICLE 19, *The Public's Right to Know: Principles on Freedom of Information Legislation* (London, 1999).

ARTICLE 19, *The Free Flow Principles: Freedom of Expression and the Rights to Water and Sanitation* (London, 20 March 2014).

Centre on Housing Rights and Evictions, *Litigating Economic, Social and Cultural Rights: Achievements, Challenges and Strategies* (Geneva, 2003).

Beatson, J. and Y. Cripps (eds.), *Freedom of Expression and Freedom of Information, Essays in Honour of Sir David Williams* (Oxford University Press, 2000).

Coliver, S. 'The Right to Information Necessary for Reproductive Health and Choice under International Law', *American University Law Review* 44 (1994–5), 1279–303.

Daruwala, M. and V. Nayak (eds.), *Our Rights, Our Information. Empowering Peoples to Demand Rights through Knowledge, Commonwealth Human Rights Initiative* (Paris: UNESCO, 2007).

Feldman, D. 'Information and Privacy', in J. Beatson and Y. Cripps (eds.), *Freedom of Expression and Freedom of Information, Essays in Honour of Sir David Williams* (Oxford University Press, 2000), 299–324.

Hartlev, M. 'Patient Rights', in B. Toebes, M. Hartlev, A. Hendriks and J. Rothmar Herrmann (eds.), *Health and Human Rights in Europe* (Antwerp: Intersentia, 2012), 111–44.

Hoffman, G. A. 'In Search of an International Human Rights to Receive Information', *International and Comparative Law Review* 25 (2002–3), 165–204.

International Commission of Jurists, *Courts and the Legal Enforcement of Economic, Social and Cultural Rights – Comparative Experiences of Justiciability* (Geneva, 2008).

Jagwanth, S. 'The Right to Information as a Leverage Right', in R. Calland and A. Tilley (eds.), *The Right to Know, The Right to Live: Access to Information and Socio-Economic Justice* (Cape Town: Open Democracy Advice Centre, 2002), 3–16.

Lemmens, T. and C. Telfer, 'Access to Information and the Right to Health: the Human Rights Case for Clinical Trials Transparency', *American Journal of Law and Medicine* 38 (2012), 63–631.

Mendel, T. *Freedom of Information, a Comparative Legal Study*, 2nd edn (Paris: UNESCO, 2008).

Perritt, H. H. and C. J. Lhulier, 'Information Access Rights Based on International Human Rights Law', *Buff. Law Review* 45 (1997), 899–929.

Rothmar Herrmann, J. 'Reproductive Health', in B. Toebes, M. Hartlev, A. Hendriks and J. Rothmar Herrmann (eds.), *Health and Human Rights in Europe* (Antwerp: Intersentia, 2012), 145–76.

Scott, R. 'Confidentiality', in J. Beatson and Y. Cripps (eds.), *Freedom of Expression and Freedom of Information, Essays in Honour of Sir David Williams* (Oxford University Press, 2000), 267–74.

Sedley, S., 'Information as a Human Right', in J. Beatson and Y. Cripps (eds.), *Freedom of Expression and Freedom of Information, Essays in Honour of Sir David Williams* (Oxford University Press, 2000), 239–48.

## UN documents

### *Committee on Economic, Social and Cultural Rights*

*Guidelines on Treaty-Specific Documents to be Submitted by States Parties under Articles 16 and 17 of the International Covenant on Economic, Social and Cultural Rights*, UN Doc. E/C.12/2008/2, 24 March 2009.

General Comment No. 3 on the Nature of States Parties' Obligations (Article 2, para. 1 of the Covenant), UN Doc, E/1993/21, 1991.

General Comment No. 14: The Right to the Highest Attainable Standard of Health (Article 12 ICESCR), UN Doc. E/C.12/2000/4, 11 August 2000.

General Comment No. 15: The Right to Water (Articles 11 and 12 ICESCR), UN Doc. E/C.12/2002/11, 20 January 2003.

General Comment No. 18: The Right to Work (Article 6 ICESCR), UN Doc. E/C.12/GC/18, 6 February 2006.

General Comment No. 19: The Right to Social Security (Article 9 of the ICESCR), UN Doc. E/C.12/GC/19, 4 February 2008.

General Comment No. 20: Non-Discrimination in Economic, Social and Cultural Rights (Article 2(2) ICESCR), UN Doc. E/C.12/GC/20, 2 July 2009.

General Comment No. 21: The Right of Everyone to Take Part in Cultural Life (Article 15(1)a ICESCR), UN Doc. E/C.12/GC/21, 21 December 2009.

Concluding Observations on Brazil, UN Doc. E/C.12/BRA/CO/2, 12 June 2009.

Concluding Observations on Cameroon, UN Doc. E/C.12/CMR/CO/2–3, 23 January 2012.

Concluding Observations on China, UN Doc. E/C.12/1/Add.107, 13 May 2005.

Concluding Observations on Ecuador, UN Doc. E/C.12/ECU/CO/3, 13 December 2012.

Concluding Observations on India, UN Doc. E/C.12/IND/CO/5, 08 August 2008.

Concluding Observations on Kazakhstan, UN Doc. E/C.12/KAZ/CO/1, 01 July 2010.

Concluding Observations on Kenya, UN Doc. E/C.12/KEN/CO/1, 01 December 2008.

Concluding Observations on Mauritania, UN Doc. E/C.12/MRT/CO/1, 30 November 2012.

Concluding Observations on Serbia, UN Doc. E/C.12/UNK/CO/1, 01 December 2008.

Concluding Observations on Slovakia, UN Doc. E/C.12/SVK/CO/2, 08 June 2012.
Concluding Observations on Sri Lanka, UN Doc. E/C.12/LKA/CO/2–4, 09 December 2010.
Concluding Observations on Tanzania, UN Doc. E/C.12/TZA/CO/1–3, 30 November 2012.
Concluding Observations on the Libyan Arab Jamahiriya, UN Doc. E/C.12/LYB/CO/2, 25 January 2006.
Concluding Observations on the Philippines, UN Doc. E/C.12/PHL/CO/4, 02 December 2008.
Concluding Observations on the Republic of Korea, UN Doc. E/C.12/KOR/CO/3, 17 December 2009.
Concluding Observations on the Russian Federation, UN Doc. E/C.12/RUS/CO/5, 1 June 2011.

### *Other*

GA, Resolution 59(1): Calling of an International Conference on Freedom of Information, 14 December 1946.
Human Rights Committee, General Comment No. 34, Article 19: Freedom of Opinion and Expression, UN Doc. CCPR/C/GC/34, 21 July 2011.
*Report of the Special Rapporteur on the Promotion and Protection of the Right to Freedom of Opinion and Expression*, UN Doc. E/CN.4/2000/63, 18 January 2000.
*Report of the Special Rapporteur on the Right of Everyone to the Enjoyment of the Highest Attainable Standard of Physical and Mental Health*, Paul Hunt, UN Doc. A/HRC/7/11, 31 January 2008.
*The Right of Everyone to the Enjoyment of the Highest Attainable Standard of Physical and Mental Health, Report of the Special Rapporteur, Paul Hunt*, UN Doc. E/CN.4/2004/49, 16 February 2004.
Joint Declaration by the UN Special Rapporteur on Freedom of Opinion and Expression, the OSCE Representative on Freedom of the Media and the OAS Special Rapporteur in Freedom of Expression, adopted 6 December 2004.
Report on the Working Methods of the Human Rights Treaty Bodies Relating to the State Party Reporting Process, UN Doc. HRI/MC/2005/4, 25 May 2005.
United Nations Commission on Human Rights, Resolution 2000/38, the Right to Freedom of Opinion and Expression, 20 April 2000.

## Case law

### *European Commission and Court of Human Rights*

ECommHR, *Guerra and Others* v. *Italy* (Appl. No. 14967/89), Report adopted 29 June 1996.

*Guerra and Others* v. *Italy* (Appl. No. 116/1996/735/932), Judgment of 19 February 1998.
*Kenedi* v. *Hungary* (Appl. No. 31475/05), Judgment of 26 May 2009.
*Leander* v. *Sweden* (Appl. No. 9248/81), Judgment of 26 March 1987.
*Loiseau* v. *France* (Appl. No. 46809/99), Judgment of 18 November 2003.
*McGinley and Egan* v. *United Kingdom* (Appl. Nos. 21825/93 and 23414/94), Judgment of 8 June 1998.
*Öneryildiz* v. *Turkey* (Appl. No. 48939/99), Judgment of 30 November 2004.
*Open Door and Dublin Well Woman* v. *Ireland* (Appl. No. 14234/88; 14235/88), Judgment of 29 October 1992.
*Österreichische Vereinigung zur Erhaltung, Stärkung und Schaffung eines wirtschaftlich gesunden land-und forstwirtschaftlichen Grundbesitzes* v. *Austria* (Appl. No. 39534/07), Judgment of 28 November 2013.
*Sdruženi Jihočeské Matky* v. *Czech Republic* (Appl. No. 19101/03), Admissibility Decision of 10 July 2006.
*Sunday Times* v. *the United Kingdom* (Appl. No. 6538/74), Judgment of 26 April 1979.
*Társaság a Szabadságjogokért* v. *Hungary* (Appl. No. 37374/05), Judgment of 14 April 2009.
*Vilness and Others* v. *Norway* (Appl. No. 52806/09), Judgment of 5 December 2013.
*Women on Waves and Others* v. *Portugal* (Appl. No. 31276/05), Judgment of 3 February 2009.

## *Inter-American Court of Human Rights*

*Claude Reyes and Others* v. *Chile*, Series C No. 151, 19 September 2006.
*Compulsory Membership in an Association Prescribed by Law for the Practice of Journalism*, Advisory Opinion OC-5/85, 13 November 1985.

## *African Commission on Human and Peoples' Rights*

Res.62(XXXII)02: Resolution on the Adoption of the Declaration of Principles on Freedom of Expression in Africa (2002), 23 October 2002.

## *Council of Europe*

Committee of Ministers, Recommendation No. R(81)19 on Access to Information Held by Public Authorities, 25 November 1981.
Committee of Ministers, Recommendation No. 2 of the Committee of Ministers to Member States on access to official documents, 21 February 2002.

# 4

# International Convention on the Elimination of All Forms of Racial Discrimination: the prohibition of 'racist hate speech'

PATRICK THORNBERRY

## 1 Introduction

The relationship between freedom of speech and hate speech directed against minorities was a subject of great interest to Kevin Boyle, expressed in, *inter alia*, his outstanding contribution to the Camden Principles.[1] I regret that I did not know him better, though our paths crossed occasionally and we had academic and academically related interests in common – the latter including chairmanship of Minority Rights Group International. I benefited enormously from reading his work, including a sharply perceptive critique (with Anneliese Baldaccini) of the human rights approach to combating racism, elements of which are drawn upon for the present chapter.[2] His work lives on, as do the personal recollections of his intelligence and gentle personality. I am honoured to be able to offer this chapter in his memory.

The International Convention on the Elimination of All Forms of Racial Discrimination (ICERD/'the Convention') quintessentially deals with acts, activities and speech against minorities, even if 'minority' is not mentioned in its text. The grounds of discrimination outlined in Article 1 of the Convention – race, colour, descent, national origin, ethnic origin – have been shaped in the practice of the Committee on the Elimination of Racial Discrimination (CERD/'the Committee') to include groups that have 'a defined collective identity for the purpose of which

1 *The Camden Principles on Freedom of Expression and Equality* (London: ARTICLE 19, April 2009).

2 K. Boyle and A. Baldaccini, 'A Critical Evaluation of International Human Rights Approaches to Racism', in S. Fredman (ed.), *Discrimination and Human Rights: The Case of Racism* (Oxford University Press, 2001), 135–91.

self-identification is the relevant criterion'.[3] The primary focus of the present chapter is on the protection offered to such groups by Article 4 of ICERD,[4] which, when read as unadorned with nuance or qualification, may appear to sit awkwardly with principles of freedom of expression, particularly with regard to its call to criminalize the dissemination of racist ideas. The current state-of-the-art interpretation by CERD of Article 4 is expressed by General Recommendation 35 (GR 35) of 2013 on combating racist hate speech, a recommendation that subsumes a range of previous recommendations but without replacing them.[5] The Recommendation offers a fresh reading of Article 4 in the context of the Convention as a whole and the wider human rights framework, and also appraises its role – and the role of criminal proscription – in combating hate speech. This chapter analyses CERD's practice on Article 4, including GR 35, reflecting on the nature and quality of its approach to combating destructive forms of speech in a bewildering variety of habitats, and the continuing challenges to be faced. Article 4 addresses hate speech and the organizational context for its production:

> States Parties condemn all propaganda and all organizations which are based on ideas or theories of superiority of one race or group of persons of one colour or ethnic origin, or which attempt to justify or promote racial hatred and discrimination in any form, and undertake to adopt immediate and positive measures designed to eradicate all incitement to, or acts of, such discrimination and, to this end, with due regard to the principles embodied in the Universal Declaration of Human Rights and the rights expressly set forth in article 5 of this Convention, *inter alia*:
>
> (a) Shall declare an offence punishable by law all dissemination of ideas based on racial superiority or hatred, incitement to racial discrimination, as well as all acts of violence or incitement to such acts against any race or group of persons of another colour or ethnic origin, and also the provision of any assistance to racist activities, including the financing thereof;

[3] Boyle and Baldaccini, 'Critical Evaluation', 152.

[4] The views expressed in the present chapter by the author (a former member of CERD) aspire to represent the Committee's practice fairly, but should not be taken as the views of CERD as a whole.

[5] CERD, General Recommendation No. 35: Combating Racist Hate Speech, UN Doc. CERD/C/GC/35, 26 September 2013 (adopted by CERD at its 83rd session, 12–30 August 2013), para. 3.

(b) Shall declare illegal and prohibit organizations, and also organized and all other propaganda activities, which promote and incite racial discrimination, and shall recognize participation in such organizations or activities as an offence punishable by law;
(c) Shall not permit public authorities or public institutions, national or local, to promote or incite racial discrimination.

While the term 'hate speech' is not referred to as such in the Convention, it has been employed with considerable frequency by CERD, with or without the 'racist' epithet that makes an appearance in the preamble to the Convention – where the States Parties declare their resolve 'to prevent and combat racist doctrines and practices'.[6] Hate speech has been subject to a range of definitions,[7] to which remarks by Robert Post may be added:

> To prohibit hate speech is . . . to forbid expression of 'extreme' intolerance or 'extreme' dislike. The qualification 'extreme' is prerequisite because intolerance and dislike are necessary human emotions which no legal order could pretend to abolish. We *should* be intolerant of injustice and we *should* dislike the needless suffering of the innocent.[8]

Hate speech in this understanding is a form of intense and uncivilized discourse that targets a multiplicity of others and may serve to frame the conditions for negative consequences to rain down upon them.[9] Waldron offers an alternative perspective: 'hate' suggests that 'we are interested in correcting the passions and emotions that lie behind a particular speech

6 International Convention on the Elimination of All Forms of Racial Discrimination, New York, 21 December 1965, entered into force 4 January 1969, 660 UNTS 195, preamble, para. 10. The European Commission against Racism and Intolerance (ECRI) defines racism as the belief that 'a ground such as race, colour, language, religion, nationality or national or ethnic origin justifies contempt for a person or a group of persons, or the notion of superiority of a person or a group of persons' (CoE ECRI, General Policy Recommendation No. 7: On National Legislation to Combat Racism and Racial Discrimination, 13 December 2002, paragraph on 'Definitions').

7 According to the Council of Europe, the term covers 'all forms of expression which spread, incite, promote or justify racial hatred, xenophobia, anti-Semitism or other forms of hatred based on intolerance, including: intolerance expressed by aggressive nationalism and ethnocentrism, discrimination and hostility against minorities, migrants and people of immigrant origin' (CoE Committee of Ministers' Recommendation No. R (97) 20 on 'Hate Speech', 30 October 1997, Appendix).

8 R. Post, 'Hate Speech', in I. Hare and J. Weinstein (eds.), *Extreme Speech and Democracy* (Oxford University Press, 2009), 123 (emphasis in the original).

9 For an extensive account of national and international norms on 'hate speech', see A. Weber, *Manual on Hate Speech* (Strasbourg: Council of Europe, 2009).

act', whereas in most hate speech legislation, as distinct from legislation on hate crimes, 'hatred is relevant not as the motivation of certain actions, but as a possible *effect* of certain forms of speech'.[10] Waldron's observations on speech effects are well taken, though issues of content, tone, motivation and effects are not easily unravelled in practice, and all may figure in a determination of what constitutes an offence to be declared by law under the terms of Article 4. In GR 35, CERD states that the focus of the recommendation is 'on the ensemble of Convention provisions that cumulatively enable the identification of expression that constitutes hate speech';[11] within these parameters, coupled with the detailed analysis in GR 35 of the relevant legal terminology, hate speech is described as 'a form of other-directed speech which rejects the core human rights principles of human dignity and equality and seeks to degrade the standing of individuals and groups in the estimation of society'.[12]

Article 4 of ICERD has been taken as an exemplar of a 'hard line' against racist hate speech, vigilantly and sternly enforced by the Committee and 'harder' than in comparable human rights instruments.[13] While commending itself to most States Parties, the Committee's approach to Article 4 has not hitherto commanded general assent, as is evidenced by the reservations of a minority of States. It may be that the Committee's adoption of GR 35 will encourage States Parties to modify or withdraw their reservations to the article, a *desideratum* expressed in the recommendation itself.[14] The emergence of GR 35, with its more fully realized account of the letter and spirit of Article 4 and related articles, reminds us that an unyielding, literal interpretation of a recalcitrant text is not the only possible outcome of an interpretative practice. The text of Article 4, with all its superficial clarity, is of a generalizing nature, incomplete as a statement of its relationship to the details of domestic penal law, and situated in a complex, rapidly drafted Convention that makes reference to a human rights system of which the Convention is a part. Developments in the human rights framework are recognized in GR 35:

10 J. Waldron, *The Harm in Hate Speech* (Cambridge, MA: Harvard University Press, 2012), 34–5.

11 CERD, GR 35, para. 5.

12 *Ibid.*, para. 10.

13 T. McGonagle, *Minority Rights, Freedom of Expression and of the Media: Dynamics and Dilemmas* (Antwerp: Intersentia, 2011), 289.

14 On reservations, see CERD, GR 35, para. 23.

> By virtue of its work in implementing the Convention as a living instrument, the Committee engages with the wider human rights environment, awareness of which suffuses the Convention. In gauging the scope of freedom of expression, it should be recalled that the right is integrated into the Convention and is not simply articulated outside it: the principles of the Convention contribute to a fuller understanding of the parameters of the right in contemporary international human rights law. The Committee has integrated this right to freedom of expression into its work on combating hate speech ... drawing upon its elaboration in sister human rights bodies.[15]

## 2 Article 4 – contested *ab initio*

There is at most a limited international consensus on the relationship between the proscription of racist hate speech and freedom of expression. Western States have been the most reluctant to assimilate the Committee's recommendations in this area, and the majority of reservations to Article 4 emanate from this quarter. In drafting the Convention, Western States presented themselves as stout defenders of freedom of expression while others, notably the bloc of Communist States and the newly independent States, took a tougher stance on suppressing racist speech.[16] In the present chapter, it is possible only to recall a limited sample of drafting issues. On the discursive aspect, a proposal by the USA to sharpen the 'due regard' clause to read 'with due regard for the fundamental right of freedom of expression'[17] was not accepted: others took the view that draft texts had taken far too timid an approach to 'the question of the dissemination of racist ideas'.[18] On the proscription of racist organizations, the representative of the USA asserted that 'pernicious ideas could not be eliminated by forcing them underground ... the ideas of an organization operating in secrecy became subversive for the very reason they were not open to scrutiny.'[19] A colourful counter analogy was offered by the representative of the USSR who recalled that:

[15] CERD, GR 35, para. 4. A footnote to the paragraph makes reference to General Comment No. 34 of the Human Rights Committee on freedoms of opinion and expression.

[16] Elements in the drafting of ICERD are extensively accounted for in N. Lerner, *The International Convention on the Elimination of All Forms of Racial Discrimination* (Alphen aan den Rijn: Sijthoff and Noordhoff, 1980). The present author is preparing a legal commentary on the Convention, including details of its drafting.

[17] A/C.3/L.1243, A/6181, para. 68.

[18] A/C.3/SR.1318, para. 30: comments of the representative of Ethiopia, requesting a separate vote on the 'due regard' clause.

[19] E/CN.4/SR.792, 10.

> [T]here had been organizations which murdered for a fee; the notorious 'Murder Incorporated' was an example. That organization had been set up for a definite object: the commission of crime. It would be curious logic to consider that it had the right to exist as long as it was not actually guilty of a murder, or that it was necessary to wait for a murder to be committed before prohibiting such an organization.[20]

Despite the impassioned pleas of some representatives to give greater ballast to the 'freedoms', the *travaux préparatoires* demonstrate that a considerable majority of governments favoured a resolute stance against hate speech. As regards racist organizations, they were to be banned forthwith without reference to activities: for many representatives it was enough simply to be a kind of 'Murder Incorporated'. The critique of 'propaganda', 'ideas' and 'theories' of racial superiority was sustained throughout the drafting, even though opposition to the penalization of the expression of ideas was also significant.

## 3 CERD practice – principally on Article 4

*Intolerance needs constant attention.* (Kevin Boyle)[21]

### *3.1 General*

The provisions of Article 4 have been elaborated on in a series of General Recommendations adopted by the Committee.[22] GR 15 (1993) provides a lengthy analysis, reading the *travaux* of the Convention to the effect that the drafters regarded Article 4 as central to the struggle against racial discrimination in view of 'a widespread fear of the revival of authoritarian ideologies' when the Convention was in process of adoption.[23] The 'mandatory character' of the article is recalled, and that its implementation requires not only the enactment of legislation but its effective enforcement.[24] The approach is subsumed and restated by GR 35, where

[20] E/CN.4/SR.794, 10. 'Murder incorporated' or 'Murder Inc.' was the name given by the press for an organized crime group in the USA that carried out murders in the 1930s and 1940s. The title of the group was a striking journalistic invention.

[21] K. Boyle, 'Hate Speech: The United States versus the Rest of the World', *Maine Law Review* 53-2 (2001), 493.

[22] Para. 3 of GR 35 recalls some CERD history in this respect.

[23] CERD, General Recommendation No. 15 on Article 4 of the Convention, UN Doc. A/48/18, ch. VIII, 17 March 1993, para. 1.

[24] *Ibid.*, see also: CERD, *Mohammad Hassan Gelle* v. *Denmark*, Communication No. 34/2004, UN Doc. A/61/18, Annex IV, 10 March 2006, para. 7.3.

it is asserted that 'it is not enough to declare the forms of conduct in article 4 as offences; the provisions of the article must also be effectively implemented. Effective implementation is characteristically achieved through investigations of offences set out in the Convention and, where appropriate, the prosecution of offenders.'[25] The Committee's repeated insistence on the need to take steps to implement the article effectively means that the incorporation of the Convention into domestic law will not, without more, fully satisfy the requirements of Article 4.[26] The key role of Article 4 in combating hate speech is the staple of many CERD interventions over decades: its functions are declared to be multiple, hence the summary in GR 35 that Article 4 'serves the functions of prevention and deterrence, and provides for sanctions when deterrence fails ... [it] also has an expressive function in underlining the international community's abhorrence of racist hate speech'.[27]

### 3.2 *Chapeau*

The *chapeau* of Article 4 sets out a condemnation of propaganda and organizations underpinned by ideas or theories of racial superiority, or attempts to justify or promote racial hatred, and the undertaking to act immediately to eradicate discrimination or incitement thereto.[28] 'Justification' makes an appearance in GR 35 in the context of a paragraph on 'denial crimes', and in a significantly restricted form: 'The Committee recommends that public denials or attempts to justify crimes of genocide and crimes against humanity, as defined by international law, should be declared as offences punishable by law, provided that they clearly constitute incitement to racial violence or hatred.'[29] The Committee has also

[25] CERD, General Recommendation No. 35, extract from para. 17.

[26] CERD, *Positive Measures Designed to Eradicate all Incitement to, or Acts of, Racial Discrimination* (New York: United Nations, 1986), para. 243. The Study was originally published on the occasion of the Second World Conference to Combat Racism and Racial Discrimination held in Geneva in August 1983, and is referred to in the present chapter as the *CERD 1983 Study*.

[27] CERD, General Recommendation No. 35, para. 10. See also, General Recommendation No. 15, para. 2.

[28] The assault on racist ideas is further buttressed by para. 6 of the preamble, which recites the conviction that 'any doctrine of superiority based on racial differentiation is scientifically false, morally condemnable, socially unjust and dangerous'.

[29] CERD, General Recommendation No. 35, para. 14, citing Human Rights Committee General Comment No. 34, the paragraph underlines that '"the expression of opinions about historical facts" should not be prohibited or punished'.

welcomed legislation against 'glorification' of those found guilty of committing crimes against peace and humanity.[30] While etymologically neutral,[31] 'propaganda' has acquired a negative meaning in connection with its use in war and for political causes (isms).[32] In an assessment by one State Party to ICERD, 'propaganda' implies scale, systematic action and extensive dissemination.[33] If the essence of propaganda is persuasion rather than logic, the Committee has nonetheless commented in the *Jewish Community* case that 'the lack of logic of particular remarks is not relevant to the assessment of whether or not they violate article 4'.[34] Ambiguity of utterance has, however, been treated as relevant to such an assessment and may work to deflect the application of Article 4 to a case.[35] Careful reading of the implications of speech may also suggest that the article is applicable: hence the recall in GR 35 that racist hate speech is not confined to 'explicitly racial remarks', and that it may involve 'indirect language in order to disguise its targets and objectives'.[36]

### *3.3 The 'due regard' clause*

The due regard clause represents one aspect of the 'opening out' of the text of ICERD to the wider framework of human rights. A study by Partsch, a former member of the Committee, outlined three different views on the 'due regard' clause, the first being that States are not authorized to take

[30] CERD, Concluding Observations on Romania, UN Doc. CERD/C/ROU/CO/16–19, 13 September 2010, para. 4 (b).

[31] From the Latin *propagare*, as used for example in the Catholic Church's *Congregatio de Propaganda Fide* – Congregation for the Propagation of the Faith.

[32] Defined in the *Concise Oxford English Dictionary*, 11th edn (Oxford University Press, 2004), 1150 as 'information, especially of a biased or misleading nature, used to promote a political cause or point of view; the dissemination of such information'. See also E. S. Herman and N. Chomsky, *Manufacturing Consent: the Political Economy of the Mass Media* (New York: Pantheon, 1988).

[33] Statement in the 13th periodic report of Denmark, cited in CERD, *POEM and FASM* v. *Denmark*, Communication No. 22/2002, UN Doc. A/58/18, Annex II. A., 21 March 2003, para. 3.7.

[34] CERD, *Jewish Community of Oslo* v. *Norway*, Communication No. 30/2003, UN Doc. A/60/18, Annex III. B., 15 August 2005, para. 10.4.

[35] Hence in a case involving a Danish politician's verbal reaction to an incident outside a nightclub, 'the *statement, despite its ambiguity, cannot necessarily be interpreted as claiming that persons of Somali origin* were responsible for the attack in question. Consequently . . . the Committee cannot conclude that her statement falls within the scope of . . . article 4' (CERD, *Jama* v. *Denmark*, Communication No. 41/2008, UN Doc. A/64/18, Annex III, 21 August 2009, para. 7.4).

[36] CERD, GR 35, para. 7.

action that would impair the 'freedoms', the second being that a balance must be struck between the freedoms and the duties under the Convention, and the third being that States may not invoke the protection of civil rights as a reason to avoid implementing the Convention.[37] Two of the three positions outlined by Partsch appear to involve one right trumping another. GR 35 eschews the 'balance' metaphor in rejecting any notion that would involve nullifying or impairing a guaranteed right:

> The relationship between proscription of racist hate speech and the flourishing of freedom of expression should be seen as complementary and not the expression of a zero sum game where the priority given to one necessitates the diminution of the other. The rights to equality and freedom from discrimination, and the right to freedom of expression, should be fully reflected in law, policy and practice as mutually supportive human rights.[38]

In *Jewish Community of Oslo* v. *Norway*,[39] a case concerning public anti-Jewish statements by a leader of the 'Bootboys' during a march and demonstration in commemoration of the Nazi leader Rudolf Hess, the Committee commented that the due regard clause:

> [R]elates generally to all principles embodied in the Universal Declaration of Human Rights, not only freedom of speech. Thus, to give the right to freedom of speech a more limited role in the context of article 4 does not deprive the 'due regard' clause of significant meaning, all the more so since all international instruments that guarantee freedom of expression provide for the possibility, under certain circumstances, of limiting the exercise of this right.[40]

GR 35 refines the sentiment expressed in the above quoted extract, recalling that the due regard clause 'has been interpreted by the Committee to apply to human rights and freedoms as a whole, and not simply to freedom of opinion and expression, which should however be borne in mind as the most pertinent reference principle when calibrating the legitimacy of speech restrictions'.[41]

### 3.4 *Offences to be declared by law*

In GR 15, Article 4(a) is analytically broken down into penalizable categories that include 'incitement to racial hatred', an inclusion that

[37] K. J. Partsch, 'Racial Speech and Human Rights: Article 4 of the Convention on the Elimination of All Forms of Racial Discrimination', in S. Coliver (ed.), *Striking a Balance: Hate Speech, Freedom of Expression and Non-Discrimination* (London: ARTICLE 19, 1992), 21–8.

[38] CERD, GR 35, para. 45.

[39] CERD, *Jewish Community of Oslo* v. *Norway.*

[40] *Ibid.*, para. 10.5.

[41] CERD, GR No. 35, para. 19.

departs from the literal wording of the paragraph, which does not refer to incitement to racial hatred but to incitement to racial discrimination – the latter concept is omitted from the recommendation.[42] The express inclusion of 'incitement to racial hatred' in GR 15 has been subject to criticism in academic literature.[43] CERD however continues to employ the term, and has recommended review of legislation in order to incorporate a specific offence of incitement to racial hatred.[44] Committee references to racial hatred in Concluding Observations have been supplemented by occasional references to 'ethnic'[45] or 'tribal'[46] hatred and to offences motivated by religious hatred against immigrant communities.[47]

GR 35 recasts the speech offences under Article 4, stating that the following are to be declared by law and effectively sanctioned:

> (a) All dissemination of ideas based on racial or ethnic superiority or hatred, by whatever means;
> (b) Incitement to hatred, contempt or discrimination against members of a group on grounds of their race, colour, descent, or national or ethnic origin;
> (c) Threats or incitement to violence against persons or groups on the grounds in (b) above;
> (d) Expression of insults, ridicule or slander of persons or groups or justification of hatred, contempt or discrimination on the grounds in (b) above, when it clearly amounts to incitement to hatred or discrimination;
> (e) Participation in organizations and activities which promote and incite racial discrimination.[48]

While recalling incitement to discrimination in its exegesis of Article 4, GR 35 moves beyond a narrowly literalist reading – of Article 4(a) in particular – by:

[42] Para. 4 of General Recommendation No. 15 recalls incitement to discrimination with reference to Article 20 of the ICCPR.
[43] McGonagle, *Minority Rights*, 282–4.
[44] CERD, Concluding Observations on the Republic of Korea, UN Doc. CERD/C/63/CO/9, 10 December 2003, para. 9.
[45] CERD, Concluding Observations on Croatia, UN Doc. CERD/C/60/CO/4, 21 May 2002, para. 12.
[46] CERD, Concluding Observations on Madagascar, UN Doc. CERD/C/65/CO/4, 10 December 2004, para. 13.
[47] CERD, Concluding Observations on the United Kingdom, UN Doc. CERD/C/63/CO/11, 10 December 2003, para. 21.
[48] CERD, GR 35, para. 13.

(i) extending the dissemination offence to include ideas of ethnic as well as racial superiority;[49]
(ii) reiterating the prohibition in GR 15 of incitement to racial hatred, adding 'incitement to . . . contempt';
(iii) widening the grounds for the incitement offences to include all the grounds of discrimination in Article 1;
(iv) elaborating the incitement concepts to include 'insults, ridicule or slander' of persons or groups as well as 'justification of hatred, contempt or discrimination'.

The fresh conceptualization of the article nonetheless continues, it may be argued, to embody its essential purposes, read in the light of the Convention as a whole.[50] In a further rebuttal of literalism, GR 35 decisively rejects any suggestion of a 'strict liability' approach to dissemination and incitement that would understand 'the words on the page' (dissemination/incitement) without an attempt to marry them with principles of criminal law on mental elements in crime:

> Incitement characteristically seeks to influence others to engage in certain forms of conduct, including the commission of crime, through advocacy or threats. Incitement may be express or implied, through actions such as displays of racist symbols or distribution of materials as well as words. The notion of incitement as an inchoate crime does not require that the incitement has been acted upon, but in regulating the forms of incitement referred to in article 4, States parties should take into account, as important elements in the incitement offences, in addition to the considerations outlined in paragraph 14 above,[51] the intention of the speaker, and the imminent risk or likelihood that the conduct desired or intended by the speaker will result from the speech in question, considerations which also apply to the other offences listed in paragraph 13.[52]

[49] In this, GR 35 echoes the language of the chapeau to Article 4 which refers to ideas of superiority 'of one race or group of persons of one colour or ethnic origin'.

[50] It may be observed that the frequently repeated condemnation (in the context of dissemination of ideas) of 'stigmatization and stereotyping' as well as 'racial profiling' has not been subsumed into the account of criminal offences set out in GR 35, para. 6 of which recalls that stereotyping and stigmatization have been 'the subject of expressions of concern and recommendations' by the Committee.

[51] The initial website version of the recommendation is incorrect: the reference should be to the considerations set out in para. 15, not para. 14; a corrected version can be found in UN Doc. A/69/18, annex VIII and may be anticipated for the Committee's annual report to the UN General Assembly.

[52] CERD, GR 35, para. 16. This stands opposed to the assertions in the CERD study of 1983 (para. 83) that: 'Two things are prohibited to be disseminated under penalty of law . . . ideas based on racial superiority and ideas based on racial hatred. It is also clear that the

Besides intention for the crimes in question, CERD has added 'imminent risk', narrowing the scope of potential hate speech prosecutions. Additionally, paragraph 15 of GR 35 supplies a short list of 'contextual factors' in the 'qualification of dissemination and incitement' as offences punishable by law – and presumably in their prosecution as such – that would require legislators, judges and prosecutors to appraise speech situations carefully before proceeding to draw conclusions as to appropriate courses of action. The message is that the lines between hate speech to be prosecuted and free speech to be protected need to be carefully drawn in their details and their context.[53] GR 35 also makes it abundantly clear from its overall structure that criminalization is not a complete response to hate speech phenomena, a conclusion cemented by paragraph 12:

> The Committee recommends that the criminalization of forms of racist expression should be reserved for serious cases, to be proven beyond reasonable doubt, while less serious cases should be addressed by means other than criminal law, taking into account, *inter alia*, the nature and extent of the impact on targeted persons and groups. The application of criminal sanctions should be governed by principles of legality, proportionality and necessity.[54]

The 'dissemination of ideas' offence envisaged in the Convention has been more controversial than incitement in that the latter relates more closely to standard criminal law categories.[55] The dissemination offence is buttressed by the pronouncement in the preamble on the 'scientifically false' nature of doctrines of racial superiority, an assertion that may be understood as a response to a history of such doctrines, often described as forms of 'race science', extreme versions of which characterized the Nazi period. This raises the issue of whether serious 'scientific' or academic discussions of racial questions are caught in the net of Article 4. In *POEM and FASM* v. *Denmark*, the State Party took the view that Article 4 did not impugn 'scientific theories put forward on differences of race,

mere act of dissemination is penalized, despite lack of intention to commit an offence and the consequences of the dissemination, whether they be grave or insignificant.' Such a stance would undermine principles of criminal liability in many (most?) jurisdictions.

[53] *Ibid.*, paras. 15 and 20.

[54] *Ibid.*, para. 12. The footnote to paragraph 12 refers to General Comment No. 34 of the Human Rights Committee on freedoms of opinion and expression.

[55] For arguments regarding the difference between disseminating racist ideas and bringing them to light, see ECtHR, *Jersild* v. *Denmark* (Appl. No. 15890/89), Judgment (Grand Chamber), 22 August 1994; for reactions of the CERD, *Annual Report of the CERD*, UN Doc. A/45/18 (Supp), 1 January 1991, para. 56.

nationality or ethnicity . . . [and] . . . probably also . . . statements that were not made in a scientific context proper, but otherwise as part of an objective debate'.[56] While the previous practice of the Committee on the offence of dissemination of ideas may have inhibited a depth of reflection on 'genres of discussion' in race questions,[57] GR 35 sets out the Committee's clear view that: 'the expression of ideas and opinions made in the context of academic debates, political engagement or similar activity, and without incitement to hatred, contempt, violence or discrimination, should be regarded as legitimate exercises of the right to freedom of expression, even when such ideas are controversial.'[58]

Ideas and theories of 'superiority' should also presumably be distinguished from ethnocentric expression in general and *a fortiori* from defensive 'recognition' or 'identity' politics practised by groups seeking their place in society.[59] The Convention should not be understood as a homogenizing force but as one supporting diversity and self-expression, hostile only to certain categories of discourse. The justification of reaction against racist ideas would lose force if extended from racist hate speech uttered by those who believe in a hierarchy of separate human races to a generalized critique of assertive or defensive 'nationalisms' of various kinds. The inclusion by the Council of Europe of 'aggressive nationalism and ethnocentrism' among the avatars of hate speech is presumably distinguishable as essentially denigratory, other-directed and as possibly supporting violence.

### *3.5 Organizations and the public sphere: 4(b) and 4(c)*

The banning of organizations in Article 4(b), *ipso facto*, and without reference to the commencement of racist activities, is perhaps the most regularly contested element in Article 4, producing many exchanges between the Committee and States Parties. Despite the syntactical connection in 4(b) with regard to 'organizations . . . which promote and incite', the essence of the CERD view is that the organization is to be banned on the basis of its character without any hiatus – that is, before it

[56] CERD, *POEM and FASM* v. *Denmark*, para. 4.10.

[57] Recalled in T. McGonagle, 'An Ode to Contextualisation: *I. A.* v. *Turkey*', *Irish Human Rights Law Review* 1 (2010), 237–51.

[58] CERD, GR 35, para. 25; see also, paras. 14 and 26.

[59] Individual opinion of Mr Carlos Manuel Vazquez (dissenting), in CERD, *Turkish Union in Berlin/Brandenburg* v. *Germany*, Communication No. 48/2010, UN Doc. A/68/18/, Annex III, Appendix, 4 April 2013, para. 6.

attempts to engage in nefarious activities – like the fictive 'Murder Incorporated' of the *travaux*.[60] The Committee has, *inter alia*, insisted on 'specific',[61] 'explicit',[62] or 'specific and unambiguous'[63] criminal legislation banning racist organizations. GR 35 is succinct on this point:

> The Committee underlines that article 4 (b) requires that racist organizations which promote and incite racial discrimination be declared illegal and prohibited. The Committee understands that the reference to 'organized. . .propaganda activities' implicates improvised forms of organization or networks, and that 'all other propaganda activities' may be taken to refer to unorganized or spontaneous promotion and incitement of racial discrimination.[64]

Participation in every case is to be punished by law, a requirement that overlaps with the assistance/financing reference in 4(a).

Article 4(c) addresses the possibility of promotion or incitement of racial discrimination by the public authorities. Lerner observes that 4(c) does not impose obligations regarding internal criminal law 'but only urges them to adjust their policies to principles in accordance with the Convention and to take care that public officers, on the national and local levels, do not depart from such policies. In that sense it complements Article 2, paragraph 1.'[65] Another author comments that 4(c) adds little to the other two paragraphs though it does 'serve to illustrate the evil of public officials and bodies engaging in racist activities'.[66] As with media racism, racist expression by public figures or officials has, however, been judged by CERD to be of particular concern in view of the influence or power they exercise. The special responsibility of public figures to provide anti-racist and pro-tolerance leadership is a recurring motif in Committee work, and in GR 35.[67]

[60] CERD, General Recommendation No. 15, para. 6.

[61] CERD, Concluding Observations on Jamaica, UN Doc. CERD/C/60/CO/6, 21 May 2002, para. 6.

[62] CERD, Concluding Observations on Uganda, UN Doc. CERD/C/62/CO/11, 2 June 2003, para. 12.

[63] CERD, Concluding Observations on Fiji, UN Doc. CERD/C/FJI/CO/17, 16 May 2008, para. 20.

[64] CERD, GR 35, para. 21.

[65] Lerner, *UN Convention*, 51.

[66] T. Mendel, 'Equality and freedom of expression: an accommodative framework', background paper for the 11 December 2008 Meeting on Promoting Equality within a Free Speech framework, ARTICLE 19, n.d., www.article19.org/data/files/pdfs/other/equality-and-freedom-of-expression-an-accommodative-framework.pdf (last accessed on 4 April 2014).

[67] Para. 22 of GR 35 addresses the case of racist statements by public officials.

### 3.6 *Further resources of the Convention*

As observed, GR 35 projects the message that the use of penalties does not always represent the most productive approach to the achievement of anti-racist objectives, and that in furtherance of an effective practical strategy, the full normative resources of the Convention should be deployed.[68] In its underpinning of the role of free speech as a counter to hate speech, GR 35, citing Article 19 of the UDHR and the ICCPR, notes that freedom of expression is not unlimited, and, *inter alia*, 'should not aim at the destruction of the rights and freedoms of others, including the right to equality and non-discrimination'.[69] The Recommendation makes the broadly philosophical point that protection from hate speech is not simply a case of opposition between freedom of expression and its restriction for the benefit of protected groups: 'the persons and groups entitled to the protection of the Convention also enjoy the right to freedom of expression and freedom from racial discrimination in the exercise of that right. Racist hate speech potentially silences the free speech of its victims.'[70] In other words, racists should not pose as 'free speech heroes' unfairly constrained by authoritarian laws when the characteristic effect of such speech is to silence others. The relationship between hate speech and the rights of others is, in the view of CERD, best expressed as a relationship between two freedoms, and not as between a freedom and a constraint.

Analogously, while much Committee concern is expressed to favour speech restrictions to protect vulnerable groups from racist attack, practice also encompasses situations where restrictions reduce the ability of minorities to oppose public discourse directed against them. GR 35 includes the following caution:

> The Committee observes with concern that broad or vague restrictions on freedom of speech have been used to the detriment of groups protected by the Convention. States parties should formulate restrictions on speech with sufficient precision, according to the standards in the Convention as elaborated in the present recommendation. The Committee stresses that measures to monitor and combat racist speech should not be used as a pretext to curtail expressions of protest at injustice, social discontent or opposition.[71]

The Recommendation devotes space to the uses of anti-racist, pro-tolerance education as a counter to hate speech, focusing in particular on

[68] *Ibid.*, para. 8. [69] *Ibid.*, para. 26. [70] *Ibid.*, para. 28. [71] *Ibid.*, para. 20.

strategies marked out in Article 7. In elaborating on the importance of school systems, information campaigns, training of officials and media codes of conduct in a holistic anti-hate speech strategy, programmes of intercultural bilingual education are proposed, and teaching on the diversity of histories and cultural traditions in the States Parties. The Recommendation makes recommendations on teaching and remembering the successful resolution of inter-ethnic conflicts, and on recalling terrible events through the prism of truth and reconciliation commissions and other means. The sundry references to indigenous peoples and ethnic groups throughout the section on Article 7 and more widely in the Recommendation bring vividly to mind that ICERD is not focused on hate speech in the abstract but on violations of the rights of specific groups and the persons taken to 'represent' such groups. The Recommendation does not purport to subsume such groups under the rubric of passive victims but addresses strategies to empower them through encouraging indigenous and minority media ownership, etc. so that they can 'talk back' at their oppressors.

### *3.7 A note on racial and religious discrimination*

Article 5 recognizes the right to 'freedom of thought, conscience and religion' as a right to be protected from *racial* discrimination.[72] The Committee's approach to tackling discrimination on the ground of religion – on the basis of the 'intersectionality' of religion with other grounds in Article 1 – has arguably not been as consistent as its approach to racial discrimination.[73] In instances where there is a clear perception of an overlap between ethnicity and religion, as in discrimination against Jews and Sikhs,[74] or against Tatars – described as 'Muslim ethnic minorities',[75] etc., the Committee may experience little difficulty in applying the Convention. However, while the Committee has made reference in Concluding Observations to Islamophobia,[76] and to intolerance and

[72] *ICERD*, Article 5(d)(vii) – present author's emphasis.

[73] See the excellent discussion by S. E. Berry, 'Bringing Muslim Minorities within the International Convention on the Elimination of All Forms of Racial Discrimination – Square Peg in a Round Hole?', *Human Rights Law Review* 11–3 (2011), 423–50.

[74] CERD, Concluding Observations on the United Kingdom, para. 20.

[75] CERD, Concluding Observations on Moldova, UN Doc. CERD/C/MDA/7, March 2008, para. 15.

[76] CERD, Concluding Observations on the United Kingdom, para. 21. Paras. 20 and 21, *ibid.*, are contextualized as relating to 'immigrant communities', an implicit ethnic connection.

hatred against 'Muslims',[77] the case law is more conservative. *PSN* v. *Denmark*[78] concerned alleged violations of, *inter alia*, Article 4 of the Convention in relation to statements made by an MP against immigrants and Muslims. The State Party argued against admissibility in that the statements referred to Muslims and not a group covered by the Article 1 'grounds', while acknowledging that 'it is possible to argue to a certain extent that the statements refer to second-generation immigrants and set up a conflict between 'the Danes' and them, thereby falling to some degree within the scope of the Convention.'[79] The petitioner contended that 'Islamophobia, just like attacks against Jews, has manifested itself as a form of racism in many European countries'.[80] Hatred, it was claimed, had been stirred up against peoples of Arab and Muslim background, and 'culture and religion are connected in Islam'.[81] In its admissibility decision, CERD observed that the impugned statements specifically referred to the Koran, to Islam and to 'Muslims in general', and not to the grounds in Article 1 of the Convention.[82] Thus, no 'specific national or ethnic groups were directly targeted', bearing in mind that Muslims in Denmark currently living in the State party are of heterogeneous origin.[83] The communication was accordingly based on religion alone and was therefore inadmissible.[84]

The result, it may be argued, leaves a gap in protection under ICERD from discrimination in that the targeted groups were essentially the same as previously, while the speech targeting them had undergone a subtle change that escaped the grasp of the Committee. As already observed,[85] the notion of indirect hate speech is alluded to by GR 35, without reference to the race/religion nexus, though the Committee's choice of

[77] Examples include CERD, Concluding Observations on Australia, UN Doc. CERD/C/AUS/CO/14, 14 April 2005, para. 13, CERD, Concluding Observations on Canada, UN Doc. CERD/C/61/CO/3, 12 August 2002, para. 24, and CERD, Concluding Observations on Switzerland, UN Doc. CERD/C/60/CO/14, 21 May 2002, para. 9.

[78] CERD, *PSN* v. *Denmark*, Communication No. 36/2006, UN Doc. A/62/18, Annex V, 8 August 2007. A more detailed account of the *PSN* case is given in Patrick Thornberry, 'Forms of Hate Speech and the Convention on the Elimination of all Forms of Racial Discrimination', *Religion and Human Rights* 5 (2010), 102–4.

[79] CERD, *PSN* v. *Denmark*, para. 4.1. [80] *Ibid.*, para. 5.3.

[81] *Ibid.*, para. 5.3. The petitioner cited the Committee's Concluding Observations of 2002 and 2006 on Denmark linking people of 'Arab and Muslim' background.

[82] *Ibid.*, para. 6.2. [83] *Ibid.*, para. 6.2.

[84] Cf. CERD, *AWRAP* v. *Denmark*, Communication No. 37/2006, UN Doc. A/62/18, Annex V, 8 August 2007.

[85] See above, text preceding n. 36.

words is open enough to include it.[86] 'Islamophobia' appears in GR 35, if only in the context of a broad recall of the forms of racist hate speech already addressed by CERD. Following a list of groups targeted by hate speech – indigenous peoples, descent-based groups, etc., paragraph 6 adds:

> In the light of the principle of intersectionality, and bearing in mind that 'criticism of religious leaders or commentary on religious doctrine or tenets of faith' should not be prohibited or punished, the Committee's attention has also been engaged by hate speech targeting persons belonging to certain ethnic groups who profess or practice a religion different from the majority, including expressions of Islamophobia, anti-Semitism and other similar manifestations of hatred against ethno-religious groups.

The formulation in the new paragraph is cautious in its phrasing on religious leaders and doctrine, in case the Committee might be understood as endorsing the contentious concept of 'defamation of religions';[87] it is also cautious on 'intersectionality', insisting on the link between ethnicity and religion, employing the inelegant compound term 'ethno-national'.[88]

## 4 Concluding reflections

> If we want things to stay as they are, things will have to change. (Giuseppe Tomasi di Lampedusa)[89]

In an earlier version of the present chapter, drafted before the emergence of GR 35, the emphasis was squarely placed on the 'hard line' against racist hate speech adopted by CERD, a line that was not, however, fully determinate, in that the text presented itself differently to different members of the Committee over four decades of operation. In GR 35, the Committee maintains its resolute stance against hate speech in significant respects: examples include its accounting of the range of

[86] CERD, GR 35, para. 7.

[87] There is an excellent critical account of this concept in McGonagle, *Minority Rights*, 363–75. See also Chapter 12 in this book. The footnote to paragraph 6 cites General Comment No. 34 of the Human Rights Committee to support the proposition regarding religious leaders and tenets of religion.

[88] The term does not show up under 'CERD' in the Universal human rights Index – www.universalhumanrightsindex.org (last accessed 7 February 2014).

[89] 'Se vogliamo che tutto rimanga come è, bisogna che tutto cambi' (*Il Gattopardo* (the Leopard), English translation by A. Colquhoun).

crimes to be declared and rigorously enforced under Article 4(a), the reiteration that Article 4 remains central to the struggle against racial discrimination, in the continuing castigation of racist organizations, and the concern for the amplified effects of hate speech by public officials.

The emergence of the Recommendation on the back of a thematic discussion in 2012 on racist hate speech also signals that the CERD archive is in the process of being replenished. The Committee has considered it an obligation to 'ensure the coherence of the interpretation of the provisions of article 4',[90] a difficult obligation towards an article that is not a model of clarity. On the relationship of Article 4 to the Convention as a whole, it is preferable to assume that the elements in a convention have complementary functions; interpretation should keep in mind the *desideratum* of reading the text as more than a casual montage of fragments. GR 35 presents itself as a rounded articulation of the Convention, subsuming elements of earlier readings by the Committee into a fresh normative synthesis, upgrading the anti-racist currency through clearer integration with libertarian speech principles, understood as both within and without the Convention. External points of reference in GR 35 include General Comment No. 34 of the Human Rights Committee, already integrated into CERD practice;[91] the range of influences goes beyond the work of the Human Rights Committee to encompass in particular the results of expert workshops organized by the Office of the High Commissioner for Human Rights.[92]

GR 35 makes the claim that the alignment or further integration of international norms has not been bought at the expense of ICERD standards, especially as it endorses the notion that freedom from racial discrimination has a human rights value at least equal to that of freedom of speech. The introduction to Camden Principles, part-authored by Kevin Boyle, expressed a similar understanding of the interrelationship between the protection of free speech and the liberation of minorities

[90] CERD, *Jewish Community of Oslo* v. *Norway*, para. 10.3.

[91] CERD, Concluding Observations on Ukraine, UN Doc. CERD/C/UKR/CO/19 21, 14 September 2011, para. 13 and Concluding Observations on Turkmenistan, UN Doc. CERD/C/TKM/CO/6-7, 13 April 2012, para. 16.

[92] The published version of the Recommendation includes a number of references to the Rabat Plan of Action on the Prohibition of Advocacy of National, Racial or Religious Hatred that Constitutes Incitement to Discrimination, Hostility or Violence, 5 October 2012, text available at www.ohchr.org/EN/NewsEvents/Pages/TheRabatPlanofAction.aspx (last accessed at 7 February 2014). See further on the Rabat Plan of Action, Chapter 12 in this book.

from discrimination and hate speech, asserting 'the affirmative relationship between freedom of expression and equality [and] the complementary and essential contribution they make to the securing and safeguarding of human dignity'.

Decision-making in the post-GR 35 era may be more fully articulated but is likely to remain challenging. The unprecedented dissenting opinion by Committee member Vazquez in *Turkish Union* v. *Germany*,[93] demonstrates that even the basic question of whether a text disseminates ideas 'based on racial superiority or hatred' may not be susceptible to quick, consensus-commanding resolution. To the majority of the Committee, statements made by Sarrazin against Turkish immigrants to Germany contained 'ideas of racial superiority, denying respect as human beings and depicting generalized negative characteristics of the Turkish population',[94] and contained elements of incitement to racial discrimination.[95] The dissenting opinion found that the same statements did not assert 'the inferiority of Turkish culture or Turks as a nationality or ethnic group' but merely criticized some aspects of their cultural practices and their attitude towards Germany.[96] The majority and dissent also diverge on the preconditions of criminal punishment for the dissemination of ideas offence in light of the 'due regard' clause of Article 4. The overall effect of GR 35 is difficult to gauge on these issues and the present chapter will not attempt their definitive resolution; the proponents in *Turkish Union* did not have the assistance of the Recommendation to articulate and ground their arguments.

The divergences in Turkish Union stand however as reminders that diversity of opinion on the hot-button issue of racist speech also characterizes the situation in 'the real world'. In addition to the intrinsic technicalities of text interpretation, the application of the Convention to local circumstances adds further dimensions to the natural complexity of the hate speech issue. Attention to locality includes the history of the country, the area and the groups implicated as oppressors and victims; locality penetrates the construction of what counts as 'hate'; thus GR 35 states that: 'Discourses which in one context are innocuous or neutral may take on a dangerous significance in another.'[97] Locality is also culture, bearing in mind that different societies take different views on

[93] CERD, *Turkish Union in Berlin/Brandenburg* v. *Germany*, Appendix.
[94] *Ibid.*, para. 12.6. [95] *Ibid.*, para. 12.8.
[96] *Ibid.*, Vazquez dissenting opinion, para. 8.
[97] CERD, General Recommendation No. 35, para. 15.

dignity and freedom, acceptable and unacceptable speech, and that all societies, even the most 'liberal', have their speech taboos: what works as cathartic speech in the African tradition of 'joking cousins' might function only as a provocation to violence elsewhere.[98]

Ethnicity or 'race' are still causes of significant and tragic disputes that result in discrimination or worse. If, as elsewhere in human affairs, the question of causation remains open to argument, it is characteristic of many tragedies that are genocidal or approach the parameters of genocide that hate speech frames the action. In less extreme cases, the standard victims of discrimination identified in CERD practice – ethnic minorities, indigenous peoples, caste groups, non-citizens, women and others subject to double or multiple discrimination, etc. – continue to feel the negative force of objectification and hostility in so many countries of the world.[99] In attempting to resolve real hate speech problems, cosmopolitan international standards do not provide blueprints for the immediate resolution of many situations, and we should, accordingly, recognize their limits. In this sense, it is more productive to regard ICERD and cognate instruments less as detailed codes and more as intelligent frameworks or springboards for practical action. Human rights standards provide signposts towards the resolution of disputes and reparation for the injured dignity of victims of violations, issue warnings as to the consequences of failure, and refurbish the necessary optimism of the will to negotiate differences. The provisions of ICERD and the work of its monitoring committee stand to be judged against such a background, in order to see better whether they truly 'make a difference'.

## Literature

Berry, S. E. 'Bringing Muslim Minorities within the International Convention on the Elimination of All Forms of Racial Discrimination – Square Peg in a Round Hole?', *Human Rights Law Review* 11(3) (2011), 423–50.

Boyle, K. 'Hate Speech: The United States versus the Rest of the World', *Maine Law Review* 53(2) (2001), 488–502.

[98] M. Davidheiser, 'Special Affinities and Conflict Resolution: West African Social Institutions and Mediation' (2005), available at www.beyondintractability.org/print/2596 (last accessed 7 February 2014).

[99] It is now a commonplace of CERD 'doctrine' that no country is free from racial discrimination, even though denials of such discrimination still reach the ears of the Committee.

Boyle, K. and A. Baldaccini, 'A Critical Evaluation of International Human Rights Approaches to Racism', in S. Fredman (ed.), *Discrimination and Human Rights: The Case of Racism* (Oxford University Press, 2001), 135–91.

*Concise Oxford English Dictionary*, 11th edn (Oxford University Press, 2004).

Davidheiser, M. 'Special Affinities and Conflict Resolution: West African Social Institutions and Mediation', in G. Burgess and H. Burgess (eds.), *Beyond Intractability, Conflict Information Consortium*, University of Colorado, BO. Posted: December 2005 at www.beyondintractability.org/essay/joking-kinship (last accessed on 4 April 2014).

Herman, E. S. and N. Chomsky, *Manufacturing Consent: the Political Economy of the Mass Media* (New York: Pantheon, 1988).

Lerner, N. *The International Convention on the Elimination of All Forms of Racial Discrimination* (Alphen aan den Rijn: Sijthoff and Noordhoff, 1980).

McGonagle, T. *Minority Rights, Freedom of Expression and of the Media: Dynamics and Dilemmas* (Antwerp: Intersentia, 2011).

'An Ode to Contextualisation: *I. A.* v. *Turkey*', *Irish Human Rights Law Review* 1 (2010), 237–51.

Mendel, T. 'Equality and freedom of expression: an accommodative framework', background paper for 11 December 2008 Meeting on Promoting Equality within a Free Speech framework, ARTICLE 19, n.d., www.article19.org/data/files/pdfs/other/equality-and-freedom-of-expression-an-accommodative-framework.pdf (last accessed on 4 April 2014).

Partsch, K. J. 'Racial Speech and Human Rights: Article 4 of the Convention on the Elimination of All Forms of Racial Discrimination', in S. Coliver (ed.), *Striking a Balance: Hate Speech, Freedom of Expression and Non-Discrimination* (London: ARTICLE 19, 1992), 21–8.

Post, R. 'Hate Speech', in I. Hare and J. Weinstein (eds.), *Extreme Speech and Democracy* (Oxford University Press, 2009), 123–38.

Thornberry, P. 'Forms of Hate Speech and the Convention on the Elimination of all Forms of Racial Discrimination', *Religion and Human Rights* 5 (2010), 97–117.

Waldron, J. *The Harm in Hate Speech* (Cambridge, MA: Harvard University Press, 2012).

Weber, A. *Manual on Hate Speech* (Strasbourg: Council of Europe Publishing, 2009).

## Miscellaneous

*Camden Principles on Freedom of Expression and Equality* (London: ARTICLE 19, April 2009).

CERD, *Positive Measures Designed to Eradicate All Incitement to, or Acts of, Racial Discrimination* (New York: United Nations Publications, 1986).

*Rabat Plan of Action on the Prohibition of Advocacy of National, Racial or Religious Hatred that Constitutes Incitement to Discrimination, Hostility or Violence*, 5 October 2012.

## UN documents

### *CERD General Recommendations*

General Recommendation No. 35: Combating Racist Hate Speech, UN Doc. CERD/C/GC/35, 26 September 2013 (adopted by CERD at its 83rd session (12–30 August 2013)), also in UN Doc. A/69/18, annex VIII.

General Recommendation No. 15 on Article 4 of the Convention, UN Doc. A/48/18, ch. VIII, 17 March 1993.

### *CERD Individual communications*

*AWRAP* v. *Denmark*, Communication No. 37/2006, UN Doc. A/62/18, Annex V, 8 August 2007.

*Jama* v. *Denmark*, Communication No. 41/2008, UN Doc. A/64/18, Annex III, 21 August 2009.

*Jewish Community of Oslo* v. *Norway*, Communication No. 30/2003, UN Doc. A/60/18, Annex III. B., 15 August 2005.

*Mohammad Hassan Gelle* v. *Denmark*, Communication No. 34/2004, UN Doc. A/61/18, Annex IV, 10 March 2006.

*POEM and FASM* v. *Denmark*, Communication No. 22/2002, UN Doc. A/58/18, Annex II. A., 21 March 2003.

*PSN* v. *Denmark*, Communication No. 36/2006, UN Doc. A/62/18, Annex V, 8 August 2007.

*Turkish Union in Berlin/Brandenburg* v. *Germany*, Communication No. 48/2010, UN Doc. A/68/18, Annex III.

### *CERD Concluding Observations*

Concluding Observations on Australia, UN Doc. CERD/C/AUS/CO/14, 14 April 2005.

Concluding Observations on Canada, UN Doc. CERD/C/61/CO/3, 12 August 2002.

Concluding Observations on Croatia, UN Doc. CERD/C/60/CO/4, 21 May 2002.

Concluding Observations on Fiji, UN Doc. CERD/C/FJI/CO/17, 16 May 2008.

Concluding Observations on Jamaica, UN Doc. CERD/C/60/CO/6, 21 May 2002.

Concluding Observations on Madagascar, UN Doc. CERD/C/65/CO/4, 10 December 2004.

Concluding Observations on Moldova, UN Doc. CERD/C/MDA/7, March 2008.
Concluding Observations on the Republic of Korea, UN Doc. CERD/C/63/CO/9, 10 December 2003.
Concluding observations on Romania, UN Doc. CERD/C/ROU/CO/16–19, 13 September 2010.
Concluding Observations on Switzerland, UN Doc. CERD/C/60/CO/14, 21 May 2002.
Concluding Observations on Turkmenistan, UN Doc. CERD/C/TKM/CO/6–7, 13 April 2012.
Concluding Observations on Uganda, UN Doc. CERD/C/62/CO/11, 2 June 2003.
Concluding Observations on Ukraine, UN Doc. CERD/C/UKR/CO/19–21, 14 September 2011.
Concluding Observations on the United Kingdom, UN Doc. CERD/C/63/CO/11, 10 December 2003.

## Case law

### *ECtHR*

*Jersild* v. *Denmark* (Appl. No. 15890/89), Judgment (Grand Chamber), 22 August 1994.

# 5

# Convention on the Rights of the Child: freedom of expression for children

LUCY SMITH

## 1 No exception for children

In a small Norwegian town, it was decided some years ago to build a cultural centre on a site that was used as a playground for children. The children of a primary school near the intended site organized a campaign against the plan to build a culture house on their playground and circulated a protest letter for signing. Some parents protested against the campaign and the school made the children withdraw the letter. A teacher in the school, upset by the school's intervention, contacted me asking whether children do not have freedom of expression. Of course they do, but this was an example of how their freedom is often ignored.

The present chapter is about freedom of expression for children, and I will concentrate on the special issues regarding the understanding of this freedom for children, the Convention on the Rights of the Child and the approach of the Committee on the Rights of the Child in this regard. General issues concerning freedom of expression will only be discussed when of special relevance for children's rights.

Human rights are not only for adults: 'Universal human rights are the travelling companions that support every human being, from the first sigh to the last sigh.'[1] The human rights conventions make no exception for children. This was made clear already in Article 1 of the Universal Declaration of Human Rights (UDHR) from 1948: '*All human beings* are born free and equal in dignity and rights' (emphasis added). The UDHR is not a binding legal instrument, but it provided the model for human rights treaties, such as the International Covenant on Civil and Political Rights (ICCPR) from 1966, which sets out the right to freedom of expression in its Article 19.

[1] C. Smith, 'Human Rights as the Foundation of Society', in P. Lødrup and E. Modvar (eds.), *Family Life and Human Rights* (Oslo: Gyldendal, 2004), 15.

In its General Comment (GC) No. 17 on the rights of the child (1989), the Human Rights Committee states that 'children benefit from all of the civil rights enunciated in the Covenant'.[2] However, it is a fact that political rights and freedoms traditionally have not been associated with children. Even today this connection is often ignored, as illustrated by the example above.

The Convention on the Rights of the Child (CRC) includes provisions on the most important civil rights in Articles 13–17, among them the right to freedom of expression in Article 13. It was important to make clear that civil rights are also rights for children. These civil rights may be characterized as active rights, rights that must be exercised by the children themselves, while the protective rights will usually be exercised by the parents on behalf of the child.[3] However, several countries already had legislation that recognized certain active rights for children, depending on the age of the child, for example the right to be heard and even autonomy on certain issues, most commonly health decisions, from a certain age.[4] Article 13 reads:

> 1. The child shall have the right to freedom of expression; this right shall include freedom to seek, receive and impart information and ideas of all kinds, regardless of frontiers, either orally, in writing or in print, in the form of art, or through any other media of the child's choice.
> 2. The exercise of this right may be subject to certain restrictions, but these shall only be such as are provided by law and are necessary:
>    (a) For respect of the rights or reputations of others; or
>    (b) For the protection of national security or of public order (ordre public), or of public health or morals.

The *ideological underpinnings* of freedom of expression, as set out in Article 13, CRC are the same as for Article 19, ICCPR and freedom of

[2] HRC, General Comment No. 17: Article 24 (Rights of the Child), UN Doc. A/44/40, 7 April 1989, para. 2.

[3] The proposal was originally submitted by the US delegation to the working group, together with the right to privacy and access to information; see, OHCHR, *Legislative History of the Convention on the Rights of the Child*, 2 vols. (2007), UN Doc. HR/PUB/07/1, vol. I, 450.

[4] See, for example, the Danish Health Act of 13/07/20: 'When the child reaches the age of 15 he/she can give informed consent to medical treatment', first introduced in Danish Act on the Legal Position of Patients, Act No. 482, 01.07.1998, Art. 8(1), Austrian Civil Code (s. 146 c (1)): 'A child who is capable of understanding the situation and making its own judgments can decide on its own whether to consent to medical treatments. If the child is over 14 years of age, it will be assumed that the child understands the situation and can form judgments.'

expression in general. In my opinion there is no reason why children should not have this freedom, and it should not be necessary to substantiate this especially. Democracy and participation are valid arguments also for minors. The Special Rapporteur on the promotion and protection of the right to freedom of opinion and expression has underlined the importance of freedom of expression for marginalized groups, including children. In his Report of 2010 to the UN Human Rights Council, the Special Rapporteur writes: 'Freedom of expression is the primary channel for participation and serves as a mechanism for inclusion; this right is therefore necessarily linked to the recognition of and respect for human dignity from childhood onward.'[5] In its General Comment No. 34 on Article 19, ICCPR, the Human Rights Committee states: 'Freedom of opinion and freedom of expression are indispensable conditions for the development of the person.'[6] This is exactly why the right to freedom of opinion and expression is so important for children. Moreover, as Herdis Thorgeirsdóttir emphasizes, freedom of expression is also important for the development of the child.[7]

The *capacity* of children to express themselves may be limited, depending on the age of the child and the issue in question, but their *right* to freedom of expression is not. The fact that children do not have the same capacities and information as most adults does not affect the right itself. Sylvie Langlaude writes: 'Thus, the extent of the child's right to freedom of expression does not depend on their evolving capacities, but the extent of their exercise of their right may do.'[8] Many adults will also have a limited basis for their expressions, but nobody would argue that freedom of expression should depend on their capacity to express meaningful ideas.

For the society at large, it is important to hear the children's voices, even on fundamental political principles. Since 22 July 2011, we have read the expressions and heard the voices of the child survivors of the Utøya massacre in Norway; their stories and their thoughts. The

[5] HRC, *Promotion and Protection of the Right to Freedom of Opinion and Expression*, UN Doc. A/HRC/14/23, 20 April 2010, paras. 50–3.

[6] HRC, General Comment No. 34: Article 19 (Freedoms of Opinion and Expression), UN Doc. CCPR/C/GC/34, 12 September 2011, para. 2.

[7] H. Thorgeirsdóttir, 'Article 13: The Right to Freedom of Expression', in A. Alen and J. VandeLanotte *et al.* (eds.), *A Commentary on the United Nations Convention on the Rights of the Child* (Leiden: Martinus Nijhoff, 2006), 19.

[8] S. Langlaude, 'On How to Build a Positive Understanding of the Child's Right to Freedom of Expression', *Human Rights Law Review* 10 (2010), 33–66.

massacre was directed at a summer camp of young social democrats, many of the participants were under 18. It was heartbreaking, but the reactions of the survivors were so impressive. Their use of words, their strong belief in democracy, their thoughts about how this shall lead to an even more open and strong democracy are convincing arguments for the importance of freedom of expression for children. The same applies to the thousands of messages from young children that were laid down among the flowers in front of the Oslo Cathedral and in many other places in Norway after the massacre.[9]

## 2 The Committee on the Rights of the Child – membership, mandate and working methods

Article 43 of the CRC establishes the Committee on the Rights of the Child ('the Committee') as the monitoring body of the Convention. The Committee examines 'the progress made by States Parties in achieving the realization of the obligations undertaken in the present Convention',[10] on the basis of reports submitted by the States Parties, first after two years, and then every five years. In the guidelines for periodic reports the States Parties are asked to:

> [P]rovide information on the measures adopted to ensure that the civil rights and freedoms of children set forth in the Convention, in particular those covered by articles 7, 8, 13 to 17 and 37 (a), are recognized by law specifically in relation to children and implemented in practice, including by administrative and judicial bodies, at the national, regional and local levels, and where appropriate at the federal and provincial levels.[11]

This illustrates that the Committee expects the right to freedom of expression for children to be expressly guaranteed in legislation and also implemented by administrative and judicial bodies.

To be able to assess the approach of the Committee it is necessary to have a certain knowledge about the Committee and its working methods. The Committee has eighteen members with 'recognized competence in

[9] All this material is housed at the National Archives of Norway (Riksarkivet).

[10] Convention on the Rights of the Child, New York, 20 November 1989, entered into force 2 September 1990, 1577 UNTS, Article 43(1).

[11] CRC, *General Guidelines Regarding the Form and Contents of Periodic Reports to Be Submitted by States Parties under Article 44, para. 1(b) of the Convention*, UN Doc. CRC/C/58, 20 November 1996, para. 48.

the field covered by this Convention'.[12] The members are elected by the States that have ratified the convention; that is all Member States represented in the UN General Assembly minus the USA and Somalia. The members will have different professional backgrounds; usually there will be lawyers, physicians, educationalists, psychologists, persons having worked for NGOs, but also former or present civil servants. The majority are therefore not lawyers, as distinct from the UN Human Rights Committee. They will not necessarily be experts in human rights. The Committee meets three times a year for four very busy weeks. Members receive no remuneration for their work and most of them have a full job besides their Committee membership, and little time to spend on the UN work outside the sessions.

The Committee on the Rights of the Child has a complaints procedure. On 19 December 2011, the 66th UN General Assembly adopted the third Optional Protocol to the CRC on a communications procedure. The Protocol will enter into force in April 2014 having been ratified by ten States. It is to be hoped that, after some years, the Protocol will contribute to strengthening the body of international jurisprudence which could, in turn, lead to the further development and reform of national legislation protecting the rights of children.

The Concluding Observations (COs) of the Committee to States Parties are drawn up on the basis of the States Parties' reports and other information from NGOs and different UN organizations. They express the most important concerns of the Committee and include recommendations to the States Parties on how to best realize their obligations under the Convention. These recommendations often go beyond the strict legal obligations of the State, but it should then appear from text that they are only recommendations. If the Committee goes further than the strict meaning of the Convention, it will usually use the words 'encourage' or 'recommend'.

The CRC Committee has published seventeen so-called General Comments. The General Comments from all the treaty bodies are first and foremost interpretations of the respective conventions regarding specific thematic issues or specific articles. In addition to providing strict interpretations of the conventions, general comments often include recommendations and examples of good practice. The interpretations are based on, among other things, experiences the committees have gathered through the State Party reports, the dialogue with the States Parties and

[12] Article 43(2) of the UN Convention on the Rights of the Child.

input from UN organizations and NGOs. Behind the publishing of General Comments from the CRC is a broad and participatory process, with many experts, institutions and organizations taking part (but not the States Parties). It could be said, though, that most of the persons involved in the drafting process are working in the field of child rights and will tend to give preference to a wide interpretation of the rights of the child. It could therefore be fruitful to also consult with leading independent human rights scholars.

The General Comments of the Committee are not legally binding. Assessments of the Comments vary. The general opinion is, however, that they are of importance as guiding texts and interpretative tools. There is, however, very little information regarding the use of General Comments by the State Parties. The General Comments of the Human Rights Committee, where almost all the members are legal experts, may have greater weight than those of the Committee on the Rights of the Child. In Norway, the General Comments of the Committee on the Rights of the Child have nevertheless in recent years been discussed in some Supreme Court cases, and there seems to be a general agreement that although they are not legally binding, they will carry a considerable weight in legal decisions.[13] Thus, one decision from 2001 is about a 17-year-old boy found guilty of robbery, bordering on aggravated robbery, which usually does not allow for community service, but requires incarceration. The Supreme Court referred to and cited from General Comment No. 10, Children's Rights in Juvenile Justice, and decided on community service.[14] In several cases about deporting asylum seeking children, General Comment No. 6, Treatment of Unaccompanied and Separated Children outside their Country of Origin has been invoked and discussed in the reasoning of the Supreme Court.[15]

## 3 Article 13 CRC and Article 19 ICCPR – two articles on freedom of expression

Article 13, CRC, is a derivative of Article 19, ICCPR, and this must have a bearing on the interpretation of the former article. The general issues and

[13] See also M. Verheyde and G. Goedertier, 'Articles 43–45: The UN Committee on the Rights of the Child', in A. Alen and J. VandeLanotte *et al.* (eds.), *A Commentary on the United Nations Convention on the Rights of the Child* (Leiden: Martinus Nijhoff, 2006), 40.

[14] Norwegian Supreme Court Reports 2001, 1313.

[15] See for example: Norwegian Supreme Court Reports 2009, 1261 and Supreme Court Reports 2012, 1985.

problems regarding freedom of expression and the interpretations of Article 19 are relevant also for Article 13, CRC. This includes the Human Rights Committee's General Comment No. 34 on Article 19. Of special relevance for children is that the General Comment emphasizes that freedom of expression includes a 'global network for exchanging ideas and opinions that does not necessarily rely on the traditional mass media intermediaries' and that the States Parties 'should take necessary steps to foster the independence of these new media and to ensure access of individuals thereto'.[16]

Article 13, CRC, does not explicitly provide for the right to hold an opinion as Article 19, ICCPR does. The reason for this is unclear; it does not appear from the *travaux préparatoires* why it was not included. One could suspect that this had something to do with scepticism regarding children's capacities to form opinions, but it could also be that the drafters assumed that the right to hold opinions was already covered in Articles 12, 13 and 14 about the child's freedom of thought.[17] The right to freedom of opinion is quite often mentioned in the Concluding Observations.[18] Children's right to freedom of opinion is in any case also enshrined in Article 19, ICCPR. The right to hold an opinion without interference is important also for children as they are especially vulnerable to manipulation.

The limitations regarding freedom of expression mentioned in Article 13(2), CRC, are the same as those in Article 19(3), ICCPR, except that the first sentence of the latter ('The exercise of the rights provided for in paragraph 2 of this article carries with it special duties and responsibilities') is omitted from Article 13 of the former. This probably has to do with children's limited capacity to undertake legal responsibilities and duties.

More important than these textual differences between Article 19, ICCPR and Article 13, CRC, is the fact that freedom of expression for children raises some special issues, taking into consideration the limited capacities of children and children's need for protection, both of which depend on the age of the child. The child has a need to be protected from harmful information, and also to a certain extent from the effect of her or

[16] HRC, General Comment No. 34: Article 19 (Freedoms of opinion and expression), UN Doc. CCPR/C/GC/34, 12 September 2011, para. 15.

[17] See also, Torgeirsdóttir, 'Right to Freedom of Expression', paras. 42–52.

[18] See for example, HRC, Concluding Observations on Equatorial Guinea, UN Doc. CRC/C/C15/Add.245, 3 November 2004, para. 343.

his own utterances or other forms of expression. Thus, the right to freedom of expression for children will sometimes need to be limited in order to protect them from serious harm. This is especially relevant as regards social media. With children's increasing use of Web 2.0 technology, it is necessary to safeguard both the security and the privacy of children who are too young to be digitally responsible, see further section 6.

## 4 The interpretation of the CRC: general remarks

### *4.1 The sources of interpretation*

Many of the articles in the CRC are vague with broad wording and thus difficult to interpret. The *travaux préparatoires* are not of great help. The drafters were an open-ended working group, there were different opinions on many important issues, and the final draft in many ways represented a compromise. This implies that the individual statements of the delegates in the working group are of limited interest, and that the text as it stands must first and foremost be the basis for the interpretation.

The CRC Committee's General Comments are the main source of interpretation of the Convention.[19] The Concluding Observations are also important in this regard. Often, they will clearly be based on a certain interpretation of an article. However, many of the Concluding Observations are recommendations and as such are not based on an exact interpretation of the Convention.

The reports from the Days of General Discussion (with participants from, among others, academia, NGOs and governments) do not have the same interpretative authority for the CRC as General Comments. It should further be emphasized that the *summary records of the meetings with the States Parties* cannot be regarded as an authoritative source of law. They do not necessarily represent the views of the whole Committee and they are not subjected to the same thorough scrutiny as the General Comments and Concluding Observations. The Concluding Observations are based on consensus. This means that there will be give and take before the final result is achieved.

The fact that Article 13 is part of a convention specially tailored for children will influence the interpretation of the Article. Many of the other articles of the CRC affect the interpretation of Article 13, as will be seen in sections 7 and 8.

[19] For a more detailed analysis of General Comments, see section 2.

### 4.2 A living instrument

The Concluding Observations undoubtedly contribute to a certain dynamic in the interpretation of the Convention. The Committee is sometimes criticized for not being consistent.[20] However, child law is a young branch of jurisprudence and one that is under rapid development. As already mentioned, some of the CRC's articles are quite vague with broad wording. It follows from this combination of vagueness and development that the CRC is to a certain extent to be regarded as a living instrument. The difficulties connected with changing this Convention – as with most other Conventions – necessitate to a certain degree a dynamic interpretation.

One of the arguments *against* a dynamic interpretation is that the CRC is relatively young. On the other hand, in the field of child rights much has happened since the Convention was adopted in 1989. The Committee must find a balance between a static interpretation and the boldest interpretation, sometimes described as 'legislation by Committee'. The interpretation must at least be in accordance with general developments in society. Several of the General Comments adopted by the Committee demonstrate that the Committee considers the Convention to be a living instrument. One example is General Comment No. 8 on corporal punishment, in which the Committee states that any sort of corporal punishment is in conflict with the CRC.[21] The Committee further states that this does not follow from the *travaux préparatoires*, but the Convention 'like all human rights instruments, must be regarded as a living instrument, whose interpretation develops over time'.[22]

### 4.3 Right to expression from day one

In its General Comment No. 7 (2005) on early childhood, the Committee states that one of the General Comment's objectives is to 'encourage recognition of young children as social actors from the beginning of

[20] See, for example, S. Langlaude, 'Children and Religion under Article 14 UNCHR: A Critical Analysis', *International Journal of Children's Rights* 16 (2008), 475–504; see also section 4.1.

[21] CRC, General Comment No. 8: The Right of the Child to Protection from Corporal Punishment and Other Cruel or Degrading Forms of Punishment, UN Doc. CRC/C/GC/8, 7 March 2007, para. 18.

[22] *Ibid.*, para. 20.

life'.[23] Later in the same General Comment, it states that children: 'make choices and communicate their feelings, ideas and wishes in numerous ways, long before they are able to communicate through the conventions of spoken or written language'.[24] This view of the Committee has been consistent over the years. In its General Comment No. 12 (2009) on the right of the child to be heard, the Committee states:

> The Committee emphasizes that article 12 imposes no age limit on the right of the child to express her or his views, and discourages States parties from introducing age limits either in law or in practice which would restrict the child's right to be heard in all matters affecting her or him. Research shows that the child is able to form views from the youngest age, even when she or he may be unable to express them verbally.[25]

This is relevant also for freedom of expression. The child has a right to freedom of expression 'from the first cry to the last sigh' – as is the case for all human rights. However, freedom of expression obviously becomes more important with the evolving capacities of the child, as the child attains a broader knowledge and information base.

### *4.4 The Committee's accentuation of the right to freedom of expression*

The Committee has repeatedly emphasized the importance of freedom of expression for children. A typical Concluding Observation is the one to Georgia in 2003:

> The Committee is concerned at the lack of legal guarantees for the freedom of expression for children below 18 years of age. It is also concerned at the inadequate attention being given to the promotion of and respect for the right of the child to freedom of expression and that prevailing traditional societal attitudes, in the family and in other settings regarding the role of children, appear to make it difficult for children to seek and impart information freely.[26]

The right to freedom of expression must be fully and expressly guaranteed in domestic legislation: 'The Committee further urges the State party

[23] CRC, General Comment No. 7: Implementing Child Rights in Early Childhood, CRC/C/GC/7Rev.1, 20 September 2006, para. 2.

[24] *Ibid.*, para. 14.

[25] CRC, General Comment No. 12: The Right of the Child to Be Heard, UN Doc. CRC/C/GC/12, 20, 20 July 2009, para. 21.

[26] CRC, Concluding Observations on Georgia, UN Doc. CRC/C/15/Add. 222, 27 October 2003, para. 28.

to undertake a comprehensive review of the Act on Youth and Children's Public Organizations to ensure its compatibility with the right of the child to freedom of association and to peaceful assembly as guaranteed under article 15 of the Convention.'[27] The Committee has also repeatedly emphasized that the States Parties have an obligation not to interfere with the child's access to information.[28]

The Committee also underlines the importance of making children aware of their right to freedom of expression. For example, where it recommended to Syria in 2003 that the State Party actively promote the implementation of these rights (Articles 13–17), by making children more aware of their rights and by facilitating their active use in daily practice.[29]

### 4.5 *More than a negative right*

Freedom of expression has traditionally been seen as a *negative* right to use freedom of expression without any interference. But the obligation not to interfere also requires *positive legislation* and other measures from the State Parties to ensure that the right to freedom of expression is not obstructed in any way, be it by public bodies or private organizations or persons. In its Concluding Observations to Singapore in 2011, the Committee expressed its concern regarding these issues: 'While noting that children are encouraged to express their views in some forums, the Committee is concerned that these forums are very limited and that the right of the child to freedom of expression, including to file complaints publicly and to receive information, and to freedom of association and peaceful assembly are, in practice, not fully guaranteed.'[30] In its Concluding Observations to the Democratic People's Republic of Korea in 2004, the Committee was concerned about the 'lack of information on civil and political rights and persistent reports of limitations on the civil and political rights of citizens, including children, in particular freedoms of opinion, expression, thought, conscience, religion, and movement, as well as the right to privacy'.[31]

[27] CRC, Concluding Observations on Ukraine, UN Doc. CRC/C/UKR/CO/3-4, 21 April 2011, para. 40.
[28] See further section 5.
[29] CRC, Concluding Observations on the Syrian Arabic Republic, UN Doc. CRC/C/15/Add. 212, 6 June 2003, paras. 34–5.
[30] CRC, Concluding Observations on Singapore, UN Doc. CRC/C/SGP/CO/2-3, 4 May 2011, para. 37.
[31] CRC, Concluding Observations on the Democratic People's Republic of Korea, UN Doc. CRC/C/15/Add.239, 1 July 2004, para. 32.

To the Republic of Korea, the Committee in 2004 expressed its concerns at the limitations on students' freedom of expression and association:

> due to strict administrative control of student councils and school regulations that limit or prohibit outside political activities of students in elementary and secondary schools. It is further concerned about allegations that Internet chat rooms, set up independently by teenagers, have been arbitrarily closed down by the authorities.[32]

## 5 The 'freedom to seek, receive and impart information and ideas of all kinds'

The phrase about the right to seek, receive and impart information in the first paragraph of Article 13 is a copy of Article 19, ICCPR. The phrase obliges States to refrain from interfering with access to information and to protect the right of access to means of communication and public dialogue. The Human Rights Committee's General Comment No. 34 emphasizes that this phrase 'embraces a right of access to information held by public bodies' and that '[s]uch information includes records held by a public body, regardless of the form in which the information is stored, its source and its date of production'.[33]

The Committee recommended to Uzbekistan in 2001 that the State: 'take(s) all effective measures, including enacting or rescinding legislation where necessary, to ensure that the right of access to information are guaranteed and implemented'.[34]

Article 13 of CRC is supplemented by Article 17 about the role of mass media, and the duty of the State to ensure that children have access to information and material from diverse sources – especially those aimed at promoting their social, spiritual and moral well-being and physical and mental health. Article 17 reads:

> States Parties recognize the important function performed by the mass media and shall ensure that the child has access to information and material from a diversity of national and international sources, especially

[32] CRC, Concluding Observations on the Republic of Korea, UN Doc. CRC/C/15/Add.197, 18 March 2003, para. 36.

[33] HRC, General Comment No. 34, 12 September 2011, para. 18. See Chapters 3 and 9 in this book.

[34] CRC, Concluding Observations on Uzbekistan, UN Doc. CRC/C/15/Add.167, 7 November 2001, para. 38.

those aimed at the promotion of his or her social, spiritual and moral well-being and physical and mental health.

To this end, States Parties shall:

(a) Encourage the mass media to disseminate information and material of social and cultural benefit to the child and in accordance with the spirit of article 29;
(b) Encourage international co-operation in the production, exchange and dissemination of such information and material from a diversity of cultural, national and international sources;
(c) Encourage the production and dissemination of children's books;
(d) Encourage the mass media to have particular regard to the linguistic needs of the child who belongs to a minority group or who is indigenous;
(e) Encourage the development of appropriate guidelines for the protection of the child from information and material injurious to his or her well-being, bearing in mind the provisions of articles 13 and 18.

Article 13 and Article 17 partly overlap, but while Article 13 is primarily about the child's right to actively seek and receive information, Article 17 is about the role of mass media towards children in general, and especially indigenous children and children of minority groups. Traditionally, the mass media have only to a limited degree written for children and offered space for children. With the Internet, the situation has changed radically as regards the possibility for many children to express themselves, communicate with others and gather information. However, the majority of the world's children do not have access to Internet, and all children still need information specially tailored for them.

Article 17 underlines the importance for children to have the necessary information for their development. It is also the opinion of the Committee that the States Parties have an obligation to encourage the media to give room for active participation of children. As regards public television, the State Party should: 'Ensure that public television takes the initiative and assumes leadership in creating responsible programming during children's prime time, giving priority to child development and not economic profit, including children's participation in the development, content and design of children's programmes.'[35] There is no reference here to any specific article, but the recommendation is most relevant in connection with Article 17, which obliges the States Parties to actively contribute to the availability of information and material based on a diversity of national and international sources. This obligation does, of course, include an

35 CRC, Concluding Observations on Spain, UN Doc. CRC/C/ESP/CO/3–4, 3 November 2010, para. 33.

obligation to use the Internet as a source of information and also as a platform for communication. In its General Comment No. 12, 'The right of the child to be heard', the Committee points out that the fulfilment of the child's right to information consistent with Article 17 is, to a large degree, a prerequisite for the effective realization of the right to express his or her views.[36] The Committee frequently refers to Articles 13 and 17 together. Most often this is reasonable, but sometimes it gives the impression that the Committee does not distinguish properly between the two articles, and the motivation behind them.

The Committee has mostly mentioned the children's use of the Internet as a source of concern and not so much as the important tool that it is for children to receive information and express opinions. This is due partly to the fact that the concerns are real and the protection necessary, and partly to the novelty of the social media where the competence of children – in rich countries at least – is superior to that of adults. However, it seems obvious that education about the limits of freedom of expression regarding Internet and telephone messages is necessary, for parents, teachers and children, alike (see further, section 7).

In its General Comment No. 34, the Human Rights Committee states that 'every individual should have the right to ascertain in an intelligible form, whether, and if so, what personal data is stored in automatic data files, and for what purposes'.[37] It has been indicated that 'seek information' in Article 13 of the CRC embraces the right of children to seek information about their origin, especially in cases of sperm donation. In my opinion, this is not an issue that concerns children specifically, but a more general issue about a person's right to know his or her origin, as a child of his or her parents. I believe that this should be an absolute right. However, to what extent a person under 18 should have this right, might depend on the age of the child and this will usually be regulated in national legislation. It is not obvious that this should be a right for a child independent of age.[38]

[36] CRC, General Comment No. 12, 20 July 2009, para. 82.

[37] HRC, General Comment No. 34, 12 September 2011, para. 18.

[38] The Committee has on a few occasions indicated that Article 7 establishes a right for the child to be informed about the identity of the sperm donor. In my opinion, it is clear from the context and the wording of Article 7 that 'the right to know and be cared for by his or her parents', is about social parents and not genetic parents. However, this is in contradiction with the general opinion, see R. Hodgkin and P. Newell, *UNICEF Implementation Handbook for the Convention on the Rights of the Child*, 3rd edn (New York: United Nations, 2007), 108. See for example, CRC, Concluding Observations on Switzerland, UN

## 6 Restrictions on the right to freedom of expression

The exercise of the right to freedom of expression for children is not unlimited, and may be subject to certain restrictions. According to Article 13(2) these restrictions 'shall only be such as are provided by law, and are necessary: (a) For respect of the rights or reputations of others; or (b) For the protection of national security or of public order (*ordre public*), or of public health or morals'. These are – word for word – the same restrictions envisaged by Article 19(3), ICCPR.

In the context of permissible restrictions generally, the Human Rights Committee recommends extreme caution and provides many examples of situations where the urge to restrict freedom of expression should be resisted. Any restrictions that might be applied to websites, blogs or other internet-based networks or support systems should be limited to content only and should not be applied to entire sites and systems.[39] It follows from the jurisprudence regarding Article 19, ICCPR, that the restrictions must conform to the strict tests of necessity and proportionality.[40] This difficult balance between freedom of expression and the protection of other interests is one of the core issues in the jurisprudence regarding freedom of expression, and will not be discussed in this chapter, except for special problems regarding children.

The strict interpretation of these restrictions in Article 19, ICCPR, is also relevant for Article 13, CRC. The Committee has emphasized this on several occasions. A typical example is its Concluding Observation to Belize in 2005:

> The Committee is concerned about the limitations on the exercise of the right to freedom of expression by children. The Committee recommends that the State party encourage and facilitate the exercise by children of their right to freedom of expression, including their right to freedom of association and of peaceful assembly, so that they can freely discuss, participate and express their views and opinions on all matters affecting them.[41]

In 2004 the Committee reiterated its earlier recommendation to Iran, expressed in its previous Concluding Observations, that the State Party establish clear criteria for determining whether a given action or

Doc. CRC/C/15/Add.182, 7 June 2002, paras. 28–9; CRC, Concluding Observations on France, UN Doc. CRC/C/FRA/CO4, 22 June 2009, para. 44.

[39] HRC, General Comment No. 34, 12 September 2011, para. 43. [40] *Ibid.*, para. 22.

[41] CRC, Concluding Observations on Belize, UN Doc. CRC/C/15/Add.252, 31 March 2005, paras. 38–9.

expression is in accordance with interpretations of Islamic texts, and consider appropriate and proportionate means to protect public morals while safeguarding the right of every child to freedom of expression and assembly.[42]

In 2003 the Committee recommended to the Republic of Korea that it amend legislation, guidelines and school regulations 'to facilitate children's active participation in decision-making processes and in political activities both within and outside schools and ensure that all children fully enjoy their right to freedom of association and expression'.[43]

However, the right to freedom of expression for children must to a certain extent be restricted to protect the child itself, both as regards his or her own expressions, and against harmful information from others. This does not follow from the text of Article 13, but it does follow from Article 3(1) and the best-interest principle.[44] It also follows from Article 17(e), according to which the State Party shall encourage 'the development of appropriate guidelines for the protection of the child from information and material injurious to his or her well-being'. Article 17(e) has been interpreted by the Committee as imposing on the State Parties a duty to protect children from harmful information. The Committee expressed concern to France in 2009 regarding children's access to harmful material, and recommended that: 'The State party takes measures to protect children from the access to harmful information, including electronic and audio-visual exposure. It further recommends that effective measures are taken to exercise control on accessibility of written, electronic and audio-visual media, including video and internet games harmful to children.'[45]

Much has happened in this area in the last years, an example here is the European Commission's Safer Internet Programme 2009–13.[46] The programme aims at empowering and protecting children and young

[42] CRC, Concluding Observations on the Islamic Republic of Iran, UN Doc. CRC/C/15/Add.254, 31 March 2005, paras. 39–40.

[43] CRC, Concluding Observations on the Republic of Korea, UN Doc. CRC/C/15/Add.197, 18 March 2003, para. 36.

[44] Article 3(1) of the Convention on the Rights of the Child: 'In all actions concerning children, whether undertaken by public or private social welfare institutions, courts of law, administrative authorities or legislative bodies, the best interests of the child shall be a primary consideration.' See further section 9.

[45] CRC, Concluding Observations on France, 22 June 2009, paras. 52–3.

[46] See J. Savirimuthu, 'The EU, Online Child Safety and Media Literacy', *International Journal of Children's Rights* 19 (2011), 59ff.

people online by awareness-raising initiatives and by fighting illegal and harmful online content and conduct. This will have a bearing also on material that children are seeking according to Article 13. The latest version of the programme will fight not only illegal content but also harmful conduct such as grooming and bullying.

## 7 Freedom of expression (Article 13) and the right to be heard (Article 12)

Article 12 about the right to be heard and Article 13 about freedom of expression are often confused. Article 13 is about the right to express opinions and to seek, receive and impart information of all kinds. This is a right to express views about anything and there is no requirement of capacities, as under Article 12. The obligation of States under Article 13 is first and foremost to refrain from interference, but there are also other obligations, as outlined in section 4.5. Article 13 does not create an obligation to listen to children or to give weight to their opinions.

Article 12 is about a right that is specially tailored for children, based on the fact that they do not have a general right to decide for themselves. This is a right for a child who is capable of forming his/her own views, to express his/her views freely in all matters that affect him/her. The article imposes a positive obligation on the State to safeguard the right of the child to be heard in all matters that affect him/her, and that due weight is given to the expressed opinions. This includes an obligation to introduce the necessary legal framework and mechanisms for the right to be heard. The core issue of this article is the right of the individual child to have a voice in decisions that affect him/her. However, it is often interpreted in a broader way, as a right for children to have a say on issues that concern children in general. Interpreted in this way, there will be a closer connection to Article 13. As stated by the Committee in its General Comment No. 12: 'creating an environment of respect for children to express their views, consistent with article 12, also contributes towards building children's capacities to exercise their right to freedom of expression'.[47]

From the point of view of the Committee, both of these articles are important prerequisites for realizing the participation of children. The Committee's strong emphasis on the right of the child to participate in general and to be a member of society forms important background

[47] CRC, General Comment No. 12, 20 July 2009, para. 81.

when interpreting Article 13. It should be underlined, however, that the right guaranteed by Article 12 is limited to matters that *affect the child*, and establishes a right to *be heard*, while Article 13 has no restrictions as regards the subject matter of the expression, and does not provide for a right to be heard. There is therefore a fundamental difference between the two provisions, and they should not be confused. However, over the years, the Committee has not always been very precise about the difference between Articles 12 and 13 and has sometimes mixed them up and also used the term 'participation' indiscriminately.

## 8 'The CRC is indivisible and its articles interdependent'[48]

The Committee has repeatedly emphasized that the CRC must be looked upon as a whole and that several other articles of the CRC influence the interpretation of Article 13. The most important Articles – 5, 3, 28 and 29 – in this connection will be discussed in the following paragraphs.

Article 5, which concerns the rights and responsibilities of parents to give appropriate direction and guidance in the exercise by the child of his or her rights, has a direct bearing on the interpretation of Article 13. It is obvious that parents will usually have a great influence on the thoughts and opinions of their children and that the capacity of the child to form opinions and express them will to a large extent depend on the parents. The problem in this connection will usually be to strike the right balance between the right of the parents to direct the child, and respect for the child's right to freedom of opinion and expression. This is an area where the right of privacy for the family will be relevant, and where the State as a general rule will not interfere. However, the State Parties have an obligation to encourage parents to respect their children's freedom of expression, as is often underlined by the Committee. The Committee has expressed concern where countries have shown that they do not fully accept children as active subjects of rights, and it is fair to say that the Committee has focused more on the child's rights in the family than on the parents' right to direct their children. However, the Committee has also emphasized that the rights of the child within the family should not be exercised at the expense of others' rights, in particular those of the parents.[49]

[48] Hodgkin and Newell, *Implementation Handbook*, 45. [49] *Ibid.*, 90.

Article 3 about the best interests of the child is one of the most important articles in the Convention. The Committee has classified Article 3(1) as one of the four general principles of the Convention, alongside Article 2 about the right to non-discrimination, Article 6 about the right to life, survival and development, and Article 12 about the child's right to express his or her views freely in 'all matters affecting the child', those views being given due weight.[50]

The best-interest principle should, however, be used with caution in connection with the civil and political rights of children, as it may serve as an excuse to restrict these rights unduly. Still, there will be some cases where there is a risk that the expression will have serious harmful consequences for the child, and where the child needs to be protected against him or herself. An example is when the child is talking to the media or using social media. My home country, Norway, has introduced regulations that make it possible for the authorities to stop or delete statements on social media – also statements from the child – that might be harmful for the child. Here, as in many other situations, there will be difficult choices between the right of the child and the need to protect the child. Depending on the age of the child and the seriousness of the risk of harm, the best interest of the child must sometimes be given preference over the wishes of the child. It follows from Article 13(2) that the right to freedom of expression is not a non-derogable right; it may be restricted if the restrictions are provided for by law and for respect of rights and reputation of others, or for the protection of national security or of public order or of public health or morals. In addition to these restrictions mentioned in Article 13(2), Article 3 may thus provide a basis for the limitation of the child's right to freedom of expression in order to protect the child him/herself.[51]

Articles 28 and 29 concerning the right to education supplement Article 13, especially regarding the right to seek and receive information. For children the school will normally be the main arena for acquiring knowledge and information and the child's right to education is important in this connection. Article 29, which sets out the goals of education, includes in para. 1(a) the development of the child's talents to their fullest potential. This includes the ability for children to express themselves orally and in writing and also take part in discussions. Further, Article

[50] CRC, General Comment No. 5: General Measures of Implementation of the Convention on the Rights of the Child (Arts. 4, 42 and 44 (para. 6)), UN Doc. CRC/GC/2003/5, 27 November 2003, para. 128.

[51] See also in this connection section 5.

29(d) is highly relevant as it provides that education shall be directed to: 'The preparation of the child for responsible life in a free society'. It is important that the CRC is part of the curriculum in school, and also in all education for professions that work with children.

Article 17 about the important function of mass media has a close relationship with Article 13, and the Committee often refers to these articles together. Article 13 includes the right to receive information, and this is further elaborated in Article 17. The media is also important for promoting awareness of the right of the child to express their views, and offering children the possibility of expressing themselves.

The Committee often bundles together civil and political rights in Articles 12 to 16, and it pays great attention to the right of the child to participate in society in general. These articles are about active rights that must be exercised first and foremost by the child him/herself, and not about protection and rights that are exercised on behalf of the child by others. Article 13 to 16 belong to the most fundamental human rights, and they are interconnected in such a way that if one of them is not respected, this will usually also be the case for the others. Articles 13 and 14 are particularly closely connected, as freedom of expression includes the display of religious symbols. The Committee has expressed concerns about the restriction of wearing religious symbols or clothing, but this is primarily viewed as a question of freedom of religion. The issue of wearing religious clothing and symbols was touched upon by the Committee in its Concluding Observations to France in 2004:

> The Committee is also concerned that the new legislation (Law No. 2004-228 of 15 March 2004) on wearing religious symbols and clothing in public schools may be counterproductive, by neglecting the principle of the best interests of the child and the right of the child to access to education, and not achieve the expected results. The Committee welcomes that the provisions of the legislation will be subject to an evaluation one year after its entry into force.[52]

In 2009 the Committee again took up this question and on this occasion it concurred with a Concluding Observation from the Human Rights Committee noting that respect for a public culture of *laïcité* would not seem to require forbidding the wearing of such common religious

[52] CRC, Concluding Observations on France, UN Doc. CRC/C/15/Add.240, 30 June 2004, para. 25.

symbols as head covering such as a skullcap (or kippah), a headscarf (or hijab), or a turban.[53] The Committee recommended that:

> The guarantees of article 14 of the Convention concerning the right of the child to freedom of thought, conscience and religion, including the right to manifest one's religion in public as well as private, be upheld and that particular attention be paid to avoid discrimination on the grounds of thought, conscience or religion.[54]

## 9 Some conclusions

All children have the right to freedom of expression. This follows both from Article 13, CRC and Article 19, ICCPR. The possibilities for the exercise of this right will change in accordance with the evolving capacities of the child, but the freedom is there for the child from day one. What is special for children is that they have a positive right of access to information and that States have a duty to provide them with information. Another difference between the approaches to freedom of expression under both treaties is that the best-interests principle, laid down in Article 3, CRC, might restrict the right to freedom of expression to protect the child from any harmful consequences of their own utterances.

The Committee has been criticized for not paying enough attention to freedom of expression, and also for an unsatisfactory analysis of Article 13.[55] This may be partly due to a lack of information available to the Committee about the situation in the individual States, as freedom of expression has not been the most-favoured topic for the NGOs in their reporting to the Committee. But it is also a fact that other concerns have appeared more important for the Committee. It seems that the right to freedom of expression and Article 13 have more or less drowned in the great attention paid by the Committee to the right of participation in general, and Article 12 in particular. This is not surprising, taking into consideration that Article 12 represents an innovation in international law. However, the Committee could, in my opinion, have been clearer about the difference between these two articles.[56] The Committee also

[53] HRC, Concluding Observations on France, UN Doc. CCPR/C/FRA/CO/4, 31 July 2008, para. 23.
[54] CRC, Concluding Observations on France, UN Doc. CRC/C/FRA/CO4, 22 June 2009, para. 46.
[55] Langlaude, 'Positive Understanding', 65.
[56] See section 6.

too often clusters together all the civil rights without mentioning any of them.

Maybe as a result of this criticism, the Committee has in later years taken up civil and political rights with the States Parties more often than before, especially Article 13 and Article 15 on freedom of association. For example, the Committee addressed the following comments to the Ukraine in 2011:

> With respect to freedom of association and peaceful assembly, the Committee is concerned that the Act on Youth and Children's Public Organizations prohibits children's participation in political rallies and demonstrations as well as the establishment of children's associations along political and religious lines. In the light of article 13 of the Convention, the Committee calls upon the State party to ensure that its domestic legislation expressly protect the right of the child to freedom of expression.[57]

The Committee expressed its concerns to Belarus, also in 2011, regarding limitations on the right to freedom of expression for children, and recommended that the State Party take all necessary measures to ensure guarantees for the full implementation of the rights to freedom of expression, freedom of association and peaceful assembly and access to appropriate information, in accordance with Articles 13, 15 and 17 of the Convention.[58] The Committee expressed its deep concern to Bahrain, again in 2011, that civil and political rights are not always respected, particularly for children.[59]

The Committee expressed the same concerns to Egypt, and recommended especially that the State Party:

> (a) Enforce article 3(c) of the Child Law (2008) concerning the right of the child to freedom of expression, including the freedom to receive, seek and impart information; (b) Increase budgetary allocation to promote children's right to freely express themselves and encourage their active involvement in the media, and thereby consolidate their position in society as subjects of rights.[60]

[57] CRC, Concluding Observations on Ukraine, UN Doc. CRC/C/UKR/CO/3–4, 21 April 2011, paras. 39–40.

[58] CRC, Concluding Observations on Belarus, UN Doc. CRC/C/BLR/CO/3–4, 4 February 2011, paras. 35–6.

[59] CRC, Concluding Observations on Bahrain, UN Doc. CRC/BHR/CO/2–3, 17 June 2011, para. 41.

[60] CRC, Concluding Observations on Egypt, UN Doc. CRC/C/EGY/CO/3–4, 17 June 2011, para. 46.

On the other hand, there are countries that obviously do not have full freedom of expression, but where this is not discussed or mentioned in the Concluding Observations. This is probably partly due to a lack of comprehensive information. In some countries, the Committee is to a large extent dependent on information from NGOs, and for some of these organizations other problems will often be more urgent. In Afghanistan, for example, with a very high level of violence against children, infant mortality that remains among the highest in the world, where two-thirds of children are chronically malnourished, and where the girls continue to be subject to multiple discrimination from the earliest stages of their life, freedom of expression will not be the most important issue.

Part of the criticism of the Committee regarding its application of Article 13 seems to build on a misunderstanding of what Concluding Observations are meant to be and of how the Committee works. For example, Sylvia Langlaude writes: 'The committee's analysis of the child's right to freedom of expression under article 13 is unsatisfactory. What is regrettable is that the Committee has not developed a clear theoretical underpinning of why the child has a freedom of expression and how the right applies to all ages but in different ways.'[61] It is not possible for the Committee to develop the analysis called for here through the Concluding Observations. The Concluding Observations must be produced during a very short period of time – a few days after the dialogue – without much secretariat support on legal issues. For a group of eighteen people with a majority of non-legal persons, it is not really possible to go deeply into difficult legal issues, at least not with the scarce resources of the secretariat. Also, the Concluding Observations are a consequence of the information the Committee receives. The members are not specialists on any country except their own (and they are supposed not to take part in the dialogue or the work on Concluding Observations of their own country).

The *legal interpretations* of the Convention by the Committee will first and foremost appear in the General Comments, although sometimes the Concluding Observations clearly presuppose a legal interpretation. However, so far other themes have been considered more important for the General Comments; there is at all times a wish-list of themes for General Comments sent in from different organizations.

[61] S. Langlaude, 'Positive Understanding', 65.

In my opinion, the task to interpret and analyse the provisions in the Convention is an obligation as much for human rights scholars as for the Committee with its very limited resources. As Langlaude mentions, more research is necessary on many of the articles. She cites Linda Kirchke from 1999: '[T]here is a sense in which the CRC is itself still in its childhood as international law. This is demonstrated by the lack of clear jurisprudence about what key provisions of the CRC should mean. Without such jurisprudential guidance, it is difficult for States Parties to know what they need to do if they are to meet their obligations.'[62] I agree with the last sentence. In turn, it will sometimes be difficult for the Committee to monitor the implementation in a meaningful fashion without jurisprudential guidance based on scholarly analysis.

One of the reasons for the meagre jurisprudence regarding the Convention compared to, for example, the ICCPR has been the lack of a complaints procedure. But even with the entry into force of the third Optional Protocol on a communications procedure in April 2014, it will take several years before the communications will offer much support in the interpretation of the Convention. It is important that more human rights scholars take an interest in the many questions of interpretation raised by this Convention.

## Literature

Hodgkin, R. and P. Newell, *UNICEF Implementation Handbook for the Convention on the Rights of the Child*, 3rd edn (New York: United Nations Publications, 2007).

Kirschke, L. *Kid's Talk: Freedom of Expression and the UN Convention on the Rights of the Child* (London: ARTICLE 19, 1999).

Langlaude, S. 'Children and Religion under Article 14 UNCHR: A Critical Analysis', *International Journal of Children's Rights* 16 (2008), 475–504.

'On How to Build a Positive Understanding of the Child's Right to Freedom of Expression', *Human Rights Law Review* 10 (2010), 33–66.

Savirimuthu, J. 'The EU, Online Child Safety and Media Literacy', *International Journal of Children's Rights* 19 (2011), 547–69.

Smith, C. 'Human Rights as the Foundation of Society', in P. Lødrup and E. Modvar (eds.), *Family Life and Human Rights* (Oslo: Gyldendal, 2004).

[62] L. Kirschke, *Kid's Talk: Freedom of Expression and the UN Convention on the Rights of the Child* (London: ARTICLE 19, 1999), 1, as cited by Langlaude, 'Positive Understanding', fn. 192.

Thorgeirsdóttir, H. 'Article 13: The Right to Freedom of Expression', in A. Alen and J. VandeLanotte *et al.* (eds.), *A Commentary on the United Nations Convention on the Rights of the Child* (Leiden: Martinus Nijhoff, 2006).

Verheyde, M. and G. Goedertier, 'Articles 43–45: The UN Committee on the Rights of the Child', in A. Alen and J. VandeLanotte *et al.* (eds.), *A Commentary on the United Nations Convention on the Rights of the Child* (Leiden: Martinus Nijhoff, 2006).

## UN documents

### *Committee on the Rights of the Child*

### General Comments

General Comment No. 5: General Measures of Implementation of the Convention on the Rights of the Child (Arts. 4, 42 and 44 (para. 6)), UN Doc. CRC/GC/2003/5, 27 November 2003.

General Comment No. 7: Implementing Child Rights in Early Childhood, CRC/C/GC/7Rev.1, 20 September 2006.

General Comment No. 8: The Right of the Child to Protection from Corporal Punishment and Other Cruel or Degrading Forms of Punishment, UN Doc. CRC/C/GC/8, 7 March 2007.

General Comment No.12: The Right of the Child to Be Heard, UN Doc. CRC/C/GC/12, 20, 20 July 2009.

### Concluding Observations

Concluding Observations on Bahrain, UN Doc. CRC/BHR/CO/2–3, 17 June 2011.

Concluding Observations on Belarus, UN Doc. CRC/C/BLR/CO/3–4, 4 February 2011.

Concluding Observations on Belize, UN Doc. CRC/C/15/Add.252, 31 March 2005.

Concluding Observations on Egypt, UN Doc. CRC/C/EGY/CO/3–4, 17 June 2011.

Concluding Observations on France, UN Doc. CRC/C/15/Add.240, 30 June 2004.

Concluding Observations on France, UN Doc. CRC/C/FRA/CO4, 22 June 2009.

Concluding Observations on Georgia, UN Doc. CRC/C/15/Add. 222, 27 October 2003.

Concluding Observations on the Islamic Republic of Iran, UN Doc. CRC/C/15/Add.254, 31 March 2005.

Concluding Observations on the Democratic People's Republic of Korea, UN Doc. CRC/C/15/Add.239, 1 July 2004.

Concluding Observations on the Republic of Korea, UN Doc. CRC/C/15/Add.197, 18 March 2003.

Concluding Observations on Spain, UN Doc. CRC/C/ESP/CO/3–4, 3 November 2010.

Concluding Observations on Singapore, UN Doc. CRC/C/SGP/CO/2-3, 4 May 2011.
Concluding Observations on Switzerland, UN Doc. CRC/C/15/Add.182, 7 June 2002.
Concluding Observations on the Syrian Arabic Republic, UN Doc. CRC/C/15/Add. 212, 6 June 2003.
Concluding Observations on Ukraine, UN Doc. CRC/C/UKR/CO/3-4, 21 April 2011.
Concluding Observations on Uzbekistan, UN Doc. CRC/C/15/Add.167, 7 November 2001.

### *Human Rights Committee*

### General Comments

General Comment No. 17: Article 24 (Rights of the Child), UN Doc. A/44/40, 7 April 1989.
General Comment No. 34: Article 19 (Freedoms of Opinion and Expression), UN Doc. CCPR/C/GC/34, 12 September 2011.

### Concluding Observations

Concluding Observations on France, UN Doc. CCPR/C/FRA/CO/4, 31 July 2008.

6

# Convention on the Rights of Persons with Disabilities: ensuring full and equal access to information

ELIZA VARNEY

## 1 Introduction

This chapter explores the role of the Convention on the Rights of Persons with Disabilities (CRPD)[1] in promoting and protecting the human rights of persons with disabilities, focusing on the right to freedom of expression and access to information. It assesses the effectiveness of the CRPD in safeguarding this right and questions the potential of this instrument to tackle the barriers encountered by persons with disabilities in accessing information and communication technologies (ICTs).

Section 2 discusses the reasons for adopting a thematic convention on the rights of persons with disabilities and reflects on the effectiveness of other instruments of the United Nations (UN), including the International Covenant on Civil and Political Rights,[2] in protecting the exercise of the right to freedom of expression and access to information by persons with disabilities. It also explores the key objectives of the CRPD and emphasises the human rights approach adopted by this Convention.

Section 3 analyses the provisions of the CRPD with particular relevance to the right to freedom of expression and access to information (including Article 9 on accessibility and Article 21 on freedom of

I would like to thank Mike Varney, Tarlach McGonagle and Yvonne Donders for constructive comments on an earlier draft. Any errors and omissions are my own. The issues discussed in this chapter are developed in E. Varney, *Disability and Information Technology: A Comparative Study in Media Regulation* (Cambridge University Press, 2013).

[1] International Convention on the Rights of Persons with Disabilities (CRPD), New York, 13 December 2006, entered into force 3 May 2008, 2515 UNTS, 3.

[2] International Covenant on Civil and Political Rights (ICCPR), New York, 16 December 1966, entered into force 23 March 1976, 999 UNTS, 171.

expression and opinion, and access to information). It stresses the role of this right in the exercise of other human rights, including the right to participate in political and public life (protected under Article 29) and the right to participate in cultural life, recreation, leisure and sport (protected under Article 30).

Section 4 explores the potential impact of the CRPD on the regulatory frameworks of States Parties to the Convention, in tackling accessibility barriers in the ICT sector. This section also discusses the potential impact of the Convention in mainstreaming disability issues in UN standards and mechanisms[3] and questions whether the UN Human Rights Committee's 2011 General Comment No. 34 (on Article 19 of the ICCPR on freedoms of opinion and expression),[4] sufficiently takes into account the rights of persons with disabilities.

Finally, section 5 explores implementation and monitoring mechanisms advanced under the CRPD to ensure and promote the full and equal enjoyment of human rights by persons with disabilities, including the right to freedom of expression and access to information. The discussion stresses that the impact of the CRPD goes beyond tackling accessibility barriers and has the potential to bring about wider positive changes in society.[5]

## 2 Background to the adoption of the CRPD

The CRPD and the associated Optional Protocol were adopted by the General Assembly of the UN on 13 December 2006[6] and they entered into force on 3 May 2008.[7] The CRPD is the first global human rights treaty of the twenty-first century. The CRPD was the fastest negotiated human rights treaty and it received the highest number of signatures on

[3] G. Quinn and T. Degener (eds.), *Human Rights and Disability: The Current Use and Future Potential of United Nations Human Rights Instruments in the Context of Disability* (New York and Geneva: United Nations, 2002), 297.

[4] HRC, General Comment 34: Article 19 (Freedoms of Opinion and Expression), 21 July 2011, UN Doc. CCPR/C/GC/34.

[5] G. Quinn, 'The United Nations Convention on the Rights of Persons with Disabilities: Toward a New International Politics of Disability', *Texas Journal on Civil Liberties and Civil Rights* 15–1 (2009), 33–52.

[6] The Optional Protocol to the International Convention on the Rights of Persons with Disabilities, 13 December 2006, UN Doc. A/61/611.

[7] The Secretariat for the Convention on the Rights of Persons with Disabilities (SCRPD), *UN Enable: Entry into Force*, 2011a; see: www.un.org/disabilities/default.asp?id=210 (last accessed 21 February 2014).

the opening day.[8] The adoption of this instrument is argued to be the most inclusive process witnessed by the UN,[9] as it relied on a high level of participation from persons with disabilities and organisations representing their interests.[10] The CRPD is also the first binding international human rights instrument that focuses specifically on the rights of persons with disabilities.[11] The Convention covers 'the full spectrum of human rights'[12] and focuses on the application of these rights to the specific circumstances of persons with disabilities,[13] seeking also to clarify the obligations that States Parties have in the promotion and protection of these rights.[14] The CRPD, therefore, seeks to 'protect and consolidate rights which, in theory, already exist'[15] and aims to ensure the equal enjoyment of these rights by persons with disabilities.[16]

The CRPD aims to complement the protection of human rights[17] provided under other international treaties such as the International Covenant on Civil and Political Rights (ICCPR) and the International Covenant on Economic, Social and Cultural Rights (ICESCR).[18] Yet, despite the universal application of the ICCPR and the ICESCR in safeguarding human rights, these instruments have failed to provide an effective level of protection for persons with disabilities[19] and were

[8] UN SCRPD, *UN Enable*, Convention on the Rights of Persons with Disabilities, 2011b; see: www.un.org/disabilities/default.asp?navid=14&pid=150 (last accessed 21 February 2014).

[9] A. S. Kanter, 'The Promise and Challenge of the United Nations Convention on the Rights of Persons with Disabilities', *Journal of International Law and Commerce* 34 (2007), 308.

[10] F. Gibson, 'The Convention on the Rights of Persons with Disabilities: The Response of the Clinic', *International Journal of Clinical Legal Education* (summer 2011), 12.

[11] Kanter, 'Promise and Challenge', 288.

[12] OHCHR, 'Monitoring the Convention on the Rights of Persons with Disabilities: Guidance for Human Rights Monitors', Professional Training Series no. 17, New York, United Nations, 2010, 24.

[13] M. A. Stein and J. A. Lord, 'Participatory Justice, and the UN Convention on the Rights of Persons with Disabilities', *Texas Journal on Civil Liberties and Civil Rights* 13 (2008), 174.

[14] OHCHR, 'Monitoring the Convention', 24.

[15] A. Lawson, 'The United Nations Convention on the Rights of Persons with Disabilities: New Era or False Dawn?', *Syracuse Journal of International Law and Commerce* 34(2) (2007), 616.

[16] Quinn, 'United Nations Convention', 43.

[17] Quinn and Degener, *Human Rights and Disability*, 296.

[18] International Covenant on Economic, Social and Cultural Rights (ICESCR), New York, 16 December 1966, entered into force 3 January 1976, 993 UNTS, 3.

[19] D. MacKay, 'The United Nations Convention on the Rights of Person with Disabilities', *Syracuse Journal of International Law and Commerce* 34(2) (2007), 323.

underused in safeguarding disability equality.[20] The drafting of these instruments relied on a vision of human rights rooted in an able-bodied norm, which limited their effectiveness in tackling human rights violations affecting persons with disabilities.[21] This approach did not place sufficient emphasis on tackling accessibility barriers faced by persons with disabilities. In the words of Kayess and French, '[i]n most cases it is not self-evident how traditional human rights are to be interpreted and applied in a manner that will penetrate to the specific human rights violations to which persons with disability are subject'.[22] Furthermore, these instruments failed to make specific reference to *disability* under the prohibited grounds for differential treatment, the situation of persons with disabilities falling within the prohibition of discrimination on grounds of *other status*.[23] This has been attributed to a limited understanding, at the time when these instruments were drafted, of the need to address these issues explicitly.[24] Stein stresses that in order to avail themselves of the protection of the ICCPR or the ICESCR, persons with disabilities had to either possess a characteristic that was explicitly referred to as a prohibited ground for differential treatment, or had to rely on the omnibus provision that was seldom enforced.[25] Consequently, persons with disabilities have made only limited use of channels such as the individual complaints mechanism established under the first Optional Protocol to the ICCPR.[26] Quinn and Degener comment that these difficulties resulted from the invisibility of persons with disabilities as subjects of human rights, caused by the absence of a strong voice in the democratic process.[27] The absence of persons with disabilities from

20 Quinn and Degener, *Human Rights and Disability*, 2.

21 R. Kayess and P. French, 'Out of Darkness into Light? Introducing the Convention on the Rights of Persons with Disabilities', *Human Rights Law Review* 8(1) (2008), 14.

22 *Ibid.*

23 ICCPR, Art. 2(1) and ICESCR, Art. 2(2). See M. A. Stein, 'A Quick Overview of the United Nations Convention on the Rights of Persons with Disabilities', *Mental and Physical Disability Law Report* 31(5) (2007), 679.

24 Committee on Economic, Social and Cultural Rights (UN CESCR), General Comment No. 5: Persons with Disabilities, 9 December 1994, UN Doc. E/1995/22, para. 6.

25 Stein, 'Quick Overview', 679.

26 Optional Protocol to the International Covenant on Civil and Political Rights, 16 December 1966, 999 UNTS, 302. See Stein, 'Quick Overview', 679. Please note that an optional protocol to the ICESCR, which establishes an individual complaints mechanism, has been adopted after the entry into force of the CRPD. See Optional Protocol to the International Covenant on Economic, Social and Cultural Rights, 10 December 2008, UN Doc. A/RES/63/117.

27 Quinn and Degener, *Human Rights and Disability*, 23.

political processes reinforced stereotypical attitudes about their powerlessness and consequently, persons with disabilities were left without the power to shape policy-making.[28] Similarly, Lawson notes that persons with disabilities have not been perceived by policy-makers as subjects of human rights entitled to full and equal protection of their rights, and sees this as an unavoidable result of their separation from the mainstream due to the barriers encountered when interacting with society.[29]

The UN has attempted to tackle these barriers through the adoption of policy guidelines such as the World Programme of Action Concerning Disabled Persons (WPA)[30] and the Standard Rules on the Equalization of Opportunities for Persons with Disabilities (Standard Rules).[31] Unlike previous disability-specific instruments adopted by the UN[32] (which relied on a medical definition of disability focused on the condition of individuals),[33] the WPA focuses on disability from an equality perspective[34] and the Standard Rules emphasise equality and full participation in society.[35] For example, Rule 5 of the Standard Rules recognises 'the overall importance of accessibility in the process of the equalization of opportunities in all spheres of society' by, *inter alia*, calling on States to 'undertake measures to provide access to information and communication'.[36] Nevertheless, these instruments are not legally binding, which has limited their impact in improving the lives of persons with disabilities.[37]

The adoption of a thematic convention on the rights of persons with disabilities was necessary, given the failure of universal human rights instruments such as the ICCPR and the ICESCR to protect effectively their human rights[38] and given the limited impact of soft law instruments

[28] *Ibid.* [29] Lawson, 'United Nations Convention', 583–4.

[30] UN GA, Resolution 37/52: World Programme of Action Concerning Disabled Persons, 3 December 1982, UN Doc. A/RES/37/52.

[31] UN GA, Resolution 48/69: Standard Rules on the Equalization of Opportunities for Persons with Disabilities, 20 December 1993, UN Doc. A/RES/48/69 [hereafter 'Standard Rules'].

[32] Examples include UN GA, Resolution 2856 (XXVI): Declaration on the Rights of Mentally Retarded Persons, 20 December 1971; UN GA, Resolution 3447 (XXX): Declaration on the Rights of Disabled Persons, 9 December 1975.

[33] See, for example, R. Scotch, 'Models of Disability and the Americans with Disabilities Act', *Berkley Journal of Employment and Labor Law* 21 (2000), 214.

[34] Lawson, 'United Nations Convention', 581. [35] *Ibid.*, 582.

[36] UN GA, Resolution 48/69, Rule 5(b). [37] Lawson, 'United Nations Convention', 582.

[38] MacKay, 'United Nations Convention', 323.

such as the WPA or the Standard Rules.[39] Stein indicates that before the CRPD, there was no international human rights instrument that was both enforceable by and applicable to persons with disabilities based on their disability status.[40] The CRPD constitutes a significant landmark in the path towards reframing the interest of persons with disabilities in terms of human rights[41] and represents a move away from a perception of persons with disabilities as objects of care.[42] The focus on persons with disabilities as holders of human rights is reflected in Article 1 of the CRPD, which stresses that the purpose of this instrument is to 'promote, protect and ensure the full and equal enjoyment of all human rights and fundamental freedoms by all persons with disabilities, and to promote respect for their inherent dignity'.[43] Furthermore, the process for drafting the CRPD and the significant involvement of persons with disabilities and their representative organisations in this process has seen an increased presence of persons with disabilities in the human rights field.[44]

While the CRPD does not define 'disability', the Convention recognises that this is 'an evolving concept'[45] and provides guidance on the concept by stating that persons with disabilities 'include those who have long-term physical, mental, intellectual or sensory impairments which in interaction with various barriers may hinder their full and effective participation in society on an equal basis with others'.[46] Nevertheless, the absence of a definition of disability in the CRPD could risk the consistent protection of persons of disabilities that was sought by the Convention.[47] The language employed in Article 1 of the CRPD poses further challenges. The guidance on the concept of disability put forward in this article is non-exhaustive, but the explicit reference to persons with 'long-term. . .impairments' and the absence of an explicit reference to persons with temporary or recurrent conditions poses the risk that States will restrict the protection conferred on persons with disabilities to the examples provided in this article.[48]

39 Lawson, 'United Nations Convention', 582.
40 Stein, 'Quick Overview', 679.
41 Kayess and French, 'Out of Darkness', 1.
42 Lawson, 'United Nations Convention', 584.
43 CRPD, Art. 1.
44 Lawson, 'United Nations Convention', 617.
45 CRPD, para. (e), preamble.
46 *Ibid.*, Art. 1.
47 A. C. Hendriks, 'UN Convention of the Rights of Persons with Disabilities', *European Journal of Health Law* 14 (2007), 277.
48 Lawson, 'United Nations Convention', 595.

Despite these concerns, the CRPD reaffirms the move away from the medical model of disability, in favour of a predominantly social model[49] that perceives disability as a socially constructed phenomenon[50] resulting from 'the interaction between persons with impairments and attitudinal and environmental barriers that hinders their full and effective participation in society on an equal basis with others'.[51] Bielefeldt rightly welcomes this approach and comments that this is necessary for recognising the injustice and human rights violations caused by discriminatory practices.[52] Thus, the focus is no longer on adapting individuals to society, but on adapting society to accommodate the full spectrum of abilities.[53] The CRPD, therefore, calls for 'respect for difference' and for 'acceptance of persons with disabilities as part of human diversity and humanity'.[54] This approach protects the interests of persons with disabilities as people will full entitlements in society, rather than as disempowered victims.[55]

The CRPD tailors the application of established human rights to circumstances particular to persons with disabilities.[56] This process has led to the transformation of some of the fundamental rights, as well as the development of novel or strengthened formulations of human rights[57] in order to facilitate the practical enjoyment of these rights by persons with disabilities.[58] As suggested by Quinn and Degener, such a process does not undermine established human rights, but instead it bestows these rights with life in order to ensure their equal enjoyment by persons with disabilities.[59] The next section explores one such transformation of established human rights: the Convention's approach to the protection and promotion of the right to freedom of expression and opinion and access to information.

49 S. Fraser Butlin, 'The UN Convention on the Rights of Persons with Disabilities: Does the Equality Act 2010 Measure up to UK International Commitments?', *Industrial Law Journal* 40(4) (2011), 428.

50 Lawson, 'United Nations Convention', 572.

51 CRPD, para. (e), preamble.

52 H. Bielefeldt, 'New Inspiration for the Human Rights Debate: The Convention on the Rights of Persons with Disabilities', *Netherlands Quarterly of Human Rights* 52(3) (2007), 398.

53 Lawson, 'United Nations Convention', 573.

54 CRPD, Art. 3(d).

55 D. M. Smith, 'Who Says You're Disabled? The Role of Medical Evidence in the ADA Definition of Disability', *Tulane Law Review* 82(1) (2007), 71–2.

56 Kayess and French, 'Out of Darkness', 3.

57 *Ibid.*, 32.

58 Quinn and Degener, *Human Rights and Disability*, 296.

59 *Ibid.*

## 3 The right to freedom of expression and opinion and access to information under the CRPD

Persons with disabilities seeking to enforce their right to freedom of expression and access to information could rely on the ICCPR as a universal human rights instrument. Article 19 of the ICCPR seeks to protect the right to 'hold opinions without interference'[60] and the right to freedom of expression, which includes 'freedom to seek, receive and impart information and ideas of all kinds'.[61] Nevertheless, as noted in the previous section of this chapter, the ICCPR has been underused by persons with disabilities seeking to enforce their rights, given the absence of an express reference to disability under the prohibited grounds for differential treatment[62] and the fact that this instrument was developed based on an understanding of human rights from an able-bodied perspective.[63] The CRPD sought to remedy this limitation[64] by trying to clarify how existing human rights apply in a disability-specific context,[65] including with regard to the right to freedom of expression and access to information.

While Article 19 of the ICCPR relies on a negative formulation of this right (referring, for example, to the right to hold opinions without interference),[66] the CRPD modifies this into a positive obligation incumbent on States Parties to ensure the equal enjoyment of this right by persons with disabilities.[67] According to Article 21 of the CRPD, States Parties are required to 'take all appropriate measures to ensure that persons with disabilities can exercise the right to freedom of expression and opinion, including the freedom to seek, receive and impart information and ideas on an equal basis with others and through all forms of communication of their choice' by, *inter alia*, 'providing information intended for the general public. . .in accessible formats and technologies appropriate to different kinds of disabilities in a timely manner and without additional cost'.[68] Article 21 of the CRPD also requires States Parties to 'accept and facilitate' in official interactions the use of 'accessible means, modes and formats of communication', including Braille and

[60] ICCPR, Art. 19(1). [61] *Ibid.*, Art. 19(2).
[62] *Ibid.*, Art. 2(1); Stein, 'Quick Overview', 679.
[63] Kayess and French, 'Out of Darkness', 14.
[64] MacKay, 'United Nations Convention', 323.
[65] Kayess and French, 'Out of Darkness', 32. [66] ICCPR, Art. 19(1).
[67] CRPD, Art. 21; see Kayess and French, 'Out of Darkness', 32–3. [68] CRPD, Art. 21(a).

sign languages,[69] and to 'recognise and promote' the use of sign languages.[70] The imposition of positive obligations on States Parties to ensure the access of persons with disabilities to information and to facilitate the use of alternative means of communication is necessary for tackling the accessibility barriers faced by persons with disabilities.[71] As Dhanda rightly stresses, the absence of such provisions would render the right to freedom of expression and access to information meaningless for persons with disabilities.[72] Article 21 of the CRPD also calls on private actors to enable the access of persons with disabilities to information, although the language adopted in this regard is not mandatory. The mass media (including providers of information via the Internet) are merely encouraged to promote accessible services to persons with disabilities,[73] while private undertakings that offer services to the general public (including via the Internet) are urged to make their services accessible to persons with disabilities.[74] Relying on the mere encouragement of private actors to provide accessible services is unlikely to overcome the accessibility barriers faced by persons with disabilities, due to the lack of economic incentives for private actors to search for accessibility solutions.[75]

The CRPD recognises the important role of accessible ICTs in enabling persons with disabilities 'to live independently and participate fully in all aspects of life'.[76] Therefore, in addition to the specific obligations put forward under Article 21, States Parties are also required to comply with general provisions on accessibility under Article 9. This article calls on States Parties to, *inter alia*, 'take appropriate measures' to ensure that persons with disabilities enjoy equal access to ICTs.[77] This is to be ensured, among other means, through the identification and elimination of accessibility barriers.[78] States Parties are also required to ensure that private actors providing services to the general public 'take into account all aspects of accessibility for persons with disabilities'.[79] In addition,

[69] *Ibid.*, Art. 21(b). [70] *Ibid.*, Art. 21(e).

[71] A. Dhanda, 'Constructing a New Human Rights Lexicon: Convention on the Rights of Persons with Disabilities', *Sur: International Journal of Human Rights* 5–8 (2008), 49.

[72] *Ibid.* [73] CRPD, Art. 21(d). [74] *Ibid.*, Art. 21(e).

[75] European Commission Communications Committee (Cocom), *Report from the Inclusive Communications Subgroup*, 27 January 2004, Doc. No. COCOM04-08, 42. Cocom assists the EU Commission in exercising its executive powers in the communications sector; see: www.umic.pt/images/stories/publicacoes/COCOM04-08_subgroup.pdf (last accessed 21 February 2014).

[76] CRPD, Art. 9(1). [77] *Ibid.* [78] *Ibid.* [79] *Ibid.*, Art. 9(2)(b).

States Parties must promote 'appropriate forms of assistance and support' for ensuring that persons with disabilities can access information[80] and promote the accessibility of new ICTs (including the Internet)[81] and the integration of accessibility features at an early stage in the design and development of ICT products and services.[82] These provisions must be read alongside Articles 3 and 4 of the CRPD. Article 3 includes accessibility as one of the general principles of the Convention.[83] Under Article 4, the general obligations on States Parties include the requirement to 'undertake or promote research and development of universally designed' ICT products and services,[84] which are 'usable by all people, to the greatest extent possible, without the need for adaptation or specialized design'.[85]

Effective access to information can play an important role in enabling a wider range of human rights,[86] including the right to participate in political and public life (Article 29) and cultural life, recreation, leisure and sport (Article 30). For example, Article 30 of the CRPD requires States Parties to ensure, *inter alia*, that persons with disabilities 'enjoy access to television programmes. . .in accessible formats'.[87] These provisions recognise the important contribution that persons with disabilities can make to the life of the community and they are designed to enable the participation of persons with disabilities in society.[88] They seek to ensure 'an enhanced sense of belonging' for persons with disabilities[89] through 'full and effective participation and inclusion in society',[90] while at the same time respecting the inherent dignity and individual autonomy of these citizens.[91] As appropriately noted by Bielefeldt, these provisions are focused towards safeguarding the mutually complementary goals of social inclusion and respect for individual autonomy.[92] Furthermore, Stein and Lord emphasise the value of participation in society as an agent for inclusion and as an instrument for social change,[93] with the aim to tackle attitudinal barriers faced by persons with disabilities in society. Similarly, MacKay notes that the best approach for challenging stereotypes is through interactions between persons with and without disabilities.[94] The full participation of persons with

[80] *Ibid.*, Art. 9(2)(f). [81] *Ibid.*, Art. 9(2)(g). [82] *Ibid.*, Art. 9(2)(h).
[83] *Ibid.*, Art. 3(f). [84] *Ibid.*, Art. 4(1)(f). [85] *Ibid.*, Art. 2.
[86] *Ibid.*, para. (v), preamble. [87] *Ibid.*, Art. 30(1)(b). [88] *Ibid.*, para. (m), preamble.
[89] *Ibid.* [90] *Ibid.*, Art. 3(c) [91] *Ibid.*, Art. 3(a).
[92] Bielefeldt, 'New Inspiration', 398–9. [93] Stein and Lord, 'Participatory Justice', 178.
[94] MacKay, 'United Nations Convention', 329.

disabilities in society is crucial for tackling stereotypical perceptions and prejudice and for safeguarding human dignity.[95]

Ensuring the 'full and effective participation' of persons with disabilities in society[96] requires reliance not only on civil and political rights (such as the right to freedom of expression and opinion and access to information)[97] but also on economic, social and cultural rights (such as the right to education,[98] health,[99] participation in cultural life, recreation, leisure and sport).[100] Achieving this objective also depends on the availability of an infrastructure that enables full participation in society.[101] Therefore, the CRPD adopts a comprehensive approach to disability,[102] which reaffirms 'the universality, indivisibility, interdependence and interrelatedness of all human rights and fundamental freedoms'[103] and which brings together civil and political rights as well as economic, social and cultural rights,[104] resulting in 'hybrid rights'.[105]

The CRPD seeks to move away from the artificial distinction between these two sets of rights, which derives from the incorporation of civil and political rights into the ICCPR and of economic, social and cultural rights into the ICESCR.[106] The adoption of two separate covenants in 1966 has created a false separation between these sets of rights,[107] with the former framed predominantly in negative terms (preventing State interference with these rights) and subject to immediate realisation.[108] In contrast, economic, social and cultural rights rely mainly on positive formulations (calling for State action) and are subject to progressive realisation, due to resource implications.[109] This distinction undermines the interrelationship and interdependence between these categories of human rights.[110] It also overlooks the fact that the nature of these categories of rights (positive/negative) is not so strict. Economic, social and cultural rights may also prevent State interference, such as the requirement on States Parties to the ICESCR to respect the liberty of parents/legal guardians to

95 D. G. Réaume, 'Discrimination and Dignity', *Louisiana Law Review* 63 (2003), 28.

96 CRPD, Art. 3(c). 97 *Ibid.*, Art. 21. 98 *Ibid.*, Art. 24. 99 *Ibid.*, Art. 25.

100 *Ibid.*, Art. 30; see Stein, 'Quick Overview', 680. 101 CRPD, Art. 9.

102 Quinn and Degener, *Human Rights and Disability*, 296; Stein, 'Quick Overview', 680

103 CRPD, para. (c), preamble. 104 Kayess and French, 'Out of Darkness', 33.

105 MacKay, 'United Nations Convention', 330; Lawson, 'United Nations Convention', 576.

106 Dhanda, 'Constructing a New Human Rights Lexicon', 55. 107 *Ibid.*, p. 48.

108 ICCPR, Art. 2.

109 ICESCR, Art. 2(1); see Dhanda, 'Constructing a New Human Rights Lexicon', 55.

110 P. Weller, 'Human Rights and Social Justice: the Convention on the Rights of Persons with Disabilities and the Quiet Revolution in International Law', *Public Space: The Journal of Law and Social Justice* 4 (2009), 74 (referring to work by Amartya Sen).

choose schools for their children which conform with their own convictions, subject to minimum educational standards.[111] Furthermore, civil and political rights may also demand State action, such as the requirement on States Parties to the ICCPR to guarantee the free expression of the will of the electors at genuine periodic elections by universal and equal suffrage held by secret ballot.[112]

The CRPD marks a positive step towards addressing these concerns by, *inter alia*, explicitly putting an end to the strict distinction between negative rights and positive rights[113] and by acknowledging the connection between the exercise of the right to freedom of expression and access to information and the development of accessible infrastructures.[114] Yet, the success of the CRPD in this respect is potentially weakened by the inclusion of Article 4(2) in the Convention, which maintains the approach of progressive realisation for economic, social and cultural rights and adds that this is without prejudice to Convention obligations subject to immediate realisation.[115] This provision, which has been included as part of the general obligations of States Parties, has been criticised for being too ambiguous[116] as the CRPD does not state explicitly which provisions are subject to immediate realisation and which provisions are to be implemented progressively.[117] The reference in Article 4(2) of the CRPD to the progressive realisation of economic, social and cultural rights is most likely due to cost-related considerations associated with the implementation of the Convention.[118] Quinn comments that the notion of progressive realisation reflects 'an inescapable reality that resources are finite and some changes take time' but stresses that States Parties must put in place measures aimed towards a 'positive dynamic' of change.[119] Similarly, MacKay argues that the reference to the progressive realisation of certain rights should not be read as 'a free pass for governments' to overlook accessibility, given that States Parties are expected to take 'concrete steps' in meeting their obligations under the CRPD.[120]

111 ICESCR, Art. 13(3).
112 ICCPR, Article 25(b); I am grateful to Yvonne Donders for this point.
113 Kayess and French, 'Out of Darkness', 32.
114 Dhanda, 'Constructing a New Human Rights Lexicon', 49; see CRPD, Arts. 21(b), 9(2)(g) and (h).
115 *Ibid.*, Art. 4(2); see also ICESCR, Art. 2(1).
116 Dhanda, 'Constructing a New Human Rights Lexicon', 55.
117 Quinn, 'United Nations Convention', 44. 118 *Ibid.* 119 *Ibid.*
120 MacKay, 'United Nations Convention', 330.

Parallels can be drawn with the call on States Parties to the ICESCR to 'take steps, individually and through international assistance and co-operation, especially economic and technical, to the maximum of its available resources, with a view to achieving progressively the full realization of the rights recognized in the present Covenant by all appropriate means, including particularly the adoption of legislative measures'.[121] As clarified by the Committee on Economic, Social and Cultural Rights in its General Comment No. 3, the call for the 'progressive realisation' of economic, social and cultural rights requires a commitment on the part of States Parties to take steps towards the full realisation of these rights 'within a reasonably short time after the Covenant's entry into force' and these steps 'should be deliberate, concrete and targeted as clearly as possible towards meeting the obligations recognized in the Covenant'.[122] A similar call for 'deliberate, concrete and targeted measures' can be made with regard to the implementation of the accessibility provisions put forward under the CRPD, especially if we consider the urgency in tackling accessibility barriers in the ICT sector, as technology progresses.

The CRPD reinforces the fact that the full and equal enjoyment of the right to freedom of expression and access to information by persons with disabilities[123] requires the imposition of a positive obligation on States Parties.[124] This includes, *inter alia*, a requirement on States Parties to provide information intended for the general public 'in accessible formats and technologies appropriate to different kinds of disabilities in a timely manner and without additional cost'.[125] This section stressed the importance of access to information as 'a prerequisite' for the exercise of other citizenship rights,[126] including the right to participate in the political and public life (Article 29) and in cultural life, recreation, leisure and sport (Article 30). The next section explores in more detail the potential of the CRPD in tackling the barriers encountered by persons with disabilities in accessing information and communication technologies.

121 ICESCR, Art. 2(1).

122 UN CESCR, General Comment No. 3: Article 2(1): The Nature of States Parties Obligations, 14 December 1990, UN Doc. E/1991/23 (SUPP) [hereafter GC 3].

123 CRPD, Arts. 1 and 21.

124 Kayess and French, 'Out of Darkness', 32.

125 CRPD, Art. 21(a).

126 M. Feintuck and M. Varney, *Media Regulation, Public Interest and the Law*, 2nd edn (Edinburgh University Press, 2006).

## 4 The potential impact of the CRPD in tackling accessibility barriers in the ICT sector

Despite technological advances that can facilitate access to and the use of ICTs (including audio description (video description),[127] closed signing[128] and the availability of subtitles (captions)[129] in live broadcasts enabled by speech-to-text technologies[130]), persons with disabilities continue to encounter a wide range of barriers to accessibility.[131] Such barriers include, *inter alia*, on-screen displays (such as electronic programme guides – EPGs)[132] that are difficult to navigate, the absence or

[127] Audio description (video description) consists of a commentary during pauses in the soundtrack to explain on-screen action or to describe details such as locations or characters. See Ofcom, *Code on Television Access Services*, 20 December 2010, http://stakeholders.ofcom.org.uk/binaries/broadcast/other-codes/ctas.pdf (last accessed 23 February 2014). Technically, the term video description refers to 'the provision of verbal description of on screen visual elements that are provided during natural pauses in dialogue', while audio description refers to 'verbal descriptions provided during a live (non-recorded) performance'. See J. Simpson, 'Inclusive Information and Communication Technologies for People with Disabilities', *Disability Studies Quarterly* 29(1) (2009), http://dsq-sds.org/article/view/167/167 (last accessed 23 February 2014). For the purpose of the present chapter, rather than focusing on the technical details that may differentiate between these terms, the analysis is concerned with the principles associated with the regulation of ICTs and as a result the terms audio description and video description are used interchangeably.

[128] Closed signing allows the public to switch the sign interpreter on and off. See M. George and L. Lennard, 'Ease of Use Issues with Domestic Electronic Communications Equipment', Ofcom Research Audit, 17 July 2007, 4.17, http://stakeholders.ofcom.org.uk/binaries/research/tv-research/easeofuse.pdf (last accessed 23 February 2014).

[129] Subtitles (captions) refer to the display of text on-screen, representing the speech and the sound effects from a particular programme. See Ofcom Code (2010). Technically, the terms subtitles and captions are different. Subtitles are intended for hearing people who need a translation of the dialogue while captions are intended for persons with hearing disabilities who need to be provided information about the dialogue and the accompanying sound effects. See http://screenfont.ca/learn/ (last accessed 23 February 2014). As the present chapter focuses on the principles associated with the regulation of ICTs rather than on the technical details that may differentiate between these terms, the discussion uses the terms 'subtitles' and 'captions' interchangeably.

[130] Speech-to-text technologies enable the availability of subtitling in live broadcasts. See 'MeAC: Measuring Progress of eAccessibility in Europe: Assessment of the Status of eAccessibility in Europe', Empirica, Work Research Centre, October 2007, 49 [hereafter MeAC report].

[131] CRPD, para. (k), preamble.

[132] An electronic programme guide (EPG) provides information on the services available and enables viewers to navigate between different programmes. See OFTEL, 'Digital Television and Interactive Services: Ensuring Access on Fair, Reasonable and Non-discriminatory Terms', March 1998.

poor quality of captions and audio descriptions and websites designed without accessibility features.[133] These barriers are likely to hinder participation in society and 'undermine the effective enjoyment of a wider range of human rights'.[134] In addition to these concerns, regulatory frameworks for the ICT sector do not go far enough in protecting the interests of persons with disabilities and seem to respond more to industry voices rather than the voices of the people.[135] If implemented effectively, the CRPD has the potential to address some of these challenges. It may deliver a regulatory framework that is focused on tackling accessibility barriers and responsive to the voices of persons with disabilities.[136]

The accessibility of ICT products and services is often approached as an afterthought by relying on add-on solutions such as software, hardware or peripheral devices designed to make mainstream products accessible for persons with disabilities.[137] The installation of these devices requires additional expense from persons with disabilities and may exclude some people from accessing ICTs.[138] On the other hand, accessibility solutions integrated into mainstream products at the outset reduce the cost of accessibility and share this cost among all consumers.[139] Integrated solutions also send the message that manufacturers of ICT products have the interests of persons with disabilities in mind when developing a product and service.[140] Unfortunately, regulatory frameworks tend to confer a significant degree of flexibility on industry players in addressing accessibility. Consequently, regulatory frameworks have failed to tackle the barriers faced by persons with disabilities in the ICT sector. For example, in the USA (a signatory to

133 George and Lennard, 'Ease of Use Issues', 4.17.

134 Lawson, 'United Nations Convention', 567.

135 E. Varney, 'Disability Rights in the Communications Sector: An Examination of Digital Television Regulation in the United Kingdom', *Communications Law* 13(6) (2008), 187–96. See also E. Varney, *Disability and Information Technology: A Comparative Study in Media Regulation* (Cambridge University Press, 2013).

136 Quinn, 'United Nations Convention', 43.

137 47 USC §§ 617(a)(2)(B) and (b)(2)(B).

138 K. Peltz Strauss, 'Past and Present: Making the Case for a Regulatory Approach to Addressing Disability Discrimination in the Provision of Emerging Broadband and Cable Technologies', Broadband and Cable Television Law 2010, Developments in Cable Technology, Practising Law Institute, New York, 2010, 943.

139 Canadian Association of the Deaf (CAD), Reply Comment to CRTC's Public Hearing 2008-8: Unresolved Issues related to the Accessibility of Telecommunications and Broadcasting Services to Persons with Disabilities, 10 June 2008, Doc. 961675, paragraph 18.

140 G. Goggin and C. Newell, 'The Business of Digital Disability', *Information Society* 23 (2007), 160.

the CRPD),[141] section 716 of the Communications Act (as added by the Twenty-First Century Communications and Video Accessibility Act),[142] places too much discretion in the hands of the industry, as it allows market players to satisfy the requirement for accessible ICT products and services by either integrating accessibility solutions or by relying on add-on solutions.[143] A similar approach has been adopted by the European Union (EU), which has signed and ratified the CRPD[144] in a development seen as having significant constitutional importance.[145] The influence of the Convention can be seen, among others, in the proposed Directive 'on implementing the principle of equal treatment between persons irrespective of [*inter alia*] disability',[146] which makes explicit reference to the accessibility principles established in the CRPD (e.g., independent living, full participation in all areas of life).[147] Recital 19d of the proposed Directive states that accessibility 'can be provided by a variety of means, including the application of the "universal design" principle'.[148] The Citizens' Rights Directive[149] (which was adopted as part of the EU regulatory framework for electronic communications

141 The CRPD was signed by the USA on 30 July 2009. See UN SCRPD, UN Enable: Convention and Optional Protocol Signatures and Ratifications, 2011c; see: www.un.org/disabilities/countries.asp?id=166 (last accessed 23 February 2014).

142 47 USC § 613; Communications Act of 1934, Pub. L. 416, 48 Stat. 1064 (1934), codified at 47 USC §§ 151ff.; Pub. L. 111–260, 124 Stat. 2751, 8 October 2010 [hereafter CVAA].

143 47 USC §§ 617(a)(2)(B) and (b)(2)(B).

144 The EU signed the CRPD on 30 March 2007 and ratified the Convention on 23 December 2010. See UN SCRPD (2011c); *Council Decision of 24 November 2009 Concerning the Conclusion, by the European Community, of the United Nations Convention on the Rights of Persons with Disabilities*, OJ No. L23/35, 27 January 2010. See G. de Búrca, 'The EU in the Negotiations of the UN Disability Convention', *European Law Review* 35(2) (2010), 174–96; L. Waddington, 'The European Union and the United Nations Convention on the Rights of Persons with Disabilities: A Story of Exclusive and Shared Competences', *Maastricht Journal of European and Comparative Law* 18(4) (2011), 431–53.

145 O. M. Arnardóttir and G. Quinn (eds.), *The UN Convention on the Rights of Persons with Disabilities: European and Scandinavian Perspectives*, vol. 100 (Leiden: Martinus Nijhoff, Brill, 2009), xvi.

146 European Commission (EC), Proposal for a Council Directive on implementing the Principle of Equal Treatment between Persons irrespective of Religion or Belief, Disability, Age or Sexual Orientation, 2 July 2008, Doc. No. COM(2008)426 [hereafter the proposed Directive].

147 *Ibid.*, recitals 19b–d. See CRPD, Art. 9.

148 Proposed Directive, recital 19d, 10511/2/10 REV 2.

149 Directive 2009/136/EC of 25 November 2009 (Citizens' Rights Directive), OJ No. L337/11, 18 December 2009.

networks and services[150] and which amends the Universal Service Directive)[151] recognises the need to create 'a market for widely available products and services incorporating facilities for disabled end-users'.[152] Nevertheless, this provision is included in the non-binding preamble of the Directive, it merely requires Member States to 'promote' the creation of such a market and makes no specific reference to the development of products based on universal design principles.[153] More could be done to promote integrated accessibility solutions as preferable to add-on solutions, as the latter entail additional expense for persons with disabilities and risks leaving them behind, as technology progresses.[154]

The CRPD sets a higher threshold, as universal design is the preferred approach, with add-on solutions being relied on if necessary.[155] As noted by Kayess and French, this approach focuses on promoting the full and equal participation of all citizens in society, by building environments that can adapt to the full range of abilities present in society.[156] The CRPD sends the message that accessibility is an integral part of the design and development of ICT products and services. Yet, the diverse accessibility requirements of persons with disabilities and the limited consumer power of these individual groups mean that market players often lack the economic incentives to integrate accessibility features at the design stage.[157] This situation is unlikely to improve in the near future without regulatory intervention.[158]

Persons with disabilities are disadvantaged by the reliance in some jurisdictions on a medical model of disability. In the USA, although the Americans with Disabilities Act (ADA)[159] reflects the social model of disability, the courts have reinforced the medical model by conditioning

150 This framework includes Directive 2002/21/EC (Framework Directive); Directive 2002/19/EC (Access Directive); Directive 2002/20/EC (Authorisation Directive); Directive 2002/22/EC (Universal Service Directive); Directive 2002/58/EC (Data Protection Directive), as amended by Directive 2009/140/EC (Better Law-making Directive) and Directive 2009/136/EC (Citizens' Rights Directive).

151 Directive 2002/22/EC of 7 March 2002 (Universal Service Directive), OJ No. L108/51, 24 April 2002.

152 Citizens' Rights Directive, recital 9.

153 *Ibid.*

154 Peltz Strauss, 'Past and Present', 943.

155 CRPD, Art. 4(1)(f).

156 Kayess and French, 'Out of Darkness', 10–11.

157 Peltz Strauss, 'Past and Present', 950.

158 Alliance for Equality of Blind Canadians (AEBC), Final Reply to CRTC's Public Hearing 2008-8: Unresolved Issues related to the Accessibility of Telecommunications and Broadcasting Services to Persons with Disabilities, 1 February 2009, Doc. No. 1004715, para. 16.

159 42 USC § 12101ff.

the application of the ADA on the provision of medical evidence.[160] This could be due to the use of the term 'impairment' in the ADA[161] (also preserved in the ADA Amendments Act of 2008)[162] which, according to Smith, creates a tension between social and medical visions of disability.[163] Although the CRPD employs the term 'impairment',[164] the Convention relies on a predominantly social vision of disability,[165] which seeks to tackle the societal barriers encountered by persons with disabilities[166] and for society to accommodate a wide range of abilities.[167] Organisations representing the interests of persons with disabilities have expressed unease regarding the use of the term 'impairment', a preferable term being 'condition', as this is perceived to be 'more inclusive and less stigmatising'.[168] However, despite these concerns (which can be addressed through guidance from the Committee on the Rights of Persons with Disabilities),[169] the CRPD has a lot to offer in strengthening the social vision of disability. The CRPD calls for 'a positive appreciation'[170] of disability as 'part of human diversity and humanity',[171] with the ultimate goal of creating a society without barriers, which accommodates the whole spectrum of abilities.[172]

Quinn has argued that in the context of disability, effective equality provisions must go beyond ensuring respect for differences and must accommodate such differences through positive measures.[173] Unfortunately, at national and supranational levels, the provisions pursuing these objectives are often subject to hardship defences. These defences tend to limit the application of provisions that require, *inter alia*, the removal of accessibility barriers, on the basis of factors such as costs. For example, the Canadian Human Rights Act[174] expects the accommodation of the interests of persons with disabilities up to the point of 'undue hardship',

160 Scotch, 'Models of Disability', 218.
161 Smith, 'Who Says You're Disabled?', 7.
162 Americans with Disabilities Amendments Act of 2008, Public Law 110-325 (2008). See 42 USC section 12102(4)(A).
163 Smith, 'Who Says You're Disabled?', 11.
164 CRPD, Art. 1.
165 Fraser Butlin, 'UN Convention', 428.
166 CRPD, paras. (e) and (k), preamble and Art. 1.
167 *Ibid.*, Art. 3(d). See discussion in Lawson, 'United Nations Convention', 573.
168 Lawson, 'United Nations Convention', 594.
169 *Ibid.*, 595; Hendriks, 'UN Convention', 277. The role of this Committee is discussed in section 5.
170 Bielefeldt, 'New Inspiration', 397.
171 CRPD, Art. 3(d).
172 Hendriks, 'UN Convention', 279.
173 Quinn, 'United Nations Convention', 43.
174 Canadian Human Rights Act, RSC 1985, c. H.-6.

to be assessed in light of factors such as 'health, safety and cost'.[175] The test adopted under the Canadian Broadcasting Act[176] requires that accessibility programming for persons with disabilities (e.g., captions, video description) should be provided 'as resources become available' for this purpose.[177] Similarly, in the USA, the removal of accessibility barriers to places of public accommodation is required only where this is 'readily achievable'[178] (defined as 'easily accomplishable and able to be carried out without much difficulty or expense').[179] Exemptions may also be allowed if access would require 'fundamental alteration' of a business or would impose an 'undue burden'[180] (i.e. a 'significant difficulty or expense').[181] Limitations on accessibility requirements have also been included in the proposed EU directive 'on implementing the principle of equal treatment between persons irrespective of [*inter alia*] disability',[182] which states that such requirements do not apply if they impose 'a disproportionate burden',[183] to be assessed, *inter alia*, in light of estimated costs.[184] The above-mentioned defences rely on vague terms, leading to disagreement on the precise meaning of terms such as 'undue hardship', 'undue burden' or 'disproportionate burden'.[185] Furthermore, a threshold on accessibility that is set too low or that can be evaded easily can have only a limited impact (if at all) in tackling accessibility barriers.[186] The above-mentioned limitations also reflect a perception of accessibility through an economic lens (concerned with cost implications) rather than a human rights lens (focused on equality of access to information as a citizenship right).[187] Such limitations fail to give sufficient weight to wider social benefits of accessibility, including the participation of persons with disabilities in society, as citizens.

[175] *Ibid.*, § 15(2). See B. D. Pooran and C. Wilkie, 'Failing to Achieve Equality: Disability Rights in Australia, Canada, and the United States', *Journal of Law and Social Policy* 20 (2005), 6.

[176] Canadian Broadcasting Act, SC 1991, c. 11. [177] *Ibid.*, § 3(1)(p).

[178] 42 USC § 12182(b)(2)(A)(iv). See K. J. Coco, 'Beyond the Price Tag: An Economic Analysis of Title III of the Americans with Disabilities Act', *Kansas Journal of Law and Public Policy* 20(1) (2010), 64.

[179] 42 USC § 12102(2)(A). [180] *Ibid.*, § 12182(b)(2)(A)(ii).

[181] 28 Code of Federal Regulations (CFR), § 36.104. See C. Burke Robertson, 'Providing Access to the Future: How the Americans with Disabilities Act can Remove Barriers in Cyberspace', *Denver University Law Review* 79(2) (2001), 220.

[182] Proposed Directive. [183] *Ibid.*, Arts. 4(1) and 4a(1). [184] *Ibid.*, Art. 4b.

[185] L. Kerzner and D. Baker, 'Law Reform Analysis: A Canadians with Disabilities Act?', Council of Canadians with Disabilities, 14 May 1999.

[186] Kayess and French, 'Out of Darkness', 9. [187] *Ibid.*

The implementation of the CRPD should lead to an increased perception of accessibility through a human rights lens. The Convention stresses that persons with disabilities are entitled to the equal enjoyment of all human rights and freedoms (including the right of access to information)[188] and calls on States Parties to 'take all appropriate steps' to provide reasonable accommodation for the requirements of persons with disabilities.[189] Furthermore, the denial of reasonable accommodation is recognised as a form of discrimination based on disability.[190] In exercising the duty to provide reasonable accommodation, States Parties are expected, *inter alia*, to engage proactively in identifying and removing accessibility barriers.[191] In the ICT sector, this could produce systemic changes to accommodate the requirements of persons with disabilities.[192] Nevertheless, this potential is limited by Article 2 of the CRPD, which states that reasonable accommodation requires 'necessary and appropriate modification and adjustments not imposing a disproportionate or undue burden'.[193] As stressed by Kayess and French, the limitations based on either disproportionate or undue burdens pose the risk that the obligations will be avoided whenever the lower of these thresholds apply.[194] Further unease is caused by the use of the term 'undue burden', as reference to the term *burden* can activate stereotypical perceptions and prejudice with regard to persons with disabilities and can undermine the wider objectives of the CRPD for promoting equality for persons with disabilities[195] and the understanding of disability as part of human diversity.[196] The limitations to reasonable accommodation stated under Article 2 of the CRPD can be particularly problematic in the ICT sector, as regulators have often proven to be more sympathetic to industry concerns regarding accessibility costs, rather than citizenship concerns raised by persons with disabilities, calling for equal access to information.[197]

National and supranational provisions addressing the accessibility of ICTs tend to reflect a hierarchy of disabilities, concentrating more on protecting the rights of persons with sensory disabilities (including blind and partially sighted people and deaf and hard-of-hearing people),

[188] CRPD, Arts. 1 and 21. [189] *Ibid.*, Art. 5(3). [190] *Ibid.*, Art. 2.

[191] Lawson, 'United Nations Convention', 598.

[192] A. Lawson, 'Disability and Employment in the Equality Act 2010: Opportunities Seized, Lost and Generated', *Industrial Law Journal* 40(4) (2011), 369.

[193] Article 2, CRPD. [194] Kayess and French, 'Out of Darkness', 27. [195] *Ibid.*

[196] CRPD, Art. 3(d).

[197] E. Varney, 'The Protection of Age and Disability Rights in the Regulation of Digital Television in the European Union', *Utilities Law Review 2007/2008* 17(1) (2008), 6–16.

overlooking the rights of persons with dexterity and cognitive disabilities.[198] Therefore, while provisions tend to be put in place to ensure the availability of closed captions and audio description, these provisions tend to miss out on accessibility measures such as the design of keypads with well-spaced buttons or the design of easy-to-navigate on-screen displays.[199] For example, in Canada (which has signed and ratified the CRPD),[200] the Broadcasting and Telecommunications Policy CRTC 2009-430 adopted by the Canadian Radio-television and Telecommunications Commission,[201] addresses the accessibility concerns of persons with sensory disabilities by putting forward provisions on closed captioning, video description and audio description.[202] These provisions tend to be more favourable to deaf and hard-of-hearing people (requiring the captioning of 100 per cent of programming),[203] than for blind and partially sighted people (with a minimum threshold of four hours per week of described programming).[204] This is due to higher costs involved in producing described programming.[205] Unfortunately, this instrument overlooks the accessibility concerns of persons with cognitive and dexterity disabilities. Similar challenges can be identified in the United States of America, where the provisions on closed captioning under section 713 (a–e) of the Communications Act (requiring that 100 per cent of programming broadcast since the start of 1998 be captioned)[206] are more generous than the requirements for video description under section 713 (f–h) (with a minimum threshold of four hours per week of described programming).[207] In the EU, Article 7 of the Audiovisual Media Services Directive[208] aims to facilitate the access of blind and partially sighted people and deaf and hard-of-hearing people to audiovisual media

198 E. Varney, 'A Hierarchy of Disability Rights? A Comparative Examination of the Regulation of Digital Television in the United States of America and the United Kingdom', *Northern Ireland Legal Quarterly* 60(4) (2009), 421–42.
199 MeAC report, 6.
200 Canada signed the CRPD on 30 March 2007 and ratified the Convention on 11 March 2010. See SCRPD (2011c).
201 Canadian Radio-television and Telecommunications Commission, Broadcasting and Telecom Regulatory Policy CRTC 2009-430: Accessibility of Telecommunications and Broadcasting Services, 21 July 2009, File: 8665-C12-200807943.
202 *Ibid.*, para. 4. 203 *Ibid.*, paras. 73–7. 204 *Ibid.*, paras. 103–13.
205 *Ibid.*, para. 105. 206 47 USC § 613(a–e). 207 *Ibid.*, section 613(f–h).
208 Directive 2010/13/EU of 10 March 2010 on the Coordination of Certain Provisions Laid Down by Law, Regulation or Administrative Action in Member States Concerning the Provision of Audiovisual Media Services (AMS Directive), OJ No. L95/1, 14 April 2010.

services,[209] although no reference is made to protecting the interests of persons with cognitive or dexterity disabilities. A similar approach is taken in the provisions on 'must carry' obligations put forward under Article 31(a) of the Universal Service Directive (as amended by the Citizens' Rights Directive),[210] which enable EU Member States to impose obligations for the transmission of, *inter alia*, accessibility services.[211] Although Recital 48 of the Citizens' Rights Directive provides a non-exhaustive list of services concerned, the examples listed are confined to services designed to assist persons with sensory disabilities.[212] More needs to be done to ensure that all persons with disabilities can enjoy effective access to information, in order to enable the effective participation in society of all citizens[213] and to ensure that advances in technology do not lead to the disempowerment and isolation of persons with disabilities.[214]

The CRPD promotes the interests of all persons with disabilities[215] and its effective implementation should lead to a move away from the hierarchy of disabilities currently experienced across jurisdictions.[216] For example, Articles 9 and 21 of the CRPD refer to the rights of *all* persons with disabilities. In fact, Article 21 calls for information intended for the general public, to be provided 'in accessible formats and technologies appropriate to different kinds of disabilities in a timely manner and without additional cost'.[217] Furthermore, by calling for the protection and promotion of the full range of human rights and fundamental freedoms and their full and equal enjoyment by 'all persons with disabilities', as well as the promotion of 'respect for their inherent dignity',[218] the CRPD emphasises the equal worth of all human beings, irrespective of abilities.[219] This is vital for defeating exclusion.[220]

209 *Ibid.*, Art. 7. 210 Universal Service Directive, Art. 31(1). 211 *Ibid.*
212 Citizens' Rights Directive, recital 48.
213 J. L Gregg, 'Policy-making in the Public Interests: A Contextual Analysis in the Passage of Closed-captioning Policy', *Disability and Society* 21(5) (2006), 537.
214 L. Johnson and E. Moxon, 'In Whose Service? Technology, Care and Disabled People: the Case for a Disability Politics Perspective', *Disability and Society* 13(2) (1998), 246 (quoting Oliver).
215 CRPD, Art. 1.
216 J. Campbell, 'Valuing Diversity: The Disability Agenda – We've Only Just Begun', *Disability and Society* 17(4) (2002), 471–8; M. Deal, 'Disabled People's Attitudes towards Other Impairment Groups: A Hierarchy of Impairments', *Disability and Society* 18(7) (2003), 898.
217 CRPD, Art. 21(a). 218 *Ibid.*, Art. 1.
219 Kayess and French, 'Out of Darkness', 11. 220 *Ibid.*

One further challenge associated with national and supranational frameworks for regulating the ICT sector concerns the absence or limited involvement of persons with disabilities in policy-making. For example, in Canada, the Canadian Radio-television and Telecommunications Commission has been criticised for its reactive stance towards disability issues and for limited leadership on these issues,[221] leading to calls for a more proactive approach and for regular consultation with organisations representing the interests of persons with disabilities.[222] In the EU, the proposed Directive 'on implementing the principle of equal treatment between persons irrespective of [*inter alia*] disability'[223] sets a low threshold for consultation with organisations representing the interests of persons with disabilities, merely requiring Member States to 'encourage dialogue with relevant stakeholders' that have a legitimate interest in combating disability discrimination,[224] while the call for involving these organisations in policy-making is confined to the non-binding preamble.[225] A more proactive approach is put forward in Article 33(1) of the Universal Service Directive (as amended by the Citizens' Rights Directive), which requires Member States to ensure that national regulatory authorities take into account, 'as far as appropriate', the views of 'disabled consumers' and establish a consultation mechanism in which consumer interests in ICTs are given 'due consideration'.[226] Yet, this provision relies on a perception of persons with disabilities as economic actors and makes no reference to the need to involve persons with disabilities in policy-making. An example of good practice at national level can be provided by the United Kingdom (which has signed and ratified the CRPD and the Optional Protocol),[227] as section 304 of the

221 Connectus Consulting Inc., *Stakeholder Consultations on Accessibility Issues for Persons with Disabilities*, Final Report submitted to the Canadian Radio-television and Telecommunications Commission, 18 April 2008.

222 The Neil Squire Society (NSS), *Initial Response to CRTC's Public Hearing 2008–8: Unresolved Issues related to the Accessibility of Telecommunications and Broadcasting Services to Persons with Disabilities*, 24 July 2008, Doc. No. 930960, para. 12. See also A. Clement *et al.*, 'Debating Universal Access in the Canadian Context: The Role of Public Interest Organizations', in M. Moll and L. R. Shade (eds.), *Ecommerce vs. E-commons: Communications in the Public Interest* (Ottawa: Canadian Centre for Policy Alternatives, 2002), 23–48.

223 Proposed Directive. 224 *Ibid.*, Art. 11. 225 *Ibid.*, recital 26.

226 Universal Service Directive, Art. 33(1).

227 The UK signed the CRPD on 30 March 2007 and ratified it on 8 June 2009. In addition, the UK signed the Optional Protocol on 26 February 2009 and ratified it on 7 August 2009. See SCRPD (2011c).

Communications Act requires the Communications Regulator Ofcom to consult, *inter alia*, persons representing the interests of persons with sensory disabilities as part of the process for issuing and reviewing the Code on Television Access Services.[228] The provision could have been improved by an explicit reference to other disabilities (in addition to sensory disabilities), including cognitive and dexterity disabilities.

The CRPD raises the bar regarding the level of involvement in policy-making that should be ensured for organisations representing the interest of persons with disabilities. Under Article 4(3), one of the general obligations of States Parties is to 'closely consult with and actively involve persons with disabilities. . .through their representative organisations' in any 'decision-making processes concerning issues relating to persons with disabilities'.[229] Persons with disabilities are in the best position to identify accessibility barriers and to find solutions for eliminating these barriers.[230] This has been seen to reflect a 'transformation of the slogan 'nothing about us without us' from a campaign anthem to a non-negotiable principle of disability rights.[231] In order to be effective, any consultation process with persons with disabilities and their representative organisations must have a real impact and their views must be adequately taken into account to shape policy-making. Furthermore, the active involvement of persons with disabilities in policy-making increases the presence of these citizens in the political arena[232] and promotes respect for their dignity.[233]

The visibility of persons with disabilities in policy-making will gradually increase as the Convention is implemented. Lawson, for example, refers to the enhanced capacity of organisations representing the interests of persons with disabilities to engage in continuing efforts to ensure the full and equal enjoyment of human rights.[234] Kayess and French comment further that the CRPD has empowered persons with disabilities to participate on an equal basis with others in shaping policies at both national and international levels.[235] Similarly, Quinn and Degener note

228 Communications Act of 2003, c. 21, s. 304. 229 CRPD, Art. 4(3).
230 AEBC, Final Reply, 2009.
231 Dhanda, 'Constructing a New Human Rights Lexicon', 50.
232 Quinn and Degener, *Human Rights and Disability*, 294.
233 Council of Canadians with Disabilities (CCD), *Initial Response to CRTC's Public Hearing 2008-8: Unresolved Issues related to the Accessibility of Telecommunications and Broadcasting Services to Persons with Disabilities*, 24 July 2008, Doc. No. 931981, para. 2.1.3.
234 Lawson, 'United Nations Convention', 618.
235 Kayess and French, 'Out of Darkness', 4.

that the Convention could provide an important channel for the mainstreaming of disability in the monitoring machinery of international human rights treaties, given that the CRPD was intended to complement rather than replace international human rights instruments such as the ICCPR and the ICESCR.[236]

So far, the objective of mainstreaming disability concerns into UN standards and processes for safeguarding the right to freedom of expression and opinion and access to information, has led to mixed results. In a report on the promotion and protection of the right to freedom of opinion and expression (focused on access to the Internet), Special Rapporteur La Rue[237] recognised that persons with disabilities 'often face barriers to accessing the Internet in a way that is meaningful, relevant and useful to them in their daily lives'[238] and called on States to 'adopt effective and concrete policies and strategies, developed in consultation with individuals from all segments of society… to make the Internet widely available, accessible and affordable to all'.[239] However, the issue of access to the Internet by persons with disabilities is framed as a call for assisting a 'disadvantaged group'[240] rather than as a citizenship right to enjoy equal access to information.

Of more pressing concern, however, is the limited reference to the rights of persons with disabilities in the Human Rights Committee's General Comment No. 34.[241] The communicative needs of persons with disabilities are acknowledged under paragraph 12, which clarifies that Article 19(2) of the ICCPR 'protects all forms of expression and the means of their dissemination' including, *inter alia*, sign language.[242] Nevertheless, while paragraph 15 calls on States Parties to 'take all necessary steps' to ensure the access of the public to new ICTs (such as 'internet and mobile based electronic information dissemination systems'), no specific reference is made to the availability of accessibility provisions for persons with disabilities[243] and no express link is made to Article 21 of the CRPD. Unfortunately, an amendment suggested by the International Disability Alliance (which highlighted that Article 19(2) of the ICCPR was supplemented by Article 21 of the CRPD), failed to be

236 Quinn and Degener, *Human Rights and Disability*, 295–7.
237 HR Council, *Report of the Special Rapporteur on the Promotion and Protection of the Right to Freedom of Opinion and Expression*, UN Doc. A/HRC/17/27, 16 May 2011.
238 *Ibid.*, para. 61. 239 *Ibid.*, para. 66. 240 *Ibid.*, para. 61.
241 HRC, General Comment No. 34, 2011. See further Chapter 2 in this book.
242 *Ibid.*, para. 12. 243 CRPD, Arts. 9 and 21.

incorporated into the final text of the General Comment.[244] Further concerns are associated with the Joint Declaration on 'Ten Key Challenges to Freedom of Expression in the Next Decade' (adopted in 2010 by the four special international mandates for protecting freedom of expression).[245] Although this document refers to discrimination in the enjoyment of this right by 'historically disadvantaged groups', persons with disabilities are not expressly mentioned in the examples listed.[246] Furthermore, although inaccessible ICTs are included in the list of challenges, there is no express reference to accessibility barriers for persons with disabilities.[247]

We have seen that while the CRPD has the potential to influence the mainstreaming of disability issues into UN mechanisms for the protection of human rights, so far this has produced mixed results concerning mechanisms for promoting Article 19 of the ICCPR. This section has also emphasised the potential of the CRPD to provide a framework for enhancing the protection of the right of persons with disabilities to access information and for addressing current challenges faced by States Parties. The next section focuses on the implementation and monitoring mechanisms that will assist in transforming the potential impact of the CRPD into reality.

## 5 Implementation and monitoring

The CRPD has great potential for improving the lives of persons with disabilities.[248] As part of their general obligations under Article 4 of the CRPD, States Parties are required 'to ensure and promote the full realisation of all human rights and fundamental freedoms for all persons with disabilities'[249] (including the right to freedom of expression and opinion and access to information).[250] To achieve this objective, States

[244] International Disability Alliance (IDA), *Submission on the Human Rights Committee's Draft General Comment on Article 19*, 22 October 2010, UN Doc. CCPR/C/GC/34/CRP.4, 3.

[245] UN Special Rapporteur on Freedom of Opinion and Expression, the Organization for Security and Co-operation in Europe Representative on Freedom of the Media, the Organization of American States Special Rapporteur on Freedom of Expression and the African Commission on Human and Peoples' Rights Special Rapporteur on Freedom of Expression and Access to Information, *Joint Declaration: Ten Key Challenges to Freedom of Expression in the Next Decade*, 3 February 2010. For discussion, see Chapter 8 in this book.

[246] *Ibid.*, para. 5. [247] *Ibid.*, para. 10. [248] Kanter, 'Promise and Challenge', 308.

[249] Art. 4(1), CRPD. [250] *Ibid.*, Art. 21.

Parties are required, *inter alia*, to adopt new measures implementing the rights enshrined in the CRPD,[251] and to modify or abolish any provisions that discriminate against persons with disabilities.[252] Nevertheless, the success of the CRPD depends on the way in which these objectives are implemented, and on the effectiveness of monitoring mechanisms.[253]

The national implementation and monitoring mechanism put forward under Article 33 of the CRPD has been praised for providing an institutional architecture for change, which operates at domestic level.[254] This article requires States Parties to designate focal points and coordination mechanisms within government for the implementation of the CRPD.[255] This was necessary to overcome a problem common to most governments, where the responsibility for disability issues is dispersed across various government departments, resulting in a chaotic system.[256] Under Article 33, States Parties are also required to ensure the presence of independent mechanisms (such as national human rights institutions) to monitor the implementation of the CRPD.[257] As stressed by Quinn, this will ensure positive steps in the reform process.[258] Finally, States Parties are required to ensure the full involvement and participation of civil society in the monitoring process, 'in particular persons with disabilities and their representative organisations'.[259] A link can be made between this provision and Article 4(3) of the CRPD, which requires States Parties to 'closely consult with and actively involve persons with disabilities' in the implementation of the CRPD and in other policy-making processes affecting their interests.[260] Quinn commends the national implementation and monitoring mechanism provision, as it requires cooperation between governments, human rights agencies and persons with disabilities. He rightly notes that the triangulation between these actors provides hope for a workable process of disability law reform.[261] This is particularly important, as the barriers faced by persons with disabilities in various environments including ICTs, can be dismantled only with the involvement of persons with disabilities and their representative organisations in shaping policy-making.

251 *Ibid.*, Art. 4(1)(a) CRPD. 252 *Ibid.*, Art. 4(1)(b) CRPD.

253 Kanter, 'Promise and Challenge', 296; M. A. Stein and J. E. Lord, 'Monitoring the Convention on the Rights of Persons with Disabilities: Innovations, Lost Opportunities, and Future Potential', *Human Rights Quarterly* 32(3) (2010), 689–728.

254 Quinn, 'United Nations Convention', 47. 255 CRPD, Art. 33(1).

256 Quinn, 'United Nations Convention', 48. 257 CRPD, Art. 33(2).

258 Quinn, 'United Nations Convention', 48. 259 CRPD, Art. 33(3).

260 *Ibid.*, Art. 4(3). 261 Quinn, 'United Nations Convention', 37.

Monitoring at international level relies on the Committee on the Rights of Persons with Disabilities (CRPD Committee)[262] and on the Conference of States Parties.[263] The latter brings together the States Parties to the CRPD, for consideration of matters regarding the implementation of the Convention.[264] This has the potential to guide the collective endeavours of the States Parties.[265] The CRPD Committee is a body of independent experts entrusted with overseeing the implementation of the CRPD.[266] The Committee considers reports periodically submitted by States Parties on their progress in implementing the CRPD,[267] makes suggestions and recommendations[268] and is required to report on its activities to the General Assembly and the Economic and Social Council.[269] This monitoring mechanism has been welcomed, although, as Gibson points out, the CRPD lacks detail on the standards that should be employed for evaluating these implementation efforts.[270] Furthermore, under the Optional Protocol to the CRPD, the CRPD Committee is entrusted with receiving complaints ('communications') from individuals or groups of individuals that have exhausted domestic remedies, concerning violations of Convention rights.[271] The potential of this mechanism for safeguarding the rights of persons with disabilities is illustrated in the decisions in *HM* v. *Sweden*[272] and *Szilvia Nyusti, Péter Takács and Tamás Fazekas* v. *Hungary*.[273] The CRPD Committee found States Parties to be in breach of specific obligations under the Convention, including in the latter case a failure to comply with obligations under Article 9(2)(b) CRPD (which requires States Parties to ensure that private actors providing services to the general public 'take into account all aspects of accessibility for persons with disabilities').[274] The CRPD Committee is also entrusted with conducting inquiries into 'grave or systematic violations' of the Convention rights by States Parties.[275] Lawson comments that although these mechanisms can play an important role in ensuring an effective implementation of the CRPD, the impact of these provisions is reduced by their inclusion into an optional protocol

[262] CRPD, Art. 34. [263] *Ibid.*, Art. 40. [264] *Ibid.*
[265] Quinn, 'United Nations Convention', 46. [266] CRPD, Art. 34. See SCRPD (2011a).
[267] CRPD, Arts. 35 and 36. See Lawson, 'United Nations Convention', 615.
[268] Art. 36(1), CRPD. [269] *Ibid.*, Art. 39.
[270] Gibson, 'Convention on the Rights of Persons with Disabilities', 12.
[271] Optional Protocol to the CRPD, Arts. 1 and 2. See Kayess and French, 'Out of Darkness', 31.
[272] CRPD/C/7/D/3/2011. [273] CRPD/C/9/D/1/2010. [274] *Ibid.*, para. 9.6.
[275] Optional Protocol to the CRPD, Art. 6.

rather than as part of the main body of the Convention.[276] While the inclusion of a communication procedure in an optional protocol[277] or to be accepted by a separate declaration[278] is common in UN human rights law, it is regrettable that to date, only 92 States Parties have signed the Optional Protocol to the CRPD (compared with 158 signatories to the Convention) and there are only 80 ratifications and accessions of the Protocol (compared with 143 ratifications and accessions to the Convention).[279] The practical impact of communications procedures under optional protocols can be open to debate. For example, this procedure under the Optional Protocol to the Convention on the Elimination of All Forms of Discrimination against Women (CEDAW) has been underused due to, *inter alia*, a lack of awareness of this route on the part of individuals and mistrust in this route on the part of NGOs.[280] Murdoch comments with regard to the CEDAW Optional Protocol that States Parties' recognition of the right of complaint had indiscernible practical benefits in shaping policy-making, tackling systemic forms of discrimination or mainstreaming women's rights in UN standards and mechanisms.[281] Notwithstanding these limitations, the States Parties' recognition of the right of complaint under the Optional Protocol procedures had an important symbolic value, showing commitment to the protection of human rights.[282]

In addition to national and international monitoring efforts, the CRPD also has provisions requiring States Parties to 'undertake appropriate and effective measures' to facilitate international cooperation.[283] Such measures include the sharing of information and best practices[284] and cooperation in research.[285] In the ICT sector, such international cooperation can play an important role in the regulation of private service providers operating beyond national confines, in eliminating accessibility barriers

[276] Lawson, 'United Nations Convention', 616.

[277] See, for example, Optional Protocol to the ICESCR, Art. 1; Optional Protocol ICCPR, Art. 1; Optional Protocol to the Convention on the Elimination of All Forms of Discrimination against Women (OP-CEDAW), 6 October 1999, 2131 UNTS 83, Arts. 1 and 2.

[278] See, for example, International Convention on the Elimination of All Forms of Racial Discrimination, 21 December 1965, entered into force 4 January 1969, 660 UNTS 195.

[279] SCRPD (2011c).

[280] J. Murdoch, 'Unfulfilled Expectations: The Optional Protocol to the Convention on the Elimination of All Forms of Discrimination against Women', *European Human Rights Law Review* 1 (2010), 26–46, at 45.

[281] *Ibid.* [282] *Ibid.* [283] CRPD, Art. 32(1). [284] *Ibid.*, Art. 32(1)(b).

[285] *Ibid.*, Art. 32(1)(c).

that cut across borders and in the harmonisation of standards for the accessibility of ICT products.[286] International cooperation is vital, given the challenges associated with regulating transnational undertakings.[287]

As we have seen, the success of the CRPD rests on collaborative efforts. These include the triangulation between coordination mechanisms within governments, independent monitoring mechanisms under bodies such as national human rights institutions and the involvement of the civil society in the monitoring process as part of national monitoring efforts.[288] They also include international cooperation between States Parties[289] and cooperation between these and the CRPD Committee.[290] The effective implementation of this instrument requires commitment from States Parties to ratify the Convention and to bring national laws up to the standards set by the CRPD.[291] It also requires dedication from the CRPD Committee.[292] A strong level of commitment is also required from organisations representing the interests of persons with disabilities, as they need to show unceasing dedication in their work for the full and equal enjoyment of human rights by persons with disabilities.[293] The success of the Convention requires the establishment of partnerships between persons with disabilities and policy-makers[294] and such partnerships have the potential to bring about real change.[295]

Achieving the full potential of the CRPD will take time.[296] Kayess and French comment that the CRPD must be received with both enthusiasm and realism,[297] while Hendriks questions whether the objective of creating a society that is accessible to all, is a realistic goal.[298] This is due to fundamental changes required for the effective implementation of the CRPD, including in the design and development of ICT products and services and the format in which information is provided.[299] Furthermore, the success of the CRPD is dependent on fundamental changes in attitudes towards persons with disabilities, from both policy-makers and the general public.[300] This process of change will require increased awareness throughout society in recognising and respecting the full and equal rights of persons with disabilities and their inherent dignity,[301] and

[286] Kayess and French, 'Out of Darkness', 32. [287] *Ibid.*
[288] CRPD, Art. 33. See Quinn, 'United Nations Convention', 37. [289] *Ibid.*, Art. 32.
[290] *Ibid.*, Art. 37. [291] *Ibid.*, Art. 4; Lawson, 'United Nations Convention', 618.
[292] *Ibid.* [293] *Ibid.* [294] Kanter, 'Promise and Challenge', 293.
[295] Quinn, 'United Nations Convention', 39.
[296] Lawson, 'United Nations Convention', 618.
[297] Kayess and French, 'Out of Darkness', 33. [298] Hendriks, 'UN Convention', 297.
[299] Lawson, 'United Nations Convention', 618. [300] *Ibid.* [301] CRPD, Art. 8(1).

it will also require financial commitments towards eliminating the accessibility barriers faced by persons with disabilities in society.[302] The CRPD, however, represents an opportunity which cannot be missed.[303] As the CRPD promotes a more inclusive society that respects the inherent dignity and worth of every human being,[304] the impact of this instrument goes beyond improving the lives of persons with disabilities and can play an important role in inspiring a renewed commitment to human rights in general.[305]

## 6 Conclusion

The CRPD has been praised for 'reconstruct[ing] both "human" and "rights" in human rights'.[306] The Convention reframes the interests of persons with disabilities in terms of human rights[307] and reaffirms their entitlement to 'the full and equal enjoyment' of those rights and to 'respect for their inherent dignity'.[308] The CRPD seeks to complement the protection of human rights[309] provided under other international instruments (such as the ICCPR) by clarifying the application of those rights in the context of disability.[310] The Convention transforms some of those rights and develops novel or strengthened formulations of human rights.[311] The CRPD explicitly puts an end to the strict distinction between negative (civil and political) rights and positive (economic, social and cultural) rights[312] and acknowledges the connection between the exercise of the right to freedom of expression and access to information and the development of accessible infrastructures,[313] in order to ensure the full and equal enjoyment of this right by persons with disabilities.[314] The CRPD adopts 'a holistic approach to disability'[315] that reaffirms the 'universality, indivisibility, interdependence and interrelatedness' of

302 Kanter, 'Promise and Challenge', 296.
303 Lawson, 'United Nations Convention', 546.
304 Fraser Butlin, 'UN Convention', 438. 305 Bielefeldt, 'New Inspiration', 397.
306 Dhanda, 'Constructing a New Human Rights Lexicon', 55.
307 Kayess and French, 'Out of Darkness', 1.
308 CRPD, Art. 1. See Lawson, 'United Nations Convention', 584.
309 Quinn and Degener, *Human Rights and Disability*, 296.
310 Lawson, 'United Nations Convention', 585.
311 Kayess and French, 'Out of Darkness', 3. 312 *Ibid.*, 32.
313 Dhanda, 'Constructing a New Human Rights Lexicon', 49. See CRPD, Arts. 21(b), 9(2)(g) and (h).
314 CRPD, Art. 21; Kayess and French, 'Out of Darkness', 32–3.
315 Quinn and Degener, *Human Rights and Disability*, 296.

human rights[316] and has a lot to offer to the development of human rights in general.[317] The Convention also provides persons with disabilities and their representative organisations with a focused route for engaging with UN mechanisms and processes, enabling these organisations to direct their attention and resources on one thematic Convention.[318] Further engagement with democratic processes is likely to increase the visibility of persons with disabilities in the human rights sphere,[319] which should lead ultimately to the mainstreaming of disability into UN standards and mechanisms for safeguarding human rights.[320]

The impact of the CRPD may be limited, *inter alia*, by the fact that enforcement mechanisms allowing the submission of complaints from individual or groups of individuals (alleging violations of rights comprised in the Convention) are confined to the Optional Protocol to the CRPD, rather than comprised in the main body of the Convention.[321] While the inclusion of a communication procedure in an optional protocol is not uncommon in the UN system,[322] an increase in the number of States Parties who signed and ratified the Optional Protocol would, at the very least, have an important symbolic value[323] about commitment to the full and equal enjoyment of human rights by persons with disabilities. Further challenges are posed by the language adopted by the CRPD, including the fact that the guidance on the concept of disability put forward under Article 1 relies on non-exhaustive examples that only mention persons with 'long-term impairments.'[324] Also, the obligation to provide reasonable accommodation for the requirements of persons with disabilities is limited to situations that do not impose 'a disproportionate or undue burden'[325] and the use of the term 'burden' risks activating negative perceptions of persons with disabilities.[326] In addition, the process of mainstreaming disability issues into wider UN processes for safeguarding human rights has led to mixed results. While the UN Human Rights Committee's General Comment No. 34 (on Article 19 of the ICCPR) recognises sign language as a form of expression protected under Article 19(2) ICCPR,[327] the remainder of the document

[316] CRPD, preamble (c); MacKay, 'United Nations Convention', 330.

[317] Bielefeldt, 'New Inspiration', 399. [318] Lawson, 'United Nations Convention', 585.

[319] *Ibid.* [320] Quinn and Degener, *Human Rights and Disability*, 297.

[321] Optional Protocol to the CRPD, Arts. 1 and 2; Lawson, 'United Nations Convention', 616.

[322] See nn. 277–8 and accompanying text. [323] Murdoch, 'Unfulfilled Expectations'.

[324] CRPD, Art. 1. See Lawson, 'United Nations Convention', 595. [325] CRPD, Art. 2.

[326] Kayess and French, 'Out of Darkness', 27. [327] GC 34, para. 12.

fails to address explicitly issues regarding the exercise of the right to freedom of expression and access to information by persons with disabilities. Furthermore, the General Comment makes no express reference to the potential relevance of Article 21 of the CRPD for the interpretation of Article 19 of the ICCPR.[328]

Time and resources – among other things – are required to overcome the accessibility barriers faced by persons with disabilities in the ICT sector (including environmental and attitudinal barriers).[329] Yet, it is important not to underestimate the urgency in tackling accessibility barriers and the overall significance of this issue, given that persons with disabilities represent approximately 10 per cent of the world's population.[330] Furthermore, it is important not to overlook the key role played by access to information as an enabler of a wider range of human rights,[331] including the right to participate in political and public life[332] and in cultural life, recreation, leisure and sport.[333] The provisions examined in this chapter (including the general obligation under Article 9 on accessibility and the specific obligations under Article 21 on the right to freedom of expression and opinion and access to information) have emphasised the need to enable the full participation of persons with disabilities as equal citizens in mainstream society.[334] The effective implementation of these provisions will benefit persons with disabilities, by facilitating the 'full and equal enjoyment' of their human rights[335] and by resulting in an 'enhanced sense of belonging' in society.[336] Equally important, it will ensure that society is not missing out on the wide range of skills that persons with disabilities have to offer to the wider community.[337]

## Postscript

In 2014, the CRPD Committee adopted General Comment 2 on Article 9 (Accessibility).[338] This document stresses, *inter alia*, the importance of

328 IDA, *Submission on the HRC's General Comment No. 34*.
329 Lawson, 'United Nations Convention', 618.
330 OHCHR, 'Monitoring the Convention'. 331 CRPD, preamble (v).
332 *Ibid.*, Art. 29. 333 *Ibid.*, Art. 30. 334 Lawson, 'United Nations Convention', 599.
335 CRPD, Art. 1. 336 *Ibid.*, preamble (m).
337 SCRPD, 'The Convention is in Force: What Next?', 2008. See www.un.org/disabilities/default.asp?id=477 (quoting Akiko Ito, Chief of the UN Secretariat for the CRPD); CRPD, preamble (m).
338 UN CRPD Committee, General Comment 2: Article 9 (Accessibility), 22 May 2014, UN Doc. CRPD/C/GC/2.

accessible ICTs as a precondition for the full and equal enjoyment by persons with disabilities of the right to freedom of expression and opinion.[339] All services provided to the public (by private or public providers) should be accessible to all, and persons with disabilities should enjoy equal access to these services 'in a manner that . . . respects their dignity'.[340] The General Comment distinguishes between the 'duty to provide accessibility' and the 'duty to provide reasonable accommodation', clarifying that the latter focuses on individuals, requires service providers to react to the particular circumstances of an individual and is subject to an 'undue burden' defence.[341] On the other hand, the duty to provide accessibility is related to groups, requires the anticipatory adoption of accessibility standards and is 'unconditional' (as it cannot be avoided by reference to an 'undue burden' defence).[342] The General Comment recognises that States Parties 'can ensure that access is achieved through gradual implementation, when necessary' and that the removal of accessibility barriers is a gradual and steady process.[343] While the clarifications put forward by the General Comment are to be welcomed, this document could have done more to stress the urgency in tackling accessibility barriers.

## Literature

Arnardóttir, O. M. and G. Quinn (eds.), *The UN Convention on the Rights of Persons with Disabilities – European and Scandinavian Perspectives, International Studies in Human Rights*, vol. 100 (Leiden: Martinus Nijhoff, Brill, 2009).

Bielefeldt, H. 'New Inspiration for the Human Rights Debate: The Convention on the Rights of Persons with Disabilities', *Netherlands Quarterly of Human Rights* 52(3) (2007), 397–400.

De Búrca, G. 'The EU in the Negotiations of the UN Disability Convention', *European Law Review* 35(2) (2010), 174–96.

Burke Robertson, C. 'Providing Access to the Future: How the Americans with Disabilities Act can Remove Barriers in Cyberspace', *Denver University Law Review* 79–2 (2001), 199–227.

Campbell, J. 'Valuing Diversity: The Disability Agenda – We've Only Just Begun', *Disability and Society* 17(4) 2002, 471–8.

Clement, A. *et al.* 'Debating Universal Access in the Canadian Context: The Role of Public Interest Organizations', in M. Moll and L. R. Shade (eds.), *Ecommerce vs. E-commons: Communications in the Public Interest* (Ottawa: Canadian Centre for Policy Alternatives, 2002).

[339] *Ibid.*, para. 21. [340] *Ibid.*, para. 13. [341] *Ibid.*, paras. 25 and 26.
[342] *Ibid.*, para. 25. [343] *Ibid.*, para. 27.

Coco, K. J. 'Beyond the Price Tag: An Economic Analysis of Title III of the Americans with Disabilities Act', *Kansas Journal of Law and Public Policy* 20(1) 2010, 58–97.

Deal, M. 'Disabled People's Attitudes towards Other Impairment Groups: A Hierarchy of Impairments', *Disability and Society* 18(7) (2003), 897–910.

Dhanda, A. 'Constructing a New Human Rights Lexicon: Convention on the Rights of Persons with Disabilities', *Sur: International Journal of Human Rights* 5(8) (2008), 43–59.

Feintuck, M. and M. Varney, *Media Regulation, Public Interest and the Law*, 2nd edn (Edinburgh University Press, 2006).

Fraser Butlin, S. 'The UN Convention on the Rights of Persons with Disabilities: Does the Equality Act 2010 Measure up to UK International Commitments?', *Industrial Law Journal* 40(4) (2011), 428–38.

Gibson, F. 'The Convention on the Rights of Persons with Disabilities: The Response of the Clinic', *International Journal of Clinical Legal Education* summer (2011), 11–24.

Goggin, G. and C. Newell, 'The Business of Digital Disability', *Information Society* 23 (2007), 159–68.

Gregg, J. L. 'Policy-making in the Public Interests: A Contextual Analysis in the Passage of Closed-captioning Policy', *Disability and Society* 21(5) (2006), 537–50.

Hendriks, A. C. 'UN Convention of the Rights of Persons with Disabilities', *European Journal of Health Law* 14 (2007), 273–98.

Johnson, L. and E. Moxon, 'In Whose Service? Technology, Care and Disabled People: the Case for a Disability Politics Perspective', *Disability and Society* 13(2) (1998), 241–58.

Kanter, A. S. 'The Promise and Challenge of the United Nations Convention on the Rights of Persons with Disabilities', *Journal of International Law and Commerce* 34 (2007), 287–321.

Kayess, R. and P. French, 'Out of Darkness into Light? Introducing the Convention on the Rights of Persons with Disabilities', *Human Rights Law Review* 8(1) (2008), 1–34.

Lawson, A. 'Disability and Employment in the Equality Act 2010: Opportunities Seized, Lost and Generated', *Industrial Law Journal* 40–4 (2011), 359–383.

'The United Nations Convention on the Rights of Persons with Disabilities: New Era or False Dawn?', *Syracuse Journal of International Law and Commerce* 34(2) (2007), 563–619.

MacKay, D. 'The United Nations Convention on the Rights of Persons with Disabilities', *Syracuse Journal of International Law and Commerce* 34(2) (2007), 323–31.

Murdoch, J. 'Unfulfilled expectations: the Optional Protocol to the Convention on the Elimination of All Forms of Discrimination against Women', *European Human Rights Law Review* 1 (2010), 26–46.

Pooran, B. D. and C. Wilkie, 'Failing to Achieve Equality: Disability Rights in Australia, Canada, and the United States', *Journal of Law and Social Policy* 20 (2005), 1–34.

Quinn, G. 'The United Nations Convention on the Rights of Persons with Disabilities: Toward a New International Politics of Disability', *Texas Journal on Civil Liberties and Civil Rights* 15(1) (2009), 33–52.

Quinn, G. and T. Degener (eds.), *Human Rights and Disability: The Current Use and Future Potential of United Nations Human Rights Instruments in the Context of Disability* (New York and Geneva: United Nations Publications, 2002).

Réaume, D. G. 'Discrimination and Dignity', *Louisiana Law Review* 63 (2003), 1–57.

Scotch, R. 'Models of Disability and the Americans with Disabilities Act', *Berkley Journal of Employment and Labor Law* 21 (2000), 213–22.

Simpson, J. 'Inclusive Information and Communication Technologies for People with Disabilities', *Disability Studies Quarterly*, 29–1 (2009).

Smith, D. M. 'Who Says You're Disabled? The Role of Medical Evidence in the ADA Definition of Disability', *Tulane Law Review* 82(1) (2007), 1–76.

Stein, M. A. 'A Quick Overview of the United Nations Convention on the Rights of Persons with Disabilities', *Mental and Physical Disability Law Report* 31(5) (2007), 679–83.

Stein, M. A. and J. E. Lord, 'Monitoring the Convention on the Rights of Persons with Disabilities: Innovations, Lost Opportunities, and Future Potential', *Human Rights Quarterly* 32(3) (2010), 689–728.

'Participatory Justice, and the UN Convention on the Rights of Persons with Disabilities', *Texas Journal on Civil Liberties and Civil Rights* 13(2) (2008), 167–85.

Varney, E. *Disability and Information Technology: A Comparative Study in Media Regulation* (Cambridge University Press, 2013).

'A Hierarchy of Disability Rights? A Comparative Examination of the Regulation of Digital Television in the United States of America and the United Kingdom', *Northern Ireland Legal Quarterly* 60(4) (2009), 421–42.

'Disability Rights in the Communications Sector: An Examination of Digital Television Regulation in the United Kingdom', *Communications Law* 13(6) (2008), 187–96.

'The Protection of Age and Disability Rights in the Regulation of Digital Television in the European Union', *Utilities Law Review 2007/2008* 17(1) (2008), 6–16.

Waddington, L. 'The European Union and the United Nations Convention on the Rights of Persons with Disabilities: A Story of Exclusive and Shared Competences', *Maastricht Journal of European and Comparative Law* 18(4) (2011), 431–53.

Weller, P. 'Human Rights and Social Justice: the Convention on the Rights of Persons with Disabilities and the Quiet Revolution in International Law', *Public Space: The Journal of Law and Social Justice* 4 (2009), 74–91.

## UN documents

Committee on Economic, Social and Cultural Rights (UN CESCR), General Comment No. 5: Persons with Disabilities, 9 December 1994, UN Doc. E/1995/22.

CESCR, General Comment No. 3: Article 2(1): The Nature of States Parties' Obligations, 14 December 1990, UN Doc. E/1991/23 (SUPP).

CRPD Committee, General Comment No. 2: Article 9 (Accessibility), 22 May 2014, UN Doc. CRPD/C/GC/2.

GA, Resolution 37/52: World Programme of Action Concerning Disabled Persons, 3 December 1982, UN Doc. A/RES/37/52.

GA, Resolution 48/69: Standard Rules on the Equalization of Opportunities for Persons with Disabilities, 20 December 1993, UN Doc. A/RES/48/69.

GA, Resolution 2856 (XXVI): Declaration on the Rights of Mentally Retarded Persons, 20 December 1971.

GA, Resolution 3447 (XXX): Declaration on the Rights of Disabled Persons, 9 December 1975.

HR Council, Report of the Special Rapporteur on the Promotion and Protection of the Right to Freedom of Opinion and Expression, UN Doc. A/HRC/17/27, 16 May 2011.

HRC, General Comment 34: Article 19 (Freedoms of Opinion and Expression), UN Doc. CCPR/C/GC/34, 12 September 2011.

## EU documents

*Council Decision of 24 November 2009 Concerning the Conclusion, by the European Community, of the United Nations Convention on the Rights of Persons with Disabilities*, OJ No. L23/35, 27 January 2010.

Directive 2002/22/EC of 7 March 2002 (Universal Service Directive), OJ No. L108/51, 24 April 2002.

Directive 2009/136/EC of 25 November 2009 (Citizens' Rights Directive), OJ No. L337/11, 18 December 2009.

Directive 2010/13/EU of 10 March 2010 on the Coordination of Certain Provisions Laid Down by Law, Regulation or Administrative Action in Member States Concerning the Provision of Audiovisual Media Services (AMS Directive), OJ No. L95/1, 14 April 2010.

European Commission Communications Committee (Cocom), *Report from the Inclusive Communications Subgroup*, Doc. no. COCOM04–08, 27 January 2004.

European Commission (EC), Proposal for a Council Directive on implementing the Principle of Equal Treatment between Persons irrespective of Religion or Belief, Disability, Age or Sexual Orientation, Doc. No. COM(2008)426, 2 July 2008.

# 7

# UNESCO: freedom of expression, information and the media

SYLVIE COUDRAY

## 1 Introduction

Freedom of expression is central to dialogue, democracy and development worldwide. Without it, an informed, engaged and responsible citizenry is impossible; corruption and crime cannot be exposed; and societies cannot hope to implement the social and economic programmes that will enable their future prosperity. When freedom of expression is upheld and championed, however, a whole host of objectives become possible, ranging from democratic governance and poverty reduction to gender equality and the empowerment of women. It is, therefore, not just an individual right, but a collective one that constitutes a prerequisite for the exercise of a number of other fundamental human rights and the attainment of the internationally endorsed Millennium Development Goals (MDGs), to which world leaders and development institutions have committed since the adoption of the United Nations Millennium Declaration in September 2000.[1]

Since its foundation, the United Nations Educational, Scientific and Cultural Organization (UNESCO) has placed freedom of expression and press freedom at the core of its mission. Indeed, its Constitution, adopted in November 1945, calls on UNESCO Member States to 'collaborate in the work of advancing the mutual knowledge and understanding of all peoples, through all means of mass communication'. UNESCO is the

[1] The eight MDGs, set time-bound targets, to be achieved by 2015, in regard to eradicating extreme poverty and hunger; achieving universal primary education; promoting gender equality and women's empowerment; reducing child mortality; improving maternal health; combating HIV/AIDS, malaria and other diseases; ensuring environmental sustainability; and fostering a global partnership for development. UN GA, Resolution 55/2: United Nations Millennium Declaration, 18 September 2000, UN Doc. A/RES/55/2. For more information, see www.un.org/millenniumgoals/bkgd (last accessed 27 January 2014).

only specialized agency within the United Nations (UN) with a mandate to 'promote the free flow of ideas by word and image'.[2]

UNESCO is governed by two bodies: the General Conference and the Executive Board. The General Conference consists of the Organization's Member States and meets every two years. It determines the policies and the main lines of work of the Organization. The Executive Board, which meets every six months and consists of fifty-eight members elected by the General Conference, assures the overall management of UNESCO.

In carrying out its mandate, the Organization's priorities are determined by a (six-year) Medium Term Strategy, broken down into (two-year) 'biennium' cycles.[3] They are also designed to reflect, incorporate and contribute to the UN's human rights-based approach to programming, gender and disability sensitivity, and wider development commitments. The resulting activities in the area of freedom of expression and media development, undertaken in partnership with civil society organizations, may be divided according to five key approaches:

- advocacy and awareness-raising and monitoring;
- safety of media professionals;
- media law and regulatory framework;
- ethical and professional standard-setting; and
- promoting media diversity.

In what follows, each of these activity areas will be addressed in turn, with a view to providing a concrete and comprehensive overview of UNESCO's role in the promotion of freedom of expression, as well as forward-looking reflections about emerging trends and challenges.

## 2 Advocacy and awareness-raising and monitoring

UNESCO's advocacy, awareness-raising and monitoring activities are designed to sensitize Member States, public institutions and civil society to the importance of freedom of expression and press freedom.

In 1993, the UN General Assembly proclaimed World Press Freedom Day, in order to remind governments worldwide of their duty to respect Article 19 of the Universal Declaration of Human Rights. Since then,

[2] Constitution of the United Nations Educational, Scientific and Cultural Organization, London, 16 November 1945, Art. 1.

[3] Beginning in 2014, UNESCO has moved to an eight-year Medium Term Strategy (2014–21) and a four-year biennium cycle (2014–17).

World Press Freedom Day has been celebrated every year on 3 May, the anniversary of the historic Declaration of Windhoek, a statement of free press principles prepared by a number of African journalists on the occasion of a UNESCO seminar entitled 'Promoting an Independent and Pluralistic African Press', held in Windhoek, Namibia in 1991.[4]

UNESCO celebrates World Press Freedom Day by bringing together media professionals, press freedom organizations and UN agencies to assess the state of press freedom worldwide and discuss ways of addressing new and enduring challenges. Each conference focuses on a theme related to press freedom, from media in violent conflict and countries in transition (2000, 2002 and 2004) to freedom of information and empowerment of people (2008, 2010).[5]

On the 20th anniversary of the proclamation of World Press Freedom Day in 2013, the spotlight was on the theme of 'Safe to Speak: Securing Freedom of Expression in All Media'. In particular, the main commemoration and others held around the world focused on issues related to the safety of journalists, combating impunity for crimes against freedom of expression, and securing a free and open Internet as the precondition for safety online.[6]

Since 1997, as a result of an initiative by UNESCO's Executive Board, UNESCO has also marked World Press Freedom Day by awarding the UNESCO/Guillermo Cano World Press Freedom Prize, named after assassinated Colombian journalist Guillermo Cano Isaza. The prize, which comes in the form of $25,000, is intended to honour the work of an individual or an organization defending or promoting freedom of expression anywhere in the world, especially when this has been achieved in the face of danger.

Regional and international organizations, as well as professional and non-governmental organizations working in the field of journalism and freedom of expression, and UNESCO Member States, are invited to nominate candidates for the prize. The prize is then awarded on the

[4] See www.un.org/en/events/pressfreedomday/windhoek.shtml (last accessed 27 January 2014).

[5] For a review of the focus themes of World Press Freedom Day celebrations over the years, see W. Horsley, *Pressing for Freedom: 20 Years of World Press Freedom Day* (Paris: UNESCO, 2013), 20–4; See http://unesdoc.unesco.org/images/0022/002205/220525E.pdf (last accessed 27 January 2014).

[6] See www.unesco.org/new/en/unesco/events/prizes-and-celebrations/celebrations/international-days/world-press-freedom-day/previous-celebrations/2013/2013-themes (last accessed 27 January 2014).

basis of the recommendation of a twelve-person international jury of distinguished media professionals.

In 2013, the UNESCO/Guillermo Cano World Press Freedom Prize was given to imprisoned Ethiopian journalist Reeyot Alemu. Ms Alemu could not attend the ceremony in person since she is currently serving a five-year sentence in Kality prison. Her message, read by Alana Barton of the International Women's Media Foundation that proposed her candidature, stated: 'The award is not only for me, but also for all individuals and institutions that struggle for press freedom around the world ... I am very worried for those who are labeled as terrorists and imprisoned only because they struggle for their rights in a peaceful way ... Since the journalists are in prison, exile or trouble, who will expose the hidden truths?'[7]

UNESCO's Director-General (DG) publicly highlights the plight of persecuted journalists frequently. Resolution 29 entitled 'Condemnation of Violence against Journalists' and adopted at the 29th Session of UNESCO's General Conference in November 1997, called upon the Director General 'to condemn assassination and any physical violence against journalists as a crime against society, since this curtails freedom of expression and, as a consequence, the other rights and freedoms set forth in international human rights instruments'. In addition, it recommended that the DG 'urge that the competent authorities discharge their duty of preventing, investigating and punishing such crimes and remedying their consequences'. In accordance with these stipulations, the DG now publicly condemns the murders of journalists and media professionals, and mobilizes against the impunity of such crimes, by urging the relevant authorities to prevent, investigate and punish them.

Alongside the DG's efforts, UNESCO's International Programme for the Development of Communication (IPDC), the only multilateral forum in the UN system designed to mobilize the international community to discuss and promote media development in developing countries, also plays a crucial role in raising awareness on journalist safety.[8]

On 27 March 2008, at its 26th session, the intergovernmental council of the IPDC adopted a 'Decision on the Safety of Journalists and the Issue of Impunity' which requested the DG 'to provide, after consultation with

[7] 'Who will expose the hidden truths?', message to be found at: www.unesco.org/new/en/unesco/resources/who-will-reveal-the-hidden-truths (last accessed 27 January 2014).

[8] See www.unesco.org/new/en/communication-and-information/intergovernmental-programmes/ipdc/special-initiatives/safety-of-journalists (last accessed 27 January 2014).

the UN Secretary-General, the Intergovernmental Council of IPDC ... with an analytical report on the basis of responses received from Member States concerned, including updated information on the Director-General's condemnations, and [to] make this report widely available'.[9] This happens every two years. Moreover, in 2010, the IPDC Council unanimously adopted a second 'Decision on the Safety of Journalists and the Issue of Impunity', which reiterated the request for governments to report to the UNESCO DG on their investigations into the killings of journalists. This Decision also requests that the General Conference of UNESCO encourages newsrooms around the world to observe one minute's silence every year on World Press Freedom Day to denounce the murders of journalists.[10]

The report presented to the IPDC Council at its 28th session in March 2012 concerned the 2010–11 biennium. During this period, UNESCO condemned the murder of 127 journalists, a tally comparable to 2008–9 when the organization had reported and condemned 123 murders. A noteworthy evolution during 2008–9 was that the percentage of killings not linked to conflict situations had dramatically increased, and the great majority of casualties were not international war correspondents, but local journalists mostly working in peacetime, covering local stories and being attacked for doing so. This trend was confirmed during the 2010–11 period, in which the number of journalists targeted for murder represented at least 75 per cent of the killings condemned by the Director-General. As for the action taken by Member States with regard to these killings, out of the thirty-eight countries and territories concerned by the killings of journalists condemned in 2006–7 and 2008–2009, only eighteen responded to the Director-General. Of the twenty-seven countries included in the list of killings in 2008–9, nine provided information on judicial follow-up.[11]

[9] UNESCO, Intergovernmental Council of IPDC, *Decision on the Safety of Journalists and the Issue of Impunity*, 27 March 2008; see www.unesco.org/new/fileadmin/MULTIMEDIA/HQ/CI/CI/pdf/ipdc2008_decision_safety_of_journalists.pdf (last accessed 27 January 2014).

[10] UNESCO, Intergovernmental Council of IPDC, *Decision on the Safety of Journalists and the Issue of Impunity*, 24–26 March 2010; see: www.unesco.org/new/fileadmin/MULTIMEDIA/HQ/CI/CI/pdf/ipdc2010_safety_decision_final.pdf (last accessed 27 January 2014).

[11] UNESCO IPDC, *Report on the Safety of Journalists and the Issue of Impunity presented by the UNESCO Director-General to the Intergovernmental Council of the IPDC*, UN Doc. CI-08/CONF.202/7, 3 March 2008 at www.unesco.org/new/fileadmin/MULTIMEDIA/HQ/CI/CI/pdf/ipdc2008_safety_of_journalists_report.pdf (last accessed 27 January

Besides its special initiative focusing on the safety of journalists, the IPDC also plays a more general role in monitoring freedom of expression, having initiated the development of a set of Media Development Indicators (MDIs) for evaluating national media landscapes, which have gained widespread recognition among UN agencies, development partners, intergovernmental bodies, media professionals and civil society groups (see further below).

Following a two-year consultation process involving a variety of experts and organizations from all over the world, the MDIs were finalized and unanimously endorsed by the IPDC Intergovernmental Council at its 26th session in 2008. The 1991 Windhoek Declaration and subsequent regional declarations on 'Promoting Independent and Pluralistic Media' adopted in Almaty, Santiago, Sana'a and Sofia, served as the theoretical framework for the MDIs. In this context, they were structured around five media development categories:

- *Category 1: a system of regulation conducive to freedom of expression, pluralism and diversity of the media:* existence of a legal, policy and regulatory framework which protects and promotes freedom of expression and information, based on international best practice standards and developed in participation with civil society.
- *Category 2: plurality and diversity of media, a level economic playing field and transparency of ownership:* the State actively promotes the development of the media sector in a manner which prevents undue concentration and ensures plurality and transparency of ownership and content across public, private and community media.
- *Category 3: media as a platform for democratic discourse:* the media, within a prevailing climate of self-regulation and respect for the journalistic profession, reflects and represents the diversity of views and interests in society, including those of marginalized groups. There is a high level of information and media literacy.

2014); UNESCO IPDC, *Report on the Safety of Journalists and the Issue of Impunity presented by the UNESCO Director-General to the Intergovernmental Council of the IPDC*, UN Doc. CI-10/CONF.202/4/BIS REV, 30 March 2010 at http://unesdoc.unesco.org/images/0018/001874/187491e.pdf (last accessed 27 January 2014); UNESCO IPDC, *Report on the Safety of Journalists and the Issue of Impunity presented by the UNESCO Director-General to the Intergovernmental Council of the IPDC*, UN Doc. CI-12/CONF.202/4 REV, 27 March 2012 at www.unesco.org/new/fileadmin/MULTIMEDIA/HQ/CI/CI/pdf/IPDC/ipdc28_dg_safety_report_final_rev.pdf (last accessed 27 January 2014).

- *Category 4: professional capacity building and supporting institutions that underpin freedom of expression, pluralism and diversity:* media workers have access to professional training and development, both vocational and academic, at all stages of their career, and the media sector as a whole is both monitored and supported by professional associations and civil society organizations.
- *Category 5: infrastructural capacity is sufficient to support independent and pluralistic media:* the media sector is characterized by high or rising levels of public access, including among marginalized groups, and efficient use of technology to gather and distribute news and information, appropriate to the local context.

These categories are intended to be taken together to create a holistic picture of the media environment, and enable a comprehensive map of the media ecology to be constructed.

Since their endorsement, the MDIs, which were originally published in English, have been made available in eight different languages, with the number of countries concerned by their application steadily increasing. At the present time, studies having been launched or completed by UNESCO in Bhutan, Bolivia, Brazil, Côte d'Ivoire, Croatia, Ecuador, Egypt, Gabon, Iraq, Jordan, the Maldives, Mauritania, Mozambique, Nepal, Palestine, South Sudan, Timor Leste, Togo, Tunisia, Uganda and Uruguay, as well as a regional project in South-East Europe. The United Nations is also using the MDIs as a basis for the elaboration of a common approach in the fields of communication development and good governance and collaboration is ongoing with the UNESCO Institute for Statistics (UIS) to apply a new set of internationally standardized media statistics that will help address gaps in available country-specific data.

## 3 Safety of media professionals

In the words of Barry James: 'Every journalist killed or neutralized by terror is an observer less of the human condition. Every attack distorts reality by creating a climate of fear and self-censorship.'[12] UNESCO works at the local, regional and international level in order to promote

[12] B. James, *Press Freedom: Safety of Journalists and Impunity* (Paris: UNESCO, 2007), 7; see www.unesco.org/new/en/communication-and-information/resources/publications-and-communication-materials/publications/full-list/press-freedom-safety-of-journalists-and-impunity (last accessed 27 January 2014).

the safety of media professionals. It does so following a gender-sensitive approach, for example taking into account the specific challenges faced by female journalists.

At the local level, the organization, often in collaboration with civil society, supports safety and risk awareness training for journalists and media workers on the ground. Indeed, as the IPDC Council's 2010 and 2012 Reports (referenced above) highlight, the vast majority of journalists killed undertaking their professional duties are local. While international journalists are well equipped and heavily protected, local ones are often untrained and underprepared for the violence they have to cover and confront. As a result, a significant percentage of IPDC-funded projects aims to provide journalists in conflict-sensitive regions with the necessary instruction.

UNESCO also works at the international and regional levels, with public authorities, private enterprises and journalists' organizations, to systematically seek ways to reduce risks involved. For example, in 2002, UNESCO supported the consultation process for the Reporters Without Borders Charter for the Safety of Journalists Working in War Zones or Dangerous Areas.[13] This theme was later to be addressed by the UN Security Council in 2006 with the adoption of Resolution 1738 on the safety of journalists in conflict situations.[14] This includes a commitment by the media, public authorities and journalists to systematically seek ways to reduce the risks involved.

On a more practical level, UNESCO has collaborated with Reporters Sans Frontières (RSF) to publish a regularly updated practical handbook for journalists working in conflict zones, available in ten languages. This *Handbook for Journalists*, first published in 1998, recalls key documents, charters and declarations, which spell out the principles of press freedom. These come from all over the world, from the African Charter on Human and Peoples' Rights to the Munich Charter on the rights and duties of journalists, which was adopted by representatives of the Journalists Unions of Belgium, France, Italy, Luxembourg, the Netherlands and West Germany in 1971. The handbook contains useful advice on precautions to be taken in dangerous situations, from how to save a

[13] Reporters Without Borders (RSF), Reporters Without Borders Charter for the Safety of Journalists Working in War Zones or Dangerous Areas, March 2002.

[14] UN SC, Resolution 1738 on the Safety of Journalists in Conflict Situations, UN Doc. S/RES/1738, 23 December 2006.

wounded or injured person to how to go about investigating press freedom violations.

In addition, UNESCO works to encourage the inclusion of journalist safety in the curricula of journalism and mass communication schools. With this in mind, a team of four UNESCO experts, on the basis of consultations with a wide variety of journalism educators, published the *Model Curricula for Journalism Education* for distribution in journalism schools worldwide. This is an Open Educational Resource (OER), in that it can be copied, shared and altered at will. The book is available via UNESCO's OER online platform, the world's largest online OER community, and is available in all six UN languages and Portuguese.[15]

UNESCO collaborates with other UN agencies to advance freedom of expression, for instance contributing to information relevant to this fundamental right in the framework of the Universal Periodic Review (a process led by the UN Human Rights Council to survey the state of human rights around the world). Moreover, UNESCO plays a central role in promoting the importance of the safety of journalists across the rest of the UN system, by promoting the incorporation of the issue into the strategies of all relevant UN agencies, funds and programmes, as well as at Member State level. Indeed, in September 2011 UNESCO hosted the first-ever UN Inter-Agency Conference on the Safety of Journalists and the Issue of Impunity,[16] convened by the Director General of UNESCO at the request of the Intergovernmental Council of the International Programme for the Development of Communication.[17] This inter-agency meeting sought to formulate a comprehensive, coherent and action-oriented approach to the issue. A Plan of Action was drafted on the conference's second day by representatives from UNESCO; the Food and Agriculture Organization (FAO); the United Nations Development Programme (UNDP); the United Nations Environment Programme (UNEP); the United Nations High Commissioner for Refugees (UNHCR); the United Nations Office on Drugs and Crime (UNODC);

[15] M. Cobden, G. S. Adam, H. H. Holm and M. Abu-Fadil, *Model Curricula for Journalism Education* (Paris: UNESCO, 2007), at www.unesco.org/new/en/communication-and-information/resources/publications-and-communication-materials/publications/full-list/model-curricula-for-journalism-education; for OERs, see www.oerplatform.org (both last accessed 27 January 2014).

[16] See www.unesco.org/new/en/communication-and-information/events/calendar-of-events/events-websites/inter-agency-meeting-on-the-safety-of-journalists-and-the-issue-of-impunity (last accessed 27 January 2014).

[17] UNESCO IPDC, *Decision on the Safety of Journalists*.

the United Nations Office of the High Commissioner for Human Rights (UN OHCHR); the World Bank Institute (WBI); and the World Food Programme (WFP). It included recommendations for the UN, Member States and civil society.[18]

The UN Plan of Action on the Safety of Journalists and the Issue of Impunity was endorsed by the UN Chief Executives Board on 12 April 2012. Following this key development, UNESCO convened a 2nd UN Inter-Agency Meeting on the Safety of Journalists and the Issue of Impunity, which took place at the United Nations Office in Vienna on 22–23 November 2012.[19] The meeting was co-hosted by UNESCO, the Office of the High Commissioner for Human Rights (UN OHCHR), the United Nations Office on Drugs and Crime (UNODC) and the United Nations Development Programme (UNDP). It brought together representatives from fifteen UN bodies and more than forty non-governmental and intergovernmental organizations, independent experts, media groups and professional associations. The purpose of this gathering was to formulate a concrete implementation strategy at global and national levels by outlining more than one hundred areas of work by UN bodies and civil society groups to secure the safety of journalists.

At the time of writing, an implementation strategy to operationalize the UN Plan at the global, regional and local level in 2013–14 had been developed, and it was being adapted to a selection of countries for a first roll-out phase (including Iraq, Nepal, Pakistan and South Sudan, as well as Latin America). The strategy makes clear that when referring to journalists, it 'includes media workers and social media producers who produce significant amounts of public-interest journalism'. Its appendix focuses on the UN's track record on safety and impunity issues and recognizes General Comment No. 34 by the Human Rights Committee on Article 19 of the International Covenant on Civil and Political Rights as constituting 'an authoritative clarification of the scope of States' obligations, calling on them to adopt adequate laws and practices together with national enforcement mechanisms to protect the right to

[18] UNESCO IPDC, *UN Plan of Action on the Safety of Journalists and the Issue of Impunity*, UN Doc. CI-12/CONF.202/6, 12 April 2012, at www.unesco.org/new/fileadmin/MULTIMEDIA/HQ/CI/CI/pdf/official_documents/UN_plan_on_Safety_Journalists_EN.pdf (last accessed 27 January 2014).

[19] See www.unesco.org/new/en/communication-and-information/freedom-of-expression/safety-of-journalists/2nd-un-inter-agency-meeting-on-the-safety-of-journalists-and-the-issue-of-impunity (last accessed 27 January 2014).

freedom of expression and opinion', also citing it among the basic texts on the subject matter.[20]

## 4 Media laws and regulatory frameworks

Media laws and regulatory frameworks are also necessary instruments in ensuring enabling environments for freedom of expression and press freedom. This is a matter of both form and substance. A country may have good laws relating to freedom of expression and the right to information, but they may not be implemented. Their function may be hampered by a culture of secrecy or corruption, institutional resistance, or a lack of technical or institutional capacity. In addition, constitutional guarantees may be eroded by exceptions and derogations from international treaty obligations or by contradictory laws covering, for example, State secrecy or defamation. The 'war on terror', for example, has seen the introduction of laws and regulations relating to national security that infringe the right to freedom of expression and erode the assumption of information access.

Citizens' awareness and empowerment is also vital: there may be inhibitions against seeking information or a reluctance to assert the right to freedom of expression, either in the public at large, or among marginalized or minority groups. Laws need to be backed up by systematic measures to make citizens aware of their right, and to make officials aware of their obligations.

In order to facilitate these goals, UNESCO provides expert advice to Member States, from Brazil to Timor Leste, on how best to ensure that media legislation complies with international standards and to raise awareness on the importance of such legislation in the media industry and among the wider public.

UNESCO's Communication and Information work in Brazil is an excellent example. Brazil's regulatory framework regarding freedom of expression and press freedom is severely outmoded, dating from 1962. Two challenges exist, in particular: the lack of media pluralism which characterizes Brazil's highly concentrated, privately owned media landscape and the absence of an independent regulator. In this context,

[20] UNESCO, OHCHR, UNDP, *Implementation Strategy 2013–2014 on the UN Plan of Action on the Safety of Journalists and the Issue of Impunity*, 2, 24 and 26, at www.unesco.org/new/fileadmin/MULTIMEDIA/HQ/CI/CI/pdf/official_documents/Implementation_Strategy_2013-2014_REV8march.pdf.

UNESCO's office in Brasilia, in partnership with the Ford Foundation, has been highly active in contributing to the ongoing debate in Brazilian society about the role of the communication industry in strengthening democracy. In March 2011, it released three studies on the Brazilian media system.

The first study, *The Regulatory Environment for Broadcasting: An International Best Practice Survey for Brazilian Stakeholders*,[21] written by international experts Toby Mendel and Eve Salomon, is an investigation of the regulatory situation of the Brazilian media system in comparison with current practices in ten other democracies (Canada, Chile, France, Germany, Jamaica, Malaysia, South Africa, Thailand, the UK and the USA) and with recommendations based on international law. The second paper, *Freedom of Expression and Broadcasting Regulation*,[22] also by Mendel and Salomon, provides content for reflection on the centrality of regulation for the protection, promotion and guarantee of the right to receive, seek and impart information, ideas and opinions. The third publication, written by Andrew Puddephatt, focuses on different angles of self-regulation applied to the media sector. *The Importance of Self-Regulation of the Media in Upholding Freedom of Expression*[23] summarizes the intersections of the theme with the practice of journalism, the editorial principles and strategies for corporate social responsibility.

Although the texts focus more on traditional media, the core principles reaffirmed by the authors can be applied to new (or innovative) media, including the Internet. For the Representative of the Ford Foundation in

[21] T. Mendel and E. Salomon, *The Regulatory Environment for Broadcasting: An International Best Practice Survey for Brazilian Stakeholders*, Series CI debates: Communication and Information, vol. 7 (Brasilia: UNESCO Office Brasilia, 2011); at www.unesco.org/new/en/communication-and-information/resources/publications-and-communication-materials/publications/full-list/the-regulatory-environment-for-broadcasting-an-international-best-practice-survey-for-brazilian-stakeholders (last accessed 27 January 2014).

[22] T. Mendel and E. Salomon, *Freedom of Expression and Broadcasting Regulation*, Series CI debates: Communication and Information, vol. 8 (Brasilia: UNESCO Office Brasilia, 2011); at www.unesco.org/new/en/communication-and-information/resources/publications-and-communication-materials/publications/full-list/freedom-of-expression-and-broadcasting-regulation (last accessed 27 January 2014).

[23] A. Puddephatt, *The Importance of Self-Regulation of the Media in Upholding Freedom of Expression*, vol. 9 (Brasilia: UNESCO Office Brasilia, 2011); at www.unesco.org/new/en/communication-and-information/resources/publications-and-communication-materials/publications/full-list/the-importance-of-self-regulation-of-the-media-in-upholding-freedom-of-expression (last accessed 27 January 2014).

Brazil, Ana Toni, 'the goal of these important studies is to contribute to the public debate that gained weight last year in Brazil regarding media regulation and freedom of expression'.[24] The three publications bring regulatory and self-regulatory best practices from other countries that seek to strengthen freedom of expression and to guarantee the development of a pluralistic and democratic media, in accordance with UNESCO's mandate.

UNESCO also supported the adoption of the Freedom of Information Law in Brazil, and is assisting the government in its implementation and in meeting a number of Brazil's commitments under the Open Government Partnership.[25] UNESCO has further supported civil society organizations, via an IPDC project, to prepare, monitor and use the new law.

Activities in Liberia also encapsulate the main thrust of UNESCO's activities in support of a regulatory environment in accordance with international standards. In 2011, UNESCO supported two Freedom of Information Stakeholders Forums, coordinated by the Centre for Media Studies and Peace Building (CEMESP) and intended to increase the visibility and understanding of Liberia's freedom of information legislation. The first forum, which took place on 5 September 2011, was held in Monrovia and aimed at law-makers, media executives and CSOs. The second, held in the rural town of Gbarnga on 12 September, targeted local county authorities and community radio journalists from the surrounding areas of Lofa, Bong, Nimba and Margibi. In a series of interactive workshops and discussions, participants highlighted the enduring need to fully implement existing freedom of information legislation. The two sessions peaked with the drafting, signing and reading of a communiqué that captured stakeholders' commitment to provide the impetus for effective implementation of Liberia's Freedom of Information Law. These actions were implemented in the lead-up to the second post-conflict legislative and presidential elections in Liberia, which were held in October 2011 (with the run-off presidential election held in November). The project, financed by the Danish International Development Agency, also included a component of training journalists on conflict-sensitive reporting; monitoring media output in regards to electoral

[24] See www.unesco.org/new/en/communication-and-information/resources/news-and-in-focus-articles/all-news/news/unesco_releases_three_publications_analyzing_media_regulation_and_freedom_of_expression_in_brazil-1 (last accessed 27 January 2014).

[25] See www.opengovpartnership.org/country/brazil (last accessed 27 January 2014).

coverage and freedom of information; and capacity-building efforts contributing to financially sustainable media.

The activities in Liberia, implemented between June 2011 and December 2012, represented a pilot phase of a broader project that is in the process of being implemented in other countries of the Manor River Union: Sierra Leone, Guinea and Côte d'Ivoire. Indeed, in the context of media laws and regulatory frameworks, freedom of information legislation is a high priority. Freedom of Information is recognized by both Resolution 59 of the UN General Assembly adopted in 1946, and Article 19 of the Universal Declaration of Human Rights (1948), which states that the fundamental right of freedom of expression encompasses the freedom 'to seek, receive and impart information and ideas through any media and regardless of frontiers'. In the words of the African Commission on Human and People's Rights' 2002 Declaration of Principles on Freedom of Expression in Africa, 'public bodies hold information, not for themselves but custodians of the public good and everyone has a right to access this information, subject only to clearly defined rules established in law'.[26]

However, in the face of calls for freedom of information, many political leaders and civil servants spring immediately to a defensive posture of stressing the need to limit the circulation of 'sensitive' information. But there are also many others, especially when newly elected, who see the value in democratizing access as a way to reform the State by exposing those officials appointed under a previous regime to the light of a new day. When executive behaviour occurs in the sunlight, its excesses are more easily exposed, valuable public input can be heard and integrated in policy design and implementation.

Like most human rights, that to freedom of information can be qualified – but such limitations should be secondary, rather than primary, considerations when it comes to legislation provision for access to information. There is substantial jurisprudence, and valuable standards proposed by NGOs such as ARTICLE 19, around this issue. Key among these is the principle of maximum disclosure, which dictates that individuals should be granted access to all information held by public bodies, except for very limited and clearly specified categories, subject to harm and public interest tests. In practice, however, it is not unusual for

[26] ACHPR, Declaration of Principles on Freedom of Expression in Africa, Banjul, the Gambia, 17–23 October 2002, Principle IV(1).

exceptions, along with the reference to official secret acts, to unduly justify arbitrary denials of information access.[27]

In terms of encouraging the empowerment of citizens, freedom of information is at the heart of a participatory democracy. Consider the consequences of an uninformed electorate going to the polls; consider the consequences when information flows are curbed or manipulated in times of political crisis or ethnic strife. Freedom of information promotes a true sense of empowerment within society and therefore gives meaning to the concept of citizenship.

In the context of the profound transformations that have taken place in the Arab region in the past few years, UNESCO has also placed special attention to facilitating support towards strengthening the legal and regulatory frameworks conducive to freedom of expression, press freedom and freedom of information in countries such as Egypt, Libya, Lebanon, Morocco, Tunisia and Jordan, among others. It is critical to support freedom of expression in fostering democratic governance, development and sustained peace, in a region where the enhanced exercise of this right has enabled social and political change, promising to transform societies in ways perhaps unimaginable only a few years ago.

Looking to the future, another priority for the next biennium is likely to be the decriminalization of defamation laws. Criminal defamation is an affront to free speech. It has enormous personal impact on the accused journalist, and may deprive him/her of his career, income and liberty. It puts a burden on journalists' families and, by definition, brands them criminals. Furthermore, it has what has been called a 'chilling effect' on other journalists and media professionals working in the jurisdiction, encouraging a climate of fear and self-censorship.

There is a trend towards decriminalization. Countries such as Ghana, Liberia and Niger have decriminalized speech, for example. Sri Lanka did the same in 2002. In Latin America, decriminalization of speech related to critical expressions against public functionaries or institutions have been almost completely eliminated through a process that started in the 1990s. However, in several countries in the region, the remaining figures

[27] For a review of international standards and case studies focused on freedom of information, see T. Mendel, *Freedom of Information: A Comparative Legal Survey*, 2nd edn (Paris: UNESCO, 2008); http://portal.unesco.org/ci/en/ev.php-URL_ID=26159&URL_DO=DO_TOPIC&URL_SECTION=201.html (last accessed 27 January 2014). See Chapters 3 and 9 in this book.

established to protect the honour of individuals are still being unduly used to restrict debate on matters of public interest (that is, public officials, acting in their personal capacity, file penal charges related to expressions critical of the exercise of their public functions).

Progress around the world in regards to this matter is linked to strong efforts of press freedom advocates. In Africa, important milestones have been the 2007 Declaration of Table Mountain,[28] and a resolution by the African Commission on Human and Peoples' Rights in 2010,[29] which called for repealing laws that criminalize speech. The African Special Rapporteur on Freedom of Expression and Access to Information is leading advocacy efforts focused on this matter in the region, in partnership with different key stakeholders. Moreover, the Pan African Parliament adopted a resolution launching a campaign to protect press freedoms in 2012.[30] In Latin America, the work of the organs of the Inter-American system of human rights and several CSOs has been critical. However, criminal defamation laws persist, and there is still much work to be done, often in some of the most progressive nations.

Finally, in a digital age characterized by prospering user-generated content, UNESCO recognizes that the principle of freedom of expression must apply not only to traditional media, but to the Internet too. Providing an unprecedented volume of resources for information and knowledge, the Internet opens up new opportunities for expression and participation and holds enormous potential for development. This is undoubtedly a blessing for creativity, exchange and dialogue. Yet the digital age also creates the need for updated legal and regulatory measures which balance a variety of potentially conflicting values and interests.

With this in mind, and within the framework of the follow-up process to the 2003 and 2005 World Summit on the Information Society (WSIS) conferences in Geneva and Tunis,[31] UNESCO has

[28] WAN-IFRA, Declaration of Table Mountain: Abolishing 'Insult Laws' and Criminal Defamation in Africa and Setting a Free Press Higher on the Agenda, 3–6 June 2007; at www.wan-ifra.org/articles/2011/02/16/the-declaration-of-table-mountain (last accessed on 27 January 2014).

[29] ACHPR, Resolution 169 on Repealing Criminal Defamation Laws in Africa, 24 November 2010. See: www.achpr.org/sessions/48th/resolutions/169 (last accessed 27 January 2014).

[30] Pan African Parliament, Resolution to Protect Media Freedoms, 18 October 2012, Doc. No. PAP/P(3)/RES/08(I); at www.wan-ifra.org/articles/2012/12/19/pan-african-parliament-resolution-to-protect-media-freedoms (last accessed 27 January 2014).

[31] These Summits brought together representatives of States, as well as representatives from international organizations, the private sector and civil society. At the first meeting in

recently launched a series on Internet freedom. The first publication, *Freedom of Connection, Freedom Of Expression: The Changing Legal and Regulatory Ecology Shaping the Internet*,[32] examines the changing legal and regulatory ecology that has shaped the internet over the years, with a view to providing a reference tool that can inform and stimulate the current debate on the global trends that have shaped freedom of expression on the internet. The second publication, *Global Survey on Internet Privacy and Freedom of Expression*,[33] seeks to identify the relationship between freedom of expression and Internet privacy, assessing where they support or compete with each other in different circumstances. The book maps out the issues in the current regulatory landscape of Internet privacy from the viewpoint of freedom of expression and provides an overview of legal protection, self-regulatory guidelines, normative challenges and case studies relating to the topic.

Freedom of expression and media development emerged as key issues in the First WSIS+10 Review Event, held at UNESCO Headquarters in Paris from 25 to 27 February 2013 ten years after the first WSIS in Geneva. The programme included a dozen sessions devoted to media,[34] and the Final Statement, adopted in the closing session of the conference, recommends that all stakeholders 'further promote universal access to information and knowledge with due respect for free flow of

Geneva in 2003 the Geneva Declaration of Principles and the Geneva Plan of Action were adopted, confirming political will to take steps to establish the foundations for an Information Society for all (Geneva Declaration of Principles and Geneva Plan of Action, WSIS-03/GENEVA/DOC/0004 and, WSIS-03/GENEVA/DOC/0005 (10–12 December 2003)). At the second meeting in Tunis in 2005, the Tunis Commitment and Tunis Agenda for the Information Society were adopted to put Geneva's Plan of Action into action (Tunis Commitment and Tunis Agenda for the Information Society, WSIS-05/TUNIS/DOC/6 (rev. 1) and WSIS-05/TUNIS/DOC/7 (16–18 November 2005)).

32 W. Dutton *et al.*, *Freedom of Connection, Freedom of Expression: The Changing Legal and Regulatory Ecology Shaping the Internet* (Paris: UNESCO, 2011), 103; at www.unesco.org/new/en/communication-and-information/resources/publications-and-communication-materials/publications/full-list/freedom-of-connection-freedom-of-expression-the-changing-legal-and-regulatory-ecology-shaping-the-internet (last accessed 27 January 2014).

33 T. Mendel *et al.*, *Global Survey on Internet Privacy and Freedom of Expression* (Paris: UNESCO, 2012), 144; at www.unesco.org/new/en/communication-and-information/resources/publications-and-communication-materials/publications/full-list/global-survey-on-internet-privacy-and-freedom-of-expression (last accessed 27 January 2014).

34 For summaries of sessions related to media, see www.unesco.org/new/fileadmin/MULTIMEDIA/HQ/CI/CI/pdf/news/media_session_reports.pdf (last accessed 27 January 2014).

information'.[35] During WSIS+10, UNESCO called for feedback on a new concept of 'Internet Universality', meaning an open, accessible, free and rights-based Internet, developed in a multi-stakeholder environment. Additionally, the safety of online journalists, bloggers and human rights activists as a precondition for freedom of expression was recognized in the Final Statement and in a UNESCO session on the Digital Safety of Journalists.

UNESCO also plays an active role in the Internet Governance Forum (IGF), designed to support the United Nations Secretary-General in carrying out the mandate from the WSIS and provide an interactive, collaborative space where all stakeholders can share their views and exchange ideas. The 7th Annual IGF Meeting was held in Baku, Azerbaijan from 6 to 9 September 2012, with its main theme 'Internet Governance for Sustainable Human, Economic and Social Development'. In this context, UNESCO organized a workshop on privacy and freedom of expression,[36] and co-hosted an open forum on the safety of online media actors.[37]

As part of its work in the area of Internet freedom, UNESCO has commissioned a study on cases around the world linked to guaranteeing the safety of journalists using digital media. The research will analyse the role of governments, intergovernmental organizations, civil society and the media in the protection of online media actors. It will also provide guidelines, good practices and policy recommendations related to respect for the right to freedom of expression in the digital environment. At the same time, UNESCO is also conducting a study on the role of Internet intermediaries, such as Internet service providers (ISPs), hosting

[35] WSIS, Final Statement, Information and Knowledge for All: An Expanded Vision and Renewed Commitment, created for the project Towards Knowledge Societies for Peace and Sustainable Development on the first WSIS+10 review event, 25–27 February 2013; at www.unesco.org/new/fileadmin/MULTIMEDIA/HQ/CI/CI/pdf/wsis/WSIS_10_Event/wsis10_final_statement_en.pdf (last accessed 27 January 2014).

[36] See www.unesco.org/new/en/communication and information/resources/news and in-focus-articles/all-news/news/unesco_launches_global_survey_on_internet_privacy_and_freedom_of_expression_at_the_internet_governance_forum/ and http://wsms1.intgovforum.org/content/no59-internet-privacy-and-freedom-expression-unesco-launches-global-survey-legal-frameworks (both last accessed 27 January 2014).

[37] See www.unesco.org/new/en/communication-and-information/resources/news-and-in-focus-articles/all-news/news/affirming_the_safety_of_online_media_actors_at_the_internet_governance_forum/ and http://wsms1.intgovforum.org/2012/Meetings/joint-open-forum-ebu-coe-osce-safety-online-media-actors (both last accessed 27 January 2014).

providers, search engines, social media platforms and other entities, in the protection of freedom of expression. Internet intermediaries function as the new and global gatekeepers of information flow in cyberspace and increasingly play a fundamental role in enabling Internet users to enjoy their right to freedom of expression and access to information on the Internet. This project aims to identify those good practices and processes related to Internet intermediaries that can encourage or protect freedom of expression by ensuring that any of its limitations are consistent with international standards.

## 5 Ethical and professional standard-setting

In addition to formal legal frameworks, any system of regulation must also include self-regulatory mechanisms that promote freedom of expression, including codes of conduct, press councils and standard-setting bodies operated by the press communities themselves.[38] Indeed, too much State intervention negates the independence of the media as a watchdog that speaks truth to power and acts as a channel through which democratic deliberation and debate can take place.

Self-regulation, on the other hand, preserves independence of the media and protects it from partisan governmental interference. It can also be more efficient than State regulation as the media often understand their own environment better than government and more effective given that it requires organizations to think about and even develop their own standards of behaviour. It also fulfils a norm-setting function where peer pressure fosters compliance. Finally, as the media environment becomes global (through the development of the internet and digital platforms) and questions of jurisdiction become more complex, self-regulation has the potential to fill the gaps that State regulation cannot cover.

There is, however, no single model suitable for all contexts. The apparatus of self-regulation is ineffective without a prevailing culture of public and peer scrutiny. Conversely, self-regulation can sometimes be effectively achieved without formal national structures or bodies, through local and international vigilance, responsiveness and transparency on questions of news ethics and accuracy. Self-regulation is most successful where it properly engages all stakeholders within the media (including publishers, owners, editors and journalists) as well as the broader public.

[38] See Chapter 11 in this book for further discussion of these and related topics.

UNESCO contributes to ethical and professional standard-setting through trainings, workshops and technological capacity-building, as well as through public knowledge resource sharing. At the global level, for instance, the conference 'The Media World after WikiLeaks and *News of the World*', held at UNESCO headquarters in Paris, gathered leading media representatives, media professionals, citizen journalists and media law experts to discuss good practices in traditional professional journalism and citizen journalism in the digital era.[39]

Regionally, between August 2008 and February 2011, UNESCO implemented the EC-funded project 'Alignment to International Standards in the Media Sector of South-East European Countries' in Albania, Bosnia and Herzegovina, Croatia, Montenegro, Serbia, the Former Yugoslav Republic of Macedonia, Turkey and Kosovo (as understood under UN Security Council Resolution 1244). The initiative was implemented in collaboration with the South-East European Network for Professionalization of Media, the Organization for Security and Co-operation in Europe and the Alliance of Independent Press Councils of Europe. It aimed to support the development of self-regulation mechanisms and the adoption of media accountability best practices.

Press council members, new ombudsmen, editors and journalists, academics, representatives from media institutes, civil society and international organizations were brought together through two series of local roundtables, two region-wide meetings and a closing conference organized in Paris in January 2011,[40] to debate the issues the media currently faces, most notably how media accountability can be supported in the digital age. Information was also shared through a publication entitled *Professional Journalism and Self-Regulation: New Media, Old Dilemmas in South East Europe and Turkey*[41] and a database[42] on the UNESCO

39 See www.unesco.org/new/en/communication-and-information/events/calendar-of-events/events-websites/the-media-world-after-wikileaks-and-news-of-the-world (last accessed 27 January 2014).

40 See www.unesco.org/new/en/communication-and-information/events/calendar-of-events/events-websites/journalism-ethics-and-self-regulation-in-europe-new-media-old-dilemmas (last accessed 27 January 2014).

41 Z. Ognian, *Professional Journalism and Self-Regulation: New Media, Old Dilemmas in South East Europe and Turkey* (Paris: UNESCO, 2011); at www.unesco.org/new/en/communication-and-information/resources/publications-and-communication-materials/publications/full-list/professional-journalism-and-self-regulation-new-media-old-dilemmas-in-south-east-europe-and-turkey (last accessed 27 January 2014).

42 See www.unesco.org/new/en/communication-and-information/freedom-of-expression/professional-journalistic-standards-and-code-of-ethics/, database can be found at www.

website. This virtual resource concerns media accountability and its various mechanisms in Europe, Africa, the Americas and South-East Asia. In 2012, UNESCO launched a three-year follow-up project, also funded by the European Commission, which will continue to build awareness and capacities to strengthen media accountability and transparency in South East Europe and Turkey.

At the country level, UNESCO launched an initiative to build capacities for strengthened media accountability in Egypt, including through the establishment of a media self-regulatory body. Moreover, in partnership with USAID, International Research and Exchanges Board (IREX), the Africa Elections Project and the International Media Centre (IMC), the Organization has supported the Liberian Media Centre in implementing an elections support programme, 'Strengthened Media for Transparent Elections', for local journalists covering the 2011 Liberian elections.[43]

This programme established a multipurpose Elections Reporting Centre (ERC) for local journalists and provided training and logistical support for media coverage of elections and conflict-sensitive reporting. It also provided daily online services for local reporters through the use of ICTs and social media applications and delivered monitoring services for media coverage and incidence of violence through a Call Centre jointly run with the Africa Elections Project. The Election Reporting Centre was furnished with a state-of-the-art E-News Lab for training and online reporting purposes. It was also equipped with a television, radio and newspaper monitoring platform, as well as 50 audio recorders; 10 video cameras; and 10 motorcycles for 300 reporters covering the elections across the country for four months.

Free resource and training handbooks on topics such as conflict-sensitive reporting[44] and investigative journalism,[45] published by

unesco.org/shs/ethics/geo/user/?action=search&db=GEO5 (last accessed 27 January 2014).

43 These actions were implemented in the framework of the project supporting media in the Manor River States, mentioned previously in this chapter.

44 See R. Howard, *Conflict-Sensitive Reporting: State of the Art; A Course for Journalists and Journalism Educators* (Paris: UNESCO, 2009); at www.unesco.org/new/en/communication-and-information/resources/publications-and-communication-materials/publications/full-list/conflict-sensitive-reporting-state-of-the-art-a-course-for-journalists-and-journalism-educators (last accessed 27 January 2014).

45 See M. L. Hunter, *Story Based Inquiry: A Manual for Investigative Journalists* (Paris: UNESCO, 2011); see www.unesco.org/new/en/communication-and-information/resources/publications-and-communication-materials/publications/full-list/story-based-inquiry-a

UNESCO, also constitute vital instruments for fostering ethical journalism and professionalism.

## 6 Promoting media diversity

The final approach that underpins UNESCO's strategy on freedom of expression is the goal of promoting diversity in media content, production and consumption. The media should reflect the diversity of society, in all its facets (including gender, age, race, ethnicity, caste, language, belief, sexual orientation, social class, etc.), in order to avoid the marginalization of minority groups. This means that media pluralism, in both form and content, is of paramount importance. Community media and public service broadcasting (PSB) are particularly relevant in this regard.

PSB is broadcasting made, financed and controlled by the public, for the public. The defining characteristic of PSBs is that they are protected from interference, of a commercial or political nature, in respect of their financing, governance and editorial independence. Their public service remit usually includes obligations to ensure that the public receives politically balanced information, especially at election times. In addition, they typically strive to ensure that their transmission system covers the whole territory of a country and that they serve all regions, cultures and linguistic groups.

Through PSB, citizens are informed, educated and also entertained. When guaranteed with pluralism, programming diversity, editorial independence, appropriate funding, accountability and transparency, public service broadcasting can serve as a cornerstone of democracy. Community media typically concerns media at the local level. In this context, radio broadcasting plays a key role as the most economical and universal means of communication meeting community needs in the context of globalization and high illiteracy rates (indeed, the importance of radio broadcasting was highlighted at the 2011 Executive Board when it was decided that World Radio Day was to be celebrated annually on 13 February). Community media increase the opportunities of rural communities to produce, acquire, contextualize

-manual-for-investigative-journalists and M. L. Hunter, *The Global Investigative Journalism Casebook* (Paris: UNESCO, 2012); at www.unesco.org/new/en/communication-and-information/resources/publications-and-communication-materials/publications/full-list/the-global-investigative-journalism-casebook (both last accessed 27 January 2014).

and share locally relevant content. This, in turn, offers the basic tools for introducing and managing community-centred, sustainable development.

UNESCO actively promotes community media through a wide range of initiatives. Both through its publications and through various international and national events, it provides a forum for best-practice sharing. The UNESCO publication *Community Media: A Good Practice Handbook*[46] is organized according to three key themes:

- The enabling environment for community media, with ten country case studies of good practice in policies, laws, regulations, funding and support structures that enable community media to establish and to flourish.
- Sustainability, with ten case studies of community media practice that demonstrate such characteristics as longevity, consistency and adaptability.
- Social impact, with ten case studies of community media contributing to social change, improvement in lives and livelihoods, social cohesion in the face of conflict, humanitarian protection, strengthened governance and accountability, increased participation in democracy and development, reduced discrimination and other benefits.

In addition, UNESCO's International Initiative for Community Multimedia Centres (CMCs) promotes community empowerment and addresses the digital divide by combining community broadcasting with the Internet and related technologies.

The CMC programme offers a global strategy for addressing the digital divide in the poorest communities of the developing world and also among countries in transition. The CMC opens a gateway to active membership of the global knowledge society by making information and communication the basic tools of the poor in improving their own lives. It combines community radio by local people in local languages with community telecentre facilities (computers with Internet and e-mail, phone, fax and photocopying services). The radio – which is low cost and easy to operate – not only informs, educates and

[46] S. Buckley, *Community Media: A Good Practice Handbook* (Paris: UNESCO, 2011); at www.unesco.org/new/en/communication-and-information/resources/publications-and-communication-materials/publications/full-list/community-media-a-good-practice-handbook (last accessed 27 January 2014).

entertains, but it also empowers the community by giving a strong public voice to the voiceless, and thus encouraging greater accountability in public affairs.

In the field of PSB, UNESCO's endeavours centre around enhancing the utility of PSB as an educational and cultural vehicle, especially for disadvantaged communities; promoting best PSB practices and professional standards and contributing to relevant revisions of national legislation; strengthening PSB as a gateway to information and knowledge for all; fostering the indigenous content quality and technological upgrading of public service broadcasting; encouraging innovative and creative improvements in programming to captivate larger audiences; and upholding discussions between media professionals, decision-makers, and other stakeholders on major PSB-related issues.

In pursuit of these objectives, the organization has worked with a number of regional broadcasting unions such as the Asian Broadcasting Union (ABU), the Caribbean Media Corporation (CMC), the European Broadcasting Union (EBU) and the Arab States Broadcasting Union (ASBU), as well as associations of broadcasters, including the South African Broadcasting Association (SABA), the Commonwealth Broadcasting Association (CBA), the International Council of French-speaking Radio and Television (CIRTEF), the International Association of Educational and Discovery Television Companies (AITED) and the International Radio and Television University (URTI), among others. Priorities for the future will include contributing to capacity-building and providing training in modern broadcasting, particularly in issues related to ICTs and stimulating an international debate on the significant PSB-related issues and its impact on education, culture and civil society.

Furthermore, especially in light of the designation of gender equality as one of two global priorities in the organization's Medium-Term Strategy for 2008–13, and reaffirmed for the 2014–21 Medium-Term Strategy, UNESCO is dedicated to ensuring that media development initiatives are gender sensitive. This means combining the promotion of gender-specific programming and the battle against female stereotypes in media content with drives to include women as members of the workforce at all levels of the media. In the words of Aidan White, former Secretary General of the International Federation of Journalists:

> [F]air gender portrayal is a professional and ethical aspiration, similar to respect for accuracy, fairness and honesty. It is the other side of the coin

> that says women need to be more present at higher levels of news business, both at work and in the unions. In a world where hard news is still mainly reported by men, journalists need to stand up for gender equality. This equality is not just a women's issue; everyone benefits from eliminating discrimination.[47]

Through a consultative process launched in 2010, UNESCO produced the Gender-Sensitive Indicators for Media (GSIM), to contribute to gender equality and women's empowerment in and through media of all forms, irrespective of the technology used.[48] On the basis of these indicators, UNESCO promotes a more balanced representation of women and men in the media and fostering gender equality in Morocco, under projects financed by the Swedish and Finnish governments. In partnership with the High Authority of the Audiovisual Communication (HACA), the Permanent Conference of the Mediterranean Audiovisual Operators (COPEAM) and the National Society of Radio and Television (SNRT), the project seeks to sensitize media professionals and reinforce their capacities for the production of audiovisual content that follows a gender-sensitive approach, as well as to support the development of internal policies towards the institutionalization of gender equality considerations within participating media outlets.

Globally, UNESCO and its partners continue to launch the Women Make the News initiative, aimed at calling attention to issues relating to gender equality in and through the media, driving debate and encouraging action-oriented solutions until global objectives are met.[49] Importantly, in November 2013, UNESCO and partner institutions convened a 'Global Forum on Media and Gender', which is expected to strengthen international cooperation, leading to the establishment of a Global Alliance on Media and Gender.

[47] A. White, *Getting the Balance Right: Gender Equality in Journalism* (Brussels: International Federation of Journalists, 2009), v; at www.unesco.org/new/en/communication-and-information/resources/publications-andcommunication-materials/publications/full-list/getting-the-balance-right-gender-equality-in-journalism (last accessed 27 January 2014).

[48] See www.unesco.org/new/en/communication-and-information/resources/publications-and-communication-materials/publications/full-list/gender-sensitive-indicators-for-media-framework-of-indicators-to-gauge-gender-sensitivity-in-media-operations-and-content (last accessed 27 January 2014).

[49] See www.unesco.org/new/en/communication-and-information/crosscutting-priorities/gender-and-media/women-make-the-news/about (last accessed 27 January 2014).

## 7 Conclusion

This chapter has outlined five key approaches employed by UNESCO in the fight for freedom of expression and, hence, development, dialogue and democracy. The challenges to freedom of expression are multiple and ever-changing. George Orwell once wrote that 'if liberty means anything at all, it means the right to tell people what they do not want to hear'.[50] Freedom of expression means, indeed, the right to inform, whatever the context, however difficult the situation. Protecting this fundamental human right, and thus upholding the UDHR, is a process without an end. The case must be continually argued; violation of this right should never be accepted; and States and societies must be helped to move forward. This is a central tenet of UNESCO's mandate.

### Literature


Buckley, S. *Community Media: A Good Practice Handbook* (Paris: UNESCO, 2011).

Cobden, M., G. S. Adam, H. H. Holm and M. Abu-Fadil, *Model Curricula for Journalism Education* (Paris: UNESCO, 2007).

Dutton, W. *et al. Freedom of Connection, Freedom of Expression: the Changing Legal and Regulatory Ecology Shaping the Internet* (Paris: UNESCO, 2011).

Horsley, W. *Pressing for Freedom: 20 Years of World Press Freedom Day* (Paris: UNESCO, 2013).

Howard, R. *Conflict-Sensitive Reporting: State of the Art; A Course for Journalists and Journalism Educators* (Paris: UNESCO, 2009).

Hunter, M. L. *Story Based Inquiry: A Manual for Investigative Journalists* (Paris: UNESCO, 2011).

*The Global Investigative Journalism Casebook, UNESCO Series on Journalism Education* (Paris: UNESCO, 2012).

James, B. *Press Freedom: Safety of Journalists and Impunity* (Paris: UNESCO, 2007).

Mendel, T. *Freedom of Information: A Comparative Legal Survey*, 2nd edn (Paris: UNESCO, 2008).

Mendel, T. and E. Salomon, *The Regulatory Environment for Broadcasting: An International Best Practice Survey for Brazilian Stakeholders, Series CI debates: Communication and Information*, vol. 7 (Brasilia: UNESCO Office Brasilia, 2011).


[50] George Orwell, 'The freedom of the press', *Times Literary Supplement*, 15 September 1972.

*Freedom of Expression and Broadcasting Regulation, Series CI debates: Communication and Information*, vol. 8 (Brazil: UNESCO Office Brasilia, 2011).

Mendel, T. *et al. Global Survey on Internet Privacy and Freedom of Expression, UNESCO Series on Internet Freedom* (Paris: UNESCO, 2012).

Ognian, Z. *et al. Professional Journalism and Self-Regulation: New Media, Old Dilemmas in South East Europe and Turkey* (Paris: UNESCO, 2011).

Puddephatt, A. *The Importance of Self-Regulation of the Media in Upholding Freedom of Expression, Series CI debates: Communication and Information*, vol. 9 (Brazil: UNESCO Office Brasilia, 2011).

White, A. *Getting the Balance Right: Gender Equality in Journalism* (Brussels: International Federation of Journalists, 2009).

## Newspaper articles

Orwell, G. 'The freedom of the press', *Times Literary Supplement*, 15 September 1972.

# 8

# The UN Special Rapporteur on freedom of opinion and expression: progressive development of international standards relating to freedom of expression

TOBY MENDEL

## 1 Introduction

The office of the United Nations (UN) Special Rapporteur on the promotion and protection of the right to freedom of opinion and expression is the only specialised UN mandate that focuses exclusively or even primarily on the fundamental right to freedom of expression. Created in 1993, in response to the growing recognition of the importance of freedom of expression not just in its own right, but also as an underpinning for all other rights, the mandate has steadily grown in importance and recognition.

This chapter explores the development of the mandate of the Special Rapporteur, and the ways in which it has been changed over the twenty years since it was created. It also outlines the main types of activities undertaken by the Special Rapporteur, whether these are formally required by the mandate or additional activities.

An important part of this chapter examines one of the most important and controversial activities of the Special Rapporteur, namely his standard-setting work. The global relevance of this work and, in particular, the fact that it is presented as an elaboration of binding international guarantees of freedom of expression, give it enormous potential to lever change. As the chapter makes clear, this work has in practice made a very important contribution to our understanding of the scope and nature of the right to freedom of expression.

As used in this chapter, the term 'standard-setting' refers to various efforts by the Special Rapporteur to elaborate on the meaning and content of the right to freedom of expression. The most explicit and classical forms of this are the Joint Declarations the Special Rapporteur adopts on an annual basis with his counterparts at the Organization for Security and Co-operation in Europe (OSCE), Organization of American States (OAS) and African Commission on Human and Peoples' Rights (ACHPR), which contain statements along the lines of 'States should…' and 'States should not…'.

Formally, these statements are not legally binding, since they are not a source of international law as envisaged in Article 38 of the Statute of the International Court of Justice.[1] At the same time, these statements represent an interpretation, by the Special Rapporteur, of the legally binding guarantees of freedom of expression found in international law. While the Special Rapporteur does not have the power to impose these interpretations on States, they provide convincing, effectively authoritative, evidence as to the content of international law, based on the status of the post of the Special Rapporteur, the respect that he commands, and the quality of those statements. Put differently, just as national courts often refer to and follow the interpretations of courts from other countries when faced with complex and otherwise unclear legal issues, many people and institutions use the standard-setting work of the Special Rapporteur in the same way. As such, and as elaborated on in more detail below, this body of work by the Special Rapporteur has had a significant impact on global understandings of the meaning and content of the right to freedom of expression, including by bodies which are more formally imbued with the power to interpret international law. In this sense, this work by the Special Rapporteur can be said to be standard-setting in nature.

## 2 Establishment and mandate

The office of the UN Special Rapporteur on the promotion and protection of the right to freedom of opinion and expression was established by a resolution of the UN Commission on Human Rights in 1993.[2] The Commission had already established a number of working groups and special rapporteurs to address various country and thematic concerns,

[1] Although the work of the Special Rapporteur arguably falls within the scope of Article 38(1)(d) of the Statute of the International Court of Justice.

[2] UN CHR, Resolution 1993/45, UN Doc. E/CN.4/1993/122, 5 March 1993. See, in particular, para. 11. The Commission was created by the UN Economic and Social Council (ECOSOC) in 1946 to promote human rights, and was replaced by the UN Human Rights Council in 2006.

and the issue of freedom of expression had for some time been a candidate for special attention by the UN.[3]

Four individuals have occupied the position of UN Special Rapporteur on freedom of opinion and expression since the creation of the mandate in 1993. Mr Abid Hussain (India) held the post for nine years from his appointment in April 1993 until July 2002, he was followed by Mr Ambeyi Ligabo (Kenya), who held the post from August 2002 to July 2008 and then Mr Frank La Rue (Guatemala), who held the post from August 2008 to October 2014. The current Special Rapporteur, Mr David Kaye (United States), was appointed in October 2014.

The original mandate of the Special Rapporteur was set out in the 1993 Resolution and remained essentially fixed until it was substantially revised in 2008, although the annual resolutions on freedom of opinion and expression of the Commission on Human Rights sometimes directed the Special Rapporteur's attention to certain issues and concerns. The following paragraphs, taken from the 1993 Resolution, describe the core of the mandate:

> The Commission on Human Rights,
>
> 12. Requests the Special Rapporteur to gather all relevant information, wherever it may occur, of discrimination against, threats or use of violence and harassment, including persecution and intimidation, directed at persons seeking to exercise or to promote the exercise of the right to freedom of opinion and expression as affirmed in the Universal Declaration of Human Rights and, where applicable, the International Covenant on Civil and Political Rights, taking into account the work being conducted by other mechanisms of the Commission and Sub-Commission which touches on this right, with a view to avoiding duplication of work;
> 13. Also requests the Special Rapporteur, as a matter of high priority, to gather all relevant information, wherever it may occur, of discrimination against, threats or use of violence and harassment, including persecution and intimidation, against professionals in the field of information seeking to exercise or to promote the exercise of the right to freedom of opinion and expression, as affirmed in the

[3] Prior to the establishment of the freedom of expression rapporteurship, for example, two Special Rapporteurs, Mr Danilo Türk and Mr Louis Joinet, had been appointed by the Sub-Commission on Prevention of Discrimination and Protection of Minorities to study this issue, and they prepared a number of reports on freedom of expression. See UN Docs. E/CN.4/Sub.2/1990/11, E/CN.4/Sub.2/1991/9 and E/CN.4/Sub.2/1992/9 and Add.1.

Universal Declaration of Human Rights and, where applicable, the International Covenant on Civil and Political Rights;

14. Further requests the Special Rapporteur to seek and receive credible and reliable information from Governments, non-governmental organisations and any other parties who have knowledge of these cases;

18. Requests the Special Rapporteur to submit to the Commission, beginning at its fiftieth session, a report covering the activities relating to his or her mandate, noting the work being conducted by other mechanisms of the Commission and Sub-Commission which touches on the right to freedom of expression and opinion, containing recommendations to the Commission and providing suggestions on ways and means to better promote and protect the right to freedom of opinion and expression in all its manifestations, as affirmed in the Universal Declaration of Human Rights and, where applicable, the International Covenant on Civil and Political Rights.

The guarantees of freedom of opinion and expression found in the Universal Declaration of Human Rights (UDHR)[4] and the International Covenant on Civil and Political Rights (ICCPR)[5] lie at the heart of the mandate of the Special Rapporteur. The UDHR, as a resolution of the UN General Assembly, is not formally legally binding, but many of its provisions, including Article 19, guaranteeing freedom of expression, are generally considered to be binding on all States as a matter of customary international law.[6] The ICCPR is a legally binding international treaty. In the above resolution, reference to the ICCPR is qualified by the term 'where applicable', since only those Member States of the UN which have ratified the ICCPR are bound by it. As of January 2015, there were 168 States Parties to the ICCPR, along with seven additional signatories.

[4] UN GA, Resolution 217A(III): Universal Declaration of Human Rights, 10 December 1948.

[5] International Covenant on Civil and Political Rights, New York, 16 December 1966, entered into force 23 March 1976, 999 UNTS 171.

[6] See, for example, *Barcelona Traction, Light and Power Company Limited Case (Belgium* v. *Spain) (Second Phase)*, ICJ Reports (1970) 3; *Namibia Opinion*, ICJ Reports (1971) 16, Separate Opinion, Judge Ammoun; *Filartiga* v. *Pena-Irala*, 630 F. 2d 876 (1980) (US Court of Appeals, 2nd Circuit). Generally, see M. S. McDougal, H. D. Lasswell and L. C. Chen, *Human Rights and World Public Order* (New Haven, CT: Yale University Press, 1980), 273–4 and 325–7.

The ICCPR guarantees freedom of expression at Article 19 as follows:

> (1) Everyone shall have the right to hold opinions without interference.
> (2) Everyone shall have the right to freedom of expression; this right shall include freedom to seek, receive and impart information and ideas of all kinds, regardless of frontiers, either orally, in writing or in print, in the form of art, or through any other media of his choice.
> (3) The exercise of the rights provided for in paragraph 2 of this article carries with it special duties and responsibilities. It may therefore be subject to certain restrictions, but these shall only be such as are provided by law and are necessary:
> (a) For respect of the rights or reputations of others;
> (b) For the protection of national security or of public order (*ordre public*), or of public health or morals.[7]

The scope of the mandate is delimited by these guarantees and it would not be appropriate for the Special Rapporteur to consider other human rights issues. However, widespread patterns of human rights abuse almost always involve serious abuses of the right to freedom of expression. Furthermore, the violation of certain other human rights, such as freedom of assembly and association, almost always also involve a breach of the right to freedom of expression.

As noted, the formal mandate of the Special Rapporteur essentially remained fixed until 2008. At the same time, the Commission on Human Rights, in its annual resolutions on freedom of expression, sometimes requested the Special Rapporteur to direct his attention to certain freedom of expression themes.

In the Commission's 1995 resolution, the Rapporteur was asked to refer cases of serious concern to the UN High Commissioner for Human Rights, to pay particular attention to the right of women to freedom of expression, free of discrimination, and to elaborate further on the right to seek and receive information.[8] These requests were essentially repeated in the 1996 resolution, and then expanded in 1997 to refer to cooperation with the Special Rapporteur on Violence Against Women, and to consider the impact of new information technologies on freedom of

[7] Article 19 of the UDHR contains a very similar positive guarantee for freedom of expression, although the scope of exceptions to this right, found at Article 29 of the UDHR, is somewhat different in nature. See further Chapter 1 in this book.

[8] UN CHR, Resolution 1995/40: Right to Freedom of Opinion and Expression, UN Doc. E/CN.4/RES/1995/40, 3 March 1995, paras. 11, 12 and 17.

expression.[9] This package of recommendations was repeated in each of the subsequent resolutions until 2003, in what can only be described as a somewhat unimaginative approach on the part of the Commission on Human Rights.

In 2000, the resolution also called on the Special Rapporteur to provide recommendations to the High Commissioner for Human Rights as part of the preparatory process for the World Conference against Racism, Racial Discrimination, Xenophobia and Related Intolerance,[10] and this was repeated in 2001.[11] The 2003 resolution also called for the Special Rapporteur to participate in the (first phase of the) World Summit on the Information Society,[12] while the 2004 and 2005 resolutions called for his participation in the second phase.[13] Otherwise, these latter two resolutions did not include the list of focus areas that had essentially been repeated since 1995.

An interesting development in 2001 was that, for the very first time, the resolution went to a vote (all of the previous resolutions had been adopted unanimously and the subsequent resolutions adopted by the Commission went back to this approach). The main reason for this was paragraph 18 of the resolution, which affirmed the 'vital importance' for the protection of freedom of expression of compliance by States with their obligations under the 'International Convention on the Elimination of All Forms of Racial Discrimination [ICERD], in particular article 4'.[14] Article 4 of ICERD calls on States to adopt broad prohibitions on the dissemination of racist statements, including 'all dissemination of ideas based on racial superiority'. This is deemed by many States to go too far in terms of limiting freedom of

[9] UN CHR, Resolution 1997/27: Right to Freedom of Opinion and Expression, UN Doc. E/CN.4/1997/27, 11 April 1997, para. 12.

[10] UN CHR, Resolution 2000/38: Right to Freedom of Opinion and Expression, UN Doc. E/CN.4/RES/2000/38, 20 April 2000, para. 13(g).

[11] UN CHR, Resolution 2001/47: Right to Freedom of Opinion and Expression, UN Doc. E/CN.4/RES/2001/47, 23 April 2001, para. 19.

[12] UN CHR, Resolution 2003/42: Right to Freedom of Opinion and Expression, UN Doc. E/CN.4/RES/2003/42, para. 17(g).

[13] UN CHR, Resolution 2004/42: Right to Freedom of Opinion and Expression 19 April 2004, UN Doc. E/CN.4/RES/2004/42, 23 April 2003, para. 10 and UN CHR Resolution 2005/38: Right to Freedom of Opinion and Expression, UN Doc. E/CN.4/RES/2005/38, 19 April 2005, para. 11.

[14] International Convention on the Elimination of All Forms of Racial Discrimination, 21 December 1965, entered into force 4 January 1969, 660 UNTS 195.

expression.[15] The result was a vote of forty-four in favour,[16] none against and eight abstentions.[17]

There were no dedicated resolutions on freedom of expression in 2006 and 2007, presumably due to the institutional transition from the Commission to the Human Rights Council, and the 2008 resolution, the first one on this topic to be adopted by the UN Human Rights Council, basically put in place a new mandate for the Special Rapporteur. Indeed, it was entitled 'Mandate of the Special Rapporteur on the promotion and protection of the right to freedom of opinion and expression'.[18] The resolution was extremely controversial, once again largely due to the way it proposed to deal with the issue of 'hate speech'.

The main controversy was the inclusion, for the first time, in the mandate of the Special Rapporteur of an obligation to report on abuses of the right to freedom of expression. Specifically, the fifteen abstaining States objected to paragraph 4(d) of the resolution, which requests the Special Rapporteur:

> To report on instances in which the abuse of the right of freedom of expression constitutes an act of racial or religious discrimination, taking into account articles 19 (3) and 20 of the International Covenant on Civil and Political Rights, and general comment No. 15 of the Committee on the Elimination of All Forms of Racial Discrimination, which stipulates that the prohibition of the dissemination of all ideas based upon racial superiority or hatred is compatible with the freedom of opinion and expression.

Canada originally sponsored the resolution, as it had sponsored all of the previous resolutions. However, Canada, along with all of the other

[15] Twenty-one States have entered reservations or declarations against this article, which is far more than is the case for any other article in ICERD. These are: Antigua and Barbuda, Austria, Bahamas, Barbados, Belgium, Fiji, France, Guyana, Ireland, Italy, Jamaica, Japan, Malta, Monaco, Nepal, Papua New Guinea, Switzerland, Tonga, Thailand, the UK and USA.

[16] Algeria, Argentina, Belgium, Brazil, Burundi, Cameroon, Canada, Colombia, Costa Rica, Czech Republic, Democratic Republic of the Congo, Ecuador, France, Germany, Guatemala, India, Indonesia, Italy, Latvia, Madagascar, Malaysia, Mauritius, Mexico, Niger, Nigeria, Norway, Pakistan, Peru, Poland, Portugal, Republic of Korea, Romania, Russian Federation, Senegal, South Africa, Spain, Swaziland, Thailand, the UK, Uruguay, the USA, Venezuela, Vietnam and Zambia.

[17] China, Cuba, Japan, Kenya, Libyan Arab Jamahiriya, Qatar, Saudi Arabia and Syrian Arab Republic.

[18] UN HR Council, Resolution 7/36: Mandate of the Special Rapporteur on the Promotion and Protection of the Right to Freedom of Opinion and Expression, UN Doc. A/HRC/RES/7/36, 28 March 2008.

members of the Western European and Others Group (WEOG), abstained from voting, leading to a total of fifteen abstentions, compared to only thirty-two votes in favour (and none against).[19]

Apart from sub-paragraph 4(d), the resolution largely reiterated the general mandate contained in the original 1993 resolution, calling on the Special Rapporteur to gather information on violations of the right to freedom of expression, to respond to credible reports about such cases, to make recommendations on ways to improve respect for freedom of expression, and to contribute to the provision of technical or advisory services by the High Commissioner for Human Rights.[20] Paragraph 4 of the resolution, apart from its sub-paragraph 4(d), largely reiterates the specific calls to direct his attention to those issues that had been included in the 1995–2003 resolutions noted above. Recent resolutions have not changed the mandate of the Special Rapporteur.

## 3 Activities

The 1994 Annual Report of the Special Rapporteur, the first to be produced, focused largely on elaborating on the scope and working methods of the mandate. Thus, paragraph 25 referred to the need to advert to both general and individual situations; paragraph 28 indicated that the Rapporteur would send credible reports of problems to governments for their responses; paragraph 29 indicated that an urgent action approach would be used where appropriate, and paragraph 32 referred to the importance of on-site visits.[21]

In practice, the activities of the Special Rapporteur can generally be divided into six categories:

1 The annual reports which the Special Rapporteur presents to the Human Rights Council.
2 Formal country visits, about which the Special Rapporteur also presents reports to the Human Rights Council.
3 Communications in relation to incidents and situations.

[19] The abstaining States were Bosnia and Herzegovina, Canada, France, Germany, Guatemala, Italy, Japan, Netherlands, Philippines, Republic of Korea, Romania, Slovenia, Switzerland, Ukraine and the UK.

[20] *Ibid.*, para. 3.

[21] UN CHR, *Report of the Special Rapporteur on the Promotion and Protection of the Right to Freedom of Opinion and Expression*, UN Doc. E/CN.4/1994/33, 26 January 1994, para. 25.

4 Press releases and other public statements.
5 Attendance at conferences, seminars and other meetings.
6 Standard-setting activities.

### *3.1 Annual reports*

One of the Special Rapporteur's most important activities is his submission of reports, formerly to the Commission on Human Rights and now to the Human Rights Council.[22] Over time, these annual reports have assumed a consistent format, starting with a summary, followed by an outline of the activities of the Rapporteur (broken down roughly into communications, country visits, press releases and participation in meetings). These reports also include a substantial section addressing a thematic freedom of expression issue, and they end with conclusions and recommendations.

Until 2001, these reports also included detailed country sections, outlining problems with freedom of expression in a number of different countries. This necessarily took up some space, and the 2001 report was a record ninety-one pages, including annexes. The country section was dropped in 2002, due largely to increasing pressure to keep reports limited in length for volume and administrative reasons, which has now become a strict requirement. The early reports were also different inasmuch as many did not include thematic sections, and this started to take on more importance in the reports once the country reports were dropped.

The thematic sections of these reports cover different issues each year, and represent an important contribution to our understanding of the key challenges facing freedom of expression globally, along with some possible solutions. In 2014, for example, the report focused on freedom of expression and elections.[23] In 2011, the main focus of the thematic section of the report was freedom of expression and the Internet.[24] In both of these cases, the thematic section was coordinated with the

[22] The reports are all available on the website of the Special Rapporteur, at: www.ohchr.org/EN/Issues/FreedomOpinion/Pages/OpinionIndex.aspx (last accessed 5 January 2015).

[23] UN HR Council, *Report of the Special Rapporteur on the Promotion and Protection of the Right to Freedom of Opinion and Expression*, UN Doc. A/HRC/26/30, 2 July 2014, paras. 10–74.

[24] UN HR Council, *Report of the Special Rapporteur on the Promotion and Protection of the Right to Freedom of Opinion and Expression*, UN Doc. A/HRC/17/27, 26 April 2011, paras. 19–66.

Joint Declaration issued by the Special Rapporteur and his regional counterparts (see section 4).

Otherwise, the thematic issues addressed in the reports vary widely. Some themes come up repeatedly, including:

- defamation (and especially criminal defamation) (2012, 2008, 2007, 2006, 2000, 1999);
- safety of media workers and others exercising their right to freedom of expression (2012, 2009, 2008, 2007, 2006, 2005, 2002, 1999);
- the right to information (2008, 2005, 2004, 2000, 1999, 1998);
- the Internet and new technologies (2011, 2007, 2006, 2002, 2001, 2000, 1999, 1998); and
- national security restrictions on freedom of expression (2009, 2004, 2003, 2002, 1998).

A large number of other thematic issues have also been addressed in the annual reports. A sample of these includes:

- freedom of expression and elections;
- surveillance;
- the rights of minorities and different groups to freedom of expression;
- poverty and freedom of expression;
- the right to information about HIV;
- religion and freedom of expression;
- women's right to freedom of expression;
- administrative measures and freedom of expression;
- impact of non-State actors on freedom of expression;
- media in countries of transition and elections;
- the police and the criminal justice system; and
- regulation of broadcasting.

In discussing these issues, the Special Rapporteur highlights problems, sets out relevant international standards and notes any best practices in the area. In recent years, the thematic parts of these reports also contain conclusions and recommendations, with the latter setting out the views of the Special Rapporteur as to what various actors should do to resolve the problems.

### *3.2 Country visits*

An important part of the work of the Special Rapporteur is official in-country visits, which are taken every year (between two and three per annum in recent years). In 2013, for example, the Special Rapporteur visited Montenegro, the former Yugoslav Republic of Macedonia and Italy, while in 2012 he visited Honduras. An attempt is made to visit a geographically and otherwise representative sample of countries, and not only to target countries with particularly serious problems regarding freedom of expression. The choice of countries is influenced by the fact that the Special Rapporteur needs an invitation from the authorities before he may make an official visit.

During these visits, the Special Rapporteur meets with a wide variety of relevant actors – including officials, media professionals, NGO representatives, academics and others – and collects information from various sources. He then provides an in-depth report on the situation regarding freedom of opinion and expression in that country to the Human Rights Council, as addendums to his main report.[25] Although these reports differ slightly in structure, they follow a similar format, namely international standards, domestic legal framework, situation of the right to freedom of expression and conclusions and recommendations. In substance, they provide an overview of the laws, policies and practices affecting freedom of opinion and expression, highlight concerns and individual cases, and provide concrete recommendations as to how to resolve any failures in respect of these rights.

### 3.3 *Communications*

The Special Rapporteur uses what are known as 'communications' to respond to situations which appear to disclose a breach of the right to freedom of expression. These involve sending a letter (communication) to the government of the country concerned and asking it to respond to the allegations. These are often made in response to credible reports of serious instances of human rights abuse received by the Special Rapporteur from individuals or NGOs, but information may also come from other sources (such as the media or other UN bodies).

Upon receipt of a communication, some governments enter into a dialogue with the Special Rapporteur, sending written responses and

[25] For example, the report on the visit to Israel, UN HR Council, *Report of the Special Rapporteur on the Promotion and Protection of the Right to Freedom of Opinion and Expression, Addendum: Mission to Israel and the Occupied Palestinian territory*, UN Doc. A/HRC/20/17/Add.2, 11 June 2012.

sometimes even taking concrete action to remedy the abuse. Other governments are less cooperative, but even then the Special Rapporteur's inquiries are important. They highlight the abuse, which is usually embarrassing to the respective country, and may protect the individual concerned or others from further abuse. They also provide an authoritative record of the fact of the abuse which, over time, can help establish a pattern of abuse, lead to redress if the situation changes or provide support to those advocating for change in the country.

Previously, the Special Rapporteur used to distinguish between regular communications and urgent actions, with the aim of an urgent action being to prevent the ongoing perpetration of serious human rights abuses, for example where a journalist has been imprisoned wrongly. Thus, in his 2005 Annual Report, the Special Rapporteur noted that between 1 January and 17 November 2004, he had made 610 communications, of which 449 were urgent actions.[26] In recent years, the distinction between regular communications and urgent actions has waned.[27] A large percentage of all communications are now made jointly with other special procedures. Thus, in his 2012 Annual Report, the Special Rapporteur indicated that he had issued 218 communications between 1 April 2011 and 20 March 2012, of which 213 were made jointly with other mandate holders.[28] In part as a result of that, these communications are now published in a central report by all of the special procedures.[29]

### 3.4 *Press releases and other statements*

Press releases and statements are different from communications inasmuch as they are intended for wide public distribution, rather than simply being reported in summary form through the formal information

[26] UN CHR, *Report of the Special Rapporteur on the Promotion and Protection of the Right to Freedom of Opinion and Expression*, UN Doc. E/CN.4/2005/64, 17 December 2004, para. 11.

[27] No such distinction, for example, has been made since the Special Rapporteur's 2008 annual Report.

[28] UN HR Council, *Report*, 4 June 2012, para. 7.

[29] See, for example, UN HR Council, *Communications Report of Special Procedures: Communications Sent, 1 December 2010 to 31 May 2011; Replies received, 1 February 2011 to 31 July 2011*, UN Doc. A/HRC/18/51, 9 September 2011.

systems of the procedures (such as the annual report). In the early days of the mandate, press releases were not used as a means to publicise freedom of expression issues. The first annual report to document a press release by the Special Rapporteur was the 2001 Annual Report, which refers to a joint press release with the OSCE Representative on freedom of the media and the OAS Special Rapporteur on freedom of expression on the subject of attacks on journalists.[30] The 2002 Annual Report chronicles four press releases and statements.[31]

This form of action has become far more common in recent years, with the 2012 Annual Report listing some twenty press releases and other statements. The vast majority of these relate to country situations. However, in the period covered by the 2012 Report, the Special Rapporteur also issued press releases on World Press Freedom Day (3 May), on the occasion of the release of his Joint Declaration with the other special mandates on freedom of expression (see below) and urging States to meet their human rights commitments in the context of the United Nations Rio+20 Conference on Sustainable Development.[32]

### 3.5 *Meetings*

The Special Rapporteur participates in a large number of conferences, seminars and similar events around the world each year, often giving presentations on various freedom of opinion and expression issues. For example, in his 2012 Annual Report, the Special Rapporteur lists some fifteen major meetings that he attended, in addition to official country visits and meetings associated directly with the functioning of his mandate. Those meetings touched on a wide variety of subjects and were hosted by a number of different actors, including several by official bodies and others by NGOs.[33]

30 UN CHR, *Report of the Special Rapporteur on the Promotion and Protection of the Right to Freedom of Opinion and Expression*, UN Doc. E/CN.4/2001/64, Annex IV, 13 February 2001.

31 UN CHR, *Report of the Special Rapporteur on the Promotion and Protection of the Right to Freedom of Opinion and Expression*, UN Doc. E/CN.4/2002/75, 30 January 2002, paras. 9–10.

32 UN HR Council, *Report*, 4 June 2012, paras. 13–32. The Rio+20 Conference was a follow-on from the 1992 Rio Conference on Environment and Development.

33 *Ibid.*, paras. 33–47.

## 4 Standard-setting

### *4.1 Relevance and importance*

The guarantees of freedom of expression in the UDHR and ICCPR are very general in nature, and, as a result, provide only very general guidance as to the scope and implications of this right. These texts have to some extent been clarified through the decisions of international judicial and quasi-judicial bodies such as the UN Human Rights Committee and the regional human rights courts and bodies (primarily the European Court of Human Rights, the Inter-American Court of Human Rights and the African Commission on Human and Peoples' Rights).[34] However, this body of law remains relatively small. It is also structurally limited inasmuch as it only addresses certain kinds of issues, namely the types of issues that affect individuals sufficiently to motivate them to appeal cases all the way through their national court systems and then on to these international bodies. Thus, while there are numerous defamation cases, there is relatively little jurisprudence on issues like the responsibility of the State to ensure diversity in the media or to respect the independence of public broadcasters.[35]

Some of the most important work of the Special Rapporteur has been to clarify the precise nature of this right through what might be described as standard-setting work. This set of activities provides a wide range of actors – civil society, the media, academics, legislators and other decision-makers, officials, judges and lawyers – with an expert and authoritative perspective on the meaning of the right to freedom of expression in different contexts.

While all of the work of the Special Rapporteur is important, the standard-setting activities are particularly so, given the ability of other players to lever this work to promote respect for freedom of expression. Inasmuch as standard-setting by the Special Rapporteur represents an authoritative interpretation of the binding international guarantees of freedom of expression found in the UDHR and ICCPR, it is far more than simply a statement of his particular views. It is essentially a

[34] See further Chapter 14 in this book.

[35] There are a couple of cases on these issues at the European Court of Human Rights. See, for example: *Centro Europa 7 SRL and Di Stefano* v. *Italy* (Appl. No. 38433/09), Judgment (Grand Chamber), 7 June 2012 and *Manole and Others* v. *Moldova* (Appl. No. 13936/02), Judgment, 17 September 2009.

statement of what he believes States must do to comply with their international legal obligations.

It is this characteristic – namely its claim to being an authoritative interpretation of international law – that imbues the standard-setting work with its real power and relevance. The persuasive power of international law remains strong in many countries, even if its enforcement mechanisms remain weak. Inasmuch as the standards proposed by the Special Rapporteur are accepted as authoritative interpretations of international law, for example by legislators and civil society groups, they carry at least part of that persuasive force.

There is also a more formal aspect to it. In the constitutions of many countries around the world, the status of international law, and sometimes specifically international human rights guarantees, ranks above that of ordinary national laws (although not normally the constitution).

Perhaps more powerful in practice is the idea that international guarantees should inform the interpretation and understanding of national constitutional human rights guarantees, at least in the area of freedom of expression. In most countries, constitutional guarantees of freedom of expression are just as brief as those found in international law. Courts thus often have very little guidance as to how to interpret these guarantees, especially when faced with novel issues (which is most issues in the context of the new constitutions adopted after the processes of democratisation that have taken place in almost all of Eastern and Central Europe and in many countries in Asia, Africa and Latin America since the early 1990s). It therefore makes sense for courts to give some weight to authoritative international sources when interpreting national guarantees. This is particularly so in the many countries in which national guarantees are cast in very similar terms to their international counterparts.

For example, when the Special Rapporteur first declared criminal defamation to be a breach of the right to freedom of expression in 2000,[36] this provided campaigners with an invaluable and hitherto unavailable source of authority on this issue. It also gave a boost to legislators and others who had been promoting the decriminalisation of defamation. Finally, it provided judges facing legal challenges with a strong argument in favour of striking down criminal defamation rules

[36] UN Special Rapporteur on Freedom of Opinion and Expression, OSCE Representative on Freedom of the Media and OAS Special Rapporteur on Freedom of Expression, Joint Declaration of 30 November 2000.

or at least interpreting them restrictively. The same is true for the many other issues about which the Special Rapporteur has adopted clear standard-setting statements.

### *4.2 Types of standard-setting activities*

The Special Rapporteur has engaged in a number of different types of standard-setting activities. At the least assertive level, it may be said that the communications and press releases issued by the Special Rapporteur are a form of standard-setting, for his mandate is formally limited to the right to freedom of expression, and it would not be appropriate for the Special Rapporteur to question a State about a matter if he did not believe that it fell within the scope of the right. However, this is at best a weak form of standard-setting for four reasons.

First, the rule cited above is only weak authority for the conclusion averred; i.e., the fact that the Special Rapporteur raises an issue represents only a rather weak assertion on his part that he believes the issue is one of freedom of expression. Second, a large majority of these statements do not contain any assertion of a specific standard. Thus, inquiring into the circumstances regarding the laying of defamation charges against a journalist is not an assertion of any specific standard. Third, even where such statements do state or imply a standard, they are rarely asserting a new (i.e., standard-setting) norm. This is because, even where inquiries into State behaviour (or failure to act) do imply a breach of the right to freedom of expression, this is often based on established standards (in the case above about defamation this might, for example, be because the charges were politically motivated or because the subject matter of the statements was clearly protected). Finally, even where an inquiry states or implies a breach of the right to freedom of expression and this is not (obviously) based on an established standard, it is still not a standard-setting statement unless it also asserts a positive norm, which is rarely the case.

The Annual and Country Reports contain far more important standard-setting statements, in particular in the Recommendations sections which are now routinely found in those reports. For example, in his 2014 Annual Report, among many other things, the Special Rapporteur stated: 'In order to secure a diverse and pluralistic political process which is hospitable to candidates and parties from across the political spectrum, States should:', and this was followed by a number of specific recommendations.

These are clearly normative statements. Furthermore, the language used – in particular the terms 'must' and 'should' – seems to imply that they are derived from a binding source, i.e., international law. However, this is not entirely clear and one of the shortcomings of these sorts of statements from a standard-setting perspective is that they are rarely presented explicitly as elaborations or interpretations of international law, even if this seems likely from the context.

## 4.3 *Joint Declarations*

Without a doubt, the most explicit and important standard-setting work of the Special Rapporteur is found in the Joint Declarations that he adopts annually with his counterparts at the OSCE, the Inter-American Commission on Human Rights (IACHR) and the ACHPR. Following on from the creation of the global mandate in the form of the UN Special Rapporteur on freedom of opinion and expression, in 1993, the Permanent Council of the OSCE created an analogous mandate, namely the Representative on Freedom of the Media, in late 1997.[37] Around the same time, in October 1997, the IACHR created the Organisation of American States (OAS) Special Rapporteur on Freedom of Expression.[38]

The genesis of the Joint Declarations was the bringing together of these three special international mandates on freedom of expression – the UN Special Rapporteur, the OSCE Representative and the OAS Special Rapporteur – for the very first time in November 1999, in London, under the auspices of ARTICLE 19, Global Campaign for Free Expression.[39] The meeting was planned primarily to provide the three mandates with an opportunity to share information and ideas, to hear the views of other experts and NGOs, and to plan future cooperation and activities.

However, the fact that having these three special mandates together in one place presented a unique opportunity quickly became apparent. In particular, the meeting came up with the idea of having them come together to make a normative statement about international standards relating to freedom of expression. Speaking as one, their voices, and

[37] OSCE Permanent Council (PC), Decision No. 193: Mandate of the OSCE Representation on Freedom of the Media, 5 November 1997, para. 1.
[38] This office was created at its 97th Regular Session in October 1997. For a report on the nature and status of these mechanisms, see T. Mendel, 'Official Mechanisms for Freedom of Expression' (London: ARTICLE 19, 2001).
[39] See www.article19.org (last accessed 28 January 2015).

hence the impact of the statement, would clearly be amplified. In this way, the idea of the Joint Declaration of the International Mechanisms for Promoting Freedom of Expression was born.

The first Joint Declaration was adopted on 26 November 1999, the last day of the November meeting of the special mandates in London. At that time, no one envisaged that the Joint Declarations would become an annual event. As a result, the 1999 Joint Declaration addresses a wide range of important freedom of expression issues, often at a fairly general level. Thus, the very first statement in the Joint Declaration states: 'We recall that freedom of expression is a fundamental international human right and a basic component of a civil society based on democratic principles.'

Although general in tone, this first Joint Declaration is impressive for its breadth. Among other things, it addresses issues such as the right to information, the decriminalisation of defamation, the promotion of an independent and pluralistic media, harassment of the media, the need for the media to refrain from engaging in hate speech, and the need for an impartial judiciary and respect for the rule of law as essential conditions for respect for freedom of expression.

Although the initial Joint Declaration does not explicitly or formally state that it is an elaboration of international law, this was implicit in the very nature of the exercise, as well as the language of at least some of the statements. Thus, the bullet point on the right to information starts with the phrase: 'Implicit in freedom of expression…', while the one on criminal defamation states that these laws 'unduly restrict the right to freedom of expression' and refers to States' 'international obligations'. The bullet point on hate speech is largely a quote from Article 20(2) of the ICCPR.

The first meeting was followed up by a second meeting a year later, in November 2000, also in London. Based on the positive reception the first Joint Declaration had enjoyed, it was agreed at that point to make this an annual event. A more-or-less logical consequence of this was to address a small number of themes in the Joint Declarations, and they have focused on between one and three themes since that time. The exception was the 2010, 10th anniversary, Joint Declaration, which took an entirely different approach, focusing on the ten key challenges for freedom of expression over the next ten years.[40] In recent years, the Joint Declarations have

[40] Joint Declaration: Ten Key Challenges to Freedom of Expression in the Next Decade of 3 February 2010.

become more specialised, with all of the last five focusing on just one theme. They have also gradually started to creep up in length, going from two to three pages to four pages in each of 2010 and 2011,[41] to five pages in each of 2012[42] and 2013.[43]

In addition to their annual Joint Declarations, the special mandates have adopted a few other joint statements. Thus, in February 2001, they adopted a Joint Statement on Racism and the Media,[44] as part of their contribution to the World Conference Against Racism, Racial Discrimination, Xenophobia and Related Intolerance (held in Durban). On a couple of occasions two of the mandates have adopted a statement on their own.[45]

There is no question that the substantive portions of these Joint Declarations (i.e., not including the preambles) represent an interpretation, by the special mandates, of international legal guarantees of freedom of expression, at least inasmuch as they are directed at official actors (for they sometimes direct recommendations at other actors, such as businesses, the media or civil society). They consistently use the term 'should' in reference to States, and the process by which they are developed makes this very clear.

At the same time, the special mandates have sometimes used the Joint Declarations, and in particular their preambles, to promote other objectives. For example, the three original mandates used the Joint Declarations of 2000 to 2003 to support the adoption of regional mechanisms on freedom of expression in Africa and Asia. Thus, the preamble to the 2001 Joint Declaration noted: '[T]he importance of regional mechanisms in promoting the right to freedom of expression and the need to promote such mechanisms in every region of the world, including in Africa and Asia.'[46]

In 2002, the African Commission on Human and Peoples' Rights adopted the Declaration of Principles on Freedom of Expression in

41 *Ibid.*, and Joint Declaration on Freedom of Expression and the Internet of 1 June 2011.
42 Joint Declaration on Crimes Against Freedom of Expression of 25 June 2012.
43 Joint Declaration on the Protection of Freedom of Expression and Diversity in the Digital Terrestrial Transition of 3 May 2013.
44 Joint Statement on Racism and the Media of 27 February 2001.
45 For example, on 21 December 2010, the UN and OAS mandates adopted a Joint Statement on WikiLeaks.
46 Joint Declaration: Challenges to Freedom of Expression in the New Century, 20 November 2001.

Africa,[47] and this was followed in 2004 by a resolution establishing the Special Rapporteur on Freedom of Expression (later changed to the Special Rapporteur on Freedom of Expression and Access to Information in Africa).[48] Since 2006, the Joint Declarations have been adopted by all four special mandates. Originally supported by ARTICLE 19, since 2010, the Declarations have been adopted 'with the assistance of' both ARTICLE 19 and the Centre for Law and Democracy.[49]

### *4.4 Standard-setting role*

For standard-setting activities to both advance traditional understandings of freedom of expression and yet maintain credibility as authoritative interpretations of that right requires a delicate balancing. If the Special Rapporteur, and the other special mandates, had 'played it safe' by only advancing perspectives on freedom of expression that were already accepted – for example because they had been proclaimed by an international court – the significance of this body of work would have been far more limited than has in fact been the case.

Certainly the Joint Declarations and other standard-setting work have consistently reaffirmed established understandings of the right to freedom of expression. For example, the 2000 Joint Declaration reiterated the well-established principle that public figures should tolerate a greater degree of criticism than ordinary citizens,[50] while the 2011 Joint Declaration included the uncontroversial statement that, 'Freedom of expression applies to the Internet, as it does to all means of communication.'[51] These sorts of statements are useful, among other things, because the Joint Declarations are very clear and accessible to people who are not experts on international law regarding the right to freedom of expression.

[47] ACHPR, *Declaration of Principles on Freedom of Expression in Africa*, Banjul, the Gambia, 17–23 October 2002.

[48] ACHPR, Resolution 71 on the Mandate and Appointment of a Special Rapporteur on Freedom of Expression in Africa, 7 December 2004.

[49] The Centre for Law and Democracy is a Canadian-based international human rights organisation specialising in foundational rights for democracy.

[50] Joint Declaration of 30 November 2000. That principle has, for example, repeatedly been asserted by the ECtHR. See, for example, *Lingens* v. *Austria* (Appl. No. 9815/82), Judgment of 8 July 1986, para. 42.

[51] Joint Declaration on Freedom of Expression and the Internet of 1 June 2011. This follows directly from Article 19(2) of the ICCPR, which protects the exercise of freedom of expression 'through any other media'.

But the standard-setting work of the Special Rapporteur has not been limited to repackaging established standards. Instead, the Special Rapporteur has advanced the understanding of freedom of expression in three key ways through his standard-setting work. First, he has filled in many of the most important 'gaps' in international jurisprudence. These gaps arise in part because of the brevity of international treaty guarantees of rights, along with the structural reasons noted above, namely that only certain kinds of issues are of a nature to give rise to individual grievances of a sufficiently weighty nature to motivate appeals all the way through to international courts. They also arise because international courts have a formal mandate only to decide the specific issue before them. This, combined with a natural tendency on the part of these bodies to be cautious – justifiable in part because of the binding nature of their decisions – has often led to court decisions which contain only rather narrow normative conclusions.

The Joint Declarations have, for example, elaborated in some detail on the ideas of diversity and independence of public broadcasters,[52] the two examples given above of areas where the implications of the right to freedom of expression have not been elaborated by international courts. They have also clarified standards in relation to many other 'gap' issues, including the following:

- Standards for protection of freedom of expression in the context of the fight against terrorism, including in the early days following on from the attacks of 11 September 2001.[53]
- Standards relating to the regulation of broadcasting and other media sectors (including journalists).[54]
- The obligation of States to take measures to counter undue commercial influence over the media.[55]

[52] See, for example, Joint Declaration on Challenges to Freedom of Expression in the New Century of 20 November 2001, Joint Declaration of 18 December 2003 and Joint Declaration on Diversity in Broadcasting of 12 December 2007.

[53] See the Joint Declaration on Challenges to Freedom of Expression in the New Century of 20 November 2001, Joint Declaration of 21 December 2005 and Joint Declaration on Defamation of Religions, and Anti-Terrorism and Anti-Extremism Legislation of 10 December 2008.

[54] See the Joint Declaration on Challenges to Freedom of Expression in the New Century of 20 November 2001, Joint Declaration of 18 December 2003 and Joint Declaration on Diversity in Broadcasting of 12 December 2007.

[55] Joint Declaration of 10 December 2002.

- Indicating that the concept of 'defamation of religions' does not accord with international law.[56]
- Standards relating to preserving media diversity in the digital terrestrial transition.[57]

In each of these cases, there were structural reasons why standards had not been developed through other systems, in particular international jurisprudence. In most cases, this is because the issues simply do not lend themselves to being advanced through the complaints system that drives international jurisprudence. Thus, issues such as promoting diversity in broadcasting, protecting the independence of public broadcasters, general regulatory standards for the media, countering undue commercial influence over the media and preserving diversity in the digital terrestrial transition largely exist to protect the right of the public as a whole to seek and receive a wide range of information and ideas. It is difficult to distil these into individual issues which might be the subject of a court appeal.

In terms of terrorism, a key value added of the Joint Declarations was that they asserted clear standards early on, before cases had wended their way through national legal systems and to international courts. The first Joint Declaration to address this issue was adopted in December 2001, just three months after the 11 September 2001 attacks.

The issue with 'defamation of religions' was again different. In that case, the issue could not be addressed by international courts largely because the main country sponsors of these declarations were not subject to the jurisprudence of international courts.[58]

Second, and closely related, the Joint Declarations have presented a holistic understanding of standards in a number of thematic areas. Issues which have received more comprehensive treatment in the Joint Declarations include defamation,[59] freedom of expression and the

[56] Joint Declaration on Defamation of Religions, and Anti-Terrorism and Anti-Extremism Legislation of 10 December 2008.

[57] Joint Declaration on the Protection of Freedom of Expression and Diversity in the Digital Terrestrial Transition, 3 May 2013.

[58] Thus, Resolution 7/19 of the Human Rights Council on Combating Defamation of Religions of 27 March 2008 was sponsored by Pakistan, on behalf of the Organization of the Islamic Conference (OIC). Although eight of the twenty-one States that voted in favour of this resolution at the Human Rights Council were at the time subject to the jurisprudence of one or another international court or quasi-judicial system, most of those countries did not have in place national laws protecting religion against defamation. See also Chapter 12 in this book.

[59] Joint Declaration of 30 November 2000.

administration of justice,[60] media regulation,[61] the right to information,[62] diversity in broadcasting[63] and during the digital terrestrial transition,[64] elections,[65] the Internet[66] and attacks on freedom of expression.[67] In many cases, these Declarations involve a combination of reiterating established standards, filling in some gaps, and engaging in the progressive development of international standards.

This latter represents the third way in which the standard-setting work of the Special Rapporteur has advanced our understanding of the right to freedom of expression. This is perhaps the most controversial, and by the same token the most exciting, role played by the Joint Declarations and other standard-setting work.

On the one hand, it is almost inherent in the nature of the mandate of the Special Rapporteur and those of his regional counterparts that they should push the envelope in terms of global understandings of freedom of expression. If they were not to do this, whom among official international actors would? Furthermore, failing to press for more progressive interpretations of international guarantees of freedom of expression would somehow represent a betrayal of the fact that they represent the only official mandates dedicated to this key right.

On the other hand, going too far in this regard – by asserting understandings of the scope of freedom of expression that were too radical or not based on solid reasoning – would arguably be outside of the mandate of these mechanisms, which is specifically limited by reference to the right. It could also seriously undermine the credibility of the mandates. This risk would be particularly high should the mandates take a position on an issue which was in direct contradiction to that of an international court.

### 4.5 *The balancing exercise: two examples*

A very good, and ultimately successful, example of the development of our understanding of the scope and nature of the right to freedom of

[60] Joint Declaration of 10 December 2002.

[61] Joint Declaration of 18 December 2003.

[62] Joint Declaration of 6 December 2004 and Joint Declaration of 19 December 2006.

[63] Joint Declaration on Diversity in Broadcasting of 12 December 2007.

[64] Joint Declaration on the Protection of Freedom of Expression and Diversity in the Digital Terrestrial Transition of 3 May 2013.

[65] Joint Statement on the Media and Elections of 15 May 2009.

[66] Joint Declaration on Freedom of Expression and the Internet of 1 June 2011.

[67] Joint Declaration on Crimes Against Freedom of Expression of 25 June 2012.

expression by the Joint Declarations is in relation to the right to information (the right to access information held by public bodies). As noted above, the very first Declaration, adopted in 1999, already asserted a right to access information, in the following (rather flowery) terms: 'Implicit in freedom of expression is the public's right to open access to information and to know what governments are doing on their behalf, without which truth would languish and people's participation in government would remain fragmented.'[68]

The issue was addressed again, and in a much more comprehensive way, in the 2004 Joint Declaration, which focuses exclusively on the right to information and secrecy legislation.[69] If the 1999 Joint Declaration had left any doubt as to the international law status of this right, this was surely not the case with the 2004 Declaration, which stated: 'The right to access information held by public authorities is a fundamental human right which should be given effect at the national level through comprehensive legislation (for example Freedom of Information Acts) based on the principle of maximum disclosure, establishing a presumption that all information is accessible subject only to a narrow system of exceptions.'

The rest of the Declaration went on to elaborate the specific characteristics of this right, and then the ways in which secrecy laws should be amended, or interpreted, to conform to those standards.

The issue was addressed again in the Joint Declaration of 2006, which went beyond the earlier statements by extending the scope of the obligation to respect the right to information to intergovernmental organisations.[70] This was both something that could not, by definition, come before international courts, given that these bodies do not fall within their jurisdiction, and also something which was clearly cutting edge in terms of its interpretation of the scope of the right to freedom of expression.

It is significant that, at the time of the 2004 Joint Declaration, no international court had held that the right to freedom of expression encompassed a right to information. The preamble to the Joint Declaration provides some indication of the reasoning upon which the special mandates based their interpretation. It refers, among other things, to the growing recognition of the right in 'authoritative international statements and declarations', the increase in recognition of the right at the national level, and the 'fundamental importance' of the right

[68] Joint Declaration of 26 November 1999.
[69] Joint Declaration of 6 December 2004.
[70] Joint Declaration of 19 December 2006.

'to democratic participation, to holding governments accountable and to controlling corruption, as well as to personal dignity and business efficiency'. It would seem that their interpretation was based on a combination of a principled analysis of international guarantees of the right to freedom of expression – which include the rights to 'seek' and 'receive' as well as to 'impart' information and ideas – as well as the centrality of the right to many of the most fundamental goals served by wider protection of freedom of expression.

Several cases claiming a right to information based on the right to freedom of expression had gone to the European Court of Human Rights before the adoption of the 2004 Joint Declaration, but the Court consistently refused to accept these claims,[71] although in some cases it found a right to access the information based on other rights.[72] In these cases, the Court consistently maintained the following position in relation to the right to freedom of expression (as guaranteed in Article 10 of the European Convention on Human Rights):[73]

> [T]he right to freedom to receive information basically prohibits a Government from restricting a person from receiving information that others wish or may be willing to impart to him. Article 10 does not, in circumstances such as those of the present case, confer on the individual a right of access... nor does it embody an obligation on the Government to impart... information to the individual.[74]

By using the words 'in circumstances such as those of the present case', the Court did not absolutely rule out the possibility of a right to information under Article 10, although it left itself only a narrow window of possibility to recognise such a right.

The situation was thus one in which the special mandates had taken a clear position on the status of the right to information, which was quite

[71] See, for example: ECtHR, *Leander* v. *Sweden* (Appl. No. 9248/81), Judgment, 26 March 1987; *Gaskin* v. *United Kingdom* (Appl. No. 10454/83), Judgment (Grand Chamber), 7 July 1989; *Guerra and Ors.* v. *Italy* (Appl. No. 14967/89), Judgment (Grand Chamber), 19 February 1998; *McGinley and Egan* v. *United Kingdom* (Appl. Nos. 21825/93 and 23414/94), Judgment, 9 June 1998; *Odièvre* v. *France* (Appl. No. 42326/98) Judgment (Grand Chamber), 13 February 2003; and *Sîrbu and Others* v. *Moldova* (Appl. Nos. 73562/01, 73565/01, 73712/01, 73744/01, 73972/01 and 73973/01), Judgment, 15 June 2004.

[72] Basically the right to respect for private and family life (as guaranteed by Article 8 of the ECHR).

[73] Convention for the Protection of Human Rights and Fundamental Freedoms (as amended), ETS No. 5, 4 November 1950, entered into force 3 September 1953.

[74] ECtHR, *Leander* v. *Sweden*, para. 74.

different from that taken by international courts, and yet not in direct and irreconcilable contradiction to their rulings.

The bold position taken by the special mandates back in 1999, and reaffirmed in 2004, was vindicated when the Inter-American Court of Human Rights, in the case of *Claude Reyes and Others* v. *Chile*, decided on 19 September 2006,[75] essentially repudiated the European Court's position and explicitly recognised a 'right of all individuals to request access to State-held information, with the exceptions permitted by the restrictions established in the Convention'.[76] Under pressure from different quarters, the European Court of Human Rights also recognised a right to information based on the right to freedom of expression in 2009.[77] Finally, in its 2011 General Comment on Article 19 of the ICCPR, the UN Human Rights Committee also finally clearly recognised the right to information.[78]

On the right to information, the special mandates took a bold position very early on, at a time when very few other actors were claiming that international guarantees of the right to freedom of expression included this right. Over time, all of the key players have come to accept their position. This therefore represents an excellent example of an issue where they can be said to have engaged in a successful attempt to progressively develop international standards.

A second example of a bold and clear position taken by the Special Rapporteur through the Joint Declarations is in relation to criminal defamation. Once again, the issue had already come up in the very first, 1999 Joint Declaration, which states: 'In many countries laws are in place, such as criminal defamation laws, which unduly restrict the right to freedom of expression. We urge States to review these laws with a view to bringing them into line with their international obligations.'[79]

If this statement left any doubt as to the views of the special mandates on the matter, this was clarified by subsequent references to the issue in

[75] IACtHR, *Claude Reyes and Others* v. *Chile*, 19 September 2006, Series C No. 151.

[76] *Ibid.*, para. 77.

[77] ECtHR, *Társaság A Szabadságjogokért* v. *Hungary* (Appl. No. 37374/05), Judgment, 14 April 2009. See also ECtHR, *Youth Initiative for Human Rights* v. *Serbia* (Appl. No. 48135/06), Judgment, 25 June 2013, ECtHR, *Österreichische Vereinigung zur Erhaltung, Stärkung und Schaffung eines wirtschaftlich gesunden land- und forstwirtschaftlichen Grundbesitzes* v. *Austria* (Appl. No. 39534/07), Judgment, 28 November 2013 and ECtHR, *Roşiianu* v. *Romania* (Appl. No. 27329/06), Judgment, 24 June 2014.

[78] UN HRC, General Comment 34: Article 19 (Freedoms of Opinion and Expression), UN Doc. CCPR/C/GC/34, 12 September 2011, para. 18.

[79] Joint Declaration of 26 November 1999.

the 2000 and 2002 Joint Declarations, with the latter stating: 'Criminal defamation is not a justifiable restriction on freedom of expression; all criminal defamation laws should be abolished and replaced, where necessary, with appropriate civil defamation laws.'[80]

Once again, these statements were made in the absence of any clear support from international courts for these positions. Indeed, as early as 1997, the (former) European Commission of Human Rights[81] appeared to approve of criminal defamation laws, albeit indirectly, by not finding a breach of the right to freedom of expression in a case where a suspended sentenced was imposed on the applicant in a criminal defamation case brought by a private party.[82]

Since then, the European Court of Human Rights has on a number of occasions upheld the imposition of criminal sentences for defamation. For example, in a case against Finland decided in 2010, the Court did not find a breach of the right to freedom of expression in a case in which fines were imposed after a criminal conviction of the applicant for defamation.[83] The Inter-American Court of Human Rights has also not gone so far as to declare criminal defamation per se to be a breach of the right to freedom of expression, instead stating, in a case involving criminal sanctions for defamation:

> [I]t has not been shown in the instant case that the abovementioned criminal punishment was the outcome of alleged deficiencies in the rules framing crimes against honor in Panamá. So, the State has not failed to comply with the general obligation to give domestic legal effects to the American Convention established in Article 2 thereof.[84]

However, the position of the special mandates is not without support. It is perhaps notable that in the case from Finland at the European Court, noted above, there were strong dissenting opinions by two judges who placed considerable emphasis on the disproportionate nature of the criminal sanction, even though it was limited to rather modest fines,[85]

[80] Joint Declaration of 10 December 2002.
[81] The Commission was a body of independent experts charged with determining whether cases should be admitted for consideration on their merits by the ECtHR. It was disbanded on 1 November 1998 upon entry into force of Protocol No. 11 to the Convention for the Protection of Human Rights and Fundamental Freedoms, which restructured the control machinery established by the Convention, CETS No. 155, 11 May 1994.
[82] ECtHR, *Panev* v. *Bulgaria* (Appl. No. 35125/97), Judgment, 3 December 1997.
[83] ECtHR, *Ruokanen and Others* v. *Finland* (Appl. No. 45130/06), Judgment, 6 April 2010.
[84] IACtHR, *Tristán Donoso* v. *Panama*, 27 January 2009, Series C No. 193, para. 131.
[85] Of, respectively, €3,450 and €1,920.

along with a (more significant) award of compensation.[86] The Inter-American Court of Human Rights, in the case noted above, easily found a breach of the right to freedom of expression, even though the penalty was a minor fine,[87] stating: '[T]he Court finds that the criminal punishment imposed upon Mr. Tristán Donoso was evidently unnecessary.'[88]

The Court also noted that while criminal proscriptions were not per se a breach of the right to freedom of expression, justification of such proscriptions would be difficult:

> The Court does not deem any criminal sanction regarding the right to inform or give one's opinion to be contrary to the provisions of the Convention; however, this possibility should be carefully analyzed, pondering the extreme seriousness of the conduct of the individual who expressed the opinion, his actual malice, the characteristics of the unfair damage caused, and other information which shows the absolute necessity to resort to criminal proceedings as an exception. At all stages the burden of proof must fall on the party who brings the criminal proceedings.[89]

Finally, the Court also cited with support changes to the Penal Code that prevented public officials from bringing criminal defamation cases, stating:

> The Court views favorably the fact that, among other modifications, the promulgation of the new Penal Code eliminated certain procedural privileges hitherto enjoyed by public officials and established that no criminal punishment may be imposed in those cases where a public official considers his or her honor has been attained; such officer shall resort to the civil jurisdiction to determine the possible subsequent liability in the event of abuse in the exercise of freedom of expression.[90]

Although the Inter-American Court of Human Rights has never taken an unequivocal position against criminal defamation, it has also never upheld a conviction for criminal defamation.

A growing number of countries from all regions of the world have also done away entirely with their criminal defamation laws, while these laws have fallen into desuetude in many more countries. Furthermore, a number of IGOs and international NGOs working in the area of freedom

[86] ECtHR, *Ruokanen and Others* v. *Finland*, dissenting Opinions of Judges Bratza and Bianku.
[87] Of 750 balboas, which is equal to US$750.
[88] IACtHR, *Tristán Donoso* v. *Panama*, para. 130.
[89] *Ibid.*, para. 120.
[90] *Ibid.*, para. 134.

of expression and freedom of the media have taken a clear position against criminal defamation laws.[91]

The situation is thus one in which, although international courts have failed to take an unequivocal position against criminal defamation, they are clearly not very favourably disposed towards it, while an increasing number of national decision-makers have taken precisely such an unequivocal position (i.e., by repealing criminal defamation rules). It may, therefore, be concluded that while the special mandates have taken a strong position on this issue, it is one which still respects the balancing they must achieve, by being progressive and yet eminently defensible.

### 4.6 *Use of the Joint Declarations*

It is, almost by definition, difficult to do comprehensive research on the use to which the Joint Declarations have been put by others actors.[92] They have repeatedly been referred to by international NGOs, usually in support of their own work to promote freedom of expression.[93]

The Joint Declarations have also been used by official bodies, including inter-governmental bodies. They have, for example been referred to quite extensively in research conducted by and for those bodies. For example, in its publication, *Democracy Revisited: Which Notion of Democracy for*

[91] See, for example, ARTICLE 19, *Defining Defamation: Principles on Freedom of Expression and Protection of Reputation* (London, July 2000); International Federation of Journalists (IFJ), *Decriminalising Defamation: An IFJ Campaign Resource for Defeating Criminal Defamation*, 2005; and World Association of Newspapers and News Publishers, *Declaration of Table Mountain: Abolishing 'Insult Laws' in Africa and Setting Free Press Higher on the Agenda*, 2007.

[92] It is even difficult to search for this online, because of the huge number of hits which key words such as 'special rapporteur' or even 'joint declaration' generate and because different actors describe these documents in different ways (so that searching on unique strings such as: 'Joint Declaration of 25 June 2012' does not necessarily return the references).

[93] See, for just a couple of random examples, World Association of Community Radio Broadcasters (AMARC), *Anniversary of the AMARC Declaration*, referring to the 2007 Joint Declaration, at: http://deepdishwavesofchange/org/2008/11/21/anniversary-of-the-amarc-declaration; and Reporters without Borders (RSF), *UN Rapporteur Presents Report on Online Free Expression*, referring to the 2011 Joint Declaration, at: http://en.rsf.org/un-rapporteur-presents-report-on-03-06-2011,40399.html (both last accessed 28 January 2015).

*the EU's External Relations?*,[94] the Office for Promotion of Parliamentary Democracy (OPPD) quoted from the 2007 Joint Declaration on Diversity in Broadcasting. The report, *Draft General Comment No. 34 (Article 19 ICCPR)*, published by the European Centre for Law and Justice at the request of the Office of the High Commissioner for Human Rights, quoted from the 2010 Joint Declaration on Ten Key Threats to Freedom of Expression.

Perhaps more significantly, the Joint Declarations have been referred to in the standard-setting exercises conducted by these bodies. For example, the Inter-Parliamentary Union referred extensively to all of the Joint Declarations addressing the right to information (1999, 2004 and 2006) in its 2009 Resolution on Freedom of Expression and the Right to Information, which set out a number of principles on these fundamental rights.[95] The Council of Europe's Declaration of the Committee of Ministers on the role of community media in promoting social cohesion and intercultural dialogue refers to the 2007 Joint Declaration on Diversity in Broadcasting.[96] Similarly, the 2007 Joint Declaration is referred to by the European Parliament in its Resolution on Community Media in Europe.[97]

The Joint Declarations have also been referred to by courts, including international courts. For example, the issue before the European Court of Human Rights in the case of *Stoll* v. *Switzerland* was whether the criminal conviction of a journalist for publishing secret documents was legitimate. By a holding of four votes to three, the Court initially held that there had been a violation of the right to freedom of expression. The matter was then referred to a Grand Chamber of seventeen judges, which decided by a vote of twelve to five that there had been no such violation. In its very carefully reasoned decision, the Grand Chamber referred, among other things, to the 2006 Joint Declaration.[98]

[94] European Parliament, *Democracy Revisited: Which Notion of Democracy for the EU's External Relations?* (Brussels: Office for Promotion of Parliamentary Democracy, September 2009).

[95] Inter-Parliamentary Union Assembly, Resolution: Freedom of Expression and the Right to Information, Addis Ababa, 10 April 2009.

[96] CoE Committee of Ministers, Declaration on the Role of Community Media in Promoting Social Cohesion and Intercultural Dialogue, 11 February 2009.

[97] European Parliament (EP), Resolution on Community Media in Europe, Doc. P6_TA (2008)0456, 25 September 2008.

[98] ECtHR, *Stoll* v. *Switzerland* (Appl. No. 69698/01), Judgment (Grand Chamber), 10 December 2007, para. 39.

In another case before the European Court of Human Rights, *Editorial Board of Pravoye Delo and Shtekel* v. *Ukraine*, the Court addressed a case of defamation arising from the republication in a newspaper of a letter which had been posted anonymously on the World Wide Web. The Court quoted from the 2005 Joint Declaration, specifically regarding the degree of protection that should be afforded to freedom of expression online, and concluded that Ukrainian law lacked adequate safeguards for journalists using material obtained over the Internet and that, as a result, it was not sufficiently clear to meet the 'prescribed by law' part of the test for restrictions on freedom of expression.[99]

The case of *Yildirim* v. *Turkey*, also before the European Court of Human Rights, involved the blocking of websites hosted by Google Sites, including that of the applicant. The majority decision found a breach of Article 10 of the ECHR holding that the restriction was not prescribed by law. A concurring opinion by Judge Pinto De Albuquerque, however, went further, holding that the wholesale blocking of websites could never be justified, relying in part on the statement to this effect in the 2011 Joint Declaration on Freedom of Expression and the Internet.[100]

Perhaps the most extensive reliance on the Joint Declarations by an international court was in the case of *Youth Initiative for Human Rights* v. *Serbia*, involving a claim for access to information from an intelligence agency. The European Court quoted extensively from ten paragraphs of the 2004 Joint Declaration and again from the 2006 Joint Declaration in finding a breach of Article 10.[101]

The above is a rather limited and somewhat random selection of instances in which the Joint Declarations have been used by other actors, and it does not reach beyond that to refer to the use made of other standard-setting by the UN Special Rapporteur. At the same time, it is already clear from the above that these standard-setting documents have influenced and continue to influence the work of both activists and decision-makers on freedom of expression issues.

[99] ECtHR, *Editorial Board of Pravoye Delo and Shtekel* v. *Ukraine* (Appl. No. 33014/05), Judgment, 5 May 2001. The Joint Declaration was referred to in para. 32, while the final conclusion of the Court on this point is found at para. 66.

[100] ECtHR, *Yildirim* v. *Turkey* (Appl. No. 3111/10), Judgment, 18 December 2012, fn. 19.

[101] ECtHR, *Youth Initiative for Human Rights* v. *Serbia* (Appl. No. 48135/06), Judgment, 25 June 2013, paras. 14 and 15.

## 5 Conclusion

The office of the UN Special Rapporteur on the promotion and protection of the right to freedom of opinion and expression plays an extremely important role in promoting and protecting the fundamental rights which define its mandate. Freedom of expression is a complex right, and through his various activities, the Special Rapporteur contributes to the development of a more profound contemporary understanding of the nature of the right and its implications, both generally and in various country contexts. His work also highlights specific instances of abuse of this right and, in that way, helps both to improve respect for it and to provide protection to those who are at risk.

The standard-setting work of the Special Rapporteur is perhaps the most controversial and important work that he undertakes. It has enormous leveraging potential, given the strong inherent power of this work through its claim to be an elaboration of international law, which is formally binding on States. But this is precisely wherein lies its controversial element. If the Special Rapporteur were unduly conservative in his elaboration of international standards, this work would make a correspondingly muted contribution. If, however, he were too radical in his approach, his claim to be developing our understanding of international law, wherein lies the force of this work, would be undermined.

It is submitted that the Special Rapporteur has struck a largely appropriate balance between developing international law and respecting more traditional understanding in his standard-setting work. There is no doubt that by joining together with his colleagues from regional human rights bodies, the Special Rapporteur has significantly bolstered the impact of his standard-setting work. There is also little question that the Joint Declarations, in particular, have promoted a strong and progressive interpretation of the right to freedom of expression. At the same time, as the two examples above demonstrate, at least the main standards they promote have strong persuasive force. In some cases, the Special Rapporteur has managed to convince even relatively careful international courts that his shared position is correct. In other cases the standards have at least come to be accepted by many other key players. In this way, the Special Rapporteur has fostered the progressive development of international standards, while maintaining the credibility of this office.

## Literature

McDougal, M. S., H. D. Lasswell and L. C. Chen, *Human Rights and World Public Order* (New Haven, CT: Yale University Press, 1980).

Mendel, T. *Official Mechanisms for Freedom of Expression* (London: ARTICLE 19, 2001).

## Case law

### *ECtHR*

*Centro Europa 7 SRL and Di Stefano* v. *Italy* (Appl. No. 38433/09), Judgment (Grand Chamber) of 7 June 2012.

*Editorial Board of Pravoye Delo and Shtekel* v. *Ukraine* (Appl. No. 33014/05), Judgment of 5 May 2001.

*Gaskin* v. *the United Kingdom* (Appl. No. 10454/83), Judgment of 7 July 1989.

*Guerra and Others* v. *Italy* (Appl. No. 14967/89), Judgment (Grand Chamber), 19 February 1998.

*Leander* v. *Sweden* (Appl. No. 9248/81), Judgment of 26 March 1987.

*Lingens* v. *Austria* (Appl. No. 9815/82), Judgment of 8 July 1986.

*McGinley and Egan* v. *the United Kingdom* (Appl. Nos. 21825/93 and 23414/94), Judgment of 9 June 1998.

*Manole and Others* v. *Moldova* (Appl. No. 13936/02), Judgment of 17 September 2009.

*Odièvre* v. *France* (Appl. No. 42326/98) Judgment (Grand Chamber) of 13 February 2003.

*Österreichische Vereinigung zur Erhaltung, Stärkung und Schaffung eines wirtschaftlich gesunden land- und forstwirtschaftlichen Grundbesitzes* v. *Austria* (Appl. No. 39534/07), Judgment of 28 November 2013.

*Panev* v. *Bulgaria* (Appl. No. 35125/97) Judgment of 3 December 1997.

*Roşiianu* v. *Romania* (Appl. No. 27329/06), Judgment of 24 June 2014.

*Ruokanen and Others* v. *Finland* (Appl. No. 45130/06), Judgment of 6 April 2010.

*Sîrbu and Others* v. *Moldova* (Appl. Nos. 73562/01, 73565/01, 73712/01, 73744/01, 73972/01 and 73973/01), Judgment of 15 June 2004.

*Stoll* v. *Switzerland* (Appl. No. 69698/01), Judgment (Grand Chamber) of 10 December 2007.

*Társaság A Szabadságjogokért* v. *Hungary* (Appl. No. 37374/05), Judgment of 14 April 2009.

*Yildirim* v. *Turkey* (Appl. No. 3111/10), Judgment of 18 December 2012.

*Youth Initiative for Human Rights* v. *Serbia* (Appl. No. 48135/06), Judgment of 25 June 2013.

### *ICJ*

*Barcelona Traction, Light and Power Company Limited Case (Belgium* v. *Spain) (Second Phase)*, ICJ Reports (1970) 3.

*Namibia Opinion*, ICJ Reports (1971) 16.

### *IACtHR*

*Claude Reyes and Others* v. *Chile*, Series C No. 15119, September 2006.

*Tristán Donoso* v. *Panama*, Series C No. 193, 27 January 2009.

### *US*

*Filartiga* v. *Pena-Irala*, 630 F. 2d 876 (2nd Circ. 1980).

# PART II

## Selected thematic focuses

# 9

# Ten challenges for the right to information in the age of mega-leaks

HELEN DARBISHIRE

## 1 Is transparency working?

Government transparency is on the march, with 98 countries now having laws which give a right of access to information, and of these over 50 having constitutional provisions confirming this right as a fundamental right.[1] International human rights bodies, including the Inter-American Court of Human Rights (2006) and the European Court of Human Rights (2009) have ruled that access to information from public bodies is a human right, something confirmed in July 2011 by the United Nations Human Rights Committee. Governments around the world are taking up the challenge of opening up to the public, out of the recognition that enlightenment ideas of a public right to scrutinise how power is being exercised is a *sine qua non* of a twenty-first-century democracy. In 2011, a new global alliance of democratic countries was formed, the Open Government Partnership, which is predicated on the principles of promoting transparency, accountability and participation, and to date has sixty-three participating States as well as active involvement of civil society.[2] There is a vibrant global civil society movement promoting transparency, with activists, journalists and members of the public reporting daily on successes in obtaining information, as well as denouncing obstacles and frustrations in the implementation of this right.

Yet, in spite of all this progress, in recent years some of the most significant disclosures of information about government behaviour – certainly those which made the biggest headlines – have come through massive leaks rather than in responses to access to information requests.

[1] For the full list of laws, including analysis of Constitutional Provisions, see www.RTI-Rating.org (last accessed 28 April 2014).

[2] Open Government Partnership: www.opengovpartnership.org (last accessed 28 April 2014), sixty-three participating Member States as at January 2014.

The mega-leaks era started in 2010 with bulk disclosures of sensitive information about the war on terror by WikiLeaks,[3] followed in 2013 by the Snowden disclosures which ripped the lid off massive surveillance operations invading the privacy of private individuals and public figures the world over.[4] Also in 2013, the Offshore leaks finally gave us a true picture of tax avoidance and hidden dealings of the mega-rich, politicians and criminals, through a leaked cache of over 2.5 million files on over 120,000 offshore companies and trusts.[5]

These highly controversial leaks have led to greater accountability for the war on terror, reforms of law and practice on protection of privacy, public pressure for changes in the behaviour of intelligence agencies, and revision of legislation about the information companies should disclose to regulators. At the national level, investigative journalists, civil society researchers, academics and others continue to rely on leaked information to find out what is really going on inside government, how public money is being spent and how power is being exercised. The media seem to report leaks as often as they report about documents obtained through legal channels in response to access to information requests or through proactive disclosure of information by public bodies.

Some sceptics have suggested that as access to information laws get stronger, public officials simply get more creative at avoiding scrutiny. Government in the age of transparency has been described as akin to

[3] In April 2010, WikiLeaks published the 'Collateral Murder' video footage from the 12 July 2007 Baghdad airstrike in which Iraqi journalists were among those killed. In July 2010, WikiLeaks released Afghan War Diary, a compilation of more than 76,900 documents about the War in Afghanistan not previously available to the public. In October 2010, the group released a set of almost 400,000 documents called the 'Iraq War Logs' in coordination with major commercial media organisations. In November 2010, WikiLeaks collaborated with major global media organisations to release US State Department diplomatic cables in redacted format. Source: http://en.wikipedia.org/wiki/WikiLeaks (last accessed 28 April 2014).

[4] The full story on the Snowden Disclosures can be found on the *Guardian* newspaper website: www.theguardian.com/world/the-nsa-files (last accessed 28 April 2014).

[5] The International Consortium for Investigative Journalists' Offshore Leaks page has the details: www.icij.org/offshore (last accessed 28 April 2014). Before these leaks, no journalist had been able to crack the secret offshore money system on a global scale. The *Columbia Journalism Review* called the revelations 'a landmark series on offshore tax havens that has law enforcement scrambling and scofflaws sweating from Mongolia to Germany, Greece to the US' (The Editors, 'Darts and Laurels', Columbia Journalism Review, 1 May 2013); at www.cjr.org/darts_and_laurels/darts_laurels_mj2013.php (last accessed 28 April 2014). An example of the legislative reforms are the revisions to the EU's Anti-Money Laundering Directive, currently being debated by the European Parliament which would require companies to reveal who are their beneficial owners.

'how gangsters in crime movies talk when they know that the police are listening. They speak clearly and offer banalities while exchanging notes under the table.'[6] This cynicism does reflect real challenges: in 2013, Canada's Information Commissioner expressed concern that the use of around 98,000 Blackberry telephones by Canadian public officials was putting information out of the reach of the Freedom of Information Act.[7]

There is still far too little empirical data available to be able to measure and track levels of transparency over time and to reach compelling conclusions about how access to information is working in different countries. There are, however, multiple anecdotal examples of how access to information is having a positive impact on the relationship between civil society and government.

There is also a growing body of evidence that access to information laws do make a difference in practice. In addition to monitoring by civil society at the national level, comparative studies such as the fourteen-country Transparency and Silence monitoring (2006)[8] and the eighty-country Ask Your Government! 6 Question Campaign (2011)[9] have found that countries with access to information laws consistently performed better in responding to the same or comparable information requests than those without.

This chapter summarises the current status of the right of access to information from a human rights perspective and then sets out ten unresolved challenges facing this still-emerging right.

## 2 The right of access to information as we know it

To understand the nature and contours of the right of access to information as currently reflected in national and international law, it is

[6] I. Krastev, 'The Transparency Conspiracy', 29 January 2013; www.project-syndicate.org/commentary/the-false-promise-of-transparent-government-by-ivan-krastev (last accessed 28 April 2014).

[7] J. Bronskill, 'Info Czar Suzanne Legault: ban instant messaging on government BlackBerrys', *Huffington Post*, 28 November 2013; www.huffingtonpost.ca/2013/11/28/suzanne-legault-instant-messaging_n_4356163.html (last accessed 28 April 2014).

[8] *Transparency and Silence: A Survey of Access to Information Laws in 14 Countries* (New York: Open Society Justice Initiative, 2006); www.opensocietyfoundations.org/publications/transparency-and-silence-survey-access-information-laws-and-practices-14-countries (last accessed 28 April 2014).

[9] 'Ask Your Government! 6 Question Campaign', Access Info Europe and Centre for Law and Democracy, October 2011; www.access-info.org/en/anti-corruption/200–6-question-campaign (last accessed 28 April 2014).

essential also to understand the history of the right as it developed over the past two centuries and, in particular, during the second half of the twentieth century.

The world's first access to information law was the Swedish Freedom of the Printing Press Act in 1766. This law was a product of enlightenment thinking. The benefits of openness had been posited during the eighteenth century when the word 'transparency' was used in the works of political philosophers such as Jean-Jacques Rousseau (1712–78), who promoted openness in his plans for the government of Poland in 1772, proposing that all public officeholders should operate 'in the eyes of the public' and even wear a uniform so that they could never be anonymous.[10] France's Declaration of the Rights of Man and of the Citizen of 1789 provides that citizens have the right to determine and follow the spending of taxes (Article 14) and that society has the right to demand accountability from all public bodies (Article 15).[11] Yet, while limited versions of these principles were enshrined in administrative codes and good government practice, only Sweden had a specific act until 1951 when Finland, an independent country since 1917, caught up with its own history: the drafter of the Swedish Act of 1766, Anders Chydenius, had in fact come from Finland.

With such limited development of access to information laws, the right was not included in the catalogue of rights in the Universal Declaration of Human Rights (1948). The focus at the time was on 'the advent of a world in which human beings shall enjoy freedom of speech and belief' and hence Article 19 of the Declaration established that

> everyone has the right to freedom of opinion and expression; this right includes freedom to hold opinions without interference and to seek, receive and impart information and ideas through any media and regardless of frontiers.[12]

[10] C. Hood, 'What Happens When Transparency Meets Blame-Avoidance?', *Public Management Review* 9(2) (2007), 193–4. Hood cites Rousseau and states that philosophers Jeremy Bentham, Immanuel Kant and, earlier, Baruch de Spinoza put forward similar ideas. It should be noted that these pre-twentieth-century concepts of transparency also include the notion of government according to stable and known rules, and the notion of maximum social openness (everyone under scrutiny by everyone else), as well as the notion of open government in the sense of public access to government documents.

[11] Assemblée Nationale, *Déclaration des droits de l'homme et du citoyen* (1789), www.assemblee-nationale.fr/histoire/dudh/1789.asp (last accessed 28 April 2014).

[12] GA, Resolution 217 (III): Universal Declaration of Human Rights, 10 December 1948.

The post-Second World War years saw a strengthening in a handful of countries of the mechanisms for accessing government information. The USA with the first iteration of the Freedom of Information Act in 1966 (it was upgraded after the Watergate scandal in 1974), was followed by France and the Netherlands in 1978.

These laws continued to reflect a paradigm of administrative responsiveness to the 'administered' or 'citizens' of a particular country.[13] An example of this is France's 1978 law, which was adopted with the title of the law on 'improving relations between the administration and the public'[14] and which only applies to the administrative activities of government. This law also typifies the earlier laws in the sense that it was a top-down instrument, part of a package of laws necessary for the functioning of a modern democracy and a service-oriented bureaucracy, but not a response to popular demand for a broad fundamental right to be enshrined in law.

In line with this approach, the Council of Europe in 1981 adopted a Recommendation to Member States on Access to Information Held by Public Bodies which limits the scope of the right: 'Everyone within the jurisdiction of a Member State shall have the right to obtain, on request, information held by the public authorities *other than* legislative bodies and judicial authorities.'[15]

The Canadian Freedom of Information Law, adopted in 1983, also reflects this more restricted view of an administrative right: it can be exercised only by Canadian citizens and residents and only upon payment of an up-front C$5 fee for each request. The Canadian law does not apply to the legislative or administrative branches, nor to private bodies performing public functions or operating substantially with public funds.

By the end of the 1980s, just a handful of countries had access to information or freedom of information laws, and these were the Nordic countries (Denmark, Finland, Norway and Sweden), some Anglo-Saxon

[13] For example, Australia's 1982 Freedom of Information Act establishes 'the right of the Australian community to access to information in the possession of the Government'; www.austlii.edu.au/au/legis/cth/consol_act/foia1982222/s3.html (last accessed 28 April 2014).

[14] Loi n° 78-753 du 17 juillet 1978 portant diverses mesures d'amélioration des relations entre l'administration et le public et diverses dispositions d'ordre administratif, social et fiscal, Version consolidée au 20 décembre 2013.

[15] Council of Europe, Recommendation No. R (81) 19 of the Committee of Ministers to Member States on the Access to Information Held by Public Authorities, 25 November 1981.

countries (the USA, Canada, Australia and New Zealand), as well as the Netherlands, France and Italy.

This initial batch of laws, while in many respects powerful tools for citizens to hold government accountable, were designed primarily to regulate communications between citizens and an increasingly large public administration. By 1990, only Finland and Sweden recognised access to information as a right in their constitutions, Norway subsequently did so (2004), whereas in none of the others was access to information a fully-fledged constitutional right.[16]

The big push forward for access to information, which led to defining and broadening the scope of the right of access to information came after the fall of the Berlin Wall, with a strong and coordinated civic reaction to counter the information control exercised by the authoritarian regimes behind the Iron Curtain. Just as the Swedish Freedom of the Press Act was adopted in reaction to the suppression of free thought and pamphleteering in an earlier time, it was a response to the information inequalities of the Soviet bloc which led to the demand for a right to information in Central and Eastern Europe. It was this movement which led to the development of access to information as a right in the sense of a fundamental human right. As early as 1992, Hungary's Constitutional Court ruled that access to information is a right essential for citizen oversight, stating that:

> the publicity and accessibility of data of public interest is a fundamental right guaranteed by the Constitution ... Free access to information of public interest promotes democratic values in elected bodies, the executive power, and public administration by enabling people to check the lawfulness and efficiency of their operations.[17]

[16] In New Zealand, s. 14 of the Bill of Rights Act 1990 reads: 'Everyone has the right to freedom of expression, including the freedom to seek, receive, and impart information and opinions of any kind in any form.' Prior to the passage of this Act, the New Zealand Court of Appeal had already described New Zealand's freedom of information legislation as 'an Act of constitutional significance'. See case of *Commissioner of Police* v. *Ombudsman* [1988] 1 NZLR 385. The Bill of Rights affirms and extends that position, for example, influencing public access to court records. See *Mafart* v. *Television New Zealand Ltd.*, Sup. Ct. No. SC70/2006 [2006] NZSC 78 (2006) 18 PRNZ 394; www.Right2INFO.org (last accessed 29 April 2014).

[17] Decision 32/1992 (V.29) AB, 183–4 (as translated by the Office of the Hungarian Parliamentary Commissioner for Data Protection and Freedom of Information). In 1994, the Hungarian Court struck down a State secrets law, ruling that it imposed impermissible restrictions on the right to information. In so doing, the Court found that free access to data of public interest, including those held by the State, is one of the preconditions for the exercise of the right to free expression (Decision 34/1994 (VI.24) AB).

All of the eight former communist countries which joined the European Union on 1 May 2004 had an access to information law, as did Romania and Bulgaria, which joined on 1 January 2007, and Croatia, which by the time it joined the EU on 1 July 2013, had already had an access to information law in force for ten years. All eleven of these countries also have constitutional provisions establishing the right.

As with post-communist Eastern Europe, the democratic transitions in Latin America played a significant role in advancing the right to information. In Mexico, the Grupo Oaxaca, a gathering of intellectuals, academics, journalists and activists, promoted and helped to draft Mexico's Federal Law on Transparency and Access to Public Information.[18] The Mexican law was adopted in 2002 by the government of President Vicente Fox who in 2000 had become the first president of Mexico to be elected from an opposition party, ending the seventy-one years of one-party rule by Mexico's Institutional Revolutionary Party, the PRI.

Mexico's Constitution at Article 6 establishes the right of free access to information and details its scope as well as its oversight mechanisms. Since 2002, thirteen countries in Latin America have adopted access to information laws. Africa followed with ten laws, and the global total is now ninety-eight.

These developments not only expanded the number of countries recognising a public right to obtain information from public bodies, but they also expanded the scope of the right itself, applying it to all information held by administrative, legislative and judicial bodies as well as often private bodies performing public functions. Indeed, the South African Constitution and law went even further to apply the right to private bodies who hold information necessary for the defence of other rights.[19]

In this way, as often happens in the development of human rights, progress on the national level impacted on international standard-setting, which in turn fuelled the advance of national standards, setting up a virtuous circle which accelerated the speed of acceptance of access to information laws as an essential underpinning of a democratic State.

[18] See I. Luna Pla, 'Movimiento social del derecho de acceso a la información en México', published by the Universidad Nacional Autónoma de México (2009); http://biblio.juridicas.unam.mx/libros/libro.htm?l=2629 (last accessed 29 April 2014).

[19] Constitution of the Republic of South Africa, 1996, Article 32; '(1)Everyone has the right of access to: (a) any information held by the state; and (b) any information that is held by another person and that is required for the exercise or protection of any rights. (2) National legislation must be enacted to give effect to this right, and may provide for reasonable measures to alleviate the administrative and financial burden on the state.'

A strong and well-organised international civil society movement pushed forward the standard-setting, through national, regional, and international declarations on the main elements of access to information laws, starting with the 1998 Principles on Freedom of Information Legislation from the human rights organisation ARTICLE 19.[20] These standard-setting exercises were complemented by conferences and debates and multiple other advocacy initiatives to promote this emerging right. Civil society worked closely with government officials, key staff in intergovernmental organisations (IGOs), and the Special Rapporteurs on Freedom of Expression to further define the standards.[21]

In the context of these developments, the Council of Europe embarked in 2006 on the exercise of converting a political recommendation of 2002[22] into the world's first binding treaty on access to information held by public bodies, which would become the Council of Europe Convention on Access to Official Documents and which was formally adopted in June 2009, although it has yet to enter into force.[23]

The process of drafting the Convention laid bare the disagreements over the nature of the right, as many of the government representatives who drafted the Convention between January 2006 and February 2008, roundly rejected the idea that access to information is a fundamental right. There was a tension in the drafting group between countries with constitutional provisions on the right of access to information (Nordic countries and new democracies such as Slovenia) and those without such clarity or with national laws which had a more limited scope (notably France).[24] One of the main consequences of this is that the Convention applies only to administrative information and it is left up to ratifying States to extend it on an optional basis to the legislative and judicial powers.

[20] A list of some of the key texts, principles and declarations can be found on the Access Info Europe website at www.access-info.org/en/principles (last accessed 29 April 2014).

[21] See Chapter 8 in this book.

[22] Council of Europe, Recommendation No. 2 of the Committee of Ministers to Member States on Access to Official Documents, 21 February 2002.

[23] Convention on Access to Official Documents, Tromsø, 18 June 2009, not entered into force yet, CETS 205. Signed as of 21 April 2014 by fourteen countries and ratified by six countries; the treaty will enter into force when it has ten ratifications.

[24] This author was present at the drafting sessions as a civil society observer and the French representative clearly stated that his mandate was to negotiate a Convention which did not set a higher standard for the right than that set by French law. The law is limited to access to administrative information. Germany did not participate actively in the drafting, having sent an official communication at the outset of the process doubting the necessity of such an instrument.

A major change in the human rights standards on the right came in September 2006 when the Inter-American Court of Human Rights ruled in the case of *Claude Reyes et al.* v. *Chile* that the protection of freedom of expression and information under Article 13 of the American Convention on Human Rights:

> protects the right of all individuals to request access to State-held information, with the exceptions permitted by the restrictions established in the Convention. Consequently, this article protects the right of the individual to receive such information and the positive obligation of the State to provide it, so that the individual may have access to such information or receive an answer that includes a justification when, for any reason permitted by the Convention, the State is allowed to restrict access to the information in a specific case.[25]

It is interesting to note that the linking by the Inter-American Court of the right of access to information to freedom of expression is consistent with the approach taken by the world's first access to information law, the Swedish Freedom of the Printing Press Act of 1766. The European Court of Human Rights adopted similar reasoning in 2009 in the case of *Társaság a Szabadságjogokért* [Hungarian Civil Liberties Union, TASZ] v. *Hungary*, when it argued that when a public body holds information which is essential either for the media to play their role as 'public watchdogs' or for civil society to play a 'social watchdog' function, then to withhold that information is an interference with freedom of expression, and hence is protected by Article 10 of the European Convention on Human Rights which protects freedom of expression.[26] The judges arrived at this conclusion using the logic that when a public body holds information and refuses to release it, it is exercising the 'censorial power of an information monopoly' and hence the interference with freedom of expression.[27]

In parallel with these developments, political declarations expanding on the nature of this right were also adopted. These include Model Laws from the Organization of American States (OAS)[28] and the African

[25] IACtHR, *Claude Reyes and Others* v. *Chile*, Series C No. 151, 19 September 2006, para. 77.
[26] ECtHR, *Társaság a Szabadságjogokért* v. *Hungary* (Appl. No. 37374/05), Judgment of 14 April 2009, paras. 36 and 38.
[27] *Ibid.*, para. 36.
[28] Organization of American States, *Model Inter-American Law on Access to Public Information*, Doc. No. AG/RES. 2607 (XL-O/10), 8 June 2010; www.oas.org/dil/AG-RES_2607-2010_eng.pdf (last accessed 29 April 2014).

Union[29] which further define in detail what an access to information law should look like. These soft law instruments go further than the Council of Europe Convention on Access to Official Documents. For example, the OAS Model Law has a section dedicated to promoting openness which includes an extensive list of information which should be made available proactively, as well as other features such as information officers and the establishment of an Information Commissioner.

These progressive and significant changes in the global hard and soft law framework for the right of access to information were picked up by the UN Human Rights Committee which in July 2011 in its General Comment No. 34 confirmed that there exists a fundamental human right to access information held by public bodies and private bodies performing public functions, and that it is linked to the well-established right to freedom of expression set out in Article 19 of the International Covenant on Civil and Political Rights (ICCPR).[30] In other words, our right to free expression is contingent on information and when this information is held by public bodies, we have a right to access it, with only limited exceptions.

The importance of General Comment No. 34 for the right of access to information should not be underestimated. It is a milestone in the development of human rights because, rather than being a mere interpretation of established rights, it confirms the existence of an emerging human right. It is more generic than the finding in a particular case before a human rights tribunal and goes further than the jurisprudence, in particular with respect to the obligation to publish information proactively. Hence it contributes to a redefinition of a modern democratic society, and the relationship between the people and the governments they elect.

At the same time, the very belated recognition of access to information as a fundamental right by international human rights bodies also highlights how not all are convinced that it is or should be seen as such. Indeed, one UN member and party to the ICCPR, Germany, urged the Human Rights Committee not to conclude that access to information is a right, as there is nothing in the German legal or constitutional framework

[29] African Union, Draft Model Law for AU Member States on Access to Information, 24 November 2010; www.achpr.org/files/instruments/access information/achpr_instr_draft_model_law_access_to_information_2011_eng.pdf (last accessed 29 April 2014).

[30] HRC, General Comment No. 34: Article 19 (Freedoms of opinion and expression), UN Doc. CCPR/C/GC/34, 12 September 2011, paras. 18 and 19. See further, Chapter 2 in this book.

which sees access to information from public bodies as a fundamental right.[31] The German position is at odds with many other European countries which do have constitutional provisions recognising the right (twenty-eight in the Council of Europe region),[32] and even the European Union, which recognises a fundamental right of access to its documents,[33] but nevertheless illustrates how this is not yet universally taken as a given, and even in countries where there is a constitutional provision on the right to information, what this means in practice is not always clear.

It was therefore particularly important at this juncture to have a further confirmation of the right of access to information from the European Court of Human Rights. This came in June 2013 in the case of the *Youth Initiative for Human Rights* v. *Serbia*. The case concerned the refusal of the Serbian intelligence agency to provide the appellant civil society organisation with information about electronic surveillance, even after it had been ordered to do so by the Serbian Information Commissioner.[34] In finding a violation of Article 10, the Court underscored the existence of a right of access to information and cited the Human Rights Committee General Comment No. 34, as well as declarations by the United Nations Special Rapporteur on Freedom of Opinion and Expression, the Organization for Security and Co-operation in Europe (OSCE) Representative on Freedom of the Media, the Organization of American States (OAS) Special Rapporteur on Freedom of Expression, and the African Commission on Human and Peoples' Rights (ACHPR) Special Rapporteur on Freedom of Expression, which also confirm the existence and scope of the right of access to information.[35]

A further European Court of Human Rights decision of 28 November 2013 in a case against Austria again confirmed the right of access to information. In this case a civil society organisation (hereafter, CSO) was seeking information about land records from a regional land register,[36]

[31] 'Germany's comments on Draft General Comment No. 34 on Article 19 of the International Covenant on Civil and Political Rights', n.d., at http://home.broadpark.no/~wkeim/files/German_comments_on_Draft_General_Comment_No.34.pdf (unofficial source, last accessed 19 April 2014).

[32] See country details on the RTI Rating; www.rti-rating.org (last accessed 29 April 2014).

[33] Consolidated version of the Treaty on the Functioning of the European Union, Art. 15.

[34] ECtHR, *Youth Initiative for Human Rights* v. *Serbia* (Appl. No. 48135/06), Judgment of 25 September 2013.

[35] *Ibid.*, paras. 13–15. See further, Chapter 8 in this book.

[36] ECtHR, *Österreichische Vereinigung zur Erhaltung, Stärkung und Schaffung eines wirtschaftlich gesunden land-und forstwirtschaftlichen Grundbesitzes* v. *Austria* (Appl. No. 39534/07), Judgment of 28 November 2013, para. 46.

the Tyrolean Real Property Transactions Commission (the Commission). Not only did the court rule that the refusal to provide this information was a violation of freedom of expression, it stated that, given the 'considerable public interest' in the land records, it 'finds it striking that none of the Commission's decisions was published, whether in an electronic database or in any other form'.[37] In this way, the Court for the first time hinted, if only in the most subtle way, at the possibility of obligations to proactively publish information.

An important feature of the international jurisprudence linking the right of access to information to freedom of expression is not simply that a convenient 'hook' was needed, but that the tribunals have made the connection between information, expression, and active engagement in public affairs as an essential aspect of democratic societies.[38] Such a linkage has also been made in the jurisprudence of the Court of Justice of the European Union, for example, in the case of *Council of the European Union* v. *Access Info Europe*, where the Court underscored the relationship between accessing documents and participation in EU decision-making, stating that 'if citizens are to be able to exercise their democratic rights, they must be in a position to follow in detail the decision-making process' and that they should 'have access to all relevant information'.[39]

From the collected body of national laws and international standards, it is possible to identify some core elements of the right of access to information, namely that it is a right of all persons, that it should apply to all information held by all public bodies, that the right may be exercised free of charge and without having to give reasons, that requests should be answered as rapidly as possible and in no more than a maximum of twenty working days, that exceptions should be limited and should be subject to both harm and public interest tests, and that there should be oversight by some independent body, often an ombudsman or information commissioner, in addition to there being recourse to the judicial authorities.

In spite of these tremendous advances, there remain various areas in which there is still too little clarity about the precise nature and normative content of the right of access to information and the consequences of its inclusion in the pantheon of fundamental rights have not as yet been fully explored. The remainder of this chapter maps out ten key challenges

[37] *Ibid.* [38] See also Chapters 1 and 3 in this book.

[39] EU Court of Justice, *Council of the EU* v. *Access Info Europe*, Final Judgment in Case 280/11 P, 17 October 2013.

facing the right of access to information which are likely to be at the heart of debates about this right in coming years.

## 3 Ten unresolved challenges for the right to know

### *3.1 A right of all persons*

A fundamental right is one which should apply to all persons, irrespective of their nationality, place of residence or other criteria. This would be consistent with the 'without frontiers' nature of the right to freedom of expression.

In total 89 of the world's 98 access to information laws recognise that the right may be exercised by 'all persons' or 'everyone'. Indeed, 64 of these laws extend the right to legal persons such as businesses, civil society organisations or political parties. Yet, as noted above, some countries limit the exercise of the right to the population directly served by the administration. These countries include Canada where only citizens and residents may make freedom of information requests,[40] Malta[41] and Turkey.[42]

The European Union similarly limits the right to citizens and residents, doing so in the treaties which establish that '[A]ny citizen of the Union, and any natural or legal person residing or having its registered office in a Member State, shall have a right of access to documents of the Union institutions.'[43] It will be interesting to see whether a legal challenge taken in one of these countries resting upon the UN Human Rights Committee standard or the jurisprudence of one of the regional courts could result in changes to national law.

[40] Canadian Access to Information Act, last modified 2010, Article 4.1; 'Subject to this Act, but notwithstanding any other Act of Parliament, every person who is (a) a Canadian citizen, or (b) a permanent resident within the meaning of subsection 2(1) of the Immigration and Refugee Protection Act, has a right to and shall, on request, be given access to any record under the control of a government institution.'

[41] Malta's 2008 Freedom of Information Act at Article 2 defines a person eligible to submit a request as a resident, citizens from Malta, EU citizens or citizens from other countries with which there is a treaty that includes the right of access to information. See www.rti-rating.org/view_country.php?country_name=Malta (last accessed 29 April 2014).

[42] Turkish law on the Right to Information, Law 4982 of 2003, states at Article 4 that 'Foreigners domiciled in Turkey and the foreign legal entities operating in Turkey can exercise the right in this law, on the condition that the information that they require is related to them or the field of their activities.' See www.rti-rating.org/view_country.php?country_name=Turkey (last accessed 29 April 2014).

[43] Consolidated version of the Treaty on the Functioning of the European Union, Art. 15.

There are some practical implications to the universal nature of access to information, not least the barrier posed by language. Even in countries with a broad definition of the right, there is usually a requirement that it be exercised in one of the official languages of the administration. The degree of flexibility which public administrations show on the language issue varies between countries and often depends on national culture rather than law.[44] There is a reasonableness test to be applied here and it is clearly unreasonable to expect national administrations around the world to provide translations into any of the world's 7,105 living languages, or even the 80 languages spoken by more than 10 million people.[45] This is particularly the case as in most countries a response to an access to information request is itself an official document and hence needs to be in the working languages of the administration. A pragmatic solution might be to make it acceptable to submit requests and obtain information in one of the UN languages, namely Arabic, Chinese, English, French, Russian and Spanish.[46] Such practical challenges still lie ahead of this new right and in the future it is likely that more consideration will have to be given to how it can be exercised in an increasingly globalised but still multicultural and multilingual world.

### 3.2 *Definition of Information*

What the public can ask for when exercising the right is also an issue where greater clarity is needed. What is information precisely?

The UN Human Rights Committee has stated that the information to which the right applies 'includes records held by a public body, regardless

[44] This author has experience of submitting requests in English to and receiving information from northern European countries such as Denmark, Finland, the Netherlands, Norway and Sweden, whereas in other countries the response to an English-language request has come variously in French, German, Greek or Polish, for example. See also Chapter 3 in this book.

[45] Ethnologue reports that there are 7,105 living languages, see: www.ethnologue.com. Wikipedia reports that there are 1,300 languages with 100,000 speakers or more, 750 with 300,000 or more, some 400 with a million or more, 200 with at least 3 million, 80 with 10 million, and 40 with 30 million; see http://en.wikipedia.org/wiki/List_of_languages_by_number_of_native_speakers (both last accessed 29 April 2014).

[46] In addition to this, a good practice would be to supply information in electronic, machine-readable, format wherever possible, thus permitting the use of online translators which – although not always reliable and no substitute for official translations – often provide a good indication of the content of documents received. When information is provided in a foreign language in a locked, scanned, PDF, this seriously impedes obtaining even a gist of what it contains.

of the form in which the information is stored, its source and the date of production'.[47] Such a broad definition is essential in the modern era in which information is stored in a wide variety of formats. As both the right to information and technology have advanced, there has been a gradual expansion of the definition of information and a combination of law, jurisprudence, and practice is giving access to a greater variety of types of information. It is now generally agreed that 'information' recorded in formats such as photographs, and audiovisual recordings is included in the scope of the right. Hence, use of the right can be made by, for example, documentary film-makers.[48]

In an increasing number of countries e-mail communications also come under the scope of the right of access to information. It is increasingly common to receive copies of e-mails as part of answers to requests for information. In some jurisdictions the use of private e-mail accounts will not always take messages out of the scope of the right to information, with a high-profile example of this being the 13,000 e-mails from former US presidential candidate and Alaskan Governor, Sarah Palin.[49]

At the other end of the spectrum, handwritten documents also fall within the definition of information. This is particularly important where the only notes of a meeting are those taken by a public official, jotted on his or her notepad. An example of such a document which contains the notes of a UK public official from a meeting held in the Council of the EU can be found on the Access Info Europe website.[50]

Some jurisdictions, however, cling to their historical roots, still referring to a right of access to 'documents' rather than to 'information'.

47 HRC, General Comment No. 34, para. 18.

48 A nice example of this is the Spanish documentary *Flecha Rota* ('Broken Arrow') about the 1966 crash of a B52 plane carrying nuclear warheads onto the coast of Almería in southern Spain. The documentary makers made an FOI request in the USA to get original footage shot by marines involved in the clean-up of the spilled plutonium. See the documentary at www.documentalesonline.com/operacion-flecha-rota-el-accidente-nuclear-de-palomares-video_688839aa5.html and read more at http://en.wikipedia.org/wiki/1966_Palomares_B-52_crash (both last accessed 29 April 2014).

49 The emails were released as over 24,000 printed pages, which were then scanned and put online by the *Guardian* newspaper and analysis of them was crowd-sourced, permitting some new information to emerge about the relationship with BP in negotiations over an oil pipeline. See the page from which the scan documents are accessible www.theguardian.com/world/sarah-palin-emails (last accessed 29 April 2014).

50 The document, which consists of handwritten notes taken during a meeting of the Council of the European Union's Working Party on Information, is available at www.access-info.org/documents/notas_uk.jpg (last accessed 29 April 2014).

Indeed, the very name of the Council of Europe Convention on Access to Official Documents reflects this, although the Convention found a solution by defining 'official documents' as 'all information recorded in any form, drawn up or received and held by public authorities'.[51]

Defendants of a documents-based approach argue that it is essential to protect public bodies from an obligation to make any additional effort to compile information in response to an information request. One of the starkest examples of this is at the EU level where the right of access to its documents was first recognised in 1997 by the Treaty of Amsterdam, just on the cusp of the modern information age. The EU's 2001 access to documents rules contain a broad definition of 'document' as 'any content whatever its medium (written on paper or stored in electronic form or as a sound, visual or audio-visual recording)'.[52] Current EU policy, however, is to draw a line between requests for documents and requests for information, which will be answered under the non-binding code of good administrative practice.[53]

Hence, EU officials will apply a distinct legal basis for responding to a request asking 'please provide documents which detail spending on official travel in 2013' and asking 'how much was spent on official travel in 2013?'. While a well-prepared requester can easily find a way around this in the way the question is framed, it remains a formal obstacle placed in the way of a fundamental right and it places an undue burden on the requester to know how to formulate their request.

The conceptual divide between 'documents' and 'information' in some jurisdictions has led open data activists to call for a complementary 'right to data'.[54] This author strongly believes that such a new right is not necessary, and could even be unhelpful, muddying the waters just as clarity about the right of access to information is being established. Such proposals do, however, highlight the need to upgrade both legislation and

[51] Convention on Access to Official Documents, Art. 1.2.b.

[52] European Parliament and Council of the European Union, Regulation 1049/2001 Regarding Public Access to European Parliament, Council and Commission Documents, OJ No. L145/43, 31 May 2001, Art. 3.a; www.europarl.europa.eu/register/pdf/r1049_en.pdf (last accessed 29 April 2014).

[53] The EU's rules concerning access to documents and to general information can be found at http://ec.europa.eu/transparency/access_documents/index_en.htm (last accessed 29 April 2014).

[54] The 'Right to Data' agenda was taken up by the UK government and set out in a White Paper on Open Data published in June 2012; http://data.gov.uk/sites/default/files/Open_-data_White_Paper.pdf (last accessed 29 April 2014).

bureaucratic attitudes to the digital era if full access is going to be provided to all information held by public bodies.

### 3.3 *Scope: the legislative and judicial branches*

The extension of the right of access to information from core administrative bodies to all branches of power, including the legislative and judicial branches, has been tracked in section 2 as part of the evolution of the right of access to information. The UN Human Rights Committee in its General Comment No. 34 specifically confirmed that right of access to information is part of an obligation which falls upon:

> All branches of the State (executive, legislative and judicial) and other public or governmental authorities, at whatever level – national, regional or local – are in a position to engage the responsibility of the State party.[55]

Three years earlier, in 2008, the Council of Europe Member States had been unable to reach agreement on this and hence the Convention on Access to Official Documents establishes a right of access only to the administrative information held by the legislative and judicial branches but not to all other information they hold. The Convention makes it optional for States to grant a wider right of access.[56]

For those countries with older laws, the right remains limited. In France, for example, the distinction between administrative and non-administrative information means in practice that while it may be possible to find out about the budgets and organisation of the Parliament or the court system, it is not possible to obtain information using the right of access to information or other documents such as documents used by parliamentary committees when discussing draft laws (the laws themselves are normally public by democratic tradition) or records of voting (in France the voting records of the National Assembly are not published).[57]

One problem here is that there is no clear international definition of what administrative functions are. The Council of Europe Convention on

[55] HRC, General Comment No. 34, para. 7.

[56] Convention on Access to Official Documents, Art. 1.2.a.ii.

[57] It is very rare that the votes of deputies in the French Assemblée Nationale are published, and according to the CSO Regards Citoyens, for 93 per cent of votes it is impossible to know how each deputy voted. See: www.regardscitoyens.org/la-transparence-des-votes-de-lassemblee-nationale-cest-possible (last accessed 29 April 2014).

Access to Official Documents ducked this issue saying that administrative functions are 'as defined by national law'.[58] At the EU level a number of bodies – including the European Court of Justice, European Central Bank and European Investment Bank – only have an obligation to provide administrative information but without a definition of what this means.

One of the arguments invoked in favour of sustaining a distinction between administrative and other functions is that it is necessary to preserve the impartiality and independent functioning of certain bodies, such as the court system. The problem with this approach is that accountability and citizen oversight is blocked in the name of impartiality and due process. In fact, there are well-established exceptions which can be invoked when information should be withheld. For example, the Convention on Access to Official Documents, establishes an exception to protect 'the equality of parties in court proceedings and the effective administration of justice'.[59]

With an appropriate regime of exceptions in place, there should be no need for blanket exclusions of certain bodies from the reach of the right of access to information. This is something which still has to be worked through in a number of jurisdictions and clarified further by international human rights bodies.

### 3.4 *Scope: private bodies*

The fourth major and, as yet, still barely explored, consequence of the right of access to information being recognised as a fundamental human right is that this could mean that it applies, at least to some extent, to private bodies. After all, other rights should be upheld by private bodies as well: the right to privacy as articulated in data protection laws applies to information held by all legal entities that hold personal data.

There was more agreement on this point during drafting of the Council of Europe Convention on Access to Official Documents than on the legislative and judicial branches, and as a result the Convention requires that the right extend to 'natural or legal persons insofar as they exercise administrative authority' while making it optional to also extend

[58] *Explanatory Report to the Convention on Access to Official Documents*, para. 8; http://conventions.coe.int/Treaty/EN/Reports/Html/205.htm (last accessed 29 April 2014).
[59] Convention on Access to Official Documents, Art. 3.1.i.

it to 'natural or legal persons insofar as they perform public functions or operate with public funds, according to national law'.[60] For the UN Human Rights Committee 'such bodies may also include other entities when such entities are carrying out public functions'.[61]

The full consequences of the right applying to private bodies have not yet been addressed, in part because the right-to-information community still has so many challenges securing information from public bodies. The only legal regime which extends this right more broadly to public bodies is the South African law which applies to all private bodies if the information relates to or can be used for protection of other human rights.[62] The European Court of Human Rights' concept of 'information monopolies' which hold information necessary for freedom of expression could also serve here as the basis for exploring when the public has a right to obtain information from private information holders.

### 3.5 *Scope: intergovernmental organisations*

A universal right is clearly one which should also be upheld by intergovernmental and supranational bodies. At present, however, only the European Union has recognised a fundamental right of access to the documents it holds (and, as noted above, this right is limited to citizens and residents of the EU area). First established in the 1997 Treaty of Amsterdam, in 2009 this right was moved by the Lisbon Treaty to the fundamental rights section of the Treaty on the Functioning of the European Union. This right is reinforced by also being included in Article 42 of the Charter of Fundamental Rights of the European Union.[63]

Apart from this, not one of the world's other major intergovernmental organisations has formally recognised the right of access to information as binding upon them. It is a particular irony that not one of the intergovernmental bodies that have led the way in promoting a recognition of the right of access to information has explicitly applied the right

[60] *Ibid.*, Arts. 2.a.i.3 and 2.a.ii.3 respectively.

[61] HRC, General Comment No. 34, para. 18.

[62] South Africa's Promotion of Access to Information Act 2000, s. 50, states there is a right to ask for a 'record [that] is required for the exercise or protection of any rights'.

[63] Charter of Fundamental Rights of the European Union, OJ, 30 March 2010, 2010/C 83/289.

to itself: not the United Nations,[64] nor UNESCO, nor the Council of Europe, nor the OAS, nor the ACHPR, nor the OSCE.

In addition, there have been limited efforts to introduce rules which would resolve this anomalous situation. At issue here is not merely the failure to establish that the right to ask for information applies to these organisations, but also the simple failure to establish formal mechanisms by which the public can request and receive information as well as the failure to establish a comprehensive proactive publication policy.

The consequences of this lack of access to information held by intergovernmental organisations are of particular concern given that many decision-making processes are now taken forward in intergovernmental negotiations carried out in forums about which even representatives of national parliaments do not always have information.

An example of the consequences of such bodies not providing information to the public is that of Eurocontrol, a stand-alone intergovernmental body which regulates European airspace. Eurocontrol has refused to provide human rights researchers with the information it holds about CIA extraordinary rendition flights, even when the information was needed for ongoing human rights litigation.[65]

There is a pressing need to resolve the issue of the right of access to information applying to IGOs. The UN would in theory be best placed to take the lead given the unequivocal interpretation of international law by the Human Rights Committee, but agreeing to adopt such a norm would not be easy. Much more probable is having the Council of Europe apply its Convention on Access to Official Documents to itself, thereby taking the lead and establishing a model for IGOs. It would also be appropriate for the OSCE to adopt the Convention on Access to Official Documents. If the OAS could apply its model law to itself, that would also be a significant step forward in reinforcing a right to ask at the intergovernmental organisation level, and all such moves would help encourage other bodies to adopt similar standards.

[64] The UN Development Programme on the other hand does have an Information Disclosure Policy, first adopted in 1997 and last updated in 2013; at www.undp.org/content/undp/en/home/operations/transparency/information_disclosurepolicy.html. UNICEF also has a disclosure policy, available here: www.unicef.org/about/legal_disclosure.html (both last accessed 29 April 2014).

[65] More information on this research conducted by Reprieve, the Global Rendition Project and Access Info Europe can be found at: www.access-info.org/en/human-rights/397-global-rendition-system-mapping (last accessed 29 April 2014).

### 3.6 *An obligation to publish information proactively*

The next challenge for the right of access to information is to move beyond a right to ask and receive information to an obligation on public bodies to make such information available proactively.[66]

If the only channel for access to information were via requests filed by individuals, huge information inequalities would rapidly arise with different people knowing different things about the functioning of government and with large sections of the population remaining ill-informed, to the detriment of society as a whole.

Such a system would also place an intolerable burden on public officials who would have to strive to answer huge volumes of requests from information-hungry citizens. Proactive disclosure therefore levels the playing field for access to government-held information. The Human Rights Committee General Comment No. 34 takes this into account, stressing that proactive publication is essential to achieve full enjoyment of the right to information. It states:

> To give effect to the right of access to information, States parties should proactively put in the public domain Government information of public interest. States parties should make every effort to ensure easy, prompt, effective and practical access to such information.[67]

In spite of the importance of proactive publication, this dimension of the right to information was not the focus of campaigners' attention, at least not until the last five years when 'open data' – the proactive release of entire government data sets – came into vogue. Democratic governments have always made some information available proactively. For example, the principle of the rule of law requires that laws be known and hence be published.[68] Yet this pre-existing tradition of proactive publication was not sufficient to do away with the demand for specific mechanisms by which members of the public could request specific documents,

[66] See also in this connection Chapter 3 in this book.

[67] HRC, General Comment No. 34, para. 19.

[68] In Europe this principle was affirmed in 2009 by the European Court of Justice which struck down a secret regulation adopted by the European Union about what passengers may and may not carry onto aircraft. The Court stated that 'the principle of legal certainty requires that … rules enable those concerned to know precisely the extent of the obligations which are imposed on them. Individuals must be able to ascertain unequivocally what their rights and obligations are and take steps accordingly' (Case C-345/06 *Gottfried Heinrich* (Reference for a preliminary ruling from the Unabhängiger Verwaltungssenat im Land Niederösterreich), 10 March 2009).

particularly in the transitional democracies of Central and Eastern Europe and of Latin America, which shaped the right to information movement over the past two decades.

In this context the emphasis was on the right to ask rather than on securing proactive obligations. Very few constitutional references exist and they tend to be vague. For example, Estonia's 1992 Constitution states at Article 44 that '[E]veryone has the right to freely obtain information disseminated for public use'. The Estonian Constitution thus creates equality of access to proactively published materials, without explicitly requiring or defining the scope of such publication.[69] Similarly, the Constitution of Chile, amended in 2008 following the *Claude Reyes* case, is rather ambiguous, stating that: 'The acts and decisions of the State authorities, as well as their reasoning and the procedures they use, shall be public', without prescribing how this publicity is to come about.[70]

An undoubted obstacle to securing constitutional provisions or laws which clearly set out proactive publication obligations is the complexity of legislating in this area: to define and secure political consensus around the precise nature and scope of the proactive disclosure is not an easy task.

As a result, even the newer and more comprehensive access to information laws such as those of Mexico (2002)[71] and India (2005)[72] have relatively limited provisions, requiring that core or basic information be published by government bodies, but deferring to sector-specific laws and to good bureaucratic practice to determine which other information should be disclosed without the need for a member of the public to submit a request.

In a typical reflection of developments at the national level, the drafters of international standards on the right of access to information have also been hesitant to define the scope of proactive publication. So while sector-specific standards such as the Aarhus Convention on

[69] Constitution of the Republic of Estonia 1992 obtained from the Office of the President of Estonia, Art. 44. Article 44 also established in its second paragraph the right to request information: 'All state agencies, local governments, and their officials have a duty to provide information about their activities, pursuant to procedure provided by law, to an Estonian citizen at his or her request, except information the disclosure of which is prohibited by law, and information intended exclusively for internal use.'

[70] Constitution of the Republic of Chile 1980 as amended, Art. 8.

[71] Mexico's Federal Transparency and Access to Public Information Act, adopted 11 June 2002, Art. 7.XVII.

[72] India's Right to Information Act, 21 June 2005, No. 22 of 2005, s. 4.

access to environmental information,[73] or the UN Convention against Corruption[74] do identify classes of information that should be made public, the drafters of the Council of Europe Convention on Access to Official Documents rejected proposals by civil society to require parties to the future convention to have minimum proactive publication obligations in place, and instead opted for rather general language in its Article 10 which has the tone more of a recommendation than of a binding treaty as it suggests that:

> At its own initiative and where appropriate, a public authority shall take the necessary measures to make public official documents which it holds in the interest of promoting the transparency and efficiency of public administration and to encourage informed participation by the public in matters of general interest.[75]

The Explanatory Memorandum to the Convention elaborates on the rationale for this, stating that citizens need information 'to form an opinion on the authorities that govern them and to become involved in the decision-making process. National rules on proactive publication are thus encouraged.'[76] The Explanatory Memorandum includes a short list of examples of the classes of information which should be published proactively:

> Information about their structures, staff, budget, activities, rules, policies, decisions, delegation of authority, information about the right of access and how to request official documents, as well as any other information of public interest.[77]

The OAS Model Law, adopted in 2010, contains much more elaborate proactive disclosure provisions. Although not a binding treaty, it does set

[73] Aarhus Convention on Access to Information, Public Participation in Decision-making and Access to Justice in Environmental Matters, Aarhus, Denmark, adopted 25 June 1998.

[74] United Nations Convention against Corruption, New York, adopted by UN General Assembly Resolution 58/4 of 31 October 2003.

[75] Convention on Access to Official Documents, Art. 10. Opened for signature on 18 June 2009, to date the Convention has been signed by twelve States out of the forty-seven members of the Council of Europe, of which two – Norway and Hungary – had ratified by 31 January 2010.

[76] *Explanatory Report to the Convention on Access to Official Documents*, para. 71. It will be noted that the recommendation from the OSCE Representative on Freedom of the Media which was submitted to the drafters of the Convention has been taken into consideration in defining the classes of information.

[77] *Ibid.*, para. 72.

a soft standard which is a valuable reference for the scope of the proactive obligation.[78]

A useful forum for further defining the nature and reach of proactive publication obligations is the Open Government Partnership, where debates are taking place over the standards for open data and which data sets governments should prioritise. Civil society is responding to this challenge by measuring the availability of such data sets, with initiatives such as the Open Data Index[79] and through the Open Government Standards, a civil society initiative to define what is meant by open government.[80]

### *3.7 A duty to collect information*

For information to be made public, it must first be collected. Where national legal frameworks contain proactive publication provisions, this places an obligation on public bodies to collect the relevant information.

Sometimes this obligation is implicit in the requirement to publish, at other times it is explicitly set out. For example, under the Aarhus Convention, there is an obligation to produce and publish Environment Impact Assessments.[81] There is, however, no obligation to collect specific information in response to requests for information. The Explanatory Report to the Council of Europe Convention explains that the right to information 'does not oblige Parties to create new documents upon requests for information, although some Parties recognise this wider duty to some extent'.[82]

Indeed, it is often argued and even stated in some laws that the right of access is limited to existing information and that there is no obligation to collect or compile information. The European Court of Human Rights has stated that 'the right to receive information cannot be construed as imposing on a State positive obligations to collect and disseminate information of its own motion'.[83]

[78] OAS, Model Inter-American Law on Access to Information.

[79] The Open Knowledge Foundation's Open Data Index: https://index.okfn.org and Access Info Europe's Open Government Standards: www.opengovstandards.org (both last accessed 29 April 2014).

[80] *Ibid.* [81] Aarhus Convention on Access to Information.

[82] *Explanatory Report to the Convention on Access to Official Documents*, para. 14.

[83] ECtHR, *Österreichische Vereinigung zur Erhaltung, Stärkung und Schaffung eines wirtschaftlich gesunden land-und forstwirtschaftlichen Grundbesitzes* v. *Austria*, para. 41.

The mechanism by which the right of access to information currently leads to the collection or creation of information is when critical voices from the media or civil society question why certain information does not exist.

There is much work to be done in defining which information should be collected by public bodies in the course of their duties. Current multilateral and multi-stakeholder initiatives, including the Open Government Partnership and sector-specific processes such as the International Aid Transparency Initiative Standard are now resulting in a focus on which information should be generated. In the field of anti-corruption, there is a focus on how much detail should be included in specific types of information such as assets declarations or public procurement contracts. The same is true in other areas ranging from budget data to crime statistics to epidemiological data.[84] This is one of the most interesting challenges for the right of access to information in the coming period, as it also relates to the efficiency and effectiveness of public bodies and what information is at their disposal when decisions are taken and hence the quality of those decisions.

### *3.8 Limited exceptions*

All national laws place some exceptions on the right of access to information in order to protect other rights – such as privacy – and a series of societal interests – such as national security and public order. Such limitations are consistent with the right to information being linked to freedom of expression, which is a fundamental but not an absolute right, and which may be limited provided that the limitations are defined by law, and necessary for the protection of legitimate aims. The question then arises whether the right of access to information should be subject to exactly the same limitations as freedom of expression and also – importantly – whether these are the only permissible exceptions.

During the drafting of the Council of Europe Convention on Access to Official Documents – between 2006 and 2008 and hence before the European Court's recognition of access to information as a right – the Member States had little difficulty in agreeing on a list of eleven exceptions to the right. These exceptions are commonly found in national access to information laws and are broad enough to encompass some

[84] For more details, see the Open Government Standards.

national nuances, while remaining within what civil society activists engaged in the drafting found to be an acceptable set of limitations on the right of access. Indeed, the list of exceptions was one of the least controversial aspects of defining the Convention language.[85]

Some of the exceptions to the right of access to information fit with what the main international human rights treaties agree on. For example, the 'protection of the rights and reputations of others' is a legitimate ground for limiting freedom of expression and it is clear in the context of access to information that privacy should be protected by government bodies, which hold huge volumes of personal data about private individuals.

The Convention reflects this by permitting an exception where harm would be caused to 'privacy and other legitimate private interests' (Article 3.1.f), provided that the public interest in knowing the information is duly considered before refusing to release it. Hence, for example, information on the detailed health of private individuals would not be released, even if these were public officials, with possible exceptions for very senior politicians such as ministers or the head of State.

In spite of the broad agreement, however, a problem arises when trying to derive the full list of exceptions to access to information from the treaty provisions on freedom of expression. Indeed, only about half of the exceptions set out in the Council of Europe Convention and found in a majority of national access to information laws, can be found in the international human rights instruments. Of the exceptions which do not form part of the standard list for freedom of expression, a number only have a bearing on access to information. For example, the inspection functions of a public authority, which refers to activities ranging from inspecting restaurants to university exams, all of which requires withholding information from the public during a limited period of time, particularly before the activity has taken place. Such a limitation is

[85] There was also a basis in the Council of Europe Recommendation (2002)2 of the Committee of Ministers to Member States on access to official documents and hence there had already been thorough negotiations on the exceptions. The one controversial exception was the additional, optional, exception, added during the development of the Convention which permits States to declare upon ratification that 'communication with the reigning Family and its Household or the Head of State shall also be included among the possible limitations'. This exception was proposed for royal families by various monarchies (Norway and the UK, but not Sweden) and then at the instigation of Ireland extended to heads of State. Source: the author's own notes from participation in the drafting meetings.

reasonable from a transparency perspective but would be meaningless if applied to freedom of expression more widely.

The difficulty in fitting the access to information exceptions with those developed for freedom of expression begs the question as to whether access to information would not be better served by being a stand-alone right with its own set exceptions. If access to information were separated, then the very specific exceptions could be catered for without blurring the boundaries of the significant body of law and jurisprudence relating to the rights to opinion and expression, and media freedom.

### 3.9 *Charges for obtaining and using public information*

In spite of the basic principle that fundamental rights can normally be exercised free of charge, in particular the right to opinion and expression, a handful of countries still charge requesters to make information requests. More seriously, most others charge for reusing at least some public information.

Those few countries which do charge for making information requests tend to be those with older laws, such as Canada (C$5) and Ireland (€15). Such charges are a vestige of the concept that a request for information is not the exercise of a right but rather that the requester is requiring a service of the administration. This thinking is out of line with a rights-based approach and has been rejected in most countries and in international standards such as the Council of Europe Convention on Access to Official Documents which stipulates that filing requests should be free of charge.[86] Here the Human Rights Committee's General Comment No. 34 lacks clarity when it states '[f]ees for requests for information should not be such as to constitute an unreasonable impediment to access to information' because it does not specify if these are fees for filing requests or for receiving information pursuant to requests.[87] Charging for copying

[86] Convention on Access to Official Documents, Art. 7 which establishes that '(1) Inspection of official documents on the premises of a public authority shall be free of charge . . . (2) A fee may be charged to the applicant for a copy of the official document, which should be reasonable and not exceed the actual costs of reproduction and delivery of the document. Tariffs of charges shall be published.' This provision was adopted in spite of lobbying from the Irish government to permit fees; Ireland is the only country in the wider European region to have mandatory fees for making a request for information. For more information on the current situation in Ireland, see www.access-info.org/en/national-campaigns/516-irish-minister-letter (last accessed 29 April 2014).

[87] HRC, General Comment No. 34, para. 19.

or delivery costs actually incurred is widely regarded as acceptable. All access to information laws without exception make a provision for this and it is supported by the Council of Europe Convention which states that a fee may only be charged to the applicant 'for a copy of the official document, which should be reasonable and not exceed the actual costs of reproduction and delivery of the document' in other words, only photocopying and postage charges are permitted.[88]

In practice, at least in established access to information regimes, requesters often receive even paper copies of documents free of charge and information delivered electronically (including scanned copies of hard-copy documents) is in most countries and in most circumstances free of charge. There are of course reports of abuses and sometimes requesters need to turn to information commissioners or the courts to challenge charges. An example of such a case comes from Peru where a requester was charged above the market rate by the Ministry of Justice for hard copies of court decisions. The case was taken to Peru's Constitutional Court which ordered the Ministry of Justice to adjust its fees to conform with Article 20 of Peru's 2002 Law on Transparency and Access to Public Information which requires copy rates to be no more than the market rate.[89]

A more significant issue is that of charging for access to large government data sets which have traditionally been sold to commercial reusers for often significant fees. Examples of such data sets include statistical, geospatial and meteorological data, and databases such as company and land registers. The charges for such data can be significant. Access Info Europe in 2013 carried out a survey[90] which found that company registers are sold for prices ranging from €10,000 in Macedonia, to €75,000 in the Netherlands, to €250,000 in Estonia.[91] An Austrian commercial data

[88] *Ibid.*

[89] The case of *Jenny Cabrera* v. *Ministry of Justice*, Decision of 9 January 2007, at: www.right2info.org/cases/plomino_documents/r2i-jenny-cabrera-v.-ministry-of-justice (last accessed 29 April 2014).

[90] Survey as yet unpublished, but on file with the author.

[91] In Europe selling of government data is permitted by the EU Directive on Re-use of Public Sector Information, first adopted in 2003 and revised in 2013. Designed to break monopolistic sales arrangements, the impact of the Directive as transposed into national law has been to encourage public officials to ask why requesters want information and what they plan to do with it, even when requests are for smaller chunks of data. Directive 2013/37/EU of the European Parliament and of the Council of 26 June 2013 amending Directive 2003/98/EC on the re-use of public sector information, OJ No. L175/1, 26 June 2013.

user reported paying around €800,000 for the company register. While for some businesses based on the reuse of government data it is worth paying the fees, such charges put the data out of the reach of the average civil society organisation and journalist, let alone the individual citizen.

Such an approach drives a wedge between accessing ('knowing') information and making use of it, and is out of synch with the idea that access to government-generated information, including large data sets, is part of freedom of expression and hence is a violation of the right of access to information. There is as yet no international court jurisprudence on this. There is a need for greater clarity on the standards and for reform of any laws which permit charging in line with an interpretation of access to information as a fundamental right.[92]

### 3.10 *The right to reuse information obtained*

The last but perhaps the most important unresolved challenge which currently faces the right of access to information is whether requesters have a right to do what they will with the information obtained using access to information laws.

It might seem logical that if the human rights basis for obtaining information from public bodies is the right to freedom of expression, then once information has been released to a member of the public – and hence by extension into the entire public domain – the recipient of the information is free to use it in any way consistent with freedom of expression principles, and hence has a right to disseminate the information to willing recipients.

Such uses would presumably include the publication of information received pursuant to an information request in any format (in broadcast media, newspapers, on the Internet), presentation of information at a public forum to inform a debate, or inclusion of the information in publications and other packaging of information intended for commercial distribution, be it a book, database, video or other format which is being sold. It should also include the extraction of data and the inclusion of that data in, for example, a mobile phone application or on a website which permits people to know everything from the time of their next bus to school exam results to spending on a particular aspect of health care.

[92] In addition to solving the legal issues around charging for government data, there will be a challenge of restructuring the budgets of the public bodies which currently rely on data sales for part of their income.

The two main limitations on reuse are laws on the processing of personal data and by copyright restrictions, whether it be the public body or third parties which hold the copyright.

Both limitations are signalled as acceptable by the Council of Europe Convention on Access to Official Documents which, in the Explanatory Report, states that

> generally requestors are free to use the information [obtained] for any lawful purpose. This includes disseminating the information and, for example, publishing it. Such use may for example be determined by laws such as those regulating intellectual property or data protection.[93]

No attempt is made in the Convention to explain this further nor to suggest how such limitations might be applied in practice, nor to give guidance to Member States about how to ensure that any such limitations do not unduly restrict free expression rights. The Human Rights Committee's General Comment No. 34 does not explicitly address the right to reuse information obtained.

With respect to processing of personal data, some limitations may be legitimate but others are not. The public interest test may argue for the release of information about public officials which would not be made available about private individuals. Such data might include the name, position, contact information, salary and career information, details of travel, even original receipts of meals eaten, as well as often their work email addresses. If, for example, a list of salaries and e-mail addresses were to be obtained, it would not be acceptable under data protection rules to spam all those earning over €50,000 a year with advertisements for luxury goods. But to use that same information about salaries to have a debate about public spending would be perfectly legitimate, as it would be to post the names of the highest earners on a website.

There is a need for greater clarity as to when personal data obtained pursuant to information requests may be used and how. At present in most European countries where this author has experience, remarkably little guidance is given to requesters when information is released, leaving the recipient to second guess the authorities as to whether and how they may process or publish the information received.

With respect to intellectual property there is currently a serious lack of clarity about what kinds of limitations can be placed on reuse of copyrighted documents. This results in some absurd problems, such as the

[93] *Explanatory Report to the Convention on Access to Official Documents*, para. 19.

2014 case of the German Ministry of Interior asking a civil society website to take down a document created by the Ministry because it was the copyright of that body.[94] The website – Fragdenstaat.de – refused, and meanwhile the document was replicated on other websites globally. The absurdity comes from the fact that if a document can be released to one requester under the right of access to information, it has been deemed to be in the public domain, and hence should be released to all other requesters. Trying to prevent web publication in such a circumstance does not make sense.

The right to make full use of documents obtained from public bodies is an issue to be worked through in the coming years, as public authorities become accustomed to accepting that the right of access to information is indeed an inherent part of freedom of expression.

## 4 Conclusions: the way ahead

With all these challenges facing the right to information, there is much work to be done by the transparency community in consolidating the phenomenal progress made during past two decades as this right has developed from one respected in a few isolated democracies to a fundamental human right with global reach.

The challenges mapped out here are about how the right of access to information should be interpreted. These are questions of law and jurisprudence, but they are also very much practical, cultural, and political challenges. The history of the right of access to information shows how it has evolved at the national level through pro-transparency victories which are then mirrored, supported, clarified and endorsed by international human rights standard-setting bodies, which in turn feeds back into national standards.

Much of the work done by civil society activists promoting and defending this right is to convince political leaders and bureaucrats of the benefits of the right of access to information and to use the existing tools of access to information laws, information commissioners, and the courts to turn these arguments into changes in transparency in practice. There is still much resistance, particularly from those who still perceive the right as something instrumental which serves to deliver

[94] The story of this incident and the take-down notice sent to the website Fragdenstaat.de can be found at www.access-info.org/en/national-campaigns/533-fragdenstaat-statement (last accessed 29 April 2014).

administrative information to citizens, to voters and tax payers, but not one which gives the public full sovereignty over the ruling political class. Further progress in entrenching the right of access to information will depend upon the success of the rights advocates engaged in the fight for transparency in securing acceptance of open government as a feature of modern democratic societies.

## Literature

Hood, C. 'What Happens When Transparency Meets Blame-Avoidance?', *Public Management Review* 9(2) (2007), 191–210.

*Transparency and Silence: A Survey of Access to Information Laws in 14 Countries* (New York: Open Society Justice Initiative, 2006).

## UN

GA, Resolution 217 (III): Universal Declaration of Human Rights, 10 December 1948.

HRC, General Comment No. 34: Article 19 (Freedoms of opinion and expression), UN Doc. CCPR/C/GC/34, 12 September 2011.

United Nations Convention against Corruption, New York, adopted by UN General Assembly Resolution 58/4 of 31 October 2003.

## Council of Europe

Convention on Access to Official Documents, Tromsø, 18 June 2009, not entered into force yet, CETS 205 and the corresponding Explanatory Report.

Committee of Ministers, Recommendation No. R (81) 19 of the Committee of Ministers to Member States on the Access to Information Held by Public Authorities, 25 November 1981.

Committee of Ministers, Recommendation Rec. (2002)2 of the Committee of Ministers to Member States on access to official documents, 21 February 2002.

## European Union

Directive 2013/37/EU of the European Parliament and of the Council of 26 June 2013 amending Directive 2003/98/EC on the reuse of public sector information, OJ No. L175/1, 26 June 2013.

European Parliament and the Council of the European Union, Regulation 1049/2001 Regarding Public Access to European Parliament, Council and Commission Documents, OJ No. L145/43, 31 May 2001.

## Other documents

Aarhus Convention on Access to Information, Public Participation in Decision-making and Access to Justice in Environmental Matters, Aarhus, Denmark, Adopted at 25 June 1998.

African Union, Draft Model Law for AU Member States on Access to Information, 24 November 2010.

Organization of American States, Model Inter-American Law on Access to Public Information, Doc. No. AG/RES. 2607 (XL-O/10), 8 June 2010.

## Case law

### *European Court of Human Rights*

*Österreichische Vereinigung zur Erhaltung, Stärkung und Schaffung eines wirtschaftlich gesunden land-und forstwirtschaftlichen Grundbesitzes* v. *Austria* (Appl. No. 39534/07), Judgment of 28 November 2013.

*Társaság a Szabadságjogokért* v. *Hungary* (Appl. No. 37374/05), Judgment of 14 April 2009.

*Youth Initiative for Human Rights* v. *Serbia* (Appl. No. 48135/06), Judgment of 25 September 2013.

### *Court of Justice of the European Union*

*Council of the EU* v. *Access Info Europe*, Final Judgment in Case 280/11 P, 17 October 2013.

*Gottfried Heinrich*, Case C-345/06 (Reference for a preliminary ruling from the Unabhängiger Verwaltungssenat im Land Niederösterreich), 10 March 2009.

### *Inter-American Court of Human Rights*

*Claude Reyes and Others* v. *Chile*, Series C No. 151, 19 September 2006.

# 10

# Early days: the UN, ICTs and freedom of expression

KAROL JAKUBOWICZ

## 1 Introduction

Many more people than in the past now have the desire, communication competence and above all the technical means to engage in mediated communication, in the creation of content and its distribution to a broad audience. They can do so with the use of new information and communication technologies (ICTs), including particularly the Internet and mobile telephony, and with the new media created on their basis. Digitalization and computerization of telecommunications and the media drive a process of convergence (integration of media industries with the technological infrastructure of telecommunications) that reshapes social communication and the traditional mass media.

The Council of Europe notes in Recommendation CM/Rec(2011)7 on a New Notion of Media that traditional media actors are being complemented or replaced by other actors, including content aggregators, application designers and users who are also producers of content.[1] The latter profit from the 'deinstutionalization' and 'disintermediation' of mediated communication. The new communicators are thus able to operate simply as individuals, unprofessional communicators and address their content directly to users, bypassing media-related intermediaries. Let us, however, also note the process of 'neo-intermediation', i.e., the emergence of new intermediaries, especially on the Internet (portals, search engines, social networks), capable of offering new services or aggregating and packaging content in new ways.

The democratic potential of these new media and technologies is undeniable. In December 2011, UN Secretary-General Ban Ki-moon said in a statement that 'Many of the people seeking their legitimate

[1] Recommendation CM/Rec(2011)7 of the Committee of Ministers to Member States on a New Notion of Media, 21 September 2011.

aspirations [are] linked through social media'.[2] A similar idea was expressed by the Council of Europe in the 2011 Declaration on the Protection of Freedom of Expression and Freedom of Assembly and Association with Regard to Privately Operated Internet Platforms and Online Service Providers:

> People, notably civil society representatives, whistleblowers and human rights defenders, increasingly rely on social networks, blogging websites and other means of mass communication in aggregate to access and exchange information, publish content, interact, communicate and associate with each other. These platforms are . . . a significant part of the public sphere.[3]

According to Latzer, communications policy has failed to keep abreast of the technological change that helps drive these processes and to transform itself into what he believes should be 'mediamatics policy'.[4] Digitalization, computerization and convergence challenge the traditional categorizations, analytical frameworks, traditionally separated regulatory bodies and regulatory models for telecommunications and the mass media.[5] The first order of business in developing a new regulatory framework was thus to overcome the technology-oriented subdivision into media and telecommunications, into mass communication and individual communication. In the European Union, for example, this has led to the development of technology-neutral, horizontal and graduated regulatory frameworks in the 2002 directives on electronic communication networks and services[6] and in the Audiovisual Media Services Directive of 2007.[7]

[2] UN Secretary-General, Ban Ki-moon, Message for Human Rights Day, UN Doc. SG/SM/13994, 5 December 2011, available at: www.un.org/News/Press/docs/2011/sgsm13994.doc.htm (last accessed 7 March 2014).

[3] Declaration of the Committee of Ministers on the protection of freedom of expression and freedom of assembly and association with regard to privately operated Internet platforms and online service providers, 7 December 2011, para. 2.

[4] M. Latzer, 'Convergence Revisited: Toward a Modified Pattern of Communications Governance', *Convergence* 15(4) (2009), 411–26; see also P. Samuelson, 'Five Challenges for Regulating the Global Information Society', no date; www.asc.upenn.edu/courses/comm334/Docs/samuelson.regs.pdf (last accessed 7 March 2014).

[5] S. Verhulst, 'About Scarcities and Intermediaries: The Regulatory Paradigm Shift of Digital Content Reviewed', in L. Lievrouw and S. Livingstone (eds.), *The Handbook of New Media* (London: Sage, 2002), 432–47.

[6] Later amended, see European Commission, *Regulatory Framework for Electronic Communications in the European Union: Situation in December 2009* (Brussels: Publications Office of the European Union, 2010).

[7] See P. Valcke *et al.*, 'European approaches to future content regulation. The new European Directive for Audiovisual Media Services: a "next generation framework" or "old wine in new barrels"?', paper presented at the EuroCPR Conference 2007, *Policies for the Content Industries* (Seville, 25–27 March 2007).

That, however, was only the first step. Many more are needed. As concerns the issue at hand, the UN Special Rapporteur on the promotion and protection of the right to freedom of opinion and expression argues that Article 19 of the Universal Declaration of Human Rights and of the International Covenant on Civil and Political Rights was 'drafted with foresight to include and to accommodate future technological developments through which individuals can exercise their right to freedom of expression'.[8] True, but this does not obviate the need to develop a response to new technologically driven opportunities and challenges to the exercise of freedom of expression or of other human rights.[9]

What we will concentrate on here is the fact that free speech online is challenged in new ways, such as distributed denial-of-service attacks against websites of independent media, human rights defenders, dissidents, whistleblowers and other new media actors. It has accordingly been suggested that digital communications 'require recognition that there are new forms of censorship, new questions of jurisdiction, and new norms and standards to develop'.[10] The legal and regulatory response to that challenge may involve reinterpreting and 'translating' existing norms and standards to make them relevant and effective in the new technological and other circumstances. Examples of such efforts are provided by the Internet Rights Charter, developed by the Association for Progressive Communications, and the draft Charter of Human Rights and Principles for the Internet, developed by the Dynamic Coalition on Internet Rights and Principles, operating *inter alia* within the UN-sponsored Internet Governance Forum. Mention could also be made here of the European Union's *eYou Guide to Your Rights Online.* But what may also be required – as suggested in the 2011 Joint Declaration on Freedom of Expression and the Internet issued by the Special Rapporteurs on freedom of expression or the media of the UN, the Organization for Security and Cooperation in Europe (OSCE), Organization of American States and the African Commission on Human and Peoples'

[8] *Report of the Special Rapporteur on the Promotion and Protection of the Right to Freedom of Opinion and Expression*, UN Doc. A/HRC/17/27, 16 May 2011, para. 21.

[9] See e.g., C. J. Hamelink, 'Human Rights for the Information Society', in B. Girard and S. Ó Siochrú (eds.), *Communicating in the Information Society* (Geneva: United Nations Research Institute for Social Development, 2003), 121–65; K. Jakubowicz, 'Human Rights and The Information Society: A Preliminary Overview', in K. Jakubowicz, *Media Revolution in Europe: Ahead of the Curve* (Strasbourg: Council of Europe Publishing, 2011), 135–64.

[10] A. Puddephatt, 'Freedom of Expression Rights in the Digital Age', Mapping Digital Media Reference Series No. 6, London: Open Society Media Program, Open Society Foundation, April 2011, 6.

Rights (they are known collectively as 'the IGO Special Mandates') – is that any forms of Internet regulation should be 'specifically designed' for the purpose.[11] Also contributors to the UN consultation on enhanced cooperation on public policy issues pertaining to the Internet suggested that 'international law might need to be updated on occasion, taking into account the unique attributes of [the Internet]'.[12]

Any discussion of the protection of human rights and implementation of other public policy objectives in the convergent digital media has to begin with the question whether or not particular policy concerns still retain their relevance. Napoli has, for example, identified 'diminished, enduring, and emergent' policy concerns in relation to media diversity in the present technological context.[13]

As for freedom of expression, some observers have no doubt that it is very much an enduring and growing concern in the ICT age: 'Neither the possibility that the internet can democratize freedom of expression, nor the potential for a new form of authoritarianism should be underestimated, but at the moment *no single direction is certain* ... Defending freedom of expression online has become a *vital task* for the modern human rights movement.'[14]

Puddephatt contrasts democratic and authoritarian approaches as determinants of ICT policy. Benkler posits a different opposition: between a business approach and what he calls a 'social production' approach.[15] The former seeks to 'colonize' the Internet[16] and to 'sell you and your clicks'.[17] It benefits from 'political and judicial pressures to

[11] The IGO Special Mandates, Joint Declaration on Freedom of Expression and the Internet, 1 June 2011.

[12] Economic and Social Council, *Report of the Secretary General on Enhanced Cooperation on Public Policy Issues Pertaining to the Internet*, UN. Doc. A/66/77-E/2011/103, 4 May 2011; http://unpan1.un.org/intradoc/groups/public/documents/un/unpan045826.pdf (last accessed 7 March 2014).

[13] P. M. Napoli, 'Diminished, Enduring, and Emergent Diversity Policy Concerns in an Evolving Media Environment', *International Journal of Communication* 5 (2011), 1182–96; http://ijoc.org/ojs/index.php/ijoc/article/view/1074/595 (last accessed 7 March 2014).

[14] [emphasis added] Puddephatt, 'Freedom of Expression Rights', 16.

[15] Y. Benkler, *The Wealth of Networks How Social Production Transforms Markets and Freedom* (New Haven, CT and London: Yale University Press, 2006).

[16] L. Dahlberg, 'The Corporate Colonization of Online Attention and the Marginalization of Critical Communication?', *Journal of Communication Inquiry* 29(2) (2005), 160–80 and 'The Internet as Public Sphere or Culture Industry? From Pessimism to Hope and Back', *International Journal of Media and Cultural Politics* 1(1) (2005), 93–6.

[17] H. Kang and M. P. McAllister, 'Selling You and Your Clicks: Examining the Audience Commodification of Google', *tripleC – Cognition, Communication, Co-operation* 9(2) (2011), 141–53.

form an institutional ecology [of the ICTs] that is decidedly tilted in favor of proprietary business models'.[18] The latter seeks to promote 'nonmarket and nonproprietary' production, a new information environment: 'as a platform for better democratic participation; as a medium to foster a more critical and self-reflective culture; and, in an increasingly information-dependent global economy, as a mechanism to achieve improvements in human development everywhere'.[19] These two sets of determinants are reflected to some extent in policy-making in this field in general, as well as in the process leading to the development of the UN's stand and policy response to the challenges of the ICT age.

If there is any doubt whether freedom of expression is a growing concern, it is enough to compare two UN documents on the subject. In the 1983 General Comment No. 10: Freedom of expression (Art. 19), the Human Rights Committee needed barely a page to interpret Article 19 of the International Covenant on Civil and Political Rights and to flag, in fairly general terms, problems with its observance. In 2011, the Human Rights Committee needed no fewer than fifteen pages of dense text to do the same in its General Comment No. 34 on Article 19 (Freedoms of opinion and expression), replacing the 1983 document.[20]

In May 2011, Frank La Rue, the then UN Special Rapporteur on the promotion and protection of the right to freedom of opinion and expression, for the first time devoted his annual report to the Human Rights Council primarily to challenges to freedom of expression in the field of the Internet.[21] Recognition that freedom of expression (including the right to information and access to information) includes Internet-based expression is also a signal that Member States' human rights obligations, assessed during the Human Rights Council's Universal Periodic Review procedure, extend to taking steps to ensure access to the Internet and that limitations or restrictions on freedom of Internet-based expression comply with agreed international standards.

Also in 2011, Mr La Rue signed the Joint Declaration on Freedom of Expression and the Internet, together with the other IGO Special Mandates. One of the concerns listed there was that 'even when done in good faith, many of the efforts by governments [that impose restrictions which are prescribed by law to prevent crime and protect the fundamental

[18] Benkler, *Wealth of Networks*, 471. [19] *Ibid.*, 2.

[20] HRC, General Comment No. 34: Article 19 (Freedoms of Opinion and Expression), UN Doc. CCPR/C/GC/34, 12 September 2011.

[21] *Report of the Special Rapporteur on Freedom of Opinion and Expression.*

rights of others, including children] fail to take into account the special characteristics of the Internet, with the result that they unduly restrict freedom of expression'.[22]

This flurry of activity, all in one year, clearly shows the UN, while very much aware of the relationship between the ICTs and freedom of expression, sees the new technologies not only as a solution to freedom of expression issues, but also as part of the problem.

Media/communications policy incorporates a number of levels and fields including 'systemic policy', when the job is to develop or wholly change a media/communication system. Clearly, the job facing governments, other stakeholders and the international community in relation to the ICTs and new media is of a systemic nature: to develop or adapt a complete framework within which human rights standards and public policy goals can successfully be implemented in a new technological environment.

## 2 Enabling and safeguarding freedom of expression in the ICT environment

Below, we will assign policy approaches and measures to particular stages of the process of (Internet) communication. A great deal depends on the receiver/user, but regrettably this element of the process is rarely given sufficient attention in policy approaches. We will conclude with a look to the future and the policy challenges it may potentially bring.

We will briefly deal with technical issues in each case, then review policy stances developed by selected countries and international organizations (with special emphasis on European ones) and conclude each segment by presenting the UN system's recent response to these challenges.

Contrary to frequent practice, we will not focus here on violations or abuses of freedom of expression on the ICTs. We will also leave aside the all-too-obvious results of political interference with freedom of expression via these technologies. Instead, we will concentrate on what policymakers in *democratic countries and in international organizations* need to do to safeguard this freedom.

The general normative, policy and legal elements of an enabling environment for freedom of expression are well known.[23] Here, we will

[22] Preamble, Joint Declaration on Freedom of Expression and the Internet, 2011.

[23] For an overview, see T. McGonagle, *Minority Rights, Freedom of Expression and of the Media: Dynamics and Dilemmas* (Antwerp: Intersentia, 2011), 130–4.

provide *examples* of policy and regulatory approaches and measures designed to create primarily technical conditions that are favourable for freedom of expression, or deal with particular technologically driven obstacles to it. This will be a patchwork of ideas and measures developed in different places, illustrating the slow and gradual emergence in piecemeal fashion of a normative and legal framework in this area.[24]

### *2.1 Access*

In Resolution 12/16 on freedom of opinion and expression, adopted in 2009, the UN Human Rights Council called on all Member States to 'facilitate equal participation in, access to and use of, information and communications technology, such as the Internet'.[25]

Van Cuilenburg and McQuail define access as control over deciding who gets access to what communications resources, when, where, how and on what conditions. In short, they say, access is about 'being able to receive and to send'.[26] We must thus consider both user and communicator access to electronic communications networks. This is in line with Tambini's definition of access as 'access to networks', 'access to content' and 'access to the shared forum'.[27] An important element is the quality of Internet access, measured in terms of speed, bandwidth, affordability and openness.

The job of ensuring physical access to the networks is universally supported and interpreted as eliminating the digital divide and promoting digital inclusion. The Council of Europe in its Recommendation CM/Rec(2007)16 of the Committee of Ministers to Member States on Measures to Promote the Public Service Value of the Internet listed a number of practical policy measures needed to 'promot[e] affordable access to the

[24] For an example, see D. Korff and I. Brown, 'Social Media and Human Rights', in T. Hammarberg *et al.*, *Human Rights and a Changing Media Landscape* (Strasbourg: Council of Europe Publishing, 2011), 175–206, for a discussion of 'emerging Internet governance standards'.

[25] HR Council, Resolution 12/16, 'Freedom of Opinion and Expression', UN Doc. A/HRC/12/L.14/Rev.1, 30 September 2009, para. 5(m).

[26] J. van Cuilenburg and D. McQuail, 'Media Policy Paradigm Shifts: Towards a New Communications Policy Paradigm', *European Journal of Communication* 18(2) (2003), 204.

[27] D. Tambini, 'What Citizens Need to Know: Digital Exclusion, Information Inequality and Rights', in E. Richards, R. Foster and T. Kiedrowski (eds.), *Communications: The Next decade A Collection of Essays Prepared for the UK Office of Communications* (London: OFCOM, 2006), 117.

Internet for individuals, irrespective of their age, gender, ethnic or social origin', including those on low incomes; those in rural and geographically remote areas; and those with special needs.[28]

Access, as a way of enabling full enjoyment of human rights and accelerated development, was given great prominence in the 2000 United Nations Millennium Declaration ('ensure that the benefits of new technologies, especially information and communication technologies ... *are available to all*')[29] and later in the outcome documents of the UN-organized World Summit on the Information Society (2003–5). The UN-sponsored Internet Governance Forum has highlighted access as one of the key policy goals in developing the Information Society. In 2011, the UN Special Rapporteur once again reminded States of their 'positive obligation to promote or to facilitate the enjoyment of the right to freedom of expression and the means necessary to exercise this right, including the Internet'.[30] According to the IGO Special Mandates, States should, at a minimum:

- Put in place regulatory mechanisms (e.g., pricing regimes and licensing agreements – that foster greater access to the Internet, including for the poor and in 'last mile' rural areas);
- Provide direct support to facilitate access
- ...
- Put in place special measures to ensure equitable access to the Internet for the disabled and for disadvantaged persons.[31]

Promoting (and partly funding) the creation of electronic communications networks is one important feature of public policy, but another part of the equation is to ensure people have the equipment, i.e., computers, needed to use them. Examples of such measures abound. In 2005, the International Telecommunication Union, a UN agency, launched the 'Connect the World' project. Another initiative, the 'One Laptop Per Child' project, has been supported by the United Nations Development Programme.

[28] Recommendation CM/Rec(2007)16 of the Committee of Ministers to Member States on measures to promote the public service value of the Internet, 7 November 2007, Appendix, section II, 'Access'.
[29] [emphasis added] UN GA Resolution 55/2, 'United Nations Millennium Declaration', UN Doc. A/55/L.2, 8 September 2000, para. 20.
[30] *Report of the Special Rapporteur on Freedom of Opinion and Expression*, para. 66.
[31] Joint Declaration on Freedom of Expression and the Internet, 2011, para. 6(e).

Apart from ensuring access, action is also needed to prevent, or minimize the use of measures to deny, or deprive of, access. We will return to this below when discussing the role of ISPs and other intermediaries.

### 2.1.1 Universal service obligation (USO)

The USO is seen in the European Union as a tool for inclusion, a social safety net, guaranteeing the availability, affordability and accessibility of basic telecommunications services.[32] Directive 2002/22/EC of 7 March 2002 on universal service and users' rights relating to electronic communications networks and services (as amended) defines the scope of USO in Article 4 as including 'functional [narrowband] Internet access'. However, Member States have the flexibility to define, where necessary and if they so wish, the data rates at national level, which may include broadband speeds.

An important step forward towards access would be to include provision of broadband Internet connectivity in regulations on the scope of USO. In 2011, the European Commission did not think that the time was right to mandate provision, as part of the USO, of mobile telecommunications services and broadband connections.[33] Nor was the European Parliament, while strongly supporting in its goal of broadband for all, convinced that 'making broadband availability obligatory [would] automatically result in higher take-up'.[34]

The UN Broadband Commission is more convinced of the need for this: one of the targets it has set for broadband development is that by 2015 'all countries should have a national broadband plan or strategy or *include broadband in their Universal Access/Service Definitions*' (emphasis added).

### 2.1.2 Access to the Internet as a human right

A further step forward would be to recognize access to the Internet as not just a mere policy goal, but as a human right, with a corresponding obligation on the State to ensure its exercise. It has been so defined (or

[32] European Commission, *Universal Service in E-Communications: Report on the Outcome of the Public Consultation and the Third Periodic Review of the Scope in Accordance with Article 15 of Directive 2002/22/E*, Doc. No. COM(2011) 795 final, 23 November 2011 and European Parliament, Resolution of 5 July 2011 on Universal Service and the 112 Emergency Number, Doc. No. 2010/2274(INI); www.europarl.europa.eusides/getDoc.do?type=TA&language=EN&reference=P7-TA-2011-0306 (last accessed 6 March 2014).

[33] *Ibid.*, European Commission. [34] *Ibid.*, European Parliament.

mandated in law as a service that must be available to everyone) in Estonia, France, Costa Rica, Finland, Malta, Switzerland and Spain, with different technical specifications in each country as to what it entails in practice. The European Union, too, has to all intents and purposes recognized Internet access as a human right in Article 1.3a of Directive 2002/21/EC of 7 March 2002 on a common regulatory framework for electronic communications networks and services (as amended).

The UN Special Rapporteur does not go so far as to recognize access to the Internet as a human right, perhaps because he is 'acutely aware that universal access to the Internet for all individuals worldwide cannot be achieved instantly'.[35]

## 2.2 *Internet governance*

The issue of Internet governance[36] best reflects the systemic nature of the emerging policy framework concerning the Internet and other ICTs, as well as the difficulties this process encounters. The issue is becoming intensely political and hotly debated in various international forums.

The main Internet governance body is the Internet Corporation for Assigned Names and Numbers (ICANN), a non-profit corporation established in 1998 under the laws of the State of California, in the USA and answerable only to the US Department of Commerce. It is responsible for the management of Internet Protocol (IP) address space allocation, protocol identifier assignment, top-level domain name system management, and root-server system management functions. This organization refers the associated technical work to the Internet Assigned Numbers Association (IANA) or the Word Wide Web Consortium (W3C), which function as the international standards organizations for the Internet.

The challenges facing Internet governance are in part due to the uncertain legitimacy of existing bodies, such as ICANN, and the degree to which these institutions focus on only one of many areas of policy and regulation shaping the future of the Internet – the efficient working of the system, its functionality.[37] The resulting vacuum of authority has,

[35] *Report of the Special Rapporteur on Freedom of Opinion and Expression*, 16 May 2011, para. 66.

[36] For a detailed explanation of the technical issues involved, see Council of Europe, Media and Information Society Division, *Internet Governance and Critical Internet Resources*, a report prepared by the Council of Europe Secretariat, April 2009.

[37] W. H. Dutton *et al.*, *Freedom of Connection, Freedom of Expression: The Changing Legal and Regulatory Ecology Shaping the Internet* (Paris: UNESCO, 2011).

according to Puddephatt, been filled by frequently arbitrary actions with a number of adverse consequences.[38]

Specific technical matters can present implications for freedom of expression and the openness of the Internet. Matters related to Internet address space, e.g., the transition from Internet Protocol Version 4 (IPv4) to IPv6, the scarce resource of IP addresses, address hijacking and the sometimes unstable change of protocols, or the Domain Name System are by nature regulating the Internet and access to it. Limitations to the American Standard Code for Information Interchange (ASCII) or the exclusion of non-Latin letters in using top-level domain can be seen as a constraint to freedom of expression. Innovations aimed at addressing these limitations are being developed.

It is argued that the neutral character of the Internet is a key element in maintaining a free and open approach to Internet-based communication, speech and expression. Yet, domination by 'the West' and the exclusion of governments or international organizations from Internet governance have long been criticized, with the USA staunchly defending the present arrangement. IBSA, the coalition of India, Brazil and South Africa, has noted in a statement submitted in 2010 that the legal status of ICANN remains problematic: 'The fact that only one country, instead of the international community of States, is the provider and guarantor of the management of names and numbers of the Internet in all countries contravenes established UN principles and universally accepted tenets of multilateralism.'[39] Also the European Commission has pointed to 'the limited possibilities that ICANN stakeholders, including governments and public authorities, have to contest ICANN Board decisions if they feel they are inconsistent with either ICANN's own by-laws or applicable law'. According to the Commission, 'ICANN . . . does not meet the required standards of independence, transparency and accountability'.[40]

Both the European Union and the Council of Europe have pointed to ICANN's Governmental Advisory Committee (GAC) as the vehicle for

[38] Puddephatt, 'Freedom of Expression Rights'.

[39] IBSA Joint Statement, 'Open consultations on Enhanced Cooperation', 14 December 2010, para. 5.

[40] European Commission, 'Informal Background Paper on ICANN New gTLD Process', Brussels: European Union, 1 September 2011; www.bof.nl/live/wp-content/uploads/EC-TLD-censorship.pdf (last accessed 6 March 2014).

stronger governmental involvement.[41] It is called upon to provide ICANN with substantive public policy advice, though the ICANN Board has been known to reject such advice. The European Commission has proposed that consensus GAC advice should be accepted as reflecting the global public interest, and should ICANN wish to reject such advice, then the Board and the GAC should agree an alternative approach to meet the public policy issues concerned.

For its part, the Council of Europe in the 2010 Declaration on Enhanced Participation of Member States in Internet Governance Matters – Governmental Advisory Committee (GAC) of the Internet Corporation for Assigned Names and Numbers (ICANN) argues that GAC can play a key role in ensuring that technical decisions on, and activities and can also contribute to promoting transparency and accountability in the management of those resources.

In a separate Declaration on Internet Governance Principles, the Council of Europe spelled out the principles that should be observed and pursued in Internet governance: human rights, democracy and the rule of law; multi-stakeholder governance; responsibilities of States; empowerment of Internet users; universality and integrity of the Internet; decentralized management; architectural principles (such as open standards, interoperability and the end-to-end nature of the Internet); open network; cultural and linguistic diversity. Let us also note the Council of Europe's 2011 Declaration on the Protection of Freedom of Expression and Information and Freedom of Assembly and Association with regard to Internet Domain Names and Name Strings.[42] It argues that individuals or operators of websites should benefit from a presumption in their favour when they choose a particular domain name or name string in order to identify and describe content hosted in their websites, to disseminate a particular point of view or to create spaces for communication, interaction, assembly and association for various societal groups or communities. Expressions contained in the names of Internet websites are also covered by the legal standards on freedom of expression and the right to receive and impart information.

[41] European Commission, *Internet Governance: the Next Steps*, Doc. No. COM(2009) 277 final, 18 June 2009.

[42] Committee of Ministers, Declaration on the Protection of Freedom of Expression and Information and Freedom of Assembly and Association with regard to Internet Domain Names and Name Strings, 21 September 2011.

The OSCE Representative on Freedom of the Media believes that 'the multi-stakeholder approach the UN Internet Governance Forum is pursuing, which includes civil society, can serve as a good-practice example for the OSCE region for Internet governance'.[43]

The multi-stakeholder approach was also advocated during the UN-organized World Summit on the Information Society (WSIS). The Tunis Agenda for the Information Society, adopted during the second phase of the Summit, recognized that all stakeholders, including governments, should be involved in their respective roles. However, neither the WSIS itself, nor the Working Group on Internet Governance, nor the Internet Governance Forum (both created as a result of WSIS), have produced solutions on how this should be done.

During the above-mentioned UN consultation on enhanced cooperation several ideas were advanced.[44] Some argued that enhanced cooperation should involve entities from various stakeholder groups, through, for example, meetings of the Internet Governance Forum or in bilateral or multilateral arrangements. An example of such an arrangement is provided by the December 2009 cooperation agreement between the ICANN and the United Nations Educational, Scientific and Cultural Organization (UNESCO) on Internet multilingualism. Others called for a new mechanism, such as a discrete intergovernmental platform with a strict mandate to discuss Internet governance. IBSA has proposed that 'governments [be] provided a formal platform under the UN that is mandated to discuss [Internet governance] issues'.[45] It would oversee existing bodies and develop global Internet policies. No consensus was reached, however. In October 2011, India submitted a proposal to the UN General Assembly regarding the formation of a UN Committee for Internet-Related Policies. Surprisingly, the reform process of ICANN itself was not discussed during the 2011 Internet Governance Forum, as it was overshadowed by the IBSA proposal.

The matter remains unresolved, and as long as it does, the systemic job of creating a complete new framework for protecting freedom of expression on the Internet will remain unfinished.

[43] OSCE Representative on Freedom of the Media, 'Internet Freedom Why It Matters', position paper, 11 January 2012, 2; www.osce.org/fom/86003 (last accessed 7 March 2014).

[44] Economic and Social Council, *Report of the Secretary General*, 2011.

[45] IBSA Joint Statement, 'Open consultations on Enhanced Cooperation', para. 6.

### 2.3 *Communicator*

The role of active communicators assumed by many former passive receivers is widely supported. The European Parliament in its 2009 Recommendation on Strengthening Security and Fundamental Freedoms on the Internet pointed to the right of individuals to express themselves freely on the Internet (for instance through user-generated content, blogs and social networking).[46] Council of Europe Member States were also called upon in Recommendation CM/Rec(2007)16 on Measures to Promote the Public Service Value of the Internet to 'promot[e] the active participation of the public in using, and contributing content to, the Internet and other ICTs'.[47]

This process has been recognized by the UN Special Rapporteur: 'the Internet has become a key means by which individuals can exercise their right to freedom of opinion and expression'.[48] Web 2.0 services or intermediary platforms facilitate participatory information sharing and collaboration in the creation of content, so that individuals are no longer passive recipients, but also, he says, active publishers of information.

In terms of the normative aspect of policy, the question becomes whether recognition of the role of users as active communicators goes so far as to recognize their right to communicate. This concept has, of course, been the subject of intense debate within the international community for several decades.[49]

#### 2.3.1 Right to communicate?

Acceptance of a form of this right seems to be suggested to some extent by van Cuilenburg and McQuail who explain that in its positive aspect, for which there should be provision, freedom of communication refers to all those activities people in society can be enabled to do, e.g., to contribute to the civic debate on politics or to express artistic creativity.[50] Tambini interprets 'access to the shared forum' as a situation in which

46 European Parliament Recommendation of 26 March 2009 to the Council on Strengthening Security and Fundamental Freedoms on the Internet (2008/2160(INI)).

47 Recommendation on Measures to Promote the Public Service Value of the Internet (2007), Appendix, section III, 'Openness'.

48 *Report of the Special Rapporteur on Freedom of Opinion and Expression*, 16 May 2011, para. 20.

49 M. L. Mueller, B. N. Kuerbis and C. Pagé, 'Democratizing Global Communication? Global Civil Society and the Campaign for Communication Rights in the Information Society', *International Journal of Communication* 1 (2007), 267–96.

50 van Cuilenburg and McQuail, 'Media Policy Paradigm Shifts'.

citizens 'have a voice and access to the relevant forum in which to make themselves heard'.[51] He also highlights the importance of public policy to ensure this type of access.

Graham Murdock has proposed a 'complex' notion of full and equal citizenship, encompassing, in addition to civil, political and social rights, also 'cultural rights', including access to deliberation, representation and participation, also via the Internet.[52] For their part, McIver and Birdsall identify three 'generations' of human rights: civil and political rights; economic, social, and cultural rights; and – in addition – collective or solidarity rights, including in the area of communication.[53] The development of global interactive communication networks in the last half of the twentieth century, say McIver and Birdsall, has generated the need for a right to communicate.

Efforts to secure formal recognition of the right to communicate at the international or national level have been unsuccessful.[54] Many questions as to what precisely it entails still remain unanswered.[55] In any case, ICTs now deliver potential solutions to the technical aspects of the right to communicate and enable countless individuals to enjoy it, so emphasis is shifting to what Tambini calls 'the right to have one's speech heard'. In his view, however, freedom of expression 'does not entail a positive right to access to expression, i.e. the right to have one's speech heard, or to have access to key media for expression'.[56]

[51] Tambini, 'What Citizens Need to Know', 117.

[52] G. Murdock, 'Rights and Representations: Public Discourse and Cultural Citizenship', in J. Gripstrud (ed.), *Media and Knowledge: The Role of Television, Department of Media Studies*, papers from a seminar at the University of Bergen, 1996 and G. Murdock, 'Building the Digital Commons: Public Broadcasting in the Age of the Internet', Spry Memorial Lecture, 2004; https://pantherfile.uwm.edu/type/www/116/Theory_OtherTexts/Theory/Murdock_BuildingDigitalCommons.pdf (last accessed 7 March 2014).

[53] W. J. McIver Jr. and W. F. Birdsall, 'Technological evolution and the right to communicate: the implications for electronic democracy', presented at Euricom Colloquium: Electronic Networks & Democracy, 2002; www.cs.duke.edu/courses/spring05/cps182s/readings/McIver-Birdsall.pdf; S. Marks, 'The Human Right to Development: Between Rhetoric and Reality', *Harvard Human Rights Journal* 17 (2004), 137–68; www.hsph.harvard.edu/stephen-marks/files/2012/10/spm_the_human_right_development.pdf (both last accessed 7 March 2014).

[54] On Canada, see W. F. Birdsall, 'A Canadian Right to Communicate?', Government Information in Canada/Information Gouvernementale au Canada, No. 15, September 1998; http://library2.usask.ca/gic/15/birdsall.html (last accessed 6 March 2014).

[55] C. J. Hamelink and J. Hoffmann, 'The State of the Right to Communicate', *Global Media Journal* 7(1)3 (2008), http://lass.purduecal.edu/cca/gmj/fa08/gmj-fa08-hamelink-hoffman.htm (last accessed 7 March 2014).

[56] Tambini, 'What Citizens Need to Know', 117.

Discussion of a potential 'right to have one's speech heard', or indeed 'right to public expression',[57] would require us to examine models and concepts of democracy that in one way or another do seek to provide a guarantee of direct individual and group involvement in, or contribution to, the process of governance.[58] That, however, would take us beyond the scope of this chapter. In any case, though UNESCO was for many years the scene of the battle for recognition of the right to communicate, neither that organization nor the UN itself are committed to supporting it today.

### 2.3.2 Media and information literacy

This is another important aspect of policy regarding freedom of expression, since 'connectivity doesn't end the digital divide, skills do'.[59]

The Council of Europe (in Recommendation CM/Rec(2007)16 on Measures to Promote the Public Service Value of the Internet) recognizes promotion of media and information literacy as an element of human rights protection in the convergent digital media environment for an overview of media education policies around the world.[60] A similar view is expressed by the OSCE Representative on Freedom of the Media who also says that 'an educated mind is the best filter'.[61]

The European Commission proposes a definition of 'media literacy for online' as including empowering users with tools to critically assess online content; extending digital creativity and production skills and encouraging awareness of copyright issues; ensuring that the benefits of the information society can be enjoyed by everyone (e-Accessibility and eInclusion); raising awareness about how search engines work and learning better to use search engines.[62] Under Article 33 of the Audiovisual Media Services Directive, the European Commission is required to

57 K. Jakubowicz, 'The Right to Public Expression. A Modest Proposal for an Important Human Right', London: Media Program, Open Society Foundation, 2010.

58 See e.g., A. Fung and E. Olin Wright, 'Deepening Democracy: Innovations in Empowered Participatory Governance', *Politics & Society* 29(1) (2001), 5–41.

59 D. Radovanovic, 'Digital divide and social media: connectivity doesn't end the digital divide, skills do', *Scientific American.com*, 14 September 2011; http://blogs.scientificamerican.com/guest-blog/2011/12/14/digital-divide-and-social-media-connectivity-doesnt-end-the-digital-divide-skills-do (last accessed 7 March 2014).

60 D. Frau-Meigs and J. Torrent (eds.), *Mapping Media Education Policies in the World. Visions, Programmes and Challenges* (New York: United Nations Alliance of Civilizations and Huelva, Spain: Grupo Comunicar, 2009).

61 OSCE Representative on Freedom of the Media, 'Why Internet Freedom Matters'.

62 European Commission, *A European Approach to Media Literacy in the Digital Environment*, Doc. No. COM(2007) 833 final, 20 December 2007.

submit a report every three years on the levels of media literacy in all EU Member States.

The UN Special Rapporteur touched on this point in his report, calling on States to 'include Internet literacy skills in school curricula, and support similar learning modules outside of schools'. In his view, in addition to basic skills training, 'modules should clarify the benefits of accessing information online, and of responsibly contributing information. Training can also help individuals learn how to protect themselves against harmful content.'[63]

In the UN system, the agency dealing with this issue is UNESCO. In addition to developing policies and promoting research,[64] UNESCO concentrates on teacher education in this field.[65] UNESCO-related events have produced a series of documents (Grünwald Declaration on Media Education of 1982; Alexandria Proclamation on Information Literacy and Lifelong Learning of 2005; Paris Agenda or 12 Recommendations for Media Education of 2007) on the subject. The Paris Agenda defined three main objectives of what it calls an 'inclusive concept of media education': to give access to all kinds of media that are potential tools to understand society and to participate in democratic life; to develop skills for the critical analysis of messages, whether in news or entertainment, in order to strengthen the capacities of autonomous individuals and active users; and to encourage production, creativity and interactivity in the different fields of media communication.

The 2011 Fez Declaration on Media And Information Literacy, issued by UNESCO together with partner bodies and organizations, highlights the individual's creative role by calling on all interested parties to 'include the production and distribution of user generated content (UGC), particularly youth-produced media' as part of the overall framework of media and information literacy.[66]

[63] *Report of the Special Rapporteur on Freedom of Opinion and Expression*, 16 May 2011, para. 88.

[64] F. W. Horton, Jr., *Understanding Information Literacy: A Primer* (Paris: UNESCO, 2007); R. Catts and J. Lau, *Towards Information Literacy Indicators. Conceptual framework paper* (Paris: UNESCO, 2008).

[65] See e.g., C. Wilson *et al.*, *Media and Information Literacy. Curriculum for Teachers* (Paris: UNESCO, 2011); P. Hine (ed.), *UNESCO ICT Competency Framework for Teachers* (Paris: UNESCO, 2011).

[66] First International Forum on Media and Information Literacy, Fez Declaration on Media and Information Literacy, 17 June 2011, para. 4.

## 2.4 *Message*

Content issues are largely the same online as offline.[67] Some ways of enforcing norms and standards in the digital media world are themselves seen as new violations of these standards. The UN Special Rapporteur notes that:

> [D]ue to the unique characteristics of the Internet, regulations or restrictions which may be deemed legitimate and proportionate for traditional media are often not so with regard to the Internet. For example, in cases of defamation of individuals' reputation, given the ability of the individual concerned to exercise his/her right of reply instantly to restore the harm caused, the types of sanctions that are applied to offline defamation may be unnecessary or disproportionate.[68]

International law-making and standard-setting in this area can be said to proceed in three directions: legitimate restrictions on content on the ICTs; prevention of unjustified restrictions on content; positive rules or action regarding content that should be present on ICTs.

### 2.4.1 Legitimate restrictions on content

As regards binding international legal instruments, the Convention on Cybercrime and its additional protocol put Parties to the Convention under an obligation to 'adopt such legislative and other measures as may be necessary to establish [dissemination of child pornography, racist and xenophobic material] as criminal offences'.

The UN Special Rapporteur lists 'legitimate types of information which may be restricted' on the Internet as including child pornography (to protect the rights of children), hate speech (to protect the rights of affected communities), defamation (to protect the rights and reputation

[67] For an extensive OSCE overview of efforts to combat Internet child pornography, racist content, extremism, glorification of violence and terrorist propaganda, libel, internet piracy, etc., see: Y. Akdeniz, 'Freedom of Expression on the Internet: A Study of Legal Provisions and Practices Related to Freedom of Expression, the Free Flow of Information and Media Pluralism on the Internet in OSCE Participating States' (Vienna: OSCE Representative on Freedom of the Media, 2010); H. Dutton *et al.*, *Freedom of Connection* (2011) and A. Finlay (ed.), *Global Information Society Watch 2011: Internet Rights and Democratization, Focus on Freedom of Expression and Association Online* (South Africa: Association for Progressive Communications (APC) and Humanist Institute for Cooperation with Developing Countries (Hivos), 2011); www.apc.org/en/system/files/gisw2011_en.pdf (last accessed 7 March 2014).

[68] *Report of the Special Rapporteur on Freedom of Opinion and Expression*, 16 May 2011, para. 27.

of others against unwarranted attacks), direct and public incitement to commit genocide (to protect the rights of others), and advocacy of national, racial or religious hatred that constitutes incitement to discrimination, hostility or violence (to protect the rights of others, such as the right to life).[69]

Apart from banning 'illegal' content, various instruments also call for limiting 'harmful' or 'inappropriate' content, while maintaining a balance with freedom of expression.[70] One such example is the European Union's Recommendation of 20 December 2006 on the Protection of Minors and Human Dignity and on the Right of Reply in relation to the Competitiveness of the European Audiovisual and On-Line Information Services Industry.

### 2.4.2 Preventing unjustified restrictions on content

The UN Special Rapporteur emphasizes in his report to the Human Rights Council that there should be as little restriction as possible to the flow of information via the Internet, except in a few, exceptional and limited circumstances prescribed by international human rights law. When a restriction is imposed as an exceptional measure on online content, it must pass a three-part, cumulative test prescribed by Article 19, paragraph 3, of the International Covenant on Civil and Political Rights. In addition, any legislation restricting the right to freedom of expression must be applied in a manner that is neither arbitrary nor discriminatory by a body which is independent of any political, commercial or other unwarranted influences. There should also be adequate safeguards against abuse, including the possibility of challenge and remedy against its abusive application.[71]

In his report to the Human Rights Council, the UN Special Rapporteur lists the following methods of curtailing freedom of expression on the Internet that should be eliminated: arbitrary blocking or filtering of content on the Internet; criminalization of legitimate expression (e.g., defamation); imposition of intermediary liability; disconnecting users from Internet access, including on the basis of violations of intellectual property rights law; cyber-attacks; inadequate protection of the right to privacy and data protection. We will return to some of these issues below.

[69] *Ibid.*, para. 25.

[70] See R. O'Connell, 'Harmful content', Group of Specialists on Human Rights in the Information Society, Council of Europe, Doc. No.MC-S-IS(2005)007, 2005.

[71] *Report of the Special Rapporteur on Freedom of Opinion and Expression*, para. 24.

### 2.4.3 Promoting needed content on the ICTs

There are different types of such content and different reasons for its promotion. The OECD 2008 Seoul Declaration for the Future of the Internet Economy calls on Member States to foster creativity in the development, use and application of the Internet, through policies that: (1) make public sector information and content, including scientific data, and works of cultural heritage more widely accessible in digital format; (2) encourage universities, governments, public research, users and business to work together in collaborative innovation networks and to make use of shared experimental Internet facilities; (3) encourage new collaborative Internet-based models and social networks for the creation, distribution and use of digital content that fully recognize the rights of creators and the interests of users.

Mr Jānis Kārkliņš, UNESCO Assistant Director-General for Communication and Information, stated during the opening session of the 2011 IGF in Nairobi, Kenya, that 'in many parts of the world, local content production, including services, usually lags behind [ICT] infrastructure development and does not generate sufficient returns to the investment made in infrastructure'. Insufficient presence of local content on the Internet is a major concern in most countries of the world. The Council of Europe in its Recommendation CM/Rec(2007)16 on Measures to Promote the Public Service Value of the Internet encourages Member States to ensure that Internet and ICT content is contributed by all regions, countries and communities so as to ensure over time representation of all peoples, nations, cultures and languages. To this end, governments should encourage and promote the growth of national or local cultural industries, especially in the field of digital content production, including all potential content creators and other stakeholders. Efforts should be undertaken to preserve the digital heritage of lasting cultural, scientific, or other values. User- and community-generated content should be promoted. The multilingualization of the Internet should be assisted and facilitated, so that everyone can use it in their own language. By implication, this is also the objective of two other Council of Europe legal instruments, the Framework Convention for the Protection of National Minorities and the European Charter for Regional and Minority Languages.

The European Union, for its part, is seeking practical solutions needed to promote the presence of European content online, including, in the case of audiovisual content, the resolution of copyright issues which may be an obstacle in this respect.[72] The Audiovisual Media Services Directive provides an example of a specific content-related regulation, designed to promote European works on the ICTs. Under Article 13 of the Directive, EU Member States are to 'ensure that on-demand audiovisual media services provided by media service providers under their jurisdiction promote, where practicable and by appropriate means, the production of and access to European works'. Such promotion could take the form of the financial contribution made by such services to the production and rights acquisition of European works or of a share and/or prominence of European works in the catalogue of programmes offered by the on-demand audiovisual media service.

All these issues are also very much alive in the work of the United Nations system.[73] UNESCO's 2003 Recommendation concerning the Promotion and Use of Multilingualism and Universal Access to Cyberspace calls on Member States to develop multilingual content and systems as well as to develop public domain content and has set the agenda for similar efforts and policies elsewhere. UNESCO also has a special mandate to ensure exercise of the rights enshrined in the Universal Declaration on Cultural Diversity and the Convention on the Protection and Promotion of the Diversity of Cultural Expressions, such as the right to cultural expression in the language of one's choice, and to have the right to access the means of expression and dissemination of their culture. A special project, ICTS for Intercultural Dialogue. Developing communication capacities of indigenous peoples (ICT4ID), was launched in 2004 to promote this aim.

### *2.5 Intermediaries/ISPs*

Technical intermediaries include 'digital gateways' located along the way of the digital television (or radio) signal (including the multiplex, electronic programme guide, the application programme interface in the set-top-box, pay-TV and conditional access system and subscriber management system). Each of them could be used as a bottleneck to

[72] European Commission, Green Paper on the Online Distribution of Audiovisual Works in the European Union: Opportunities and Challenges Towards a Digital Single Market, COM(2011) 427 final, 13 July 2011.

[73] For an extensive review of the UN record on freedom of expression, media freedom and the rights of indigenous peoples, see L. M Graham, 'A Right To Media?', *Columbia Human Rights Law Review* 41(2) (2010), 429–507.

hinder or block a broadcaster's content or a service provider's access to the audience.[74] For example, the use of proprietary technical standards developed by one company could prevent competitors from being able to use a network or pass through some of these gateways, or enable them to pass only on terms dictated by the owner. Hence the strong emphasis in the European Union telecommunication directives, for example, on the principle of 'fair, reasonable and non-discriminatory terms' for access or for use of technology. Another crucial element is the interoperability of technologies and equipment, again heavily promoted in the EU, to eliminate the possibility of abuse with the help of proprietary standards.

Internet intermediaries include Internet service providers (ISPs, acting as access providers or as providers applications, or content), hosting providers, search engines, e-commerce intermediaries, Internet payment systems and participative Web platforms. They can (and sometimes do) interfere with freedom of expression and access to information, either of their own volition, or under pressure from the State or other stakeholders.

Most democratic countries apply one of two broad principles as concerns intermediary liability for illegal or actionable content or activity by third parties.[75] According to one of them, intermediaries are not responsible for third-party content distributed or conveyed on the Internet without modification by the intermediary, or for transactions taking place through their platform outside of their knowledge or control, nor do they have a general monitoring and surveillance obligation. This type of system was first implemented in the USA in section 230 of the Communications Act. The second principle is that there may nevertheless be specific obligations (and liability for their execution), such as identifying users, preserving traffic data in response to requests, removing ('taking down') content upon receipt of a valid notice, etc. Such 'limited liability' or 'safe harbour', providing limitation of remedies, was implemented in the European Union in Directive 2000/31/ of 8 June 2000 on Certain Legal Aspects of Information Society Services, in

[74] On such gatekeeping, see P. O. Looms, 'Gatekeeping in Digital Media', Mapping Digital Media Reference Series No. 8. London: Open Society Media Program, Open Society Foundation, April 2011.

[75] Organization for Economic Co-operation and Development (OECD), *The Role of Internet Intermediaries in Advancing Public Policy Objectives. Forging Partnerships for Advancing Policy Objectives for the Internet Economy Part II*, Doc. No. DSTI/ICCP(2010)11/FINAL, 22 June 2011.

Particular Electronic Commerce, in the Internal Market, and in the United States in the Digital Millennium Copyright Act (DMCA, for copyright-infringing material only).

We may additionally distinguish two types of 'private censorship', performed by the intermediaries themselves.

### 2.5.1 'Self-regulatory' and 'co-regulatory' private censorship

'Self-regulatory' private censorship (also called 'hidden censorship') by intermediaries[76] takes place when they seek to avoid legal problems (as when a British ISP was hoaxed into removing a section of John Stuart Mill's *On Liberty*, upon receiving unfounded copyright complaints against it), or to pursue their business interests in an environment that forces them to exercise such a form of censorship: 'This illustrates the problem with self-censorship procedures, which rely on hidden judgments being made by unaccountable bodies.'[77]

According to Braman and Roberts, contracts between ISPs and users (terms of service and acceptable use policies) introduce a vast array of rules pertaining to content and expression on the Internet. Seeking to avoid legal content-related problems, ISPs assume 'regulatory' functions and introduce rules that have a 'media law-like effect'. The result, say the authors, is a speech environment significantly more restrictive than that developed through two centuries of judicial consideration of the type of communications environment intended by the US Constitution.[78]

'Co-regulatory' private censorship may emerge in situations when governments – often under pressure e.g., from copyright holders[79] – find that 'going after the content provider is not always possible [so] a more successful strategy is to put pressure on the ISPs in charge of the

[76] I. Rorive, 'Freedom of Expression in the Information Society', Working Paper for the Preparatory Group on Human Rights, the Rule of Law and the Information Society, IP 1 (2004) 49, Integrated Project 1: Making Democratic Institutions Work, Strasbourg: Council of Europe.

[77] C. Ahlert, 'How liberty was lost on the Internet', 1 June 2004, *Spiked*; www.spiked-online.com/Articles/0000000CA553.htm (last accessed 6 March 2014).

[78] S. Braman and S. Roberts, 'Advantage ISP: Terms of Service as Media law', *New Media & Society* 5(3) (2003), 422–48. On 'privatization of censorship', see also D. Tambini, D. Leonardi and C. Marsden, *Codifying Cyberspace: Communications Self-Regulation in the Age of Internet Convergence* (London and New York: Routledge, 2008).

[79] M. Humeau, 'European Parliament: Raising Awareness On "Self"-Regulation', EDRi-gram newsletter – Number 9.24, 14 September 2011; http://edri.org/edrigramnumber9-24self-regulation-workshop-european-parliament/ (last accessed 7 March 2014).

communication process'.[80] This may have the effect of turning the ISPs and other intermediaries (search engines, credit card companies and advertisers) into 'the new cyber police', as the private sector 'is being pressured, compelled, and even incentivized to 'police the internet' by governments looking to download their growing cyberspace controls'.[81] A special, and rather questionable, initiative in this respect is the 'Clean IT Project', organized as a public–private partnership between the European Commission, government departments and ISPs in a number of countries where a 'non-legislative framework' will be developed to counter illegal use of the Internet from a counter-terrorism perspective.

### 2.5.2 Filtering and blocking

In establishing a technical filtering regime, a State has several initial options: domain name system (DNS) filtering, Internet protocol (IP) address filtering, or URL filtering. Most States implement URL filtering, as this method can be the most accurate.[82]

Several dozen States (including Italy, Ireland and the UK), many of them undemocratic, have gone beyond a legal ban on citizen publication or access of undesirable material online and have set up technical means of filtering its citizens' access to the Internet. National judges have imposed monitoring on ISPs and right-holders in several countries. Another solution is the 'three-strikes' procedure introduced in France, as a result of which internet access subscribers downloading pirated content may have access suspended for a specified period from two months to one year.

Intellectual property protection is also, at the time of writing, the goal of the controversial draft Protect-IP Act (PIPA) and Stop online Piracy Act (SOPA) bills in the USA that would mandate Domain Name System (DNS) blocking and filtering by ISPs to protect the interests of copyright holders.

True, in some countries, such as Ireland and Germany, earlier attempts to introduce laws or measures obliging ISPs to filter content have been dropped. In Germany, after more than two years of debate,

80 B. Frydman and I. Rorive, 'Regulating Internet Content through Intermediaries in Europe and the USA', *Zeitschrift für Rechtssozologie* 23(1) (2002), 41–59.

81 Finlay (ed.), *Global Information Society Watch.*

82 For a detailed description and analysis of Internet content filtering, see R. Deibert *et al.* (eds.), *Access Denied: The Practice and Policy of Global Internet Filtering* (Cambridge, MA: MIT Press, 2008).

Parliament finally decided on 1 December 2011, to abolish the Access Impediment Act. That law provided for blocking access to websites deemed to have child pornographic content and required ISPs to ban a list of websites compiled and considered as 'dubious' by the Federal Criminal Police office.

Yet, international organizations seem to have accepted that some forms of filtering will not go away. The European Union in recital 3 of Directive 2002/21/EC of 7 March 2002 on a Common Regulatory Framework for Electronic Communications Networks and Services (as amended) recognizes that it may be necessary to take 'measures regarding end-users' access to, or use of, services and applications through electronic communications networks liable to restrict those fundamental rights or freedoms'. In a later ruling, the Court of Justice of the European Union took a much tougher line, namely that EU law precludes an injunction made against an internet service provider requiring it to install a system for filtering all electronic communications passing via its services which applies indiscriminately to all its customers, as a preventive measure, exclusively at its expense, and for an unlimited period.[83] This may not exclude such action in situations which do not meet all the criteria listed by the Court, but it certainly severely limits any remaining scope for imposing such measures.

The OECD in its Communiqué on Principles for Internet Policy-Making speaks only of 'limiting Internet intermediary liability', noting that Internet intermediaries can and do play an important role by addressing and deterring illegal activity, fraud and misleading and unfair practices conducted over their networks and services as well as advancing economic growth.[84]

For its part, the Council of Europe seems to have reconciled itself to the idea that filtering or blocking content or access to the Internet may, in special circumstances, be necessary. In the 2008 Recommendation CM/Rec(2008)6 on Measures to Promote the Respect for Freedom of Expression and Information with regard to Internet Filters, the Council noted that 'the voluntary and responsible use of Internet filters (products, systems and measures to block or filter Internet content) can promote

[83] Case 70/10, *Scarlet Extended SA* v. *SABAM*, Judgment of the Court of Justice of the European Union, 24 November 2011, Reports of cases, 2011-I-11959.

[84] Adopted at an OECD High Level Meeting on the Internet Economy, Paris, 28–29 June 2011.

confidence and security on the Internet for users, in particular children and young people'.[85]

Interestingly, the Council of Europe seems to have won at least some of the ISPs themselves over to its approach. The 2008 *Human Rights Guidelines for Internet Service Providers*, developed by the Council in cooperation with the European Internet Services Providers Association (EuroISPA), advises ISPs to be transparent about the fact that 'any filtering or blocking software installed on your servers . . . may lead to a removal or inaccessibility of content' and about all aspects of the method of filtering applied.[86] Also, the ISP should verify the illegality of the content, for instance by contacting the competent law enforcement authorities.[87] The *Guidelines* accept that users may be cut off from the Internet for law enforcement or other legitimate and strictly necessary reasons (such as 'a violation of contractual obligations or intentional abuse').[88] Still, it leaves some hope: 'The customer should . . . be instructed of *the steps to be taken to re-establish the access*'.[89]

As for the UN, Secretary-General Ban Ki-moon said in a statement in December 2011 that 'governments must not block access to the Internet and various forms of social media as a way to prevent criticism and public debate'.[90]

The UN Special Rapporteur seeks in his report to spell out circumstances and processes that need to be in place for any filtering or blocking of content. In this, he refers to the fact that the UN seeks to involve business in human rights protection.[91] In June 2011, the Human Rights Council endorsed the *Guiding Principles on Business and Human Rights: Implementing the United Nations 'Protect, Respect and Remedy' Framework*, developed by John Ruggie, the Special Representative of the Secretary-General on the issue of human rights and transnational corporations and other business enterprises. The document calls on business enterprises to avoid infringing on the human rights of others and to perform a human rights due-diligence process to identify, prevent,

[85] Recommendation CM/Rec(2008)6 of the Committee of Ministers to Member States on Measures to Promote the Respect for Freedom of Expression and Information with regard to Internet Filters, 26 March 2008, preamble.

[86] Council of Europe, in cooperation with EuroISPA, *Human Rights Guidelines for Internet Service Providers*, para. 20.

[87] *Ibid.*, para. 21. [88] *Ibid.*, para. 19. [89] [emphasis added] *Ibid.*

[90] UN Secretary-General, Ban Ki-moon, Message for Human Rights Day.

[91] *Report of the Special Rapporteur on Freedom of Opinion and Expression*, 16 May 2011.

mitigate and account for how they address their impacts on human rights and provide redress, where necessary.[92]

With reference to these principles, the Special Rapporteur says ISPs should not prevent access to content, or disclose private information without a court order. They should be transparent to the user involved and to the wider public about measures taken; warn users before the implementation of restrictive measures; and minimize the impact of restrictions strictly to the content involved. Finally, there must be effective remedies for affected users, including the possibility of appeal through the procedures provided by the intermediary and by a competent judicial authority.

The IGO Special Mandates consider denying individuals the right to access the Internet 'an extreme measure' and defend the 'mere conduit principle' ('No one who simply provides technical Internet services ... should be liable for content generated by others ... as long as they do not specifically intervene in that content or refuse to obey a court order to remove that content, where they have the capacity to do so').[93] At a minimum, intermediaries should not be required to monitor user-generated content and should not be subject to extrajudicial content takedown rules which fail to provide sufficient protection for freedom of expression (which is the case with many of the 'notice and takedown' rules currently being applied).[94]

The IGO Special Mandates also call for the promotion of self-regulation by service- and content-providers via the ICTs, noting that it can be 'an effective tool in redressing harmful speech'.[95] As we have seen, Finlay calls this 'the downloading of cyberspace controls' by governments,[96] though perhaps this could more appropriately be called the 'outsourcing of regulation' in an area where traditional methods of regulation and oversight are not effective. Both self-regulation[97] and co-regulation[98] help further with 'codifying cyberspace' and establishing rules for expression via the new communication services.

[92] For an overview of the 'Ruggie' Framework, see www.business-humanrights.org/SpecialRepPortal/Home/Protect-Respect-Remedy-Framework (last accessed 7 March 2014).

[93] Joint Declaration: Freedom of Expression and the Internet, 1 June 2011, para. 2(a).

[94] *Ibid.*, para. 2(b). [95] Joint Declaration, para. 1(e).

[96] Finlay (ed.), *Global Information Society Watch.*

[97] Tambini *et al.*, *Codifying Cyberspace.*

[98] Hans Bredow Institut, 'Final Report: Study on Co-Regulation Measures in the Media Sector', study for the European Commission, Directorate Information Society and Media, Hans Bredow Institut for Media Research, University of Hamburg, June 2006; http://ec.europa.eu/avpolicy/info_centre/library/studies/index_en.htm (last accessed 7 March 2014).

Here let us mention only one such scheme, the Global Network Initiative: Protecting and Advancing Freedom of Expression and Privacy in Information and Communications Technologies,[99] launched in October 2008 by a number of leading players in the field, with the United Nations Special Representative of the Secretary-General on Business and Human Rights acting as an observer. Here, self-regulation is perceived as a weapon against possible oppressive action by governments, in that parties undertake to avoid or minimize the impact of government restrictions on freedom of expression, including restrictions on the information available to users and the opportunities for users to create and communicate ideas and information. This also applies to government demands, laws and regulations to suppress freedom of expression, remove content or otherwise limit access to information and ideas in a manner inconsistent with internationally recognized laws and standards.

## 2.6 *Channel*

In the context of a communication explosion, the electromagnetic spectrum is becoming even more of a strategic resource than before. In addition to spectrum management, ultimately the responsibility of the International Telecommunication Union (ITU), the digital switchover, the allocation of the resulting 'digital dividend', as well as the development of broadband networks are necessary elements of a policy package oriented towards boosting channel availability.

### 2.6.1 Digital switchover

The digital switchover of terrestrial television (and radio) – a process planned, managed and overseen by the UN agency, the ITU Digital – involves the use of compression systems to multiplex a number of programme services into a single integrated signal and its transmission over the spectrum previously used by a single analogue channel. The result is what is known as the 'digital dividend' which in the simplest terms can be defined as the amount of radio spectrum released by the transition to digital television and radio.[100] Within the EU, it has been

[99] For details, see: https://www.globalnetworkinitiative.org (last accessed 7 March 2014).

[100] G. Pogorel, 'The Digital Dividend: Radio Spectrum, Mobile Broadband, and the Media', Mapping Digital Media Reference Series No. 10, London: Open Society Media Program, Open Society Foundation, April 2011.

established that as digital TV replaces analogue TV, four-fifths of the airwaves that used to carry TV broadcasts will be freed up.

### 2.6.2 Digital dividend

The digital dividend spectrum can be used for innovative services, from improved and new interactive television broadcasting to mobile communications and wireless broadband Internet access.

Which of these services should be able to profit more from the 'digital dividend' is the subject of intense debate worldwide.[101] Broadcasters argue that digital technologies must be used to create more over-the-air channels, so as to provide greater choice for the public, in terms of more diversity in information, entertainment and culture, enhanced prospects for the exercise of freedom of expression, media pluralism, growth in media content production. They also point at the need for bandwidth to accommodate high-definition (HD) television, and 3D television.

On the other hand, the telecommunications industry has hugely expanded over the past twenty years, and the massive uptake by consumers of mobile internet access has provoked an explosive growth in data traffic, stimulating an escalating appetite for capacity and bandwidth. Moreover, the frequency bands used until now by over-the-air television enjoy physical qualities of propagation and indoor penetration that would translate into low deployment costs for mobile telecommunications operators.

The European Commission has repeatedly called for a coordinated approach to the use of the digital dividend, with the implication that it should be dedicated mostly to industrial and economic uses in the field of telecommunications.[102]

The Council of Europe said in a 2008 Declaration on the allocation and management of the digital dividend and the public interest that 'technical and legislative choices involved in the switch-over to the digital environment should not be determined by economic factors alone but ought also

[101] For an overview of the European debate, see D. Korteweg and T. McGonagle, 'The Digital Dividend: Opportunities and Obstacles', in S. Nikoltchev (ed.), *Switchover to the Digital Dividend*, IRIS plus 2010–6 (Strasbourg: European Audiovisual Observatory, 2010), 7–26.

[102] European Commission, *Reaping the Full Benefits of the Digital Dividend in Europe: A Common Approach to the Use of the Spectrum Released by the Digital Switchover*, Doc. No. COM(2007) 700 final, 13 November 2007 and European Commission, *Transforming the Digital Dividend into Social Benefits and Economic Growth*, Doc. No. COM(2009) 586 final, 28 October 2009.

to take account of social, cultural and political factors'.[103] The Council called on Member States to 'pay special attention to the promotion of innovation, pluralism, cultural and linguistic diversity, and access of the public to audiovisual services' and to 'take in due account the needs of broadcasters and of the media at large, both public service and commercial media, as well as those of other existing or incoming spectrum users'.[104] In another declaration, the Council additionally drew attention to the desirability of allocating a sufficient number of frequencies, both in analogue and digital environments, to community media.[105]

Also the IGO Special Mandates, including the UN Special Rapporteur, have concentrated on securing the benefits of the digital dividend for broadcasting. In their Joint Declaration on Diversity in Broadcasting, they said that at least part of the spectrum released through the digital dividend should be reserved for broadcasting uses, including public interest and community broadcasters.[106] Then, in their Joint Declaration, Ten Key Challenges to Freedom of Expression in the Next Decade, they expressed concern 'that the benefits from the switchover to digital frequencies will go largely to existing broadcasters, and other uses such as telecommunications, to the detriment of greater diversity and access, and public interest media'.[107]

Approaching the digital dividend conundrum from a freedom of expression perspective, it would appear that the insistence of the IGO Special Mandates and of the Council of Europe on its use for broadcasting purposes is more conducive to its promotion. However, given that the Internet and other ICTs are increasingly being used for the many modes of mediated social communication, its use for telecommunication purposes might actually create better conditions for the exercise of this right.

## *2.7 Channel capacity*

Channel capacity naturally determines how many users can communicate and what types of content – with what bandwidth needs – they can

[103] Preamble, Declaration of the Committee of Ministers on the allocation and management of the digital dividend and the public interest, 20 February 2008.

[104] *Ibid.*, para. (ii).

[105] Declaration of the Committee of Ministers on the role of community media in promoting social cohesion and intercultural dialogue, 11 February 2009, para. (ii).

[106] IGO Special Mandates, Joint Declaration on Diversity in Broadcasting.

[107] IGO Special Mandates, Joint Declaration: Ten Key Challenges to Freedom of Expression in the Next Decade, para. 6.

use for the purpose. After Bar and Sandvig we may say that 'network control' is the power to decide how the communication network will be used and by whom, and also how much capacity will be available to particular users.[108] Policies and measures in two areas, development of broadband networks and the issue of 'net neutrality', can promote greater channel capacity.

### 2.7.1 Broadband

Broadband can be generally defined as the range of technologies making possible high-speed and high-capacity data communication through fixed or mobile connections. This includes cable modem, DSL, fibre-to-the-home/building and other fixed (wired) broadband technologies. Mobile broadband connections include wireless Internet access through a portable modem, mobile phones, or other mobile device. It has been said that 'broadband networks will be as critical to the 21st century as railroads were to the 19th century and the basic telephone lines were to the 20th century'.[109]

Broadband development[110] has been very much in the focus of attention at both the international[111] and national level. A number of countries have set benchmarks or legal requirements for network capacity, designed to ensure high quality of service and high speeds. Switzerland was the first country in the world to provide broadband universal service with download/upload 600/100 kbps data speed to its citizens. Finland has made 1-megabit broadband Web access a legal right, with the goal of a 100Mb broadband connection by 2015. The European Union envisages in the Digital Agenda for Europe that basic broadband networks will cover 100 per cent of EU citizens by 2013 and that by 2020 there should be 30 Mbps coverage for all EU citizens, with 50 per cent or more of EU households having subscriptions above 100 Mbps. The Danish government plans for all homes and enterprises to have access to a broadband connection of at least 100 Mbps by 2020.

[108] F. Bar and C. Sandvig, 'US Communication Policy after Convergence', *Media, Culture & Society* 30(4) (2008), 531–50.

[109] P. L. Parcu *et al.*, *Study on Broadband Diffusion: Drivers and Policies*, Florence School of Regulations, Communications and Media, European University Institute, 2011, 11.

[110] On ways of promoting it, see *ibid.*

[111] E.g., within the EU, see European Commission, Body of European Regulators for Electronic Communications (EC BEREC), *Broadband Promotion Report*, Doc. No. BoR (11) 70, 2011.

Estonia's EstWin project targets at least 100 Mbps availability for the whole population by 2015.

As far as the United Nations is concerned, the Broadband Commission for Digital Development, launched in May 2010 by the ITU and UNESCO, has issued a report entitled *A 2010 Leadership Imperative: Towards a Future Built on Broadband*, including a 2010 Declaration of Broadband Inclusion for All. As he presented the report, ITU Secretary-General Hamadoun Touré called for a 'broadband boom' and urged all governments to ensure that more than half of all the world's people have access to broadband networks by 2015, and make access to high-speed networks a basic civil right. Among other things, the report stresses the importance of promoting cultural diversity and multilingualism in the online world.

In 2011, the Broadband Commission issued another report, *Broadband: A Platform For Progress*, calling on governments rapidly to formulate and implement national multi-sectoral broadband plans. In a special section on freedom of expression, the report notes that with the development of the broadband Internet, 'there is a need to continually *expand and adapt* policies and regulatory frameworks, and to explore the relationships between freedom of expression and other key values and rights'.[112] Some of the specific problem areas that must be considered include: technical measures for controlling Internet flows, such as content filtering; fraud, child protection, human trafficking (especially of women and children), decency, libel, and control of hate speech; network regulation, including particularly regulation of Internet service providers, and security.

In 2011, the Broadband Commission set four targets for broadband development:

- Target 1: Making broadband policy universal. By 2015, all countries should have a national broadband plan or strategy or include broadband in their Universal Access/Service Definitions.
- Target 2: Making broadband affordable. By 2015, entry-level broadband services should be made affordable in developing countries through adequate regulation and market forces (amounting to less than 5% of average monthly income).

[112] [emphasis added] Broadband Commission for Digital Development, *Broadband: A Platform for Progress. A Report by the Broadband Commission for Digital Development* (Geneva: ITU, Paris: UNESCO, 2011).

- Target 3: Connecting homes to broadband. By 2015, 40% of households in developing countries should have Internet access.
- Target 4: Getting people online. By 2015, Internet user penetration should reach 60% worldwide, 50% in developing countries and 15% in Less Developed Countries.

### 2.7.2 Net neutrality

Channel capacity available to particular users can also depend on what is known as traffic management by network operators. This issue has spawned a major international debate on the issue of 'network [or net] neutrality',[113] understood as a situation of open, end-to-end Internet, allowing all data flows to be transmitted without any form of priority. It thus amounts to a general and *ex ante* obligation of non-discrimination for network operators when granting access to providers of online services, with the aim of excluding practices such as blocking access to non-affiliated content, degrading the quality of transmission, imposing unreasonable restrictions or prioritizing affiliated content.[114]

Network administrators who manage networks can control, prioritize or block specific data transmissions, either to improve quality of service on the network, or – in an anti-competitive manner – to block or disadvantage competing services.[115] They can inspect data and subsequently prioritize or deprioritize packets in a tiered fashion at the middle of the network. This process is known as 'access-tiering'.[116]

Forms of infringing on net neutrality include 'blocking' (either making it difficult to access or outright restricting certain services or websites on the internet), or 'throttling' (a technique employed to manage traffic and minimize congestion by degrading, i.e. slowing down certain types of traffic and so affecting the quality of content, such as video streaming provided to consumers by a competitor).

[113] N. van Eijk, 'Net Neutrality and Audiovisual Services', in S. Nikoltchev (ed.), *Why Discuss Network Neutrality?, IRIS plus* 2011-5 (Strasbourg: European Audiovisual Observatory, 2011), 7–20.

[114] P. Valcke *et al.*, 'Guardian Knight or Hands Off: The European Response to Network Neutrality. Legal Considerations on the Electronic Communications Reform', *Communications & Strategies* 72(4) (2008), 89–112.

[115] OECD, *Internet Traffic Prioritisation: An Overview*, Doc. No. DSTI/ICCP/TISP(2006)4/FINAL, 6 April 2007.

[116] S. G. Verhulst, 'Net Neutrality and the Media', Mapping Digital Media Reference Series No. 7., London: Open Society Media Program, Open Society Foundation, April 2011.

The British Office of Communications has compiled the following 'Traffic management continuum':

1 Best efforts: no traffic management by the ISP, no charging for tiered traffic;
2 Traffic management only applied during periods of high congestion;
3 Priority always given to most vulnerable types of services e.g., voice, video streaming, games;
4 Blocking content e.g., spam, illegal website content;
5 Throttling/degrading of some types of traffic, e.g., peer-to-peer;
6 Priority given to some service providers content or applications over others (perhaps for a fee as a potential revenue stream for ISPs);
7 Blocking rival's content or applications, e.g., rival IPTV service.[117]

Traffic management, especially of the kinds listed under items 4–7, may have major implications for free speech, individual autonomy and democratic participation.

Paradoxically, both supporters and opponents of net neutrality see a similar threat looming on the horizon. Supporters argue that net neutrality is essential in order to prevent telecom companies from restricting access to blogs, wikis and independent podcasts. An individual blog, small business site, or independent media outlet should have the same access to the Internet (and the public) as major news outlets and media sites. The advent of access-tiering or other similar schemes could limit this free flow of information, and thus undermine what is widely agreed to be one of the main contributions of the Internet. Proponents of this approach say that traffic management may ultimately lead to the networks and online media being dominated by a small set of conglomerates (able to foreclose all competition in an increasing range of services provided over broadband lines), driving out this profusion of independent voices that should be a hallmark of ITC-enabled social communication.[118]

Some supporters of net neutrality have gone so far as to write it into the statute books. Legislation adopted in 2010 made Chile the first country in the world to mandate network neutrality in law. Pursuant to this law, ISPs must 'ensure access to all types of content, services or applications available on the network and offer a service that does not distinguish content, applications or services, based on the source of it or

[117] OFCOM, 'Traffic Management and "Net Neutrality": A Discussion Document', London: Office of Communications, 24 June 2010.
[118] Verhulst, 'Net Neutrality and the Media'.

their property'. In June 2011, the Netherlands became the first country in Europe to enshrine the concept of network neutrality into national law by banning its mobile telephone operators from blocking or charging consumers extra for using Internet-based communications services and from giving preference to their own content.

Opponents of the net neutrality principle argue that it boils down to promoting a Darwinian competition among every conceivable use of the Internet, so that only the best survive, leading to very much the same consolidation of the industry.[119] They also contend that limitations placed on operators' private property interests could eventually prove too burdensome to be commercially viable. Without the ability to adapt and develop business models that include a certain level of discrimination, service providers could, it is claimed, become unprofitable.

The matter is not cut and dried, however. It seems to be the general conclusion that clinically pure net neutrality is not possible or indeed desirable.

The Charter of Human Rights and Principles for the Internet, developed by a Dynamic Coalition on Internet Rights and Principles says that the Internet architecture should be 'a vehicle for free, open, equal and non-discriminating exchange of information, communication and culture', but this does not preclude '*positive discrimination* to promote equity and diversity on and through the Internet'.[120]

The Federal Communications Commission of the USA has adopted three basic rules on this question:

1. Transparency. Broadband providers must disclose the network management practices, performance characteristics, and terms and conditions of their broadband services;
2. No blocking. Broadband providers may not block lawful content, applications, services, or non-harmful devices; and
3. *No unreasonable discrimination.* Fixed broadband providers may not unreasonably discriminate in transmitting lawful network traffic.[121]

The European Commission says that any regulation that might more strictly impose net neutrality 'should avoid deterring investment, or

[119] T. Wu, 'Network Neutrality, Broadband Discrimination', *Journal of Telecommunications and High Technology Law* 2 (2003), 141–78.

[120] [emphasis added] See http://internetrightsandprinciples.org/wpcharter (last accessed 11 June 2014).

[121] [emphasis added] Federal Communications Commission (FCC), *Report and Order: Preserving the Open Internet, Broadband Industry Practices*, Doc. No. GN Docket No. 09-191, WC Docket No. 07-52, Washington, DC, 23 December 2010.

innovative business models, lead to a more efficient use of the networks and to creating new business opportunities at different levels of the internet value chain while preserving for consumers the advantages of a choice of internet access products tailored to their needs'.[122] Also the Body of European Regulators for Electronic Communications (BEREC), operating within the European Union, proposes to approach the issue from the point of view of transparency.[123] This suggests that the best that can be achieved is full transparency about traffic restrictions, and appears to reflect the industry's view of the matter. For its part, the European Parliament, in its 2011 Resolution on the Open Internet and Net Neutrality in Europe, recognizes that 'reasonable traffic management' is required to enable operators to shape internet traffic in order to maintain networks' functional capacity and stability and to meet quality-of-service requirements.[124] The Council of Europe's 2010 Declaration on Network Neutrality and the above-mentioned *Human Rights Guidelines for Internet Service Providers* affirm the principle of net neutrality, but also warn ISPs: 'If you apply bandwidth caps, filter or block certain traffic, make sure that your customers are *informed about such service restrictions in a clear manner beforehand.*'[125]

A similar approach is adopted by the IGO Special Mandates, including the UN Special Rapporteur. They said in their 2011 Joint Declaration On Freedom of Expression and the Internet that 'there should be no discrimination in the treatment of Internet data and traffic, based on the device, content, author, origin and/or destination of the content, service or application'.[126] Still, they also noted that 'Internet intermediaries should be required to be transparent about any traffic or information management practices they employ, and relevant information on such practices should be made available in a form that is accessible to all stakeholders.'[127]

[122] European Commission, Communication from the Commission to the European Parliament, the Council, the Economic and Social Committee and the Committee of the Regions: the Open Internet and Net Neutrality in Europe, Doc. No. COM(2011) 222 final, 19 April 2011, 9–10.

[123] BEREC, Draft Guidelines on Net Neutrality and Transparency: Best Practices and Recommended Approaches, Doc. No. BoR (11) 44, October 2011.

[124] European Parliament Resolution on the Open Internet and Net Neutrality in Europe, Doc. No. P7_TA-PROV(2011)0511, 17 November 2011.

[125] [emphasis added] *Human Rights Guidelines for Internet Service Providers*, para. 18.

[126] Joint Declaration on Freedom of Expression and the Internet, para. 5(a).

[127] *Ibid.*, para. 5(b).

## 3 Looking to the future

User behaviour patterns, which receive scant attention in policy texts, as well as a number of other factors – social and economic, cultural and technological – will play a major role in determining the future of ICT-enabled communication. Two forecasts of the future of the Internet may be cited as illustrations of what may be in store.

One forecast on the evolving Internet[128] envisages the possibility that one of the following scenarios will unfold:

- 'Fluid Frontiers': This is a world in which 'the Internet becomes pervasive and centrifugal. Technology continues to make connectivity and devices more and more affordable while global entrepreneurship – and fierce competition – ensure that the wide range of needs and demands from across the world are met quickly and from equally diverse setups and locations.'[129]
- 'Insecure Growth': 'This is a world in which users – individuals and business alike – are scared away from intensive reliance on the Internet. Relentless cyber attacks driven by wide-ranging motivations defy the preventive capabilities of governments and international bodies. Secure alternatives emerge but they are expensive.'[130]
- 'Short of the Promise': 'This is a frugal world in which prolonged economic stagnation in many countries takes its toll on the spread of the Internet. Technology offers no compensating breakthroughs and protectionist policy responses to economic weakness make matters worse – both in economic terms and with regard to network technology adoption.'[131]
- 'Bursting at the Seams': This is a world in which 'the Internet becomes a victim of its own success. Demand for IP-based services is boundless but capacity constraints and occasional bottlenecks create a gap between the expectations and reality of Internet use. . .'[132]

Another forecast of the 'future Internet'[133] envisages quite different scenarios:

- 'Smooth Trip' – the rise of the Internet economy as a whole life and work style;

[128] E. Rueda-Sabater, D. Derosby, J. Johnston and N. Murphy, 'The Evolving Internet: Driving Forces, Uncertainties, and Four Scenarios to 2025', Cisco, Global Business Network, 2010; http://newsroom.cisco.com/dlls/2010/ekits/Evolving_Internet_GBN_Cisco_2010_Aug.pdf (last accessed 7 March 2014).

[129] *Ibid.*, 15. [130] *Ibid.*, 19. [131] *Ibid.*, 23. [132] *Ibid.*, 27.

[133] I. Brown *et al.*, 'Towards a Future Internet: Interrelation between Technological, Social and Economic Trends', final report for DG Information Society and Media, Oxford Internet Institute, University of Oxford, SCF Associates, 17 November 2010.

- 'Going Green' – the Internet combats the growing environmental challenges;
- 'Commercial Big Brother' – an authoritarian/commercial consumer platform;
- 'Power to the People' – emergence of the e-Demos, a forum for democracy and freedom.

As can be seen, each of those scenarios would pose very different policy challenges and necessitate radically different policy responses in terms of creating an enabling environment for the exercise and protection of the right to free expression in the new technological landscape. The UN would have a very important role to play in developing and promoting such policy responses.

## 4 Conclusion

Freedom of expression and free flow of information issues have been at the forefront of attention at the United Nations since its inception. These issues, approached from an Information Society perspective, were also centre stage at the UN-sponsored World Summit on the Information Society in 2003 and 2005. So, it is remarkable that the Human Rights Council and the UN Special Rapporteur only really came to grips with these issues in the ICT context in 2011. It does not appear that, as of the time of writing in December 2011, the UN High Commissioner for Human Rights has yet taken up these matters.

An attempt was made in this paper to piece together the response of the UN system to the ICT-related policy challenges in relation to freedom of expression and to show it in a comparative perspective. In general terms, it has turned out to be relatively full and complete, except in those areas where Member States' interests diverged too much for consensus to be possible. Still, the UN has a long way to go before it can match the much more detailed and wide-ranging *acquis* in this field of the European Union and especially the Council of Europe (in terms of human rights standards). A sign of recognition that more needs to be done can be found in the Human Rights Council's decision, in Resolution 18/119 of October 2011, to convene at its 19th session, 'a panel discussion on the promotion and protection of freedom of expression on the Internet, with a particular focus on the ways and means to improve its protection in accordance with international human rights law'.

The need for the UN to become much more actively involved is clear: with the global reach of the Internet, only solutions on a global scale have any chance of being effective (but are also the most difficult to achieve). This is all the more so that if Tim Wu (author of *The Master Switch: The Rise and Fall of Information Empires*) is right, the 'Commercial Big Brother' scenario may have a good chance of coming true. According to Wu, the threat not only of political, but also of large-scale commercial censorship of the Internet is very real. In his view, we are in a critical period for the Internet. It is now about fifteen years into its cycle as an open 'medium' and at that moment in their cycle, most open media tend to turn to closed media. The telephone, radio, cinema and television all went from being technologies used by lots of different individuals and companies, to ones controlled by just a few monopolies.[134] A similar consolidation of power may be about to happen to the Internet. Amazon, Google, Apple and Facebook are so large that one or more of them could team up with a mobile network and end net neutrality, by privileging that network's clients above all others. It is something that is already partly happening, with more potentially to come: 'Monopolies such as Google and Apple may soon decide to choose which parts of the internet to give us – or switch off – and in some cases have already started to do so.'[135]

The UN, to its credit, has been instrumental in starting a worldwide debate about these issues. It is clearly time to go further and act to secure and safeguard freedom of expression and freedom of the media in the ICT environment.

## Literature

Bar, F. and C. Sandvig, 'US Communication Policy after Convergence', *Media, Culture & Society* 30(4) (2008), 531–50.

Benkler, Y. *The Wealth of Networks How Social Production Transforms Markets and Freedom*, (New Haven, CT and London: Yale University Press, 2006).

Braman, S. and S. Roberts, 'Advantage ISP: Terms of Service as Media law', *New Media & Society* 5(3) (2003), 422–48.

Catts, R. and J. Lau, *Towards Information Literacy Indicators: Conceptual Framework Paper* (Paris: UNESCO, 2008).

[134] P. Kingsley, 'The Wu master', *Guardian*, 17 March 2011; www.theguardian.com/technology/2011/mar/17/the-master-switch-tim-wu-internet (last accessed 7 March 2014); much the same point about the 'rise and stall of the generative net', amounting to an end of what Benkler calls 'social production' on the Internet, is made by J. Zittrain, *The Future of the Internet and How to Stop It* (New Haven, CT and London: Yale University Press, 2008).

[135] *Ibid.*

Dahlberg, L. 'The Corporate Colonization of Online Attention and the Marginalization of Critical Communication?', *Journal of Communication Inquiry* 29(2) (2005), 160–80.

'The Internet as Public Sphere or Culture Industry? From Pessimism to Hope and Back', *International Journal of Media and Cultural Politics* 1(1) (2005), 93–6.

Deibert, R. *et al.* (eds.), *Access Denied: The Practice and Policy of Global Internet Filtering* (Cambridge, Massachusetts: MIT Press, 2008).

Dutton, W. H. *et al. Freedom of Connection, Freedom of Expression: The Changing Legal and Regulatory Ecology Shaping the Internet* (Paris: UNESCO, 2011).

Finlay, A. (ed.), *Global Information Society Watch 2011: Internet Rights and Democratization, Focus on Freedom of Expression and Association Online* (South Africa: Association for Progressive Communications (APC) and Humanist Institute for Cooperation with Developing Countries (Hivos), 2011); www.apc.org/en/system/files/gisw2011_en.pdf (last accessed 7 March 2014).

Frau-Meigs, D. and J. Torrent (eds.), *Mapping Media Education Policies in the World. Visions, Programmes and Challenges* (New York: United Nations Alliance of Civilizations and Huelva, Spain: Grupo Comunicar, 2009).

Frydman, B. and I. Rorive, 'Regulating Internet Content through Intermediaries in Europe and the USA', *Zeitschrift für Rechtssozologie* 23(1) (2002), 41–59.

Fung, A. and E. Olin Wright, 'Deepening Democracy: Innovations in Empowered Participatory Governance', *Politics & Society* 29(1) (2001), 5–41.

Graham, L. M. 'A Right To Media?', *Columbia Human Rights Law Review* 41(2) (2010), 429–507.

Hamelink, C. J. 'Human Rights for the Information Society', in B. Girard and S. Ó Siochrú (eds.), *Communicating in the Information Society* (Geneva: United Nations Research Institute for Social Development, 2003), 121–65.

Hamelink, C. J. and J. Hoffmann, 'The State of the Right to Communicate', *Global Media Journal* (2008), 7–13.

Hine, P. (ed.), *UNESCO ICT Competency Framework for Teachers* (Paris: UNESCO, 2011).

Horton, F. W., Jr., *Understanding Information Literacy: A Primer* (Paris: UNESCO, 2007).

Jakubowicz, K. 'Human Rights and the Information Society: A Preliminary Overview', in K. Jakubowicz, *Media Revolution in Europe: Ahead of the Curve* (Strasbourg: Council of Europe, 2011), 135–64.

Kang, H. and M. P. McAllister, 'Selling You and Your Clicks: Examining the Audience Commodification of Google', *tripleC – Cognition, Communication, Co-operation* 9(2) (2011), 141–53.

Korff, D. and I. Brown, 'Social Media and Human Rights', in T. Hammarberg *et al.*, *Human Rights and a Changing Media Landscape* (Strasbourg: Council of Europe, 2011), 175–206.

Korteweg, D. and T. McGonagle, 'The Digital Dividend: Opportunities and Obstacles', in S. Nikoltchev (ed.), *Switchover to the Digital Dividend, IRIS plus 2010-6*, (Strasbourg: European Audiovisual Observatory, 2010), 7–26.

Latzer, M. 'Convergence Revisited. Toward a Modified Pattern of Communications Governance', *Convergence* 15(4) (2009), 411–26.

Marks, S. 'The Human Right to Development: Between Rhetoric and Reality', *Harvard Human Rights Journal* 17 (2004), 137–68.

McGonagle, T. *Minority Rights, Freedom of Expression and of the Media: Dynamics and Dilemmas* (Antwerp: Intersentia, 2011).

Mueller, M. L., B. N. Kuerbis and C. Pagé, 'Democratizing Global Communication? Global Civil Society and the Campaign for Communication Rights in the Information Society', *International Journal of Communication* 1 (2007), 267–96.

Napoli, P. M. 'Diminished, Enduring, and Emergent Diversity Policy Concerns in an Evolving Media Environment', *International Journal of Communication* 5 (2011), 1182–96; http://ijoc.org/ojs/index.php/ijoc/article/view/1074/595 (last accessed 7 March 2014).

Tambini, D. 'What Citizens Need to Know: Digital Exclusion, Information Inequality and Rights', in E. Richards, R. Foster, T. Kiedrowski (eds.), *Communications: The Next Decade: A Collection of Essays Prepared for the UK Office of Communications* (London: OFCOM, 2006), 112–24.

Tambini, D., D. Leonardi and C. Marsden, *Codifying Cyberspace: Communications Self-Regulation in the Age of Internet Convergence* (London and New York: Routledge, 2008).

Valcke, P. *et al.* 'Guardian Knight or Hands Off: The European Response to Network Neutrality. Legal Considerations on the Electronic Communications Reform', *Communications & Strategies* 72(4) (2008), 89–112.

Van Cuilenburg, J. and D. McQuail, 'Media Policy Paradigm Shifts: Towards a New Communications Policy Paradigm', *European Journal of Communication* 18(2) (2003), 181–207.

Van Eijk 'Net Neutrality and Audiovisual Services in S. Nikoltchev (ed.), *Why Discuss Network Neutrality?*, IRIS Plus 2011-5 (Strasbourg: European Audiovisual Observatory, 2011), 7–20.

Verhulst, S. 'About Scarcities and Intermediaries: The Regulatory Paradigm Shift of Digital Content Reviewed', in L. Lievrouw and S. Livingstone (eds.), *The Handbook of New Media* (London: Sage, 2002), 432–47.

Wilson, C. *et al. Media and Information Literacy: Curriculum for Teachers* (Paris: UNESCO, 2011).

Wu, T. 'Network Neutrality, Broadband Discrimination', *Journal of Telecommunications and High Technology Law* 2 (2003), 141–78.

Zittrain, J. *The Future of the Internet and How to Stop It* (New Haven, CT and London: Yale University Press, 2008).

## Journalistic articles

Ahlert, C. 'How Liberty was lost on the internet', *Spiked*, 1 June 2004; www.spiked-online.com/Articles/0000000CA553.htm (last accessed 6 March 2014).

Kingsley, P. 'The Wu master', *The Guardian*, 17 March 2011; www.theguardian.com/technology/2011/mar/17/the-master-switch-tim-wu-internetKorff (last accessed 7 March 2014).

Radovanovic, D. 'Digital divide and social media: connectivity doesn't end the digital divide, skills do', *Scientific American.com*, 14 September 2011, http://blogs.scientificamerican.com/guest-blog/2011/12/14/digital-divide-and-social-media-connectivity-doesnt-end-the-digital-divide-skills-do/ (last accessed 7 March 2014).

## Miscellaneous

Broadband Commission for Digital Development, *Broadband: A Platform for Progress. A Report by The Broadband Commission for Digital Development* (Geneva: ITU, Paris: UNESCO, 2011).

Brown, I. *et al. Towards a Future Internet: Interrelation between Technological, Social and Economic Trends. Final Report for DG Information Society and Media* (Oxford Internet Institute, University of Oxford, SCF Associates, 17 November 2010).

Hans Bredow Institut, *Final Report: Study on Co-Regulation Measures in the Media Sector*, study for the European Commission, Directorate Information Society and Media, Hans Bredow Institut for Media Research, University of Ham burg, June 2006 http://ec.europa.eu/avpolicy/info_centre/library/studies/index_en.htm (last accessed 7 March 2014).

Humeau, M. 'European Parliament: raising awareness on "self"-regulation', EDRi-gram newsletter - Number 9.24, 14 September 2011, http://edri.org/edrigramnumber9–24self-regulation-workshop-european-parliament (Last accessed 7 March 2014).

Jakubowicz, K. *The Right to Public Expression: A Modest Proposal for an Important Human Right* (London: Media Program, Open Society Foundation, 2010).

Looms, P. O. *Gatekeeping in Digital Media: Mapping Digital Media Reference Series No. 8* (London: Open Society Media Program, Open Society Foundation, April 2011).

McIver, W. J. Jr. and W. F. Birdsall, 'Technological evolution and the right to communicate: the implications for electronic democracy', presented at Euricom Colloquium: Electronic Networks & Democracy, 2002; www.cs.duke.edu/courses/spring05/cps182s/readings/McIver-Birdsall.pdf (last accessed 7 March 2014).

Murdock, G. 'Rights and Representations: Public Discourse and Cultural Citizenship', in J. Gripstrud (ed.), *Media and Knowledge: The Role of Television* (Department of Media Studies, Papers from a Seminar at the University of Bergen, 1996).

'Building the digital commons: public broadcasting in the age of the Internet', 2004 Spry Memorial lecture, 2004; https://pantherfile.uwm.edu/type/www/116/Theory_OtherTexts/Theory/Murdock_BuildingDigitalCommons.pdf (last accessed 7 March 2014).

OFCOM, *Traffic Management and 'Net Neutrality': A Discussion Document* (London: Office of Communications, 24 June 2010).

Parcu, P.L. *et al. Study on Broadband Diffusion: Drivers and Policies* (Florence School of Regulations, Communications and Media, European University Institute, 2011).

Pogorel, G. *The Digital Dividend: Radio Spectrum, Mobile Broadband, and the Media – Mapping Digital Media Reference Series No. 10* (London: Open Society Media Program, Open Society Foundation, April 2011).

Puddephatt, A. *Freedom of Expression Rights in the Digital Age, Mapping Digital Media Reference Series No. 6* (London: Open Society Media Program, Open Society Foundation, April 2011).

Rorive, I. 'Freedom of Expression in the Information Society', working paper for the Preparatory Group on Human Rights, the Rule of Law and the Information Society, IP 1 (2004) 49, Integrated Project 1: Making Democratic Institutions Work, Strasbourg: Council of Europe.

Rueda-Sabater, E., D. Derosby, J. Johnston and N. Murphy, *The Evolving Internet: Driving Forces, Uncertainties, and Four Scenarios to 2025'* (Cisco, Global Business Network, 2010); http://newsroom.cisco.com/dlls/2010/ekits/Evolving_Internet_GBN_Cisco_2010_Aug.pdf (last accessed 7 March 2014).

Samuelson, P. 'Five Challenges for Regulating the Global Information Society', n.d.; www.asc.upenn.edu/courses/comm334/Docs/samuelson.regs.pdf (last accessed 7 March 2014).

Valcke, P. *et al.* 'European approaches to future content regulation. The New European Directive for Audiovisual Media Services: a "next generation framework" or "old wine in new barrels"?', paper presented at the EuroCPR Conference 2007, Policies for the Content Industries (Seville 25–27 March 2007).

Verhulst, S. G. *Net Neutrality and the Media: Mapping Digital Media Reference Series No. 7* (London: Open Society Media Program, Open Society Foundation, April 2011).

## Legal and political documents

### *Council of Europe*

#### Committee of Ministers

Declaration of the Committee of Ministers on the protection of freedom of expression and freedom of assembly and association with regard to privately operated Internet platforms and online service providers, 7 December 2011.

Recommendation CM/Rec(2011)7 of the Committee of Ministers to member States on a new notion of media, 21 September 2011.

Declaration of the Committee of Ministers on the role of community media in promoting social cohesion and intercultural dialogue, 11 February 2009.

Recommendation CM/Rec(2008)6 of the Committee of Ministers to Member States on measures to promote the respect for freedom of expression and information with regard to Internet filters, 26 March 2008.

Declaration of the Committee of Ministers on the allocation and management of the digital dividend and the public interest, 20 February 2008.

Recommendation CM/Rec(2007)16 of the Committee of Ministers to Member States on measures to promote the public service value of the Internet, 7 November 2007.

#### Miscellaneous

O'Connell, R. 'Harmful content', Group of Specialists on Human Rights In the Information Society, Council of Europe, Doc. No. MC-S-IS(2005)007, 2005.

Council of Europe, in cooperation with EuroISPA, *Human Rights Guidelines for Internet Service Providers*, 2008.

Council of Europe, Media and Information Society Division, *Internet Governance and Critical Internet Resources*, Report prepared by the Council of Europe Secretariat, April 2009.

### *EU*

BEREC, *Broadband Promotion Report*, Doc. No. BoR (11) 70, 2011.

BEREC, *Draft Guidelines on Net Neutrality and Transparency: Best Practices and Recommended Approaches*, Doc. No. BoR (11) 44, 2011.

#### European Commission

*A European Approach to Media Literacy in the Digital Environment*, Doc. No. COM(2007) 833 final, 20 December 2007.

European Commission, 'Informal Background Paper on ICANN New gTLD Process', Brussels: European Union, 1 September 2011; www.bof.nl/live/wp-content/uploads/EC-TLD-censorship.pdf (last accessed 6 March 2014).

*Reaping the Full Benefits of the Digital Dividend in Europe: A Common Approach to the Use of the Spectrum Released by the Digital Switchover*, Doc. No. COM (2007) 700 final, 13 November 2007.

*Internet Governance: The Next Steps*, Doc. No. COM(2009) 277 final, 18 June 2009.

*Transforming the Digital Dividend into Social Benefits and Economic Growth*, Doc. No. COM(2009) 586 final, 28 October 2009.

*Regulatory Framework for Electronic Communications in the European Union: Situation in December 2009*, Publications office of the European Union, 2010.

*Communication from the Commission to the European Parliament, the Council, the Economic and Social Committee and the Committee of the Regions: the Open Internet and Net Neutrality in Europe*, Doc. No. COM(2011) 222 final, 19 April 2011.

*Green Paper on the Online Distribution of Audiovisual Works in the European Union: Opportunities and Challenges Towards a Digital Single Market*, COM (2011) 427 final, 13 July 2011.

*Universal Service in E-Communications: Report on the Outcome of the Public Consultation and the Third Periodic Review of the Scope in Accordance with Article 15 of Directive 2002/22/E*, Doc. No. COM(2011) 795 final, 23 November 2011.

## European Parliament

Recommendation of 26 March 2009 to the Council on strengthening security and fundamental freedoms on the Internet (2008/2160(INI).

Resolution of 5 July 2011 on Universal Service and the 112 Emergency Number, Doc. No. 2010/2274(INI).

Resolution on the open internet and net neutrality in Europe, Doc. No. P7_TA-PROV(2011)0511, 17 November 2011.

## *UN*

Economic and Social Council, *Report of the Secretary General on Enhanced Cooperation on Public Policy Issues Pertaining to the Internet*, UN. Doc. A/66/77-E/2011/103, 4 May 2011; http://unpan1.un.org/intradoc/groups/public/documents/un/unpan045826.pdf (last accessed 7 March 2014).

HRC, General Comment No. 34: Article 19 (Freedoms of opinion and expression), UN Doc. CCPR/C/GC/34, 12 September 2011.

*Report of the Special Rapporteur on the Promotion and Protection of the Right to Freedom of Opinion and Expression*, UN Doc. A/HRC/17/27, 16 May 2011.

## *OCSE*

Akdeniz, Y. *Freedom of Expression on the Internet: A Study of Legal Provisions and Practices Related to Freedom of Expression, the Free Flow of Information and Media Pluralism on the Internet in OSCE Participating States* (Vienna: OSCE Representative on Freedom of the Media, 2010).

OSCE Representative on Freedom of the Media, 'Internet freedom: why it matters', position paper, 11 January 2012; www.osce.org/fom/86003 (last accessed 7 March 2014).

## *OECD*

*Internet Traffic Prioritisation: An Overview*, Doc. No. DSTI/ICCP/TISP(2006)4/FINAL, 6 April 2007.

*The Role of Internet Intermediaries In Advancing Public Policy Objectives. Forging Partnerships for Advancing Policy Objectives for the Internet Economy Part II*, Doc. No. DSTI/ICCP(2010)11/FINAL, 22 June 2011.

## *IGO Special Mandates*

Joint Declaration on Diversity in Broadcasting, 12 December 2007.

Joint Declaration: Ten Key Challenges to Freedom of Expression in the Next Decade, 3 February 2010.

Joint Declaration on Freedom of Expression and the Internet, 1 June 2011.

11

# A new vision of values, accountability and mission for journalism

AIDAN WHITE

## 1 Introduction

After 150 years in which traditional media have largely controlled the information people receive and how they receive it, journalism is being dismantled and rebuilt raising compelling questions about the role and responsibility of media in the future.

The information revolution has transformed the landscape of journalism raising new questions about who is a journalist and what is journalism in an age when all citizens have access to the tools that allow them to publish freely across different platforms of communication.

The legal conditions in which journalism operates are on the whole much the same as those enjoyed by all citizens who have the right to free expression, yet the growth of the open information landscape has created a new debate about what distinguishes journalism from free expression and how journalists and media professionals maintain attachment to notions of responsible communications through a traditional regime of ethical conduct, good governance and self-regulation.

The legal protections for journalism are limited to references in international law regarding accreditation rights, protection of pluralism, freedom of movement or limited rights to protect sources of information, such as those noted in the United Nations (UN) Human Rights Committee's General Comment No. 34 on freedom of opinion and expression.[1]

But beyond the narrowly defined parameters of international protection, the future of journalism has become a major talking point for professionals and policymakers alike as online media, blogging and social networks have invaded the newsroom and transformed the culture of traditional news gathering, adding new layers of user-generated content

[1] HRC, General Comment No. 34: Article 19 (Freedoms of opinion and expression), UN Doc. CCPR/C/GC/34, 12 September 2011. See further, Chapter 2 in this book.

and raising questions about how traditional values hitherto used to define responsible use of information can be applied across the new information landscape.

Journalism in many countries has been a game dictated by elite professionals and egocentric political power brokers. Now the rules have been changed by the creation of an open information environment which is unruly, unpredictable and refreshingly liberated.

This media makeover has been tumultuous. A mix of economic recession, technological convergence and a seismic shift in media markets has devastated the newspaper industry, particularly in the USA and Europe. More than 100,000 jobs have been lost and hundreds of newspapers have closed or switched online. In broadcasting, too, the digital revolution has laid waste to traditional norms of production, marketing and news reporting.

In other parts of the world it is a different story. In India, Brazil and China, for example, traditional media have seen growth, but this may be only a temporary phenomenon. Everywhere the Internet has given millions of people access to the public information space and in the process has rewritten the script for how journalism works. The pace of change in Europe and North America has been rapid; in other regions it has been more measured; but there is a sense that the global information revolution will overwhelm media markets and the public information space everywhere. The power of mass circulation newspapers and primetime broadcasting to influence captive audiences is in decline and is being replaced by systems of online communication driven by individuals and special interest groups.

This transformation has not gone unnoticed within political circles as governments, many of them shaken by the impact of WikiLeaks and its uncovering of the secret world of diplomacy in 2010, and the revelations by Edward Snowden of global surveillance by the US National Security Agency in 2013, are scrambling to monitor and control social networks and the Internet. Some of them, even in democratic countries, have turned to restrictive laws to limit the chaotic growth of unrestrained speech and ever-expanding public access to information.

But new laws and other measures to control media and the Internet which add to existing forms of censorship can have a chilling effect on journalism and a negative effect on society as a whole. With this in mind, the debate about the future of communications and the role of journalism is firmly focused on how to rebalance the relationship between free speech and the law.

At the same time, within media, there is fresh debate about how to strengthen the ethical craft of journalism, to promote good governance and transparency in media and to build public trust in forms of self-regulation of journalism over overt political interference and legal controls of media content.

Journalists want to embrace the full potential of connected and open societies, and they have an interest in promoting ethics, but they prefer to keep the law at arm's length. If there is to be a rekindling of the notion of mission in journalism, as many of them want, they prefer to do it themselves, particularly through credible and effective forms of self-regulation.

The former Human Rights Commissioner of the Council of Europe, Thomas Hammarberg, in the book, *Human Rights and a Changing Media Landscape*,[2] has spelled out the priorities of his own office in this area, calling for constitutional support for freedom of expression; a deeper discussion on how to promote ethical journalism; encouragement to media to develop a system of effective self-regulation; and more action to help media satisfy the public's right to know with laws on access to information.

Hammarberg's call is recognition that journalists themselves have a vested interest in the defence and promotion of human rights, particularly the right to free expression. Importantly, his statement also highlights a concern within media that, although there is greater access to other kinds of information, the decline in the availability of public-spirited journalism means people no longer have access to quality journalism in the quantity and quality required for democracy to function.

A key element of the change overtaking media is how information technology, particularly through the Internet and the sophisticated hardware of mobile telephones, now allows the audience to play an active and decisive role in newsgathering. More people are doing journalistic work, but most of them are not in regular media employment. Some do not even regard themselves as journalists.[3] Not surprisingly, the mass of these new players are largely untrained, and have little sense of professional or ethical responsibility.

[2] Council of Europe Commissioner for Human Rights, *Human Rights and a Changing Media Landscape* (Strasbourg: Council of Europe, 2011), 12–13.

[3] International Federation of Journalists (FDJ), *IFJ Congress Report: Journalism, In Touch with the Future*, 25–29 May 2010; see: www.ifj.org/assets/docs/032/066/7c74420-9dfce42.pdf (last accessed 28 January 2014).

Rapidly expanding social networks such as Facebook and Twitter now drive the news agenda and are also influential distributors of news. The typical editorial crisis facing media today is not so much to find news, but how to verify and moderate the superabundance of information and comment flooding into newsrooms.

There is a growing belief, even among liberal supporters of internet freedom, that unrestrained expression without any sense of responsibility must have limits, but the challenge for journalists, bloggers and social networkers alike is how to set boundaries without resorting to expansion of legal rules and controls that might stifle free speech and discipline dissent.

Today most media insiders, including editors and media owners, recognize that the challenges facing journalism will not be overcome without a bold prescription to cure the ills of media.

Among solutions currently being looked at are an urgent return to professional values inside the industry, an overhaul of official media policies and even the discreet use of law to underpin and promote journalism as a public good.[4]

A return to the basics of journalism would strengthen enormously the work of media as watchdogs over the exercise of power and protectors of rights and the public interest. Wearing its robe as the 'fourth estate', journalism has always been an essential addition to the powers of the executive, the legislature and the judiciary, but this power can also be misused. It can become a blunt instrument in the service of narrow, political interests even posing a threat to the functioning of democracy.

Some media in Europe, Africa and the Middle East provide propaganda for their political friends, to stir up rivalries and conflict. Others routinely incite xenophobic hatred as they seek scapegoats among migrant communities and other vulnerable groups to blame for austerity. As always in times of uncertainty and recession, journalism can quickly come under the influence of unscrupulous politics.[5]

[4] In 2011 a new international group, the Global Editors Network, was launched. It brings together news executives across all media platforms. One key objective is the revival of ethical journalism. See: www.globaleditorsnetwork.org (last accessed 28 January 2014).

[5] See, for instance *The Leveson Report: An Inquiry into the Culture, Practices and Ethics of the Press* (2012 HC 779) in the UK which condemned politically biased reporting and the unhealthy relationship between politics and the press; www.official-documents.gov.uk/document/hc1213/hc07/0779/0779.pdf (last accessed 28 January 2014) and, more directly, the propaganda and incitement to violence of Radio Mille Collines in the 1993 Rwandan

But it is not just external conditions that shape the way media work. When media have no sense of corporate responsibility; when they grow ever stronger through concentration of ownership and when they play politics on the global stage, corruption can flourish.

As the behaviour of the companies in the media empire owned by Rupert Murdoch over the last thirty years shows, without a rights-based corporate culture unaccountable media can subvert international standards both of journalism and free expression.

In the 1990s Murdoch sold Hong Kong's *South China Morning Post*, one of the world's most profitable newspapers, because its China reporting was too negative. He dropped the BBC from satellite broadcasts into China and broke a contract with Hong Kong's ex-Governor, Chris Patten, whose book, including critical discussion of China's government, was due to be published by the group's publishing arm, HarperCollins.[6]

The company's casual censorship to please China's communist leaders is matched by its betrayal of ethical journalism half a world away in London and New York. In the United States the company's flagship Fox News abandoned journalistic norms on behalf of its political allies, developing a curious revenue model based upon populist, biased and 'attack dog' journalism. Its generosity to right-wing politics has extended beyond the newsroom. In 2010 the company donated a million dollars to help elect Republican governors to office.[7]

In this context, the bribery of police officers, undue political influence and illegal phone hacking exposed in the group's London newspaper operations in 2011 should surprise no one. This behaviour flows from a well-established corporate culture that has consistently run counter to the values of ethical conduct in media.[8]

Genocide, D. Yanagizawa-Drott, *Propaganda and Conflict: Theory and Evidence from the Rwandan Genocide* (Cambridge, MA: Harvard University, 2012); see www.hks.harvard.edu/fs/dyanagi/Research/RwandaDYD.pdf (last accessed 28 January 2014).

6 Stories of self-censorship in the Murdoch empire are well documented, not least by journalists who have worked for him in the past. See R. Greenslade, 'How Self-censorship works in the empire of Rupert Murdoch', *Guardian*, 4 March 2008; see: www.theguardian.com/media/greenslade/2008/mar/04/howselfcensorshipworksinth (last accessed 28 January 2014).

7 H. Kurtz, 'News Corp. defends 1$ million donation to Republican Governors Association', *Washington Post*, 17 August 2010, see: www.washingtonpost.com/wpdyn/content/article/2010/08/17/AR2010081704338.html (last accessed 28 January 2014).

8 Almost every editor employed by Murdoch has a story if not a book to write or already written on these stories, but the comments by Jonathan Mirsky in the *New York Review of Books* are particularly revealing on relations with China ('Murdoch's Chinese Adventure',

It is wishful thinking to imagine, therefore, that the burden of ethical responsibility in media can be assumed by working journalists alone. Ethical conduct in journalism is not just about cleaning up malpractice on the part of editors and reporters; it is also about promoting good governance at the top of the media pyramid. The boardroom, as well as the newsroom, has to change its way of working.

There has to be more transparency, more attachment to standards of good conduct and more accountability to curb the overweening power of media magnates such as Murdoch and Silvio Berlusconi in Italy, and the equally offensive but largely unreported behaviour of regional media networks elsewhere such as the powerful *Times of India* group. All of this makes a powerful case for a radically new approach to corporate governance in media.[9]

Organizations that occupy the public information space and with enormous power to influence democracy must be kept in check by rules that oblige them to respect the rights of others. Such obligations might usefully include public declarations of attachment to universal principles of human rights including free expression; commitments to transparency and rules to avoid conflicts of interest; and signing up to industry-wide systems of self-regulation and codes of professional conduct.[10]

Having said that, no amount of worthy declarations and commitments to good behaviour will compensate or solve the problem of general economic pressures, shrinking markets and competition for audience across media which have squeezed editorial departments and reduced the scope for public interest journalism.

In these conditions important stories are not being told, corruption goes unreported; the voices of minorities are unheard; racist and xenophobic messages are increasingly in play; privacy is breached; and there is

*New York Review of Books*, 26 July 2011), see: www.nybooks.com/blogs/nyrblog/2011/jul/26/truth-about-murdoch-china (last accessed 27 January 2014).

9 The *Times of India* has controversially struck secret deals with business partners that guarantee them favourable news coverage and many Indian newspapers have been condemned for the practice of 'paid news' when politicians pay for positive editorial coverage, particularly at election time.

10 There are more than 400 codes of conduct worldwide. Two of the most recognized are IFJ, *Code of Principles on the Conduct of Journalism*, 1954, see: http://ethicaljournalism-initiative.org/en/contents/ifj-code-of-principles-on-the-conduct-of-journalism, and Society for Professional Journalists (SPJ), *Code of Ethics*, 1996, see: www.spj.org/ethicscode.asp (both last accessed 27 January 2014).

scant analysis of complex issues that often lead to conflict such as security issues, migration, or religious and cultural differences.

The collapse of investment in editorial work in recent years, particularly in editing, checking, training and investigative journalism, has had a palpable impact – standards have fallen and public confidence has diminished.

The question of how to fill the vacuum created by private media which no longer invest in news journalism raises new and tricky dilemmas, not least that of how to attract new forms of funding for public interest journalism.

In recent years scores of networks of investigative journalists have sprung up around the world. Like many online media initiatives, such as the Pulitzer-prize winning network *Propublica* in the United States, these groups are run by freelance reporters or journalists exiled from the traditional media and are subsidized by foundations and philanthropists. These new players help to keep the flame of public interest journalism alive, but they rarely make money.

Across the globe there is a rush to develop new market models, but so far there is little evidence that good journalism, the sort of ethical, fact-based reporting that democracy needs to function can be made profitable. Even the much-acclaimed online site *Huffington Post*, bought in 2011 by the Internet giant AOL, only makes money because it relies upon the goodwill of more than 2,000 correspondents who give their services for free.

Many people argue that public interest journalism will only survive with new forms of public support and a complete rewriting of the public service model of media. But many traditional journalists argue that extending the use of tax-payers' money to keep journalism afloat will risk more political interference and compromise editorial independence.

It is against this background of economic, technological and political turbulence that a new and focused public debate is now taking place over the challenges facing the future of media and journalism; about media policy and the use of law; about how journalism is organized and paid for; and, most crucially, on the need for a revival of ethical conduct and credible systems of self-regulation, and for new rules of good governance.

## 2 The legal challenge

Even with sound codes and models of good practice to follow there can be no consistent body of ethical or quality journalism unless the principles of media freedom are defined in law, protected by the State and upheld in practice. Creating an ethical environment for journalism is, therefore, a duty of government as well as a responsibility of media practitioners.

The law is a necessary part of journalism insofar as it is needed to protect human rights standards relevant for media freedom. Free expression is guaranteed under Article 19 of the Universal Declaration of Human Rights, Article 19 of the International Covenant on Civil and Political Rights and Article 10 of the European Convention of Human Rights. The right to free expression also forms part of the Charter of Fundamental Rights of the European Union, in Article 11, and in Article 13 of the American Convention on Human Rights of the Organization of American States.

The right to freedom of expression is subject to certain restrictions and may be overridden by decisions taken in the interest of national security, prevention of disorder or crime, or protection of an individual's reputation.

It is these potential limitations that worry journalists, who object to laws that provide unacceptably broad definitions of what constitutes 'security' or 'disorder' or 'reputation', which can limit free speech, increase self-censorship and reduce legitimate scrutiny of public affairs.

Of course, human rights are sometimes conflicting. The need to balance competing rights provides potential traps for law-makers and journalists alike. When media freedom and privacy rights come into conflict, for instance, there is no easy way to make judgments, either in the courtroom or the newsroom, without giving one priority over the other.

Editors are regularly forced to make editorial judgements that often mean making hard choices between competing rights. But to make judgements that are morally and legally defensible, the law has to be narrowly defined and unambiguous and journalists themselves must be informed, competent, and able to work freely.

Of course, this is easier said than done. The lack of a legally acceptable international definition of hate-speech, for instance, makes life difficult for journalism and for law enforcement. Journalists find themselves having to make judgement calls in the midst of professional and political pressures that lead inevitably to allegations of bias or unprofessionalism and police, faced with interpretation of what constitutes incitement to hatred may fall back on more coherent legal instruments, such as laws on public order or breach of the peace.

In most countries, unfortunately, neither the law nor the conditions in which media work give encouragement to journalists to act ethically.

In the case of *access to information* laws, for instance, although there has been a global flourishing of freedom of information over the past decade with dozens of countries enacting rules to guarantee people's right to know, the battle for open government has only been partly won. Often political and official institutions construct bureaucratic obstacles to transparency by demanding heavy fees or reducing the number of staff available to deal with requests, which leads to lengthy delays in providing information.[11]

Equally troubling is the use of powerful *defamation* laws to punish legitimate journalism. These laws are often used to protect public figures from press criticism even though human rights law requires people in public life to be ready to accept more critical examination of their affairs than ordinary people. Politicians in particular have to accept that their words and actions are open to a higher degree of scrutiny from both journalists and the public at large.[12]

In 43 of the 57 participating States of the OSCE, journalists can still go to prison for defamation.[13] The OSCE says that imprisonment for defamation should be abolished without delay and its Representative on Freedom of the Media has recommended that offences against 'honour and dignity' be decriminalized and instead dealt with in civil law courts. As long as punitive defamation laws remain in place they will intimidate journalists and lead to self-censorship.[14]

Similar problems exist with *insult laws.* For journalists, *blasphemy* laws are particularly difficult to navigate, especially when they provide special protection for a particular religion, but fail to extend the same immunity to other beliefs. Blasphemy laws exist in many democratic countries where, even if application of the law is rare, and convictions rarer still, there is often still a strong link between religion and the State and the law only protects one religion.

[11] BBC World Service Documentaries, *The Right to Know*, 16 August 2008, see www.bbc.co.uk/worldservice/documentaries/2008/08/080807_right_to_know1.shtml (last accessed on 27 January 2014).

[12] See ECtHR, *Lingens* v. *Austria* (Appl. No. 9815/82), Judgment of 8 July 1986.

[13] The thirteen participating States in the OSCE region which, as per 11 July 2011, had fully decriminalized defamation are Armenia, Bosnia and Herzegovina, Cyprus, Estonia, Georgia, Kyrgyzstan, Moldova, Romania, Ireland, the UK, Ukraine, Montenegro and the USA.

[14] See OSCE Representative on Freedom of the Media, *Regular Report to the Permanent Council of the OSCE*, Doc. No. FOM.GAL/5/10/Rev.1, 16 December 2010.

But perhaps the most difficult tasks facing journalists come when they have to balance competing rights such as the people's right to know and the individual's right to *privacy.* Human rights law determines that every human being has a right to respect for private life but in countries where democratic traditions are weak, legitimate journalistic invasion of privacy is constrained by law.[15]

Journalists understand very well the need for privacy, but they draw the line at confidentiality being used to limit accountability or to draw a curtain around hypocrisy and misconduct in public life. However, too rigorous application of privacy rules often makes it impossible for media to publish anything touching on fundamental aspects of a person's private life such as their sexual behaviour or medical conditions, even where publication is in the public interest.

Journalists do well to have a convincing public interest defence when they delve into other peoples' lives. The public does not mind much when media expose the indiscretions of political or show business celebrities; after all, these people hunger for the glare of publicity when it suits them, but if media take liberties with the privacy of ordinary people they can expect the whirlwind of public outrage.

The most perfect illustration of how reckless and intrusive journalism can provoke public anger is the illegal phone hacking by News Corporation journalists in the United Kingdom, leading to the closure of one of Europe's best-selling newspapers, *News of the World.*

In 2011 a story of scandalous behaviour by journalists and news executives inside News Corporation that had simmered for almost a decade boiled over with public admissions that journalists had illegally hacked telephones, including that of a murdered teenager, and revelations of bribery of police, cover-up of malpractice at the highest level, hush-money and pay-offs to victims, and systematic lying to regulators and parliamentarians.

This predatory culture of intrusion caused widespread revulsion and an unprecedented public backlash. The government announced an investigation into media conduct and, for the first time in half a century, the possibility of legal regulation of the press was thrust on to the policy agenda in the United Kingdom.

In the event the publication of the *Leveson Report* into press ethics, which roundly condemned media owners and proposed a system

[15] A key global organization campaigning for privacy is Privacy International, see www.privacyinternational.org (last accessed 27 January 2014).

of independent legal regulation, did not resolve the question on how to regulate the press.[16]

Government proposals backed by all leading parties which proposed the creation of a Royal Charter for the press – an ancient mechanism for granting legal status – were strongly opposed by most of the British press which announced plans in 2014 to launch a new self-regulation system, but without any statutory underpinning.[17] Despite the mischief at the *News of the World* and elsewhere in the tabloid press, many people, and not just those inside journalism, see dangers in media policy being driven by anger over cases like this. Of course, public outrage is legitimate when the ethics of journalism are abandoned in pursuit of money and political influence, and when the press exercises power without responsibility, but it is no basis for curtailing media freedom.

Certainly, there is something to be said for curbing the power of media oligarchies – of which News Corporation is a prime example – but that needs to be done in the name of pluralism, freedom and respect for privacy.

The News International case, disgraceful though it is, should not be used as an excuse to impose heavy media regulation which would inhibit the capacity of investigative journalism.

Importantly, the case highlights the challenge facing editors and journalists. They have to recognize that public anger will not be quelled by glib assurances of declarations of a return to ethical values. Unless media begin to demonstrate commitment to respect people's rights they cannot hope to win public support for notions of self-regulation.

Journalists need to demonstrate in particular more attachment to privacy rights. They must show commitment to transparency and fairness in their methods. They need to put in place new forms of (self-) regulation that will restore public confidence.

This process was started in 2012 with the launch of the Ethical Journalism Network which brings together more than twenty-five regional and international media professional groups working across all platforms of media. This group aims to promote a fresh debate inside journalism on how to confront the challenges not just of privacy but about building a more responsible structure for public information and media that will restore public trust and strengthen the craft of journalism.

[16] *Leveson Report*; see www.levesoninquiry.org.uk (last accessed 28 January 2014).

[17] See the Independent Press Standards Organisation: www.ipso.co.uk (last accessed 28 January 2014).

When media do this it will encourage States to exempt the media for acts of journalism which might otherwise be controversial, but which seen in an ethical spotlight can be justified as legitimate reporting. The key commitment must be not to intrude into anybody's private life unless there is an overriding consideration for the public interest.

This should also be the benchmark for laws regarding privacy on the Internet, and particularly involving people's rights to control the information being collected about them by companies such as Google and social networks like Facebook, YouTube and Twitter. The European Union, for instance, plans to put sweeping new rules in place that will force companies to obtain permission from individuals about the use of their personal data or face fines if they refuse to delete that data at the consumer's request.[18]

Such a law may limit the degree of commercial exploitation of personal information by corporations and will certainly challenge the extensive secrecy which surrounds how these companies work, but even so, journalists worry that new rules like this may be used to restrict reporters gathering personal information for legitimate journalism.

The former European Commissioner for Justice, Fundamental Rights and Citizenship, Viviane Reding, says that strengthening citizen's rights 'to be forgotten' and to have personal data deleted by social networks will not take precedence over freedom of the media, but it is not clear how protections for journalists will be put in place.[19]

Another area where journalists routinely come up against the law is the *protection of sources*. Although around 100 countries, in one way or another, recognize in law the right of journalists to protect people who provide them with information, there is increasing pressure on reporters to reveal the names of whistle-blowers and confidential sources. During the past ten years the European Federation of Journalists has identified numerous instances of where there have been overt and covert attempts to obtain information on journalists' sources of information and in 2012 they launched a specific campaign to highlight these problems.[20]

[18] European Commission, Reform of Data Protection Legislation, see http:/ec.europa.eu/justice/data-protection (last accessed on 28 January 2014).

[19] K. J. O'Brien, 'Europe weighs tough law on online privacy', *International New York Times* (former *Herald Tribune*), 24 January 2012. The EC proposal can be viewed at http:/ec.europa.eu/justice/data-protection (last accessed 28 January 2014).

[20] See http://europe.ifj.org/en/pages/protection-of-sources (last accessed on 28 January 2014).

Governments in the United Kingdom, Germany, Italy, the Netherlands and Denmark, for instance, have been among those condemned in recent years for a range of offences, including tapping the telephones of journalists, planting spies in newsrooms, and prosecuting editors and reporters to gather information about journalists, their work and their sources.

Since the European Court of Human Rights' groundbreaking verdict of 1996 in the *Goodwin* case,[21] when it ruled that protection of sources was a right guaranteed in European human rights law, the Court has repeatedly reaffirmed the importance of this right.[22] In a memorable phrase, the Court said that an order to disclose a source had a 'potentially chilling effect' on the exercise of press freedom and continued: 'Without such protection sources may be deterred from assisting the press in informing the public on matters of public interest'.[23]

The Court's recognition of this right is critical, but generally judges do not give reporters an absolute right to protect their sources and in recent years there have been numerous cases, some in the name of counter-terrorism, where the authorities have applied pressure, both open and covert, to obtain the names of those who gave confidential material to journalists. In 2006, journalists protested over actions by the authorities in Germany and the United States to tap telephones and to send spies into newsrooms to obtain information on the contacts of journalists.[24]

Many journalists recognize the need in certain circumstances for exceptions to the principle of protection of sources, but they argue these should be applied in strictly controlled circumstances. In Belgium, for instance, the law provides that only a judge can decide to ask a journalist to disclose a source and then only when there is a serious threat to the physical integrity of the source; when the information sought is crucial to prevent any physical harm to people; and when the information cannot be obtained by other means. This set of guidelines may be as good as it gets for source protection, and given that these benchmarks are not

[21] ECtHR, *Goodwin* v. *the United Kingdom* (Appl. No. 17488/90), Judgment of 27 March 1996.

[22] ECtHR, *Sanoma Uitgevers* v. *the Netherlands* (Appl. No. 38224/03), Judgment (Grand Chamber) of 14 September 2010 and ECtHR, *Telegraaf Media Nederland and Others* v. *the Netherlands* (Appl. No. 39315/06), Judgment of 22 November 2012.

[23] *Goodwin*, para. 39.

[24] Scoop Media, 'Phone taps in US and newsroom spying in Germany', 22 May 2006, see: www.scoop.co.nz/stories/WO0605/S00428.htm (last accessed 28 January 2014).

properly recognized in most countries, Belgium's legislation may provide inspiration for efforts to strengthen legal protection in other countries.[25]

The use of law to ban *hate speech* provides another minefield of legal threats to unwary reporters and editors. These laws arise from the painful evidence of how propaganda can be used to incite hatred and violence, most recently twenty years ago in the genocide and ethnic cleansing in Rwanda and during the recent Balkan wars.

Although hate speech laws are a legitimate antidote to racism, incitement to hostility, discrimination or violence, in some countries these laws go beyond protection from objective harm and prohibit publication of any statements which are perceived as offensive. In particular, these can be laws which protect the State, its institutions and its leading representatives from insult or defamation or other forms of hatred. The prevalence of these laws led to an international campaign calling for their repeal.[26]

Not surprisingly, journalists say that general and vague definitions of hatred in the law stifles legitimate, if dissenting, opinion and opens the door to prosecutions over content that does not pose a serious threat to people but is regarded as offensive.

Additionally, many journalists oppose the use of '*denial laws*' to limit speech arguing that those who deny the Holocaust, for instance, should be exposed to public ridicule rather than being imprisoned, as the history of this era is too well documented for it to be seriously questioned. Unfortunately these laws tend to proliferate. In January 2012 a law prohibiting denial of genocide, including the 1915 Armenian genocide, was adopted in France, but was later overturned by the country's constitutional court.[27]

Meanwhile, in Turkey journalists and writers languish in jail or face prosecution for questioning of the country's official version of the Armenian story. Even worse, the journalist Hrant Dink who referred to the

[25] Belgian Act of 7 April 2005 on the protection of journalistic sources, Official Journal of 27 April 2005; D. Voorhoof, 'Belgium: Law on the Protection of Journalistic Sources May Inspire Other Countries', University of Ghent, version 2 (2008), see: www.psw.ugent.be/Cmsglobal/uploads/publications/dv/05recente_publicaties/Belgium.Lawsources.version2008.pdf (last accessed 28 January 2014).

[26] World Press Freedom Committee, Campaign against Insult Laws, see www.wpfc.org/CampaignAgainstInsultLaws.html (last accessed 28 January 2014).

[27] Constitutional Council, Decision No. 2012–647 DC of 28 February 2012 on the Loi visant à réprimer la contestation de l'existence des génocides reconnus par la loi. For a news report, see CNN Wire Staff, 'French court overturns Armenian genocide denial law', CNN, 28 February 2012, at http://edition.cnn.com/2012/02/28/world/europe/france-armenia-genocide/index.html (last accessed 28 January 2014).

Armenian genocide in his writings was convicted in 2005 and then murdered two years later by nationalist extremists.[28]

The process of legally ring-fencing official versions of history is both ludicrous and dangerous, raising the prospect of different States pursuing their own version of history by demanding that writers, journalists and all citizens keep to a script that is approved by the government. It opens the way to subjugating freedom of expression to nationalist agendas all over the world.

## 3 The ethical challenge

Given the enormous opportunities for bare-knuckle courtroom battles between media and the law it is hardly surprising that most journalists yearn for media policy which supports the voluntary principle for rules on ethical conduct and good governance.

However, to give their argument more weight, journalists must do more to put their own house in order. They need to isolate and expose those who betray the principles and standards of their trade and they need to regulate their work in a credible manner.

Ethical journalism, unlike media freedom, does not require a legal framework – although journalists who practise it do need the law to guarantee their rights to work freely.

To build credibility, journalism must be responsible and adhere to codes of conduct and norms of ethical behaviour. More than 30 years ago the landmark Seán MacBride Report for UNESCO in 1980 made this point when it laid emphasis on 'professional integrity and standards' in its recommendations for better international communications. The report concluded that:

> For the journalist, freedom and responsibility are indivisible. Freedom without responsibility invites distortion and other abuses. But in the absence of freedom there can be no exercise of responsibility. . .The adoption of codes of ethics at national and, in some cases, at the regional level is desirable, provided that such codes are prepared and adopted by the profession itself – without governmental interference.[29]

[28] ECtHR, *Dink* v. *Turkey* (Appl. Nos. 2668/07, 6102/08, 30079/08, 7072/09 and 7124/09), Judgment of 14 September 2010.

[29] Seán MacBride *et al.*, *Many Voices One World: Towards a New More Just and More Efficient World Information and Communication Order* (Paris: UNESCO, 1980), Recommendations, Part III, Introduction and para. 43.

Put grandly, ethical journalism is rooted in moral values and serves the public's right to know; it favours truth and resists pressure to distort reality whether it comes from media owners, business interests or political forces.

Put simply, the ethical newsroom works around principles of truth-telling, independence, accountability and respect for the audience. These are standards that define the essential elements of what we might call journalism as a public good; they raise awareness of what is acceptable and unacceptable, and remind us of moral responsibilities. Good journalism reinforces attachment to acceptable standards of behaviour and, in this sense, is an ally of everyone striving for democracy and human rights.

Ethical journalism is more often than not spelled out in a *code of conduct* which sets out the values and obligations of people working in a media enterprise. Sometimes the code will form part of a journalist's contract of employment. More often, it will be the mission statement of the media organization itself.

Most codes are aspirational and a statement of commitment from journalists to be responsible and accountable. In this way they provide protection for media owners and journalists from criticism and legal action. There are more than 400 codes of one form or another in existence, most of which reflect a consistent set of common values and principles of journalism.[30]

Codes are the guarantor of value-based journalism and allegiance to a code is a benchmark for quality. They are also an important way of defining who is and who is not a journalist. Today that distinction is important not least because many new players in the world of information do not feel bound by any framework of values but sometimes demand the same rights as media professionals.

Many codes are developed to cover special areas of reporting – the rights of children, for instance, or health reporting, or environmental issues. Sometimes they arise when journalists and media find themselves under criticism, as was the case when Italian publishers and journalists issued an industry code in 2008 to promote ethical reporting of refugee and

[30] The most extensive collection of available codes of conduct has been assembled by Media Accountability Systems and can be found at www.rjionline.org/codes-ethics. A list of 50 codes in 30 European countries has been assembled by Ethicnet at http://ethicnet.uta.fi. There is also a list developed in conjunction with the IFJ by the MediaWise Trust, www.mediawise.org.uk/codes-of-conduct/codes (all last accessed 28 January 2014).

immigration issues. This initiative followed protests by the United Nations High Commissioner for Refugees over racist media coverage of a multiple murder. The code sets out ethical guidelines and is part of a programme that includes awareness raising, training and the creation of an independent observatory monitoring media coverage of discrimination.[31]

However, a code is only a starting point. Detailed guidelines and training are also needed to illustrate how ethical journalism works in practice. In this way good journalists are able, for example, to avoid hate speech, sexual stereotyping, or discrimination in reporting on minorities, and they have standards to follow when identifying and resolving conflicts of interest.

The codes and guidelines of well-established media which can be found on their web-sites – such as the BBC, or the Associated Press, for example – are often detailed and require regular monitoring and that often obliges media to establish elaborate internal systems to monitor editorial performance. This is one of the key elements in creating a culture of effective and credible self-regulation.

*Self-regulation* is a solemn promise by quality-conscious journalists and media to correct their mistakes and to make themselves accountable. But for this promise to have meaning there must be two conditions: journalists and media have to behave ethically, and governments should not interfere in journalism or use legal means to monitor and control media.

However, defining where to draw the legal line in the regulation of the expanding public information space, including journalism, has become increasingly urgent as countries seek their own remedies for what they perceive to be the dangers posed by the information chaos of the Internet.

Some countries, such as South Africa and Hungary have recently passed controversial laws that seek to restrain irresponsible speech and in Britain there is an ongoing forensic examination of the British press by the Leveson Inquiry, launched in the wake of the phone-hacking scandal.[32]

[31] The Code of Conduct is a protocol to the Italian Charter of Duties of Journalists (*La Carta dei Doveri del Giornalista*).

[32] A useful international comparative analysis of hate speech in this area was produced out of South Africa, S. Fredman *et al.*, 'Comparative Hate Speech Law: Memorandum', Pro Bono Publico, University of Oxford (2012), see: http://denning.law.ox.ac.uk/news/events_files/2012_-_LRC_Hate_Speech_Memorandum.pdf (last accessed 28 January 2014).

Increasingly, media professionals recognize the need for new mechanisms that will give bite to the principle of self-regulation. Some leading media figures are now calling for co-regulation, whereby some legal authority is provided for a self-regulator to carry out investigations and to enforce judgments.[33]

Such narrowly defined and limited legal powers for regulators could well be enough to bring serial offenders in media to heel, and will certainly raise the credibility of self-rule in journalism in the eyes of the public. This approach may also help solve a wider problem of setting standards at a time when digital convergence has rendered traditional forms of content control increasingly obsolete.

Almost every country operates a dual system of regulation of media content, one covering broadcasting (almost always statutory) and another for the press which may be statutory but which may also involve a voluntary process including, for instance, press councils.

However, given that journalism in the integrated newsroom is disseminated, often simultaneously, on different platforms, maintaining different systems of control over the same content is outmoded if not absurd. When the press and broadcasting operated in different worlds it made sense, but today newspapers tell their stories in video packages and online services as well as in print, and broadcasters' networks are major players in providing online news.

So which is the route to follow – the straight and narrow statutory path or the more winding voluntary road? Most journalists and editors remain convinced that the law should keep out of the newsroom. The principle of self-rule is, they argue, a bulwark against the threat of political interference in editorial independence. But to be convincing, both to insiders and the outside world, voluntary principles of self-regulation need to operate through a system that will promote standards, support pluralism and, may even need to be strengthened with some legal underpinning. This could lead to a framework which could usefully extend self-rule in journalism into areas where in the past legal controls have prevailed such as broadcasting.

Of course, there are good arguments – including from people inside journalism – for keeping statutory regulation that works (such as at the BBC, for instance) or for encouraging voluntary press council systems to absorb responsibility for monitoring all journalistic works including

[33] Including UK editors who have given evidence to the *Leveson Report*, see: www.leveson-inquiry.org.uk

online and broadcasting content (such as in Norway),[34] but these are exceptions. In most countries where democratic structures are weak, the evidence of scores of press freedom advocacy groups over the years is that use of law alone inevitably leads to governmental interference, and weakens efforts to build respect for voluntary systems.

In order to resolve this dilemma we need to rework notions of media accountability, inviting a new vision of media regulation, one which goes beyond bureaucratic frameworks for policing journalism, and which encourages self-regulation as a positive force for setting high standards and defending them.

There may be a need for new architecture or radical alteration of existing structures. Already some new models are emerging. In Indonesia, for instance, the press council plays a role in monitoring media performance, raises awareness about the responsible use of information, and steers disputes over content into forms of mediation rather than courtroom confrontation.[35]

Adapting existing press councils or State media structures will help, but at the same time, we should not disregard the importance of less complex forms of ethical standard-setting through peer-review, the use of readers' editors or ombudsmen, or the building of an ethical culture through professional journals and the systematic monitoring and reporting on media by non-governmental organizations and human rights bodies.

One key question is that of funding. Who pays for media accountability? In some countries, such as Germany and Sweden, taxpayers do pay some of the costs, but the media also pay their share. Public subsidies wherever they are made usually cover the 'public interest' activities of a press council. In Germany, for instance, this includes the administrative costs of handling complaints from readers. Any budgetary support from the State for self-regulation must be provided according to principles which ensure transparency and accountability, and which provide safeguards against governmental or political interference.[36]

[34] The Norwegian Press Association, see www.presseforbundet.no (last accessed 28 January 2014).

[35] See further http://gfmd.info/images/uploads/Independent_Press_Council_of_Indonesia.pdf (last accessed 28 January 2014).

[36] A useful international survey of press councils and how they work and are financed was published in 2012 (L. Fielden, 'Comparing the Press: A Comparative Study of International Press Councils', Reuters Institute for Journalism, University of Oxford (2012)); see: https://reutersinstitute.politics.ox.ac.uk/fileadmin/documents/Publications/Working_Papers/Regulating_the_Press.pdf (last accessed 28 January 2014).

Media accountability, in whatever form it comes, must balance the rights of the individual and the community and the rights of journalists and the press. But it must not be self-serving. It is vital that press or media councils act on behalf of the public and the profession and are not perceived to be only in place to shield media owners from criticism or scrutiny. One of the primary roles of new or reformed institutions to regulate media content will be to apply rules of corporate governance to media ensuring, for instance, transparency on political affiliation and ownership.

In short, a media accountability system[37] needs to:

- mediate complaints from the public in a transparent service, free of charge, and provide remedies for unethical conduct by journalists;
- help build trust between journalists and the public to ensure that the media can resist political and economic pressure;
- protect journalistic independence and media freedom in society;
- ensure the right of the public to be informed;
- support social and professional conditions that will enable journalists to serve their public better;
- foster better understanding within society at all levels about the role played by independent journalism in democratic life; and
- support journalists in their work and encourage professional solidarity.

This is not a manifesto for policing. It is about mediation, advocacy and education and seeking opportunities for fresh dialogue within society about the media and the need to support ethical journalism.

## 4 Conclusions: towards a coalition for ethical journalism

In this chapter I argue that journalism itself is a necessary part of the means by which power is held to account, but on its own, even with the best architecture for self-regulation, it is not enough.

The fabric of accountability requires a healthy policy environment, an independent judiciary and trustworthy law-makers as well as statutory watchdogs, public auditors to ensure financial transparency, ombudsmen, independent privacy authorities, and active and independent civil

[37] See C. J. Bertrand (ed.), *An Arsenal for Democracy: Media Accountability Systems* (Cresskill, NJ: Hampton Press, 2003) and *Media Ethics & Accountability Systems* (New Brunswick, NJ and London: Transaction, 2000).

society institutions all play a role in making society transparent and sensitive to rights.

In particular, law is important in helping to ensure a proper balancing of individual rights and the public interest and in creating legal safeguards for journalism. With this in mind a coherent national media policy should:

- provide constitutional support for freedom of expression with narrowly defined limits reflected in law;
- review legislation affecting the media and journalism and repeal outdated and unused statutes that have the potential to intimidate, silence or otherwise stifle legitimate expression in the public interest;
- enact effective and useful rules on access to information from public bodies with limited and narrowly defined exceptions;
- decriminalize defamation and avoid punitive fines in civil cases;
- review funding and technical assistance programmes for media to support pluralism and diversity and structures for self-regulation but do so without compromising editorial independence; and
- strengthen and update systems of media accountability and reinforce principles of self-regulation in an integrated and open media environment.

Above all, media policy at all levels needs to be defined according to principles of pluralism and independence which prohibit all forms of political interference in journalism and which also encourage social dialogues and provide a minimum level of social protection to eliminate corrupt and precarious employment.

Within this framework, media professionals need to play their part. One recent actor is the Ethical Journalism Network (EJN), a programme for responsibility and transparency in media that claims to be a unifying voice of journalists, editors and publishers and a forum for open debate on the future of media. The intention is to rekindle the confidence of citizens in the positive force of independent journalism.[38]

This is the latest effort in a growing movement to revive the ethical spirit and values in journalism. In 2006 the International Federation of Journalists launched the Ethical Journalism Initiative, a campaign to promote practical training in ethical journalism and to encourage debate about the future of journalism.[39]

[38] See www.ethicaljournalismnetwork.org (last accessed 29 January 2014). [39] *Ibid.*

The coalition calls for a wholesale review of how journalism works to strengthen principles of transparency, good governance and respect for the audience. It was formally launched in June 2012 at a meeting held in UNESCO and outlined a vision guided by the following principles:

1 That ethical journalism, investigative reporting and media pluralism are essential for the function of democracy;
2 That connectedness and openness are an essential remedy to unreliable sources of information;
3 That the digital revolution provides a unique and historic opportunity to secure the information rights of all citizens.

The coalition reinvigorates the notion of journalism as a public good and outlines three new elements in the debate about ethics:

Firstly, it seeks commitment to ethical conduct from the top to the bottom of media. By emphasizing promotion of corporate social responsibility it throws down a challenge to media owners and managers. Ethics in the newsroom are important, and have been the focus of media development work for many years, but now the spotlight needs to be turned equally fiercely on the boardroom.

Second, it recognizes how the media world has changed. By reaching out to people who work in journalism across all platforms, it opens up opportunities for professional solidarity in a notoriously divided industry. It also provides an opportunity for traditional media and new players to work together in defining how to promote responsibility in the use of information.

Third, it provides a new vision of self-regulation, or co-regulation, including some limited legal underpinning. It revives the notion of self-rule in media as a positive and dynamic feature of journalism through advocacy, education and conflict resolution. As such, it is a blueprint for setting standards in tune with the age which, in the right hands, can be used to underpin democracy and strengthen humanitarian values in society.[40]

## Literature

Bertrand, C. J. *Media Ethics & Accountability Systems* (New Brunswick, NJ and London: Transaction, 2000).

[40] See: http://ethicaljournalismnetwork.org/en/contents/founding-text (last accessed 29 January 2014).

(ed.), *An Arsenal for Democracy: Media Accountability Systems* (Cresskill, NJ: Hampton Press, 2003).

Council of Europe Commissioner for Human Rights, *Human Rights and a Changing Media Landscape* (Strasbourg: Council of Europe, 2011).

Fielden, L. *Comparing the Press: A Comparative Study of International Press Councils* (Reuters Institute for Journalism, University of Oxford, 2012).

Fredman, S. *Comparative Hate Speech Law: Memorandum* (Pro Bono Publico, University of Oxford, 2012).

MacBride, S. *et al. Many Voices One World: Towards a new more just and more efficient world information and communication order* (Paris: UNESCO, 1980).

Voorhoof, D. 'Belgium: law on the protection of journalistic sources may inspire other countries', University of Ghent, version 2 (2008).

Yanagizawa-Drott, D. *Propaganda and Conflict: Theory and Evidence from the Rwandan Genocide* (Cambridge, MA: Harvard University Press, 2012).

## Newspaper articles

Greenslade, R. 'How self-censorship works in the empire of Rupert Murdoch', *Guardian*, 4 March 2008.

Kurtz, H. 'News Corp. defends 1$ million donation to Republican Governors Association', *Washington Post*, 18 August 2010.

Mirsky, J. 'Murdoch's Chinese adventure', *New York Review of Books*, 26 July 2011.

O'Brien, K. J. 'Europe weighs tough law on online privacy', *International New York Times* [former *Herald Tribune*], 24 January 2012.

## ECtHR case law

*Dink* v. *Turkey* (Appl. Nos. 2668/07, 6102/08, 30079/08, 7072/09 and 7124/09), Judgment of 14 September 2010.

*Goodwin* v. *the United Kingdom* (Appl. No. 17488/90), Judgment of 27 March 1996.

*Lingens* v. *Austria* (Appl. No. 9815/82), Judgment of 8 July 1986.

*Sanoma Uitgevers* v. *the Netherlands* (Appl. No. 38224/03), Judgment (Grand Chamber) of 14 September 2010.

*Telegraaf Media Nederland and Others* v. *the Netherlands* (Appl. No. 39315/06), Judgment of 22 November 2012.

12

# Uprooting 'defamation of religions' and planting a new approach to freedom of expression at the United Nations

SEJAL PARMAR

## 1 Introduction

There is little doubt that the most controversial issue concerning freedom of expression at the United Nations (UN) Charter-based human rights bodies over the past decade has been that of 'defamation of religions'. From 1999 to 2010, resolutions of UN bodies – specifically the General Assembly, the Human Rights Council and its predecessor, the Commission on Human Rights – on 'combating defamation of religions' preoccupied and polarised the international community. Their proponents, the Organisation of Islamic Cooperation (OIC), argued that such resolutions served to protect religious minorities from discriminatory acts; this was disputed by European States, the United States and many human rights NGOs who argued that these resolutions instead undermined international human rights law on freedom of expression as well as global efforts to combat discrimination against religious minorities.[1] Outside the UN, meanwhile, the resolutions provoked a growing tide of criticisms from a disparate community of human rights NGOs and a burgeoning commentary in academic journals.[2] In March 2011, there came a remarkable breakthrough in this seemingly intractable debate at the 16th session of

[1] The Organisation for Islamic Cooperation was known as the Organisation of Islamic Conference until its name was changed on 28 June 2011 at the 38th session of the Council of Foreign Ministers of the Organization of the Islamic Conference in Astana, Kazakhstan.

[2] M. Grinberg, 'Defamation of Religions, v Freedom of Expression: Finding the Balance in a Democratic Society', *Sri Lanka Journal of International Law* 18 (2006), 197–222; J. Rivers, 'Guest Editorial: The Question of Freedom of Religion or Belief and Defamation', *Religion and Human Rights* 2 (2007), 113–8; J. Temperman, 'Blasphemy, Defamation of Religions and Human Rights Law', *Netherlands Quarterly of Human Rights* 26 (2008), 527–45; J. Cerone, 'Inappropriate Renderings: The Danger of Reductionist Resolutions', *Brooklyn Journal of International Law* 33 (2008), 357–78; R. J. Dobras, 'Is the United Nations

the Human Rights Council: after several years of declining support for the resolutions, the OIC decided not to present a Resolution on combating defamation of religions. Instead the OIC proposed a Resolution on 'combating intolerance, negative stereotyping and stigmatisation of, and discrimination, incitement to violence, and violence against persons based on religion or belief'. This Resolution was subsequently adopted by members of the Human Rights Council on the basis of consensus (i.e. without a vote). Resolution 16/18 of the Human Rights Council embodied a de facto rejection of the concept of defamation of religions. It has since been consolidated through similar Resolutions adopted by the Human Rights Council in subsequent years – through resolution 19/25 of 23 March 2012 and Resolution 22/31 of 22 March 2013 – and the Third Committee of the General Assembly – through Resolution 66/167 of 19 December 2011 and Resolution 67/178 of 20 December 2012. The Human Rights Committee's General Comment No. 34 on Article 19 of the International Covenant on Civil and Political Rights (ICCPR), which was finalised in July 2011, embedded the rejection of defamation of religions by stating 'prohibitions of displays of lack of respect for a religion or other belief system, including blasphemy laws, are incompatible with the Covenant'.[3] The Rabat Plan of Action, which was adopted by experts in October 2012 following a series of

Endorsing Human Rights Violations? An Analysis of the United Nations' Combating Defamation of Religions, Resolutions and Pakistan's Blasphemy Laws', *Georgia Journal of International and Comparative Law* 37 (2009), 339–80; J. Foster, 'Prophets, Cartoons, and Legal Norms: Rethinking the United Nations Defamation of Religion Provisions', *Journal of Catholic Legal Studies* 49 (2009), 19–57; L. B. Graham, 'Defamation of Religions: the End of Pluralism', *Emory International Law Review* 23 (2009), 69–84; S. Parmar, 'The Challenge of 'Defamation of Religions to Freedom of Expression and the International Human Rights System', *European Human Rights Law Review* 3 (2009), 353–75; L. Langer, 'The Rise (and Fall?) of Defamation of Religions, *Yale Journal of International Law* 35 (2010), 257–63; N. McLaughlin, 'Spectrum of Defamation of Laws and the Possibility of a Universal International Standard', *Loyola of Los Angeles International and Comparative Law Review*, 32 (2010) 395–426; T. McGonagle, *Minority Rights, Freedom of Expression and of the Media: Dynamics and Dilemmas* (Antwerp: Intersentia, 2011), 363–75; R. A. Kahn, 'A Margin of Appreciation for Muslims? Viewing the Defamation of Religions Debate through *Otto-Preminger v Austria*', *Charleston Law Review* 5 (2011), 401–54; R. C. Blitt, 'The Bottom up Journey of "Defamation of Religion" from Muslim States to the United Nations: A Case Study of the Migration of Anti-Constitutional Ideas', in *Special Issue on Human Rights: New Possibilities/New Problems, Studies in Law, Politics and Society* 36 (2011), 121–211; B. G. Scharffs, 'International Law and the Defamation of Religion Conundrum', *Review of Faith and International Affairs* 11 (2013), 66–75.

[3] Human Rights Committee (HRC), General Comment No. 34, UN Doc. CCPR/C/GC/34, 11 September 2011, para. 48. For commentary on the General Comment, see Chapter 2 of this book and M. O'Flaherty, 'Freedom of Expression: Article 19 of the International

workshops organised by the Office of the High Commissioner for Human Rights (OHCHR) later lent express support to Resolution 16/18 and General Comment No. 34 by fleshing out the implications of the prohibition of incitement to national, racial, or religious hatred under international law.[4]

This chapter tells the story of what appears to be the decline of 'defamation of religions' as a legal concept and the rise of a 'new approach' to the protection of freedom of expression in its complex interaction with the protection of the right to equality and freedom of religion or belief. UN resolutions on defamation of religions, though not legally binding and essentially recommendatory in nature, were highly significant from an international human rights law perspective. They had gathered clear normative value, even if they could not be taken to represent *opinio juris* on the issue[5] and they had embedded a discourse that was strongly contested by many authorities as being deeply at odds with the protection of the right to freedom of expression in international human rights law. This chapter highlights the key characteristics of the resolutions on defamation of religions (section 2). It then reviews the arguments put forward in favour of and against such resolutions (section 3) before analysing the resolutions of the Human Rights Council and General Assembly on combating intolerance, negative stereotyping, stigmatisation, discrimination, incitement to violence and violence on religious grounds as evidence of a 'new approach' to freedom of expression at the UN (section 4). The chapter finally assesses the significance of this new approach, in terms of its impact upon other processes within and outside the framework of the UN human rights system (section 5).

## 2 The 'defamation of religions' Resolutions

The Commission on Human Rights was the first UN human rights body to adopt a resolution on the subject of defamation of religions in 1999.[6]

Covenant on Civil and Political Rights and the Human Rights Committee's General Comment No 34', *Human Rights Law Review* 12(4) (2012), 627–54.

4 *Rabat Plan of Action on the Prohibition of Advocacy of National, Racial or Religious Hatred that Constitutes Incitement to Discrimination, Hostility or Violence*, Appendix, Annual Report of the United Nations High Commissioner for Human Rights, UN Doc. A/HRC/22/17/Add.4, 11 January 2013, paras. 17, 13 and 41.

5 See A. Clapham, *Human Rights Obligations of Non-State Actors* (Oxford University Press, 2006), 104.

6 Commission on Human Rights (CHR), Resolution 1999/82, 30 April 1999.

Resolutions on defamation of religions were adopted by the Commission on Human Rights and afterwards by its successor, the Human Rights Council, under the agenda item on 'racism, discrimination, xenophobia and related intolerance' every year until 2011, except in 2006, the year when the Council was established. The General Assembly followed the example of the Human Rights Council, adopting similar resolutions on defamation of religions from 2005 to 2011.[7] This section examines the content of these resolutions on defamation of religions by distinguishing several features that characterised them and suggesting what these characteristics reveal about their underpinning rationales. This section focuses more on the resolutions adopted by the Human Rights Council than on those of the General Assembly mainly because, as the UN's principal human rights organ, the Council has been the venue of the most fraught and high-profile tussles, involving groups of States and NGOs, concerning the resolutions in recent years.

### 2.1 *Attributes and rationales*

The *first* and most obvious feature of the series of resolutions is their centrepiece concept.[8] At first sight, defamation of religions looks as if it is 'an actionable legal concept'.[9] Yet its meaning is never clearly defined in any of the resolutions.[10] Although the content of the concept may be drawn from national laws on the same subject, its meaning in the resolutions should be adduced from the resolutions themselves.[11] The series of resolutions presented defamation of religions as a matter in need of the attention of the international community, as inconsistent with the

[7] General Assembly (GA), Resolution 60/150, 16 December 2005, Resolution 61/164, 19 December 2006, Resolution 61/154, 18 December 2007 and Resolution 63/170, 18 December 2008.

[8] The OIC proposed a resolution on 'vilification' rather than 'defamation religions' at the 65th session of the General Assembly in November 2010. See ARTICLE 19 and the Cairo Institute for Human Rights Studies, 'UN General Assembly: UN Member States Should Vote Against Resolution on Vilification of Religions', Statement, 19 November 2010.

[9] Rivers, 'Question of Freedom of Religion', 115.

[10] However, this lack of definition of the concept of defamation of religions is also a feature of States' domestic laws. See *Report of the High Commissioner for Human Rights on the Implementation of Human Rights Council Resolution 7/19 entitled 'Combating Defamation of Religion'*, UN Doc. A/HRC/97, September 2008, para. 58.

[11] The term does not appear in substantive text of the resolution until the third Commission on Human Rights in 2001; see CHR, Resolution 2001/4: Combating Defamation of Religions, 18 April 2001.

protection of human rights, and as incompatible with broader UN 'objectives of a truly globalized world and the promotion and maintenance of international peace and security'.[12] 'Defamation of religions' appeared as a term of art to infer a distinct phenomenon that is a 'serious affront to human dignity leading to a restriction on the freedom of religion of their adherents and incitement to religious hatred and violence'.[13] The term gathered significance through the negative consequences to which it apparently gives rise, such as: 'social disharmony and ... violations of human rights';[14] 'negative' and 'deliberate stereotyping of religions';[15] 'instances of intolerance, discrimination; and acts of violence against followers of certain faiths occurring in many parts of the world' and 'the negative projection of certain religions in the media and the introduction and enforcement of laws and administrative measures that specifically discriminate against and target persons with certain ethnic and religious backgrounds'.[16] The seriousness of defamation of religions as a human rights issue was further conveyed through the actions prescribed by the resolutions, notably 'adequate protection against acts of hatred, discrimination, intimidation and coercion resulting from defamation of religions'.[17]

While it is true that laws on defamation of religions, blasphemy or religious insult exist at the national level, the fact that UN bodies were adopting annual resolutions on this particular concept was hugely significant.[18] The recurrent proposal of the resolutions indicates a real

[12] CHR, Resolution 2002/9: Combating Defamation of Religions, 15 April 2002, para. 15 of preamble; Resolution 2003/4: Combating Defamation of Religions, 14 April 2003, para. 13 of preamble and Resolution 2004/6: Combating Defamation of Religions, 13 April 2004, para. 13 of preamble.

[13] See for example, Human Rights Council (HR Council), Resolution 10/22: Combating Defamation of Religions, 26 March 2009 and Resolution 13/16: Combating Defamation of Religions, 25 March 2010.

[14] CHR, Resolution 2005/3: Combating Defamation of Religions, 12 April 2005, para. 14 of preamble; HR Council, Resolution 4/9: Combating Defamation of Religions, 30 March 2007, para. 9 of preamble; Resolution 7/19: Combating Defamation of Religions, 27 March 2008, para. 14 and Resolution 10/22, 26 March 2009, para. 11 of preamble.

[15] For example: HR Council, Resolution 7/19, 27 March 2008, paras. 1 and 4.

[16] HR Council, Resolution 10/22, 26 March 2009, para. 9 of preamble.

[17] See CHR, Resolution 2005/3, 12 April 2005, para. 10; HR Council, Resolution 4/9, 30 March 2007, para. 8; Resolution 7/19, 27 March 2008, para. 9 and Resolution 10/22, 26 March 2009, para. 13.

[18] See Temperman, 'Blasphemy, Defamation of Religions and Human Rights Law', 522–5. Pakistan, Iran, Bahrain, Morocco, the Maldives, Afghanistan, Algeria, Jordan, Kuwait, Malaysia, Oman, Saudi Arabia and Yemen all have laws which restrict freedom of

attempt by their proponents to integrate the concept into the discourse of UN human rights bodies and thereby accord it the sense of legitimacy that it might not have gained otherwise.[19] The entrenchment of the concept in international law was the essential objective of the proposal of the resolutions. Indeed, Pakistan publicly acknowledged that their proposal at the Human Rights Council and General Assembly was 'an annual initiative of the OIC',[20] which was also reinforced through other initiatives.[21] Moreover, it was widely accepted that the OIC's annual proposal of draft resolutions on combating defamation of religions was part of the organisation's long-term strategy of building momentum towards its ultimate objective – drafting and adoption of a legally binding instrument, such as a treaty amendment, on the subject.[22] In any event,

expression in the interest of respect for Islam. Blasphemy remains an offence in Australia, Austria, Canada, New Zealand, Ireland, Greece, Finland and Norway. In Germany, there is a provision in the Penal Code for penalising both insulting religions as well as insults aimed at secular beliefs.

19 Parmar, 'Challenge of "Defamation of Religions" to Freedom of Expression', 375.

20 Introduction by Pakistan on behalf of the Organisation of the Islamic Conference (OIC) of Resolution A/HRC/7/L.15 on 'Combating defamation of religion', 27 March 2008.

21 For example, at the Human Rights Council's 7th session in March 2008, the OIC successfully argued for a change to the mandate of the Special Rapporteur on Freedom of Opinion and Expression, requiring that mandate-holder to 'report on instances where the abuse of the right to freedom of expression constitutes an act of racial or religious discrimination'; HR Council Resolution 7/36: Mandate of the Special Rapporteur on the Promotion and Protection of the Right to Freedom of Opinion and Expression, 28 March 2008; ARTICLE 19, 'Press release: UN Human Rights Council undermines freedom of expression', 31 March 2008. An OIC news release referring to the amendment stated: 'The OIC attaches great importance to freedom of expression and opinion. . . However, it firmly believes that rights carry with them certain responsibilities . . . the OIC, once again, condemns printing of insulting caricatures and making of hate documentaries against Islam and Muslims. The OIC also stresses the responsibility of States to curb this trend. Incitement to hatred on religious and racial ground and defamation of religions by individuals, groups or State must not be tolerated' (*OIC Weekly Newsletter*, 17 (2008), 23 April 2008 (17 Rabie Al-Thani 1429)).

22 Some States at the Ad Hoc Committee on the elaboration of complementary standards have supported the development of 'new internationally binding normative standards' concerning the 'abuse of the right to freedom of expression' (para. 23) including '(a) Defamation of religions, religious personalities, holy books, scriptures and symbols; (b) Provocative portrayals of objects of religious veneration as a malicious violation of the spirit of tolerance; (c) Prohibition of publication of material with the aim of protecting the rights of others and against seriously or gratuitously offensive attacks on matters regarded as sacred by the followers of any religion' (para. 26). Such standards should *inter alia* provide for '[l]egal prohibition of publication of material that negatively stereotypes, insults, or uses offensive language on matters regarded by followers of any religion or belief as sacred or inherent to their dignity as human beings, with the aim of protecting

the proposal and defence of the UN resolutions on defamation of religions quickly became *a*, if not *the*, key element of the OIC's agenda at the UN; as such, the resolutions also developed into a fundamental part of its political identity and hence that of its members.

The *second* characteristic of the resolutions is the connections that they draw between the concept of defamation of religions, on the one hand, and violations of human rights – particularly the rights to non-discrimination and to freedom of religion and belief – on the other. The relationship with the right to non-discrimination, and more broadly speaking the right to equality irrespective of religion or belief, are especially emphasised.[23] The opening paragraph of the preamble to all resolutions recalled 'all States have pledged themselves, under the Charter of the United Nations, to promote and encourage universal respect for and observance of human rights and fundamental freedoms for all without distinction as to race, sex, language or religion'. Subsequent paragraphs asserted, for example, that 'discrimination against human beings on the grounds of religion or belief constitutes an affront to human dignity' as well as a 'disavowal of those principles'.[24] The March 2010 resolution of the Human Rights Council expressed a 'deep concern' about 'the manifestations of intolerance and discrimination in

their fundamental human rights' (para. 27(e)). See Ad Hoc Committee on the elaboration of complementary standards, *Outcome Referred to in Para. 2(d) of the Road Map on the Elaboration of Complementary Standards*, UN Doc. A/HRC/AC.1/2/2, 26 August 2009, paras. 23, 26, 27(e). See also *Report of the Ad Hoc Committee on the Elaboration of Complementary Standards on Its Second Session*, UN Doc. A/HRC/13/58, 21 January 2010, para. 38. On the establishment of the Ad Hoc Committee on the elaboration of complementary standards, see HRC, *Decision 3/103: Global Efforts for the Total Elimination of Racism, Racial Discrimination, Xenophobia and Related Intolerance and the Comprehensive Follow-up to the World Conference Against Racism, Racial Discrimination, Xenophobia and Related Intolerance and the Effective Implementation of the Durban Declaration and Programme of Action*, 8 December 2006, paras. (a) and (i) and HR Council, Resolution 6/21: Elaboration of International Complementary Standards to the International Convention on the Elimination of All Forms of Racial Discrimination, 28 September 2007.

[23] It is interesting to note that the 2009 and 2010 Resolutions add 'general welfare', presumably derived from Article 29 of the UDHR, as grounds for a permissible restriction to those included in Article 19. 'General welfare' appears used as a term to cover efforts against defamation of religions; HR Council, Resolution 10/22, 26 March 2009, para. 10 and Resolution 13/16, 25 March 2010, para. 11.

[24] CHR, Resolution 1999/82, 30 April 1999, para. 2 of the preamble; Resolution 2000/84: Combating Defamation of Religion, 26 April 2000, para. 3 of the preamble; Resolution 2002/9, 15 April 2002, para. 3 of the preamble; Resolution 2003/4, 14 April 2002, para. 3 of the preamble and Resolution 2004/6, 13 April 2004, para. 3 of the preamble.

matters of religion or belief still evident in the world, which have led to intolerance against the followers of these religions'. It goes on to urge 'all States to provide, within their respective legal and constitutional systems, adequate protection against acts of hatred, discrimination, intimidation and coercion resulting from defamation of religions and incitement to religious hatred in general, and to take all possible measures to promote tolerance and respect for all religions and beliefs'.[25] The series of resolutions also sought to promote 'understanding, tolerance and respect in matters relating to the freedom of religion or belief'.[26] There was an even greater emphasis in later resolutions on the positive promotion of rights, associated values and supporting actions. Notably, the March 2010 Resolution welcomed 'all international and regional initiatives to promote cross-cultural and interfaith harmony', underlined 'the important role of education in the promotion of tolerance, which involves acceptance by the public of and its respect for diversity', reaffirmed 'the commitment of the international community to promote, among other things, a culture of peace and respect for all religions, beliefs, and cultures', urged States 'to take all possible measures to promote tolerance and respect for all religions and beliefs' and called for 'strengthened international efforts to foster a global dialogue for the promotion of a culture of tolerance and peace at all levels, based on respect for human rights and diversity of religions and beliefs, and ... States, non-governmental organizations and religious leaders as well as the print and electronic media to support and foster such a dialogue'.[27]

The connections drawn in the resolutions between fighting defamation of religions, on the one hand, and targeting human rights violations and positively advancing human rights, on the other, show that they were drafted with the aim of countering what their proponents saw as real abuses of human rights. The promotion of the rights and values as described above are, *in and of themselves*, laudable – particularly in the light of evidence of heightened levels of discrimination against religious minorities in the world;[28] this was not contested by the many NGOs who

[25] HR Council, Resolution 13/16, 25 March 2010, para. 14.

[26] CHR, Resolution 1999/82, 30 April 1999, para. 4; Resolution 2000/84, 26 April 2000, para. 4. See also: HR Council, Resolution 4/9, 30 March 2007, para. 9 of the preamble and Resolution 7/19, 27 March 2008, para. 8 of the preamble.

[27] HR Council, Resolution 13/16, 25 March 2010, paras. 7 and 13 of the preamble and paras. 9, 14, 18.

[28] Numerous reports of Minority Rights Group reveal that religious intolerance has joined racism in many parts of the world as the leading cause of the persecution of minorities.

criticised the resolutions.[29] Indeed, some of the language in these resolutions resonates with the *Camden Principles on Freedom of Expression and Equality*, adopted in April 2009, which call for the promotion of intercultural understanding through dialogue and a detailed understanding of the proper relationship between freedom of expression and equality.[30] Some of the language also resonates with the recognition by the Special Rapporteur on freedom of religion or belief that '[i]nterreligious dialogue constitutes one of the principal means of countering sectarian attitudes and enhancing religious tolerance worldwide.'[31] However, it is wrong to draw such direct connections with defamation of religions because neither the Camden Principles nor the reports of the Special Rapporteur on freedom of religion or belief ever endorsed the concept of defamation of religions.

A *third* trait of all the resolutions is the attention they gave to discriminatory practices against Islam and Muslims.[32] This is unsurprising given

See, for example, Minority Rights Group, 'The State of the World's Minorities and Indigenous Peoples: Events of 2010', July 2011; Minority Rights Group, 'Peoples Under Threat, Online Briefing', May 2011.

29 See ARTICLE 19, 'UN HRC: Over 100 Organisations Urge Council to Reject Defamation of Religions and Protect Freedom of Expression', 10 March 2011; www.article19.org/resources.php/resource/1733/en/un-hrc:-over-100-organisations-urge-council-to-reject-'defamation-of-religions'-and-protect-freedom-of-expression (last accessed 3 March 2014); letter of 100 civil society organisations (led by ARTICLE 19, the Cairo Institute for Human Rights Studies and Human Rights Watch) of 9 March 2011; www.ifex.org/international/2011/03/09/defamation_of_religions (last accessed 3 March 2014).

30 The Camden Principles on Freedom of Expression and Equality are a set of international standards which were developed on the basis of discussions involving high level experts on freedom of expression from the UN, regional organisations, civil society and academia. These experts included the UN Special Rapporteurs on freedom of opinion and expression and on contemporary forms of racism, racial discrimination, xenophobia and related intolerance. The development of the principles was facilitated by ARTICLE 19. See the Camden Principles on Freedom of Expression and Equality, April 2009; www.article19.org/data/files/pdfs/standards/the-camden-principles-on-freedom-of-expression-and-equality.pdf (last accessed 3 March 2014). The Camden Principles have been referred to in the following documents of UN human rights bodies: *The Rabat Action Plan on the Prohibition of Incitement to National, Racial or Religious Hatred*; *Report of the Special Rapporteur on Freedom of Religion or Belief*, Heiner Bielefeldt, UN Doc. A/HRC/19/60, 22 December 2011; *Report of the Special Rapporteur on the Promotion and Protection of the Right to Freedom of Opinion and Expression*, Frank La Rue, UN Doc. A/HRC/66/290, 10 August 2011.

31 *Report of the Special Rapporteur on Freedom of Religion or Belief*, Asma Jahangir, 10th Session of the Human Rights Council, UN Doc. A/HRC/10/8, 6 January 2009, para. 18.

32 The focus on Islamophobia was a major point of criticism from States opposing the resolutions for a number of years. At the debates on the 2007 resolution, for example, the representatives of India, Guatemala, Japan, Peru, Brazil, Canada and Germany on behalf

that the resolutions were initiated by the OIC largely on the basis of 'manifestations of intolerance and misunderstanding, not to say hatred, of Islam and Muslims in various parts of the world'.[33] Interestingly, a draft of the first resolution adopted by the Commission on Human Rights in 1999 was 'defamation of Islam' but, following negotiations, the OIC agreed to make the title inclusive of all religions, even though that text focused on Islam.[34] The focus on Islam within the texts remained even as the resolutions grew more elaborate. References to the targeting of Islam and Muslims reached a high point in the 2002 Resolution which for the first time noted 'the intensification of the campaign of defamation of religions and the ethnic and religious profiling of Muslim minorities' in the aftermath of 9/11.[35] However, all the resolutions, including the final March 2010 Resolution and, interestingly, those that pre-date 9/11, express a 'deep concern that Islam is frequently and wrongly associated with human rights violations and terrorism'.

While the resolutions may have been justified as necessary for the protection of religious minorities against discrimination, this third feature of the resolutions suggests that they were actually intended to raise awareness of discriminatory practices against Muslims, in particular, and enhance protection against them by the UN human rights bodies. Yet the resolutions' real target is defamation of *religions*, rather than religious adherents. They condemn and require responses to actions against not only individuals and groups but also religious symbols and personalities. This can be seen from the 2009 and 2010 Resolutions. These deplore 'the targeting of ... venerated personalities of all religions' and 'religious symbols'.[36] They then condemn 'deliberate stereotyping of religions, their

of the EU all expressed concern that the resolution focused excessively on a single religion. Yet the emphasis on Islam and Muslims endured till the end. Grinberg argues that the resolutions also served to insulate Muslim States from international scrutiny (M. Grinberg, 'Defamation of Religions v Freedom of Expression: Finding the Balance in A Democratic Society' (2006)).

33 *Summary of Record of 61st meeting*, Commission on Human Rights 55th session, UN Doc. E/CN.4/1999/SR.61 19 October 1999.

34 *Ibid.* The representative of Pakistan in 1999 argued that 'no other religion received such constant negative media coverage' whereas the representative of Germany indicated that the then draft resolution's overall design was 'not balanced, since it referred exclusively to the negative stereotyping of Islam'.

35 CHR, Resolution 2002/9, 15 April 2001, para. 3 and para. 9 of the preamble.

36 HR Council, Resolution 10/22, 26 March 2009, paras. 5 and 6 and Resolution 13/16, 25 March 2010, paras. 3 and 10.

adherents and sacred persons', and call upon States to exert 'the utmost effort ... to ensure that religious ... symbols are fully respected and protected'.[37] The Preambles to the 2009 and 2010 Resolutions also noted the 'need to adopt a comprehensive and non-discriminatory approach to ensure respect for all races and religions'.[38] It must be observed that any limits on the scope of such terms as 'venerated personalities', 'sacred persons' and 'symbols' would be deeply contested by individuals and groups within and across religions.

A *fourth* attribute of the resolutions is their identification with various, mainly UN, sources including: the conclusions of the World Conference on Human Rights;[39] the UN Millennium Declaration;[40] the Durban Declaration and Programme of Action;[41] the Global Agenda for Dialogue among Civilisations;[42] the reports of Special Rapporteurs on contemporary forms of racism, racial discrimination, xenophobia and related intolerance;[43] a report of the High Commissioner for Human Rights on the subject of 'combating defamation of religions';[44] General Comment No. 15 of the Committee on the Elimination of Racial Discrimination;[45] the UN Global Counter-Terrorism Strategy;[46] the Alliance of Civilizations, the International Dialogue on Interfaith Cooperation for Peace and Harmony and the Dialogue among the

37 HR Council, Resolution 10/22, 26 March 2009, paras. 4 and 14 and Resolution 13/16, 25 March 2010 paras. 4 and 16.

38 HR Council, Resolution 10/22, 26 March 2009 and Resolution 13/16, 25 March 2010.

39 CHR, Resolution 1999/82, 30 April 1999, para. 3 of preamble.

40 CHR, Resolutions 2001/4, 18 April 2001, para. 4 of preamble and Resolution 2002/9, 15 April 2002, para. 5 of preamble; Resolution 2003/4, 14 April 2002, para. 5 of preamble; Resolution 2004/6, 13 April 2004, para. 5 of preamble; Resolution 2005/3, 12 April 2005, para. 3 of preamble and HR Council, Resolution 10/22, 26 March 2009, para. 5 of preamble.

41 CHR, Resolution 2002/9, 15 April 2002, para. 7 of preamble; Resolution 2004/6, 13 April 2004, para. 5 of preamble; Resolution 2005/3, 12 April 2005, para. 5 of preamble; HR Council, Resolution 4/9, 30 March 2007, para. 2 of preamble; Resolution 7/19, 27 March 2008, para. 2 of preamble and Resolution 10/22, 26 March 2009, para. 6 of preamble.

42 CHR, Resolution 2000/84, para. 8 of preamble; Resolution 2002/9, para. 4 of preamble, Resolution 2003/4, para. 6 of preamble; Resolution 2004/6, para. 6 of preamble; Resolution 2005/3, para. 4 of preamble and HR Council, Resolution 10/22, para. 5 of preamble.

43 HR Council Resolution 4/9 recalls the report on 'Situation of Muslims and Arabs in various parts of the world' E/CN.4/2006/17 and the *Report of the Special Rapporteur on Defamation of Religions*; HR Council, Resolution 10/22, para. 1.

44 HR Council, Resolution 4/9, para. 5.

45 HR Council, Resolution 7/19, para. 13 and Resolution 10/22, para. 11.

46 HR Council, Resolution 10/22, para. 8 and Resolution 13/16, para. 9.

Followers of World Religions and Cultures.[47] Independent sessions of the OIC[48] and joint initiatives of the OIC and the OHCHR[49] and of the OIC and the EU[50] are also referenced in earlier resolutions; but the later Resolutions of March 2009 and March 2010 refrain from making any references to OIC sources or meetings, suggesting a conscious attempt to distance the text from the OIC. The 2009 and 2010 resolutions instead welcome initiatives of the High Commissioner for Human Rights, specifically 'a seminar on freedom of expression and advocacy of religious hatred that constitutes incitement to discrimination, hostility and violence'[51] and 'a series of expert workshops to examine legislation, judicial practices and national policies in different regions, in order to assess different approaches to prohibiting incitement to hatred, as stipulated in article 20 of the International Covenant on Civil and Political Rights'.[52]

This final key attribute suggests a conscious attempt to ensure that the resolutions gained legitimacy from processes and initiatives of the intergovernmental organisations, within the UN and beyond. Such referencing to relevant UN and other sources is not unusual in the resolutions of UN human rights bodies. Indeed, it is a regular feature in the generation of international norms. However, the validity of such referencing to non-treaty sources must be called into question when it is done in such a context, aiming to bolster a concept that has been authoritatively condemned as an erosion of the rights contained in international human rights treaties. The next part of this chapter reviews the critiques of the resolutions on defamation of religions, including, most importantly, those based on international human rights treaty law.

[47] HR Council, Resolution 13/16, para. 7.

[48] HR Council, Resolution 4/9, para. 4 of preamble (recalling the final communiqué of the Third Extraordinary Session of the Islamic Summit Conference); Resolution 7/19, para. 5 of preamble (recalling the Declaration of the Islamic Conference at its 34th session which 'condemned the growing trend of Islamophobia and systematic discrimination against adherents of Islam') and para. 6 (noting the final communiqué by the OIC at its eleventh summit).

[49] CHR, Resolution 1999/82, para. 7 of preamble and Resolution 2000/84, para. 9 of preamble.

[50] CHR, Resolution 2002/9, para. 8 of preamble; Resolution 2003/4, para. 8 of preamble; Resolution 2004/6, para. 8 of preamble; Resolution 2005/3, para. 6 of preamble and HR Council, Resolution 7/19, para. 7 of preamble.

[51] HR Council, Resolution 10/22, paras. 1 and 17.

[52] HR Council, Resolution 13/16, para. 20.

## 3 Critiques of 'defamation of religions'

The chorus of voices raised in protest against this series of UN resolutions on defamation of religions grew louder and louder until the adoption of Human Rights Council Resolution 16/18 in March 2011. For many years before, Member States of the Human Rights Council, notably members of the European Union and Canada,[53] had vociferously opposed the resolutions while voting against them. The USA, although it only became a member in 2009, added its criticism to the rest.[54] International and regional human rights authorities had also long expressed their disquiet about the resolutions on defamation of religions. At the Durban Review Conference in April 2009, the Special Rapporteur on contemporary forms of racism, racial discrimination, xenophobia and related intolerance, the Special Rapporteur on freedom of religion or belief and the Special Rapporteur on freedom of expression issued a Joint Statement highlighting their collective concern about the subject, although the statement did not refer to the series of resolutions directly.[55]

[53] The Canadian representative Paul Mayer stated: 'There was also concern that the protection of the religions themselves, rather than the protection of the adherents to the resolution, was the focus of the resolution. Canada was also concerned that one religion only appeared to be the focus of the resolution. A lack of implementation of existing obligations was the single most pressing obstacle to tackling religious discrimination [*sic*]' (*Summary Record of 4th session of Human Rights Council*, 30 March 2007; www.ohchr.org/EN/NewsEvents/Pages/DisplayNews.aspx?NewsID=2509&LangID=E (last accessed 3 March 2014)).

[54] 'The introduction of the defamation concept in effect seeks to export the blasphemy laws found in many OIC countries to the international level. While the United States discourages actions that are offensive to particular religious traditions, including Islam, the "defamation of religions" concept is inconsistent with the freedoms of religion and expression and the OIC's approach will weaken religious freedom protections, including protections for minority Muslim populations.' See also: US Department of State, *International Religious Freedom Report 2008*; www.state.gov/j/drl/rls/irf/2008 (last accessed 3 April 2014).

[55] Joint Statement by Mr Githu Muigai, the Special Rapporteur on contemporary forms of racism, racial discrimination, xenophobia and related intolerance, Ms Asma Jahangir, the Special Rapporteur on freedom of religion or belief and Mr Frank la Rue, the Special Rapporteur on the promotion and protection of freedom of opinion and expression, OHCHR side event during the Durban Review Conference, Geneva, 22 April 2009; www.ohchr.org/Documents/Issues/Religion/SRJointstatement22April09.pdf (last accessed 3 March 2014). This followed a joint declaration by the key UN and regional mandate holders on freedom of expression focusing on the subject of defamation of religions as well as anti-terrorism legislation. OCSE/UN/OAS, Joint Declaration: Anti-Defamation and Anti-Terrorism and Anti-Extremism Legislation, 10 December 2008; www.article19.org/data/files/pdfs/other/joint-declaration-on-defamation-of-religions-and-anti-terrorism-and-anti-ext.pdf (last accessed 3 March 2014).

Yet the most resounding criticisms of the resolutions came from a broad range of civil society organisations.[56] In March 2011 in advance of the 16th session of the Human Rights Council, more than one hundred organisations led by ARTICLE 19, the Cairo Institute for Human Rights Studies and Human Rights Watch undertook a 'Joint Action' under the umbrella of the International Freedom of Expression Exchange (IFEX). They resolved 'to strongly urge' States 'to engage in the negotiations' and 'to vote against any resolution which refers to 'defamation of religions' or similar terms ... and support a resolution which omits such terms and focuses on freedom of expression, freedom of religion and non-discrimination in ways that properly reflect international human rights standards'.[57] This section elaborates on two sets of critiques, one legal and one practical, which were evident in the arguments of the resolutions' opponents.

### *3.1 Legal critiques*

The *first* set of critiques of the resolutions on combating defamation of religions highlights their incompatibility with international human rights law, particularly on freedom of expression and specifically the criteria for permissible restrictions on the right to freedom of expression in Article 19 paragraph 3 and Article 20 paragraph 2 of the ICCPR.[58] This is a legal argument and as a result perhaps the most compelling. It is often found in the statements of relevant Special Procedures of the Human Rights

[56] Partnerships between NGOs in opposition to the resolutions on defamation of religions developed at the Human Rights Council, in particular. For example, ARTICLE 19 frequently worked alongside the Cairo Institute for Human Rights Studies and Human Rights Watch on the issue at the Human Rights Council. However, there were clear distinctions in the approach of various NGOs and NGO groupings in relation to, most notably, the appropriate limits to freedom of expression, with US-based NGOs rejecting the standards set by Article 20 of the ICCPR on incitement to national, racial or religious hatred.

[57] IFEX Joint Action, 'Over 100 Organisations Call on UN Human Rights Council to Reject "Defamation" and "Denigration" of Religions', www.ifex.org/international/2011/03/09/defamation_religions (last accessed 3 April 2014).

[58] See the *travaux préparatoires* of Article 20 of the ICCPR at www.ohchr.org/EN/Issues/FreedomOpinion/Articles19-20/Pages/TravauxPreparatoires.aspx (last accessed 3 March 2014). A number of States – including Australia, Belgium, Finland, Luxembourg, New Zealand, the UK and the USA – have entered reservations to Article 20 para. 1 or Article 20 as a whole. On 'hate speech' generally, see M. Herz and P. Molnar (eds.), *The Content and Context of Hate Speech: Rethinking Regulation and Responses* (Cambridge University Press, 2012).

Council. For example, the UN Special Rapporteur on the right to freedom of opinion and expression has on numerous occasions stated that limitations on the right to freedom of expression in international law 'are not designed to protect belief systems from external or internal criticism'.[59] Many human rights NGOs reflected such arguments in their criticisms of the resolutions. In the letter signed by more than one hundred NGOs of March 2011, it was stated: 'international human rights law does not and should not protect religions per se, but does and should protect individuals from discrimination, violence and hostility on the basis of their religion'. They stated, 'religious ideas, beliefs and systems should not be exempt from discussion, debate or even sharp criticism, whether from internal or external commentators'.[60]

The legal argument in relation to whether the right to freedom of expression in international law permits restrictions to combat defamation of religions is best understood by considering Articles 19 and 20 of the ICCPR in further detail.[61] Article 19 paragraph 2 of the ICCPR protects the 'freedom to seek, receive and impart information and ideas *of all kinds*, regardless of frontiers, either orally, in writing or in print, in the form of art, or through any other media of his choice' (emphasis added). As the Human Rights Committee stated in General Comment No. 34:

> This right includes the expression and receipt of communications of every form of idea and opinion capable of transmission to others, subject to the provisions in article 19, paragraph 3, and article 20. It includes political discourse, commentary on one's own and on public affairs, canvassing, discussion of human rights, journalism, cultural and artistic expression, teaching, and religious discourse ... The scope of paragraph 2 embraces even expression that may be regarded as deeply offensive.[62]

Article 19 paragraph 3 then states:

> The exercise of the rights provided for in paragraph 2 of this article carries with it special duties and responsibilities. It may therefore be subject to certain restrictions, but these shall only be such as are provided by law and are necessary:

[59] *Report of the Special Rapporteur on the Promotion and Protection of the Right to Freedom of Opinion and Expression*, Ambeyi Ligabo, to the Human Rights Council, UN Doc. A/HRC/7/14, 28 February 2008, para. 85.

[60] ARTICLE 19, 'Letter of Civil Society Organisations to State Representatives', 9 March 2011; www.article19.org/data/files/pdfs/letters/-defamation-and-denigration-of-religions-at-the-16th-session-of-the-united-n.pdf (last accessed 3 March 2014).

[61] See further in this connection, Chapters 1 and 2 in this book.

[62] Footnotes from original text omitted.

(a) For respect of the rights or reputations of others;
(b) For the protection of national security or of public order (ordre public), or of public health or morals.

Article 20 paragraph 2 of the ICCPR states:

> Any advocacy of national, racial or religious hatred that constitutes incitement to discrimination, hostility or violence shall be prohibited by law.

It is important to note that Articles 19 and 20 are compatible with and complement each other. As the Human Rights Committee has stated, the 'acts that are addressed in article 20 are all subject to restriction pursuant to article 19, paragraph 3' and '[a]s such, a limitation that is justified on the basis of article 20 must also comply with article 19, paragraph 3'.[63]

> 51. What distinguishes the acts addressed in article 20 from other acts that may be subject to restriction under article 19, paragraph 3, is that for the acts addressed in article 20, the Covenant indicates the specific response required from the State: their prohibition by law. It is only to this extent that article 20 may be considered as *lex specialis* with regard to article 19.
> 52. It is only with regard to the specific forms of expression indicated in article 20 that States parties are obliged to have legal prohibitions. In every case in which the State restricts freedom of expression it is necessary to justify the prohibitions and their provisions in strict conformity with article 19.

Although the authoritative guidance of General Comment No. 34 came after the last of the resolutions of the human rights bodies on defamation of religions, the legal position set forth in this General Comment on freedom of expression shows in specific terms why those resolutions did not meet international legal standards on freedom of expression. The most relevant section of the General Comment is paragraph 48 in which the Committee very clearly states:

> Prohibitions of displays of lack of respect for a religion or other belief system, including blasphemy laws, are incompatible with the Covenant, except in the specific circumstances envisaged in article 20, paragraph 2, of the Covenant. Such prohibitions must also comply with the strict requirements of article 19, paragraph 3, as well as such articles as 2, 5, 17, 18 and 26. Thus, for instance, it would be impermissible for any such laws to discriminate in favour of or against one or certain religions or

[63] HRC, General Comment No. 34, para. 50; see HRC, *Ross* v. *Canada*, Communication No. 736/1997, 18 October 2000.

> belief systems, or their adherents over another, or religious believers over non-believers. Nor would it be permissible for such prohibitions to be used to prevent or punish criticism of religious leaders or commentary on religious doctrine and tenets of faith.[64]

The widely hailed success of General Comment No. 34 was considerably drawn from this paragraph – one of its 'most dramatic advances' on the interpretation of freedom of expression, together with recognition of the right to information and the role of modern media and information technologies.[65] Interestingly, however, the Committee does *not* refer to 'defamation of religions' as such. One may adduce from this paragraph however that, in the Committee's opinion, prohibitions on defamation of religions are indeed covered by this paragraph. In other words, any laws that purport to restrict defamation of religions or advocate the combating of defamation of religions (as the UN human rights bodies' resolutions did) are *incompatible* with the ICCPR unless they genuinely constitute prohibitions on 'incitement to discrimination, hostility or violence' and meet the standards of Article 19 paragraph 3 of the ICCPR and other provisions of the ICCPR, including those on non-discrimination. While this statement is not the strongest that the Committee could have made against laws on defamation of religions, it sets the bar impossibly high: any law restricting defamation of religions, blasphemy or religious insult that meets the standards of paragraph 48 would fall short of its presumed purpose, the protection of religion from critical speech.

The resolutions may be also analysed under the general test for permissible restrictions in Article 19 paragraph 3 and the Human Rights Committee's authoritative interpretation of it. Under Article 19 paragraph 3, restrictions on freedom of expression must be 'provided by law'[66] and only be imposed based on one of the grounds set out in subparagraphs (a) and (b) of Article 19(3). Restrictions on freedom of expression are not allowed on grounds not specified in paragraph 3, 'even

[64] HRC, Concluding Observations on the United Kingdom of Great Britain and Northern Ireland, the Crown Dependencies of Jersey, Guernsey and the Isle of Man, UN Doc. CCPR/C/79/Add.119, 27 March 2000. See also: *Concluding Observations on Kuwait*, UN Doc. CCPR/CO/69/KWT, 27 July 2000.

[65] Open Society Justice Initiative, 'Article 19: UN Reinforces Freedom of Expression and Right to Information' 28 July 2011; See also ARTICLE 19, 'ARTICLE 19 Welcomes General Comment on Freedom of Expression', Statement, 5 August 2011.

[66] See General Comment No. 34, para. 25. See also: HRC, *De Groot* v. *the Netherlands*, Communication No. 578/1994, 14 July 1995. See HRC, General Comment No. 27: Freedom of Movement (Art. 12), UN Doc. CCPR/C/21/Rev.1/Add.9, 2 November 1999.

if such grounds would justify restrictions to other rights protected in the Covenant'.[67] They must conform to the strict tests of necessity and proportionality, in the sense they should not be overbroad.[68] Restrictions must be applied only for those purposes for which they were prescribed and must be directly related to the specific need on which they are predicated.[69] In applying the principle of proportionality, States should consider 'the form of expression at issue as well as the means of its dissemination', meaning that political speech, in particular concerning political or public figures is accorded a higher level of protection.[70] Thus, paragraph 3 'may never be invoked as a justification for the muzzling of any advocacy of multi-party democracy, democratic tenets and human rights'.[71] Furthermore, it is for the State Party to demonstrate the legal basis for any restrictions imposed on freedom of expression.[72] The Committee has stated: '[w]hen a State party invokes a legitimate ground for restriction of freedom of expression, it must demonstrate in specific and individualized fashion the precise nature of the threat, and the necessity and proportionality of the specific action taken, in particular by establishing a direct and immediate connection between the expression and the threat.'[73]

Finally, laws restricting the rights in Article 19(2) must also 'themselves be compatible with the provisions, aims and objectives of the Covenant' as well as its provisions on non-discrimination.[74]

[67] General Comment No. 34, para. 22.

[68] The Committee observed in General Comment No. 27 that 'restrictive measures must conform to the principle of proportionality; they must be appropriate to achieve their protective function; they must be the least intrusive instrument amongst those which might achieve their protective function; they must be proportionate to the interest to be protected. . .The principle of proportionality has to be respected not only in the law that frames the restrictions but also by the administrative and judicial authorities in applying the law' (General Comment No. 27, para. 14). See also: HRC, *Marques* v. *Angola*, Communication No. 1128/2002, 18 April 2005 and *Coleman* v. *Australia*, Communication No. 1157/2003, 10 August 2006.

[69] See HRC, General Comment No. 22, Official Records of the General Assembly, Forty-eighth Session, Supplement No. 40 (A/48/40), Annex VI.

[70] General Comment No. 34, para. 34. See HRC, *Bodrozic* v. *Serbia and Montenegro*, Communication No. 1180/2003, 31 October 2005.

[71] See General Comment No. 34, para. 23. See also: HRC, *Mukong* v. *Cameroon*, Communication No. 458/91, 21 July 1994.

[72] See HRC, *Korneenko et al.* v. *Belarus*, Communication No. 1553/2007, 31 October 2006.

[73] General Comment No. 34, para. 35. See HRC, *Shin* v. *Republic of Korea*, Communication No. 926/2000, 16 March 2004.

[74] General Comment No. 34, para. 26. See HRC, *Toonen* v. *Australia*, Communication No. 488/1992, 30 March 1994.

Thus, properly framed defamation laws may indeed be justified under the first of the legitimate grounds for restriction listed in paragraph 3, that of respect for 'the rights or reputations of others'. Such laws, however, must be carefully crafted so that they 'do not serve, in practice, to stifle freedom of expression', as the Committee has indicated.[75] Significantly, the Committee has indicated that the term 'others' in paragraph 3 relates to other persons individually or as members of a community,[76] including individual members of a community defined by its religious faith[77] or ethnicity,[78] but the term cannot be said to apply in respect of religions per se.[79]

Under Article 20 paragraph 2, only 'incitement to discrimination, hostility or violence shall be prohibited by law'. Terms such as 'deliberate' or 'negative stereotyping' and even the 'frequent and wrong association of Islam with human rights violations and terrorism' used in the Resolutions fall far short of the threshold of incitement put forward in Article 20 paragraph 2. It is interesting to note that later resolutions juxtapose defamation of religions with references to incitement in an apparent attempt to accord the former concept a sense of legitimacy through proximity to the latter.[80] The connection distorts international law on incitement under Article 20 paragraph 2, even though there is uncertainty about the precise scope of that provision.

International law-based criticisms of the resolutions on defamation of religions were also based on freedom of religion. The Special Rapporteurs on freedom of religion or belief and on contemporary forms of racism, racial discrimination, xenophobia and related intolerance had asserted that the right to freedom of religion or belief 'protects primarily the individual and, to some extent, the collective rights of the community concerned, but it does not protect the religions or beliefs per se'.[81] The

[75] General Comment No. 34, para. 47. HRC, Concluding Observations on the United Kingdom of Great Britain and Northern Ireland, UN Doc. CCPR/C/GBR/CO/6, 30 July 2008.

[76] See HRC, *Ross* v. *Canada*.

[77] See HRC, *Faurisson* v. *France*, Communication No. 550/93, 8 November 1996; HRC, Concluding Observations on Austria, UN Doc. CCPR/C/AUT/CO/4, 30 October 2007.

[78] HRC, Concluding Observations on Slovakia, UN Doc. CCPR/CO/78/SVK, 22 August 2003 and Concluding Observations on Israel, UN Doc. CCPR/CO/78/ISR, 5 August 2003.

[79] General Comment No. 34, para. 28.

[80] HR Council, Resolution 10/22, paras. 3, 5, 6, 11, 13, 14, 17, 19 and Resolution 13/16, paras. 1, 3, 5, 6, 12, 14, 15, 17, 19, 20.

[81] *Report to the Second Session of the Human Rights Council*, UN Doc. A/HRC/2/3, 20 September 2006, para. 38.

UN Working Group on Arbitrary Detention had also stated that: 'defamation of religions may offend people and hurt their feelings but it does not directly result in a violation of their rights to freedom of religion'.[82]

The above-mentioned critiques of the resolutions are clearly based on the content of international human rights law on freedom of expression and, to a lesser extent, freedom of religion. There is another, related though distinct, critique that questions whether it is feasible to protect religions from insult or attack at all. The resolutions on defamation of religions assume that it is possible to protect the reputation of religions, as if they are monolithic and internally uncontested systems of belief. Yet all religions have a spectrum of interpretations. They may have different understandings of divine authority and most present rival claims to the absolute truth, whereby even practising one religion may actually be viewed as a 'defamation' of another.

### 3.2 *Practical critiques*

The *second* set of critiques of the defamation of religions resolutions highlights their practical shortfalls, particularly the harm they cause to their purported general aims of promoting human rights, specifically religious freedom and equality. The proponents of the resolutions drew on the existence of national blasphemy and religious insult laws around the world as backing for the resolutions because such laws sought to protect rights and maintain social harmony among various groups, particularly religious ones. Although OIC States often referred to European States' blasphemy and religious insult provisions as evidence of their hypocrisy on the issue,[83] it was obvious that they were most influenced

[82] UN Working Group on Arbitrary Detention, Opinion No. 35/2008 (Egypt), Communication addressed to the Government on December 6 2007, U.N. Doc. A/HRC/13/30/Add.1 at 146, para. 38.

[83] Leading members of the OIC appeared especially keen to refer to domestic blasphemy and religious insult laws in European States as evidence of the hypocrisy of those States opposing the UN resolutions on the subject. A wide range of specific offences 'with a religious aspect' exists across Europe, as the Council of Europe's advisory body on constitutional matters, the Venice Commission, reported in October 2008. Such offences include: the disturbance of religious practice, blasphemy, religious insult, negationism, discrimination (including on religious grounds) and incitement to hatred. European Commission for Democracy through Law ('the Venice Commission'); *Report on the Relationship between Freedom of Expression and Freedom of Religion: the Issue of Regulation and Prosecution of Blasphemy, Religious Insult and Incitement to Religious Hatred*, adopted by the Venice Commission at its 76th Plenary Session, CDL-AD(2008)026, 23

by the existence of such laws in their own countries. So while the resolutions on defamation of religions provided a cover for national blasphemy laws, the existence of those laws conversely sustained the adoption of the resolutions over many years. For Robert C. Blitt, this phenomenon of the mutual reinforcement of international and domestic norms on the issue of defamation of religions/blasphemy demonstrates that 'the vertical axis linking international and domestic law is in fact open to two-way traffic that allows for the transmission of domestic anti-constitutional ideas from the bottom up to the international level, rather than only in a top-down manner'.[84]

Critics of the resolutions pointed to the negative, indeed counter-productive, impact of this 'bottom-up' migration of norms.[85] The March 2011 letter signed by more than 100 NGOs argued that, by supporting a resolution that omitted the term defamation of religions and instead promoted freedom of expression, freedom of religion and non-discrimination according to international human rights standards, States would: 'reflect the growing consensus that has emerged at the UN General Assembly and the Council over the past two years that the concept of "defamation" or "denigration of religions" is counterproductive to global efforts to combat discrimination against religious minorities and serves to entrench repression and violence against non-believers, members of religious minorities and political dissidents'.[86]

This echoed the Joint Statement made at the 2009 Durban Review Conference by the Special Rapporteur on contemporary forms of racism, racial discrimination, xenophobia and related intolerance, the Special Rapporteur on freedom of religion or belief and the Special Rapporteur on freedom of opinion and expression. The statement noted:[87]

October 2008, paras. 2, 22–40. Furthermore, the European Court of Human Rights has not taken a clear line on the issue of blasphemy. See, notably ECtHR, *Otto-Preminger Institute* v. *Austria* (Appl. No. 13470/87), 20 September 1994 and *Wingrove* v. *UK* (Appl. No 13470/87), 25 November 1996.

84 Blitt, 'Bottom up Journey of "Defamation of Religion"', 121.

85 S. Choudhury, 'Migration as a New Metaphor in Comparative Constitutional Law', in S. Choudhury (ed.), *The Migration of Constitutional Ideas* (Cambridge University Press, 2006), 1–35.

86 ARTICLE 19, 'Letter of Civil Society Organisations to State Representatives', 9 March 2011; www.article19.org/data/files/pdfs/letters/-defamation-and-denigration-of-religions-at-the-16th-session-of-the-united-n.pdf (last accessed 3 March 2014).

87 Joint Statement by Mr Githu Muigai, Special Rapporteur on contemporary forms of racism, racial discrimination, xenophobia and related intolerance, Ms Asma Jahangir, Special Rapporteur on freedom of religion or belief and Mr Frank la Rue, Special

> [t]he difficulties in providing an objective 'definition of the term 'defamation of religions' at the international level make the whole concept open to abuse. At the national level, domestic blasphemy laws can prove counter-productive, since this could result in the de facto censure of all inter-religious and intra-religious criticism. Many of these laws afford different levels of protection to different religions and have often proved to be applied in a discriminatory manner. There are numerous examples of persecution of religious minorities or dissenters, but also of atheists and non-theists, as a result of legislation on religious offences or overzealous application of laws that are fairly neutral.[88]

The notion that targeting defamation of religions would serve to *protect* religious minorities underpinned the resolutions, but it was a deeply flawed assumption, as has been demonstrated in recent reports produced by Freedom House, Human Rights First and the Cairo Institute for Human Rights on the impact of domestic blasphemy laws.[89] Indeed, the very opposite is true. Freedom House's March 2010 report *Policing Belief: The Impact of Blasphemy Laws on Human Rights* shows that such provisions 'typically give rise to the violation, not the protection, of fundamental human rights'.[90] The study, which assessed blasphemy and religious insult laws in a number of countries (namely, Algeria, Egypt, Greece, Indonesia, Malaysia, Pakistan and Poland), exposes the harsh penalties associated with such legislation and concludes that such

Rapporteur on the promotion and protection of freedom of opinion and expression, OHCHR side event during the Durban Review Conference, Geneva, 22 April 2009; www.ohchr.org/Documents/Issues/Religion/SRJointstatement22April09.pdf. In similar terms, the Special Rapporteur on freedom of religion and belief noted the penalising of defamation of religions can 'be counterproductive, since it may create an atmosphere of intolerance and fear and may even increase the chances of a backlash' (*Interim Report of the Special Rapporteur on Freedom of Religion or Belief*, UN Doc. A/62/280, 20 August 2007, at para. 77).

[88] The Special Procedures also debunked any assumption that 'defamation of religions' might be likened to racism. They stated: 'the elements that constitute a racist statement may not be the same as those that constitute a statement "defaming religion" as such. To this extent, the legal measures and in particular the criminal measures, adopted by national legal systems may not necessarily be applicable to 'defamation of religions' (*ibid.*).

[89] Freedom House, 'Policing Belief: The Impact of Blasphemy Laws on Human Rights', October 2010; Cairo Institute for Human Rights Studies, 'Defamation of Religions: International Developments and Challenges on the Ground', March 2011; Human Rights First, 'Blasphemy Laws Exposed: The Consequences of Criminalizing "Defamation of Religions"', March 2011; Human Rights First, 'Blasphemy Laws Exposed: The Consequences of Criminalizing "Defamation of Religions"', March 2012.

[90] *Ibid.*, at 1.

laws have a 'particularly pernicious effect' in terms of being abused both by governments to silence political opposition, government critics and other dissidents, and by private individuals to settle petty disputes.[91] It shows that in such countries religious extremists have exploited blasphemy laws to justify attacks on religious minorities, creating a culture of intolerance, and that religious institutions have used blasphemy laws to impose 'state-sanctioned interpretations of religious doctrine on members of minority sects that are deemed deviant or heretical'.[92] The report usefully identifies various human rights violations that frequently flow from the applications of domestic blasphemy laws. Individuals accused of blasphemy often face violations of: freedom of expression, both in terms of their 'direct enforcement as well as the self-censorship they engender'; the right to equal treatment and non-discrimination because 'religious minorities and heterodox sects ... are often targeted disproportionately'; the right to liberty, because alleged blasphemers are often arbitrarily arrested and detained for prolonged periods based on false or unsubstantiated accusations of blasphemy; the right to fair trial because of lax legal procedures; the right to life and the prohibition of torture, cruel, inhuman or degrading treatment or punishment, because of the treatment to which they are subjected in custody by State agents, as well as the violence perpetrated by other non-State actors.[93]

## 4 The 'new approach'

### *4.1 Emergence of the new approach*

Support for the defamation of religions resolutions reached its zenith in 2006, but had been diminishing in the years before the adoption of Resolution 16/18 in March 2011. The turning tide at the Human Rights Council and at the General Assembly was evidenced by the shifts in voting patterns against the resolutions over a number of years, as well as minor concessionary changes made to the language of the texts proposed. Opposition to the resolutions had ratcheted up at the 2009 Durban Review

[91] The report examines the application of the following provisions: Article 144 bis 2 of the Algerian Penal Code, Articles 26 and 77 of the Algerian Information Code; Articles 98(f), 161, 176 and 178 of the Egyptian Penal Code; Section 7, Articles 198 and 199 of the Greek Penal Code; Article 156(A) of the Indonesian Penal Code; Articles 295–298A of the Malaysian Penal Code; Section XV, Articles 295–98 of the Pakistan Penal Code; Article 196 of the Polish Penal Code.

[92] Freedom House, 'Policing Belief', 2. [93] *Ibid.*

Conference, whose final outcome document omitted any reference to the concept of defamation of religions, even though it was considered during the conference discussions.[94] One month before the conference, the 10th session of the Human Rights Council had seen the defamation of religions resolution adopted by a margin of 12 votes, but it was notable that the total votes of the 13 abstaining States and the 11 States against the resolution outweighed the 23 votes in its favour.[95] In December 2009, members of the Group of Latin American and Caribbean States (GRULAC), including Mexico, Chile, Panama and Uruguay voted for the first time against the resolution at the General Assembly.[96] The movement against the resolutions gathered pace at the March 2010 session of the Human Rights Council, where the resolution was adopted by the lowest margin: 20 States voted in favour of the resolution, 17 voted against it and there were 8 abstentions.[97] Interestingly, Argentina and Zambia opposed the resolution for the first time and a number of States – notably Chile, Argentina and Mexico – expressed their commitment to upholding freedom of expression while combating intolerance.[98] In November 2010, the Third

[94] Durban Review Conference, *Outcome Document*, 20–24 April 2009; www.un.org/en/durbanreview2009/pdf/Durban_Review_outcome_document_En.pdf (last accessed 3 March 2014); D. Petrova, '"Smoke and Mirrors": The Durban Review Conference and Human Rights Politics at the United Nations', *Human Rights Law Review* 10(1) (2010), 129–50.

[95] HR Council, Resolution 10/22, adopted by a recorded vote of 23 to 11, with 13 abstentions. The voting was as follows: *in favour*: Angola, Azerbaijan, Bahrain, Bangladesh, Bolivia, Cameroon, China, Cuba, Djibouti, Egypt, Gabon, Indonesia, Jordan, Malaysia, Nicaragua, Nigeria, Pakistan, Philippines, Qatar, Russian Federation, Saudi Arabia, Senegal, South Africa; *against*: Canada, Chile, France, Germany, Italy, the Netherlands, Slovakia, Slovenia, Switzerland, Ukraine, the UK; *abstaining*: Argentina, Brazil, Bosnia and Herzegovina, Burkina Faso, Ghana, India, Japan, Madagascar, Mauritius, Mexico, Republic of Korea, Uruguay, Zambia.

[96] ISHR, 'Support for "Defamation of Religions" Continues to Decline: Draft Resolution Passes by Only 12 Votes', 25 November 2010; www.ishr.ch/news/support-defamation-religion-continues-decline-draft-resolution-passes-only-12-votes (last accessed 3 March 2014).

[97] HR Council, Resolution 13/16, adopted by a recorded vote of 20 to 17, with 8 abstentions. The voting was as follows: *in favour*: Bahrain, Bangladesh, Bolivia, Burkina Faso, China, Cuba, Djibouti, Egypt, Indonesia, Jordan, Kyrgyzstan, Nicaragua, Nigeria, Pakistan, the Philippines, Qatar, Russian Federation, Saudi Arabia, Senegal, South Africa; *against*: Argentina, Belgium, Chile, France, Hungary, Italy, Mexico, Netherlands, Norway, Republic of Korea, Slovakia, Slovenia, Ukraine, the UK, the USA, Uruguay, Zambia; *abstaining*: Bosnia and Herzegovina, Brazil, Cameroon, Ghana, India, Japan, Madagascar, Mauritius.

[98] ISHR, 'Human Rights Council: Changing Dynamics on "Defamation of Religions"', 14 April 2010; www.ishr.ch/news/human-rights-council-changing-dynamics-defamation-religions (last accessed 3 March 2014).

Committee of the General Assembly adopted the resolution by a margin of 12 votes, less than half the margin of the 26 votes in the previous year.[99] Although the OIC as an organisation continued publicly to insist that it would pursue the issue of defamation of religions 'relentlessly', including by bringing the resolution to the General Assembly in 2011,[100] the voting patterns of the previous years suggested that any resolution proposed late that year on the subject of defamation of religions would run the real risk of being defeated. The OIC, led by Pakistan, knowing that it was sooner or later going to lose the battle over the resolutions, was unwilling to risk the embarrassment of such a defeat in March 2011. It therefore decided that it would be preferable to propose a resolution that could gain consensus from Western and OIC States.

The diminishing support for the defamation of religions resolutions in the years leading up to Resolution 16/18 was undoubtedly the result of the pressure exerted by Western States, international authorities (notably, the Special Procedures) and NGOs, upon those States that maintained their support for the OIC-proposed resolutions. NGOs' advocacy strategies included directly lobbying the Geneva-based delegations of States that had previously voted in favour of the resolutions or abstained in the vote on them and applying pressure on the capitals of those States themselves. It also involved challenging domestic legal provisions on defamation of religions. In March 2010, four NGOs – namely, ARTICLE 19, Amnesty International, the Cairo Institute for Human Rights Studies and the Egyptian Initiative for Personal Rights – submitted a joint *amicus curiae* brief to the Indonesian Constitutional Court arguing that Indonesia's laws on defamation of religions violated Indonesia's international human rights obligations to respect and protect freedom of expression, freedom of thought, conscience and religion, and the right to equality.[101]

[99] GA/SHC/4001, 23 November 2010.

[100] ISHR, 'Support for "Defamation of Religions"'.

[101] The organisations submitted the brief on 11 March 2010 to the Indonesian Constitutional Court in the judicial review of Law Number 1/PNPS/1965 concerning the prevention of religious abuse and/or defamation. The 1965 law prohibits 'interpretation and activities [that] are in deviation of the basic teachings' of 'a religion adhered to in Indonesia', which includes some faiths with followers in the country but not others. The Indonesian Criminal Code imposes a five-year prison sentence on anyone who publicly expresses views or engages in actions which are considered 'abuse or defamation' of these religions. See: www.article19.org/data/files/pdfs/analysis/judicial-review-of-law-number-1-pnps-1965-concerning-the-prevention-of-relig.pdf (last accessed 3 March 2014). On 19 April 2010, the Indonesian Constitutional Court upheld the 1965 law;

But there were other factors, internal and external to the Council, that contributed to the shift and these deserve recognition. *First*, the election of the United States to the Human Rights Council on 19 June 2009 brought a sense of energy and focus to the Council's work on the most controversial and difficult of global human rights challenges. In what seemed to be a refreshing change from the more belligerent approach of European States (many of which had held seats on the Human Rights Council since its inception), the USA immediately implemented the Obama administration's approach of constructive engagement by reaching out to members of the OIC, in addition to other like-minded States and NGOs.[102] Within a few months, in September 2009, the USA demonstrated that it was possible to break the traditional divide between the OIC and Western States on controversial issues by working together with Egypt, an influential member of the OIC, to propose a resolution on freedom of expression, which was later adopted by consensus and welcomed by NGOs.[103] The USA thus marked itself as a leader on freedom of expression issues at the Human Rights Council and, in doing so, persuaded others of the benefits of constructive engagement in international diplomacy.

*Second*, the grave impact of domestic blasphemy laws was put under international spotlight in early 2011 after the assassination of two prominent Pakistani politicians who opposed the country's harsh blasphemy laws. The killings of the Governor of Punjab, Salmaan Taseer, and the Minister for Minority Affairs, Shahbaz Bhatti, on 4 January and 2 March 2011 respectively, illustrated to a global audience 'how deadly the debate over blasphemy laws has become'.[104]

ARTICLE 19, 'Indonesia: Court decision upholding "defamation of religions" is a major setback', press release, 27 April 2010.

[102] The holders of the position of Deputy Assistant Secretary for International Organizations at the United States Department of State – notably Suzanne Nossel (August 2009 to November 2011) and her successor Paula Schriefer (May 2012 – present) – have held regular briefings with NGOs on the Human Rights Council. These have been a useful forum for NGOs based in Washington, DC who could attend in person, but also those based elsewhere because it is possible to attend such briefings via conference calls, unlike similar, highly useful NGO briefings of the UK Foreign and Commonwealth Office which can only be attended in person.

[103] A/HRC/RES/12/16, 2 October 2009. For ARTICLE 19's analysis of a draft of the adopted resolution, see ARTICLE 19, 'Comment on the Draft Text of the Resolution On Freedom of Expression Proposed by Egypt and the United States at the 12th session of the Human Rights Council', 23 September 2009.

[104] Human Rights First, 'Blasphemy Law Exposed', 2011, 2. See also, D. Walsh, 'Pakistan's blasphemy laws have left even judges in fear of their lives', *Guardian*, 3 October 2011;

*Third*, the OIC's decision to drop the concept of defamation of religions in early 2011 came at a time of revolution across the Arab world. The so-called Arab Awakening that began in Tunisia in late 2010 and spread to Egypt in the early months of 2011 was itself sparked by the lack of freedom of speech and political freedoms in addition to poor living conditions, corruption and rising food prices. Although the intervening period has seen blasphemy laws being enforced with vigour and freedom of expression being attacked in numerous ways, the initial Arab 'Spring' in 2011 arguably influenced OIC States towards greater flexibility in their diplomatic positions.

The mere proposal of Resolution 16/18 on 'combating intolerance, negative stereotyping and stigmatisation of, and discrimination, incitement to violence, and violence against persons based on religion or belief' at the March 2011 session of the Human Rights Council was certainly viewed as evidence of a 'seismic shift' in the attitude among influential OIC States, particularly Pakistan which submitted the resolution on the OIC's behalf.[105] The resolution's adoption was greeted with widespread political applause. In welcoming Human Rights Council Resolution 16/18 as a 'landmark achievement', US Secretary of State Hillary Clinton stated that it represented 'a significant step forward in the global dialogue on countering intolerance, discrimination, and violence against persons based upon religion or belief'. Clinton congratulated the OIC for its 'leadership' on the resolution, which 'demonstrate[d] a desire to move the debate on these shared challenges in a constructive and affirmative direction', while emphasising that the resolution needed to be 'followed by sustained commitment' against religious discrimination and violence.[106]

### 4.2 *Features of the new approach*

Resolution 16/18 is important because of its content and the consensus by which it was adopted, which was hard fought for on both sides of the

www.guardian.co.uk/commentisfree/belief/2011/oct/03/pakistan blasphemy laws (last accessed 3 March 2014).

105 ARTICLE 19 and the Cairo Institute for Human Rights Studies, 'The Demise of Defamation of Religions? Council Should Support Resolution on Religious Discrimination', statement, 22 March 2011.

106 Press statement of Hillary Rodham Clinton, 'Adoption of Resolution 16/18 Countering Religious Intolerance a "landmark achievement"', Washington, DC, 24 March 2011; http://geneva.usmission.gov/2011/03/24/adoption-of-resolution-at-human-rights-council-combating-discrimination-and-violence (last accessed 3 March 2014).

debate.[107] It was endorsed by subsequent resolutions of the General Assembly – namely, Resolution 66/167 of 19 December 2011 and Resolution 67/178 of 20 December 2012 – and of the Human Rights Council itself – namely Resolution 19/25 of 23 March 2012 and Resolution 22/31 of 22 March 2013. Though their longer preambular statements distinguish the General Assembly resolutions, the language of all these resolutions of both UN human rights bodies is strikingly similar with the substantive paragraphs of Resolution 16/18 at the core of each of them. Human Rights Council Resolution 19/25 is virtually identical to Human Rights Council Resolution 16/18, except for the addition of preambular paragraphs referring to Resolution 16/18 itself and the panel discussion held at the seventeenth session of the Human Rights Council pursuant to Resolution 16/18. General Assembly Resolution 67/178 and Human Rights Council Resolution 22/31 both contain important references to other intergovernmental and expert processes. The remainder of this section considers the essence of the series of post-'defamation of religions' resolutions and identifies the extent to which it represents a new approach to the protection of freedom of expression at the UN.[108]

*First* and foremost, the key feature of these resolutions is their omission of any reference to defamation of religions. This is essentially what makes the approach embodied in Human Rights Council Resolution 16/18 'new', and so 'conceptually and practically' significant.[109] NGOs have observed that, as a result of this omission, the UN human rights bodies '[cease] to provide cover for national blasphemy laws' as indicated above.[110]

*Second* and relatedly, the problems that the new resolutions seek to address are broadly defined as 'incidents of intolerance, discrimination and violence against persons based on their religion or belief' and 'advocacy of discrimination or violence on the basis of religion'.[111] The types of acts covered by the resolutions include, more specifically: 'acts

[107] ARTICLE 19 argued that the title, which was 'awkward and overly long', could have been made shorter without changing its substantive scope. Such drafting weaknesses, however, were viewed as 'minor in nature and should not dissuade states from supporting it'.

[108] General Assembly Resolution 66/167 of December 2011 and Human Rights Council Resolution 19/25 of 23 March 2012.

[109] M. Evans, 'Advancing freedom of religion or belief: agendas for change', Annual Lambeth Interfaith lecture, 8 June 2011; www.archbishopofcanterbury.org/articles.php/2062/archbishop-hosts-annual-lambeth-inter-faith-lecture (last accessed 3 March 2014).

[110] Human Rights First, 'Blasphemy Laws Exposed', 1.

[111] See preamble of Human Rights Council Resolution16/18 of 24 March 2011, General Assembly Resolution 66/167 of December 2011 and Human Rights Council Resolution 19/25 of 23 March 2012.

directed against ... homes, businesses, properties, schools, cultural centres or places of worship'; 'wilful [exploitation of] tensions or [targeting of] individuals'; 'discrimination against persons belonging to religious minorities ... the negative projection of the followers of religions and the enforcement of measures that specifically discriminate against persons on the basis of religion or belief'; 'derogatory stereotyping, negative profiling, stigmatization of persons based on their religion or belief, as well as programmes and agendas pursued by extremist organizations and groups aimed at creating and perpetuating negative stereotypes about religious groups, particularly when condoned by governments'; as well as 'advocacy of religious hatred against individuals that constitutes incitement to discrimination, hostility or violence'.[112] Yet, it is observed that many of these harms are the same as those previously closely associated with defamation of religions in earlier resolutions. Terms such as 'intolerance', 'stereotyping', 'negative projection' and also 'incitement' are not new but make a *re*appearance in the new resolutions.[113] What is significant is that these words are now used to describe discriminatory acts, including and most notably incitement, against individuals and groups on the grounds of religion or belief, and are no longer coupled with the notion of defamation of religions. Yet the shift of focus to the concept of incitement could have been predicted to raise new challenges for the UN human rights system. For Malcolm Evans, writing in June 2011, 'the malleable contours of that concept' and 'the forces which seek to subvert the freedom of religion and convert it into a means of repression remain alive, well, and focussed'.[114]

*Third*, these new resolutions appear to reinforce existing international human rights law on incitement to hatred, by recalling in the title and numerous provisions the concepts and language of Article 20 paragraph 2 of the ICCPR.[115] Through Resolution 16/18, for instance, the Human Rights Council condemns 'any advocacy of religious hatred against individuals that constitutes incitement to discrimination, hostility or violence'. Given that the resolutions on defamation of religions also drew support from Article 20 paragraph 2 of the ICCPR, the resolutions'

[112] Human Rights Council Resolution 16/18 of 24 March 2011, preamble and paras. 1 and 2.
[113] *Ibid.* [114] Evans, 'Advancing Freedom of Religion or Belief'.
[115] Shortly before the adoption of HR Council Resolution 16/18, ARTICLE 19 and the Cairo Institute for Human Rights Studies stated: 'the text of the resolution leaves no doubt as to the primacy of these international human rights obligations' (ARTICLE 19 and the Cairo Institute for Human Rights Studies, 'Demise of Defamation of Religions?').

significance, at least vis-à-vis Article 20 paragraph 2 of the ICCPR, is that defamation of religions is no longer juxtaposed with the concept of incitement as set out in international law. In terms of the legal measures States are required to take, the resolutions appear to embrace the legal standard of the United States, which prohibits incitement to *imminent* violence, rather than other international and regional standards on penalising incitement to hatred more broadly.[116]

*Fourth*, in various other ways the new resolutions reinforce existing international human rights standards on the rights to freedom of expression, equality and freedom of religion or belief. The resolutions call upon States to 'take effective measures to ensure public functionaries in the conduct of their public duties do not discriminate against an individual on the basis of religion or belief'.[117] However, the new resolutions emphasise the need for positive action by States in order to properly protect and promote key rights. For instance, the resolutions reaffirm 'the positive role that the exercise of the right to freedom of opinion and expression and the full respect for the freedom to seek, receive and impart information can play in strengthening democracy and combating religious intolerance'.[118] Moreover, the new resolutions suggest a deeper understanding of freedom of expression and the right to equality as mutually reinforcing and interdependent rights, and of how they may be realised simultaneously in practice. The emphasis on intercultural dialogue in the new resolutions really does echo and support the progressive standards contained in the Camden Principles on Freedom of Expression and Equality.[119] For instance, Resolution 16/18 recognises the important part that the 'open, constructive and respectful debate of ideas, as well as interfaith and intercultural dialogue . . .can play in combating religious hatred, incitement and violence'.[120] The same resolution earlier

[116] The resolutions call on States to actively adopt measures 'to criminalize incitement to imminent violence based on religion or belief' in para. 5((f), while at the same time 'understanding the need to combat . . . incitement to religious hatred' in para. 5(g). S. Nossel, Questions and Answers at JBI Meeting, 22 January 2012; www.jbi-humanrights.org/jacob-blaustein-institute/su.html (last accessed 3 March 2014).

[117] Para. 6(a). [118] Preamble para. 4.

[119] The Camden Principles on Freedom of Expression and Equality, Parts II and III (Principles 5–10).

[120] HRC, Resolution 16/18, Para 5(h); see also para. 4 which recognises that 'the open debate of ideas, as well as interfaith and intercultural dialogue . . . can be among the best protections against religious intolerance and can play a positive role . . . in combating religious hatred' (ARTICLE 19 and the Cairo Institute for Human Rights Studies, 'Demise of Defamation of Religions?').

encourages States to create 'collaborative networks to build mutual understanding, promoting dialogue'[121] and urges individual 'leaders to discuss within their communities the causes of discrimination, and evolving strategies to counter these causes'.[122] It calls on States to 'foster religious freedom and pluralism by promoting the ability of members of all religious communities to manifest their religion, and to contribute openly and on an equal footing to society'[123] as well as 'strengthened international efforts to promote tolerance and peace based on respect for human rights and the diversity of religions and beliefs'.[124]

## 5 Significance of the 'new approach'

Having analysed both the resolutions on defamation of religions and those on 'combating intolerance, negative stereotyping and stigmatisation of, and discrimination, incitement to violence, and violence against persons based on religion or belief', this chapter now turns to assessing the significance of the latter in terms of their impact upon and relationship with other processes within and outside the framework of the UN human rights system. This section also highlights some factors that are crucial to the robustness and durability of the new approach embodied by Resolution 16/18 and similar subsequent resolutions, as well as other human rights advances at the Human Rights Council.

### *5.1 UN human rights bodies*

Resolution 16/18 has produced a range of ripple effects across the UN human rights system – at the Human Rights Council and the treaty bodies, and also through the work of the OHCHR. Most obviously, there have been the subsequent resolutions – Human Rights Council Resolutions 19/25 of 23 March 2012 and 22/31 of 22 March 2013 and General Assembly Resolutions 66/167 of 19 December 2011 and 67/178 of 20 December 2012.

There are the initiatives undertaken pursuant to those resolutions: pursuant to Resolution 16/18, the OHCHR hosted a panel discussion on 'Countering Religious Intolerance' during the 17th session of the Human Rights Council;[125] pursuant to General Assembly resolution 66/167, the

[121] Para. 5(a). [122] Para. 5(d). [123] Para. 6(b). [124] Para. 9.

[125] See www.ohchr.org/EN/NewsEvents/Pages/Practicalmeasurestopromoteacultureoftolerance.aspx (last accessed 4 March 2014).

Secretary-General submitted at the 67th session of the General Assembly in 2012 a report on steps taken by States to 'combat intolerance, negative stereotyping, stigmatization, discrimination, incitement to violence and violence against persons, based on religion or belief'.[126]

The new consensus against defamation of religions achieved in Resolution 16/18 resonated in the Human Rights Committee's authoritative interpretation of Article 19 of the ICCPR, General Comment No 34. As indicated earlier, this stated that '[p]rohibitions of displays of lack of respect for a religion or other belief system, including blasphemy laws, are incompatible' with the ICCPR unless they constitute incitement under Article 20 paragraph 2 and comply with Article 19 paragraph 3.[127] However, this position of the Committee confirming the inconsistency between the protection of free speech under international law and laws on 'defamation of religions' was far from guaranteed. The ultimate formulation of paragraph 48 was agreed by the Human Rights Committee on 21 July 2011 at its very last meeting considering the General Comment during its 102nd session.[128] The wording of the paragraph was a marked improvement on earlier formulations,[129] which appeared to leave room for blasphemy or laws prohibiting defamation of religion,[130] as both States and

[126] General Assembly Resolution 66/167 of 19 December 2011, para. 10; *Report of the Secretary General on Combating Intolerance, Negative Stereotyping, Stigmatization, Discrimination, Incitement to Violence and Violence against Persons Based on Religion or Belief*, UN Doc. A/67/296, 10 August 2012.

[127] General Comment No. 34, para. 48.

[128] General Comment No. 34 was adopted at the 2820th meeting of the Human Rights Council at its 102nd session which was held from 11–29 July 2011.

[129] CCPR/C/GC/34/CRP.1, 31 August 2009, para. 49; CCPR/C/GC/34/CRP.2, 29 January 2010, para. 47; CCPR/C/GC/34/CRP.4, 22 October 2010, para. 50; CCPR/C/GC/34/CRP.6, 3 May 2011, para. 50.

[130] Notably, the latest publicly available draft version of the General Comment before its adoption, which was dated 3 May 2011, stated at its para. 50 that: 'Blasphemy prohibitions and other prohibitions of display of disrespect to a religion or other belief system may not be applied in a manner that is incompatible with the para. 3 or other provisions of the Covenant, including Articles 2, 5, 18 and 26 taking into account relevant general comments including General Comment No. 22. Thus, for instance, they may not discriminate in a manner that prefers one or certain religions or belief systems or their adherents over another, or religious believers over non-believers. Blasphemy laws should not be used to prevent or punish criticism of religious leaders or commentary on religious doctrine and tenets of faith. States parties should repeal criminal law provisions on blasphemy and regarding displays of disrespect for religion or other belief system other than in the specific context of compliance with article 20 (discussed below).'

NGOs had pointed out before the 102nd session.[131] A number of global NGOs – notably, ARTICLE 19 joined later by Human Rights Watch and Amnesty International[132] – felt further compelled to write letters to Committee members reinforcing such earlier submissions during the session itself, having learnt of the Committee's intention to finalise the General Comment at that session and concerned that the paragraph dealing with prohibitions on religious insult and blasphemy laws would not be improved.[133] These NGO letters contained critical references to consensus achieved on Human Rights Council Resolution 16/18 and its omission of the term defamation of religions.[134] Thus, the NGO advocacy strategy at the Human Rights Committee echoed the breakthrough of Resolution 16/18 and, in doing so, reinforced the value of looking to the main UN Charter-based human rights body to the principal treaty body on civil and political rights.

The momentum generated by Resolution 16/18 and General Comment No. 34 may have nudged the Committee on the Elimination of Racial Discrimination into convening, in August 2012, a 'day of thematic discussion' to reflect upon the possibility of preparing a general recommendation on the subject of racist hate speech on the basis of Articles 4(a) of the International Convention on the Elimination of Racial

131 For example, see ARTICLE 19, 'Statement on Draft General Comment No. 34 on Article 19 of the ICCPR on Freedom of Opinion and Expression upon completion of the first reading by the Human Rights Committee' 31 January 2011, paras. 47–9; see also, 'Observations of the United States of America on the Human Rights Committee's Draft General Comment 34: Article 19', 5 July 2011 (on file with author).

132 Letter from Dr Agnes Callamard, ARTICLE 19 Executive Director, to Committee Members, 13 July 2011; letter from Julie de Rivero, Geneva Director, Human Rights Watch, to Committee Members, 20 July 2011; letter from Michael Bochenek, Senior Director, International Law and Policy Programme, Amnesty International, to the Chair of the Human Rights Committee, 20 July 2011 (all on file with author).

133 The Rapporteur of the General Comment, Michael O'Flaherty, has written that he believed the earlier language to be 'rigorous' and leaving 'little or no space for the operation of blasphemy laws'. He also criticises NGOs for making 'their submissions very late in the day (during the Committee session)' and for having 'considerably overstated their case'. Yet he concedes that the NGO's 'concerted lobby afforded the Committee the occasion to revisit the language whereby it declared that blasphemy laws were only compatible with the Covenant when enacted pursuant to the requirements of Article 20'; O'Flaherty, 'Freedom of Expression', 652.

134 The letters from ARTICLE 19 and Human Rights Watch also referred to the statements of the UN Special Rapporteurs on freedom of opinion and expression, freedom of religion or belief and racism, racial discrimination, xenophobia and related intolerance.

Discrimination (ICERD) which requires States to declare as 'an offence punishable by law all dissemination of ideas based on racial superiority or hatred, incitement to racial discrimination, as well as all acts of violence or incitement to such acts against any race or group of persons of another colour or ethnic origin, and also the provision of any assistance to racist activities, including the financing thereof'.[135] Although the resulting General Recommendation No. 35 on 'combating racist hate speech', which was adopted a year later in September 2013, does not deal with 'hate speech' on the grounds of religion or belief, it is interesting that the Committee expressly draws upon the 'elaboration' of freedom of expression by its 'sister human rights bodies', notably General Comment No. 34 of the Human Rights Committee.[136]

### 5.2 *The Istanbul Process*

The new approach under Resolution 16/18 has left an impression on intergovernmental structures, specifically through the so-called 'Istanbul Process for Combating Intolerance Based on Religion or Belief'. The 'Istanbul Process' purports to operationalise Resolution 16/18 and has gained much attention from its most influential backer, the United States. In July 2011, US Secretary of State Clinton and the OIC's Secretary General Ihsanoglu co-chaired a High-Level Ministerial meeting on the implementation of Resolution 16/18 in Istanbul. The meeting, which was attended by the EU High Representative for Foreign Affairs and the ministers of foreign affairs and representatives from twenty States,[137] sought to 'turn . . . energies to seeking real and effective measures against bigotry, discrimination and violence on the basis of religion or belief in ways spelled out in resolution 16/18, which are fully consistent with freedom of expression'.[138] The Istanbul meeting led to a joint statement

[135] International Convention on the Elimination of All Forms of Racial Discrimination, summary record of the 2196th meeting, Day of thematic discussion on racist hate speech, UN Doc. CERD/C/SR.2196, 4 September 2012.

[136] Committee on the Elimination of Racial Discrimination, General Recommendation No. 35 on 'Combating racist hate speech', 26 September 2013, CERD/C/GC/35 at para. 4. See also paras. 12 and 16. For analysis, see Chapter 4 in this book.

[137] US Department of State, 'The "Istanbul Process for Combating Religious Intolerance and Discrimination Based on Religion or Belief" Implementing Human Rights Council (HRC) Resolution 16/18, December Expert Meeting', www.humanrights.gov/wp-content/uploads/2011/12/20111204-Istanbul-Process.pdf (last accessed 3 March 2014).

[138] US Department of State, 'Remarks of Hillary Rodham Clinton at Organisation of Islamic Conference High Level Meeting on Combating Religious Intolerance', Center for Islamic

by governments calling upon all relevant stakeholders throughout the world to take seriously the call for action set forth in Resolution 16/18.[139] The US Department of State subsequently held the first expert meeting on the implementation of Resolution 16/18 on 12–14 December 2011, in Washington, DC. That brought together representatives from twenty-six governments and four international organisations, including law enforcement and anti-discrimination experts. This initial meeting focused on discussing the specific steps called for in the resolution: first, the enforcement of anti-discrimination laws (in relation to discrimination based on religion or belief); and second, training government officials, including training on how to implement effective outreach to religious communities.[140] Following the Washington, DC meeting, the US Department of State compiled a report on the expert presentations and the key points put forward during the discussions. This report was publicly disseminated and also submitted to the OHCHR.[141] A further meeting on 'combating intolerance and promoting freedom of religion or belief for all: working on UN Human Rights Council Resolution 16/18' was hosted by the Canadian High Commission and the UK Foreign and Commonwealth Office in London on 3 and 5 December 2012.[142] The proposal for creating a UN observatory for monitoring religious freedom violations, which is troubling for States such as the USA, was discussed at this meeting.

The Istanbul Process may be considered as an example of the 'strengthened international efforts to foster global dialogue for the promotion of a culture of tolerance and peace at all levels' that Resolution 16/18 calls for. At the same time, the process is justifiably open to criticisms about its legitimacy. Despite the purported aim of implementing Resolution 16/18, the process is closed and lacking in transparency with access to information about the various meetings held under its

Arts and History, Istanbul, Turkey, 15 July 2011; http://iipdigital.usembassy.gov/st/english/texttrans/2011/07/20110715154318su0.647575.html#axzz2xtys7y60 (last accessed 3 March 2014).

[139] US Department of State, '"Istanbul Process"'.

[140] US Department of State, *Report of the United States on the First Meeting of Experts to Promote the Implementation of United Nations Human Rights Council Resolution 16/18*, December 2011; www.humanrights.gov/wp-content/uploads/2012/04/1618FirstMeetingReport.pdf (last accessed 3 March 2014).

[141] *Ibid.*

[142] Wilton Park Conference Report, 'Combating intolerance and promoting freedom of religion or belief for all: Working on UN Human Rights Council Resolution 16/18', 3–5 December 2012, WP 1187, February 2013.

auspices very limited indeed.[143] There are also limited possibilities for broad NGO participation and as a result inadequate provision for external scrutiny of this process.

Moreover, its relationship with the UN human rights system is unclear: the nature of the process involves the interpretation of the scope of Resolution 16/18, yet the initiative should be distinguished from the UN human rights bodies. Even though the Istanbul Process is expressly welcomed by General Assembly Resolution 67/178 of 20 December 2012 and Human Rights Council 22/31 of 22 March 2013, the existence of the process potentially offers an alternative, and inevitably rival, mechanism for the interpretation of international human rights law to UN human rights bodies and processes, such as that which led up to the Rabat Plan of Action (discussed below). This could lead to confusion among States about how to combat religious discrimination and protect freedom of expression under international law, and consequent intransigence on domestic reform. If the Istanbul Process is to provide a genuinely useful resource for States in the implementation of Resolution 16/18, these questions concerning its transparency and authority need to be fruitfully addressed.

### 5.3 *Rabat Plan of Action*

In contrast to the intergovernmental and closed nature of the Istanbul Process focusing on the action plan under Resolution 16/18, the series of expert workshops on the narrower subject of international law's prohibition of incitement which culminated in the Rabat Plan of Action in October 2012 brought together experts, UN authorities and NGO representatives and was remarkably open and transparent. The series of expert workshops on the prohibition of 'advocacy of national, racial or religious hatred that constitutes incitement to discrimination, hostility and violence' was instigated by the Durban Review Conference in 2009 when declining States' support for UN human rights bodies' resolutions defamation of religions was clearly discernible and a refocusing of the debate on the meaning of incitement looked inevitable.[144] That shift of focus

[143] The first meeting in Washington was apparently held under the 'Chatham House' rules in order to promote a 'free and candid exchange of views'. See US Department of State, 'Remarks of Hillary Rodham Clinton', 4.

[144] Para. 134 of the Durban Review Conference outcome document 'takes note of the proposal of the OHCHR, in cooperation with regional stakeholders in all parts of the

came with Resolution 16/18 which was adopted interestingly a little over a month after the European regional workshop in Vienna on 9 and 10 February. Together with General Comment No. 34, the Rabat Plan of Action presents the most important fortification of the new approach under Resolution 16/18 from within the UN human rights system.[145] Indeed, it should serve as a restraint on parties wishing to revive the concept of defamation of religions in the superficial guise of 'incitement against persons on the grounds of religion or belief' as condemned in the new resolutions. The OHCHR workshops are therefore crucial in preventing the 'transmogrification' of the discourse of defamation of religions into one of incitement.[146]

The series of workshops was organised by the OHCHR and brought together forty-five experts in Vienna, Nairobi, Bangkok and Santiago in 2011 before a final wrap-up expert meeting was held in Rabat, Morocco on 4 and 5 October 2012.[147] The workshops were intended to examine 'legislative patterns, judicial practices and ... policies' concerning the prohibition of incitement to national, racial or religious hatred around the world; produce a 'comprehensive assessment of the state of implementation of this prohibition'; and 'identify possible actions at all levels'.[148] The resulting Rabat Plan of Action envisages a holistic approach to the implementation of international obligations on incitement to discrimination, hostility and violence which includes 'criminal sanctions ... as last

world, to organize in light of the OHCHR Expert Seminar on the links between articles 19 and 20 of the International Covenant on Civil and Political Rights (ICCPR) a series of expert workshops to attain a better understanding of the legislative patterns, judicial practices and national policies in the different regions of the world with regard to the concept of incitement to hatred, in order to assess the level of implementation of the prohibition of incitement to hatred, as stipulated in article 20 of the ICCPR', *Report of the Durban Review Conference*, Geneva, UN Doc. A/CONF.211/820–24 April 2009.

145 For a more detailed analysis of the significance of the Rabat Plan of Action, see S. Parmar, 'The Rabat Plan of Action: A Global Blueprint for Combating "Hate Speech"', *European Human Rights Law Review* 1 (2014), 21–31.

146 Blitt, 'Bottom up Journey of "Defamation of Religion"'.

147 The regional workshops that were organised throughout 2011 took place in Vienna on 9–10 February 2011(for the European region), in Nairobi on 6–7 April 2011(for the African region), in Bangkok on 6–7 July 2011(for the Asia-Pacific region) and in Santiago on 12–13 October 2011 (for the Americas region).

148 Concept paper on OHCHR's expert workshops on the prohibition of incitement to national, racial or religious hatred: follow-up to the expert seminar on articles 19 and 20 of the ICCPR with regard to freedom of expression and incitement to hatred, 2011, www.ohchr.org/Documents/Issues/Expression/ICCPR/IncitementWorkshopsConcept-Paper.pdf (last accessed 4 March 2014).

resort measures to be only applied in strictly justifiable situations', 'civil sanctions and remedies ... including pecuniary and non-pecuniary damages, along with the right of correction and the right to reply' and 'administrative sanctions and remedies ... including those identified and put in force by various professional and regulatory bodies'.[149] Such legal responses also include 'comprehensive anti-discrimination legislation that includes preventive and punitive action to effectively combat incitement to hatred'.[150] At the same time, the Rabat Plan of Action acknowledges the importance of non-legal responses, specifically 'policies, practices and measures nurturing social consciousness, tolerance and understanding change and public discussion' that should also be adopted by States to '[create] and [strengthen] a culture of peace, tolerance and mutual respect among individuals, public officials and members of the judiciary ... [to render] media organizations and religious/community leaders more ethically aware and socially responsible'.[151] The plan therefore suggests that a greater level of commitment is required from a range of State and non-State actors to combat more effectively religious discrimination and violence.[152]

The Rabat Plan of Action thus fleshes out the legal and policy implications of States' international legal obligations to prohibit 'incitement', the term found at the heart of Resolution 16/18 and subsequent similar resolutions. The plan is arguably imbibed with a strong sense of legitimacy because of the transparent nature of the process leading up to its adoption by which the contributions of stakeholders were made available on the OHCHR website,[153] and the meaningful participation of a range of stakeholders.[154] The workshops each included: the presentation of a regional study of major trends in legislation, jurisprudence and policy relating to the prohibition of incitement; joint submissions of the Special Rapporteurs on freedom of opinion and expression, racism, racial discrimination and related intolerance and freedom of religion or

149 *Rabat Plan of Action*, para. 34. 150 *Ibid.*, para. 26. 151 *Ibid.*, para. 35.

152 Lecture at the London School of Economics by Ms Navi Pillay UNCHR, 'Freedom of expression and incitement to hatred in the context of international human rights law', 15 February 2013.

153 See www.ohchr.org/EN/Issues/FreedomOpinion/Articles19-20/Pages/ExpertsPapers.aspx (last accessed 4 March 2014).

154 For Franck, legitimacy was 'a property of a rule or rule-making institution which itself exerts a pull toward compliance on those addressed normatively because those addressed believe that the rule or institution has come into being and operates in accordance with generally accepted principles of right process' (T. Franck, *The Power of Legitimacy Among Nations* (New York: Oxford University Press, 1990), 24).

belief;[155] expert papers by members of human rights treaty bodies, leading academics and prominent NGOs; and contributions from stakeholders, including States, other NGOs and national human rights institutions.[156] The Rabat Plan of Action thus expressly draws on authoritative interpretations of international law by treaty bodies, namely General Comment No. 34 of the Human Rights Committee[157] and General Recommendation No. 15 of the Committee on the Elimination of Racial Discrimination,[158] as well as the Camden Principles on Freedom of Expression and Equality, a set of principles developed by ARTICLE 19, the leading international NGO working on freedom of expression globally, on the basis of multi-stakeholder discussions.[159] As part of its contribution to all of the workshops, ARTICLE 19 developed a six-part 'threshold test' that should be applied when assessing whether a particular form of expression reaches the level prohibited under Article 20 paragraph 20 of the ICCPR.[160] This proposal was reflected in the adopted action plan's identification of the following six elements to determine whether speech is severe enough to be prohibited through the criminal law as incitement.

1 *Context:* context is of great importance when assessing whether particular statements are likely to incite discrimination, hostility or

155 Interestingly, in their submissions to the workshops, the three UN mandate-holders welcomed 'the fact that the debate seems to be shifting to the concept of "incitement to national, racial or religious hatred" and cautioned "against confusion between a racist statement and an act of "defamation of religion"' (joint submission by Mr Heiner Bielefeldt, Special Rapporteur on freedom of religion or belief, Mr Frank La Rue, Special Rapporteur on the promotion and protection of the right to freedom of opinion and expression, and Mr Githu Muigai, Special Rapporteur on contemporary forms of racism, racial discrimination, xenophobia and related intolerance, OHCHR expert workshop on Europe, 9–10 February 2011, Vienna).

156 See www.ohchr.org/EN/Issues/FreedomOpinion/Articles19-20/Pages/ExpertsPapers.aspx (last accessed 4 March 2014).

157 *Rabat Plan of Action*, paras. 8, 17 and 23.

158 *Ibid.*, para. 23.

159 *Ibid.*, paras. 8 (fn.), 21 and 58.

160 See, most notably, A. Callamard, B. Bukovska and S. Parmar, 'Towards an Interpretation of Article 20 of the ICCPR: Thresholds for the Prohibition of Incitement to Hatred', study prepared for the regional expert meeting on Article 20, organized by the OHCHR, Vienna, February 8–9, 2010; www.ohchr.org/Documents/Issues/Expression/ICCPR/Vienna/CRP7Callamard.pdf (last accessed 4 March 2014) ARTICLE 19's policy brief was finalised on the basis of the comments received during the workshops and published in December 2012. See ARTICLE 19, 'Policy Brief: Prohibiting Incitement to Discrimination, Hostility or Violence', December 2012; www.article19.org/data/files/medialibrary/3548/ARTICLE-19-policy-on-prohibition-to-incitement.pdf (last accessed 4 March 2014).

violence against the target group, and it may have a direct bearing on both intent and/or causation. Analysis of the context should place the speech act within the social and political context prevalent at the time the speech was made and disseminated.

2 *Speaker:* the speaker's position or status in the society should be considered, specifically the individual's or organisation's standing in the context of the audience to whom the speech is directed.
3 *Intent:* Article 20 of the ICCPR anticipates intent. Negligence and recklessness are not sufficient for an act to be an offence under Article 20 of the Covenant, as this article provides for 'advocacy' and 'incitement' rather than the mere distribution or circulation of material. In this regard, it requires the activation of a triangular relationship between the object and subject of the speech act as well as the audience.
4 *Content and form:* the content of the speech constitutes one of the key foci of the court's deliberations and is a critical element of incitement. Content analysis may include the degree to which the speech was provocative and direct, as well as the form, style, nature of arguments deployed in the speech or the balance struck between arguments deployed.
5 *Extent of the speech act:* extent includes such elements as the reach of the speech act, its public nature, its magnitude and size of its audience. Other elements to consider include whether the speech is public, what means of dissemination are used, for example by a single leaflet or broadcast in the mainstream media or via the Internet, the frequency, the quantity and the extent of the communications, whether the audience had the means to act on the incitement, whether the statement (or work) is circulated in a restricted environment or widely accessible to the general public.
6 *Likelihood, including imminence:* incitement, by definition, is an inchoate crime. The action advocated through incitement speech does not have to be committed for said speech to amount to a crime. Nevertheless, some degree of risk of harm must be identified. It means that the courts will have to determine that there was a reasonable probability that the speech would succeed in inciting actual action against the target group, recognizing that such causation should be rather direct.

Given its credibility and legitimacy – based on the process leading up to its adoption and its substantive elaboration of obligations under international law on incitement[161] – it is positive that the Rabat Plan of Action has already influenced various UN human rights actors (who have expressly referred to the plan as a whole or to its specific provisions), notably the Human Rights Council and General Assembly,[162] the Committee on the Elimination of Racial Discrimination,[163] several Special Rapporteurs[164] and the Special Adviser to the Secretary General on the Prevention of Genocide,[165] as well as the High Commissioner for Human Rights.[166]

## 5.4 *Robustness*

The new approach towards combating religious discrimination in compliance with freedom of expression may be viewed as a demonstration of a much-needed positive shift in the institutional dynamics at the Human Rights Council during 2011.[167] On the one hand, there are many other examples of significant progress on thematic issues including the first-ever resolution on sexual orientation, gender identity and human rights, which was previously considered as 'off-limits'.[168] On the other hand, there are

[161] See Parmar, 'Rabat Plan of Action', at 24–31.

[162] HR Council Resolution 22/31 of 22 March 2013, A/HRC/RES/22/31, para. 4; General Assembly Resolution 67/178 of 20 December 2012, A/RES/67/178, preamble, para. 22.

[163] General Recommendation No. 35.

[164] *Report of the Special Rapporteur on Freedom of Religion*, Heiner Bielefeldt, A/HRC/22/51, 24 December 2012 at para. 63; *Report of the Special Rapporteur on Freedom of Opinion and Expression*, Frank La Rue, A/HRC/23/, 17 April 2013 at para. 8; *Report of the Special Rapporteur on Freedom of Opinion and Expression*, Frank La Rue, A/67/357, 7 September 2012; *Report of the Special Rapporteur on Contemporary Forms of Racism, Racial Discrimination, Xenophobia and Related Intolerance*, Mutuma Ruteere, A/HRC/23/56, 2 April 2013 at para. 9.

[165] 'Preventing Incitement: Policy Options for Action', November 2013.

[166] See, for example, N. Pillay, 'Freedom of expression and incitement to hatred in the context of international human rights law', lecture at the London School of Economics, 15 February 2013; OHCHR press release, 'Between free speech and hate speech: the Rabat Plan of Action, a practical tool to combat incitement to hatred', 21 February 2013.

[167] Human Rights Watch, 'Keeping the Momentum: One Year in the Life of the Human Rights Council', 22 July 2011, www.hrw.org/sites/default/files/reports/hrc0911ForWeb.pdf (last accessed 4 March 2014).

[168] The resolution called on the High Commissioner for Human Rights to commission a study that documents discriminatory laws and practices and acts of violence against individuals based on their sexual orientation and gender identity, in all regions of the world. The Council called on OHCHR to examine how international human rights law can be used to end violence and related human rights violations based on sexual orientation and gender identity. The Council also decided to convene a panel discussion during its March 2012 session focusing on the issue of discriminatory laws and practices and acts

active, countervailing forces to this positive development. More specifically, some of the conservative attitudes previously informing resolutions on defamation of religions appear to have been redirected into support for 'traditional values' and the 'protection of the family' being integrated into the UN human rights agenda.[169] Since 2009, the Human Rights Council has adopted resolutions on 'a better understanding of traditional values of humankind' as a mechanism for 'promoting human rights and fundamental freedoms'.[170] The discourse of 'traditional values' embraced in these resolutions has been viewed as a 'code for human rights abuse' because it undermines the human rights principles of indivisibility and universality and presents 'an immediate threat' to the rights – including and notably free speech rights – of vulnerable groups, including women and lesbian, gay, bisexual and transgender (LGBT) people.[171] It should

of violence against individuals based on their sexual orientation and gender identity. It requested the panel to discuss what would be appropriate follow-up to the recommendations of the study commissioned by the High Commissioner; HRC, Resolution 17/19: Human rights, sexual orientation and gender identity, UN Doc. A/HRC/Res/17/19, 17 June 2011; Human Rights Watch, 'Landmark Vote on Sexual Orientation', 17 June 2011; www.hrw.org/news/2011/06/17/landmark-un-vote-sexual-orientation (4 March 2014).

169 At the 22nd session of the Council in February–March 2013, Egypt presented a draft text on the 'protection of the family', though consideration of the text was postponed until the 24th session of the Council in June 2013, although it was not actually presented then. See International Service for Human Rights, 'ISHR's achievements at the Human Rights Council's 22nd session', 26 April 2013; www.ishr.ch/council/428-council-not-in-feed/1494-ishrs-achievements-at-the-human-rights-councils-22nd-session (last accessed 4 March 2014).

170 There have so far been three such resolutions at the HR Council: Resolution 12/21 of 2 October 2009; Resolution 16/3 of 24 March 2011; and Resolution 21/3 of 27 September 2012. See also the report of the High Commissioner for Human Rights in response to Resolution 21/3 of 27 September 2012: Summary of Information from States Members of the United Nations and Other Relevant Stakeholders on Best Practices in the Application of Traditional Values While Promoting and Protecting Human Rights and Upholding Human Dignity, A/HRC/24/22, 17 June 2013.

171 G. Reid, '"Traditional Values" Code for Human Rights Abuse?', 17 October 2012; http://globalpublicsquare.blogs.cnn.com/2012/10/17/traditional-values-code-for-human-rights-abuse (last accessed 4 March 2014); see also, G. Reid, 'The Trouble with Tradition: When "Values" Trample Over Rights', in *Human Rights Watch World Report: Events of 2012*; www.hrw.org/world-report/2013 (last accessed 4 March 2014). The 'traditional values' resolutions build on and bolster laws seeking to curb freedom of expression by restricting 'homosexual propaganda' on the grounds of child protection. See ARTICLE 19, 'Traditional Values? Attempts to Censor Sexuality', March 2013; www.article19.org/resources.php/resource/3637/en/what%E2%80%99s-wrong-with-tradition?-how-%E2%80%98homosexual-propaganda%E2%80%99-bans-violate-human-rights (last accessed 4 March 2014).

come as no surprise that the Russian-sponsored resolutions are backed by States such as China and Cuba, as well as members of the OIC.[172] The constituencies and cleavages within the Human Rights Council on the issue of 'traditional values' thus resemble those that dominated the debate on defamation of religions for many years.

The robustness and durability of the new approach to freedom of expression under Resolution 16/18 depends on a number of factors underlying this recent shift in dynamics. The most significant of these factors are highlighted here.

The *first* of these factors is the impact of the domestic law and policies of key States upon international cooperation on contentious human rights issues, including freedom of expression. Religious insult laws remain applicable in European States – a factor which made their strong stance against resolutions on defamation of religions smack of double standards.[173] Yet it is the preponderance of national laws and policies on blasphemy, defamation and insult of religions across much of the rest of the world that undoubtedly undercut the possibilities for meaningful implementation of Resolution 16/18. Despite the initial optimism surrounding the Arab Awakening, the protection of freedom of expression in the Middle East and North Africa region, especially with respect to speech concerning religion, has *deteriorated* since late 2010.[174] Blasphemy and religious insult laws continue to be vigorously applied in many States which previously supported the defamation of religions resolutions.[175] In May 2012, the owner of Tunisian Nessma TV, Nabil Karoui, was fined 2,300 dinars (US$1,490) for broadcasting the animated film *Persepolis*, deemed as blasphemous by some

172 The OIC States who voted in favour of Resolution 21/3 of 9 October 2012 were: Bangladesh, Cameroon, Indonesia, Jordan, Kuwait, Kyrgyzstan, Libya, Malaysia, Maldives, Mauritania, Qatar, Saudi Arabia, Senegal and Uganda.

173 Venice Commission, *Report on the Relationship between Freedom of Expression and Freedom of Religion: the Issue of Regulation and Prosecution of Blasphemy, Religious Insult and Incitement to Religious Hatred.*

174 Human Rights Watch has indicated that the climate for freedom of expression in Egypt has actually deteriorated since Hosni Mubarak was ousted in February 2011. See Human Rights Watch, 'Egypt: A Year of Attacks on Freedom of Expression', 11 February 2012; www.hrw.org/news/2012/02/11/egypt-year-attacks-free-expression (last accessed 4 March 2014); see also Human Rights First, 'Blasphemy Laws Exposed', 2012; www.humanrightsfirst.org/our-work/fighting-discrimination/blasphemy (last accessed 4 March 2014).

175 US Department of State, Bureau of Democracy, Human Rights and Labour, *International Religious Freedom Report 2012*; www.state.gov/j/drl/rls/irf/religiousfreedom/index.htm#wrapper (last accessed 4 March 2014).

Islamists.[176] Although from late 2012 the Tunisian National Constituent Assembly decided to remove from the draft constitution proposals that would have criminalised 'attacks on that which is sacred,' there is the risk – and even expectation – that existing or newly adopted laws 'could be used to increase the use of accusations of blasphemy to stifle peaceful dissent and to polarise Tunisian society along a secular versus religious axis.'[177] In relation to Egypt, Human Rights Watch reported that in 2012 at least fifteen people were interrogated or indicted for defaming religion. In September 2012, Bishoy Kamel, Coptic Christian schoolteacher, was sentenced to six years' imprisonment for 'insulting Islam' while in December 2012, Alber Saber, a blogger, was convicted and sentenced to three years' imprisonment for insulting Islam and Christianity. The new Egyptian Constitution, which was approved by referendum in December 2012, makes such prosecutions more likely. Article 44 of the Constitution prohibits insulting or criticising prophets and messengers, and the Egyptian penal code establishes the associated criminal penalties, including a minimum of six months and a maximum of five years' imprisonment for citizens who promulgate 'extremist thoughts with the aim of inciting strife, demeaning or defaming any of the heavenly religions, or inflicting damage to the national unity'.[178]

Thus, while the discourse of defamation of religions appears to have been erased from the UN agenda for now, the impact of prohibitions on defamation of religions stubbornly remains through domestic provisions on blasphemy and religious insult that remain intact in many States. There needs to be greater coherence between progressive decisions on challenging human rights issues taken by the UN human rights bodies, especially the Human Rights Council, and domestic policies and laws, in order for those steps to gain traction and survive. Put simply and in connection with the current discussion, if there is no movement towards the abolition of blasphemy and religious insult laws at national level around the world, the new international approach towards combating religious discrimination in compliance with freedom of expression will lose credibility and practical meaning. Yet it is difficult to see how such a movement will emerge anytime soon.

[176] 'Tunisia', in *Human Rights Watch World Report: Events of 2012*, 620; www.hrw.org/world-report/2013 (last accessed 4 March 2014).

[177] Human Rights First, 'Blasphemy, Freedom of Expression, and Tunisia's Transition to Democracy', May 2013, 1.

[178] As quoted in US Department of State, *International Religious Freedom Report 2012*.

The *second* factor is the openness of key States to constructive engagement. The decision to adopt Resolution 16/18 and, in doing so, to deepen the understanding of 'discrimination, incitement to violence, and violence against persons based on religion or belief' was the outcome not only of the game-changing engagement of the USA since its election to the Council, but also the OIC's own awareness that its relentless proposal of resolutions on defamation of religions discourse had gravely tarnished its reputation. Significantly, the OIC maintained this position despite calls made in 2012 for it to revive its efforts to combat defamation of religions at the UN following the publication by a French satirical weekly magazine, *Charlie Hebdo*, of a set of cartoons depicting the Prophet Mohammed and the distribution of the film, *Innocence of Muslims*.[179]

The *third* factor is the pervasiveness of 'bloc politics' at the Human Rights Council, which is also reflected in the General Assembly.[180] The story of defamation of religions and its demise shows that, while these UN human rights bodies are formally speaking statist bodies, the identity ties between States mean that voting blocs hold a powerful sway upon individual States.[181] The story also exposes the muscle and self-confidence of one particular organisation, the OIC, and the strength of the bonds between its members and those who would wish to stand in solidarity with them. Despite the erosion of support for resolutions on defamation of religions in later years, it remained a challenge for the EU and the United States to persuade States in the African Group and Latin American and Caribbean Group (GRULAC) of the problematic nature of the concept in the face of intransigent adherence to the notion by the OIC.[182] It was arguably only when key players within the OIC recognised that their advocacy of resolutions on defamation of religions was untenable that the debate really changed. The influence of bloc politics continues to be seen in the discussions following Resolution 16/18, for example in terms of

[179] T. Heneghen, 'West's free speech stand bars blasphemy ban: OIC', *Reuters*, 15 October 2012.

[180] The European Parliament, Policy Department, Directorate-General for External Policies, *Study on the European Union and the Review of the Human Rights Council*, Doc. No. EXPO/B/DROI/2010/06, February 2011, 15.

[181] B. Rajagopal, 'Lipstick on a Caterpillar: Assessing the New Human Rights Council through Historical Reflection', *Buffalo Human Rights Law Review* 13 (2007), 7–17.

[182] A 2011 policy study produced for the European Parliament in advance of the review of the Human Rights Council observed that 'moderate states in blocs opposing the EU often find it more attractive to go along with the OIC or the Africa Group or the NAM than to resist the peer pressure and vote with the EU' (NAM indicates Non-Aligned Movement). See European Parliament, *Study on the European Union*.

attitudes towards its further implementation through the establishment of a UN observatory to monitor violations of religious freedom.

The *fourth* factor relates to the possibilities for consolidating progress through other UN human rights bodies and processes. The discontinuance of resolutions on defamation of religions in March 2011 could not by itself mark a 'new approach' towards freedom of expression. It is a 'new approach' because it has been consolidated and developed in compliance with freedom of expression standards through complementary instruments and processes emanating from the UN human rights system – namely the subsequent resolutions by the General Assembly and the Human Rights Council, the Human Rights Committee's General Comment No. 34 and the Rabat Plan of Action – as well as the Istanbul Process intended to identify best practices for the implementation of Resolution 16/18.

Yet attempts to consolidate progress have not been smooth and consistent, as States' differing perspectives on the various elements of the new approach have been revealed. The process leading up to the adoption of the series of resolutions building on Resolution 16/18 has been increasingly fraught with tension. Indeed, the new approach currently appears rather fragile. Cracks in the consensus among States, which had already begun to appear, were particularly evident during the negotiations on Human Rights Council Resolution 22/31 of 22 March 2013. The USA was concerned by and initially resisted the reference to the OHCHR workshops and the Rabat Plan of Action on incitement in that resolution.[183] The biggest threat to the consensus, however, may yet result from the growing calls, particularly among OIC States, for the establishment of a UN observatory to monitor violations of freedom of religion or belief as a means to implement the action plan under Resolution 16/18. (Human Rights Council Resolution 22/31 'mentions follow-up measures for further improvement of the implementation' of the action plan, but does not actually indicate an observatory.) If the establishment of such an observatory were agreed in principle, future battles would predictably lie over its specific purposes, function, structure and scope of work.

## 6 Conclusions

This story of defamation of religions provides a highly instructive case study of the struggles within the UN human rights bodies, particularly

[183] Para 4.

the Human Rights Council, between and among States, blocs, notably the OIC, and NGOs on one of the most highly contentious contemporary human rights issues. Resolution 16/18 marked an important and positive turning point in the international protection of freedom of expression in its connection with freedom of religion or belief and equality. It remains important to understand the rationales for and against UN resolutions on defamation of religions in order to guard against the possibility of the resurrection of the concept at the UN human rights bodies or in another UN forum at a later date. More likely than the slogan of 'combating defamation of religions' being raised, however, is the prospect of attempts to undermine freedom of expression through specific measures proposed to implement the Resolution 16/18 agenda. States should now focus on further embedding the new approach by making positive efforts to implement Resolution 16/18 at the national level. For this to be done effectively, the Istanbul Process needs to be made open to broader participation and also transparent with its recommendations for best practices widely disseminated through, at minimum, a website containing documentation from all meetings held to date and future meetings, including outcome documents and submissions received. At the same time, State and non-State actors, including the media, should capitalise on the sense of momentum behind the Rabat Plan of Action by publicly endorsing and then implementing its recommendations relating to legislation and policies, while national judges should pay due attention to the plan's threshold criteria when deciding cases concerning allegations of incitement. More ambitiously, the rejection of the discourse of defamation of religions at the UN in 2011 should herald the beginning of a global campaign for the abolition of national blasphemy and religious insult laws.

## Literature

Blitt, R. C. 'The Bottom up Journey of "Defamation of Religion" from Muslim States to the United Nations: A Case Study of the Migration of Anti-Constitutional Ideas', in *Special Issue on Human Rights: New Possibilities/New Problems, Studies in Law, Politics and Society* 36 (2011), 121–211.

Cerone, J. 'Inappropriate Renderings: The Danger of Reductionist Resolutions', *Brooklyn Journal of International Law* 33 (2008), 357–78.

Choudhury, S. 'Migration as a New Metaphor in Comparative Constitutional Law', in S. Choudhury (ed.), *The Migration of Constitutional Ideas* (Cambridge University Press, 2006), 1–35.

Clapham, A. *Human Rights Obligations of Non-State Actors* (Oxford University Press, 2006).

Dobras, R. J. 'Is the United Nations Endorsing Human Rights Violations? An Analysis of the United Nations' Combating Defamation of Religions Resolutions and Pakistan's Blasphemy Laws', *Georgia Journal of International and Comparative Law* 37 (2009), 339–80.

Foster, J. 'Prophets, Cartoons, and Legal Norms: Rethinking the United Nations Defamation of Religion Provisions', *Journal of Catholic Legal Studies* 49 (2009), 19–57.

Franck, T. *The Power of Legitimacy among Nations* (New York: Oxford University Press, 1990).

Graham, L. B. 'Defamation of Religions: the End of Pluralism', *Emory International Law Review* 23 (2009), 69–84.

Grinberg, M. 'Defamation of Religions v Freedom of Expression: Finding the Balance in a Democratic Society', *Sri Lanka Journal of International Law* 18 (2006), 197–222.

Herz, M. and P. Molnar (eds.), *The Content and Context of Hate Speech: Rethinking Regulation and Responses* (Cambridge University Press, 2012).

Kahn, R. A. 'A Margin of Appreciation for Muslims? Viewing the Defamation of Religions Debate through *Otto-Preminger v. Austria*', *Charleston Law Review* 5 (2011), 401–54.

Langer, L. 'The Rise (and Fall?) of Defamation of Religions', *Yale Journal of International Law* 35 (2010), 257–63.

McGonagle, T. *Minority Rights, Freedom of Expression and of the Media: Dynamics and Dilemmas* (Antwerp: Intersentia, 2011).

McLaughlin, N. 'Spectrum of Defamation of Laws and the Possibility of a Universal International Standard', *Loyola of Los Angeles International and Comparative Law Review* 32 (2010), 395–426.

O'Flaherty, M. 'Freedom of Expression: Article 19 of the International Covenant on Civil and Political Rights and the Human Rights Committee's General Comment No 34', *Human Rights Law Review* 12(4) (2012), 627–54.

Parmar, S. 'The Challenge of "Defamation of Religions" to Freedom of Expression and the International Human Rights System', *European Human Rights Law Review* 3 (2009), 353–75.

Petrova, D. 'Smoke and Mirrors: the Durban Review Conference and Human Rights Politics at the United Nations, *Human Rights Law Review* 10(1) (2010), 129–50.

Rajagopal, B. 'Lipstick on a Caterpillar: Assessing the New Human Rights Council through Historical Reflection', *Buffalo Human Rights Law Review* 13 (2007), 7–17.

Rivers, J. 'Guest Editorial: The Question of Freedom of Religion or Belief and Defamation', *Religion and Human Rights* 2 (2007), 113–18.

Scharffs, B. G. 'International Law and the Defamation of Religion Conundrum', *Review of Faith and International Affairs* 11 (2013), 66–75.

Temperman, J. 'Blasphemy, Defamation of Religions and Human Rights Law', *Netherlands Quarterly of Human Rights* 26 (2008), 527–45.

## Miscellaneous

ARTICLE 19, 'Press release: UN Human Rights Council undermines freedom of expression', 31 March 2008.

'Indonesia: Court decision upholding "defamation of religions" is a major setback', press release, 27 April 2010.

'Statement on Draft General Comment No. 34 on Article 19 of the ICCPR on Freedom of Opinion and Expression upon completion of the first reading by the Human Rights Committee', 31 January 2011.

'UN HRC: Over 100 Organisations Urge Council to Reject Defamation of Religions and Protect Freedom of Expression', 10 March 2011; http://www.article19.org/resources.php/resource/1733/en/un-hrc:-over-100-organisations-urge-council-to-reject-'defamation-of-religions'-and-protect-freedom-of-expression (last accessed 4 March 2014).

'Letter of Civil Society Organisations to State Representatives', 9 March 2011; www.article19.org/data/files/pdfs/letters/-defamation-and-denigration-of-religions-at-the-16th-session-of-the-united-n.pdf (last accessed 3 March 2014).

'ARTICLE 19 Welcomes General Comment on Freedom of Expression', Statement, 5 August 2011.

'Comment on the Draft Text of the Resolution on Freedom of Expression Proposed by Egypt and the United States at the 12th Session of the Human Rights Council', 23 September 2009.

'Traditional Values? Attempts to Censor Sexuality', March 2013; www.article19.org/resources.php/resource/3637/en/what%E2%80%99s-wrong-with-tradition?-how-%E2%80%98homosexual-propaganda%E2%80%99-bans-violate-human-rights (last accessed 4 March 2014).

'Policy Brief: Prohibiting Incitement to Discrimination, Hostility or Violence', December 2012; www.article19.org/data/files/medialibrary/3548/ARTICLE-19-policy-on-prohibition-to-incitement.pdf (last accessed 4 March 2014).

ARTICLE 19 and the Cairo Institute for Human Rights Studies, 'UN General Assembly: UN Member States Should Vote against Resolution on Vilification of Religions', Statement, 19 November 2010.

'The Demise of Defamation of Religions? Council Should Support Resolution on Religious Discrimination' Statement, 22 March 2011.

Cairo Institute for Human Rights Studies, 'Defamation of Religions: International Developments and Challenges on the Ground', March 2011.

Callamard, A., B. Bukovska and S. Parmar, 'Towards an Interpretation of Article 20 of the ICCPR: Thresholds for the Prohibition of Incitement to Hatred', study prepared for the regional expert meeting on Article 20, Organized by the Office of the High Commissioner for Human Rights, Vienna, February 8–9, 2010; www.ohchr.org/Documents/Issues/Expression/ICCPR/Vienna/CRP7Callamard.pdf (last accessed 4 March 2014).

'Concept paper on OHCHR's expert workshops on the prohibition of incitement to national, racial or religious hatred: follow-up to the expert seminar on Articles 19 and 20 of the ICCPR with regard to freedom of expression and incitement to hatred', 2011; www.ohchr.org/Documents/Issues/Expression/ICCPR/IncitementWorkshopsConceptPaper.pdf (last accessed 4 March 2014).

Evans, M. 'Advancing freedom of religion or belief: agendas for change', Annual Lambeth Interfaith lecture, 8 June 2011; www.archbishopofcanterbury.org/articles.php/2062/archbishop-hosts-annual-lambeth-inter-faith-lecture (last accessed 3 March 2014).

Freedom House, 'Policing Belief: The Impact of Blasphemy Laws on Human Rights', October 2010.

Heneghen, T. 'West's free speech stand bars blasphemy ban: OIC', *Reuters*, 15 October 2012.

Human Rights First, 'Blasphemy Laws Exposed: The Consequences of Criminalizing "Defamation of Religions"', March 2011.

Human Rights First, 'Blasphemy Laws Exposed: The Consequences of Criminalizing "Defamation of Religions"', March 2012.

Human Rights First, 'Blasphemy, Freedom of Expression, and Tunisia's Transition to Democracy', May 2013.

Human Rights Watch, 'Keeping the Momentum: One Year in the Life of the Human Rights Council', 22 July 2011; www.hrw.org/sites/default/files/reports/hrc0911ForWeb.pdf (last accessed 4 March 2014).

'Landmark Vote on Sexual Orientation', 17 June 2011; www.hrw.org/news/2011/06/17/landmark-un-vote-sexual-orientation (last accessed 4 March 2014).

IFEX Joint Action, 'Over 100 Organisations Call on UN Human Rights Council to Reject "Defamation" and "Denigration" of Religions'; www.ifex.org/international/2011/03/09/defamation_religions (last accessed 4 March 2014).

ISHR, 'Support for "Defamation of Religions" Continues to Decline: Draft Resolution Passes by Only 12 Votes', 25 November 2010; www.ishr.ch/news/support-defamation-religion-continues-decline-draft-resolution-passes-only-12-votes (last accessed 3 March 2014).

'Human Rights Council: Changing Dynamics on "Defamation Of Religions"', 14 April 2010; www.ishr.ch/news/human-rights-council-changing-dynamics-defamation-religions (last accessed 3 March 2014).

Minority Rights Group, 'The State of the World's Minorities and Indigenous Peoples: Events of 2010', July 2011.

Minority Rights Group, 'Peoples under Threat, Online Briefing', May 2011.

Nossel, S. Questions and answers at JBI Meeting, 22 January 2012; www.jbi-humanrights.org/jacob-blaustein-institute/su.html (last accessed 3 March 2014).

Open Society Justice Initiative, 'Article 19: UN Reinforces Freedom of Expression and Right to Information', 28 July 2011.

Reid, G. '"Traditional values" code for human rights abuse?', 17 October 2012; http://globalpublicsquare.blogs.cnn.com/2012/10/17/traditional-values-code-for-human-rights-abuse (last accessed 4 March 2014).

'The Trouble with Tradition: When "Values" Trample Over Rights', in *Human Rights Watch World Report: Events of 2012*; www.hrw.org/world-report/2013 (last accessed 4 March 2014).

Walsh, D. 'Pakistan's blasphemy laws have left even judges in fear of their lives', *Guardian*, 3 October 2011; www.guardian.co.uk/commentisfree/belief/2011/oct/03/pakistan-blasphemy-laws (last accessed 3 March 2014).

US Department of State, 'The 'Istanbul Process for Combating Religious Intolerance and Discrimination Based on Religion or Belief, Implementing Human Rights Council (HRC) Resolution 16/18, December Expert Meeting'; www.humanrights.gov/wp-content/uploads/2011/12/20111204-Istanbul-Process.pdf (last accessed 3 March 2014).

'Remarks of Hillary Rodham Clinton at Organisation of Islamic Conference High Level Meeting on Combating Religious Intolerance', Center for Islamic Arts and History, Istanbul, Turkey, 15 July 2011; http://iipdigital.usembassy.gov/st/english/texttrans/2011/07/20110715154318su0.647575.html#axzz2x-tys7y60 (last accessed 3 March 2014).

Wilton Park Conference Report, *Combating Intolerance and Promoting Freedom of Religion or Belief for All: Working on UN Human Rights Council Resolution 16/18*, 3–5 December 2012 WP 1187, February 2013.

## UN Documents

### *HRC*

### General Comments

General Comment No. 22: The Right to Freedom of Thought, Conscience and Religion (Art. 18), UN Doc. CCPR/C/21/Rev.1/Add.4, 27 September 1993.

General Comment No. 27: Freedom of Movement (Art. 12), UN Doc. CCPR/C/21/Rev.1/Add.9, 2 November 1999.

General Comment 34: Article 19 (Freedoms of Opinion and Expression), UN Doc. CCPR/C/GC/34, 12 September 2011.

## Concluding Observations

Concluding Observations on Austria, UN Doc. CCPR/C/AUT/CO/4, 30 October 2007.

Concluding Observations on Israel, UN Doc. CCPR/CO/78/ISR, 5 August 2003.

Concluding Observations on Kuwait, UN Doc. CCPR/CO/69/KWT, 27 July 2000.

Concluding Observations on Slovakia, UN Doc. CCPR/CO/78/SVK, 22 August 2003.

Concluding Observations on the United Kingdom of Great Britain and Northern Ireland, UN Doc. CCPR/C/GBR/CO/6, 30 July 2008.

Concluding Observations on the United Kingdom of Great Britain and Northern Ireland, the Crown Dependencies of Jersey, Guernsey and the Isle of Man, UN Doc. CCPR/C/79/Add.119, 27 March 2000.

## *HR Council*

Resolution 4/9: Combating Defamation of Religions, 30 March 2007.

Resolution 6/21: Elaboration of International Complementary Standards to the International Convention on the Elimination of All Forms of Racial Discrimination, 28 September 2007.

Resolution 7/19: Combating Defamation of Religions, 27 March 2008.

Resolution 10/22: Combating Defamation of Religions, 26 March 2009.

Resolution 13/16: Combating Defamation of Religions, 25 March 2010.

*Decision 3/103: Global Efforts for the Total Elimination of Racism, Racial Discrimination, Xenophobia and Related Intolerance and the Comprehensive Follow-Up to the World Conference against Racism, Racial Discrimination, Xenophobia and Related Intolerance and the Effective Implementation of the Durban Declaration and Programme of Action*, 8 December 2006.

*Summary Record of 4th Session of Human Rights Council*, 30 March 2007, www.ohchr.org/EN/NewsEvents/Pages/DisplayNews.aspx?NewsID=2509&LangID=E (last accessed 4 March 2014).

*Report of the Special Rapporteur on Freedom of Religion or Belief*, Asma Jahangir, 10th Session of the Human Rights Council, UN Doc. A/HRC/10/8, 6 January 2009.

*Report of the Special Rapporteur on Freedom of Religion or Belief*, Heiner Bielefeldt, UN Doc. A/HRC/19/60, 22 December 2011.

*Interim Report of the Special Rapporteur on Freedom of Religion or Belief*, UN Doc. A/62/280, 20 August 2007.

*Report of the Special Rapporteur on the Promotion and Protection of the Right to Freedom of Opinion and Expression*, Ambeyi Ligabo, to the Human Rights Council, UN Doc. A/HRC/7/14, 28 February 2008.

*Report of the Special Rapporteur on the Promotion and Protection of the Right to Freedom of Opinion and Expression*, Frank La Rue, UN Doc. A/HRC/66/290, 10 August 2011.

*Report to the Second Session of the Human Rights Council*, UN Doc. A/HRC/2/3, 20 September 2006.

## *CHR*

Resolution 1999/82: Combating Defamation of Religions, 30 April 1999.

Resolution 2000/84: Combating Defamation of Religions.

Resolution 2001/4: Combating Defamation of Religions, 18 April 2001.

Resolution 2002/9: Combating Defamation of Religions, 15 April 2002.

Resolution 2003/4: Combating Defamation of Religions, 14 April 2003.

Resolution 2004/6: Combating Defamation of Religions, 13 April 2004.

Resolution 2005/3: Combating Defamation of Religions, 12 April 2005.

*Summary Record of 61st meeting*, Commission on Human Rights 55th session, UN Doc. E/CN.4/1999/SR.61, 19 October 1999.

## *Other UN documents*

*Rabat Plan of Action on the Prohibition of Advocacy of National, Racial or Religious Hatred that Constitutes Incitement to Discrimination, Hostility or Violence*, Appendix, Annual Report of the United Nations High Commissioner for Human Rights, UN Doc. A/HRC/22/17/Add.4, 11 January 2013.

*Report of the High Commissioner for Human Rights on the Implementation of Human Rights Council resolution 7/19 entitled 'Combating Defamation of Religion'*, UN Doc. A/HRC/97, September 2008.

Ad Hoc Committee on the Elaboration of Complementary Standards, *Outcome Referred to in Para. 2(d) of the Road Map on the Elaboration of Complementary Standards*, UN Doc. A/HRC/AC.1/2/2, 26 August 2009.

*Report of the Ad Hoc Committee on the Elaboration of Complementary Standards on Its Second Session*, UN Doc. A/HRC/13/58, 21 January 2010.

*Report of the Secretary General on Combating Intolerance, Negative Stereotyping, Stigmatization, Discrimination, Incitement to Violence and Violence Against Persons Based on Religion or Belief*, UN Doc. A/67/296, 10 August 2012.

Joint Statement by Mr Githu Muigai, the Special Rapporteur on contemporary forms of racism, racial discrimination, xenophobia and related intolerance, Ms Asma Jahangir, the Special Rapporteur on freedom of religion or belief and Mr Frank la Rue, the Special Rapporteur on the promotion and protection of freedom of opinion and expression, OHCHR side event during the Durban Review Conference, Geneva, 22 April 2009.

UN Working Group on Arbitrary Detention, Opinion No.35/2008 (Egypt), UN Doc.

A/HRC/13/30/Add.1 at 146, Communication addressed to the Government on December 6 2007.

## National documents

Indonesian Constitutional Court, *Judicial Review of Law Number 1/PNPS/ 1965 Concerning the Prevention of Religious Abuse and/or;* www.article19.org/data/files/pdfs/analysis/judicial-review-of-law-number-1-pnps-1965-concerning-the-prevention-of-relig.pdf (last accessed 3 March 2014).

US Department of State, *International Religious Freedom Report 2008*; www.state.gov/j/drl/rls/irf/2008/108351.html.

US Department of State, *Report of the United States on the First Meeting of Experts to Promote the Implementation of United Nations Human Rights Council Resolution 16/18*, December 2011; www.humanrights.gov/wp-content/uploads/2012/04/1618FirstMeetingReport.pdf (last accessed 3 March 2014).

US Department of State, Bureau of Democracy, Human Rights and Labour, *International Religious Freedom Report 2012;* www.state.gov/j/drl/rls/irf/religiousfreedom/index.htm#wrapper (last accessed 4 March 2014).

## Other documents

ARTICLE 19, *Camden Principles on Freedom of Expression and Equality*, April 2009.

European Parliament, Policy Department, Directorate-General for External Policies, *Study on the European Union and the Review of the Human Rights Council*, Doc. No. EXPO/B/DROI/2010/06, February 2011, 15.

OCSE/UN/OAS, *Joint Declaration: Defamation of Religions, and Anti-Terrorism and Anti-Extremism Legislation*, 10 December 2008.

Venice Commission, *Report on the Relationship Between Freedom of Expression and Freedom of Religion: the Issue of Regulation and Prosecution of Blasphemy, Religious Insult and Incitement to Religious Hatred*, Adopted at its 76th Plenary Session, CDL-AD(2008)026, 23 October 2008.

*Report of the Durban Review Conference*, Geneva, UN Doc. A/CONF.211/8, 20–24 April 2009.

Durban Review Conference, *Outcome Document*, 20–24 April 2009; www.un.org/en/durbanreview2009/pdf/Durban_Review_outcome_document_En.pdf (last accessed 3 March 2014).

## Case law

### *HRC*

*Bodrozic* v. *Serbia and Montenegro*, Communication No. 1180/2003, 31 October 2005.
*Coleman* v. *Australia*, Communication No. 1157/2003, 10 August 2006.
*De Groot* v. *The Netherlands*, Communication No. 578/1994, 14 July 1995.
*Korneenko et al.* v. *Belarus*, Communication No. 1553/2007, 31 October 2006.
*Marques* v. *Angola*, Communication No. 1128/2002, 18 April 2005.
*Mukong* v. *Cameroon*, Communication No. 458/91, 21 July 1994.
*Ross* v. *Canada*, Communication No. 736/1997, 18 October 2000.
*Shin* v. *Republic of Korea*, Communication No. 926/2000, 16 March 2004.
*Toonen* v. *Australia*, Communication No. 488/1992, 30 March 1994.
*Faurisson* v. *France*, Communication No. 550/93, 8 November 1996.

### *ECtHR*

*Otto-Preminger Institute* v. *Austria* (Appl. No. 13470/87), 20 September 1994.
*Wingrove* v. *UK* (Appl. No. 13470/87), 25 November 1996.

13

# Limits to freedom of expression: lessons from counter-terrorism

MARTIN SCHEININ

## 1 Introduction

The relationship between the right to freedom of expression and the prevention of terrorism is particularly fraught. On the one hand, in climates and contexts where there is a heightened risk of terrorist activities being perpetrated, States' authorities often argue that it is necessary to restrict freedom of expression. The reasons presented vary from the need to criminalize incitement to violence to the argument that terrorists and the proponents of terrorism must be denied the oxygen of publicity. On the other hand, freedom of expression, especially for the media, offers an important tool for exposing governmental and terrorist propaganda and providing reliable, accurate information about conflicts and their underlying causes. This tension is adverted to in the UN Human Rights Committee's General Comment No. 34 on freedom of opinion and expression. The General Comment stresses the need for counter-terrorism measures to be fully compatible with Article 19, paragraph 3, of the International Covenant on Civil and Political Rights (ICCPR), which sets out the conditions for permissible restrictions on the right to freedom of expression. It also calls for relevant offences, such as 'praising', 'glorifying', or 'justifying' terrorism, to be clearly defined by States in order to ensure that they do not lead to unnecessary or disproportionate interference with freedom of expression.

This chapter addresses the relationship between freedom of expression and countering terrorism mainly from the perspective of international (United Nations) human rights law, based on the experience of the author first (1997–2004) as a member of the above-mentioned independent expert body, the Human Rights Committee, and subsequently (2005–11) as the Special Rapporteur on the promotion and protection of human rights and fundamental freedoms while countering terrorism, reporting as an individual academic expert to the intergovernmental Human Rights

Council. For comparative purposes, however, reference is also made to certain European instruments and their application, as well as to the role of the United Nations Security Council in combating terrorism.

## 2 The legal framework

At the universal level, the main legal framework for the human right to freedom of expression is provided by the ICCPR of 1966.[1] Article 19 guarantees the freedom of opinion and of expression and also prescribes, in paragraph 3, the conditions under which freedom of expression can be made subject to permissible restrictions. Notably, the protection of national security and public order *(ordre public)* are mentioned among the legitimate aims that justify such restrictions when the other conditions for their permissibility are met. Hence, also counter-terrorism measures may be legitimate, even if they interfere with freedom of expression, as long as they remain within the parameters set forth in paragraph 3. Further, it is also notable that the ICCPR contains other provisions that can potentially be invoked to justify counter-terrorism measures, even when they result in restrictions upon freedom of expression. Article 4 provides the State with a right to temporarily *derogate* from many human rights, including Article 19, when there is a genuine threat to the nation that calls for an officially proclaimed state of emergency. Article 5, in turn, denies protection to the abusive invocation of human rights to justify any activity aimed at the destruction of human rights. And Article 20 provides for certain mandatory restrictions upon freedom of expression, including in respect of such advocacy of national, racial or religious hatred that constitutes incitement to discrimination, hostility or violence. While all these provisions are potentially relevant in assessing the relationship between freedom of expression and counter-terrorism, States have in practice not declared derogations from Article 19, and the Human Rights Committee has been quite reluctant to apply Article 5 or Article 20. Hence, it is safe to say that by default counter-terrorism measures are assessed through the prism of the permissible limitations clause in Article 19, paragraph 3.

Save for the unique clause in Article 20 ICCPR, the above considerations would apply also to the legal framework under the European Convention on Human Rights (ECHR) of 1950, as amended by subsequent

[1] International Covenant on Civil and Political Rights, New York, 16 December 1966, entered into force 23 March 1976, 999 UNTS, 171.

Protocols.[2] Separate European instruments adopted in the post-9/11 era have, however, sought to address directly the problem of expressions that may facilitate terrorism. Similarly to Article 20 ICCPR, they basically apply the standard of *incitement* but also include important nuances. In 2005 the Council of Europe adopted a separate Convention on the Prevention of Terrorism, which obliges its parties to criminalize 'public provocation to commit terrorist offences' (Article 5), 'recruitment for terrorism' (Article 6) and 'training for terrorism' (Article 7).[3] The first of these three provisions is of interest here, and defines 'public provocation' as 'the distribution, or otherwise making available, of a message to the public, with the intent to incite the commission of a terrorist offence, where such conduct, whether or not directly advocating terrorist offences, causes a danger that one or more such offences may be committed'. The wording is a compromise between various European States, including those that by then did not at all criminalize incitement to terrorism and those that applied a broader standard of 'apology' or 'glorification' of terrorism. Strictly taken, the wording of Article 5 clearly is an incitement provision, as it requires the clear and specific subjective *mens rea* element of an 'intent to incite the commission of a terrorist offence'. That said, the subsequent part containing the objective element that refers to someone actually getting incited, includes the confusing line 'whether or not directly advocating terrorist offences'. Hence, there is a real prospect that the Convention on the Prevention of Terrorism will be used to justify criminalizations that go beyond actual incitement to terrorism and may therefore pose potential threats to freedom of expression.[4]

Despite this inherent problem in the text, Article 5 was copied verbatim into the EU Framework Decision on Combating Terrorism, in an amendment introduced in 2008. Hence, the formulation represents a common, even if unclear, Council of Europe and European Union standard.[5] For diplomatic purposes, the outcome may be one of 'constructive

[2] Convention for the Protection of Human Rights and Fundamental Freedoms as amended by Protocols no. 11 and no. 14, Rome, 4 November 1950, entered into force 3 September 1953, CETS 5, Arts. 10 (Freedom of Expression), 15 (Derogation in Time of Emergency) and 17 (Prohibition of Abuse of Rights).

[3] Convention on the Prevention of Terrorism, Warsaw, 16 May 2005, entered into force 1 June 2007, CETS 196.

[4] See below for a discussion of *Leroy* v. *France*.

[5] *Council Framework Decision 2008/919/JHA Amending Framework Decision 2002/475/JHA on Combating Terrorism*, OJ No. L330/21, 28 November 2008, Art. 1 (amending Art. 3 of the original Framework Decision).

ambiguity' but when freedom of expression and criminal punishment for its exercise are at issue, one could hope for a clearer European standard. The ambiguity is reflected in the intergovernmental Explanatory Report accompanying the Convention, where the following paragraph can be found under Article 5:

> When drafting this provision, the CODEXTER bore in mind the opinions of the Parliamentary Assembly (Opinion No. 255 (2005), paragraph 3.vii and following), and of the Commissioner for Human Rights of the Council of Europe (document BcommDH (2005) 1, paragraph 30 in fine) which suggested that such a provision could cover 'the dissemination of messages praising the perpetrator of an attack, the denigration of victims, calls for funding for terrorist organizations or other similar behaviour' which could constitute indirect provocation to terrorist violence.[6]

It can be doubted whether this formulation is faithful to the actual wording of Article 5 which includes the double requirement of a subjective intent to incite to terrorism and an objective danger that as a consequence someone else gets incited and commits an act of terrorism. That double requirement is duly repeated in paragraphs 99 and 100 of the same Explanatory Report. The paragraph may equally well be understood to reflect the view that the notion of 'indirect provocation' gets a meaning independent of actual incitement. However, such an interpretation can be dismissed with the argument that the word 'indirect' relates only to the objective element of incitement and not the subjective, *mens rea* element of an intent to incite.

Notably, the United Nations has been moving more cautiously than Europe in addressing incitement to terrorism. Among the conventions and protocols against terrorism,[7] there are instruments to combat, *inter alia*, the financing of terrorism,[8] but there is no treaty about incitement. In 2005, the Security Council adopted Resolution 1624 which addresses the issue, calling upon States 'to prohibit by law incitement to commit a terrorist act or acts'.[9] Notably, this is not a resolution under Chapter VII

[6] *Explanatory Report on the Convention on the Prevention of Terrorism*, 16 May 2005, CETS 196, para. 95, available at the Council of Europe treaty website www.conventions.coe.int (last accessed 23 January 2014).

[7] For a list and texts of international conventions and protocols against terrorism, see www.un.org/en/terrorism/instruments.shtml (last accessed 23 January 2014).

[8] International Convention for the Suppression of the Financing of Terrorism, New York, 9 December 1999, entered into force 10 April 2002, 2178 UNTS, 197.

[9] UN SC, Resolution 1624 (2005) Concerning Threats to International Peace and Security, UN Doc. S/RES/1624, 14 September 2005, para. 1(a).

of the United Nations Charter, which mandates the Security Council to decide on legally binding obligations of Member States when confronted with a threat to peace and international security. Instead, the non-Chapter VII resolution entrusts the Counter-Terrorism Committee of the Security Council, a body that itself was established through a Chapter VII resolution,[10] to receive reports from States on how they implement Resolution 1624.[11] It is also remarkable that the Security Council resolution adopts a strict incitement standard and through its preamble reaffirms the right to freedom of expression and the exhaustive nature of Article 19, paragraph 3 ICCPR, in defining the scope of permissible limitations to the right.[12]

## 3 Defining terrorism and related notions: the case of the Russian Federation

When this author in 2005–11 served as UN Special Rapporteur on human rights and counter-terrorism, a recurring theme in his work was varying national definitions of terrorism and related notions, and the resulting risks for the enjoyment of human rights when governments applied their own definitions of terrorism to stigmatize a wide range of unwanted phenomena in their countries.[13] The Special Rapporteur addressed definitions of terrorism systematically in his thematic reports to the Human Rights Council and the General Assembly, as well as in the course of his country visits.

One example of the broadening use of measures originally introduced against terrorism being used in relation to other forms of unwanted behaviour is the 2002 law on extremism in the Russian Federation.[14] Section 1, subsection 1, of the law lists twelve different categories of 'extremism' which trigger the powers of the law enforcement authorities

[10] UN SC, Resolution 1373 (2001) Concerning Threats to International Peace and Security Caused by Terrorist Acts, UN Doc. S/RES/1373, 28 September 2001.

[11] For outcomes of the work of the CTC in this area, see UN SC, *Global Survey of the Implementation by Member States of Security Council Resolution 1624 (2005)*, UN Doc. S/2012/16, 9 January 2012.

[12] UN SC, Resolution 1624 (2005), preamble.

[13] See, for instance: HR Council, *Report of the Special Rapporteur on the Promotion and Protection of Human Rights and Fundamental Freedoms While Countering Terrorism*, UN Doc. E/CN.4/2006/98/Add.1, 23 December 2005, para. 27.

[14] Russian Federal Law No. 114-FZ on Combating Extremist Activity, 25 July 2002 and amended several times in 2006–8, s. 1 subs. 1.

and ultimately a criminal punishment. The list includes, *inter alia*, the following categories of 'extremism':[15]

(1) forcible change of the foundations of the constitutional system and violation of the integrity of the Russian Federation;

(2) public justification of terrorism and other terrorist activity;

(4) propaganda of the exceptional nature, superiority or deficiency of persons on the basis of their social, racial, ethnic, religious or linguistic affiliation;

(9) propaganda and public show of Nazi emblems or symbols or of emblems or symbols similar to Nazi emblems or symbols to the point of confusion;

(10) public calls inciting the carrying out of the aforementioned actions or mass dissemination of knowingly extremist material, and likewise the production or storage thereof with the aim of mass dissemination;

(11) public, knowingly false accusation of an individual holding state office of the Russian Federation or state office of a Russian Federation constituent entity of having committed actions mentioned in the present Article.

These examples illustrate how the notion of extremism can be invoked to combat and punish very different forms of activity. While some of them (e.g., Item 2 on terrorism and Item 4 on propaganda for racial superiority) would have their basis in international law, the provision as a whole carries a risk of misuse, including in relation to the freedom of expression. While the reference in Item 1 to 'forcible change' implies the prohibited use of violence, that is not necessarily the case for Item 10 which refers to 'extremist material' and its possession or dissemination which of course do not entail the use of violence. And 'false' public accusations about public officials having committed acts of extremism is defined in Item 11 as in itself being a form of extremism, bringing this stigma upon certain forms of critical public expression.

In June 2012, the European Commission for Democracy through Law ('the Venice Commission')[16] adopted an opinion on the extremism law.[17]

[15] An English translation of the law is provided in CoE European Commission for Democracy through Law (Venice Commission), *Opinion No. 660/2011: on the Federal Law on Combating Extremist Activity of the Russian Federation*, 20 June 2012, CDL-AD(2012) 016, 7. The twelve different categories of extremism are not numbered in the law itself.

[16] The Venice Commission is the Council of Europe's advisory body on constitutional matters.

[17] CoE Venice Commission, *Opinion No. 660/2011*, 20 June 2012.

In the view of the Venice Commission, the law includes broad and imprecise provisions, particularly such as the definitions of 'extremism', 'extremist actions', 'extremist organizations' or 'extremist materials' which give too wide discretion in the interpretation and application of the law, 'thus leading to arbitrariness'.[18] The Commission criticized several provisions of the extremism law, including the list of categories of extremism in section 1, subsection 1:

> The Commission however has strong reservations about the inclusion of certain activities under the list of 'extremist' activities. Indeed, while some of the definitions in Article 1 refer to notions that are relatively well defined in other legislative acts of the Russian Federation, a number of other definitions listed in Article 1 are too broad, lack clarity and may open the way to different interpretations. In addition ... certain of the activities defined as 'extremist' in the Extremism Law seem not to require an element of violence.[19]

The Commission called for the amendment of the provisions that provide administrative and judicial authorities with far-reaching tools in combating 'extremism', including the preventive measures of warnings and notices and the related punitive measures of liquidation or ban on the activities of religious or other organizations, or closure of media outlets. In this context the Commission specifically referred to problems in respect of the freedom of expression as triggering its call for amendments.[20] In short:

> the Extremism Law has the capacity of imposing disproportionate restrictions of fundamental rights and freedoms as enshrined in the European Convention on Human Rights (in particular Articles 6, 9, 10 and 11) and infringe the principles of legality, necessity and proportionality. In the light of the above comments, the Venice Commission recommends that this fundamental shortcoming be addressed in relation to each of the definitions and instruments provided by the Law in order to bring them in line with the European Convention on Human Rights.[21]

## 4 Contributions by the Human Rights Committee

Also the Human Rights Committee, the treaty body monitoring States' compliance with the ICCPR, has been critical about Russia's law on extremism. In its consideration of periodic reports by the Russian Federation in 2003 and 2009, the Committee has been quite clear in its criticism.

[18] *Ibid.*, para. 74. [19] *Ibid.*, para. 31. [20] *Ibid.*, para. 76. [21] *Ibid.*, para. 77.

For instance, in its Concluding Observations of 2009, the Committee stated that the Russian definition of extremist activity 'remains vague, allowing for arbitrariness in its application'.[22]

In its long-awaited General Comment on freedom of expression (Article 19 ICCPR), the Human Rights Committee addressed in 2011 the context of terrorism and extremism in one carefully formulated paragraph:

> States parties should ensure that counter-terrorism measures are compatible with paragraph 3. Such offences as 'encouragement of terrorism' and 'extremist activity' as well as offences of 'praising', 'glorifying', or 'justifying' terrorism, should be clearly defined to ensure that they do not lead to unnecessary or disproportionate interference with freedom of expression. Excessive restrictions on access to information must also be avoided. The media plays a crucial role in informing the public about acts of terrorism and its capacity to operate should not be unduly restricted. In this regard, journalists should not be penalized for carrying out their legitimate activities.[23]

Clearly, the Committee was conscious of the fact that many States go beyond the mere criminalization of actual incitement to acts of terrorism, but seek to also criminalize speaking favourably about terrorism or specific manifestations of terrorism or terrorist individuals, or seek to prevent the press from even reporting neutrally on terrorism, presumably under the theory that terrorist organizations survive only because of the public attention they are getting. Instead of trying to pronounce itself directly on the permissibility of the resulting restrictions on freedom of expression, the Committee simply insists upon Article 19, paragraph 3, providing for the applicable test: any restrictions must meet the cumulative conditions of being (a) provided by law, and (b) necessary towards the legitimate aims of (c) respect of the rights or reputations of others or the protection of national security, public order or public health or morals.

Even if not a case about incitement to terrorism, the case of *Faurisson* v. *France* illustrates the approach taken by the Human Rights Committee in respect of limitations upon freedom of expression.[24] Mr Faurisson, a

[22] HRC, Concluding Observations on Russia, UN Doc. CCPR/C/RUS/CO/6, 29 October 2009, para. 24; HRC, Concluding Observations on Russia, UN Doc. CCPR/CO/79/RUS, 6 November 2003, para. 20.

[23] HRC, General Comment No. 34: Article 19 (Freedoms of Opinion and Expression), UN Doc. CCPR/C/GC/34, 12 September 2011. See Chapter 2 in this book.

[24] HRC, *Communication No. 550/1993: Robert Faurisson* v. *France*, UN Doc. CCPR/C/58/D/550/1993, 19 July 1995.

former history professor, had publicly contested the use of gas chambers for the extermination of Jews at Auschwitz and in other Nazi concentration camps. On the basis of the French Gayssot Act of 1990,[25] he had been convicted of the crime of denying crimes against humanity (*contestation de crimes contre l'humanité*), often referred to as Holocaust denial. The Human Rights Committee declared the case admissible under freedom of expression (Article 19). It did not follow the suggestion by the respondent government to declare the case inadmissible on the basis of Articles 5 (abuse of rights) and 20 (prohibition of incitement) as incompatible with the ICCPR, but proceeded to assess the conviction of Mr Faurisson under the permissible limitations test of Article 19, paragraph 3. Although the Committee might have had some misgivings about certain aspects of the Gayssot Act, it nevertheless found that the law, 'as read, interpreted and applied to the author's case by the French courts' was compatible with the ICCPR, and that the resulting restriction upon freedom of expression hence was provided by law.[26] Next, the Committee addressed whether the author's criminal conviction served a legitimate aim. It assessed that although Faurisson's statements seemingly related to historical facts, for instance about the use of asphyxiating gas in the Nazi concentration camps, they 'read in their full context, were of a nature as to raise or strengthen anti-Semitic feelings' and their curtailing therefore served the legitimate aim of respect of the right of others.[27] Finally, the Committee also held that the restriction in question was necessary, as the respondent government had asserted that the denial of the existence of the Holocaust was the principal contemporary vehicle for anti-Semitism.[28]

For the relationship between freedom of expression and incitement to terrorism under the ICCPR the lesson of the case is twofold. First, the Committee gave proper emphasis to the human right of freedom of expression by dealing with the case on the merits and through the permissible limitations test of Article 19 itself, instead of dismissing the

[25] Loi n° 90-615 of 13 July 1990 (Gayssot) tendant à réprimer tout acte raciste, antisémite ou xénophobe.

[26] HRC, *Communication No. 550/1993: Robert Faurisson* v. *France*, para. 9.5.

[27] *Ibid.*, para. 9.6.

[28] *Ibid.*, para. 9.7. Several concurring opinions by individual Committee members were appended to the views, demonstrating that within the Committee there was hesitation about the broadly formulated provisions of the Gayssot Act but that the Committee nevertheless was unanimous in concluding that the freedom of expression had not been violated in the individual case of Mr Faurisson.

case under Article 5 or Article 20. Second, the case demonstrates that human rights law is also capable of addressing symbolic speech or coded language, placing it in its actual context. Therefore, be it a case of addressing permissible limitations to freedom of expression or specific provisions on incitement to terrorism, what matters is not merely the language used but also the intent behind the expressions and the consequences they may have upon other people. This takes us back to the issue why the formulation of Article 5 of the Council of Europe Prevention of Terrorism Convention is problematic.

## 5 The case of *Leroy* v. *France*

On 11 September 2001, the French cartoonist Denis Leroy drew a cartoon depicting the attack on the twin towers of the World Trade Center in New York. He submitted it to the Basque weekly magazine *Ekaitza*. The cartoon was accompanied with a caption, which parodied the advertising slogan of a famous brand: 'We have all dreamt of it… Hamas did it'. The drawing was published in the magazine on 13 September 2001. After being convicted by the French courts of complicity in the apology of terrorism (*complicité d'apologie du terrorisme)*, Mr Leroy took his case to the European Court of Human Rights (ECtHR), alleging a violation of his freedom of expression (Article 10).

Departing from its earlier well-developed incitement standard,[29] the ECtHR concluded that there had not been a violation of Article 10. In the *Leroy* judgment, nowhere does the court imply that the drawing encourages acts of violence or terrorism. Instead, the Court stated that 'through his choice of language, the applicant commented approvingly on the violence perpetrated against thousands of civilians and diminishes the dignity of the victims'.[30] The reference to the dignity of the victims implies that the case represents a departure from an incitement standard.

[29] ECtHR, *Öztürk* v. *Turkey* (Appl. No. 22479/93), Judgment (Grand Chamber) 28 September 1999; ECtHR, *Surek* v. *Turkey (No. 1)* (Appl. No. 26682/95), Judgment (Grand Chamber) 8 July 1999.

[30] ECtHR, *Leroy* v. *France* (Appl. No. 36109/03), Judgment 2 October 2008, para. 43. The quoted translation has been taken from an excellent case comment by S. Sottiaux, '*Leroy* v. *France*: Apology of Terrorism and the Malaise of the European Court of Human Rights' Free Speech Jurisprudence', *European Human Rights Law Review* 3 (2009), 421. Comparing earlier cases, Sottiaux concludes at p. 425 that in *Leroy* v. *France* the ECtHR moved away from its earlier incitement standard and advanced a new position according to which apology of terrorism simply is a category of unprotected speech.

In the same context, the Court referred to Article 8 of the Prevention of Terrorism Convention to justify – as such correctly – that for the application of Article 5 of the same Convention (public provocation to commit a terrorist offence) it was immaterial whether an act of terrorism actually was subsequently committed. The problem, however, is that the Court failed to apply the standard of Article 5 itself, namely the double requirement of a subjective element to intentionally incite the commission of an act of terrorism and an objective element that someone else gets incited, so that there is an actual danger of the commission of an act of terrorism.

It hence appears that when departing from its own earlier incitement standard, the ECtHR was half-heartedly inspired by the Council of Europe Prevention of Terrorism Convention, even if that inspiration may represent a misunderstanding or misapplication of that Convention. It is tempting to conclude that the political agreement of Council of Europe governments that public provocation to terrorism shall be criminalized, encouraged the ECtHR to move away from its earlier incitement standard and to adopt a more tolerant view in respect of any criminalizations Member States may have in place to counter expressions seen as favourable to terrorism.

## 6 The Special Rapporteur and the case of Spain

While serving as United Nations Special Rapporteur on human rights and counter-terrorism, this author addressed the impact of counter-terrorism measures upon freedom of expression, *inter alia*, through a series of country visits. One case in point was a mission to Spain during which the impact of counter-terrorism measures upon the freedom of expression was addressed. Spain has for decades suffered from the deadly violence by the Basque separatist terrorist organization Euskadi Ta Askatasuna (ETA). As many local political parties and grass-roots organizations also have been calling for the self-determination of the Basque people, the responses by the Spanish authorities have often gone beyond addressing the actual terrorist violence and have targeted other organizations that share some of the political aims of ETA, even if rejecting violence. In his mission report, the Special Rapporteur recognized the importance of the preventive dimension of the fight against terrorism and the necessary restrictions this might impose upon certain rights, including the closely interconnected rights of freedom of expression (Article 19 ICCPR) and freedom of association (Article 22 ICCPR).

In the same breath, the Special Rapporteur emphasized that counter-terrorism measures should not be used to limit the rights of NGOs, the media or political parties: 'Any measures affecting the exercise of rights fundamental for a democratic society must be applied in accordance with precise criteria established by law, as well as in compliance with the principles of proportionality and necessity.'[31]

He made reference to the Spanish context where the activities of several associations, including media enterprises, political groups and grass-roots organizations, have been subject to court proceedings because of alleged links to terrorism, mainly pursuant to Article 516 of the Spanish Penal Code concerning membership of a terrorist organization.[32]

In the concluding section of the mission report, the Special Rapporteur also took the view that the crime of glorification of terrorism in Article 578 of the Spanish Criminal Code should be amended so as to be applied exclusively to acts intended to incite the commission of a terrorist crime and carrying the risk that such acts are subsequently committed. In his view other statements falling under the broader notion of 'apology' of terrorism should not be fought with the tool of criminal law.[33]

A much-discussed case highlighting some of the problems in the application of Spanish law was that of *Eguncaria*, the only Basque-language newspaper that was closed down in 2003 due to its alleged links with the terrorist organization ETA. The closure of the newspaper took place upon orders by Juan del Olmo, one of the investigative judges of the Audiencia Nacional, the court with nationwide jurisdiction in all terrorism cases. Documents and computers were seized, the assets of the newspaper were first frozen and then liquidated. Several individuals were arrested but later released. Officials of the newspaper, including the editor-in-chief, alleged that they were tortured during the investigation. More than seven years after the fact, Audiencia Nacional reversed its own actions and concluded that there had been no basis for the closure of the newspaper. In an exceptional – and promising – way it distanced itself from the so-called 'Octopus theory', according to which ETA has its tentacles everywhere and the fact that its control cannot be proven only supports the presumption of secret control. In 2010, the final and

[31] HR Council, *Report of the Special Rapporteur on the Promotion and Protection of Human Rights and Fundamental Freedoms while Countering Terrorism: Mission to Spain*, UN Doc. A/HRC/10/3/Add.2, 16 December 2008, para. 12.

[32] *Ibid.*, para. 13. [33] *Ibid.*, para. 53(d).

unanimous sentence by the Criminal Court of Audiencia Nacional was that there were no grounds to close the newspaper. The court rejected as erroneous the view that everything that has to do with the Basque language and culture would be controlled by ETA and also clearly stated that the closure of *Eguncaria* was an interference in the freedom of the press. It even found that the defendants' allegations about torture were credible.[34]

## 6 Conclusions and final remarks

The above illustrations and analysis justify the following two conclusions. First, the permissible limitations clauses in human rights treaty provisions on freedom of expression, including Article 19, paragraph 3, ICCPR, are the proper framework for accommodating legitimate concerns related to countering terrorism. A proper legal framework must be in place for the resulting restrictions, and any limitations placed upon the freedom of expression must be deemed necessary for the protection of a legitimate aim, such as the prevention or investigation of serious crime, including terrorism. Second, when such an analysis results in an assessment that criminal sanctions are needed in order to combat and prevent the propagation of terrorism, then incitement to commit acts of terrorism is the proper standard. Notions such as 'glorification' or 'apology' are overly broad and carry the risk of violating freedom of expression.

The final report of the current author as Special Rapporteur on human rights and counter-terrorism presented, on the basis of all earlier work, a selection of ten elements of 'best practice' in countering terrorism, the notion of best practice referring to both being effective in the actual combat of terrorism and at the same time fully respecting human rights.[35] One of the ten elements of best practice put forward in the report was the following formulation for a model clause on incitement to terrorism: 'It is an offence to intentionally and unlawfully distribute, or otherwise make available, a message to the public with the intent to incite the commission of a terrorist offence, where such conduct, whether or

[34] Audiencia Nacional (Spanish National Court), *Eguncaria*, Criminal Chamber, First Section, Judgment no. 27/2010, 12 April 2010.

[35] HR Council, *Report of the Special Rapporteur on the Promotion and Protection of Human Rights and Fundamental Freedoms while Countering Terrorism*, UN Doc. A/HRC/16/51, 22 December 2011, para. 10.

not expressly advocating terrorist offences, causes a danger that one or more such offences may be committed.'[36] As explained in the report, this formulation closely follows the text of Article 5 of the Council of Europe Prevention of Terrorism Convention. Notably, the problematic combination of indirect advocacy and an incitement standard has been modified by using the word 'expressly' in the latter part of the provision. Unlike the word 'directly', used in the same part of the definition in the Prevention Convention, the proposed wording may not be misunderstood as compromising the actual standard of incitement. In the report in question, the Special Rapporteur openly referred to the case of *Leroy* v. *France* as triggering the need to introduce this modification.[37] The proposed wording would cover the situation of using coded language or artistic expression for the purpose of communicating the incitement, but would not reduce the requirement to prove both a subjective intention to incite, as well as an objective danger that a terrorist act will be committed.

## Literature

Sottiaux, S. '*Leroy* v. *France*: Apology of Terrorism and the Malaise of the European Court of Human Rights' Free Speech Jurisprudence', *European Human Rights Law Review* 3 (2009), 415–27.

## UN documents

HRC, Communication No. 550/1993: *Robert Faurisson* v. *France*, UN Doc. CCPR/C/58/D/550/1993, 19 July 1995.

HRC, Concluding Observations on Russia, UN Doc. CCPR/CO/79/RUS, 6 November 2003.

HRC, Concluding Observations on Russia, UN Doc. CCPR/C/RUS/CO/6, 29 October 2009.

HR Council, *Report of the Special Rapporteur on the Promotion and Protection of Human Rights and Fundamental Freedoms While Countering Terrorism*, UN Doc. E/CN.4/2006/98/Add.1, 23 December 2005.

HR Council, *Report of the Special Rapporteur on the Promotion and Protection of Human Rights and Fundamental Freedoms While Countering Terrorism: Mission to Spain*, UN Doc. A/HRC/10/3/Add.2, 16 December 2008.

36 *Ibid.*, para. 32(8). 37 *Ibid.*, para. 30.

## Case law

### *ECtHR*

*Leroy* v. *France* (Appl. No. 36109/03), Judgment of 2 October 2008.
*Öztürk* v. *Turkey* (Appl. No. 22479/93), Judgment (Grand Chamber) of 28 September 1999.
*Sürek* v. *Turkey (No. 1)* (Appl. No. 26682/95), Judgment (Grand Chamber) of 8 July 1999.

### *Spain*

Audiencia Nacional (Spanish National Court), *Eguncaria,* Criminal Chamber, First Section, Judgment no. 27/2010, 12 April 2010.

14

# Tacit citing: the scarcity of judicial dialogue between the global and the regional human rights mechanisms in freedom of expression cases

ANTOINE BUYSE

## 1 Introduction

The European Convention on Human Rights (ECHR) 'cannot be interpreted and applied in a vacuum', the European Court of Human Rights famously held in the case of *Loizidou* v. *Turkey*.[1] The Court referred to the fact that, in its view, human rights treaties should be interpreted in the context of public international law. But what about the closer context of fellow human rights regimes, such as the International Covenant on Civil and Political Rights (ICCPR)?

Fundamental rights are almost inherently open norms, stated in rather general wording. This means that the way in which they are interpreted plays an even bigger role than in more detailed substantive norms, such as traffic laws or provisions of contract law. For the specific right to freedom of expression, the openness of the norm is even more pronounced in the sense that its precise limits are heavily contested. Article 19, ICCPR is the most important and influential formulation of freedom of expression at the international level. It has been interpreted by way of General Comments, Concluding Observations on specific countries and views of the Human Rights Committee in individual cases. A larger body of interpretation of the freedom of expression has, however, been established on the regional level, especially in Europe.

The question then arises to what extent adjudicative bodies at the global level (i.e., the Human Rights Committee) and the regional level (i.e., the European Court of Human Rights and to a lesser extent, the courts of other regional systems) interact by way of citing each other's

[1] ECtHR, *Loizidou* v. *Turkey* (Appl. No. 15318/89), Judgment (Grand Chamber), 18 December 1996, para. 43.

standards and interpretations. Is there a certain level of dialogue between international human rights institutions as part of a phenomenon that Anne-Marie Slaughter has dubbed a 'global community of courts'?[2] Or do these systems operate mostly in autonomous legal orders with relatively little interaction? This chapter will address these more general questions by focusing on possible interactions relating to the right to freedom of expression. After a short overview of the relationship between the Human Rights Committee and the European Court of Human Rights and the other regional mechanisms, this chapter will delve into the case law on freedom of expression of the European – and to a lesser extent the other regional – mechanisms to see whether and how they make use of the global norm contained in Article 19, ICCPR.

## 2 Interaction: possibilities and problems

The growth of the number of regional and global human rights treaties since World War II has also led to a myriad of supervisory mechanisms. Many, although not all, of these mechanisms allow for individual complaints to be lodged. This has led to a large body of (quasi-)jurisprudence. The increase in the number of official watchdogs of human rights has, as in other fields of international law, given rise to concerns of fragmentation. Since a large number of States are parties to not one, but a number of global and regional human rights conventions, there is a risk that differing or even conflicting interpretations may emerge of what are, at the core, similar standards. The judges or experts on the different human rights bodies may not always be inclined to follow the case law of their peer bodies. Precedent in and of itself is the product of a specific socio-legal culture. Easy borrowing may lead to misunderstandings. This is very much the case when one talks about national courts engaged in judicial borrowing.[3] For international human rights mechanisms, this risk may be less in so far as their memberships are typically international and their members have backgrounds in different legal systems. Nevertheless, the global and regional human rights bodies have developed in parallel rather than in inter-institutional unison.

[2] A. Slaughter, 'A Global Community of Courts', *Harvard International Law Journal*, 44 (2003), 191–219.

[3] R. J. Krotoszynski, '"I'd Like to Teach the World to Sing (in Perfect Harmony)": International Judicial Dialogue and the Muses – Reflections on the Perils and the Promise of International Judicial Dialogue', *Michigan Law Review* 104 (2006), 1321–59.

Does the risk of fragmentation indeed materialise in practice? As Slaughter has asserted, there is a judicial dialogue between international courts. This happens in two distinct ways: directly and informally on the one hand, by real meetings of judges, and through case law on the other hand, whenever references are made to the dicta or ratios of other courts.[4] Given that judicial legitimacy is founded among others on persuasive argumentation, it may help judges to consider what other jurists have found persuasive in adjudicating similar problems. Although cross-jurisdictional borrowing in this sense is always hampered by the fact that a full and perfect understanding of the 'other' system is not possible, those other systems may offer inspiration. Specifically, they may point to alternative ideas about the scope and content of rights in general and of fundamental rights in particular.[5]

The extent to which one can truly speak of a dialogue in the sense of mutual citing of each other's jurisprudence on an equal basis is debatable. Analysis of international case law in the past decades has shown that there are clear asymmetries in courts citing other courts.[6] Some courts are much more active in citing than others. This can be explained in various ways. First, the jurisprudence of a court must be persuasive, if possible supported by the positive critiques of international legal scholars.[7] After all, there is no hierarchy between the various judicial bodies in the field of human rights. Also, more generally, courts may have a greater inclination to make use of external jurisprudence for inspiration when they do not themselves yet possess a very large corpus of case law, when they have been trained in law schools in other legal systems[8] or potentially when they are well-versed in legal comparativism.

This analysis not only concerns courts in the strict sense of the word. Similar processes of dialogue may apply to a potential dialogue between regional human rights courts and the United Nations Human Rights Committee. Whereas the Committee's views on individual communications

4 Slaughter, 'Global Community of Courts', 195 and 201.

5 Krotoszynski, 'International Judicial Dialogue', 1356–8.

6 N. Miller, 'An International Jurisprudence? The Operation of "Precedent" across International Tribunals', *Leiden Journal of International Law* 15 (2002), 483–526; E. Voeten, 'Borrowing and Non-Borrowing among International Courts', *Journal of Legal Studies* 39–2 (2010), 547–76.

7 P. M. Wald, 'Tribunal Discourse and Intercourse: How the International Courts Speak to One Another', *Boston College International and Comparative Law Review* 30 (2007), 23–4.

8 D. S. Law and W. Chang, 'The Limits of Global Judicial Dialogue', *Washington Law Review* 86 (2011), 523–78.

are formally only recommendations, they do have a quasi-judicial character. The Committee itself has indicated that it perceives its views as judicial, referring to the values of impartiality and independence, the way in which it interprets the ICCPR and what it calls the 'determinative character' of its decisions: the answer to the question whether a State has violated the Covenant or not.[9]

Finally, a caveat: the following analysis bases itself mostly on explicit mentions in case law of the views or judgments of other human rights bodies. In many ways this is only a starting point for further research. The fact that jurisprudence of other bodies is not openly mentioned in a judgment does not mean it was not considered. In this respect, separate opinions, both concurring and dissenting ones, may shed some light on the extent of a possible dialogue. But to offer a fuller picture, a different kind of analysis would be necessary: research into the backgrounds of judges and Human Rights Committee members and interviews with them, to assess whether they were trained in legal comparativism or to see whether they have in some earlier capacity been active in another human rights body. With this limitation in mind, the analysis will proceed below.

## 3 A tale of two treaties

How do these more general considerations about judicial borrowing play out in the context of the Human Rights Committee's interplay with the Strasbourg system? From a normative perspective it is important to note that almost all the States Parties to the ECHR have also ratified the ICCPR and its optional protocol, which provides for an individual complaints mechanism. When adjudicating individual complaints relating to these States, it would thus in principle make sense to interpret the obligations flowing from the ECHR in harmony with the ICCPR. The opposite might be more difficult. The very fact that the ICCPR is a global treaty and that the Human Rights Committee has a global composition makes it more difficult to justify to the legal interpretations of one regional court. That may not be seen as representative. Indeed, the Committee seems determined to safeguard its interpretative autonomy,

[9] HRC, General Comment No. 33: The Obligations of States Parties under the Optional Protocol to the International Covenant on Civil and Political Rights, UN Doc. CCPR/C/GC/33, 5 November 2008, para. 11.

not just towards regional human rights case law but also vis-à-vis the findings of fellow United Nations treaty bodies.[10]

The first dimension of interplay is a procedural one. Since the two regimes stem from different organisations there is no formal link between them, nor – as already mentioned – a hierarchy. For applicants it is very difficult to go forum shopping between the Committee and the Court. Article 35 ('admissibility criteria'), ECHR, precludes this: it provides that the European Court will not deal with applications that have 'already been submitted to another procedure of international investigation or settlement.' The Optional Protocol to the ICCPR does, in principle, enable such a subsequent application, even if the matter has previously been addressed in a judgment of the Strasbourg Court. In practice, however, many European countries have entered reservations on this point. More specifically, the Committee of Ministers of the Council of Europe has even recommended such reservations to prevent a de facto appeal possibility beyond the European Court.[11] Coupled with the greater visibility and effective remedial effect of the European human rights machinery, this has driven most European applicants to bring their case to the Court rather than to the Human Rights Committee.[12]

The second dimension of interplay relates to the substance of human rights. The norms in the two treaties are also to a large extent similar, in the sense that the ECHR largely consists of civil and political rights, including the right to freedom of expression. There are, however, differences that have had an impact. Specifically, the possibilities to restrict human rights under the ECHR were perceived by many countries to be more extensive than under the ICCPR. This has led to declarations and reservations by a number of European States when ratifying the ICCPR. France, for example, declared that the rights to freedom of expression, assembly and association in the ICCPR would be implemented in accordance with the corresponding rights in the European Convention.[13] Uniformity may have seemed the main concern, but according to Yogesh Tyagi, the real reason is that the ECHR seemed to permit more leeway. Belgium, which introduced a similar declaration to the French one,

[10] Y. Tyagi, *The UN Human Rights Committee: Practice and Procedure* (Cambridge University Press, 2011), 653.

[11] Committee of Ministers of the Council of Europe, Resolution 70(17), 15 May 1970. See also: M. Nowak, *CCPR Commentary*, 2nd edn (Kehl am Rhein: Engel, 2005), 881.

[12] Tyagi, *UN Human Rights Committee*, 743.

[13] See treaties.un.org. The declaration on the freedom of assembly was withdrawn on 22 March 1988.

openly acknowledged as much.[14] This can be seen, for example, when comparing the legitimate aims under which a State can restrict the freedom of expression. Under Article 19, ICCPR the mentioned aims are the rights and reputation of others, the protection of national security or public order, and the protection of public health or morals. The restriction clause of Article 10, ECHR seems more extensive. As the second paragraph of that Article indicates:

> The exercise of these freedoms, since it carries with it duties and responsibilities, may be subject to such formalities, conditions, restrictions or penalties as are prescribed by law and are necessary in a democratic society, in the interests of national security, territorial integrity or public safety, for the prevention of disorder or crime, for the protection of health or morals, for the protection of the reputation or rights of others, for preventing the disclosure of information received in confidence, or for maintaining the authority and impartiality of the judiciary.

This is a slightly longer list than the one in the ICCPR. In addition, Article 16, ECHR ('Restrictions on political activity of aliens') allows States to restrict the freedom of political expression of aliens, irrespective of the conditions of Article 10. The reservations thus seem to weaken the slightly higher standard of the ICCPR by referring to the ECHR text.

As a result of these procedural and substantive issues, the coexistence of the two human rights protection systems, mainly due to the position taken by a number of European States, seems somewhat uneasy. The Human Rights Committee has at times expressed its dismay about the privileged position of the ECHR in many European States as compared to the ICCPR, for example in the context of the State report of Iceland:

> The Committee also expresses its concern over the apparent preference accorded, in the domestic law as well as in legal doctrine and jurisprudence, to the European Convention for the Protection of Human Rights and Fundamental Freedoms as against the International Covenant on Civil and Political Rights. In that regard, the attention of the State party is drawn to the fact that the latter guarantees a number of human rights not protected under the former and that permissible restrictions are less broad-based.[15]

[14] *Ibid.* Belgium stated: 'Articles 19, 21 and 22 shall be applied by the Belgian Government in the context of the provisions and restrictions set forth or authorized in articles 10 and 11 of the Convention for the Protection of Human Rights and Fundamental Freedoms of 4 November 1950, by the said Convention.'

[15] HRC, *Annual Report to the UN General Assembly*, UN Doc. A/49/40 vol. 1, 21 September 1994, para. 76. See also Tyagi, *UN Human Rights Committee*, 744.

A certain *jalousie de métier* towards its European counterpart seems rather apparent here. On the other hand, the constant presence of a number of Committee members from ECHR States Parties throughout the Committee's history guarantees a minimum degree of knowledge and potential 'legal empathy' with the European system of human rights protection.

## 4 The European Court of Human Rights

To what extent does dialogue, in any shape or form, or at least mutual referencing, play out in the jurisprudence of the Human Rights Committee and the European Court of Human Rights? It has been noted by commentators that the European case law has been a source of inspiration and citation by regional human rights bodies, such as the Inter-American Court of Human Rights and the African Commission on Human and Peoples' Rights, but not so much by the Human Rights Committee.[16] The European Court's approach, for its part, has not been consistent over the years. Magdalena Forowicz, in her work on the reception of international law in the European Court, distinguishes two strands of case law in this respect. First, the cases in which the reference directly followed from procedural or coexistence reasons, for example when an applicant had first applied to the Human Rights Committee and only later to Strasbourg. These cases reflect what she labels a rather 'uninhibited approach' to the Committee's case law and the ICCPR. The other strand of case law concerns cases where the European Court used the ICCPR to clarify the ECHR. In this category of cases, the 1980s reflect a more open approach than the subsequent decade in which the Court took more distance, and the last decade again shows a certain rapprochement.[17] This section will deal with the ways in which the European Court has dealt with the Human Rights Committee's work in the specific context of freedom of expression cases. The subsequent section will consider the two other regional human rights systems and the last section will assess the other side of the coin; the Committee's references to regional case law.

[16] D. Harris, M. O'Boyle, E. Bates and C. Buckley, *Harris, O'Boyle & Warbrick: Law of the European Convention on Human Rights*, 2nd edn (Oxford University Press, 2009), 30–1.

[17] M. Forowicz, *The Reception of International Law in the European Court of Human Rights* (Oxford University Press, 2010), 154.

References in the Court's case law to the ICCPR and the Human Rights Committee are both relatively recent and relatively rare. The findings here are based on a search of the Court's case law database, HUDOC, by looking for the terms 'Human Rights Committee', 'General Comment', 'ICCPR' and 'International Covenant', which yielded two handfuls of judgments.[18] Most of these date from the 1990s and especially the 2000s. This in itself does not say much about quantitative trends, since these last two decades are precisely the phase in which the volume of the Court's case law increased tremendously. Most references mention the Covenant itself, while a few later references also to the Committee's work. In freedom of expression cases, the latter concerns Concluding Observations on States Parties to the ICCPR rather than the Committee's views in individual applications. In what follows the ways in which the ICCPR features in the European Court of Human Rights' jurisprudence will be assessed.

The earliest mentions contrast rather than connect the European and global human rights protection systems. Two judgments against Germany, *Glasenapp* and *Kosiek* from 1986, are the earliest mentions of the ICCPR. These cases related to dismissals or failures to renew contracts of a schoolteacher and a university researcher respectively, for being associated with the extreme left or right. Both claimed that these State actions violated their freedom of expression. The Court however held that the access to a post in the civil service lay at the core of these two cases. It explicitly contrasted the ECHR with the ICCPR. The latter, in Article 25(c), includes a right of access on general terms of equality, to public service in one's country. The State Parties to the ECHR deliberately excluded such a right from the Convention.[19]

Another example is the media regulation case of *Groppera Radio AG and Others* v. *Switzerland*, in which the Court focused its analysis on the third sentence of paragraph 1 of Article 10, ECHR: 'This article shall not

[18] The database has been searched until 1 December 2011. Since the writing of this contribution in early 2012, developments at the Court have continued. Explicit references to the Human Rights Committee's work featured to different extents, for example, in these three cases: ECtHR, *Yıldırım* v. *Turkey* (Appl. No. 3111/10), Judgment, 18 December 2012; ECtHR, *Youth Initiative for Human Rights* v. *Serbia* (Appl. No. 48135/06), Judgment, 25 June 2013; ECtHR, *Perinçek* v. *Switzerland* (Appl. No. 27510/08), Judgment, 17 December 2013.

[19] ECtHR, *Glasenapp* v. *Germany* (Appl. No. 9228/80), Judgment (Grand Chamber), 28 August 1986, para. 48; ECtHR, *Kosiek* v. *Germany* (Appl. No. 9704/82), Judgment (Grand Chamber), 28 August 1986, para. 34.

prevent States from requiring the licensing of broadcasting television or cinema enterprises.' The Court noted that Article 19, ICCPR did not include a comparable provision:

> The negotiating history of Article 19 shows that the inclusion of such a provision in that Article had been proposed with a view to the licensing not of the information imparted but rather of the technical means of broadcasting in order to prevent chaos in the use of frequencies. However, its inclusion was opposed on the ground that it might be utilised to hamper free expression, and it was decided that such a provision was not necessary because licensing in the sense intended was deemed to be covered by the reference to 'public order' in paragraph 3 of the Article.[20]

Thus, in the Court's view, the purpose of the media regulation provision in Article 10, ECHR was to permit States to regulate through a system of licences the technical aspects of broadcasting in particular. It did not, however, exempt such measures from Article 10(2)'s requirements for limiting the right to freedom of expression.[21] In this case, the ICCPR was thus used to construct an interpretation of the ECHR, which offered the widest possible safeguards for freedom of expression.

There have also been a number of positive references to the ICCPR. The Covenant surfaces in a number of alleged hate speech cases. In *Jersild* v. *Denmark*, about a journalist convicted for spreading hate speech by having interviewed right-wing youth on television, Article 20, ICCPR, on the obligation to combat hate speech, is mentioned by the Court as a relevant source.[22] In its consideration of the merits, however, the Court refers to the Convention on the Elimination of All Forms of Racial Discrimination rather than to the ICCPR. A similar mention can be found in the case of *Gündüz* v. *Turkey*:[23] the Court mentioned Article 20, ICCPR under relevant international instruments, but when concluding in the substantive part of the judgment that hate speech is not protected by Article 10, ECHR, the ICCPR is no longer explicitly mentioned. An implicit source of inspiration at most, then. In *Balsytė-Lideikienė* v. *Lithuania* – a case about a calendar which contained hateful

[20] ECtHR, *Groppera Radio AG and Others* v. *Switzerland* (Appl. No. 10890/84), Judgment (Grand Chamber), 28 March 1990, para. 61. The Court referred to Document A/5000 of the 16th session of the United Nations General Assembly, 5 December 1961, para. 23.

[21] *Ibid.*

[22] ECtHR, *Jersild* v. *Denmark* (Appl. No. 15890/89), Judgment (Grand Chamber), 23 September 1994, para. 21.

[23] ECtHR, *Gündüz* v. *Turkey* (Appl. No. 35071/97), Judgment (Chamber), 4 December 2003.

expressions – the Court again mentioned Article 20, ICCPR as a relevant source of law to be taken into account. This time, however, it referred back to it explicitly in its assessment of whether a 'pressing social need' existed for limiting the freedom of expression in the case. In its balancing exercise, it noted the respondent State's obligation under international law to prohibit advocacy of national hatred – a direct reference to the provision in the ICCPR on this.[24]

Another positive mention of the Covenant, in the context of artworks, occurred in the case of *Müller and Others* v. *Switzerland*, a case about allegedly obscene artwork.[25] It was the first case in which the Court explicitly extended the scope of Article 10, ECHR to cover artistic expression.[26] The provision itself is silent on it, but the Court stated in rather lapidary fashion that artistic expressions are part of the concept of freedom of expression. To support it, it referred to the second sentence of Article 10, ECHR which mentions the media, 'whose activities extend to the field of art', as the Court held. Second, it found confirmation of its views in Article 19, ICCPR, which specifically mentions information and ideas 'in the form of art'.[27]

In two cases about alleged attacks on people's honour and reputation, both against Norway, the ICCPR also featured. In *Tønsbergs Blad AS* and *Haukom*, the State mentioned that under Article 17, ICCPR it was obliged to protect individuals against unlawful attacks on their reputation. The Court, for its part, reasoned that the newspaper's content was not 'capable of causing such injury to personal reputation as could weigh heavily in the balancing exercise.'[28] Thereby, Norway's invocation of the ICCPR became irrelevant. An earlier case had been more successful in that sense. In *Bladet Tromsø and Stensaas*, the State had equally invoked Article 17, ICCPR. In that case, the Court took it into account when balancing the relevant factors. It held that the seal hunters, who had been the target of criticism in a Norwegian newspaper, had a right to

[24] ECtHR, *Balsytė-Lideikienė* v. *Lithuania* (Appl. No. 72596/01), Judgment (Chamber), 4 November 2008, para. 78.

[25] ECtHR, *Müller and Others* v. *Switzerland* (Appl. No. 10737/84), Judgment (Chamber), 24 May 1988.

[26] D. Shelton, 'An Introduction to the History of International Human Rights Law', *George Washington University Law School Legal Studies Research Paper No. 346*, at ssrn.com paper no. 1010489 (2007), 25 (last accessed 21 January 2014).

[27] ECtHR, *Müller and Others*, para. 27.

[28] ECtHR, *Tønsbergs Blad AS and Haukom* v. *Norway* (Appl. No. 510/04), Judgment, 1 March 2007, para. 93.

protection of their honour and reputation, as internationally recognised in the ICCPR.[29] The Court used that element to inform its own interpretation of Article 10, ECHR.

Finally, in a small number of judgments, the Human Rights Committee's work played a role. *Lepojić* v. *Serbia* concerned a journalist found guilty of defamation of a mayor. The applicant himself pointed out that this was part of a wider pattern of pressure exerted on the press. Under the unusual heading 'relevant international standards and findings referred to by the applicant',[30] the Court mentioned the Human Rights Committee's Concluding Observations on Serbia and Montenegro. In those observations, the Committee expressed its concern about 'the high number of proceedings initiated against journalists for media-related offences, in particular as a result of complaints filed by political personalities who feel that they have been subject to defamation because of their functions.'[31] The Court itself did not return to the issue of the possible wider pattern of pressure on the press in assessing the merits of the case. What this example shows is that individual applicants can use the Committee's work to contextualise their case.

In a case about a newspaper editor who had been sentenced by a military court, *Ergin* v. *Turkey (No. 6)*, the Human Rights Committee's General Comment on Article 14 ICCPR (administration of justice)[32] and its Concluding Observations on specific countries were mentioned under 'relevant domestic and international law and practice'. These observations, on Poland and Slovakia, related to the unacceptability of trying civilians in military courts.[33] In the merits of the judgment, the Court came to a similar finding by referring to 'developments over the last decade at the international level ... which confirm the existence of a trend towards excluding the criminal jurisdiction of military courts over civilians.'[34] An

[29] ECtHR, *Bladet Tromsø and Stensaas* v. *Norway* (Appl. No. 21980/93), Judgment (Grand Chamber), 20 May 1999, para. 65.

[30] Unusual in the sense that the Court rarely explicitly states that the sources were suggested by either of the parties; applicant or respondent.

[31] HRC, Concluding Observations on Serbia and Montenegro, UN Doc. CCPR/CO/81/SEMO, 12 August 2004, as cited in ECtHR, *Lepojić* v. *Serbia* (Appl. No. 13909/05), Judgment 6 November 2007, para. 40.

[32] HRC, General Comment No. 13: Article 14 (Equality Before the Courts and the Right to a Fair and Public Hearing by an Independent Court Established by Law), UN Doc. HRI/GEN/1/Rev.9, 13 April 1984.

[33] ECtHR, *Ergin* v. *Turkey (No. 6)* (Appl. No. 47533/99), Judgment, 4 May 2006, paras. 22–23.

[34] *Ibid.*, para. 45.

even more explicit mention followed in *Stoll* v. *Switzerland*, a case about a journalist who had been convicted for publishing classified information. The Court, again under relevant international legal materials, cited Concluding Observations of the Human Rights Committee, this time criticising the overly broad application of the Official Secrets Act in the United Kingdom. The Committee asserted that the State 'should ensure that its powers to protect information genuinely related to matters of national security are narrowly utilised'.[35] In the merits of the case, the European Court explicitly referred to these findings to support its own argument along the same lines.[36]

As the above overview reflects, the number of references to the global norm of freedom of expression is limited in the jurisprudence of the European Court of Human Rights. Mostly, the Covenant has been used by the Court as an (additional) interpretative tool to give meaning to the European Convention's own freedom of expression provision. At times, the Court has used the Human Rights Committee's concluding country observations in the same way. It has not (yet) used the Committee's views in individual cases.[37] This may not only relate to a general attitude of the Court towards the Committee's work, but may also be to a large extent caused by a factor of a different, very pragmatic kind. The Committee's case law on freedom of expression is still extremely limited compared to the European Court's jurisprudence. There is in that sense less reason to engage in judicial borrowing or dialogue to solve legal issues. The same holds for why governments and applicants use the Committee's case law so sparingly: the Court's own case law is a much larger treasure trove in which to delve for the golden argument that makes or breaks a case. To put it differently, if one wants to know how a complicated high-tech espresso machine works, it is of little use to consult the manual for a simple coffee grinder, no matter how reputable that grinder may be.

## 5 The Inter-American and African human rights systems

The Inter-American human rights system has a tradition of being relatively open to other sources of law, not only human rights law but also

[35] HRC, Concluding Observations on the United Kingdom, UN Doc. CCPR/CO/73/UK, 6 December 2001, para. 21, as cited in ECtHR, *Stoll* v. *Switzerland* (Appl. No. 69698/01), Judgment (Grand Chamber), 10 December 2007, para. 42.

[36] *Ibid.*, para. 54.

[37] Nor has it yet referred to the Committee's General Comment on the right to freedom of expression.

international humanitarian law. In this section, the extent of the use of Human Rights Committee case law by the Inter-American Court of Human Rights will be assessed.[38] The primary freedom of expression provision in the American Convention on Human Rights (ACHR) is Article 13, which is the equivalent of Articles 19 and 20, ICCPR.[39] Just over twenty cases of the total jurisprudence (many thousands of cases) of the Court include references to the case law of the Human Rights Committee. This in itself reflects the Court's openness, in principle, to the work of that United Nations treaty body. Virtually all of these are positive references: invoking the work of the Committee to support an interpretation made by the Inter-American Court in the judgment at hand.[40] In only very few cases, however, is freedom of expression the core of matter. All of these cases date from after the turn of the century.

The earliest example is the judgment of *Olmedo-Bustos and Others* v. *Chile*, better known as the case of 'The Last Temptation of Christ'.[41] It concerned the decision of Chile's highest court to prohibit the showing of the movie in the country. The Inter-American Court held that this constituted censorship in violation of Article 13, ACHR. In a rather tentative start for the Court as a whole to refer to the Committee's work in freedom of expression cases, Judge Cançado Trindade stated in a concurring opinion that under international human rights law, not only national judicial bodies but also legislative bodies have obligations. To support his argument, he pointed out that the Human Rights Committee had in a freedom of expression case called for legislative changes.[42]

In *Herrera-Ulloa* v. *Costa Rica*, the Committee's case law made it to the merits of the Inter-American Court's judgment. In the case, about a journalist who had been convicted for defamation, the Court emphasized the close relationship between freedom of expression and democracy: free formation of public opinion as the 'sine qua non' for a vibrant

38 Cases have been reviewed in the case law database of the Inter-American Court of Human Rights: corteidh.or.cr until 1 June 2011.

39 In addition, Article 14 of the American Convention on Human Rights concerns a specific right to reply in cases of inaccurate or offensive statements or ideas in the media.

40 See e.g., Inter-American Court of Human Rights (IACtHR), *Heliodoro Portugal* v. *Panama*, Series C. No. 186, 12 August 2008, para. 11, positively referring to the Human Rights Committee's case law on enforced disappearances. And also IACtHR, *Caesar* v. *Trinidad and Tobago*, Series C. No. 123, 11 March 2005, para. 63, on corporal punishment.

41 IACtHR, *Olmedo-Bustos and Others* v. *Chile*, Series C. No. 73, 5 February 2001.

42 Para. 6, note 17, of his concurring opinion, citing HRC, *J. Ballantyne, E. Davidson and G. McIntyre* v. *Canada*, Nos. 359/1989 and 385/1989, 5 May 1993, para. 13.

democracy. To underline the consensus on this relationship, the judgment contains references to both regional case law – of the European Court and the African Commission on Human and Peoples' Rights – and global case law.[43] It refers, in particular, to the Human Rights Committee's views in *Aduayom and Others* v. *Togo*, which noted that in a democracy it is essential that 'its citizens must be allowed to inform themselves about alternatives to the political system/parties in power, and that they may criticize or openly and publicly evaluate their Governments without fear of interference or punishment.'[44] A month later, in August 2004, exactly the same reference was made on the same point in *Ricardo Canese* v. *Paraguay*, a case about a presidential candidate who had been convicted for slander due to remarks made about a rival candidate in an electoral debate.[45] Concerns about the need for free debate and free expression for democracies are thus widely shared among global and regional human rights supervisors.

Finally, the judgment in *Ríos and Others* v. *Venezuela* related to the hampering by State officials of the work of journalists of RCTV television station. The Court noted the following about the criteria under which the State can regulate the work of the media:

> With regard to the accreditations or authorizations for the written media to participate in official events, which imply a possible restriction on the exercise of the freedom to seek, receive, and impart information and ideas of any nature, it must be proven that their application is legal, it seeks a legitimate objective, and it is necessary and proportional in relation to the objective sought within a democratic society. The requirements for the accreditation must be clear, objective, and reasonable, and their application must be transparent.[46]

Most of these elements are directly taken from the Human Rights Committee's views in *Gauthier* v. *Canada* to which the Inter-American Court explicitly refers.[47] Specific criteria in the case law of the global mechanism were used here by its regional peer to elucidate the meaning of a regional human rights treaty.

The African Commission on Human and Peoples' Rights does not seem to refer to the work of the Human Rights Committee in its freedom

[43] IACtHR, *Herrera-Ulloa* v. *Costa Rica*, Series C. No. 107, 2 July 2004, para. 114.
[44] HRC, *Aduayom and Others* v. *Togo*, Nos. 422/1990 a.o., 12 July 1996, para. 7.4.
[45] IACtHR, *Ricardo Canese* v. *Paraguay*, Series C. No. 111, 31 August 2004, para. 84, citing the same UN HRC case of *Aduayom and Others*.
[46] IACtHR, *Ríos and Others* v. *Venezuela*, Series C. No. 194, 28 January 2009, para. 346.
[47] HRC, *Gauthier* v. *Canada*, No. 633/1995, 5 May 1999, para. 13.6.

of expression cases.[48] And the Court has not yet addressed freedom of expression cases. Any possible interaction with the African human rights system thus still lies in the future.

## 6 The Human Rights Committee

A striking feature in the Human Rights Committee's jurisprudence is the absence of any mention of regional human rights case law in the Committee's views. This seems to be in line with a broader practice. The Committee's views in cases of torture show a similar pattern.[49] Conversely, both applicants and respondent States do tend to invoke regional human rights case law, above all Strasbourg jurisprudence. This has occurred not only in cases directed against European States, but also in case law relating to Canada, Australia and Sri Lanka.

The earliest example is the leading Human Rights Committee case of Professor Robert Faurisson, who was convicted in France under the Gayssot Act,[50] which makes it an offence to question or minimise Nazi crimes, including the Shoah. Faurisson had asserted, among other things, that 'the myth of the gas chambers is a dishonest fabrication'.[51] According to France, in its arguments in the case, the Act was meant to counter modern forms of anti-Semitism. Contrary to what Faurisson himself claimed – that he was undertaking legitimate historical research – France argued that his views were directed against Jews. It invoked Article 5, ICCPR which prohibits the destruction of rights. Moreover, it argued that Article 20 of the Covenant obliged it to prohibit advocacy of racial or religious hatred. To support its first point, on the destruction or abuse of rights, France referred to the European Convention and case law of the (former) European Commission of Human Rights.[52] Article 17, ECHR, like Article 5, ICCPR, prohibits the abuse of rights. The practice of the Commission and to a certain extent the European Court had been to declare cases concerning the convictions of racist applicants inadmissible under Article 17. The Human Rights Committee, for its part, was not prepared to travel that European road.

[48] A full check of its case law up to 1 December 2011 showed no results in this respect.
[49] See Buyse (2011/2012).
[50] Official title: Loi no. 90-615 du 13 juillet 1990 tendant à réprimer tout acte raciste, antisémite ou xenophobe (Gayssot).
[51] HRC, *Robert Faurisson* v. *France*, No. 550/1993, 8 November 1996, para. 2.6.
[52] In the pre-1998 Strasbourg system, this Commission was the first port of call for applicants. It could refer cases to the Committee of Ministers of the Council of Europe or to the European Court of Human Rights.

It assessed the case of *Faurisson* on substance under Article 19 and held that the conviction had pursued a legitimate aim and was necessary. The Committee noted the possibility that measures taken under the Gayssot Act could, in other circumstances, be incompatible with the Covenant. Years later, in its new General Comment on the right to freedom of expression, adopted in 2011, the Committee became even more unequivocal on this point: 'Laws that penalise the expression of opinions about historical facts are incompatible with the obligations that the Covenant imposes on States parties in relation to the respect for freedom of opinion and expression.'[53] Notably, the Committee referred in a footnote to its 1996 *Faurisson* decision, in which it had taken a more nuanced approach. The European system has also slightly changed its position over time: cases of racism are less easily dismissed under the abuse of rights clause and increasingly dealt with on the merits under Article 10 ECHR.[54]

A similar issue of anti-Semitism surfaced in the case of *Malcom Ross* v. *Canada*.[55] The applicant was a schoolteacher who had been dismissed because of his anti-Jewish writings. He invoked the European Court case of *Vogt* v. *Germany* which concerned a schoolteacher dismissed on account of her communist activities. In that case the Court had found a violation of the right to freedom of expression.[56] Canada, a State obviously not party to the ECHR, argued that the applicant's situation differed from the *Vogt* case in that Vogt's activities were for a lawful political party and her expressions were not discriminatory. The Committee did follow the European Court case law in holding that by removing Ross from his teaching position his freedom of expression had been restricted. But it did so without explicitly referring to the *Vogt* case. The situation did not amount to a violation of Article 19, however, since the Committee argued that such a restriction could be argued to be necessary to 'protect the right and freedom of Jewish children to have a school system free from bias, prejudice and intolerance'.[57]

[53] HRC, General Comment No. 34: Article 19 (Freedoms of Opinion and Expression), UN Doc. CCPR/C/GC/34, 12 September 2011, para. 49.

[54] See e.g., ECtHR, *Féret* v. *Belgium* (Appl. No. 15615/07), Judgment, 16 July 2009 and H. Cannie and D. Voorhoof, 'The Abuse Clause and Freedom of Expression in the European Human Rights Convention: An Added Value for Democracy and Human Rights Protection?', *Netherlands Quarterly of Human Rights* 29(1) (2011), 54–83.

[55] HRC, *Malcolm Ross* v. *Canada*, No. 736/1997, 18 October 2000.

[56] ECtHR, *Vogt* v. *Germany* (Appl. No. 17851/91), Judgment (Grand Chamber), 26 September 1995.

[57] HRC, *Malcolm Ross* v. *Canada*, para. 11.6.

In *Zeljko Bodrozic* v. *Serbia and Montenegro*, the facts related to the conviction of a journalist for insulting a politician in a magazine article.[58] The applicant referred to four classic freedom-of-expression judgments of the European Court of Human Rights: *Handyside*, *Lingens*, *Oberschlick* and *Schwabe*.[59] These cases related *inter alia* to the fact that freedom of expression also protects critical utterances and that the limits of permissible criticism are wider when it targets politicians than ordinary citizens. The Human Rights Committee noted in its views that 'in circumstances of public debate in a democratic society, especially in the media, concerning figures in the political domain, the value placed by the Covenant upon uninhibited expression is particularly high.'[60] This reflects the Strasbourg case law very closely, but the Committee referred instead to its own jurisprudence – the case of *Aduayom and Others* v. *Togo*[61] – in which it emphasized the importance of possibilities for open criticism in relation to political parties and the political system. Interestingly, this jurisprudence was delivered later than the European cases mentioned in the *Bodrozic* case. There might thus be a possibility that the Committee was influenced by those cases, but such influence is implicit rather than explicit.

There have also been cases in which both parties referred to the European Court's case law. In *Avon Lovell* v. *Australia*, a contempt of court case, the applicant referred to a friendly settlement in the ECtHR case of *Harman* v. *the United Kingdom*, as a result of which Australian rules on contempt of court were also adjusted.[62] Here, the argument seems to have been incidental as it did not play any further role in the case. Australia invoked a classic freedom of expression case, the *Sunday Times (No. 1)* judgment of the European Court relating to contempt of court.[63] Again, the Committee did not examine that case law but rather concluded through its own argumentation that Article 19 had not been violated.

[58] HRC, *Zeljko Bodrozic* v. *Serbia and Montenegro*, No. 1180/2003, 31 October 2005.

[59] ECtHR, *Handyside* v. *the United Kingdom* (Appl. No. 5493/72), Judgment (Grand Chamber), 7 December 1978; ECtHR, *Lingens* v. *Austria* (Appl. No. 9815/82), Judgment (Grand Chamber), 8 July 1986; ECtHR, *Oberschlick* v. *Austria* (Appl. No. 11662/85), Judgment (Chamber), 23 May 1991; ECtHR, *Schwabe* v. *Austria* (Appl. No. 13704/88), Judgment (Chamber), 28 August 1992.

[60] HRC, *Zeljko Bodrovic* v. *Serbia and Montenegro*, para. 7.2.

[61] HRC, *Aduayom and Others* v. *Togo*, Nos. 422/1990 a.o., 12 July 1996.

[62] HRC, *Avon Lovell* v. *Australia*, No. 920/2000, 24 March 2004, para. 5.10.

[63] ECtHR, *Sunday Times* v. *the United Kingdom (No. 1)* (Appl. No. 6538/74), Judgment (Grand Chamber), 26 April 1979, para. 47.

At times the references to European case law seem to have been even more in vain: when the applicant refers to it in her or his arguments under Article 19, but the Committee declines to assess the freedom of expression aspects of a case. In *Anthony Michael Immanuel Fernando* v. *Sri Lanka*,[64] another contempt of court case, the applicant argued that the contempt powers had not been defined with sufficient precision. The quality of the legal provision itself was thus at stake. He referred to the aforementioned *Sunday Times* case and another European case on the criteria for lawfulness, *Grigoriades* v. *Greece*,[65] to argue that a legal norm should be accessible and that its effects should be foreseeable. As to the proportionality of the sentence he received – a year of imprisonment with hard labour – he referred to proportionality criteria in the Strasbourg case *De Haes and Gijsels* v. *Belgium*.[66] Unfortunately, the Committee held his Article 19 claim to be insufficiently substantiated and therefore did not probe the issue further.

In two cases the European human rights protection system featured only from a procedural perspective. In *Dobroslav Paraga* v. *Croatia* the Committee noted that the applicant had registered two complaints with the European Court of Human Rights. These related to different issues and therefore did not preclude the Committee from assessing the application at hand.[67] And in *Jacobus Gerardus Strik* v. *the Netherlands* the State noted that the European Commission of Human Rights had earlier declared the applicant's case inadmissible. Although the Committee did the same, this is a far cry from any form of judicial dialogue.[68]

Finally, references to the other two regional mechanisms by any of the parties in cases before the Human Rights Committee are almost non-existent. A survey of the Committee's views in freedom of expression cases up to 2011[69] yielded no mentions of the African system or treaties.

[64] HRC, *Anthony Michael Immanuel Fernando* v. *Sri Lanka*, No. 1189/2003, 31 March 2005.

[65] ECtHR, *Grigoriades* v. *Greece* (Appl. No. 24348/94), Judgment (Grand Chamber), 25 November 1997.

[66] ECtHR, *De Haes and Gijsels* v. *Belgium* (Appl. No. 19983/92), Judgment, 24 February 1997.

[67] HRC, *Dobroslav Paraga* v. *Croatia*, No. 727/1996, 4 April 2001.

[68] HRC, *Jacobus Gerardus Strik* v. *the Netherlands*, No. 1001/2001, 1 November 2002.

[69] By using the electronic human rights database of the Netherlands Institute of Human Rights (SIM) at www.uu.nl/sim (last accessed 27 January 2014) – and combining a search for Article 19 cases with references to the African and Inter-American regional mechanisms and treaties.

The Inter-American system surfaced in only one case. In the case of journalist *Zeljko Bodrovic*, the applicant referred to Report 22/94 of the Inter-American Commission on Human Rights on so-called 'desacato' or contempt laws in Argentina, among other references to European Court case law mentioned earlier and even United States Supreme Court jurisprudence. He used those references to substantiate his claim that Article 19 protects freedom of expression in an extensive manner, specifically in political debate.[70] Laws such as the one under review in the Inter-American Commission's report offer more rather than less protection to public officials in contempt cases. In *Bodrovic* the Human Rights Committee, as noted above, essentially granted the applicant's claim and held that Article 19 accords a high degree of protection for public debate about political figures, but did so with reference to its own case law rather than the cases from regional systems invoked by the applicant.

## 7 Conclusion

The overview of regional and global case law presented above shows a rather minimalist version of judicial dialogue. It may even be better to speak of intermittent listening to each other's findings. Moreover, the extent to which the various adjudicative human rights bodies show a willingness to openly use the jurisprudence of their peers differs widely.

The most striking difference is that regional bodies do refer to universal standards but the Human Rights Committee does not explicitly use regional standards or case law. Of all the adjudicative human rights bodies surveyed, the European Court has perhaps the least need to refer to external case law. Its own jurisprudence is extensive and detailed and its legitimacy is relatively high. This may explain why the ICCPR mostly features as a comparative standard in a small number of cases to inform, contrast or confirm a certain interpretation of the ECHR. The case law of the Human Rights Committee itself does not feature in European freedom of expression cases. In the Inter-American jurisprudence, references to the Human Rights Committee's case law do occur in some instances, mostly to strengthen the persuasive force of a certain interpretation

[70] HRC, *Zeljko Bodrovic* v. *Serbia and Montenegro*, para. 3.1.

the Court makes, in showing that this interpretation is in line with international trends, both coming from its global and its regional peers. And in the occasional case, the Human Rights Committee's jurisprudence is used to fill the rather open frame of a human rights norm from the American Convention.

A rather different pattern is to be seen in the views of the Human Rights Committee. Both applicants and States – remarkably both from Europe and outside it – do refer to European cases and these indeed may have at times informed the findings of the Committee. But this never occurs explicitly. Reflections of, for example, the European Court's interpretations of the freedom of expression norm can be found, but these are not mentioned as such. This cannot be explained by the fact that the Committee's own jurisprudence on freedom of expression cases is large – it is not. Nor could one say that it can only be caused by a lack of knowledge of regional systems – a sizeable portion of the Committee's members are from Europe and the Americas. Rather, the reason may be found in the fact that open citing could be seen to weaken rather than strengthen the persuasive force of the Committee's views. Explicit references to only one or a few regional systems may not be acceptable or convincing to Committee members and State Parties beyond Europe or Latin America. It could even fuel criticisms that the UN human rights system is Western rather than universal. In that sense, the current ways of 'tacit citing', learning from regional systems without too openly acknowledging it may be the highest attainable form of dialogue at this point in time. To turn the current soft silent one-way whispers into a fully-fledged dialogue requires more openness, especially on the part of State Parties to the various human rights systems and a recognition that using other treaties and their jurisprudence for elucidation or inspiration does not mean one automatically yields to or is bound by their views.

## Literature

Cannie, H. and D. Voorhoof, 'The Abuse Clause and Freedom of Expression in the European Human Rights Convention: An Added Value for Democracy and Human Rights Protection?', *Netherlands Quarterly of Human Rights* 29(1) (2011), 54–83.

Forowicz, M. *The Reception of International Law in the European Court of Human Rights* (Oxford University Press, 2010).

Harris, D., M. O'Boyle, E. Bates and C. Buckley, *Harris, O'Boyle & Warbrick: Law of the European Convention on Human Rights*, 2nd edn (Oxford University Press, 2009).

Krotoszynski, R. J. '"I'd Like to Teach the World to Sing (in Perfect Harmony)": International Judicial Dialogue and the Muses - Reflections on the Perils and the Promise of International Judicial Dialogue', *Michigan Law Review* 104 (2006), 1321–59.

Law, D. S. and W. Chang, 'The Limits of Global Judicial Dialogue', *Washington Law Review* 86 (2011), 523–78.

Miller, N. 'An International Jurisprudence? The Operation of "Precedent" across International Tribunals', *Leiden Journal of International Law* 15 (2002), 483–526.

Nowak, M. *CCPR Commentary*, 2nd edn (Kehl am Rhein: Engel, 2005).

Shelton, D. 'An Introduction to the History of International Human Rights Law', *George Washington University Law School Legal studies Research Paper No. 346*, at ssrn.com paper no. 1010489 (2007), 1–30 (last accessed 21 January 2014).

Slaughter, A. 'A Global Community of Courts', *Harvard International Law Journal* 44 (2003), 191–219.

Tyagi, Y. *The UN Human Rights Committee: Practice and Procedure* (Cambridge University Press, 2011).

Voeten, E. 'Borrowing and Non-Borrowing among International Courts', *Journal of Legal Studies* 39(2) (2010), 547–76.

Wald, P. M. 'Tribunal Discourse and Intercourse: How the International Courts Speak to One Another', *Boston College International and Comparative Law Review* 30 (2007), 15–29.

## Case law

### *European Court of Human Rights*

*Balsytė-Lideikienė* v. *Lithuania* (Appl. No. 72596/01), Judgment, 4 November 2008.

*Bladet Tromsø and Stensaas* v. *Norway* (Appl. No. 21980/93), Judgment (Grand Chamber), 20 May 1999.

*De Haes and Gijsels* v. *Belgium* (Appl. No. 19983/92), Judgment, 24 February 1997.

*Ergin* v. *Turkey (No. 6)* (Appl. No. 47533/99), Judgment, 4 May 2006.

*Féret* v. *Belgium* (Appl. No. 15615/07), Judgment, 16 July 2009.

*Glasenapp* v. *Germany*, (Appl. No. 9228/80), Judgment (Grand Chamber), 28 August 1986.

*Grigoriades* v. *Greece* (Appl. No. 24348/94), Judgment (Grand Chamber), 25 November 1997.

*Groppera Radio AG and Others* v. *Switzerland* (Appl. No. 10890/84), Judgment (Grand Chamber), 28 March 1990.
*Gündüz* v. *Turkey* (Appl. No. 35071/97), Judgment (Chamber), 4 December 2003.
*Handyside* v. *the United Kingdom* (Appl. No. 5493/72), Judgment (Grand Chamber), 7 December 1978.
*Jersild* v. *Denmark* (Appl. No. 15890/89), Judgment (Grand Chamber), 23 September 1994.
*Kosiek* v. *Germany* (Appl. No. 9704/82), Judgment (Grand Chamber), 28 August 1986.
*Lepojić* v. *Serbia* (Appl. No. 13909/05), Judgment, 6 November 2007.
*Lingens* v. *Austria* (Appl. No. 9815/82), Judgment (Grand Chamber), 8 July 1986.
*Loizidou* v. *Turkey* (Appl. No. 15318/89), Judgment, 18 December 1996.
*Müller and Others* v. *Switzerland* (Appl. No. 10737/84), Judgment, 24 May 1988.
*Oberschlick* v. *Austria* (Appl. No. 11662/85), Judgment, 23 May 1991.
*Perinçek* v. *Switzerland* (Appl. No. 27510/08), Judgment, 17 December 2013.
*Schwabe* v. *Austria* (Appl. No. 13704/88), Judgment, 28 August 1992.
*Stoll* v. *Switzerland* (Appl. No. 69698/01), Judgment (Grand Chamber), 10 December 2007.
*Sunday Times* v. *the United Kingdom (No. 1)* (Appl. No. 6538/74), Judgment (Grand Chamber), 26 April 1979.
*Tønsbergs Blad AS and Haukom* v. *Norway* (Appl. No. 510/04), Judgment, 1 March 2007.
*Vogt* v. *Germany* (Appl. No. 17851/91), Judgment (Grand Chamber), 26 September 1995.
*Yıldırım* v. *Turkey* (Appl. No. 3111/10), Judgment, 18 December 2012.
*Youth Initiative for Human Rights* v. *Serbia* (Appl. No. 48135/06), Judgment, 25 June 2013.

### *Human Rights Committee*

*Aduayom and Others* v. *Togo*, Nos. 422/1990 a.o., 12 July 1996.
*Anthony Michael Immanuel Fernando* v. *Sri Lanka*, No. 1189/2003, 31 March 2005.
*Avon Lovell* v. *Australia*, No. 920/2000, 24 March 2004.
*Dobroslav Paraga* v. *Croatia*, No. 727/1996, 4 April 2001.
*Gauthier* v. *Canada*, No. 633/1995, 5 May 1999.
*J. Ballantyne, E. Davidson and G. McIntyre* v. *Canada*, Nos. 359/1989 and 385/1989, 5 May 1993.
*Jacobus Gerardus Strik* v. *the Netherlands*, No. 1001/2001, 1 November 2002.
*Malcolm Ross* v. *Canada*, No. 736/1997, 18 October 2000.
*Robert Faurisson* v. *France*, No. 550/1993, 8 November 1996.
*Zeljko Bodrozic* v. *Serbia and Montenegro*, No. 1180/2003, 31 October 2005.

*Inter-American Court of Human Rights*

*Caesar* v. *Trinidad and Tobago*, Series C No. 123, 11 March 2005.
*Heliodoro Portugal* v. *Panama*, Series C No.186, 12 August 2008.
*Herrera-Ulloa* v. *Costa Rica*, Series C No. 107, 2 July 2004.
*Olmedo-Bustos and Others* v. *Chile*, Series C No. 73, 5 February 2001.
*Ricardo Canese* v. *Paraguay*, Series C No. 111, 31 August 2004.
*Ríos and Others* v. *Venezuela*, Series C No. 194, 28 January 2009.

# Human Rights Committee General Comment No. 34: Article 19: Freedoms of opinion and expression, UN Doc. CCPR/C/GC/34, 12 September 2011

102nd Session, Geneva, 11–29 July 2011

## General remarks

1. This general comment replaces general comment No. 10 (nineteenth session).
2. Freedom of opinion and freedom of expression are indispensable conditions for the full development of the person. They are essential for any society.[1] They constitute the foundation stone for every free and democratic society. The two freedoms are closely related, with freedom of expression providing the vehicle for the exchange and development of opinions.
3. Freedom of expression is a necessary condition for the realization of the principles of transparency and accountability that are, in turn, essential for the promotion and protection of human rights.
4. Among the other articles that contain guarantees for freedom of opinion and/or expression, are articles 18, 17, 25 and 27. The freedoms of opinion and expression form a basis for the full enjoyment of a wide range of other human rights. For instance, freedom of expression is integral to the enjoyment of the rights to freedom of assembly and association, and the exercise of the right to vote.
5. Taking account of the specific terms of article 19, paragraph 1, as well as the relationship of opinion and thought (article 18), a reservation to paragraph 1 would be incompatible with the object and purpose of the Covenant.[2] Furthermore, although freedom of opinion is not listed among those rights that may not be derogated from pursuant to the

[1] See communication No. 1173/2003, *Benhadj v. Algeria*, views adopted on 20 July 2007; No. 628/1995, *Park v. Republic of Korea*, Views adopted on 5 July 1996.

[2] See the Committee's General Comment No. 24 (1994) on issues relating to reservations made upon ratification or accession to the Covenant or the Optional Protocols thereto, or in relation to the declarations under Article 41 of the Covenant, *Official Records of the General Assembly, Fiftieth Session, Supplement No. 40*, vol. I (A/50/40 (Vol. I)), annex V.

provisions of article 4 of the Covenant, it is recalled that, "in those provisions of the Covenant that are not listed in article 4, paragraph 2, there are elements that in the Committee's opinion cannot be made subject to lawful derogation under article 4".[3] Freedom of opinion is one such element, since it can never become necessary to derogate from it during a state of emergency.[4]

6. Taking account of the relationship of freedom of expression to the other rights in the Covenant, while reservations to particular elements of article 19, paragraph 2, may be acceptable, a general reservation to the rights set out in paragraph 2 would be incompatible with the object and purpose of the Covenant.[5]

7. The obligation to respect freedoms of opinion and expression is binding on every State party as a whole. All branches of the State (executive, legislative and judicial) and other public or governmental authorities, at whatever level – national, regional or local – are in a position to engage the responsibility of the State party.[6] Such responsibility may also be incurred by a State party under some circumstances in respect of acts of semi-State entities.[7] The obligation also requires States parties to ensure that persons are protected from any acts by private persons or entities that would impair the enjoyment of the freedoms of opinion and expression to the extent that these Covenant rights are amenable to application between private persons or entities.[8]

8. States parties are required to ensure that the rights contained in article 19 of the Covenant are given effect to in the domestic law of the State, in a manner consistent with the guidance provided by the Committee in its general comment No. 31 on the nature of the general legal obligation imposed on States parties to the Covenant. It is recalled that States parties should provide the Committee, in accordance with reports submitted pursuant to article 40, with the relevant domestic legal rules, administrative practices and judicial decisions, as well as relevant policy

[3] See the Committee's General Comment No. 29 (2001) on derogation during a state of emergency, para. 13, *Official Records of the General Assembly, Fifty-sixth Session, Supplement No. 40*, vol. I (A/56/40 (Vol. I)), annex VI.

[4] General Comment No. 29, para. 11. [5] General Comment No. 24.

[6] See the Committee's General Comment No. 31 (2004) on the nature of the general legal obligation imposed on States Parties to the Covenant, para. 4, *Official Records of the General Assembly, Fifty-ninth Session, Supplement No. 40*, vol. I (A/59/40 (Vol. I)), annex III.

[7] See communication No. 61/1979, *Hertzberg et al. v. Finland*, Views adopted on 2 April 1982.

[8] General Comment No. 31, para. 8; See communication No. 633/1995, *Gauthier v. Canada*, Views adopted on 7 April 1999.

level and other sectoral practices relating to the rights protected by article 19, taking into account the issues discussed in the present general comment. They should also include information on remedies available if those rights are violated.

## Freedom of opinion

9. Paragraph 1 of article 19 requires protection of the right to hold opinions without interference. This is a right to which the Covenant permits no exception or restriction. Freedom of opinion extends to the right to change an opinion whenever and for whatever reason a person so freely chooses. No person may be subject to the impairment of any rights under the Covenant on the basis of his or her actual, perceived or supposed opinions. All forms of opinion are protected, including opinions of a political, scientific, historic, moral or religious nature. It is incompatible with paragraph 1 to criminalize the holding of an opinion.[9] The harassment, intimidation or stigmatization of a person, including arrest, detention, trial or imprisonment for reasons of the opinions they may hold, constitutes a violation of article 19, paragraph 1.[10]

10. Any form of effort to coerce the holding or not holding of any opinion is prohibited.[11] Freedom to express one's opinion necessarily includes freedom not to express one's opinion.

## Freedom of expression

11. Paragraph 2 requires States parties to guarantee the right to freedom of expression, including the right to seek, receive and impart information and ideas of all kinds regardless of frontiers. This right includes the expression and receipt of communications of every form of idea and opinion capable of transmission to others, subject to the provisions in article 19, paragraph 3, and article 20.[12] It includes political

[9] See communication No. 550/93, *Faurisson v. France*, Views adopted on 8 November 1996.

[10] See communication No. 157/1983, *Mpaka-Nsusu v. Zaire*, Views adopted on 26 March 1986; No. 414/1990, *Mika Miha v. Equatorial Guinea*, Views adopted on 8 July 1994.

[11] See communication No. 878/1999, *Kang v. Republic of Korea*, Views adopted on 15 July 2003.

[12] See communications Nos. 359/1989 and 385/1989, *Ballantyne, Davidson and McIntyre v. Canada*, Views adopted on 18 October 1990.

discourse,[13] commentary on one's own[14] and on public affairs,[15] canvassing,[16] discussion of human rights,[17] journalism,[18] cultural and artistic expression,[19] teaching,[20] and religious discourse.[21] It may also include commercial advertising. The scope of paragraph 2 embraces even expression that may be regarded as deeply offensive,[22] although such expression may be restricted in accordance with the provisions of article 19, paragraph 3, and article 20.

12. Paragraph 2 protects all forms of expression and the means of their dissemination. Such forms include spoken, written and sign language and such non-verbal expression as images and objects of art.[23] Means of expression include books, newspapers,[24] pamphlets,[25] posters, banners,[26] dress and legal submissions.[27] They include all forms of audio-visual as well as electronic and Internet-based modes of expression.

## Freedom of expression and the media

13. A free, uncensored and unhindered press or other media is essential in any society to ensure freedom of opinion and expression and the enjoyment of other Covenant rights. It constitutes one of the cornerstones of a democratic society.[28] The Covenant embraces a right whereby the media may receive information on the basis of which it can carry out its function.[29] The free communication of information and ideas about public and political issues between citizens, candidates and elected representatives is essential. This implies a free press and other media able to comment on public issues without censorship or restraint

[13] See communication No. 414/1990, *Mika Miha v. Equatorial Guinea*.
[14] See communication No. 1189/2003, *Fernando v. Sri Lanka*, Views adopted on 31 March 2005.
[15] See communication No. 1157/2003, *Coleman v. Australia*, Views adopted on 17 July 2006.
[16] Concluding observations on Japan (CCPR/C/JPN/CO/5).
[17] See communication No. 1022/2001, *Velichkin v. Belarus*, Views adopted on 20 October 2005.
[18] See communication No. 1334/2004, *Mavlonov and Sa'di v. Uzbekistan*, Views adopted on 19 March 2009.
[19] See communication No. 926/2000, *Shin v. Republic of Korea*, Views adopted on 16 March 2004.
[20] See communication No. 736/97, *Ross v. Canada*, Views adopted on 18 October 2000.
[21] *Ibid.* [22] *Ibid.* [23] See communication No. 926/2000, *Shin v. Republic of Korea*.
[24] See communication No. 1341/2005, *Zundel v. Canada*, Views adopted on 20 March 2007.
[25] See communication No. 1009/2001, *Shchetoko et al. v. Belarus*, Views adopted on 11 July 2006.
[26] See communication No. 412/1990, *Kivenmaa v. Finland*, Views adopted on 31 March 1994.
[27] See communication No. 1189/2003, *Fernando v. Sri Lanka*.
[28] See communication No. 1128/2002, *Marques v. Angola*, Views adopted on 29 March 2005.
[29] See communication No. 633/95, *Gauthier v. Canada*.

and to inform public opinion.[30] The public also has a corresponding right to receive media output.[31]

14. As a means to protect the rights of media users, including members of ethnic and linguistic minorities, to receive a wide range of information and ideas, States parties should take particular care to encourage an independent and diverse media.

15. States parties should take account of the extent to which developments in information and communication technologies, such as Internet and mobile based electronic information dissemination systems, have substantially changed communication practices around the world. There is now a global network for exchanging ideas and opinions that does not necessarily rely on the traditional mass media intermediaries. States parties should take all necessary steps to foster the independence of these new media and to ensure access of individuals thereto.

16. States parties should ensure that public broadcasting services operate in an independent manner.[32] In this regard, States parties should guarantee their independence and editorial freedom. They should provide funding in a manner that does not undermine their independence.

17. Issues concerning the media are discussed further in the section of this general comment that addresses restrictions on freedom of expression.

## Right of access to information

18. Article 19, paragraph 2 embraces a right of access to information held by public bodies. Such information includes records held by a public body, regardless of the form in which the information is stored, its source and the date of production. Public bodies are as indicated in paragraph 7 of this general comment. The designation of such bodies may also include other entities when such entities are carrying out public functions. As has already been noted, taken together with article 25 of the Covenant, the right of access to information includes a right whereby the media has access to information on public affairs[33] and the right of

[30] See the Committee's General Comment No. 25 (1996) on Article 25 (Participation in public affairs and the right to vote), para. 25, *Official Records of the General Assembly, Fifty-first Session, Supplement No. 40*, vol. I (A/51/40 (Vol. I)), annex V.

[31] See communication No. 1334/2004, *Mavlonov and Sa'di v. Uzbekistan.*

[32] Concluding observations on Republic of Moldova (CCPR/CO/75/MDA).

[33] See communication No. 633/95, *Gauthier v. Canada.*

the general public to receive media output.[34] Elements of the right of access to information are also addressed elsewhere in the Covenant. As the Committee observed in its general comment No. 16, regarding article 17 of the Covenant, every individual should have the right to ascertain in an intelligible form, whether, and if so, what personal data is stored in automatic data files, and for what purposes. Every individual should also be able to ascertain which public authorities or private individuals or bodies control or may control his or her files. If such files contain incorrect personal data or have been collected or processed contrary to the provisions of the law, every individual should have the right to have his or her records rectified. Pursuant to article 10 of the Covenant, a prisoner does not lose the entitlement to access to his medical records.[35] The Committee, in general comment No. 32 on article 14, set out the various entitlements to information that are held by those accused of a criminal offence.[36] Pursuant to the provisions of article 2, persons should be in receipt of information regarding their Covenant rights in general.[37] Under article 27, a State party's decision-making that may substantively compromise the way of life and culture of a minority group should be undertaken in a process of information-sharing and consultation with affected communities.[38]

19. To give effect to the right of access to information, States parties should proactively put in the public domain Government information of public interest. States parties should make every effort to ensure easy, prompt, effective and practical access to such information. States parties should also enact the necessary procedures, whereby one may gain access to information, such as by means of freedom of information legislation.[39] The procedures should provide for the timely processing of requests for information according to clear rules that are compatible with the Covenant. Fees for requests for information should not be such as to constitute an unreasonable impediment to access to information. Authorities should provide reasons for any refusal to provide access to information.

[34] See communication No. 1334/2004, *Mavlonov and Sa'di v. Uzbekistan*.
[35] See communication No. 726/1996, *Zheludkov v. Ukraine*, Views adopted on 29 October 2002.
[36] See the Committee's General Comment No. 32 (2007) on the right to equality before courts and tribunals and to a fair trial, para. 33, *Official Records of the General Assembly, Sixty-second Session, Supplement No. 40, vol. I (A/62/40 (Vol. I)), annex VI.*
[37] General Comment No. 31.
[38] See communication No. 1457/2006, *Poma v. Peru*, Views adopted on 27 March 2009.
[39] Concluding observations on Azerbaijan (CCPR/C/79/Add.38 (1994)).

Arrangements should be put in place for appeals from refusals to provide access to information as well as in cases of failure to respond to requests.

## Freedom of expression and political rights

20. The Committee, in general comment No. 25 on participation in public affairs and the right to vote, elaborated on the importance of freedom of expression for the conduct of public affairs and the effective exercise of the right to vote. The free communication of information and ideas about public and political issues between citizens, candidates and elected representatives is essential. This implies a free press and other media able to comment on public issues and to inform public opinion without censorship or restraint.[40] The attention of States parties is drawn to the guidance that general comment No. 25 provides with regard to the promotion and the protection of freedom of expression in that context.

## The application of article 19 (3)

21. Paragraph 3 expressly states that the exercise of the right to freedom of expression carries with it special duties and responsibilities. For this reason two limitative areas of restrictions on the right are permitted, which may relate either to respect of the rights or reputations of others or to the protection of national security or of public order (*ordre public*) or of public health or morals. However, when a State party imposes restrictions on the exercise of freedom of expression, these may not put in jeopardy the right itself. The Committee recalls that the relation between right and restriction and between norm and exception must not be reversed.[41] The Committee also recalls the provisions of article 5, paragraph 1, of the Covenant according to which "nothing in the present Covenant may be interpreted as implying for any State, group or person any right to engage in any activity or perform any act aimed at the destruction of any of the rights and freedoms recognized herein or at their limitation to a greater extent than is provided for in the present Covenant".

[40] See General Comment No. 25 on article 25 of the Covenant, para. 25.

[41] See the Committee's General Comment No. 27 on Article 12, *Official Records of the General Assembly, Fifty-fifth Session, Supplement No. 40*, vol. I (A/55/40 (Vol. I)), annex VI, sect. A.

22. Paragraph 3 lays down specific conditions and it is only subject to these conditions that restrictions may be imposed: the restrictions must be "provided by law"; they may only be imposed for one of the grounds set out in subparagraphs (a) and (b) of paragraph 3; and they must conform to the strict tests of necessity and proportionality.[42] Restrictions are not allowed on grounds not specified in paragraph 3, even if such grounds would justify restrictions to other rights protected in the Covenant. Restrictions must be applied only for those purposes for which they were prescribed and must be directly related to the specific need on which they are predicated.[43]

23. States parties should put in place effective measures to protect against attacks aimed at silencing those exercising their right to freedom of expression. Paragraph 3 may never be invoked as a justification for the muzzling of any advocacy of multi-party democracy, democratic tenets and human rights.[44] Nor, under any circumstance, can an attack on a person, because of the exercise of his or her freedom of opinion or expression, including such forms of attack as arbitrary arrest, torture, threats to life and killing, be compatible with article 19.[45] Journalists are frequently subjected to such threats, intimidation and attacks because of their activities.[46] So too are persons who engage in the gathering and analysis of information on the human rights situation and who publish human rights-related reports, including judges and lawyers.[47] All such attacks should be vigorously investigated in a timely fashion, and the perpetrators prosecuted,[48] and the victims, or, in the case of killings, their representatives, be in receipt of appropriate forms of redress.[49]

[42] See communication No. 1022/2001, *Velichkin v. Belarus*, Views adopted on 20 October 2005.

[43] See the Committee's General Comment No. 22, *Official Records of the General Assembly, Forty-eighth Session, Supplement No. 40* (A/48/40), annex VI.

[44] See communication No. 458/91, *Mukong v. Cameroon*, Views adopted on 21 July 1994.

[45] See communication No. 1353/2005, *Njaru v. Cameroon*, Views adopted on 19 March 2007.

[46] See, for instance, Concluding Observations on Algeria (CCPR/C/DZA/CO/3); Concluding Observations on Costa Rica (CCPR/C/CRI/CO/5); Concluding Observations on Sudan (CCPR/C/SDN/CO/3).

[47] See communication No. 1353/2005, *Njaru v. Cameroon*; Concluding Observations on Nicaragua (CCPR/C/NIC/CO/3); Concluding Observations on Tunisia (CCPR/C/TUN/CO/5); concluding observations on the Syrian Arab Republic (CCPR/CO/84/SYR); Concluding Observations on Colombia (CCPR/CO/80/COL).

[48] *Ibid.* and Concluding Observations on Georgia (CCPR/C/GEO/CO/3).

[49] Concluding Observations on Guyana (CCPR/C/79/Add.121).

24. Restrictions must be provided by law. Law may include laws of parliamentary privilege[50] and laws of contempt of court.[51] Since any restriction on freedom of expression constitutes a serious curtailment of human rights, it is not compatible with the Covenant for a restriction to be enshrined in traditional, religious or other such customary law.[52]

25. For the purposes of paragraph 3, a norm, to be characterized as a "law", must be formulated with sufficient precision to enable an individual to regulate his or her conduct accordingly[53] and it must be made accessible to the public. A law may not confer unfettered discretion for the restriction of freedom of expression on those charged with its execution.[54] Laws must provide sufficient guidance to those charged with their execution to enable them to ascertain what sorts of expression are properly restricted and what sorts are not.

26. Laws restricting the rights enumerated in article 19, paragraph 2, including the laws referred to in paragraph 24, must not only comply with the strict requirements of article 19, paragraph 3 of the Covenant but must also themselves be compatible with the provisions, aims and objectives of the Covenant.[55] Laws must not violate the non-discrimination provisions of the Covenant. Laws must not provide for penalties that are incompatible with the Covenant, such as corporal punishment.[56]

27. It is for the State party to demonstrate the legal basis for any restrictions imposed on freedom of expression.[57] If, with regard to a particular State party, the Committee has to consider whether a particular restriction is imposed by law, the State party should provide details of the law and of actions that fall within the scope of the law.[58]

28. The first of the legitimate grounds for restriction listed in paragraph 3 is that of respect for the rights or reputations of others. The term

[50] See communication No. 633/95, *Gauthier v. Canada.*

[51] See communication No. 1373/2005, *Dissanayake v. Sri Lanka,* Views adopted on 22 July 2008.

[52] See General Comment No. 32.

[53] See communication No. 578/1994, *de Groot v. The Netherlands,* Views adopted on 14 July 1995.

[54] See General Comment No. 27.

[55] See communication No. 488/1992, *Toonen v. Australia,* Views adopted on 30 March 1994.

[56] General Comment No. 20, *Official Records of the General Assembly, Forty-seventh Session,* Supplement No. 40 (A/47/40), annex VI, sect. A.

[57] See communication No. 1553/2007, *Korneenko et al. v. Belarus,* Views adopted on 31 October 2006.

[58] See communication No. 132/1982, *Jaona v. Madagascar,* Views adopted on 1 April 1985.

"rights" includes human rights as recognized in the Covenant and more generally in international human rights law. For example, it may be legitimate to restrict freedom of expression in order to protect the right to vote under article 25, as well as rights under article 17 (see para. 37).[59] Such restrictions must be constructed with care: while it may be permissible to protect voters from forms of expression that constitute intimidation or coercion, such restrictions must not impede political debate, including, for example, calls for the boycotting of a non-compulsory vote.[60] The term "others" relates to other persons individually or as members of a community.[61] Thus, it may, for instance, refer to individual members of a community defined by its religious faith[62] or ethnicity.[63]

29. The second legitimate ground is that of protection of national security or of public order (*ordre public*), or of public health or morals.

30. Extreme care must be taken by States parties to ensure that treason laws[64] and similar provisions relating to national security, whether described as official secrets or sedition laws or otherwise, are crafted and applied in a manner that conforms to the strict requirements of paragraph 3. It is not compatible with paragraph 3, for instance, to invoke such laws to suppress or withhold from the public information of legitimate public interest that does not harm national security or to prosecute journalists, researchers, environmental activists, human rights defenders, or others, for having disseminated such information.[65] Nor is it generally appropriate to include in the remit of such laws such categories of information as those relating to the commercial sector, banking and scientific progress.[66] The Committee has found in one case that a restriction on the issuing of a statement in support of a labour dispute, including for the convening of a national strike, was not permissible on the grounds of national security.[67]

[59] See communication No. 927/2000, *Svetik v. Belarus*, Views adopted on 8 July 2004.
[60] *Ibid.*
[61] See communication No. 736/97, *Ross v. Canada*, Views adopted on 18 October 2000.
[62] See communication No. 550/93, *Faurisson v. France*; concluding observations on Austria (CCPR/C/AUT/CO/4).
[63] Concluding observations on Slovakia (CCPR/CO/78/SVK); concluding observations on Israel (CCPR/CO/78/ISR).
[64] Concluding Observations on Hong Kong (CCPR/C/HKG/CO/2).
[65] Concluding Observations on the Russian Federation (CCPR/CO/79/RUS).
[66] Concluding Observations on Uzbekistan (CCPR/CO/71/UZB).
[67] See communication No. 518/1992, *Sohn v. Republic of Korea*, Views adopted on 18 March 1994.

31. On the basis of maintenance of public order (*ordre public*) it may, for instance, be permissible in certain circumstances to regulate speech-making in a particular public place.[68] Contempt of court proceedings relating to forms of expression may be tested against the public order (*ordre public*) ground. In order to comply with paragraph 3, such proceedings and the penalty imposed must be shown to be warranted in the exercise of a court's power to maintain orderly proceedings.[69] Such proceedings should not in any way be used to restrict the legitimate exercise of defence rights.

32. The Committee observed in general comment No. 22, that "the concept of morals derives from many social, philosophical and religious traditions; consequently, limitations… for the purpose of protecting morals must be based on principles not deriving exclusively from a single tradition". Any such limitations must be understood in the light of universality of human rights and the principle of non-discrimination.

33. Restrictions must be "necessary" for a legitimate purpose. Thus, for instance, a prohibition on commercial advertising in one language, with a view to protecting the language of a particular community, violates the test of necessity if the protection could be achieved in other ways that do not restrict freedom of expression.[70] On the other hand, the Committee has considered that a State party complied with the test of necessity when it transferred a teacher who had published materials that expressed hostility toward a religious community to a non-teaching position in order to protect the right and freedom of children of that faith in a school district.[71]

34. Restrictions must not be overbroad. The Committee observed in general comment No. 27 that "restrictive measures must conform to the principle of proportionality; they must be appropriate to achieve their protective function; they must be the least intrusive instrument among those which might achieve their protective function; they must be proportionate to the interest to be protected…The principle of proportionality has to be respected not only in the law that frames the restrictions but also by the administrative and judicial authorities in applying the law".[72]

[68] See communication No. 1157/2003, *Coleman v. Australia.*

[69] See communication No. 1373/2005, *Dissanayake v. Sri Lanka.*

[70] See communication No. 359, 385/89, *Ballantyne, Davidson and McIntyre v. Canada.*

[71] See communication No. 736/97, *Ross v. Canada*, Views adopted on 17 July 2006.

[72] General Comment No. 27, para. 14. See also communications No. 1128/2002, *Marques v. Angola*; No. 1157/2003, *Coleman v. Australia.*

The principle of proportionality must also take account of the form of expression at issue as well as the means of its dissemination. For instance, the value placed by the Covenant upon uninhibited expression is particularly high in the circumstances of public debate in a democratic society concerning figures in the public and political domain.[73]

35. When a State party invokes a legitimate ground for restriction of freedom of expression, it must demonstrate in specific and individualized fashion the precise nature of the threat, and the necessity and proportionality of the specific action taken, in particular by establishing a direct and immediate connection between the expression and the threat.[74]

36. The Committee reserves to itself an assessment of whether, in a given situation, there may have been circumstances which made a restriction of freedom of expression necessary.[75] In this regard, the Committee recalls that the scope of this freedom is not to be assessed by reference to a "margin of appreciation"[76] and in order for the Committee to carry out this function, a State party, in any given case, must demonstrate in specific fashion the precise nature of the threat to any of the enumerated grounds listed in paragraph 3 that has caused it to restrict freedom of expression.[77]

## Limitative scope of restrictions on freedom of expression in certain specific areas

37. Among restrictions on political discourse that have given the Committee cause for concern are the prohibition of door-to-door canvassing,[78] restrictions on the number and type of written materials that may be distributed during election campaigns,[79] blocking access during election periods to sources, including local and international media, of political commentary,[80] and limiting access of opposition parties and

[73] See communication No. 1180/2003, *Bodrozic v. Serbia and Montenegro*, Views adopted on 31 October 2005.
[74] See communication No. 926/2000, *Shin v. Republic of Korea*.
[75] See communication No. 518/1992, *Sohn v. Republic of Korea*.
[76] See communication No. 511/1992, *Ilmari Länsman et al. v. Finland*, Views adopted on 14 October 1993.
[77] See communications Nos. 518/92, *Sohn v. Republic of Korea*; No. 926/2000, *Shin v. Republic of Korea*.
[78] Concluding Observations on Japan (CCPR/C/JPN/CO/5). [79] *Ibid.*
[80] Concluding Observations on Tunisia (CCPR/C/TUN/CO/5).

politicians to media outlets.[81] Every restriction should be compatible with paragraph 3. However, it may be legitimate for a State party to restrict political polling imminently preceding an election in order to maintain the integrity of the electoral process.[82]

38. As noted earlier in paragraphs 13 and 20, concerning the content of political discourse, the Committee has observed that in circumstances of public debate concerning public figures in the political domain and public institutions, the value placed by the Covenant upon uninhibited expression is particularly high.[83] Thus, the mere fact that forms of expression are considered to be insulting to a public figure is not sufficient to justify the imposition of penalties, albeit public figures may also benefit from the provisions of the Covenant.[84] Moreover, all public figures, including those exercising the highest political authority such as heads of State and government, are legitimately subject to criticism and political opposition.[85] Accordingly, the Committee expresses concern regarding laws on such matters as, lese majesty,[86] *desacato*,[87] disrespect for authority,[88] disrespect for flags and symbols, defamation of the head of State[89] and the protection of the honour of public officials,[90] and laws should not provide for more severe penalties solely on the basis of the identity of the person that may have been impugned. States parties should not prohibit criticism of institutions, such as the army or the administration.[91]

39. States parties should ensure that legislative and administrative frameworks for the regulation of the mass media are consistent with the provisions of paragraph 3.[92] Regulatory systems should take into account the differences between the print and broadcast sectors and the

[81] Concluding Observations on Togo (CCPR/CO/76/TGO); Concluding Observations on Moldova (CCPR/CO/75/MDA).

[82] See communication No. 968/2001, *Kim v. Republic of Korea*, Views adopted on 14 March 1996.

[83] See communication No. 1180/2003, *Bodrozic v. Serbia and Montenegro*, Views adopted on 31 October 2005.

[84] *Ibid.* [85] See communication No. 1128/2002, *Marques v. Angola*.

[86] See communication No. 422-424/1990, *Aduayom et al. v. Togo*, Views adopted on 30 June 1994.

[87] Concluding Observations on the Dominican Republic (CCPR/CO/71/DOM).

[88] Concluding Observations on Honduras (CCPR/C/HND/CO/1).

[89] See Concluding Observations on Zambia (CCPR/ZMB/CO/3), para. 25.

[90] See Concluding Observations on Costa Rica (CCPR/C/CRI/CO/5), para. 11.

[91] *Ibid.*, and see Concluding Observations on Tunisia (CCPR/C/TUN/CO/5), para. 91.

[92] See Concluding Observations on Viet Nam (CCPR/CO/75/VNM), para. 18, and Concluding Observations on Lesotho (CCPR/CO/79/Add.106), para. 23.

Internet, while also noting the manner in which various media converge. It is incompatible with article 19 to refuse to permit the publication of newspapers and other print media other than in the specific circumstances of the application of paragraph 3. Such circumstances may never include a ban on a particular publication unless specific content, that is not severable, can be legitimately prohibited under paragraph 3. States parties must avoid imposing onerous licensing conditions and fees on the broadcast media, including on community and commercial stations.[93] The criteria for the application of such conditions and licence fees should be reasonable and objective,[94] clear,[95] transparent,[96] non-discriminatory and otherwise in compliance with the Covenant.[97] Licensing regimes for broadcasting via media with limited capacity, such as audiovisual terrestrial and satellite services should provide for an equitable allocation of access and frequencies between public, commercial and community broadcasters. It is recommended that States parties that have not already done so should establish an independent and public broadcasting licensing authority, with the power to examine broadcasting applications and to grant licenses.[98]

40. The Committee reiterates its observation in general comment No. 10 that "because of the development of modern mass media, effective measures are necessary to prevent such control of the media as would interfere with the right of everyone to freedom of expression". The State should not have monopoly control over the media and should promote plurality of the media.[99] Consequently, States parties should take appropriate action, consistent with the Covenant, to prevent undue media dominance or concentration by privately controlled media groups in monopolistic situations that may be harmful to a diversity of sources and views.

41. Care must be taken to ensure that systems of government subsidy to media outlets and the placing of government advertisements[100] are not

[93] Concluding Observations on Gambia (CCPR/CO/75/GMB).

[94] See Concluding Observations on Lebanon (CCPR/CO/79/Add.78), para. 25.

[95] Concluding Observations on Kuwait (CCPR/CO/69/KWT); Concluding Observations on Ukraine (CCPR/CO/73/UKR).

[96] Concluding Observations on Kyrgyzstan (CCPR/CO/69/KGZ).

[97] Concluding Observations on Ukraine (CCPR/CO/73/UKR).

[98] Concluding Observations on Lebanon (CCPR/CO/79/Add.78).

[99] See Concluding Observations on Guyana (CCPR/CO/79/Add.121), para. 19; Concluding Observations on the Russian Federation (CCPR/CO/79/RUS); Concluding Observations on Viet Nam (CCPR/CO/75/VNM); Concluding Observations on Italy (CCPR/C/79/Add. 37).

[100] See Concluding Observations on Lesotho (CCPR/CO/79/Add.106), para. 22.

employed to the effect of impeding freedom of expression.[101] Furthermore, private media must not be put at a disadvantage compared to public media in such matters as access to means of dissemination/ distribution and access to news.[102]

42. The penalization of a media outlet, publishers or journalist solely for being critical of the government or the political social system espoused by the government[103]can never be considered to be a necessary restriction of freedom of expression.

43. Any restrictions on the operation of websites, blogs or any other Internet-based, electronic or other such information dissemination system, including systems to support such communication, such as Internet service providers or search engines, are only permissible to the extent that they are compatible with paragraph 3. Permissible restrictions generally should be content-specific; generic bans on the operation of certain sites and systems are not compatible with paragraph 3. It is also inconsistent with paragraph 3 to prohibit a site or an information dissemination system from publishing material solely on the basis that it may be critical of the government or the political social system espoused by the government.[104]

44. Journalism is a function shared by a wide range of actors, including professional full-time reporters and analysts, as well as bloggers and others who engage in forms of self-publication in print, on the Internet or elsewhere, and general State systems of registration or licensing of journalists are incompatible with paragraph 3. Limited accreditation schemes are permissible only where necessary to provide journalists with privileged access to certain places and/or events. Such schemes should be applied in a manner that is non-discriminatory and compatible with article 19 and other provisions of the Covenant, based on objective criteria and taking into account that journalism is a function shared by a wide range of actors.

45. It is normally incompatible with paragraph 3 to restrict the freedom of journalists and others who seek to exercise their freedom of expression (such as persons who wish to travel to human rights-related

[101] Concluding Observations on Ukraine (CCPR/CO/73/UKR).

[102] Concluding Observations on Sri Lanka (CCPR/CO/79/LKA); and see Concluding Observations on Togo (CCPR/CO/76/TGO), para. 17.

[103] Concluding Observations on Peru (CCPR/CO/70/PER).

[104] Concluding Observations on the Syrian Arab Republic (CCPR/CO/84/SYR).

meetings)[105] to travel outside the State party, to restrict the entry into the State party of foreign journalists to those from specified countries[106] or to restrict freedom of movement of journalists and human rights investigators within the State party (including to conflict-affected locations, the sites of natural disasters and locations where there are allegations of human rights abuses). States parties should recognize and respect that element of the right of freedom of expression that embraces the limited journalistic privilege not to disclose information sources.[107]

46. States parties should ensure that counter-terrorism measures are compatible with paragraph 3. Such offences as "encouragement of terrorism"[108] and "extremist activity"[109] as well as offences of "praising", "glorifying", or "justifying" terrorism, should be clearly defined to ensure that they do not lead to unnecessary or disproportionate interference with freedom of expression. Excessive restrictions on access to information must also be avoided. The media plays a crucial role in informing the public about acts of terrorism and its capacity to operate should not be unduly restricted. In this regard, journalists should not be penalized for carrying out their legitimate activities.

47. Defamation laws must be crafted with care to ensure that they comply with paragraph 3, and that they do not serve, in practice, to stifle freedom of expression.[110] All such laws, in particular penal defamation laws, should include such defences as the defence of truth and they should not be applied with regard to those forms of expression that are not, of their nature, subject to verification. At least with regard to comments about public figures, consideration should be given to avoiding penalizing or otherwise rendering unlawful untrue statements that have been published in error but without malice.[111] In any event, a public interest in the subject matter of the criticism should be recognized as a defence. Care should be taken by States parties to avoid excessively

[105] Concluding Observations on Uzbekistan (CCPR/CO/83/UZB); Concluding Observations on Morocco (CCPR/CO/82/MAR).

[106] Concluding Observations on Democratic People's Republic of Korea (CCPR/CO/72/PRK).

[107] Concluding Observations on Kuwait (CCPR/CO/69/KWT).

[108] Concluding Observations on the United Kingdom of Great Britain and Northern Ireland (CCPR/C/GBR/CO/6).

[109] Concluding Observations on the Russian Federation (CCPR/CO/79/RUS).

[110] Concluding Observations on the United Kingdom of Great Britain and Northern Ireland (CCPR/C/GBR/CO/6).

[111] *Ibid.*

punitive measures and penalties. Where relevant, States parties should place reasonable limits on the requirement for a defendant to reimburse the expenses of the successful party.[112] States parties should consider the decriminalization of defamation[113] and, in any case, the application of the criminal law should only be countenanced in the most serious of cases and imprisonment is never an appropriate penalty. It is impermissible for a State party to indict a person for criminal defamation but then not to proceed to trial expeditiously – such a practice has a chilling effect that may unduly restrict the exercise of freedom of expression of the person concerned and others.[114]

48. Prohibitions of displays of lack of respect for a religion or other belief system, including blasphemy laws, are incompatible with the Covenant, except in the specific circumstances envisaged in article 20, paragraph 2, of the Covenant. Such prohibitions must also comply with the strict requirements of article 19, paragraph 3, as well as such articles as 2, 5, 17, 18 and 26. Thus, for instance, it would be impermissible for any such laws to discriminate in favour of or against one or certain religions or belief systems, or their adherents over another, or religious believers over non-believers. Nor would it be permissible for such prohibitions to be used to prevent or punish criticism of religious leaders or commentary on religious doctrine and tenets of faith.[115]

49. Laws that penalize the expression of opinions about historical facts are incompatible with the obligations that the Covenant imposes on States parties in relation to the respect for freedom of opinion and expression.[116] The Covenant does not permit general prohibition of expressions of an erroneous opinion or an incorrect interpretation of past events. Restrictions on the right of freedom of opinion should never be imposed and, with regard to freedom of expression, they should not go beyond what is permitted in paragraph 3 or required under article 20.

[112] *Ibid.*

[113] Concluding Observations on Italy (CCPR/C/ITA/CO/5); Concluding Observations on the Former Yugoslav Republic of Macedonia (CCPR/C/MKD/CO/2).

[114] See communication No. 909/2000, *Kankanamge v. Sri Lanka*, Views adopted on 27 July 2004.

[115] Concluding Observations on the United Kingdom of Great Britain and Northern Ireland - the Crown Dependencies of Jersey, Guernsey and the Isle of Man (CCPR/C/79/Add.119). See also Concluding Observations on Kuwait (CCPR/CO/69/KWT).

[116] So called "memory-laws", see communication No. 550/93, *Faurisson v. France*. See also Concluding Observations on Hungary (CCPR/C/HUN/CO/5), para. 19.

## The relationship between articles 19 and 20

50. Articles 19 and 20 are compatible with and complement each other. The acts that are addressed in article 20 are all subject to restriction pursuant to article 19, paragraph 3. As such, a limitation that is justified on the basis of article 20 must also comply with article 19, paragraph 3.[117]

51. What distinguishes the acts addressed in article 20 from other acts that may be subject to restriction under article 19, paragraph 3, is that for the acts addressed in article 20, the Covenant indicates the specific response required from the State: their prohibition by law. It is only to this extent that article 20 may be considered as *lex specialis* with regard to article 19.

52. It is only with regard to the specific forms of expression indicated in article 20 that States parties are obliged to have legal prohibitions. In every case in which the State restricts freedom of expression it is necessary to justify the prohibitions and their provisions in strict conformity with article 19.

[117] See communication No. 736/1997, *Ross v. Canada*, Views adopted on 18 October 2000.

# INDEX

Lightning Source UK Ltd.
Milton Keynes UK
UKOW06n2043310515

252650UK00003B/27/P